SOFTWARE SYSTEMS ARCHITECTURE

SECOND EDITION

SOFTWARE SYSTEMS ARCHITECTURE

Working with Stakeholders Using Viewpoints and Perspectives

SECOND EDITION

NICK ROZANSKI
EOIN WOODS

✦ Addison-Wesley

Upper Saddle River, NJ ▪ Boston ▪ Indianapolis ▪ San Francisco
New York ▪ Toronto ▪ Montreal ▪ London ▪ Munich ▪ Paris ▪ Madrid
Capetown ▪ Sydney ▪ Tokyo ▪ Singapore ▪ Mexico City

Many of the designations used by manufacturers and sellers to distinguish their products are claimed as trademarks. Where those designations appear in this book, and the publisher was aware of a trademark claim, the designations have been printed with initial capital letters or in all capitals.

The authors and publisher have taken care in the preparation of this book, but make no expressed or implied warranty of any kind and assume no responsibility for errors or omissions. No liability is assumed for incidental or consequential damages in connection with or arising out of the use of the information or programs contained herein.

The publisher offers excellent discounts on this book when ordered in quantity for bulk purchases or special sales, which may include electronic versions and/or custom covers and content particular to your business, training goals, marketing focus, and branding interests. For more information, please contact:

U.S. Corporate and Government Sales
(800) 382-3419
corpsales@pearsontechgroup.com

For sales outside the United States please contact:

International Sales
international@pearson.com

Visit us on the Web: informit.com/aw

Library of Congress Cataloging-in-Publication Data

Rozanski, Nick.
    Software systems architecture : working with stakeholders using viewpoints and perspectives / Nick Rozanski, Eoin Woods. 2nd ed.
        p. cm.
    Includes bibliographical references and index.
    ISBN 0-321-71833-X (hard cover : alk. paper)
1. Computer software Development. 2. Computer architecture. I. Woods, Eoin. II. Title.

    QA76.76.D47R696 2012
    005.3 dc23   2011040253

ISBN-13: 978-0-321-71833-4
ISBN-10: 0-321-71833-X
Text printed in the United States on recycled paper at Courier in Westford, Massachusetts.
First printing, October 2011

To my family, Isabel, Sophie, Alex, and Luci
—NR

*To my parents, Anne and Desmond,
and to my family, Lynda and Katherine*
—EW

CONTENTS

PREFACE TO THE SECOND EDITION

The IT landscape looks significantly different today from when we first started work on our book ten years ago. The world is a much more connected place, with computers and the Internet being a big part of many people's daily lives both at home and at work. This has led to an even greater expectation among users and other stakeholders that systems should be functionally rich and complete, easy to use, robust, scalable, and secure. We feel that the architect has an important role in achieving these goals and are heartened by the fact that this view seems to have gained fairly widespread acceptance among software development professionals and senior business and technology management.

We were delighted by the positive reception to the first edition of our book from practitioners, aspiring software architects, and academia. Our readers seemed to find it useful, comprehensive, and informative. However, architecture is a constantly changing discipline, and the second edition reflects what we have learned and improved upon in our own practice since the publication of the first edition. It also incorporates a number of very useful comments and suggestions for improvement from readers, for which we are extremely grateful.

However, our fundamental messages remain the same. Our primary focus is on architecture as a service to stakeholders and a way to ensure that an information system meets their needs. We continue to emphasize the vital importance of views as a way of representing an architecture's complexity in a way its stakeholders can understand. We are also unswerving in our belief that architecture must define how a system will provide the required quality properties—such as scalability, resilience, and security—as well as defining its static and dynamic structure, and that perspectives provide an effective way to do this.

Our main audience is practicing or aspiring architects, but we hope that other IT professionals, who may be working alongside an architect, and students, who will one day find themselves in this position, will also find it a useful read.

The most important changes in this edition are as follows.

- We have introduced a new viewpoint, which we call the Context viewpoint. This describes the relationships, dependencies, and interactions between the system and its environment (the people, systems, and external entities with which it interacts). It extends, formalizes, and standardizes the relatively brief discussion of scope and context that used to be in Chapter 8.

- We have expanded the discussion of different aspects of the role of architecture in Part II.

- We have revised most of the viewpoint and perspective definitions, particularly the Functional and Concurrency views and the Performance and Scalability perspective.

- We have revised and extended the Bibliography and the Further Reading sections in most chapters.

- We have updated the book to align with the concepts and terminology in the new international architecture standard ISO 42010 (which derives from IEEE Standard 1471).

- We have updated our UML modeling advice and examples to reflect the changes introduced in version 2 of UML.

We hope that you find the second edition of the book a useful improvement and extension of the first edition, and we invite you to visit to our Web site at www.viewpoints-and-perspectives.info for further software architecture resources or to contact us to provide feedback on the book.

ACKNOWLEDGMENTS FOR THE SECOND EDITION

In addition to the people we thanked for the first edition, we would also like to thank our second-edition reviewers—Paul Clements, Tim Cull, Rich Hilliard, Philippe Kruchten, and Tommi Mikkonen—and our diligent and thorough copy editor, Barbara Wood. In particular, we would like to thank Paul for his thorough, insightful, and challenging comments and suggestions for improvement, which we found extremely useful.

PREFACE TO THE FIRST EDITION

The authors of this book are both practicing software architects who have worked in this role, together and separately, on information system development projects for quite a few years. During that time, we have seen a significant increase in the visibility of software architects and in the importance with which our role has been viewed by colleagues, management, and customers. No large software development project nowadays would expect to go ahead without an architect—or a small architectural group—in the vanguard of the development team.

While there may be an emerging consensus that the software architect's role is an important one, there seems to be little agreement on what the job actually involves. Who are our clients? To whom are we accountable? What are we expected to deliver? What is our involvement once the architectural design has been completed? And, perhaps most fundamentally, where are the boundaries between requirements, architecture, and design?

The absence of a clear definition of the role is all the more problematic because of the seriousness of the problems that today's software projects (and specifically, their architects) have to resolve.

- The expectations of users and other stakeholders in terms of functionality, capability, time to market, and flexibility have become much more demanding.

- Long system development times result in continual scope changes and consequent changes to the system's architecture and design.

- Today's systems are more functionally and structurally complex than ever and are usually constructed from a mix of off-the-shelf and custom-built components.

- Few systems exist in isolation; most are expected to interoperate and exchange information with many other systems.

- Getting the functional structure—the design—of the system right is only part of the problem. How the system behaves (i.e., its quality properties) is just as critical to its effectiveness as what it does.

- Technology continues to change at a pace that makes it very hard for architects to keep their technical expertise up-to-date.

When we first started to take on the role of software architects, we looked for some sort of software architecture handbook that would walk us through the process of developing an architectural design. After all, other architectural disciplines have behind them centuries of theory and established best practice.

For example, in the first century A.D., the Roman Marcus Vitruvius Pollio wrote the first ever architectural handbook, *De architectura libri decem* ("Ten Books on Architecture"), describing the building architect's role and required skills and providing a wealth of material on standard architectural structures. In 1670, Anthony Deane, a friend of diarist Samuel Pepys, a former mayor of the English town of Harwich, and later a member of Parliament, published a groundbreaking textbook, *A Doctrine of Naval Architecture*, which described in detail some of the leading methods of the time for large ship design. Deane's ideas and principles helped systematize the practice of naval architecture for many years. And in 1901, George E. Davis, a consulting engineer in the British chemical industry, created a new field of engineering when he published his text *A Handbook of Chemical Engineering*. This text was the first book to define the practical principles underpinning industrial chemical processes and guided the field for many years afterward.

The existence of such best practices has a very important consequence in terms of uniformity of approach. If you were to give several architects and engineers a commission to design a building, a cruise liner, or a chemical plant, the designs they produced would probably differ. However, the processes they used, the ways they represented their designs on paper (or a computer screen), and the techniques they used to ensure the soundness of their designs would be very similar.

Sadly, our profession has yet to build any significant legacy of mainstream industrial best practices. When we looked, we found a dearth of introductory books to guide practicing information systems architects in the details of doing their jobs.

Admittedly, we have an abundance of books on specific technologies, whether it's J2EE, CORBA, or .NET, and some on broader topics such as Web services or object orientation (although, because of the speed at which software technology changes, many of these become out-of-date within a few years). There are also a number of good general software architecture books, several of which we refer to in later chapters. But many of these books aim to lay down principles that apply across all sorts of systems and so are written in quite general terms, while most of the more specific texts are aimed at our colleagues in the real-time and embedded-systems communities.

We feel that if you are a new software architect for an information system, the books that actually tell you how to do your job, learn the important things you need to know, and make your architectural designs successful are few and far between. While we don't presume to replace the existing texts on software architecture or place ourselves alongside the likes of Vitruvius, Deane, and Davis, addressing these needs was the driving force behind our decision to write this book.

Specifically, the book shows you:

- What software architecture is about and why your role is vitally important to successful project delivery
- How to determine who is interested in your architecture (your *stakeholders*), understand what is important to them (their *concerns*), and design an *architecture* that reflects and balances their different needs
- How to communicate your architecture to your stakeholders in an understandable way that demonstrates that you have met their concerns (the *architectural description*)
- How to focus on what is *architecturally significant*, safely leaving other aspects of the design to your designers, without neglecting issues like performance, resilience, and location
- What important activities you most need to undertake as an architect, such as identifying and engaging stakeholders, using scenarios, creating models, and documenting and validating your architecture

Throughout the book we primarily focus on the development of large-scale information systems (by which we mean the computer systems used to automate the business operations of large organizations). However, we have tried to present our material in a way that is independent of the type of information system you are designing, the technologies the developers will be using, and the software development lifecycle your project is following. We have standardized on a few things, such as the use of Unified Modeling Language (UML) in most of our diagrams, but we've done that only because UML is the most widely understood modeling language around. You don't have to be a UML expert to understand this book.

We didn't set out to be the definitive guide to developing the architecture of your information system—such a book would probably never be finished and would require the collaboration of a huge number of experts across a wide range of technical specializations. Also, we did not write a book of prescriptive methods. Although we present some activity diagrams that explain how to produce your deliverables, these are designed to be compatible with the wide range of software development approaches in use today.

What we hope we have achieved is the creation of a practical, practitioner-oriented guide that explains how to design successful architectures for information systems and how to see these through to their successful implementation. This is the sort of book that we wish had been available when we started out as software architects, and one that we expect to refer to even now.

You can find further useful software architecture resources, and contact us to provide feedback on the book's content, via our Web page: www.viewpoints-and-perspectives.info. We look forward to hearing from you.

ACKNOWLEDGMENTS

This book would never have appeared without the advice, assistance, and support of a lot of people.

We are very grateful to the many reviewers who commented on the text at various stages of its creation, including Gary Birch, Chris Britton, Kelley Butler, Sholom Cohen, Dan Haywood, Sallie Henry, Andy Longshaw, Robert Nord, Dan Paulish, Martyn Thomas, and Hans van Vliet.

We'd also like to thank the team members at Addison-Wesley for all of their work to make the book a reality, including Kim Boedigheimer, John Fuller, Peter Gordon, Chrysta Meadowbrooke, Simon Plumtree, and Elizabeth Ryan.

Other people who provided us with advice, encouragement, and inspiration at various times include Felix Bachmann, Dave Borthwick, David Emery, Wolfgang Emmerich, Rich Hilliard, Philippe Kruchten, Roland Leibundgut, Mike Mackay, Dave Maher, Mark Maier, Lucia Rapanotti, and Gaynor Redvers-Mutton.

We would also like to thank our families for their constant love, encouragement, and support throughout the project.

1

INTRODUCTION

Today's large-scale software systems are among the most complex structures ever built by humans, containing millions of lines of code, thousands of database tables, and hundreds of components, all running on dozens of computers. This presents some formidable challenges to software development teams—and if these challenges aren't addressed early, systems are delivered late, over budget, or with an unacceptably poor level of quality.

Most projects nowadays recognize the importance of appointing a software architect, or in some cases a group of software architects, to provide technology guidance and leadership to the rest of the team. However, as an industry, there is no generally accepted definition of what software architects do, how they do it, or what they are expected to deliver.

STAKEHOLDERS, VIEWPOINTS, AND PERSPECTIVES

This book is intended as a practical guide for software architects, whether you are experienced or just starting your career. It focuses on three fundamental concepts: stakeholders, viewpoints, and perspectives. To understand why these concepts are important to you, let's look at an example of how the practice of software architecture often unfolds.

EXAMPLE Sally is a software architect who works for a large commercial organization. As one of the most senior members of the IT staff, Sally gets involved in a lot of different activities, but her key role is leading the definition and design of the organization's information systems. One of these systems is taking most of her time and attention at present.

It all starts simply enough: Sally is asked to start looking at options for replacing the current stock management system (which is batch-based and fairly elderly) with a more modern system that would better support the changing needs of the business. In particular, the business wants the system to be more interactive and to allow employees to process stock movements in real time rather than entering data and seeing the results the next day. The time lag imposed by the current system is a real competitive disadvantage and also leads to mistakes because of the lack of immediate feedback.

At first glance, the problem doesn't seem too complicated. Sally talks to a few people around the organization about the new system's requirements, and soon she has some idea of how to get started. Interviewing the business analysts and some of the main users at the head office suggests some key requirements, which seem fairly straightforward. Sally starts to sketch possible solutions.

However, as she discusses her ideas around the company, Sally meets some people with very different ideas about the key requirements for the system. The users at the distribution depots claim to need totally different information from what the staff members at the head office need. Back at the head office, the commercial managers say it is crucial that they have real-time summary reporting throughout the day. However, this would slow the main transaction flow significantly, which isn't acceptable to the people in the logistics group that is actually paying for the system.

Sally also interviews people outside the immediate business area, and they all have opinions too. The IT operations group members are worried about adopting new technology and don't think they can administer the application server that Sally is planning to use. The IT auditors inform her that they need a two-year archive of all stock release authorizations in case of possible fraud. Leaving aside the difficulty of collecting it, that's a lot of stock movement data to keep in the system.

Sally is struggling to reconcile the conflicting requirements of many of the people she has interviewed. She is also worried that she may have left out someone important or failed to address a key requirement.

The architect in our example is working with a number of different people, each with different interests in and concerns about the new system. Traditionally, software developers have concentrated on the needs of end users and sometimes developers, but as our example illustrates, this is far too narrow a view if you want to create a system that satisfies everyone affected by it.

We call the people affected by our system its stakeholders. Because stakeholder needs are why the system is being created in the first place, meeting these needs is your chief goal as an architect. To do this, you need to clearly identify your stakeholders, work with them to understand their concerns, balance their inevitably conflicting priorities, and design an architecture that addresses their requirements as effectively as possible.

We talk about stakeholders throughout the book. We explore the concept in Part I, explain how to work effectively with them in Part II, and show you how to create architectures that meet their needs in Parts III and IV. For now, let us continue with our example.

Sally has done some work to understand and involve her stakeholders, and although she may not feel she can meet all of their concerns, at least she now feels that she has a good understanding of what those concerns are.

Based on her understanding of the important stakeholder needs, Sally starts her architectural design in earnest. She sketches the functional structure of the system, identifying the key components and planning how they will work together to provide the required functionality. While she's thinking about this, she starts grouping components into processes and working out where these processes will run in the data center. In order to meet the concerns of the operations group, Sally adds some system management components to her design that should make it more manageable. She realizes she needs to think about the data in the system, so she adds the main data stores and annotates the data flows between the key components. This sidetracks her for a while, as it's quite involved, but within a couple of weeks Sally has a detailed architecture model to show people.

She's pretty unhappy about the responses she gets from the people who received her document. Most of them don't reply at all, and those who do seem to be concerned about minor details of the system or even the way she formatted the document. Sally heads off to talk to some of the end users, developers, and IT operations staff who reviewed the architecture in order to find out why they didn't provide better feedback.

The result of her stakeholder chats is a bit demoralizing—no one seems to have grasped the most important features of her model. The developers are distracted by the operational components such as servers and disk arrays, and they worry about the way the application will be deployed to the data center, which isn't their primary responsibility. The IT operations people are pleased to see their system management software in the model, but they keep asking questions about data stores and data flows, when it seems quite obvious to Sally that this is not their concern. The end users don't really understand anything and keep asking,

"But what will it do?" Sally feels this is pretty unfair because she has taken great pains to make sure that everything the system could do is documented somewhere.

In spite of producing a detailed architectural design, Sally doesn't seem to have helped anyone understand her system. It isn't clear to her how she can reorganize it in order to get her messages across more clearly.

Sally is facing a problem familiar to many architects: How can you describe something as multifaceted as the architecture of a complex system to the different people who need to understand it? Indeed, this has been a problem for software engineers since the early days of computing.

If you read the more recent literature on software architecture, one of the first useful discoveries you will make is the concept of an architectural view. An architectural view is a description of *one aspect* of a system's architecture and is an application of the timeless problem-solving principle of "divide and conquer." By considering a system's architecture through a number of distinct views, you can understand, define, and communicate a complex architecture in a selective fashion and thus avoid overwhelming your readers with its overall complexity. Examples of architectural views include the system's functional structure, information organization, and the deployment environment.

Although describing an architecture using views helps partition the architectural description and make it easier to understand, it still leaves you with the problem of deciding which views to use and how to create each one. Again, many of us have faced this problem in the past. A proven solution is to use template views, called architectural viewpoints, to guide the process of developing the views that describe your architecture.

Using viewpoints and views to guide the architecture definition process is a core theme of this book. We introduce, explain, and contextualize them in Part I, while Part III contains a complete set of viewpoint definitions you can use directly on your own architecture projects. For now, let's see how Sally uses viewpoints in our example.

Sally decides to use a set of viewpoints to create a view-based architectural description. Because she is working to tight deadlines, she focuses her attention on the system's functionality, the important information flows, and its deployment environment. This results in an effective representation of an architecture that seems to meet the majority of the needs that her discussions with stakeholders have revealed. Her ideas are approved, and development of the first version of the system begins. The software development goes fairly well, but some new complications emerge.

Having looked at the integration test logs and talked to some of the system testers, Sally starts to worry about system performance. She didn't think much about performance earlier because no one seemed to be concerned about it, but the performance she is seeing, even with test data volumes, seems pretty poor to her.

At the same time, some of the security and audit group members are raising concerns about system security. Again, they didn't mention this when Sally was gathering requirements, but now that the system is starting to take shape, they're talking about protecting parts of the system from different users and asking how they can be sure that the system databases aren't updated by support staff without authorization. This is even more troublesome because, although Sally feels pretty confident about sorting out performance problems, she's far less sure about security.

Finally, the corporate business continuity group recently sent out a stern e-mail reminding everyone of the need for all systems to be recoverable to a physically remote disaster recovery site within eight hours of a major failure. Sally wasn't aware that this group worked with IT at all; the mainframe applications that she normally deals with inherit their disaster recovery facilities automatically from the mainframe environment, and she hasn't needed to worry about this before.

Although it looks as if the system will provide the functionality that people requested, Sally is concerned that they will still be unhappy with it because it won't be quick enough, won't address their security concerns, or won't be available after any major systems failure.

Having recognized these problems, Sally isn't sure what to do about them. She knows about performance and availability, but she's not clear about how to increase the system's level of security. Leaving aside her technical knowledge, Sally doesn't know how to redesign her system in a way that balances these different concerns—concerns that no one mentioned when she was capturing requirements.

The architect in our example has realized that *what* a system does is only part of the story and that *how* the system provides its services often has a huge impact on the perceptions that stakeholders have of it. The architecture you choose for your system dictates how quickly it runs, how secure it is, how available it is, how easy it is to modify, and many other nonfunctional factors, which we collectively term *quality properties*. Designing a system that exhibits acceptable quality properties is a crucial part of your role as an architect.

Achieving your quality goals is a cross-structural aspect of the architecture definition process (in fact, quality properties are also often known as *cross-cutting concerns*) and is likely to impact all of the different structures that make up your architecture. This means that achieving your quality goals is likely to affect all of the views in your architectural description.

We have found that the conventional view and viewpoint approach works very well for the definition of architectural structures but is less helpful when considering quality properties. We need a better way to ensure that our architecture exhibits the quality properties required of it and to organize our architectural knowledge about quality properties. In order to do this, we have defined a new concept. The *architectural perspective* is analogous to a viewpoint, but rather than addressing a type of architectural structure, a perspective addresses a particular quality property (such as performance, security, or availability).

Applying perspectives to views to ensure that they exhibit the required quality properties is another important theme of this book. We provide an overview of perspectives in Part I, while Part IV contains a complete set of perspective definitions you can use directly on your own architecture projects in order to avoid the kinds of problems that troubled the architect in our example.

Recapping, the core themes of this book are stakeholders, viewpoints, and perspectives.

- *Stakeholders* are the people for whom we build systems. A key part of your role as an architect is knowing how to work with stakeholders in order to create an architecture that meets their complex, overlapping, and often conflicting needs.

- *Viewpoints* (and views) are an approach to structuring the architecture definition process and the architectural description, based on the principle of separation of concerns. Viewpoints contain proven architectural knowledge to guide the creation of an architecture, described in a particular set of views (each view being the result of applying the guidance in a particular viewpoint).

- *Perspectives* are a complementary concept to viewpoints that we introduce in this book. Perspectives contain proven architectural knowledge and help structure the architecture definition process by separating concerns but focusing on cross-structural quality properties rather than architectural structures.

In this book we introduce, explain, and explore these three concepts and define an approach for creating effective architectures for your information systems. Of course, the approach we present is a simplification; architecture definition isn't a linear flow that can be easily written down but is in reality an incremental process involving an iterative cycle of information capture, model development, review, and refinement. What we present here is a practical, proven framework for tackling the architecture definition process and handling the challenges that make software architecture such a fascinating job.

THE STRUCTURE OF THIS BOOK

The book is divided into five parts.

- Part I provides an introduction to and review of the basic concepts we use throughout the book (e.g., stakeholder, architectural description, viewpoint, view, and perspective) and describes the role of the software architect.
- Part II describes the most important activities you need to undertake as an architect, such as agreeing on a project's scope, identifying and engaging stakeholders, using scenarios and patterns, creating models, and documenting and validating your architecture.
- Part III is a catalog of the seven most important viewpoints you will need when creating your architectural description: the Context, Functional, Information, Concurrency, Development, Deployment, and Operational viewpoints.
- Part IV is a catalog of the most important perspectives for information systems, including Security, Performance and Scalability, Availability and Resilience, Evolution, Location, Development Resource, Internationalization, and a number of others.
- Part V pulls these concepts together and explains how you can start to put our ideas into practice.

WHO SHOULD READ THIS BOOK

This book will clearly be of interest to you if you are a software architect or would like to become one. It presents a number of concepts with which you will be familiar and others that may be new to you. We hope it will help explain and clarify your role, establish your boundaries, and improve the way you do your job. For experienced architects, the reference material in Parts III and IV is likely to be particularly helpful for day-to-day use.

Parts of the book may interest some architectural stakeholders too. Sponsors and senior management on system development projects who work with architects on the demand side of the relationship will want to read Part I, the introductory chapters of Parts III and IV (about viewpoints and perspectives, respectively), and Part V. The same applies to users.

Software developers (particularly designers) and support and maintenance staff may also find much helpful material in this book and will probably want to focus on Parts III and IV in more detail in order to better understand the aspects of the architecture definition process that interest them.

CONVENTIONS USED

To help make the text easy to read and refer back to, some standard features appear throughout the book.

- We provide clear *definitions* of all of the important terms we use—either a reiteration of the accepted definition where its use is widespread or our own definition where the term (or our use of it) is new.
- We define a number of *principles* that underpin the theoretical aspects of the book. A principle is a fundamental statement of belief, approach, or intent that forms a basis for developing our ideas.
- We present *strategies* and *checklists* that will help you successfully apply our principles in your day-to-day work as an architect.
- We include a number of *examples* to illustrate the text. These are, for the most part, based on real projects with which one or the other of us has been involved in the past (with names changed to protect the innocent).
- We *summarize* the most important points at the end of most chapters in Parts I and II.
- We provide *checklists* at the end of the chapters in Parts III and IV to help you apply our guidance effectively and make sure that you don't miss anything important.
- We provide lists of *further reading* at the end of most chapters in the book.

PART I

ARCHITECTURE FUNDAMENTALS

2

SOFTWARE ARCHITECTURE CONCEPTS

One of the problems when we talk about architecture for software systems is that the terminology has been loosely borrowed from other disciplines (such as building architecture or naval architecture) and is widely used, inconsistently, in a variety of situations. For example, the term *architecture* is used to refer to the internal structure of microprocessors, the internal structure of machines, the organization of networks, the structure of software programs, and many other things.

This chapter defines and reviews some of the core concepts that underpin the discussion in the remainder of the book: *software architecture*, *architectural elements*, *stakeholders*, and *architectural descriptions*.

SOFTWARE ARCHITECTURE

Computers can be found everywhere in modern society—not just in data centers or on desks but also in cars, washing machines, cell phones, and credit cards. Whether they are big or small, simple or complex, all computer systems are made up of the same three fundamental parts: software (e.g., programs or libraries); data, which may be either transient (in memory) or persistent (on disk or ROM); and hardware (e.g., processors, memory, disks, network cards).

 DEFINITION When we refer to a computer **system**, we mean the software elements that you need to specify and/or design in order to meet a particular set of requirements and the hardware that you need to run those software elements on.

When you try to understand a system, you are interested in what its individual parts actually do, how they work together, and how they interact with the world around them—in other words, its *architecture*. A widely accepted definition of software architecture can be found in the recent international standard ISO/IEC 42010, "Systems and Software Engineering—Architecture Description" [ISO11].

 DEFINITION The **architecture** of a system is the set of fundamental concepts or properties of the system in its environment, embodied in its elements, relationships, and the principles of its design and evolution.

Let's look at three key parts of this definition in a bit more detail, namely, a system's *elements and relationships*, its *fundamental properties*, *and the principles of its design and evolution*.

System Elements and Relationships

Any system is composed of a number of pieces, which may be called things like module, component, partition, or subsystem. We deliberately avoid using any of these terms because they all have connotations suggesting certain types of implementation or deployment technology. We prefer to follow the lead of the ISO standard and a number of others and use the less familiar but semantically neutral term *elements* to refer to the pieces that constitute a system. We'll define the term *architectural element* more formally later in this chapter, but at this stage let's just agree that elements are the architecturally significant pieces of a system.

The elements that constitute a system and the relationships between them define the structure of the system that contains them. There are two types of structures that are of interest to the software architect: *static structure* (organization of design-time elements) and *dynamic structure* (organization of runtime elements).

1. The *static structures* of a system tell you what the design-time form of a system is—that is, what its elements are and how they combine to provide the features required of the system.

 DEFINITION The **static structures** of a system define its internal design-time elements and their arrangement.

Internal design-time software elements might be programs, object-oriented classes or packages, database stored procedures, services, or any other self-contained code unit. Internal data elements include classes, relational database entities/tables, and data files. Internal hardware elements include computers or their constituent parts such as disk or CPU and networking elements such as cables, routers, or hubs.

The static arrangement of these elements defines—depending on the context—the associations, relationships, or connectivity between these elements. For software modules, for example, there may be static relationships such as a hierarchy of elements (module *A* is built from modules *B* and *C*) or dependencies between elements (module *A* relies on the services of module *B*). For classes, relational entities, or other data elements, relationships define how one data item is linked to another one. For hardware, the relationships define the required physical interconnections between the various hardware elements of the system.

2. The system's *dynamic structures* show how the system actually works—that is, what happens at runtime and what the system does in response to external (or internal) stimulus.

DEFINITION The **dynamic structures** of a system define its runtime elements and their interactions.

These internal interactions may be flows of information between elements (element *A* sends messages to element *B*) or the parallel or sequential execution of internal tasks (element *X* invokes a routine on element *Y*), or they may be expressed in terms of the effect they have on data (data item *D* is created, updated many times, and finally destroyed).

Of course, a system's static and dynamic structures are closely related to one another. For example, without static structure elements such as programs or databases, there would not be any dynamic structure elements for information to flow between. However, the two types of structures are not the same. Consider a simple client/server system with one client-facing element that handles all interactions with users. This would appear once as a static structure element but would appear many times (once per active user) in a dynamic structure model. The dynamic structure model would also have to explain what caused the instances of the client element to become active or inactive (e.g., a user logging in and logging off again).

Fundamental System Properties

The fundamental properties of a system manifest themselves in two different ways: *externally visible behavior* (what the system does) and *quality properties* (how the system does it).

1. *Externally visible behavior* tells you what a system does from the standpoint of an external observer.

DEFINITION The **externally visible behavior** of a system defines the functional interactions between the system and its environment.

These external interactions form a set similar to the ones we considered for dynamic structure. This includes flows of information in and out of the system, the way that the system responds to external stimuli, and the published "contract" or API that the architecture has with the outside world.

External behavior may be modeled by treating the system as a black box so that you don't know anything about its internals (if you make request P to a system built in compliance with the architecture, you are returned response Q). Alternatively, it may consider changes to internal system state in response to external stimuli (submitting a request R causes the creation of an internal data item D).

2. *Quality properties* tell you how a system behaves from the viewpoint of an external observer (often referred to as its nonfunctional characteristics).

DEFINITION A **quality property** is an externally visible, nonfunctional property of a system such as performance, security, or scalability.

There is a whole range of quality properties that may be of interest: How does the system perform under load? What is the peak throughput given certain hardware? How is the information in the system protected from malicious use? How often is it likely to break? How easy is it to manage, maintain, and enhance? How easily can it be used by people who are disabled? Which of these characteristics are relevant depends on your circumstances and on the concerns and priorities of your stakeholders.

Principles of Design and Evolution

One of the things that is immediately obvious about a well-structured and maintainable system is that its implementation is consistent and respects a system-wide set of structuring conventions. This allows the system to be more easily understood and encourages extensions to the system to be made in a consistent and logical way, fitting into the overall form of the system without introducing unnecessary complexity.

One of the things that is necessary in order to achieve this internal implementation consistency is a clear set of *principles* to guide the system's design and evolution.

According to the *Oxford English Dictionary*, the general definition of a principle is a *fundamental truth or proposition serving as the foundation for belief or action*. In the context of architectural design, we extend this definition slightly and define an architectural principle to be a *fundamental statement of belief, approach, or intent that guides the definition of your architecture*.

Defining and following architectural principles is a powerful way of establishing a decision-making framework for a consistent, well-structured architecture. Principles expose underlying assumptions and bring them out into the cold light of day—in other words, they make the implicit explicit. They are a great way to kick off an architecture project, especially when motivation or scope is unclear. They are also useful if you suspect that there are significant but unrecognized conflicts or contradictions in the requirements of a proposed architecture. We'll have quite a lot more to say about design principles in Chapter 8.

System Properties and Internal Organization

Let's explore the idea of system properties and how they are related to the internal organization of a system by means of a simple example.

EXAMPLE An airline reservation system supports a number of different transactions to book airline seats, update or cancel them, transfer them, upgrade them, and so forth. Figure 2–1 shows the context for this system. (We have used a simplified use case notation here: The rectangle represents the system, the "stick man" represents customers who interact with the system, and the notation boxes provide additional supporting information.)

The *externally visible behavior* of the system (what it does) is its response to the transactions that can be submitted by customers, such as booking a seat, updating a reservation, or canceling a booking. The *quality properties* of the system (how it does it) include the average response time for a transaction under a specified load; the maximum throughput the system can support; system availability; and the time, skills, and cost required to repair defects.

Faced with these requirements, there are a number of ways that an architect could design a system for it. Over the next few pages we outline two possible architectural approaches for this system.

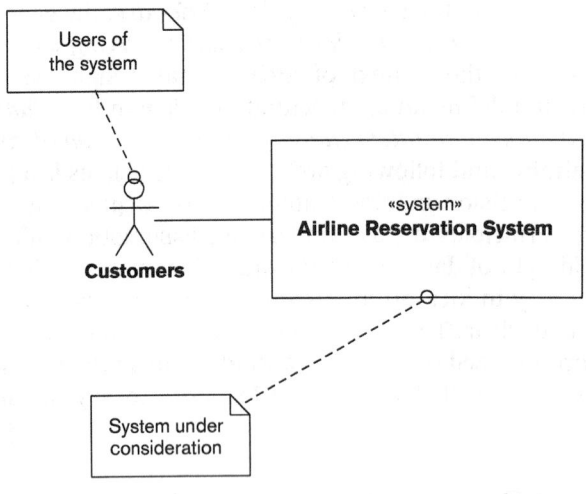

FIGURE 2–1 CONTEXT DIAGRAM FOR AN AIRLINE BOOKING SYSTEM

The architect could design a solution for the airline reservation system based around a *two-tier client/server* approach. (In fact, this is an example of the use of an *architectural style*, as we will see in Part II.) In this approach, shown in Figure 2–2, a number of clients (which present information to customers and accept their input) communicate with a central server (which stores the data in a relational database) via a wide-area network (WAN). An established architectural style like two-tier client/server has widely known benefits and pitfalls, so starting like this with a well-understood approach helps to avoid introducing unnecessary risk to the design.

As the diagram illustrates, the *static structure* (design-time organization) for this client/server architecture consists of the client programs (which in this example are further broken down into presentation, business logic, database, and network layers), the server, and the connections between them. A related architectural diagram would show that the *dynamic structure* (runtime organization) is based on a request/response model: Requests are submitted by a client to the server over the WAN, and responses are returned by the server to the client. The static elements of the architecture provide the mechanisms whereby the dynamic interactions can occur (for example, the client programs submit requests on behalf of the users and receive and display the results).

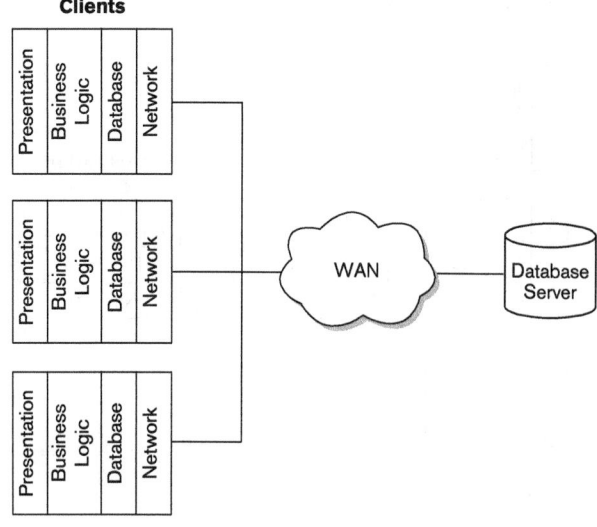

FIGURE 2-2 Two-Tier Client/Server Architecture for An airline Booking System

Alternatively, the architect could take a three-tier client/server approach, where only the presentation processing is performed on the clients, with the business logic and database access performed in an application server, as shown in Figure 2–3.

The *static structure* for this architecture consists of the client programs (which in this example are further broken down into presentation and network layers), the application server (here, business logic, database, and network layers), the database server, and the connections between them. The *dynamic structure* is based on a three-tier request/response model: Requests are submitted by a client to the application server over the WAN, the application server submits requests to the database server if necessary, and responses are returned by the application server to the client.

The architect might identify the two-tier approach as appropriate for the architecture because of its relative operational simplicity, because it can be developed quickly by the organization's software developers, because it can be delivered at lower cost than other options, or for a range of other reasons.

FIGURE 2-3 THREE-TIER CLIENT/SERVER ARCHITECTURE FOR AN AIRLINE BOOKING SYSTEM

Alternatively, the architect may consider the three-tier approach to be right for the architecture because it provides better options for scalability as workload increases, because less powerful client hardware is needed, because it may offer better security, or for other reasons.

Whichever approach the architect considers to be more appropriate, she chooses it because it provides the best match between the system properties promised by the approach and the requirements of the system.

In this example, there are two possible solutions to the problem, based around a two-tier approach and a three-tier approach, respectively. We call these *candidate architectures*.

DEFINITION A **candidate architecture** for a system is a particular arrangement of static and dynamic structures that has the potential to exhibit the system's required externally visible behaviors and quality properties.

Although the candidate architectures have different static and dynamic structures, each must be able to meet the system's overall requirements to process airline bookings in a timely and efficient manner. However, although all candidate architectures are believed to share the same important externally visible behaviors (in this case, responses to booking transactions) and general quality properties (such as acceptable response time, throughput, availability, and time to repair), they are likely to differ in the specific set of quality properties that each exhibits (such as one being easier to maintain but more expensive to build than another).

In each case, the extent to which the candidate actually exhibits these behaviors and properties must be determined by further analysis of its static and dynamic structures. For example, the two-tier candidate architecture might meet the functional requirements better because it supports functionally richer clients; the three-tier candidate architecture might deliver better throughput and response time because it is more loosely coupled.

It is part of the architect's role to derive the static and dynamic structures for each of the candidate architectures, understand the extent to which they exhibit the required behaviors and quality properties, and select the best one. Of course, what is meant by "best" may not always be clear; we will return to this issue in Part II.

We can capture the relationship between the externally visible properties of a system and its internal structure and organization as follows.

- The externally visible behavior of a system (what it does) is determined by the combined functional behavior of its internal elements.
- The quality properties of a system (how it does it) such as performance, scalability, and resilience arise from the quality properties of its internal elements. (Typically, a system's overall quality property is only as good as the property of its worst-behaving or weakest internal element.)

Of course, it's not really as simple as that! For example, a server that cannot scale to process the workload submitted to it may also become functionally constrained (for example, users may not be able to log in to it or execute some resource-heavy functions). However, we still find that this rather simplistic distinction is a useful one that has informed much of our thinking.

The Importance of Software Architecture

Every computer system, large or small, is made up of pieces that are linked together. There may be a small number of these pieces, or perhaps only one, or there may be dozens or hundreds; and this linkage may be trivial, or very complicated, or somewhere in between.

Furthermore, every system is made up of pieces that interact with each other and the outside world in a deterministic (predictable) way. Again, the behavior may be simple and easily understood, or it may be so convoluted that no one person can understand every aspect of it. However, this behavior is still there and still (in theory at least) describable.

In other words, every system has an architecture, in the same way that every building, bridge, and battleship has an architecture—and every human body has a physiology.

This is such an important concept that we will state it formally as a principle here.

PRINCIPLE Every system has an architecture, whether or not it is documented and understood.

The architecture of a system is an intrinsic, fundamental property that is present whether or not it has been documented and is understood. Every system has precisely one architecture—although, as we will see, it can be represented in a number of ways.

ARCHITECTURAL ELEMENTS

As explained previously, we standardize the term *architectural element* to refer to the pieces from which systems are built.

DEFINITION An **architectural element** (or just element) is a fundamental piece from which a system can be considered to be constructed.

The nature of an architectural element depends very much on the type of system you are considering and the context within which you are considering its elements. Programming libraries, subsystems, deployable software units (e.g., Enterprise Java Beans or .NET assemblies), reusable software products (e.g., database management systems), or entire applications may form architectural elements in an information system, depending on the system being built.

An architectural element should possess the following key attributes:

- A clearly defined set of *responsibilities*
- A clearly defined *boundary*
- A set of clearly defined *interfaces*, which define the *services* that the element provides to the other architectural elements

Architectural elements are often known informally as *components* or *modules*, but these terms are already widely used with established specific meaning. In particular, the term *component* tends to suggest the use of a programming-level component model (such as J2EE or .NET), while *module* tends to suggest a programming language construct. Although these are valid architectural elements in some contexts, they won't be the type of fundamental system element used in others.

For this reason, we deliberately don't use these terms from now on. Instead, we use the term *element* throughout the book to avoid confusion (following the lead of others, including ISO 42010 and Bass, Clements, and Kazman [BASS03]—see the Further Reading section at the end of this chapter for more details).

STAKEHOLDERS

Traditional software development has been driven by the need of the delivered software to meet the requirements of users. Although the definition of the term *user* varies, all software development methods are based around this principle in one way or another.

However, the people affected by a software system are not limited to those who use it. Software systems are not just used: They have to be *built* and *tested*, they have to be *operated*, they may have to be *repaired*, they are usually *enhanced*, and of course they have to be *paid for*. Each of these activities involves a number—possibly a significant number—of people in addition to the users. Each of these groups of people has its own requirements, interests, and needs to be met by the software system.

We refer collectively to these people as *stakeholders*. Understanding the role of the stakeholder is fundamental to understanding the role of the architect in the development of a software product or system. We define a stakeholder as follows.

DEFINITION A **stakeholder** in the architecture of a system is an individual, team, organization, or classes thereof, having an interest in the realization of the system.

The definition is based on the one from ISO Standard 42010, which we discuss in more depth in Part II. For now, let's look at a couple of key concepts from this definition.

Individual, Team, or Organization

First of all, consider the phrase "individual, team, or organization." As we shall see in this book, those with an interest in the architecture of a system stretch far more widely than just its developers, or even its developers and users. A much broader community than this is affected by the realization of the architecture as a system, such as those who have to support it, deploy it, or pay for it.

Specifying the architecture is a key opportunity for the stakeholders to direct its shape and direction. You will find, however, that some stakeholders are more interested in their roles than others, for a variety of reasons that have little to do with architecture. Part of your role, therefore, is to engage and galvanize, to persuade people of the importance of their involvement, and to obtain their commitment to the task.

As the definition notes, a stakeholder often represents a class of individual, such as user or developer, rather than a specific person. This presents some problems because it may not be possible to capture and reconcile the needs of all members of the class (all users, all developers) in the time available. Furthermore, you may not have the stakeholders at hand (e.g., when developing a new product). In either case, you need to select some representative stakeholders who will speak for the group. We'll come back to this in Part II.

Interests and Concerns

Now consider the phrase "having an interest in the realization of the system." This criterion is—deliberately—a broad one, and its interpretation is entirely specific to individual projects. As you will see when you start to develop your architecture, you are engaged in a process of discovery as much as one of capture—in other words, this early in the system development lifecycle, your stakeholders may not yet know precisely what their requirements are.

Another way that we sometimes express this idea is to say that we are interested in stakeholders who have *concerns* about the system. We find the term *concern* particularly appropriate because of the broad range of possible types of stakeholder involvement with a system.

DEFINITION A **concern** about an architecture is a requirement, an objective, a constraint, an intention, or an aspiration a stakeholder has for that architecture.

Many concerns will be common among stakeholders, but some concerns will be distinct and may even conflict. Resolving such conflicts in a way that leaves stakeholders satisfied can be a significant challenge.

FIGURE 2-4 THE QUALITY TRIANGLE

EXAMPLE Some of the important attributes of a software development project are often shown as a triangle whose corners represent cost, quality, and time to market. Ideally we would like a project to have high quality, zero cost, and immediate delivery, but we know this isn't possible. The *quality triangle* in Figure 2-4 shows that it is necessary to make compromises between these three attributes, and the best you are likely to achieve is two out of three. In this diagram, each apex of the triangle represents one of these desired qualities, and we have shown a few indicative combinations of the qualities on the diagram, to illustrate how they affect each other.

For example, a high-quality system tends to take longer to build and to cost more. Conversely, it is often possible to reduce the initial development time, but, assuming costs are kept roughly constant, this comes at the expense of reducing the quality of the delivered software.

One or more of these attributes is likely to be important to different stakeholders, and it is the architect's job to understand which of these attributes is important to whom and to reach an acceptable compromise when necessary. We'll talk more about how to do this in Part II.

The Importance of Stakeholders

Stakeholders (explicitly or implicitly) drive the whole shape and direction of the architecture, which is developed solely to create a system for their benefit and to serve their needs. Stakeholders ultimately make or direct the fundamental decisions about scope, functionality, operational characteristics, and structure of the eventual product or system—under the guidance of the architect, of course. Without stakeholders, there would be no point in developing the architecture because there would be no need for the system it will turn into, nor would there be anyone to build it, deploy it, run it, or pay for it.

PRINCIPLE Architectures are created solely to meet stakeholder needs.

It follows that if a system does not adequately meet the needs of its stakeholders, it cannot be considered a success—no matter how well it conforms to good architectural practice. In other words, architectures must be evaluated with respect to stakeholder needs as well as abstract architectural and software engineering principles.

As we've seen, it is not uncommon for the needs of different stakeholders to be in conflict with one another. There is no easy answer to such a dilemma, and it often falls to the architect to strike an effective balance in such cases (for example, by accepting higher maintenance costs in a performance-critical system, caused by the level of optimization and integration of system elements required in order to reduce request processing latency).

PRINCIPLE A good architecture is one that successfully addresses the concerns of its stakeholders and, when those concerns are in conflict, balances them in a way that is acceptable to the stakeholders.

Part II explores the concept of stakeholders in more detail and explains how they can be classified, identified, selected, and engaged in the development of the architecture.

ARCHITECTURAL DESCRIPTIONS

An architecture for a software system can be an incredibly complex thing. Part of the architect's role is to describe this complexity to the people who need to understand it. The architect does this by means of an *architectural description*.

DEFINITION An **architectural description (AD)** is a set of products that documents an architecture in a way its stakeholders can understand and demonstrates that the architecture has met their concerns.

"Products" in this context consist of a range of things—particularly *architectural models*, but also *scope definition*, *constraints*, and *principles*. We discuss each of these in more detail in Parts II and III.

A description of an architecture has to present its essence and its detail at the same time—in other words, it must provide an overall picture that summarizes the whole system, but it also must decompose into enough detail that it can be validated and the described system can be built.

Although it is true that every system has an architecture, it is unfortunately not true that every system has an AD. Even if an architecture is documented, it may be documented only in part, or the documentation may be out-of-date or unused.

Strictly speaking, therefore, our definition describes a *good* AD. However, an AD that its stakeholders cannot understand or that doesn't demonstrate to them that their concerns have been met is really not worth having—in fact, it can be more of a liability than an asset. The AD needs to contain all of (and ideally only) the information needed to communicate the architecture effectively to those stakeholders who need to understand it.

PRINCIPLE Although every system has an architecture, not every system has an architecture that is effectively communicated via an architectural description.

Of course, the chances of your architectural ideas being implemented as you envisaged them are far less if the AD is inadequate.

EXAMPLE The AD for the airline reservation system referred to earlier focused strongly on the static structure (the key hardware and software elements and how they are organized) and to a lesser extent on its external behavior (the way that those elements interact to respond to requests that users could make). Because most users would have a customer at a sales desk or on the end of a telephone, quick response time and system reliability are paramount.

If the AD for such a system does not consider the quality properties of the system in any detail—in particular, if there is no clear definition of response-time requirements nor any performance models—it is quite likely that when the system is deployed, it will deliver poor performance, particularly under peak load.

The solution to this is to identify a group of users who can agree on what the performance requirements are, and then the architect can balance these against what analysis and testing reveal is practically possible.

> This helps avoid the significant amount of enhancement and tuning inevitably required when performance problems emerge later in the lifecycle.

The architect writes the AD and is also one of its major users. You use the AD as a memory aid, a basis for analysis, a record of decisions, and so on. However, you are only one of the users of the AD. To a lesser or greater extent, all of the other stakeholders need to understand the architecture (or at least parts of it) as it relates to them. If the AD does not help with this, it has failed.

PRINCIPLE A good architectural description is one that effectively and consistently communicates the key aspects of the architecture to the appropriate stakeholders.

Nowadays there is a plethora of techniques, models, architecture description languages, and other ways to document architectures. Choosing the right ones for a particular system development is a significant challenge in its own right; you need to take into account the characteristics of the system and the skills and capabilities of its stakeholders.

Part II explores the concept of ADs in more detail, and Parts III and IV explain the different elements of an AD and how to create them.

RELATIONSHIPS BETWEEN THE CORE CONCEPTS

The important relationships between our core concepts are illustrated in the UML class diagram in Figure 2–5. The diagram brings out the following relationships among the concepts we have discussed so far.

- A system is built to address the needs, concerns, goals, and objectives of its stakeholders.
- The architecture of a system comprises a number of architectural elements and their interelement relationships.
- The architecture of a system can potentially be documented by an AD (fully, partly, or not at all). In fact, there are many potential ADs for a given architecture, some good, some bad.
- An AD documents an architecture for its stakeholders and demonstrates to them that it has met their needs.

FIGURE 2-5 CORE CONCEPT RELATIONSHIPS

We use standard UML conventions in Figure 2–5 and throughout the book. Here, rectangles represent our architectural concepts, and directed lines represent relationships from one concept to another. A filled diamond at the "from" end of a line indicates an "is composed of" relationship. The cardinality of each relationship (how many of one thing can be related to another) is shown at each end of each line. The relationships are annotated to give a brief indication of what they mean.

SUMMARY

In this chapter we laid our foundations by defining and discussing some concepts and terms we will be using throughout the rest of the book.

- The *architecture* of a system defines its *static structure*, its *dynamic structure*, its *externally visible behavior*, its *quality properties*, and the *principles that should guide its design and evolution*. Each of these aspects is important although not always addressed. Every computer system has an architecture, even if we don't understand it.

- A *candidate architecture* for a system is one that has the potential to exhibit the system's required externally visible behaviors and quality properties. Most problems have several candidate architectures, and it is the job of the architect to select the best one.

- An *architectural element* is a clearly identifiable, architecturally meaningful piece of a system.

- A *stakeholder* is a person, group, or entity with an interest in or concerns about the realization of the architecture. Stakeholders include users but also many other people, such as developers, operators, and acquirers. Architectures are created solely to meet stakeholder needs.

- An *architectural description* is a set of products that documents an architecture in a way its stakeholders can understand and demonstrates that the architecture has met their concerns. Although every system has an architecture, not every system has an effective AD.

FURTHER READING

We have aligned our language and concepts in this chapter with the most recent general standard we are aware of in the field of software architecture—ISO/IEC Standard 42010 [ISO11] (an evolution of IEEE Standard 1471-2000 for architecture description). According to its own introduction, this standard addresses "the creation, analysis and sustainment of architectures of systems through the use of architecture descriptions." Our conceptual model is based on the one presented in the standard.

Much of our thinking on software architecture concepts is based on the work done by the Software Architecture group of the Software Engineering Institute. The book by Bass, Clements, and Kazman [BASS03] is a thorough introduction to the main ideas in the field of software architecture and provides a lot more depth and background on the fundamental concepts than we provide here.

One of the original books on software architecture is by Shaw and Garlan [SHAW96]. This book provides a minimalist and elegant introduction to the fundamental ideas in software architecture, including overviews of an AD, architectural styles, and possible tool support. Even earlier than this, one of the original papers in the software architecture field, by Perry and Wolf [PERR92], is well worth reading for its clear focus on the important elements of the discipline.

If you want to take a wider view of software architecture, a useful book may be the cross-disciplinary *Art of Systems Architecting* [MAIE09]. This book is novel in that it introduces and discusses the idea of architecture (and "architecting") as a set of principles and techniques valid across all complex systems domains. A particular emphasis is placed on architecture heuristics, and a set of interesting heuristics is provided. Examples are taken from buildings, manufacturing, social systems, IT, and collaborative systems.

A number of other good introductory books on the subject have appeared in the years between the first and second editions of this book. In all of our writing, we have tried to stress that it is important to focus your architecture work on the most important aspects of the problem that you face, rather than trying to use every viewpoint and perspective in every case. George Fairbanks's book *Just Enough Software Architecture* [FAIR10] is a practical guide to doing exactly this, showing you how to practice "risk-driven architecting" in order to tailor your architecture work in response to the risks that you face. Ian Gorton's book *Essential Software Architecture* [GORT06] is a concise, practical introduction to a number of important software architecture topics; and Richard Taylor, Neno Medvidovic, and Eric Dashofy have created a very comprehensive introduction to the subject in [TAYL09].

If you are interested in defining a formal process for your software architecture work, Peter Eeles and Peter Cripps's book *The Process of Software Architecting* [EELE09] will be a useful guide to achieving this.

3

VIEWPOINTS AND VIEWS

When you start the daunting task of designing the architecture of your system, you will find that you have some difficult architectural questions to answer.

- What are the main functional elements of your architecture?
- How will these elements interact with one another and with the outside world?
- What information will be managed, stored, and presented?
- What physical hardware and software elements will be required to support these functional and information elements?
- What operational features and capabilities will be provided?
- What development, test, support, and training environments will be provided?

A common temptation—one you should strongly avoid—is to try to answer all of these questions by means of a single, heavily overloaded, all-encompassing model. This sort of model (and we've all seen them) will probably use a mixture of formal and informal notations to describe a number of aspects of the system on one huge sheet of paper: the functional structure, software layering, concurrency, intercomponent communication, physical deployment environment, and so on. Let's see what happens when we try to use an all-encompassing model in our AD, by means of an example.

As the example shows, this sort of AD is really the worst of all worlds. Many writers on software architecture have pointed out that it simply isn't possible to describe a software architecture by using a single model. Such a model is hard to understand and is unlikely to clearly identify the architecture's most

EXAMPLE   Although the airline reservation system we introduced in Chapter 2 is conceptually fairly simple, in practice some aspects of this system make it very complicated indeed.

- The system's data is distributed across a number of systems in different physical locations.
- A number of different types of data entry devices must be supported.
- The system must be able to present some information in different languages.
- The system must be able to print tickets and other documents on a wide range of printers.
- The plethora of international regulations complicates the picture even further.

After some discussion, the architect draws up a first-cut architecture for the system, which attempts to represent all of its important aspects in a single diagram. This model includes the full range of data entry devices (including various dumb terminals, desktop PCs, and wireless devices), the multiple physical systems on which data is stored or replicated data is maintained, and some of the printing devices that must be supported (the model does not cover remote printing because it is done at a separate facility). The model is heavily annotated with text to indicate, for example, where multilanguage support is required and where data must be audited, archived, or analyzed to support regulatory requirements.

However, no details of the network interfaces between the different components are included—these are abstracted out into a network icon because they are so complex. (In fact, the network design is probably the most complicated aspect of the architecture, requiring support for a number of different and largely incompatible network protocols, routing over public and private networks, synchronous and asynchronous interactions, and varying levels of service reliability and availability.) Furthermore, the model does not address any of the implications of having the same data distributed around multiple systems.

Because it is so complex and tries to address a wide mix of concerns in the same diagram, the model fails to engage any of the stakeholders. The users find it too complex and difficult to understand (particularly because of the large number of physical hardware components represented). The technology stakeholders, on the other hand, tend to disregard it because of the detail that is left out, such as the network topology. The legal team members can't use it to satisfy themselves that the regulatory aspects will be adequately handled, and the sponsor finds it completely incomprehensible.

Furthermore, the architect spends an inordinate amount of time keeping it up-to-date—every time a new type of data entry device or printer is discussed, for example, the diagram needs to be updated and reprinted on a very large sheet of paper.

Because of these problems, the diagram soon becomes obsolete and is eventually forgotten. Unfortunately, the issues that the model fails to address do not disappear and thus cause many problems and delays during the implementation and the early stages of live operation.

important features. It tends to poorly serve individual stakeholders because they struggle to understand the aspects that interest them. Worst of all, because of its complexity, a monolithic AD is often incomplete, incorrect, or out-of-date.

PRINCIPLE It is not possible to capture the functional features and quality properties of a complex system in a single comprehensible model that is understandable by, and of value to, its stakeholders.

We need to represent complex systems in a way that is manageable and comprehensible by a range of business and technical stakeholders. A widely used approach—the only successful one we have found—is to attack the problem from different directions simultaneously. In this approach, the AD is partitioned into a number of separate but interrelated *views*, each of which describes a separate aspect of the architecture. Collectively, the views describe the whole system.

To help you understand what we mean by a view, let's consider the example of an architectural drawing for one of the elevations of an office block. This portrays the building from a particular aspect, typically a compass bearing such as northeast. The drawing shows features of the building that are visible from that vantage point but not from other directions. It doesn't show any details of the interior of the building (as seen by its occupants) or of its internal systems (such as plumbing or air conditioning) that influence the environment its occupants will inhabit. Thus the blueprint is only a partial representation of the building; you have to look at—and understand—the whole set of blueprints to grasp the facilities and experience that the whole building will provide.

Another way that a building architect might represent a new building is to construct a scale model of it and its environs. This shows how the building will look from all sides but again reveals nothing about the mechanisms to be used in its construction, its interior form, or its likely internal environment.

STRATEGY A complex system is much more effectively described by a set of interrelated views, which collectively illustrate its functional features and quality properties and demonstrate that it meets its goals, than by a single overloaded model.

Let's take a look at what this approach means for software architecture.

ARCHITECTURAL VIEWS

An architectural view is a way to portray those aspects or elements of the architecture that are relevant to the concerns the view intends to address—and, by implication, the stakeholders to whom those concerns are important.

This idea is not new, going back at least as far as the work of David Parnas in the 1970s and more recently Dewayne Perry and Alexander Wolf in the early 1990s. However, it wasn't until 1995 that Philippe Kruchten of the Rational Corporation published his widely accepted written description of views, *Architectural Blueprints—The "4 + 1" View Model of Software Architecture*. This suggested four different views of a system and the use of a set of scenarios (use cases) to elucidate its behavior. Kruchten's approach has since evolved to form an important part of the Rational Unified Process (RUP).

IEEE Standard 1471 (the predecessor of ISO Standard 42010) formalized these concepts in 2000 and brought some welcome standardization of terminology. In fact, our definition of a view is based on and extends the one from the original IEEE standard.

DEFINITION A **view** is a representation of one or more structural aspects of an architecture that illustrates how the architecture addresses one or more concerns held by one or more of its stakeholders.

When deciding what to include in a view, ask yourself the following questions.

- *View scope*: What structural aspects of the architecture are you trying to represent? For example, are you trying to define the runtime functional elements and their intercommunication, or the runtime environment and how the system is deployed into it? Do you need to represent the dynamic or static elements of these structures? (For example, in the case of the functional element structure, do you wish to show the elements and the connectors between them, or the sequence of interactions they perform in order to process an incoming request, or both?)

- *Element types*: What type(s) of architectural element are you trying to categorize? For example, when considering how the system is deployed, do you need to represent individual server machines, or do you just need to represent a service environment (like Force.com SiteForce or Google AppEngine) that your system elements are deployed into?

- *Audience*: What class(es) of stakeholder is the view aimed at? A view may be narrowly focused on one class of stakeholder or even a specific individual, or it may be aimed at a larger group whose members have varying interests and levels of expertise.

- *Audience expertise*: How much technical understanding do these stakeholders have? Acquirers and users, for example, will be experts in their subject areas but are unlikely to know much about hardware or software, while the converse may apply to developers or support staff.

- *Scope of concerns*: What stakeholder concerns is the view intended to address? How much do the stakeholders know about the architectural context and background to these concerns?

- *Level of detail*: How much do these stakeholders need to know about this aspect of the architecture? For nontechnical stakeholders such as users, how competent are they in understanding its technical details?

As with the AD itself, one of your main challenges is to get the right content into your views. Provide too much irrelevant detail, for example, and your audience will be overwhelmed; too little information, and you risk your audience being confused or making assumptions that may not be valid. There are two key questions you should ask yourself when deciding what to include in a view. First of all, can the stakeholders that it targets use it to determine whether their concerns have been met? And second, can those stakeholders use it to successfully undertake their role in building the system?

We will explore the second question in more detail in Chapter 9, but for now we will summarize these questions as follows.

 STRATEGY Only include in a view information that furthers the objectives of your AD—that is, information that helps explain the architecture to stakeholders or demonstrates that the goals of the system (i.e., the concerns of its stakeholders) are being met.

VIEWPOINTS

It would be hard work if every time you were creating a view of your architecture you had to go back to first principles to define what should go into it. Fortunately, you don't quite have to do that.

In his introductory paper, Philippe Kruchten defined four standard views, namely, Logical, Process, Physical, and Development. The IEEE standard made this idea generic (and did not specify one set of views or another) by proposing the concept of a *viewpoint*.

The objective of the viewpoint concept is an ambitious one—no less than making available a library of templates and patterns that can be used off the shelf to guide the creation of an architectural view that can be inserted into an AD. We define a viewpoint (again after IEEE Standard 1471) as follows.

DEFINITION A **viewpoint** is a collection of patterns, templates, and conventions for constructing one type of view. It defines the stakeholders whose concerns are reflected in the viewpoint and the guidelines, principles, and template models for constructing its views.

Architectural viewpoints provide a framework for capturing reusable architectural knowledge that can be used to guide the creation of a particular type of (partial) AD. You may find it helpful to compare the relationship between viewpoints and views to the relationship between classes and objects in object-oriented development.

- A class definition provides a template for the construction of an object. An object-oriented system will include at runtime a number of *objects*, each of a specified *class*.

- A viewpoint provides a template for the construction of a view. A viewpoints-and-views-based architecture definition will include a number of *views*, each conforming to a specific *viewpoint*.

Viewpoints are an important way of bringing much-needed structure and consistency to what was in the past a fairly unstructured activity. By defining a standard approach, a standard language, and even a standard metamodel for describing different aspects of a system, stakeholders can understand any AD that conforms to these standards once familiar with them.

In practice, of course, we haven't fully achieved this goal yet. There are no universally accepted ways to model software architectures, and many ADs use their own homegrown conventions (or even worse, no particular conventions at all). However, the widespread acceptance of techniques such as entity-relationship models and of modeling languages such as UML takes us some way toward this goal.

In any case, it is extremely useful to be able to categorize views according to the types of concerns and architectural elements they present.

STRATEGY When developing a view, whether or not you use a formally defined viewpoint, be clear in your own mind what sorts of concerns the view is addressing, what types of architectural elements it presents, and who the viewpoint is aimed at. Make sure that your stakeholders understand these as well.

RELATIONSHIPS BETWEEN THE CORE CONCEPTS

To put views and viewpoints in context, we can now extend the conceptual model we introduced in Chapter 2 to illustrate how views and viewpoints contribute to the overall picture (see Figure 3–1).

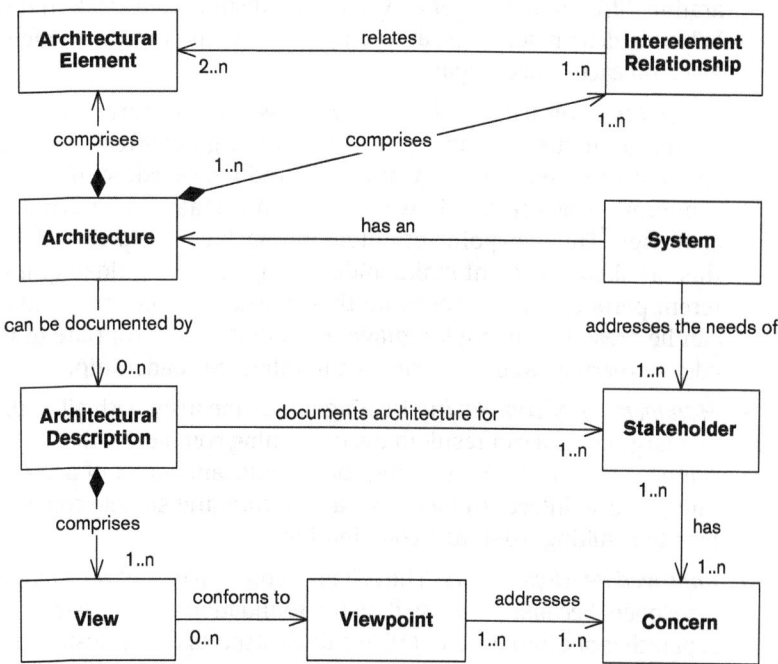

FIGURE 3–1 VIEWS AND VIEWPOINTS IN CONTEXT

We have added the following relationships to the diagram we originally presented as Figure 2–5.

- A viewpoint defines the aims, intended audience, and content of a class of views and defines the concerns that views of this class will address.
- A view conforms to a viewpoint and so communicates the resolution of a number of concerns (and a resolution of a concern may be communicated in a number of views).
- An AD comprises a number of views.

THE BENEFITS OF USING VIEWPOINTS AND VIEWS

Using views and viewpoints to describe the architecture of a system benefits the architecture definition process in a number of ways.

- *Separation of concerns:* Describing many aspects of the system via a single representation can cloud communication and, more seriously, can result in independent aspects of the system becoming intertwined in the model. Separating different models of a system into distinct (but related) descriptions helps the design, analysis, and communication processes by allowing you to focus on each aspect separately.

- *Communication with stakeholder groups:* The concerns of each stakeholder group are typically quite different (e.g., contrast the primary concerns of end users, security auditors, and help-desk staff), and communicating effectively with the various stakeholder groups is quite a challenge. The viewpoint-oriented approach can help considerably with this problem. Different stakeholder groups can be guided quickly to different parts of the AD based on their particular concerns, and each view can be presented using language and notation appropriate to the knowledge, expertise, and concerns of the intended readership.

- *Management of complexity:* Dealing simultaneously with all of the aspects of a large system can result in overwhelming complexity that no one person can possibly handle. By treating each significant aspect of a system separately, the architect can focus on each in turn and so help conquer the complexity resulting from their combination.

- *Improved developer focus:* The AD is of course particularly important for the developers because they use it as the foundation of the system design. By separating out into different views those aspects of the system that are particularly important to the development team, you help ensure that the right system gets built.

VIEWPOINT PITFALLS

Of course, the use of views and viewpoints won't solve all of your software architecture problems automatically. Although we have found that using views is really the only way to make the problem manageable, you need to be aware of some possible pitfalls when using the view-and-viewpoint-based approach.

- *Inconsistency*: Using a number of views to describe a system inevitably brings consistency problems. It is theoretically possible to use architecture description languages to create the models in your views and then cross-check these automatically (much as graphical modeling tools attempt to check structured or object-oriented methods models), but there are no such machine-checkable architecture description languages in widespread use today. This means that achieving cross-view consistency within an AD is an inherently manual process. To assist with this, Chapter 23 includes a checklist to help you ensure consistency between the standard viewpoints presented in our catalog in Part III.

- *Selection of the wrong set of views*: It is not always obvious which set of views is suitable for describing a particular system. This is influenced by a number of factors, such as the nature and complexity of the architecture, the skills and experience of the stakeholders (and of the architect), and the time available to produce the AD. There really isn't an easy answer to this problem, other than your own experience and skill and an analysis of the most important concerns that affect your architecture.

- *Fragmentation*: Having several views of your architecture can make the AD difficult to understand. Each separate view also involves a significant amount of effort to create and maintain. To avoid fragmentation and minimize the overhead of maintaining unnecessary descriptions, you should eliminate views that do not address significant concerns for the system you are building. In some cases, you may also consider creating hybrid views that combine models from a number of views in the viewpoint set (e.g., creating a combined deployment and concurrency view). Beware, however, of the combined views becoming difficult to understand and maintain because they address a combination of concerns.

OUR VIEWPOINT CATALOG

Part III of this book presents our catalog of seven core viewpoints for information systems architecture: the Context, Functional, Information, Concurrency, Development, Deployment, and Operational viewpoints. Although the viewpoints are (largely) disjoint, we find it convenient to group them as shown in Figure 3–2.

FIGURE 3-2 VIEWPOINT GROUPINGS

- The Context viewpoint describes the relationships, dependencies, and interactions between the system and its environment (the people, systems, and external entities with which it interacts).
- The Functional, Information, and Concurrency viewpoints characterize the fundamental organization of the system.
- The Development viewpoint exists to support the system's construction.
- The Deployment and Operational viewpoints characterize the system once in its live environment.

You can use the shape and position of the icons in Figure 3–2 to help understand how our viewpoints are related to one another. We have put the Context viewpoint at the top of the diagram to indicate its role as the "overarching" viewpoint that informs the scope and content of all the others. We group the Functional, Information, and Concurrency viewpoints together at the left, to highlight that between them they define how the system provides its functionality.

The viewpoints on the right-hand side are to some extent driven by those on the left; for example, the Development viewpoint defines standards and models for the construction of the architecture's functional, information, and concurrency elements. We have further grouped the Deployment and Operational viewpoints, since between them, these views define the system's production environment.

Viewpoint Overview

Table 3–1 briefly describes our viewpoints.

Of course, not all of these viewpoints may apply to your architecture, and some will be more important than others. You may not need views of all of these types in your AD, and in some cases there may be other viewpoints that you need to identify and add yourself. This means that your first job is to understand the nature of your architecture, the skills and experience of the stakeholders, and the time available and other constraints, and then to come up with an appropriate selection of views.

FIGURE 3–2 VIEWPOINT CATALOG

Viewpoint	Definition
Context	Describes the relationships, dependencies, and interactions between the system and its environment (the people, systems, and external entities with which it interacts). The Context view will be of interest to many of the system's stakeholders and plays an important role in helping them to understand its responsibilities and how it relates to their organization.
Functional	Describes the system's runtime functional elements, their responsibilities, interfaces, and primary interactions. A Functional view is the cornerstone of most ADs and is often the first part of the description that stakeholders try to read. It drives the shape of other system structures such as the information structure, concurrency structure, deployment structure, and so on. It also has a significant impact on the system's quality properties such as its ability to change, its ability to be secured, and its runtime performance.
Information	Describes the way that the system stores, manipulates, manages, and distributes information. The ultimate purpose of virtually any computer system is to manipulate information in some form, and this viewpoint develops a complete but high-level view of static data structure and information flow. The objective of this analysis is to answer the big questions around content, structure, ownership, latency, references, and data migration.
Concurrency	Describes the concurrency structure of the system and maps functional elements to concurrency units to clearly identify the parts of the system that can execute concurrently and how this is coordinated and controlled. This entails the creation of models that show the process and thread structures that the system will use and the interprocess communication mechanisms used to coordinate their operation.
Development	Describes the architecture that supports the software development process. Development views communicate the aspects of the architecture of interest to those stakeholders involved in building, testing, maintaining, and enhancing the system.

Continued on next page

FIGURE 3-2 VIEWPOINT CATALOG *(CONTINUED)*

Viewpoint	Definition
Deployment	Describes the environment into which the system will be deployed and the dependencies that the system has on elements of it. This view captures the hardware environment that your system needs (primarily the processing nodes, network interconnections, and disk storage facilities required), the technical environment requirements for each element, and the mapping of the software elements to the runtime environment that will execute them.
Operational	Describes how the system will be operated, administered, and supported when it is running in its production environment. For all but the simplest systems, installing, managing, and operating the system is a significant task that must be considered and planned at design time. The aim of the Operational viewpoint is to identify system-wide strategies for addressing the operational concerns of the system's stakeholders and to identify solutions that address these.

While it can be hard to generalize, and it is important to choose your set of views for the specific context in which you find yourself, Table 3–2 lists the relative importance that we have often found each view to have for some typical types of information systems. We suggest you use this table as a starting point when choosing the views to include in your AD.

TABLE 3-2 MOST IMPORTANT VIEWS FOR TYPICAL SYSTEM TYPES

	OLTP Information System	Calculation Service/ Middleware	DSS/MIS System	High-Volume Web Site	Enterprise Package
Context	High	Low	High	Medium	Medium
Functional	High	High	Low	High	High
Information	Medium	Low	High	Medium	Medium
Concurrency	Low	High	Low	Medium	Varies
Development	High	High	Low	High	High
Deployment	High	High	High	High	High
Operational	Varies	Low	Medium	Medium	High

SUMMARY

Capturing the essence and the detail of the whole architecture in a single model is just not possible for anything other than simple systems. If you try to do this, you will end up with a Frankenstein monster of a model that is unmanageable and does not adequately represent the system to you or any of the stakeholders.

By far the best way of managing this complexity is to produce a number of different representations of all or part of the architecture, each of which focuses on certain aspects of the system, showing how it addresses some of the stakeholder concerns. We call these *views*.

To help you decide what views to produce and what should go into any particular view, you use *viewpoints*, which are standardized definitions of view concepts, content, and activities.

The use of views and viewpoints brings many benefits, such as separation of concerns, improved communication with stakeholders, and management of complexity. However, it is not without its pitfalls, such as inconsistency and fragmentation, and you must be careful to manage these.

In this chapter, we introduced our viewpoint catalog, comprising the Context, Functional, Information, Concurrency, Development, Deployment, and Operational viewpoints, which we describe in detail in Part III.

FURTHER READING

A lot of useful guidance on creating ADs using views (including a discussion of when and how to combine views) and thorough guidance for creating the documentation for a wide variety of types of views can be found in Clements et al. [CLEM10]. Other references that help to make sense of viewpoints and views are IEEE Standard 1471 [IEEE00], ISO Standard 42010 [ISO11], and Kruchten's "4 + 1" approach [KRUC95]. One of the earliest explicit references to the need for architectural views appears in Perry and Wolf [PERR92].

Some of the other viewpoint taxonomies that have been developed over the last decade or so—including Kruchten's "4 + 1," RM-ODP, the viewpoint set by Hofmeister et al. [HOFM00], and the set by Garland and Anthony [GARL03]—are described in the Appendix, together with recommendations for further reading in this area.

Part III, where we describe our viewpoint catalog in detail, contains references for specific view-related reading.

4

ARCHITECTURAL PERSPECTIVES

In Chapter 3, we explained how we use viewpoints (such as the Context, Functional, Information, and Deployment viewpoints) to guide the process of capturing and representing the architecture as a set of views, with the development of each view being guided by the use of a specific viewpoint. When creating a view, your focus is on the issues, concerns, and solutions pertinent to that view. So, for an Information view, for example, you focus on things such as information structure, ownership, transactional integrity, data quality, and timeliness.

Many of the important concerns that are pertinent to one view are much less important when considering the others. Data ownership, for example, is not key to formulating the Concurrency view, nor is the development environment a major concern when considering the Functional view. (Of course, the *decisions* taken in one view can have a considerable impact on the others, and it is a big part of the architect's job to make sure that these implications are understood. However, the *concerns* addressed in different views are largely different.)

Although the views, when combined, form a representation of the whole architecture, we can consider them largely independent of one another—a disjoint partition of the whole architectural analysis. In fact, for any significant system, you usually *must* partition your analysis this way because the entire problem is too much to understand or describe in a single piece.

QUALITY PROPERTIES

Many architectural decisions address concerns that are common to many or all views. These concerns are normally driven by the need for the system to exhibit a certain quality property rather than to provide a particular function. In our experience, trying to address these aspects of an architecture by using viewpoints doesn't work well. Let's look at an example to understand why.

> **EXAMPLE** Security is clearly a vital quality of most systems. It has always been important to be able to restrict access to data or functionality to appropriate classes of users, and in the age of the Internet, good external and internal security is even more important. If some of your systems are exposed to the wider world, they are vulnerable to attack, and the consequences of a breach can be disastrous for finances or public relations. (The large number of high-profile Internet security failures in Europe and North America that have occurred since the early part of the millennium illustrates this clearly.)
>
> In our experience, security is often not thought through properly early in the project lifecycle. Part of the reason for this is that security is hard—the means for achieving an appropriate level of security are complex and require sophisticated analysis. Also, it may be considered to be "someone else's problem"—the responsibility of a specialist security group rather than of the organization as a whole. You may be surprised, therefore, that we have not included a Security viewpoint in our catalog to go along with the others (Functional, Information, Deployment, and so forth).
>
> We used to approach concerns such as security just like that ourselves. We used a Security viewpoint and started to consider which classes of stakeholders have concerns in this area, what this viewpoint should consist of, and how a typical Security view might actually look.
>
> However, experience taught us that security is an important factor that affects aspects of the architecture addressed by most if not all of the other viewpoints we presented in Chapter 3. Furthermore, which of the system's security qualities are significant depends on which viewpoint we are considering. Here are some examples.
>
> - From the Functional viewpoint, the system needs the ability to identify and authenticate its users (internal and external, human and mechanical). Security processes should be effective but unobtrusive, and any external processes exposed to the outside world need to be resilient to attack.
>
> - From the Information viewpoint, the system must be able to control different classes of access to information (read, insert, update, delete). The system may need to apply these controls at varying levels of granularity (e.g., defining object-level security within a database).

■ From the Operational viewpoint, the system must be able to maintain and distribute secret information (e.g., keys and passwords) and must be up-to-date with the latest security updates and patches.

When we consider the system from the Development, Concurrency, and Deployment viewpoints, we'll probably also find aspects of the architecture that will be affected by security needs.

So our overall criterion of "the system must be secure" actually breaks down *across* the viewpoints into a number of more specific criteria.

As the example shows, there is an inherent need to consider quality properties such as security in each architectural view. Considering a quality property in isolation just doesn't make sense, so using a viewpoint to guide the creation of another view for each quality property doesn't make sense either.

ARCHITECTURAL PERSPECTIVES

Going back to our example, although security is clearly important, representing it in our conceptual model of software architecture as another viewpoint doesn't really work. A comprehensive security viewpoint would have to consider process security, information security, operational security, deployment security, and so on. In other words, it would affect exactly the aspects of the system that we have considered so far using our viewpoints.

Rather than defining another viewpoint and creating another view, we need some way to modify and enhance our *existing* views to ensure that our architecture exhibits the desired quality properties. This should define the activities that we would perform to determine whether the architecture exhibits the required quality properties, some proven architectural tactics that we would apply to improve the architecture if we discover that it doesn't, and some guidelines we would follow to help us apply these tactics in the right way.

We therefore need something in our conceptual model that can be considered "orthogonal" to viewpoints, and we have coined the term *architectural perspective* (which we shorten to *perspective*) to refer to it.

 DEFINITION An **architectural perspective** is a collection of architectural activities, tactics, and guidelines that are used to ensure that a system exhibits a particular set of related quality properties that require consideration across a number of the system's architectural views.

Although our use of the term *perspective* is relatively new compared to the other concepts we discuss in the book, the ideas behind it have a very established pedigree. The issues addressed by perspectives are often referred to as *cross-cutting concerns* or *nonfunctional requirements* of the architecture, although we prefer not to use this latter term.[1]

With perspectives, we are trying to *systematize* what a good architect does anyway—understand the quality properties that are required; assess and review the architectural models to ensure that the architecture exhibits the required properties; identify, prototype, test, and select architectural tactics to address cases when the architecture is lacking; and so on.

DEFINITION An **architectural tactic** is an established and proven approach you can use to help achieve a particular quality property.

An example architectural tactic for achieving satisfactory overall system performance might be to define different processing priorities for different parts of the system's workload, and to manage this by using a priority-based process scheduler. The concept of architectural tactics was created and developed by the software architecture researchers at the Carnegie Mellon Software Engineering Institute (SEI), and although our definition is worded slightly differently from theirs, our approach to tactics is based directly on their work in this area.

Don't confuse tactics with design patterns, which we discuss in Part II. Although tactics and patterns are both valuable sources of design knowledge, a tactic is much more general and less constraining than a classical design pattern because it does not mandate a particular software structure but provides general guidance on how to design a particular aspect of your system. (See the Further Reading section at the end of this chapter for some references on tactics.)

A perspective provides a framework to guide and formalize this process. This means that you never work with perspectives in isolation but instead use them with each view of your architecture to analyze and validate its qualities and to drive further architectural decision making. We describe this as *applying* the perspective to the view.

---

1. Although it is true that the perspectives tend to address concerns that are distinct from what the system actually does, the division of concerns as *functional* or *nonfunctional* is often quite artificial, and we try to avoid the use of these terms. Perspectives can have an impact on how a system works, sometimes significantly, and using these terms can imply that these areas are somehow less important than functionality.

EXAMPLE The ability to identify and authenticate users is a key quality property of almost every software system. It is very important to be able to confirm that users really are who they claim to be and validate that they are allowed to access the system.

To meet this requirement, the architecture therefore needs sound mechanisms to identify and authenticate its users. These features manifest themselves (to a greater or lesser extent) in different architectural views; for example:

- The system needs access to an authentication service or to a list of users and their passwords or other authentication data. If authentication data is held within the application, the data must be held in such a way that it cannot be easily obtained by others (e.g., one-way encrypted passwords). Access to an external authentication service would be shown in the Context and Functional views (and possibly the Deployment view); if authentication information needs to be held securely within the system, this would be defined in the Information view.

- The system must protect access by means of login screens of some sort, which would require the user to present appropriate credentials before being allowed to access the system. It also requires the ability for operational staff to manage the list of users and to reset their passwords. The functional features would be defined in the Functional view and the operational aspects defined in the Operational view.

- In some application domains, the system might need to maintain a verifiably secure store of security keys and certificates, using specialized hardware in a secure physical environment. These features would be defined in the Deployment view.

Different quality properties, such as security, performance, availability, or usability, vary in their applicability to different types of systems. Usability, for example, is unlikely to be particularly important to an infrastructure project with little or no functionality exposed to users. However, broad categories of systems are likely to have similar overall quality property requirements and common ways of meeting them, so we intend perspectives to be defined in sets, with each set aimed at a particular category of system. In this book we focus on large-scale information systems and have therefore defined a set of perspectives for systems in that domain.

In our experience, the most important perspectives for large information systems include *Security* (ensuring controlled access to sensitive system resources), *Performance and Scalability* (meeting the system's required performance profile and handling increasing workloads satisfactorily), *Availability and Resilience* (ensuring system availability when required and coping with failures that could affect this), and *Evolution* (ensuring that the system can cope with likely changes). We define these perspectives in detail in Part IV, along with a number of less widely applicable perspectives such as *Regulation* (the ability of the system to conform to local and international laws, quasi-legal regulations, company policies, and other rules and standards).

You will find these perspective definitions useful whether you are just starting out as an architect or already have significant experience in the role. You can use the definitions in a number of different ways.

- A perspective is a useful *store of knowledge*, helping you quickly review your architectural models for a particular quality property without having to absorb a large quantity of more detailed material.

- A perspective acts as an effective *guide* when you are working in an area that is new to you and you are not familiar with its typical concerns, problems, and solutions.

- A perspective is a useful *memory aid* when you are working in an area that you are more familiar with, to make sure that you don't forget anything important.

In general, you should try to apply your perspectives, even if only informally, as early as possible in the design of your architecture. This will help prevent you from going down architectural blind alleys in which you develop a model that is functionally correct but offers, for example, poor performance or availability.

As with viewpoints, it is important to define perspectives in a standard way, to make them easy to use and to ensure that they all approach a subject area in the same general way. The perspective definitions in Part IV are all structured in the following manner.

- *Applicability*: This section explains which of your views are most likely to be affected by applying the perspective. For example, applying the Evolution perspective might affect your Functional view more than your Operational view.

- *Concerns*: This information defines the quality properties that the perspective addresses.

- *Activities*: In this section, we explain the steps for applying the perspective to your views—identifying the important quality properties, analyzing the views against these properties, and then making architectural design decisions that modify and improve the views.

- *Architectural tactics*: Each perspective identifies and describes the most important tactics for achieving its quality properties.

- *Problems and pitfalls*: This section explains the most common things that can go wrong and gives guidance on how to recognize and avoid them.

- *Checklists*: The checklists provide a list of questions to help you make sure you have addressed the most important concerns, considered the most appropriate tactics, and avoided the most common pitfalls.

- *Further reading*: Our perspective descriptions are necessarily brief, helping you understand the most important issues, problems, and proven practices. The Further Reading section provides a number of pointers to further information.

APPLYING PERSPECTIVES TO VIEWS

As we indicate in Figure 4–1, you apply each relevant perspective to some or all of the views that you are using in order to address that perspective's system-wide quality property concerns. The architectural views contain the description of the architecture, while the perspectives guide you through the process of analyzing and modifying your architecture to make sure it exhibits a particular quality property.

Although every perspective can be applied to every view (in other words, the relationship between perspectives and views is many-to-many), in practice, because of time constraints and the risks that you need to address, you usually apply only *some* of the perspectives to *some* of the views. An easy way to understand this process is to think of a two-dimensional grid, with views along one axis and perspectives along another, as shown in Figure 4–2.

Each rectangle in the grid represents the application of a perspective to a view, and the contents of the rectangle define the important qualities and concerns at that intersection. Here are some examples.

- When you apply the Security perspective to the Information view, it guides the design of your architecture so that, for example, it includes appropriate data access control and data ownership.

- When you apply the Performance perspective to the Concurrency view, it guides the design of your architecture so that, for example, a suitable process structure is used, and shared resources will not lead to contention.

- When you apply the Evolution perspective to the Functional view, it guides the design of your architecture so that, for example, you consider the types of changes that will be required and build in the right level of flexibility.

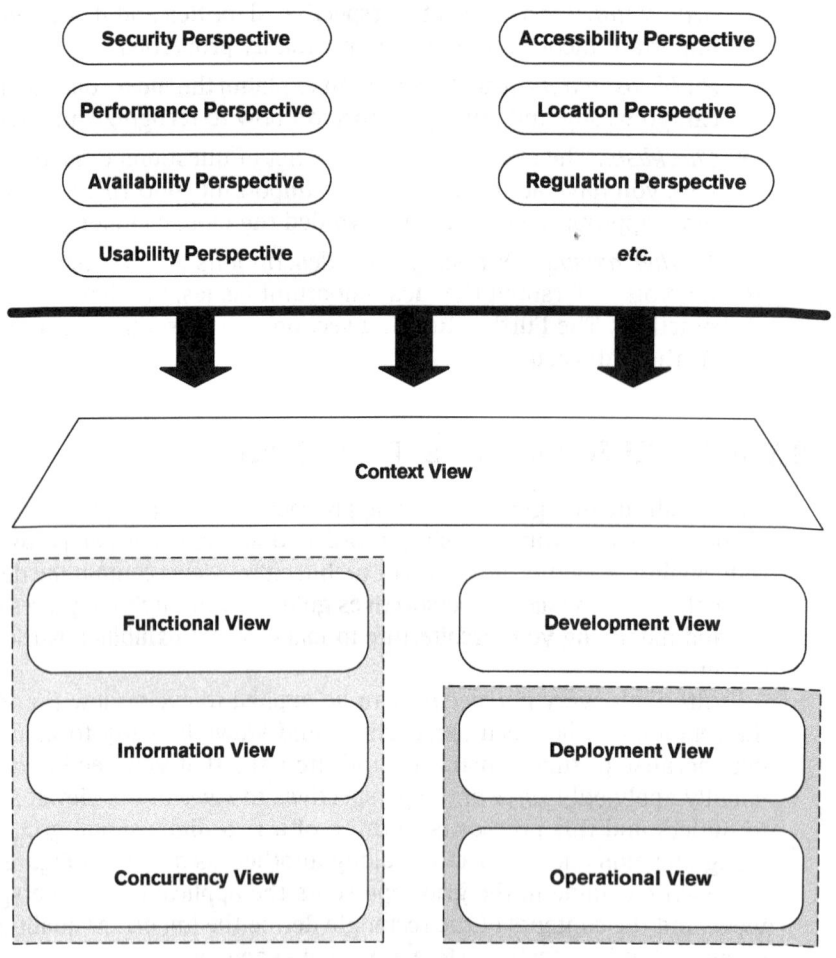

FIGURE 4–1 APPLYING PERSPECTIVES TO VIEWS

You can draw a grid like the one shown in Figure 4–2 to record which perspectives you intend to apply to which views. When you are working on a particular view, look along the rows of the grid to remind yourself of the important non-view-specific qualities and how they manifest themselves in that view. You may even want to add detail to your grid to record how important each perspective is to each view for your system, as illustrated in Table 4–1.

PERSPECTIVES

	Security	Performance	Availability	Evolution

VIEWS — Operational, Concurrency, Information, Functional

Concurrency Performance (shared resources, blocking, queuing, coordination)

Information Security (access control, access classes, object-level security)

Functional Evolution (extension points, flexible interfaces, meta-approaches)

FIGURE 4–2 EXAMPLES OF APPLYING PERSPECTIVES TO VIEWS

EXAMPLE Going back to our example of security, having decided on a candidate architecture for your system and captured it as a set of views, you would then apply the Security perspective in order to ensure that the system meets its security requirements.

To apply this perspective, you would perform a number of activities, as listed in the perspective's definition, such as identifying the sensitive resources in the system, identifying the threats that the system faces, and deciding how to mitigate each threat by using suitable security processes and technology. The result would typically be some changes to your candidate architecture such as those listed here.

- You might decide to partition the system differently in order to easily restrict access to parts of it. This would affect your Functional view.

- Your security design might introduce new hardware and software elements to the system to limit access or to add additional guarantees (such as encryption to ensure privacy). You would need to add these new elements to your Deployment view to define where they fit, and you might need to update the Development view to define how these new elements should be used.

- You might identify new operational procedures to support secure operation (e.g., certificate management) or modify existing procedures to ensure security (e.g., handling backups of sensitive data). These procedural changes will modify the Operational view.

Applying the Security perspective has not resulted in a new security view but has identified a number of modifications to your existing views that help address your stakeholders' security concerns.

TABLE 4-1 TYPICAL VIEW AND PERSPECTIVE APPLICABILITY

	Perspectives			
Views	**Security**	**Performance and Scalability**	**Availability and Resilience**	**Evolution**
Context	Medium	Low	Low	Medium
Functional	Medium	Medium	Low	High
Information	Medium	Medium	Low	High
Concurrency	Low	High	Medium	Medium
Development	Medium	Low	Low	High
Deployment	High	High	High	Low
Operational	Medium	Low	Medium	Low

CONSEQUENCES OF APPLYING A PERSPECTIVE

Applying a perspective to a view can lead to *insights*, *improvements*, and *artifacts*.

Insights

Applying a perspective almost always leads to the creation of something—usually some sort of model—that provides an insight into the system's ability to meet a required quality property. Such a model demonstrates either that the architecture meets its required quality properties or (more likely in the early stages of architecture definition) that it is deficient in some way.

EXAMPLE Applying the Security perspective might reveal the existence of a number of significant security threats that are not countered by the system in its current form. You would then need to understand these threats, understand what the risks are, and understand the impact these risks have on your architecture.

These insights normally drive further architectural design activity and are usefully recorded in their own right as rationales for significant design decisions.

Improvements

If applying the perspective tells you that the architecture will not meet one of its quality properties, the architecture needs to be improved. In this case, you may need to change an existing model in the view, create additional models to further develop the content of the view, or perhaps do both of these.

EXAMPLE Applying the Performance and Scalability perspective to your Deployment view might demonstrate that you need to replicate the application servers in order to be capable of scaling to meet expected demand. This could lead to a change to the Deployment model to show several servers instead of one and possible changes to the Functional or Information views to support this load balancing.

These improvements are, of course, integral to the AD and should be given as much prominence as your original models.

Artifacts

Some of the models and other deliverables created as a result of applying a perspective will be of only passing interest and will probably be discarded once the insight or improvement they reveal is understood. However, other outputs of applying a perspective are of significant lasting value and are important supporting architectural information. These outputs, which we term *artifacts*, are a valuable outcome of applying a perspective and should be preserved.

> **EXAMPLE** Applying the Location perspective to your Deployment view might result in a spreadsheet that models the physical network to show that there is sufficient bandwidth and capacity for the expected traffic. This spreadsheet is a useful artifact that is likely to be needed in the future to investigate the probable impact of changes to the system or the network. You should retain and reference this artifact from the AD.

Artifacts are typically captured as documents, models, or implementations, which are referenced from the AD as supporting information. Small documents can be integrated into the AD as appendices, but take care to avoid creating a huge document because this can become unwieldy and difficult to read and maintain.

RELATIONSHIPS BETWEEN THE CORE CONCEPTS

To put perspectives in context, we can now add a further piece to our conceptual model, as shown in Figure 4–3.

We have added the following relationships to update the similar diagram we showed previously as Figure 3–1.

- The content of a view can be shaped by a number of perspectives, in order to ensure the system's ability to exhibit the quality properties considered by that perspective.
- A perspective addresses a number of concerns of the system's stakeholders.

THE BENEFITS OF USING PERSPECTIVES

Applying perspectives to a view benefits your AD in several ways.

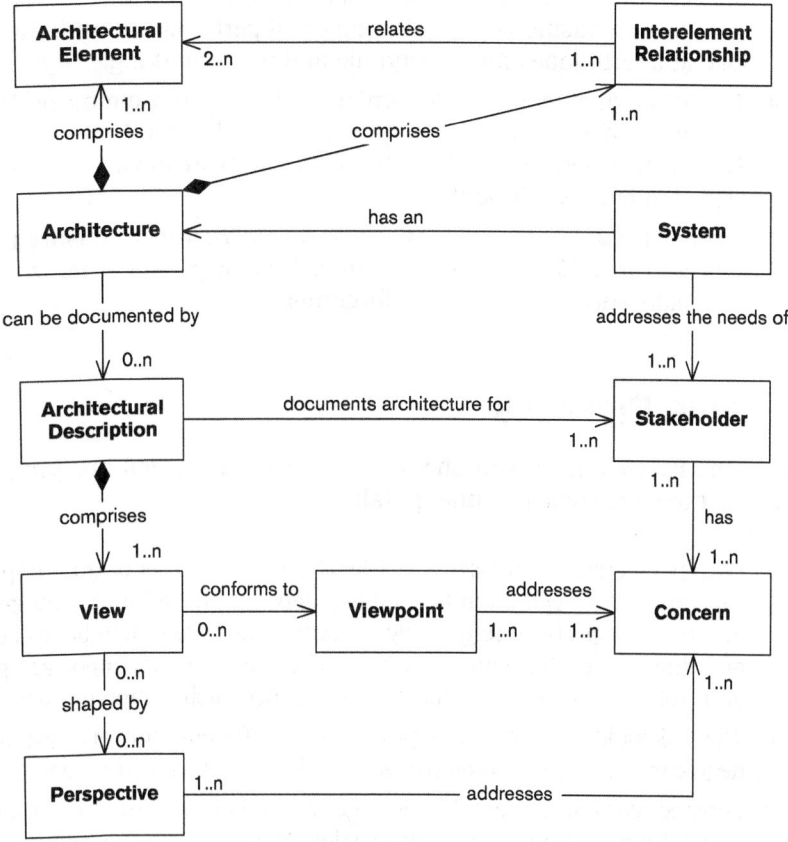

FIGURE 4-3 PERSPECTIVES IN CONTEXT

- The perspective defines *concerns* that guide architectural decision making to help ensure that the resulting architecture will exhibit the quality properties considered by the perspective. For example, the Performance perspective defines standard concerns such as response time, throughput, and predictability. Understanding and prioritizing the concerns that a perspective addresses helps you bring a firm set of priorities to later decision making.

- The perspective provides common conventions, measurements, or even a notation or language you can use to *describe* the system's qualities. For example, the Performance perspective defines standardized measures such as response time, throughput, latency, and so forth, as well as how they are specified and captured.

- The perspective describes how you can *validate* the architecture to demonstrate that it meets its requirements across each of the views. For example, the Performance perspective describes how to construct mathematical models or simulations to predict expected performance under a given load and techniques for prototyping and benchmarking.

- The perspective may offer recognized *solutions* to common problems, thus helping to share knowledge between architects. For example, the Performance perspective describes how hardware devices may be multiplexed to improve throughput.

- The perspective helps you work in a *systematic* way to ensure that its concerns are addressed by the system. This helps you organize the work and make sure that nothing is forgotten.

Perspective Pitfalls

As with any technique, you should take some care when applying perspectives as there are some potential pitfalls.

- Each perspective addresses a single, closely related set of quality property concerns. There will often be conflicts between the solutions suggested by different perspectives (e.g., a highly evolvable system may be less efficient, and thus less performant, than a less flexible one). An important part of your role as a software architect is to balance such competing needs.

- The stakeholder concerns and priorities are different for every system, so the degree to which you should consider each perspective varies considerably.

- Perspectives contain established, general advice for ensuring that a system exhibits certain quality properties. However, every situation is different, and it is important that you think about the advice and its relevance to your situation and then apply it appropriately.

Comparing Perspectives to Viewpoints

Since the first edition of the book was published, we've been asked a number of times why we introduced the idea of architectural perspectives and didn't just define a set of viewpoints that addressed system qualities. So we thought it was worth explaining in a little more detail why we introduced a new concept rather than reusing an existing one.

The ISO standard for architecture definition, ISO 42010 (formerly known as IEEE 1471), formalizes many of the concepts that we discuss in this book but does not include the concept of a perspective. It addresses the cross-cutting nature of perspectives by means of models shared across architecture views.

- Sharing architecture models between architecture views permits an architecture description to capture distinct but related concerns without redundancy or repetition of the same information in multiple views and reduces possibilities for inconsistency.

- Sharing of architecture models also permits an aspect-oriented style of architecture description: Architecture models shared across architecture views can be used to express architectural perspectives.

This approach is certainly workable and is broadly compatible with ours, but we've found it valuable to treat perspectives as a distinct and separate concept.

Both viewpoints and perspectives define concerns and the stakeholders who have an interest in them, but the other information in viewpoints and views, and describing the way it is used, is quite different. Viewpoints are focused more on guiding the production of models that describe the architecture, whereas perspectives are focused more on providing activities and tactics to ensure that the system exhibits its required quality properties. Most important, perspectives can be *applied* to one or more of the views, which makes them fundamentally different for us.

We can compare and contrast our notions of view, viewpoint, and perspective—probably the three most important concepts in this book—as follows.

- A *view* is a representation of all (or part of) an architecture—that is, a way to document its architecturally significant features according to a related set of concerns. A view captures a description of one or more of the architectural structures of the system. Architects use views to explain the architectural structure of the system to stakeholders and to demonstrate that the architecture will meet their concerns. A view comprises a set of tangible architectural products, such as principles and models; the complete set of views of an architecture forms the AD.

- A *viewpoint* guides the process of creating a particular type of view. A viewpoint defines the concerns addressed by the view and the approach for creating and describing that aspect of the architecture.

- A *perspective* guides the process of design so that the system will exhibit one or more important *qualities*. As such, a perspective can be considered analogous to a viewpoint, but for a related set of quality properties rather than a type of architectural structure. However, using a perspective usually results in changes to the architectural views (i.e., the system's structures) rather than the creation of new structures. We also use perspectives as a means of capturing common problems and pitfalls and identifying solutions to them.

So in summary, while it's certainly possible to create viewpoints that address quality property concerns, we've found a number of advantages to handling quality properties a little differently using a distinct concept, that of the architectural perspective.

OUR PERSPECTIVE CATALOG

Part IV of this book defines several perspectives (see Table 4–2) that form a set intended for application to the architectures of large-scale information systems.

As we have said, there are many perspectives, and it is not usually feasible or even desirable to consider all perspectives in the context of all of the views. Not every perspective is relevant to every system and view, and in fact it is rare that you will need to consider anywhere near the complete set of perspectives for anything other than the largest and most complex projects.

TABLE 4–2 PERSPECTIVE CATALOG

Perspective	Desired Quality
Accessibility	The ability of the system to be used by people with disabilities
Availability and Resilience	The ability of the system to be fully or partly operational as and when required and to effectively handle failures that could affect system availability
Development Resource	The ability of the system to be designed, built, deployed, and operated within known constraints related to people, budget, time, and materials
Evolution	The ability of the system to be flexible in the face of the inevitable change that all systems experience after deployment, balanced against the costs of providing such flexibility
Internationalization	The ability of the system to be independent from any particular language, country, or cultural group
Location	The ability of the system to overcome problems brought about by the absolute location of its elements and the distances between them
Performance and Scalability	The ability of the system to predictably execute within its mandated performance profile and to handle increased processing volumes in the future if required
Regulation	The ability of the system to conform to local and international laws, quasi-legal regulations, company policies, and other rules and standards
Security	The ability of the system to reliably control, monitor, and audit who can perform what actions on which resources and the ability to detect and recover from security breaches
Usability	The ease with which people who interact with the system can work effectively

TABLE 4-3 MOST IMPORTANT PERSPECTIVES FOR TYPICAL SYSTEM TYPES

	OLTP Information System	Calculation Service/ Middleware	DSS/MIS System	High-Volume Web Site	Enterprise Package
Accessibility	Varies	Low	Varies	High	High
Availability and Resilience	Varies	High	Medium	High	Medium
Development Resource	Medium	High	Medium	High	Low
Evolution	Varies	Low	High	Varies	Medium
Internationalization	Varies	Low	Varies	High	Varies
Location	Varies	Low	Low	High	Varies
Performance and Scalability	Varies	High	Varies	High	Varies
Regulation	Varies	Low	Varies	Varies	Varies
Security	Varies	Low	Medium	High	High
Usability	Medium	Low	Low	High	Medium

As with views, it is hard to provide generally applicable advice for which perspectives to concentrate on, but to act as a starting point when planning your work, Table 4–3 contains a set of suggested priorities for some typical types of information systems.

 STRATEGY Apply only the most relevant perspectives to your views. Base your selection on the needs of the stakeholders, the relative importance of the different quality properties to them, and your own experience and judgment.

SUMMARY

Viewpoints and views are an excellent way to partition your architecture into a set of interrelated models. However, these are often assessed for completeness and correctness against only functional requirements, rather than against other system qualities such as performance and scalability. This can result in a system that is functionally correct but exhibits poor response time or is insecure or unreliable. A mechanism is required to make sure this doesn't happen. It doesn't really make sense to use viewpoints to do this, because these system qualities often have implications for many if not all of the other viewpoints. A separate but related concept is required, which we call *perspectives*. We define a perspective as a collection of activities, tactics, and guidelines you use to ensure that the system will exhibit a particular set of related qualities, properties, or behaviors. Using perspectives gives you a framework for the analysis and improvement of your architectural models against the qualities the perspective addresses.

Applying a perspective to a view allows you to ensure that the architecture, as represented in that view, is fit for its purpose as far as that perspective is concerned. This is an iterative process: You create models in your views, assess these models against criteria defined in the perspective, revise your view models according to the outcome of this analysis, and iterate again.

We can compare and contrast our notions of view, viewpoint, and perspective as follows. A *view* is a representation of all (or part of) an architecture—that is, a way to document its architecturally significant features according to a related set of concerns; a *viewpoint* guides the process of creating a particular type of view; and a *perspective* guides the process of designing the architecture so that it exhibits one or more important *qualities*.

There are many perspectives, and it is not usually feasible or useful to apply all perspectives to all views.

FURTHER READING

Standard books such as *Software Architecture in Practice* [BASS03], *Evaluating Software Architectures* [CLEM02], and *Design and Use of Software Architectures* [BOSC00] all discuss quality properties and are well worth reading for more background in this area.

One particularly relevant area of software architecture research is the study of tactics being undertaken at the SEI as part of its software architecture program. The original definition of an architectural tactic can be found in an SEI technical report from 2003 [BACH03]; sets of generic tactics for various quality properties are outlined in Chapter 5 of Bass et al. [BASS03]; and the SEI Web site (www.sei.cmu.edu) contains links to a number of technical reports that discuss tactics further.

5

THE ROLE OF THE SOFTWARE ARCHITECT

If you gathered a group of software architects in a room and asked them to describe the jobs they do, you would probably end up with at least a dozen different definitions. More tellingly, if you asked the people with whom the architects work how their colleagues fill their working hours, you would probably get still more definitions.

Our own practical experience supports this. On some projects, the person with the title of architect has a very hands-on, directional involvement in the nuts and bolts of designing, coding, and testing. Alternatively, architecture may be viewed as an ivory tower from which pronouncements are handed down at intervals to the build and implementation teams. Architect is also often used as a generic title to denote a senior technical member of staff (such as the Java architect that a number of organizations have).

Architects may specialize in one area, such as networking, middleware, or database design, to the exclusion of others; occasionally, the architect may not even have a system development background at all, having entered through another route such as business analysis. The title may also be further qualified in various ways such as application architect, data architect, or even enterprise architect, without being clear what these roles involve.

So before we consider how you perform your job as an architect, we need to understand exactly what that job *is*—what your responsibilities are, where your boundaries are, what areas you should delegate to others, and how you work alongside the other members of the team to ensure a successful software delivery.

In this chapter, we establish a definition of the software architect's role, including what you are and are not expected to do to fulfill this role and what qualities you need to possess in order to be a successful architect. We also explore how this role relates to others involved in the product or system development process.

THE ARCHITECTURE DEFINITION PROCESS

The last concept in our model of software architecture captures the process used to design an architecture and create an AD for it. We call such a process *architecture definition*.

DEFINITION Architecture definition is a process by which stakeholder needs and concerns are captured, an architecture to meet these needs is designed, and the architecture is clearly and unambiguously described via an architectural description.

This process is often called *architectural design*, and we say this informally ourselves. However, in the book we tend to avoid this term because of the potential confusion between its usage as a process and as an artifact.

The goal of an architecture definition process is to design an architecture that meets the needs of its stakeholders. There are a number of aspects to this:

- *Capturing stakeholder needs*, that is, understanding what is important to stakeholders (possibly helping them reconcile conflicts such as functionality versus cost), and recording and agreeing on these needs
- Making a series of *architectural design decisions* that result in a candidate architecture
- *Assessing the candidate architecture* to determine how well it meets the stakeholder needs
- *Refining* the architecture until it is adequate
- *Capturing the architectural design decisions* made and the resulting *architectural structures* of the system in some form of AD appropriate to the environment in which you are working

These activities form the core of the architecture definition process and are normally performed iteratively. We talk more about this in Part II, in particular how stakeholder needs and concerns relate to functional and architectural requirements. For now, we'll leave you with another principle.

PRINCIPLE A good architecture definition process is one that leads to a good architecture, documented by an effective architectural description, which can be realized in a way that is time-efficient and cost-effective for the organization.

Architecture Definition Isn't Just Design

A common question that arises is whether architecture definition is "just" part of design or whether there is something more to it. It's true that architecture definition incorporates elements of design and also of requirements analysis, but as we shall see in this book, it is a separate activity from each of these.

- Design is an activity focused on the solution space and targeted primarily at one group of people—the developers. It works within a clearly defined set of constraints (the system's requirements) and is essentially a process of translating these into the specifications for a conformant system. Historically, design has tended not to focus as much on the needs of other groups such as operations or support, assuming that their needs have been captured in the requirements specifications (or often ignoring them altogether).

- Requirements analysis, on the other hand, is an activity focused on the problem space that (in its purest forms) ignores the needs and constraints of groups like developers and systems administrators because it defines what is desired rather than what is possible. It also works within a clearly defined set of constraints (the system's required scope), although within these constraints it tends to have much more freedom than the design process does.

Architecture definition resolves this tension by bridging the gap between the problem and solution spaces, as shown in Figure 5–1. Its focus is to understand the needs of everyone who has an interest in the architecture, to balance these needs, and to identify an acceptable set of tradeoffs between these where necessary. The tradeoffs take into account the constraints that exist (e.g., technical feasibility, timescales, resources, deployment environment, costs, and so on).

Although your role as a software architect incorporates elements of design and of requirements capture, there are some key differences between it and the other two roles, the most significant of which revolve around its *scope*.

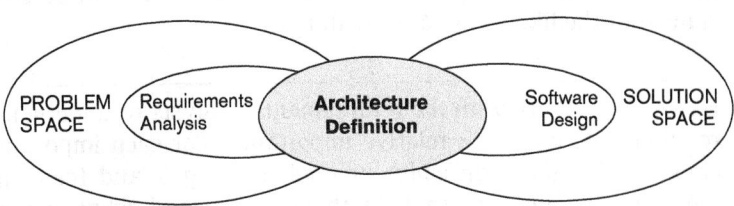

FIGURE 5–1 ARCHITECTURE DEFINITION, REQUIREMENTS ANALYSIS, AND SOFTWARE DESIGN

- You have to take input from a much wider range of people than just the user community (as we have seen in our discussion of stakeholders).
- You have to consider a much wider range of concerns than just functionality (as we have seen in our discussion of views and perspectives).
- You have to consider the big picture as well as the details.

Architecture definition is often more a process of *discovery* than of just capture. At the early stages when—with luck—you start to be involved, the stakeholders may have only hazy ideas of their expectations of the system. Furthermore, there may be a number of conflicting ideas about how the system should be built, and there are likely to be big gaps in technical knowledge and developer experience in the proposed solution elements.

Although theory says that you should not start to think about the solution until you understand the problem—and we like this approach, as a theory—in practice, stakeholders start to think about technology solutions from day one. You can't avoid this; you just have to manage it.

The Boundary between Requirements Analysis and Architecture Definition

Part of your role as an architect is to be involved in the process of analyzing, understanding, and prioritizing the system's requirements. This also allows you to start assessing the difficulty involved in implementing each requirement.

Strictly speaking, your role does not include requirements gathering, and ideally you will be presented with a complete, consistent, prioritized list of the key goals and requirements for the system. However, such a list often doesn't exist, and even when it does, requirements analysts often struggle to trade off requirements against each other; while part of this process involves understanding the relative business value of requirements, it must also take into account the associated costs and risks.

Some of the requirements specified initially are likely to be difficult to implement because the requirements analysts have little or no insight into the implementation options. As an architect, you are ideally placed to provide this insight so that the importance of each requirement can be considered in the context of the likely cost of providing it.

STRATEGY Work with the requirements analysts to understand the system's requirements and their relative importance. For each important requirement, consider the likely difficulty of implementing it and feed this back to the requirements analysts to help them understand what can and cannot be achieved.

The Boundary between Architecture Definition and Design

One of the most important decisions you will have to make as an architect is whether something is important enough for you to worry about or whether it can safely and more appropriately be left until the detailed design phase—in other words, whether it is *architecturally significant*. Philippe Kruchten neatly captured the essence of architectural significance in his definition, which we paraphrase here.

DEFINITION A concern, problem, or system element is **architecturally significant** if it has a wide impact on the structure of the system or on its important quality properties such as performance, scalability, security, reliability, or evolvability.

Predicting whether or not something will prove to be architecturally significant is difficult and requires you to use your judgment, skill, and expertise (and that of your stakeholders) to consider the circumstances of your particular project. For example, when a new technology is involved, questions around reliability and performance may be very significant, whereas they may be far less so in a system where the technologies are established and well understood by the developers.

Your job as an architect is to ensure that you focus your and your stakeholders' attention on the important questions and decisions, which are those that are likely to have a significant effect on the system's ability to meet its goals—this is something that will become easier with practice. Beware, however, of assuming that all architectural concerns are found at the abstract level; often, the devil is in the details. You need to consider aspects of your architecture at all levels, from the strategy to the code. It is also important to keep considering whether your judgment is correct and to make sure that as your architecture develops, you continue to review whether your scope is appropriate.

EXAMPLE It isn't always obvious whether something is architecturally significant because you often don't know what will end up having a big impact on the system's qualities. For example, consider the database design: Beyond defining that the system will have a third-normal-form data model and providing some guidance as to when denormalization should occur, is the design of the database schema architecturally significant? You certainly won't be able to design the entire database schema yourself except on the smallest projects.

As with many architectural decisions, this depends on the context. In systems with relatively simple, straightforward data access patterns, we would generally say that the detail of the database schema isn't architecturally significant, because it won't have a big impact on the system's abilities to meet its quality goals. However, consider the situation where a system makes extensive and complicated use of the database with many very large queries, many of which are performance-critical. In this case, we suggest that a lot of the database design detail *is* architecturally significant because many of those detailed decisions could have serious ramifications for the system's performance and stability if made wrongly.

When considering the architectural significance of a decision, try to look ahead and consider whether the different likely options for that decision are going to impact the system's key qualities. If some of the options are likely to cause trouble in the future, you've found an architecturally significant decision. You can see why we say that this can be difficult to do!

STRATEGY   As you are designing the architecture, review the areas you have determined as being architecturally significant or not, and revise these as necessary in the light of your deeper understanding of your stakeholders' concerns and of the architecture itself.

THE ROLE OF THE ARCHITECT

We can now define the role of the architect in the following principle.

PRINCIPLE   The architect is responsible for designing, documenting, and leading the construction of a system that meets the needs of all its stakeholders.

We see four aspects to this role:

1. To identify and engage the stakeholders
2. To understand and capture the stakeholders' concerns
3. To create and take ownership of the definition of an architecture that addresses these concerns
4. To take a leading role in the realization of the architecture into a physical product or system

A common theme in most descriptions of what the architect does is something along the lines of "the architect owns the big picture." We certainly support this view. One of your responsibilities as an architect is to develop and maintain a high-level view of the main elements in the product or system, which is subsequently used to guide detailed design, coding, testing, and deployment.

But this isn't all. You need to ensure that the architecture you develop is right for your situation. As we have seen, every problem has a number of possible architectural solutions, and every architecture has a number of possible representations. You must select an architecture that is fit for purpose and then document that architecture in an appropriate way.

Traditionally, the architect is viewed as making primarily an up-front contribution to system development—in other words, being heavily involved in the inception stages of the project. However, your responsibility does not end there. In fact, we find in general that the architect's involvement during the software development lifecycle conforms to the pattern illustrated in Figure 5–2.

This figure shows the architect's depth of involvement during each major development iteration of the system's delivery. During the initial phases, your involvement is intense. You are fully occupied in defining and agreeing on scope, agreeing on and validating requirements, and providing the technical leadership to make the decisions that will shape the architecture.

Your involvement typically lessens during the design, build, and test phases, while the product or system is being built, tested, and integrated. In practice, you may take a different role during this period, such as design authority or designer. If so, you are likely to be involved in mentoring,

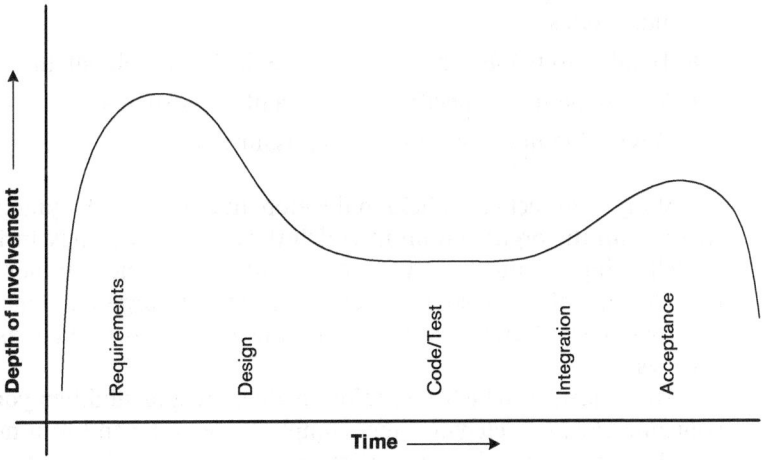

FIGURE 5–2 THE ARCHITECT'S INVOLVEMENT

reviews, problem resolution, and technical leadership. In any case, if the architecture needs any changes, you must lead the change process.

Your involvement peaks again prior to and during acceptance, as you provide support and guidance to help resolve the last-minute problems that inevitably occur and to ensure a smooth transition into the operational environment and beyond.

STRATEGY Stay involved with the development process beyond the creation of the AD and through construction, acceptance, and handover (possibly at a reduced level of involvement).

Architectural Leadership

In our experience, most organizations view "architect" as a technology leadership role, although it may not always be clear in practice what this requires you to do.

From a system standpoint, architectural leadership means the people-focused activities that help ensure successful implementation of the system. This includes the following:

- Explaining and promoting the architecture to the business and technology stakeholders, and justifying the principles and decisions that underpin it
- Providing input to and support for planning and estimating tasks
- Participating in change control processes
- Taking responsibility for and signing off on the completion of technical milestones
- Helping to resolve issues that arise during development
- Taking on more specific development roles such as design authority
- Reviewing documentation and possibly code

Many architects also help to develop and promote the practice of architecture within the organization in which they work. This may include arranging or delivering architectural training; mentoring of more junior staff, perhaps in a design role; developing viewpoints for the organization; or developing and overseeing architectural governance processes such as architectural reviews.

The extent to which you take on these responsibilities yourself, oversee someone else, or delegate them completely will depend to a major extent on the characteristics of your project and your own skills and aspirations. We discuss this in more detail in Chapter 30, which closes the book.

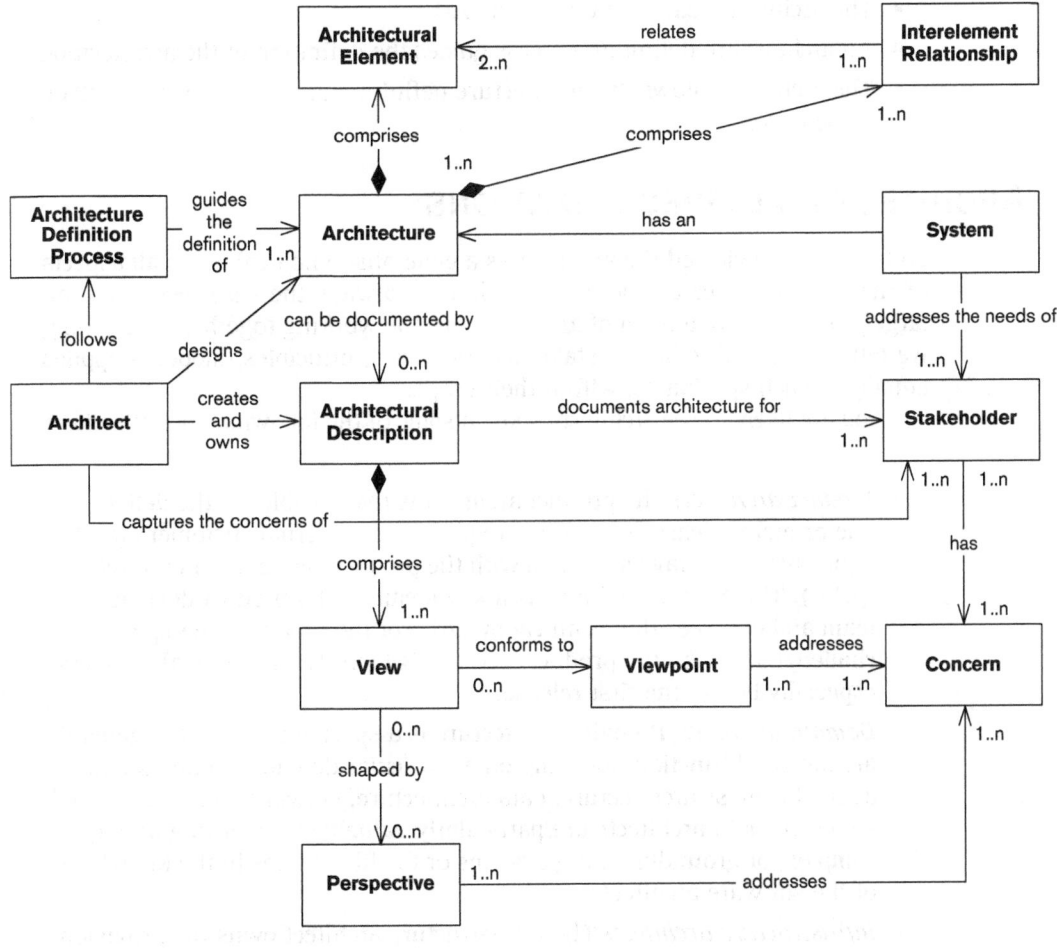

FIGURE 5-3 ARCHITECTURE DEFINITION AND THE ARCHITECT IN CONTEXT

INTERRELATIONSHIPS BETWEEN THE CORE CONCEPTS

We can now add two final pieces to our relationship diagram, namely, the process of architecture definition and the architect, as shown in Figure 5–3.

We have added the following relationships to augment the earlier versions of the model shown in previous chapters (e.g., Figure 4–3).

- The architect captures and consolidates the concerns of the stakeholders.
- The architect designs an architecture that meets these concerns.

- The architect creates and owns the AD.
- An architecture definition process guides the definition of the architecture.
- The architect follows the architecture definition process to carry out all of these tasks.

ARCHITECTURAL SPECIALIZATIONS

So far, we have viewed the architect as a generalist who deals with all aspects of the system under development. This isn't always the case, especially on large projects where a team of architects may be working together. Everything we talk about in this book—stakeholders, views, principles, models—applies equally to such specialists, within their scope.

You are likely to see architects take on some of the following specializations.

- *Product architect*: The product architect is responsible for the delivery of one or more releases of a software product to external customers (and typically would stay associated with the product over a number of release cycles). The product architect is a key member of a product development team and oversees the technical integrity of the product. One specific challenge faced by the product architect is identifying user stakeholders, especially before the first release.
- *Domain architect*: Domain architecture is a specialization of the general architectural function, focusing on a particular domain of interest, such as the business architecture, data architecture, network architecture, and so on. Domain architects are particularly valuable for working on large, complex, or groundbreaking systems or for filling gaps in the knowledge of the software architect.
- *Infrastructure architect:* The infrastructure architect owns the provision of hardware and software infrastructure to systems and often performs this activity at a company-wide level. On the hardware side this may include data centers, servers, storage and backup, desktop computers, wide-area and local-area networking, office peripherals such as printers, and specialist devices such as certificate servers. Infrastructure software includes areas such as enterprise security, database management systems, enterprise messaging, identity and security, and desktop tools such as word processing software. Information systems will often be mandated to use all or some of these company-wide elements.
- *Solution architect*: In contrast with the domain architect, the solution architect specifically takes a broad, high-level view of the entire solution. This role also focuses on wider issues than just technology, such as business process change, procurement, staffing, and so forth.

- *Enterprise architect*: Whereas the software architect concerns herself with a single (albeit probably complex and important) system, the enterprise architect has responsibility for the cross-system information systems architecture of the whole enterprise, including sales and marketing, client-facing systems, products and services, purchasing and accounts, the supply chain, human resources, and so forth. The enterprise architect is also often concerned with the definition and oversight of company-wide principles, standards, and policies and, like the solution architect, also concerns herself with wider issues such as business process change.

THE ORGANIZATIONAL CONTEXT

Let's look at how your role as a software architect compares with the roles of the other key personnel on software development projects.

Business Analysts

A business analyst is responsible for capturing and documenting detailed business requirements, typically focusing on stakeholders from the user community, and ensuring that these are correct, complete, and consistent. You will often draw on the specialized knowledge of the business analyst, especially when dealing with views of interest to acquirers, users, and assessors.

Project Managers

A project manager is responsible for ensuring delivery of the product or system and meeting commercial priorities for resources, costs, and timescales. You will often help the project manager develop plans or assess them for reasonableness. You will also provide the project manager with technical information, feedback, advice, risk assessment, and so on throughout the project lifecycle.

In our experience the most productive relationship between project managers and architects follows a *partnership* model: The project manager focuses on stakeholders, plans, budgets, staffing and resources, milestones, deadlines, and deliverables; and the architect focuses on stakeholders, concerns, scope, requirements, views, and models.

Design Authorities

A design authority (sometimes referred to as a technical design authority or a technical lead) takes overall responsibility for the quality of the internal element designs for the system. In our experience, the architect often fills this role as the project moves into the design phase. The design authority takes the architectural views as her input and acts as guide and leader to the software developers who design, build, test, and integrate the product or system.

We have found that design authority is often the role actually performed by people who have the job title of technical architect. These key people are often the primary technical points of contact for how the system is implemented and how the underlying technology platform works. This role on the project is crucial and must be filled by an extremely strong staff member. However, making tradeoffs between requirements and possibilities for the system's stakeholders is not an inherent part of being a technical design authority, although it is a key part of the architect's role. Therefore we argue that the technical design authority plays a design role rather than an architectural one.

The boundary between the design authority and the architect is probably the hardest one to define formally. One guideline we find useful when deciding whether an issue is architecturally significant is to consider its impact on stakeholders. If the outcome of a decision is likely to have a significant impact on important stakeholders or requires tradeoffs between stakeholder needs, the architect should probably be responsible for the decision. If the decision is visible only within the development team, it is probably a design authority issue.

Of course, it is not always possible to make this assessment up front, and it is essential that the two roles cooperate fully. Let's consider a couple of examples to see how this might work in practice.

EXAMPLE Architecture definition for a new system has identified the need for a relational database, from the industry-leading supplier, for persistent storage of transaction data. The imminent new release of the database server will provide some significant new technology features and potential improvements in performance.

Functionally, the system would look identical whether it were built on the current or new version of the relational database management system. However, taking on the new version presents some commercial risk related to availability of skills, confidence in the new platform, and the potential problems associated with any point-zero release.

Because of the possible commercial impact, we would tend to involve the architect in this decision.

EXAMPLE In integration tests, some end-user queries have been falling far short of their performance requirements, taking a minute or more to complete under peak load. Monitoring and analysis have suggested that some database tables need to be internally restructured, indexes modified, and objects spread more evenly across physical disks. Access to data, which occurs via stored procedures, will not be affected (other than being much faster).

Because these changes have no visible stakeholder impact (other than to make the system compliant), it seems reasonable not to involve the architect in what are essentially internal systems decisions and to instead make this the responsibility of the design authority.

Technology Specialists

A technology specialist provides detailed expertise in one specific area. Where the architect provides breadth, the technology specialist provides depth, and the combination of the two can be extremely powerful.

Broadly speaking, it is the technology specialist's responsibility to provide detailed facts, to assess the architecture for technical feasibility, and to spot pitfalls early. You should be able to take the information provided by the technology specialist and apply it to addressing the problems you need to solve.

You should always make the best use of the skills and knowledge of your colleagues in the organization. It's not possible to know everything about everything, and as an architect you aren't expected to.

PRINCIPLE The architect provides and oversees the architectural breadth and works closely with both business-focused and technology-focused specialists who provide the specialist depth.

Developers

The architect's involvement doesn't end with handing over the completed and accepted AD. Although your level of participation may decrease during the build and test phases, you will still maintain a technology leadership role to ensure that the team adheres to the spirit and the letter of the AD.

This may involve mentoring staff through the detailed design process, reviewing designs as they are completed to ensure conformance to the system's architectural principles, arbitrating technology disputes, or even developing pieces of the implementation if required. You are likely to get involved in integration and system testing to ensure that the tests exercise an appropriate selection of functional and operational characteristics.

You will also need to lead the change process if (as is likely) the AD requires any modifications during development.

The nature of your interactions with your development team will depend to some extent on the lifecycle model the team is following. An architect for a large "waterfall" development program will interact very differently with her developers than will an architect on a smaller iterative or agile development project. We address this issue in Chapter 7.

THE ARCHITECT'S SKILLS

Although the job of the architect traditionally has a technology focus, and in nearly all cases the architect herself has a strong technology background, we have seen that the role is much broader than merely drawing up technical plans and designs.

You must have an across-the-board understanding of technology at a high level and of the real-world issues and problems the system is required to solve. You should have real experience with designing and building systems, although it may not always be possible to have direct, practical knowledge of the specific technologies you plan to use. (This is an example of when you must draw on the experience of technology specialists.)

Typically you will also have one or more areas of deeper technical expertise; this may not apply to your current project but will give you the ability to recognize a good design when you see one.

As well as technology knowledge, you also need to have a good understanding of the business domain in which you are working. While you don't need to understand every detail of every process, you do need to understand the main business processes and main types of information that are found in the business area and the dependencies, importance, and criticality of each. This knowledge will allow you to communicate more effectively with your business-oriented stakeholders and will allow you to make more informed prioritization and tradeoff decisions, as you will understand their likely impact on the business.

It is also very important that you have good "soft skills" as well, more so than for many other IT roles, with the possible exception of the project manager. These skills include:

- *Information capture*: As we will see, you have to capture many types of information, from a wide variety of different stakeholders, with different interests in your architecture and different levels of business and technical expertise. You need to keep your stakeholders on track in interviews, to get them to focus on the important architectural concerns, and to "drill down" into detail where appropriate. You also need to be able to listen to their answers and take notes at the same time!

- *Facilitation*: Workshops and meetings can be a very effective way of capturing information and mapping out potential solutions. However, managing such a gathering can be quite a challenge, especially when you have a mix of senior and more junior stakeholders, or when there is hidden (or explicit) conflict.

- *Negotiation*: Reaching consensus among a wide variety of stakeholders with often conflicting or incompatible concerns can also be a challenge. Negotiation skills help you to understand and act on what is truly of value to people and what they can afford to give away.

- *Communication*: You may have the best architecture ever, but unless you can communicate it effectively to all of your different stakeholders, and get their buy-in, it is unlikely to be built. Different stakeholders have different interests and need to be communicated to in different ways—in person or through documents, concisely or in great detail.
- *Flexibility*: You need to be able to rapidly learn about unfamiliar business areas and technologies, to make quick changes of direction where appropriate, and to be ready to discard your preconceived ideas about the problem or its solution. You also need to know when to hold your ground.

Above all, you must earn and maintain the confidence of all of your stakeholders, from senior management and users to developers, third parties, and operational staff.

THE ARCHITECT'S RESPONSIBILITIES

A pro forma list of responsibilities for an architect would include the following items.

- Ensure that the scope, context, and constraints are documented and accepted.
- Identify, engage, and enfranchise your stakeholders.
- Facilitate the making of system-level decisions, ensuring that they are made on the basis of the best information and are aligned with stakeholder needs.
- Arbitrate and ensure that consensus is reached when stakeholder needs are in conflict or are incompatible.
- Arbitrate and ensure that consensus is reached when architectural compromises need to be made (for example, performance against flexibility or security against ease of use).
- Capture and interpret input from technical and domain specialists (and represent this accurately to stakeholders as needed).
- Define and document the architecture of the system.
- Define and document strategies, standards, and guidelines to direct the build and deployment of the system.
- Ensure that the architecture meets the system quality attributes.
- Develop and own the AD (i.e., manage all changes to it).
- Help ensure that agreed-upon architectural principles and standards are applied to the finished system or product.
- Provide technical leadership.

It is rare, in our experience, for such a role definition to exist in many organizations. If you find yourself without one, you may find it helpful to create one (use our list as a template) and get it agreed to and publicized with your stakeholders. It should be a simple document that defines your architectural scope (the tasks you will perform), your deliverables (the documents and other material you will produce), and possibly the way you will work (for example, that you will conduct architectural reviews with key stakeholders to ensure that you are addressing their concerns).

STRATEGY Ensure that you have clear terms of reference for your role on any project in which you are significantly involved. If this does not already exist, draw up a brief terms of reference document, and review and agree on it with your stakeholders.

In many cases, you may also have some responsibilities for developing and promoting the role of architecture in your organization, outside of your involvement on specific projects. An obvious area of focus is the definition of viewpoints; you may also find yourself involved in (or responsible for) the development of architectural processes, tools, templates, and other materials.

SUMMARY

We have discussed two distinct concepts in this chapter, the final chapter of Part I.

- *Architecture definition* is a process whereby stakeholder needs and concerns are captured, an architecture to meet these needs is designed, and the architecture is fully and unambiguously described via an AD.
- The *architect* is the person (or group) responsible for designing, documenting, and leading the construction of an architecture that meets the needs of all its stakeholders.

There is no single commonly accepted definition of the software architect's role. The role of the architect includes elements of requirements capture and high-level design but is more than either of these. In this chapter, we defined the four main responsibilities of the architect: to identify and engage the stakeholders, to understand and capture their concerns, to create and take ownership of the AD, and to take a leading role in the realization of the architecture.

We presented some architectural specializations that you may encounter (or even choose to take on) such as product architects, domain architects, infrastructure architects, solution architects, and enterprise architects. We also compared and contrasted the role of the architect with other key project roles such as business analysts, project managers, design authorities, technology specialists, and developers. We considered when the architect is important: primarily during the early stages of system development and during acceptance, with a lesser role during the build and test phases.

Finally, we discussed the skills that a good architect should possess and presented the architect's responsibilities.

FURTHER READING

Most of the architecture books we mentioned earlier in Part I contain some discussion of the architect's role, for example, [CLEM10]. In addition, McGovern et al. [MCGO04] contains a good discussion of roles related to software and enterprise architecture.

Many books are available that can help you develop good soft skills, such as information capture and communication skills, good examples being [FISH03], [PELL09], and [BREN10]. These books will help you to identify your weaknesses in these areas and give you a lot of practical ideas for improving your skills, although in our experience the best way to learn soft skills is through training, mentoring, and experience.

The definition of *architecturally significant* that we paraphrased earlier in this chapter can be found in Kruchten [KRUC03].

PART II

THE PROCESS OF SOFTWARE ARCHITECTURE

6

INTRODUCTION TO THE SOFTWARE ARCHITECTURE PROCESS

It is not our aim in this book to define another software development method or to radically change existing models of the software development lifecycle. However, many software development methods fail to clearly define the role of software architecture in the development lifecycle. If they discuss it at all, they usually view architecture definition as merely the first part of software design—and we hope this book will show you that this view is far too simplistic.

As we have seen, architecture definition is a broad, creative, dynamic activity that is much more about discovering stakeholder concerns, evaluating options, and making tradeoffs than simply capturing information. At the outset, your stakeholders may have some fundamental disagreements about scope, objectives, and priorities. It may be necessary to change direction, possibly even significantly, partway through the exercise as a result of information you have uncovered through your work.

Although every situation is different, there is a core set of activities you will usually need to perform as part of architecture definition for any project. We describe these activities in the following chapters. You may need to do other things during architecture definition too, but you will probably need to perform most of the activities we describe in Part II to avoid creating future problems.

Part II begins by presenting a generic and straightforward process for architecture definition, which you can use to help plan your own architecture definition work and to align your plans with those for the other parts of the development. The subsequent chapters look at each of the key activities of the process, namely:

- Agreeing on scope and context, constraints, and baseline architectural principles
- Identifying and engaging stakeholders
- Identifying and using architectural scenarios
- Using architectural styles and patterns
- Producing architectural models
- Documenting the architecture
- Validating the architecture

For each of these activities, we provide practical advice and guidance, including checklists to help make sure you haven't forgotten anything and pointers to further reading.

7

THE ARCHITECTURE
DEFINITION PROCESS

Architecture definition starts early in the project lifecycle, when scope and requirements are often still unclear and the current view of the system may differ substantially from what is eventually built. For this reason, architecture definition tends to be a more fluid activity than later tasks such as designing, building, and testing, when the problem you are solving is better understood. When you start, you don't fully know the size and extent of your system, where the complexity is, what the most significant risks are, or where you will encounter conflict among your stakeholders.

In this chapter, we outline a simple process of architecture definition that applies (in some way) to most software development projects, irrespective of the development approaches used. You can use the process we describe with most forms of the software development lifecycle—from the very structured and formal to those founded on iterative or agile principles.

The material in this chapter will help you plan your own architecture definition work and align your plans with those for the other parts of the development. Of course, the way you do this will vary according to the needs of your project, the method you are following, the time available, and your skills and those of your team. You will be most successful if you use this chapter as a framework or starting point for developing your own personalized architecture definition process.

GUIDING PRINCIPLES

For an architecture definition process to be successful, it must adhere to the following principles.

- It must be driven by *stakeholder concerns*, as we discussed in Part I. As we will see, stakeholder concerns are the core—but by no means the only—inputs to the process. Furthermore, the process must *balance* these concerns effectively where they conflict or have incompatible implications.

- It must encourage the effective *communication* of architectural decisions, principles, and the solution itself to stakeholders.

- It must ensure, on an ongoing basis, that the architectural decisions and principles are *adhered to* throughout the lifecycle up to the final deployment.

- It must (as much as possible, given the fluid nature of architecture definition) be *structured*. In other words, it must comprise a series of one or more steps or tasks, with a clear definition of the objectives, inputs, and outputs of each step. Typically, the outputs from one step are the inputs to subsequent steps.

- It must be *pragmatic*—that is, it must consider real-world issues such as lack of time or money, shortage of specific technical skills, unclear or changing requirements, the existing context, and organizational considerations.

- It must be *flexible* so that it can be tailored to particular circumstances. (This is sometimes referred to as a *toolkit* or *framework* approach, with the idea that you use those elements of the toolkit you need and ignore the rest.)

- It must be *technology-agnostic*. That is, the process must not mandate that the architecture be based around any specific technology, architectural pattern, or development style, nor should it dictate any particular modeling, diagramming, or documentation style.

- It must *integrate* with the chosen software development lifecycle.

- It must align with good *software engineering practices* and *quality management standards* (such as ISO 9001) so that it can integrate easily with existing approaches.

Having set out our ground rules, let's consider the context in which architecture definition operates, starting with where we want to end—its outcomes.

Process Outcomes

Clearly, the main goal of architecture definition is to develop a sound architecture and to manage the production and maintenance of all of the elements of an AD that captures it. However, there are some desirable secondary outcomes or consequences of architecture definition, such as the following.

- *Clarification of requirements and of other inputs to the process*: Your stakeholders may not be absolutely clear about what they want, and it may take some time to pin them down.

- *Management of stakeholders' expectations*: Your architecture will inevitably need to make compromises around your stakeholders' concerns. It is far better to make these compromises visible and clearly understood early in the life of the project than to let them emerge later.

- *Identification and evaluation of architectural options*: There is rarely just one solution to a problem. When there are several potential solutions, your analysis will reveal the strengths and weaknesses of each and justify the chosen solution.
- *Description of architectural acceptance criteria* (indirectly): Architecture definition should lead to a clear understanding of the conditions that must be met before the stakeholders will accept the architecture as conforming to their requirements (e.g., it must provide a particular function, achieve certain response times, or restart in less than a given time period).
- *Creation of a set of design inputs* (ideally): Such information as guidance for and constraints on the software design process will help ensure the integrity of your architecture.

Having defined the goals that our architecture definition process must meet, let us continue by considering the context within which the process must work.

THE PROCESS CONTEXT

Architecture forms the bridge between requirements and design, performing the tradeoffs necessary to satisfy the demands of both. In process terms, this means that architecture definition sits between requirements analysis and software construction (design, code, and test). A good model for the interaction between requirements, architecture, and construction is the Three Peaks model (see Figure 7–1), an extension of Bashar Nuseibeh's Twin Peaks model.

The three triangles (the peaks) in the diagram represent the major software evelopment activities of requirements analysis, architecture definition, and construction; the widening of the shapes at their bases represents an increasing amount of elaboration as time goes on while the system is developed. The curling arrows show how requirements and architecture as well as architecture and construction are intertwined to a progressively increasing degree during system development. Although the specification, architecture, andimplementation of the system are quite distinct, as the Three Peaks model illustrates, they have profound effects on each other and so cannot be considered in isolation.

The following key relationships exist between software architecture and the requirements and construction activities of the software lifecycle.

- Requirements analysis provides the context for architecture definition by defining the scope and the system's desired functionality and quality properties.

- Architecture definition often reveals inconsistent and missing requirements and also helps stakeholders understand the relative costs and complexities of meeting their concerns. This feeds back into requirements analysis to clarify and add requirements and to prioritize these when tradeoffs are made between stakeholders' aspirations and what can be achieved given time and budget constraints.

- When architecture definition has resulted in an architecture that appears to meet an acceptable set of user requirements, the construction of the system can be planned.

- Construction is often organized as a set of incremental deliveries, each of which aims to provide a useful set of functions and to leave the system in a stable, usable state (albeit an incomplete one). The construction of each increment provides further feedback to architecture definition, validating or indicating problems with the architecture as currently specified; hence, there is architecture definition activity throughout the lifecycle.

Requirements analysis, architecture definition, and software construction have a strong, interconnected set of relationships. Requirements analysis provides an initial context for architecture definition but is then itself affected by architecture definition as requirements are understood more fully. In turn, architecture definition drives the implementation process, but each piece of construction performed provides feedback about the effectiveness and utility of the architecture in use.

SUPPORTING ACTIVITIES

Our architecture definition process assumes that the following will be available to you and accepted by the sponsor and other stakeholders before you start:

- A definition of the system's baseline scope and context
- A definition of key stakeholder concerns

Our process also assumes that the right stakeholders have been identified and engaged.

In reality, it is rare for the baseline scope and concerns to be captured to an appropriate level of detail at this early stage, and it is unlikely that any stakeholders (other than perhaps developers and occasionally users) will have been brought on board and engaged in the process. It can be a big challenge to discover and consolidate these inputs and then to gain agreement on them from an engaged stakeholder community before you can even think about a solution. We present a number of techniques for doing this in Chapters 8 and 9.

At the other end of the process, once you have an AD, you will often want to deliver a skeleton system implementation as the first development increment. Such an implementation can be very valuable because it offers a practical validation of the architecture, acts as a credibility test for the system's stakeholders, and provides a framework in which the development team can work.

The slightly extended UML activity diagram in Figure 7–2 shows how architecture definition relates to the following supporting activities. The square boxes with underlined names represent key inputs to and outputs from the process. The activities are as follows.

- Define the initial scope and context.
- Engage the stakeholders.
- Capture first-cut concerns.
- Define the architecture.
- Optionally, create a skeleton system.

Having defined the initial scope and context for your system with the acquiring stakeholders, you can then identify and engage the other important stakeholders whose concerns need to be addressed by the architecture. Capturing their concerns provides a primary input, along with the scope and context, to architecture definition. (As we will see, both the scope and the concerns as defined at this point may change, subject to stakeholder agreement, during architecture definition.)

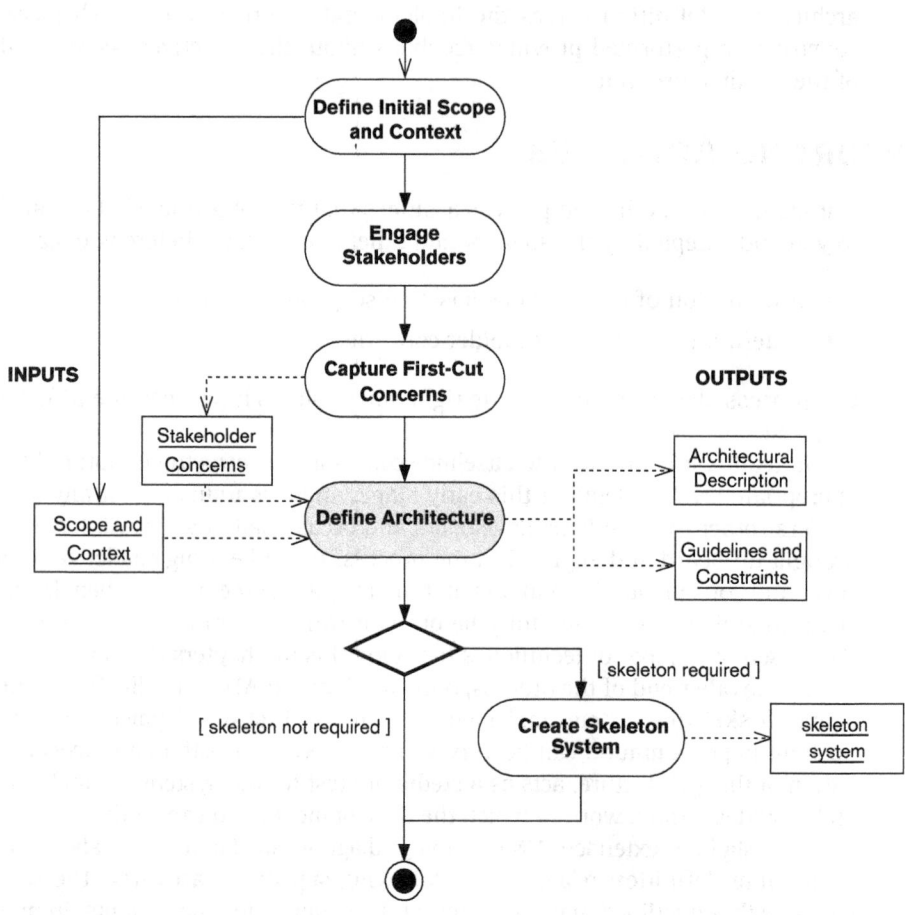

FIGURE 7–2 ACTIVITIES SUPPORTING ARCHITECTURE DEFINITION

Architecture definition results in an AD and normally a set of guidelines and constraints to guide the system construction. Once you have an AD, you can (if you have the time and resources) create a skeleton system that will act as an evolvable prototype of the system you want to build.

We describe each of these supporting activities in Tables 7–1 through 7–5.

TABLE 7–1 DEFINE THE INITIAL SCOPE AND CONTEXT

Aims	To clearly define the boundaries of the system's behavior and responsibilities and the operational and organizational context within which the system exists.
Inputs	Acquirer needs and vision; organizational strategy; enterprise IT architecture.

TABLE 7-1 DEFINE THE INITIAL SCOPE AND CONTEXT (*CONTINUED*)

Outputs	Initial statements of the goals of the system and what is included and excluded from its responsibilities, along with an initial system context definition. These can be captured in a draft Context view.
Comments	This step is primarily a process of understanding strategic and organizational objectives and how the system helps meet them, along with some analysis to understand which other systems need to interact with this one. We talk about this activity in Chapter 16. Note that the scope as defined here may change (subject to stakeholder agreement) during architecture definition.

TABLE 7-2 ENGAGE THE STAKEHOLDERS

Aims	To identify the system's important stakeholders and to create a working relationship with them.
Inputs	Scope and context from the draft Context view; organizational structure.
Outputs	Definition of each of the stakeholder groups, with one or more named, engaged people who will represent the group.
Comments	This step involves understanding the organizational context you are working in and identifying the key people who will be affected by the system. You can then start to get to know their representatives and begin building a working relationship with them. We talk more about this activity in Chapter 9.

TABLE 7-3 CAPTURE FIRST-CUT CONCERNS

Aims	To clearly understand the concerns that each stakeholder group has about the system and the priorities they place on each concern.
Inputs	Stakeholder list; scope and context.
Outputs	Initial definition of a set of prioritized concerns for each stakeholder group.
Comments	This step often starts with your initial stakeholder meetings. It normally involves a series of presentations and meetings with representatives of each stakeholder group that allow you to explain what you aim to achieve and allow the stakeholders to explain their interests in the system. We talk more about this activity in Chapter 9. Note that the concerns as defined here may change (subject to stakeholder agreement) during architecture definition.

TABLE 7-4 DEFINE THE ARCHITECTURE

Aims	To create the AD for the system.
Inputs	Stakeholder list; scope and context.
Outputs	AD; guidelines and constraints.
Comments	We describe this step in detail in the Architecture Definition Activities section of this chapter.

TABLE 7-5 CREATE THE SKELETON SYSTEM

Aims	Optional step to create a working (albeit limited) implementation of your architecture that can evolve into a delivered system during the system construction phase of the lifecycle.
Inputs	AD; associated guidelines and constraints.
Outputs	A limited working system that illustrates that the system can address at least one of your scenarios.
Comments	If you have the time and resources available to allow the creation of a skeleton system, it forms an effective bridge between architecture definition and software construction. This step allows the architect and the developers to build a working system that can execute at least a simple functional scenario the system is meant to address. The skeleton system acts as a validation of your architecture (and an important proof point for many stakeholders) as well as a framework for the software construction phase.

ARCHITECTURE DEFINITION ACTIVITIES

Your biggest difficulty as an architect is the amount of uncertainty and change you face as you bring your stakeholders together. Although you will be working from an agreed-upon scope—or if not, you will produce one as a matter of urgency—this is likely to change as the implications of including or excluding certain features emerge and as the stakeholders better understand the significance of what they are requesting. Functional and quality property requirements are also likely to evolve, perhaps significantly.

For this reason, our architecture definition process is an iterative one. In other words, you need to repeat the main steps several times before you produce a finished AD. Of course, for a small or simple architecture, you may produce the completed AD after the first iteration, but for anything complex, unfamiliar, or contentious, a single iteration is unlikely to suffice. Also, the architecture will keep evolving as the system is developed, so you will return to this cycle of activities throughout the project.

The UML activity diagram in Figure 7-3 illustrates our process, which involves the following steps.

FIGURE 7–3 DETAILS OF ARCHITECTURE DEFINITION

1. Consolidate the inputs.
2. Identify scenarios.
3. Identify the relevant architectural styles.
4. Produce a candidate architecture.
5. Explore the architectural options.

6.   Evaluate the architecture with the stakeholders.

7A. Rework the architecture

7B. Revisit the requirements.

Although it is obviously a simplification of the reality of architecture definition, you may find our model useful in discussions with management, colleagues, and stakeholders.

The curved arrows between steps 7A and 7B in the figure indicate that these steps are not done in isolation: There is often a heavy interaction between them as reworking the architecture may suggest changes to requirements and vice versa. For example, simplifying the concurrency model may necessitate changes to the order in which the system performs some tasks. Of course, all such changes should be reviewed and ratified with stakeholders.

The individual steps in this process are described in Tables 7–6 through 7–13.

TABLE 7–6 STEP 1: CONSOLIDATE THE INPUTS

Aims	To understand, validate, and refine the initial inputs.
Inputs	Raw process inputs (scope and context definition from draft Context view, stakeholder concerns).
Outputs	Consolidated inputs, with major inconsistencies removed, open questions answered, and (at a minimum) areas requiring further exploration identified.
Activities	Take the raw process inputs, resolve inconsistencies between them, answer open questions, and delve deeper where necessary, to produce a solid baseline.
Comments	It is rare for you to be provided with a consistent, accurate, and agreed-upon set of process inputs. During this step you take the information available, fill in gaps, resolve inconsistencies, and obtain formal agreement from the key stakeholders.

TABLE 7–7 STEP 2: IDENTIFY SCENARIOS

Aims	To identify a set of scenarios that illustrates the system's most important requirements.
Inputs	Consolidated inputs (as currently defined).
Outputs	Architectural scenarios.
Activities	Produce a set of scenarios that characterize the most important attributes required of the architecture and can be used to evaluate how well a proposed architecture will meet the underlying functional and quality property requirements.
Comments	A scenario is a description of a situation that the system is likely to encounter, which allows assessment of the effectiveness of the architecture in that situation. Scenarios can be identified for required functional behavior ("How does the system do X?") and for desired quality properties ("How does the system cope with load Y?" or "How can the architecture support change Z?"). We explain how to approach this step in Chapter 10.

TABLE 7-8 STEP 3: IDENTIFY THE RELEVANT ARCHITECTURAL STYLES

Aims	To identify one or more proven architectural styles that could be used as a basis for the overall organization of the system.
Inputs	Consolidated inputs (as currently defined); architectural scenarios.
Outputs	Architectural styles to consider as the basis for the system's main architectural structures.
Activities	Review existing catalogs of architectural styles, and consider system organizations that have worked well for you before. Identify those that appear to be relevant to the architecture as you currently understand it.
Comments	Using an architectural style is a way to reuse architectural knowledge that has proved effective in previous situations. This can help you arrive at a suitable system organization without having to design it from scratch and so reduces the risks involved in using new, unproven ideas. We talk more about using architectural styles in Chapter 11.

TABLE 7-9 PRODUCE A CANDIDATE ARCHITECTURE

Aims	To create a first-cut architecture for the system that reflects its primary architectural concerns and that can act as a basis for further architectural evaluation and refinement.
Inputs	Consolidated inputs (as currently defined); relevant architectural styles, viewpoints, and perspectives.
Outputs	Draft architectural views.
Activities	Produce an initial set of architectural views to define your initial architectural ideas, using guidance from the viewpoints and perspectives and any relevant architectural styles.
Comments	Although they may contain gaps, inconsistencies, or errors, the draft views form a starting point for the more detailed architecture work later.

TABLE 7-10 EXPLORE THE ARCHITECTURAL OPTIONS

Aims	To explore the various architectural possibilities for the system and make the key architectural decisions to choose among them.
Inputs	Consolidated inputs; draft architectural views; architectural scenarios, viewpoints, and perspectives.
Outputs	More detailed or accurate architectural views for some parts of the architecture.
Activities	Apply scenarios to the draft models to demonstrate that they are workable, that they meet requirements, and that there are no hidden problems. Take any areas of risk, concern, or uncertainty that are revealed and further explore the requirements, problems, and issues. Where there is more than one possible solution, evaluate the strengths and weaknesses of each (refer to Chapter 14 for guidance on how to do this) and select the best one.
Comments	The aim of this step is to fill in gaps, remove inconsistencies in the models, and provide extra detail where needed.

TABLE 7–11 STEP 4: EVALUATE THE ARCHITECTURE WITH THE STAKEHOLDERS

Aims	To work through an evaluation of the architecture with your key stakeholders, capture any problems or deficiencies, and gain the stakeholders' acceptance of the architecture.
Inputs	Consolidated inputs; architectural views and perspective outputs.
Outputs	Architectural review comments.
Activities	Evaluate your architecture with a representative collection of stakeholders. Capture and agree on any improvements to or comments on the models.
Comments	Although each group of stakeholders will have different interests, the overall objective is to confirm that stakeholder concerns are met and that the architecture is of good quality. You may have to work hard to obtain consensus if the concerns of different stakeholders conflict with one another. We talk about this activity in Chapter 14.

TABLE 7–12 REWORK THE ARCHITECTURE

Aims	To address any concerns that have emerged during the evaluation task.
Inputs	Architectural views; architectural review comments; relevant architectural styles, viewpoints, and perspectives.
Outputs	Reworked architectural views; areas for further investigation (optional).
Activities	Take the results of the architectural evaluation and address them in order to produce an architecture that better meets its objectives. This step normally involves functional analysis, the use of viewpoints and perspectives, and prototyping.
Comments	This step is done concurrently and often quite collaboratively with step 7B (Revisit the requirements). The two steps feed back into step 5 (Explore the architectural options).

TABLE 7–13 REVISIT THE REQUIREMENTS

Aims	To consider any changes to the system's original requirements that may have to be made in light of architectural evaluation.
Inputs	Architectural views; architectural review comments.
Outputs	Revised requirements (if any).
Activities	The work done so far may reveal inadequacies or inconsistencies in requirements or requirements that are infeasible or expensive to implement. In this case, you may need to revisit these requirements with stakeholders and obtain their agreement to the necessary revisions.
Comments	This step is done concurrently and often quite collaboratively with step 7A (Rework the architecture). The two steps feed back into step 5 (Explore architectural options).

PROCESS EXIT CRITERIA

In some other ideal world, architecture definition would continue until the architecture was complete, correct, and fully documented in the AD. However, the problem with this approach is that it takes a great deal of effort that, depending on the project, might be better spent elsewhere. It's also very hard to fully validate an architectural design until it's been at least partially implemented, and so trying to nail down every detail before a line of code has been written can be quite counterproductive.

The key to deciding when enough architecture work has been completed is to consider the risks your project is facing. If you have unresolved risks that are likely to endanger project success, you need to do more architecture work. If you have addressed the material risks to a sufficient level, you are likely to have performed enough architecture work.

A good indication of whether you have addressed your risks is when there are no comments, questions, or concerns outstanding from your architectural evaluation. This means that your stakeholders (including yourself) believe that the proposed system will meet their concerns, and that they believe that the risks that they are aware of have been mitigated.

Different projects will require different amounts of architecture work, depending on their scale, complexity, criticality, and technical characteristics. For example, large package implementation projects will require a lot more architecture work up front than departmental software development projects, as there is little opportunity for iteration, feedback, and correction in a large package implementation project. A midsize software development project is often less risky and more flexible, meaning that it can evolve to mitigate many of problems that may be discovered as construction progresses.

PRINCIPLE Architecture definition (or an iteration of it) can be considered complete once the material risks that the system faces have been mitigated, which can be judged by the absence of significant comments or actions after stakeholder evaluation of the architecture.

In practice, you are unlikely to achieve complete agreement, particularly when the stakeholder group is large or diverse or when requirements are complex. Usually you will finish architecture definition when most of the concerns of the more important stakeholders have been addressed and when you feel confident that the project can proceed with an acceptable level of risk. In some cases, however, you will find that some important stakeholder concerns are still outstanding when the allocated time for architecture definition ends. This is an unfortunate situation, but when time is limited, it may be unavoidable. It is essential in such cases that you prioritize your work to focus on the riskiest or most contentious areas so that at least these are resolved before you move into construction. In this way you can be relatively confident that your architecture is adequate to meet its most important challenges.

Don't forget to include yourself in the list of AD reviewers. Even if your stakeholders are happy with the architecture, if you are not, you should not consider it complete. You may have knowledge or understanding of the system that they don't, and it is your responsibility to ensure that this is reflected in the architecture.

STRATEGY Include yourself in the reviewers of the architectural description, and do not finish initial architecture definition until you are satisfied that there are no significant issues with the architecture.

It is not hard to find yourself descending into a repeating cycle of further and deeper refinement and enlargement of your AD, with the result that you never build the system or that development goes ahead without you. This worst possible outcome is to be strongly resisted. In our experience, on all but the largest projects, you should aim to complete the production of the AD in one to three months.

STRATEGY Aim to produce an architectural description that is good enough to meet the needs of its users, rather than strive for a perfect version that will take significantly more resources to complete without providing any real benefit to the system's stakeholders.

Of course, completion of the AD does not mean that you are no longer working as an architect. You'll be involved throughout, advising, leading, overseeing, resolving problems, revising the architecture as new knowledge emerges, and so on. This means that once the AD is baselined and placed under configuration control, it should continue to be a living document, kept up-to-date throughout the construction steps and into deployment.

ARCHITECTURE DEFINITION IN THE SOFTWARE DEVELOPMENT LIFECYCLE

Architecture definition does not replace the normal software development lifecycle but should be thought of as an integral part of it. In this section, we discuss how architecture definition fits into the common approaches to designing and building systems.

Waterfall Approaches

In the classic waterfall model, software development is viewed as a linear sequence of tasks, with each task using the outputs of the previous one as its inputs, and feeding into the next task in turn, as shown in Figure 7–4. So, for example, the functional specification provides the inputs to the design stage, the design provides the inputs to the build and unit test stage, and so on. When changes are required to the system, these feed backward to the preceding stage and possibly further up the waterfall. Although somewhat discredited as a development approach for large systems, due to its late feedback and inflexibility, the waterfall approach is still a useful and widely used mental model for the fundamental steps needed in a software development project.

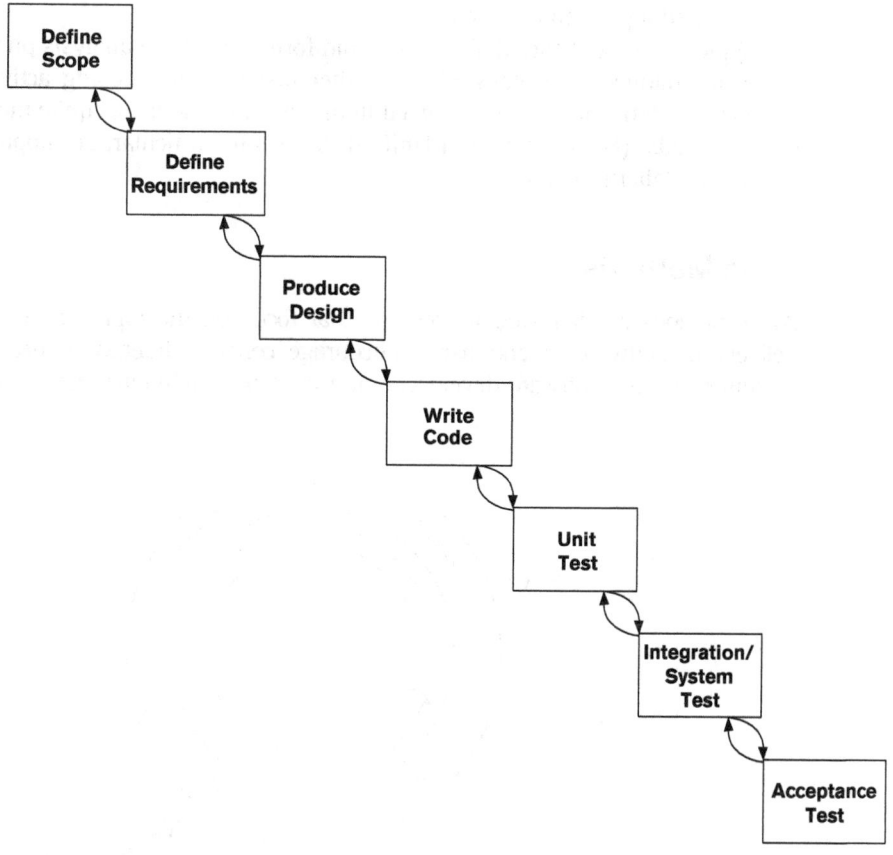

FIGURE 7–4 THE WATERFALL MODEL OF DEVELOPMENT

Architecture definition is easy to integrate with such a linear approach: It is usually viewed as a separate task early in the lifecycle (before, after, or sometimes alongside requirements definition).

Iterative Approaches

The motivation behind iterative approaches (such as Feature Driven Development and the Rational Unified Process) is to reduce risk by means of early delivery of partial functionality, as shown in Figure 7–5. Each iteration usually focuses on one area that presents significant risk because its requirements are unclear, for example, or because it is a complex or leading-edge element of the system. In most iterative approaches, the individual iterations are run as accelerated development projects in their own right, broken down into structured tasks with defined inputs and deliverables.

Typically, architecture definition would form part of the analysis phase, or it could alternatively run alongside the other tasks as an ongoing activity. Our architecture definition process is itself iterative, which dovetails quite nicely with such methods. (For the Rational Unified Process in particular, our approach fits well in its Elaboration phase.)

Agile Methods

Agile methods are lightweight methods that focus on the rapid and continuous delivery of software to end users, encourage constant interaction between the customer and the software developers, and attempt to minimize the management

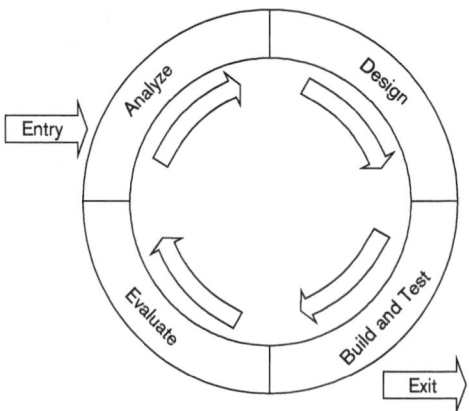

FIGURE 7–5 ITERATIVE DEVELOPMENT

overhead of the development process (in particular, a dramatic reduction in the amount of development documentation produced). The aim of agile methods is to allow a team (or a larger organization) to react and adapt to change in its environment quickly enough to deal with the change and not become overwhelmed by it. Three of the best-known agile methods for software development are Extreme Programming (XP), Scrum, and Lean Software Development.

In our experience, it can sometimes be difficult to get software architects and agile development teams to work well together. Agile developers may take little account of the architecture description, dismissing it as "big design up front," while software architects may struggle to deliver their ideas and designs in ways that agile teams are interested in and can use. This is a regrettable state of affairs, since both approaches can offer significant benefits to a system development project, and the priorities and beliefs of the two groups are much closer together than might initially appear to be the case.

Agile teams use flexible, adaptive software development approaches based on the philosophy of the *Agile Manifesto*. Typical practices include the use of short, regular development cycles, customer prioritization of work, and automated testing and retrospectives, with the aim of delivering useful working software frequently. The focus is on intensive user involvement in specifying and prioritizing requirements, and building "the simplest thing possible," and there is little for the software architect to disagree with in any of these ideas.

Well-run agile projects do a tremendous job of delivering useful software in a timely and user-focused manner, particularly when requirements are unclear or volatile. But the same teams can encounter problems as their systems become larger or more complicated and they have to cope with factors such as performance, availability, security, or systems monitoring that are of little direct interest to the end user. A good software architecture can help meet many of these challenges and ensure that agile teams don't become overwhelmed by the amount of refactoring required to meet complicated nonfunctional requirements.

When you are acting as the software architect on a project using an agile approach, there are a number of things you can do to help ensure its success.

- Deliver your architecture work incrementally. Define the basic architectural structures in the early stages, and refine this using a demand-based approach.

- Work collaboratively with the team to agree on a clear set of design principles, and ensure that they are understood and used to ensure consistency throughout the system's implementation.

- Define your components clearly and unambiguously, and document their responsibilities and interfaces to avoid confusion and rework as new functions need to be added to the system.

- Share information widely using simple tools such as wikis and presentations rather than relying on sophisticated modeling and information management tools.

- Make sure every deliverable has a customer (else why are you doing it?) and that the customers understand and agree with the value it is bringing them.

- Aim to create "good enough" documents that you can deliver as soon as they are usable rather than waiting for them to be polished to the point of perfection.

- If practicable, work with the team to create working examples or prototypes to prove ideas and guide critical or risky parts of the development work.

- Focus on cross-cutting concerns. Your position and experience as an architect give you a unique position to identify these concerns and define appropriate system-wide strategies and solutions. You can use perspectives to help you here.

- When you need to work with a number of teams simultaneously, you won't be able to spend all of your time working in one team. So make sure that you still work closely with each team to encourage a two-way flow of ideas and to make sure that they understand the architecture.

- Focus on areas of architectural significance, and leave the more detailed design to the developers.

SUMMARY

In this chapter, we outlined a simple process of architecture definition, applicable to most software development projects, which you can use to help formulate your plans and schedules.

We started the chapter by defining the principles that our process should adhere to. It should be stakeholder-driven (of course), structured, pragmatic, flexible, and technology-neutral. It must also integrate with your existing software development lifecycle and with established best practices of software engineering.

We explained the context of the process and defined its outcomes; these obviously include specifying the architecture and producing the AD but often extend into other areas, such as better understanding of the problem being solved and management of stakeholder expectations.

We defined the essential inputs to the process: a baseline definition and stakeholder concerns. The baseline definition, which includes scope and context, must be determined and accepted at the start of the process. Stakeholder concerns, which include high-level functional and technical requirements and architectural constraints, are more likely to be discovered, elaborated, and refined as your analysis progresses.

We defined a simple, iterative process of architecture definition based on drawing up a set of architectural models, exploring some of their features in more detail, reviewing these with stakeholders, and reworking the models. Finally, we explained how this process aligns with existing development lifecycles such as the waterfall, iterative, and agile models.

FURTHER READING

Most books on software architecture include a description of some form of architecture definition process. Three books listed in the Bibliography include representative examples of different processes [GARL03, BASS03, BOSC00]. The first of these also discusses how architecture can coexist with agile processes.

A number of texts discuss the various modern software development processes, including XP [BECK00], Lean Software Development [POPP03], Scrum [BEED02], Feature Driven Development [PALM02], and the Rational Unified Process [KRUC03]. The Coding the Architecture Web site (www.codingthearchitecture.com), run by the independent consultant Simon Brown, has a lot of useful material about working as a software architect with agile teams. If you'd like to see what the *Agile Manifesto* really says, you can find it at www.agilemanifesto.org.

The Twin Peaks model (on which we based our Three Peaks model) is described in an article in *IEEE Computer* [NUSE01].

8

Concerns, Principles, and Decisions

Architecture definition can often be a voyage of discovery for both the architect and the stakeholders. At the early stages of any software development project, you will find that while the project's overall goals and objectives are probably accepted and communicated, the detail is still vague. Indeed, one of your objectives as an architect is to take this detail and make it firm and ratified. As we explained in Chapter 7, there are a number of different inputs that you use to shape and define your architectural solution, and these inputs come from different places and vary in their importance and significance.

Of course, the most obvious things that shape and define your architectural solution are the scope and requirements of the system. This is so important that it is part of one of our viewpoints, the Context viewpoint, which we describe in Chapter 16. However, other things can be just as important as inputs to your architectural decision making.

- *Business and IT strategies* set the long-term business and technology priorities and direction for the organization and may also include a roadmap to get from today to the "target state."
- *Goals and drivers* are the fundamental issues and problems that prompted your stakeholders, especially the acquirers and users, to initiate the project.
- *Standards and policies* mandate certain aspects of how the organization does business or operates internally.
- There are also many other *real-world constraints* that you need to take into account, such as time and money, availability of skills, or technology pitfalls and limitations.

We collectively refer to these inputs as *concerns*. Let's remind ourselves of the definition of *concern* that we introduced in Part I.

DEFINITION A **concern** about an architecture is a requirement, an objective, a constraint, an intention, or an aspiration a stakeholder has for that architecture.

Our definition of concern is deliberately broad and wide-ranging. A concern may be specific, unambiguous, and measurable, in which case we call it a "requirement" and can use the techniques of traditional systems analysis to capture it, document it, and use it to shape the architecture. On the other hand, a concern may be vague and loosely stated but nonetheless important to your stakeholders. Indeed, such a concern may be more important to them than the specific requirements.

EXAMPLE A retailer has a strong reputation for quality of service and customer responsiveness, which must be reflected in every interaction with the customer. This translates into a number of goals and aspirations for a new online store that the retailer wants to build.

- The values, ethos, and reputation of the retailer must be reflected in the appearance and operation of the online store and its supporting processes.
- At all times, the Web site should try to present a "human" face to the customer (even those portions of it that are fully automated).
- The online store must be easy to use by customers who have limited experience with computers and e-commerce.
- The online store must be responsive (quick to load and respond to customer actions) whether or not the customer has a fast Internet connection.
- The online store must cover all aspects of the shopping experience, including an up-to-date, browseable catalog; a secure online purchasing system; order tracking; and returns handling.

Apart from the last item, none of these can be considered formal and measurable requirements, and the last one is really a statement of scope. However, if the system does not meet these goals and aspirations, it will probably be viewed as a failure.

As we can see, there is a broad range of concerns that shape or influence your architecture. We find it useful to group these into two categories: *problem-focused concerns*, which influence or constrain the problem that the system is trying to solve; and *solution-focused concerns*, which influence or constrain the possible solutions to that problem.

Solution-focused concerns are often (though not always) derived, directly or indirectly, from problem-focused concerns—for example, an organization's IT strategy is usually driven pretty explicitly from its business strategy. In some instances, there is also a flow in the other direction, with technology driving a change in business behavior or priorities (these are sometimes referred to as "technology opportunities"). For example, the prevalence of smartphones and other mobile devices significantly changed the way that retailers interacted with their customers.

This arrangement is nicely summarized in methodologies like Capgemini's IAF (see the Appendix) as "why, what, how, with what." As we shall see, the problem-focused concerns answer the "why" and "what" questions about the architecture, and the solution-focused concerns answer the "how" and "with what" questions.

We show this breakdown in Figure 8–1 along with the most important types of concerns you might have to deal with. As you can see, we have further grouped the concerns into ones that have *influence* and drive decision making in a certain direction (for example, a business or technology goal), and ones that impose *constraints* and therefore restrict the decisions you can make (such as a standard or policy that you have to follow).

FIGURE 8-1 PROBLEM-FOCUSED AND SOLUTION-FOCUSED CONCERNS

This taxonomy isn't perfect, of course, and it's not always possible to place a concern cleanly into one of the four quadrants in our diagram. But understanding whether a concern is problem- or solution-focused, and whether it is an influencer or a constraint, should help you ensure that it is appropriately addressed in your architecture.

PROBLEM-FOCUSED CONCERNS

Problem-focused concerns are those concerns that influence or constrain the problem that the system is trying to solve. A problem-focused concern may influence the architecture by suggesting or mandating a capability of the system, or by shaping or clarifying the nature and specific details of that capability. It may constrain the architecture by allowing the system to behave only in certain ways in certain circumstances, or by prohibiting the system from doing something altogether.

Problem-focused concerns address the "why" and "what" questions about the system: Why does it need to do something, or what does it need to do? They include business strategy, business goals and drivers, system scope and requirements, and business standards and policies.

Business Strategy

A *business strategy* defines the direction for the business as a whole or for some part of it. It looks at questions such as what goods and services it provides, who its customers are, how the organization differentiates itself from its competitors, and how it structures and organizes itself. It may also include a *roadmap* that describes how the business is planning to transform itself into the desired future state.

While you are unlikely to have to refer to it directly, understanding the main tenets of the business strategy is a useful way of understanding the concerns of your more business-focused stakeholders and ensuring that your architectural decisions are aligned with the priorities of the organization. In particular, the business strategy will have driven at least some of your requirements, so understanding the strategy will help you understand why these requirements are important.

You may also find that the business strategy is a useful way of justifying some of your architectural decisions or priorities. For example, if the business strategy is to move toward a customer self-service model (whether in-store or on the Internet), the customer-facing aspects of your architecture become very significant.

Business Goals and Drivers

The business goals and drivers set the business context for the project and are the fundamental reason it exists. These goals and drivers are typically defined quite informally, and in language that relates to one or more specific problems or potential opportunities facing the organization that has commissioned the system.

DEFINITION A **business goal** is a specific aim the organization has, while a **business driver** is some force acting on the organization that requires it to behave in a particular way in order to protect and grow its business.

EXAMPLE A retailer may have a specific *business goal* to achieve 15% of its sales via online purchases made through its Web site. A *business driver* acting on the organization could be the fact that it is losing market share to a competitor with a much better and easier-to-use shopping Web site.

Unfortunately, goals and drivers typically exhibit a number of characteristics that make them hard to translate into specific architectural features or capabilities.

- They are often expressed using imprecise language—indeed, the stakeholders may not really be clear about what they mean.
- They are unlikely to be quantifiable or measurable in any useful way, which means that there are no objective criteria for judging whether or not they have been met. It all comes down to gut feelings and the subjective assessments of the stakeholders.
- Since they have a strong business focus, it is often unclear how they might translate into an architectural solution.

You cannot afford to ignore goals and drivers, since they have a major influence on the nature of the architecture and what it is supposed to achieve. However, there are a number of tactics for successfully dealing with them.

- Try to turn them into requirements. For example, a goal about growing market share might translate into some sizing and performance requirements.

- Manage your stakeholders' expectations of success, especially when goals are vague or unachievable. For example, a system developed under tight budgetary constraints that has ambitious goals for 24/7 availability is unlikely to succeed. You need to make the stakeholders understand why this is the case and work with them to develop more realistic goals.

- Develop architectural principles that translate the goals into physical features and qualities of your architecture. For example, a goal related to ease of use might be translated into principles around a common look and feel, exception handling, and interfaces between automated and manual processes. (We will talk about principles shortly.)

In some cases, you may be given a formal statement of business goals and drivers, probably written on behalf of the acquirers of the system. In other cases, you will need to investigate the underlying need for the system and work closely with your acquirers in order to understand their goals. Either way, it is up to you to satisfy yourself that you understand what motivates the need for your system and that the system you intend to build will meet these underlying needs.

This normally involves asking your key stakeholders a large number of pertinent questions to help them and you understand the goals, the drivers, and their implications. This sort of activity may well be something that you have not done before, or that you don't feel confident you can do well. In this case, you should try to involve someone (a requirements analyst, for example) who understands the business domain well and can help you translate this into implications for your architecture.

System Scope and Requirements

The *system scope* defines the main responsibilities of the system, that is, the important capabilities that it will be required to provide. For clarity, it may also identify some specific exclusions, although by definition, anything not listed in the scope is excluded. As we said earlier, system scope is so important that it forms part of the Context viewpoint, which we describe in Chapter 16.

Requirements define in more detail what the system is required to do. They are usually broken down into *functional requirements* and *quality properties* (these are often referred to as "nonfunctional requirements," but as we said in Chapter 2, we are not big fans of this terminology).

In our experience, it is unusual for the architect to get involved in the specification of detailed functional requirements. You will probably need some sort of elaboration of the system's responsibilities (defined in the system scope) in order to understand the implications for your architecture. However, because it is uncommon for detailed functional requirements to significantly impact the architectural solution, you are unlikely to have the need (or the time) to capture any further detail for the purposes of your AD. Of course, it is valuable to be involved in the review of detailed functional requirements as they develop, to make sure that your design can support them.

You may well not be involved in the specification of required quality properties either. However, it is rare in our experience for there to be much in the way of consensus about or even consideration of system qualities at this early stage in the system development lifecycle, and so it will often fall to you to clarify and define these. Indeed, in many areas—internationalization, usability, accessibility—there may be little consensus as to how such requirements can even be expressed or translated into system features.

You will probably have to work hard to extract this information from your stakeholders, but using architectural perspectives can help with this process, as we discuss in detail in Part IV of the book.

Business Standards and Policies

Business standards and policies mandate certain aspects of how the organization does business or operates internally. They may be driven by regulation, by accepted best practices, or by the organization's ethos and ways of working.

You may need to refer to some business standards and policies directly, but even when this isn't the case, you may need to have an awareness of them as they may constrain some aspects of your architecture in significant ways. For example, most businesses have a data retention policy that defines in what circumstances data on their customers can be retained, for how long, and how the data must be protected from unauthorized access. These will ultimately translate into architectural features such as archiving capabilities and security controls.

Ideally you should find that business standards and policies are reflected in the system's requirements. However, this may not always be the case—in particular, things like data retention policies are often forgotten—and so standards and policies can be a useful source of information. As with business strategy, you can also use them to help justify your architectural decisions.

SOLUTION-FOCUSED CONCERNS

Solution-focused concerns are those that influence or constrain the solution to the problems defined in the problem-focused concerns. A solution-focused concern may influence the architecture by suggesting or mandating a specific approach to building the system, or by shaping and clarifying how it is built.

It may constrain the architecture by requiring that the system be constructed in a certain way.

Solution-focused concerns address the "how" and "with what" questions about the system: How should it be built to make sure it works in the right way, and with what components and technologies? They include IT strategy, technology goals and drivers, and technology standards and policies.

IT Strategy

In a comparable way to the business strategy, an organization's IT strategy defines its long-term direction for IT. It can be viewed as the "business strategy for IT," which considers IT to be a business unit in its own right, providing services to the rest of the organization, and possibly to customers and third parties as well.

As with the business strategy, you may not need to have to refer to the IT strategy directly, but it is important that you understand its main concepts and ideas so that you are aware of any implications for your architecture. It may drive some technology requirements or constraints (for example, to build systems in a loosely coupled, multitier way, or to use central services or data stores).

Technology Goals and Drivers

Technology goals and drivers set out the relevant technology objectives, intentions, or aspirations of the project. As with business goals and drivers, a technology goal is a specific aim the IT department has, while a technology driver is some force acting on the project or IT department that requires people to behave in a particular way.

EXAMPLE The retailer mentioned previously may have a specific *technology goal* to be able to scale its customer-facing systems at short notice to meet fluctuating spikes in demand. A *technology driver* might be the unpredictable and volatile usage patterns of its Internet systems.

As with business goals, technology goals and drivers are often expressed in an imprecise way, and you may find it hard to turn these into more quantitative influences or constraints. The tactics we described earlier will also be useful here.

Technology Standards and Policies

Technology standards may have a very strong technology focus, such as those that define the physical mechanisms for linking computers together; or they may have more of a business focus, such as those that define the syntax and semantics of a certain class of business messages. Adopting standards can ease the design and development process and make it easier to integrate the system with others, now and in the future.

Technology policies define processes that must be followed in order to meet stakeholder needs. You may need to comply with preexisting policies (security policies are a common example), or alternatively your architectural analysis may identify the need to produce some policies of your own.

A large number of off-the-shelf technology standards are available to you.

- *Open standards* are defined and ratified by bodies such as the International Organization for Standardization (ISO), the Institute of Electrical and Electronics Engineers (IEEE), and the World Wide Web Consortium (W3C). They are generally accepted by the community at large and typically apply across a range of hardware and software environments.
- *Proprietary standards* are created and managed by commercial companies or other large organizations. These usually apply only to a particular manufacturer's products but often gain wider acceptance because of the supplier's market dominance.
- *De facto standards* have not (yet) been ratified by an independent standards body but are widely followed. It is not always obvious which of several competing standards will ultimately be successful; in such a situation, you may want to try to isolate those parts of the architecture into a separate layer or module that can be more easily changed to comply with another standard.
- *Organizational standards* are developed for use by your organization. These may mandate the use of certain hardware or software suppliers or define standard ways to use infrastructure components such as messaging frameworks or data warehouses.

You may also have to comply with legal, statutory, or regulatory standards. Your stakeholders will be able to advise you on these, or it may be appropriate to bring in experts if the issues are complex or the consequences of noncompliance severe. We talk more about this when we discuss the Regulation perspective in Chapter 29.

You and your stakeholders may also define local technology standards, which are aimed at the specific problems you are trying to solve. Although these may involve extra work up front, they will usually save you time in the long run.

You should focus on architectural-level standards while developing your AD. Coding and unit-testing standards, for example, are probably not of concern to you at this point (although they clearly are important, and you may need to lead their formulation later as you create the Development view).

You should ensure that compliance with standards can be tested in some way. Some standards are accompanied by programs or test suites that will demonstrate a system's compliance; if not, you may want to derive tests of your own. Again, this is not primarily your concern, but you may want to work with your developers and testers to ensure that such tests are put in place, particularly if there are legal or regulatory requirements for compliance.

OTHER REAL-WORLD CONSTRAINTS

In addition to requirements, standards, and the other documentation we have already described, you will have to deal with numerous real-world constraints of one sort or another. It is very unusual for you to be given a completely free hand when making choices about your architecture—in reality, you are often constrained in various ways, although these constraints are often not written down. You need to understand these constraints up front, document the key ones in your AD, and ratify them with your stakeholders.

Real-world constraints can have important implications for your architecture. For example, a limitation in the ability of a key technical component to scale beyond a certain level means that your architecture is likewise constrained, or that you need to find another way of dealing with heavy workload (e.g., scaling out rather than scaling up).

Constraints often force you to make compromises in your architecture as well. This requires careful thought and may also require some skillful negotiation with stakeholders to explain why the compromises are necessary and to ensure that they do not fundamentally undermine your solution.

EXAMPLE Online retailers usually use third parties to validate credit cards and take payments from customers. However, this process can sometimes be slow, especially at peak periods. The implication of this constraint is that customers may be faced with unacceptably long wait times while making a purchase, which may lead to their attempting to pay twice or even abandoning their purchase. You need to ensure that the Web site delivers a positive customer experience without being vulnerable to accidental or willful misuse.

Rather than make a customer wait for a payment to be authorized, many retailers perform the authorization in the background after the purchase has completed. The customer is presented with a message saying that the purchase has gone through and may then receive an e-mail a few minutes later confirming the payment. If payment is declined, the purchase is put on hold and the customer is given the opportunity to pay using some other means.

This approach might be encapsulated in a general statement to the effect that customers should not be left waiting while slow background processes complete. Such a statement affects the system's functionality, the way it stores and manages data, and various operational processes and so should probably be documented separately from any view.

The types of constraints you should consider include the following.

- *Technical constraints*: All technologies have limitations of one form or another, around functionality, the ability to scale, or security, for example. You can use the Perspective Catalog (see Part IV) to help uncover the key constraints of the technologies you are using to build your solutions, and to understand their implications for your architecture.

- *Time*: Almost all software development projects have deadlines for their completion, often ambitious ones. These deadlines will constrain your ability to build complex solutions and to have long test cycles or deployment windows, and they may well constrain the time you have to design your architecture.

- *Cost*: Similarly, cost constraints will limit your ability to use expensive tools, deploy on expensive hardware, hire expensive staff, or build complex solutions.

- *Skills*: New or niche technologies, unusual development approaches, or specialized business domains may place constraints on the ability of the project to find appropriately skilled staff. At a minimum it may be necessary to spend time and money on training them, which will take budget from development activities. You may also have to take the skills of users into consideration, particularly for systems used by members of the public.

- *Operational constraints*: These include, for example, the need to provide service at particular times, the need to operate the system in compliance with particular organizational standards, or the need to fit into existing operational schedules such as backup cycles or regular planned network maintenance.

- *Physical constraints*: These include, for example, the distance between architectural clients and servers or the constraints imposed by time zones and calendars.

- *Organizational or cultural constraints*: For example, there may be pre-ferred development approaches such as offshoring or outsourcing, or "political" reasons why you need to make certain architectural choices. (You may need to be careful about documenting some of these, but you have to understand them!)

WHAT MAKES A GOOD CONCERN

The AD is primarily intended to document your architecture. However, it is often valuable to use it as a vehicle for recording stakeholder concerns and the other factors that led to your architectural decisions. This approach helps you explicitly demonstrate that your solution meets the needs of the stakeholders and shows where you had to make compromises because of conflicting concerns or other real-world constraints.

Concerns should be clearly stated and avoid jargon that is not understood. They are usually numbered or otherwise uniquely identified. A well-expressed concern also has the following characteristics (although they are often hard to achieve, especially at the vaguer end of the spectrum).

- It is (as far as practicable) *quantified* and *measurable*. Avoid statements like "The system must respond quickly" or "The interface must be easy to use."
- It is *testable* in a way that objectively demonstrates whether it has been achieved.
- It is *traceable*, both forward and backward. In other words, it can be justified backward to strategy or goals, for example, and can be traced forward into architectural or design features. (We explain how to do this in the next section.)

Depending on circumstances—and timescales—it may be useful to explicitly cross-reference concerns against the key features of your architecture. For example, when there is a need for high system availability, you may choose to implement hardware redundancy in parts of your architecture.

You may choose to document concerns as part of the main AD, as an appendix, or in a separate document. Remember, however, that the primary purpose of the AD is to document the architecture—it's not intended to be a requirements specification. You probably don't want to go into much detail about concerns in the AD; you can do this later as part of functional specification and design.

As with the scope, you need to get the balance right—providing too much detail will obscure the big picture, and too little detail will lead to ambiguity.

ARCHITECTURAL PRINCIPLES

As we explained in Chapter 2, your architecture exists solely to meet your stakeholders' concerns. If you have a large and varied group of stakeholders, as you usually do, understanding and reconciling all of their various concerns can be difficult. The concerns will often vary in importance, visibility, and clarity—some may have broad support and be widely understood, while others may be obscure, complicated, or of interest to only a few stakeholders—and some concerns may be in conflict with one another or even completely incompatible.

Not only that, but concerns can affect the requirements and architecture—and each other—in different ways. We have seen that solution-focused concerns influence or constrain the architecture directly, by defining or restricting the candidate architectures you can use. Problem-focused concerns generally influence or constrain the architecture more indirectly, by defining requirements or mandating behaviors that suggest suitable candidate architectures that meet those requirements.

Sometimes the influences and constraints work in the other direction—that is, from the solution space back to the problem space. For example, an IT department might mandate certain security features to protect the confidentiality and integrity of its information, which could significantly change the business interactions that users and customers have with the company's systems.

We illustrate the multifaceted interrelationships between concerns in Figure 8–2. The boxes in the diagram represent the types of concerns that you may need to address; the solid arrows represent the relationships from the problem space toward the solution space; and the dashed arrows represent the reverse relationships, from the solution space back toward the problem space.

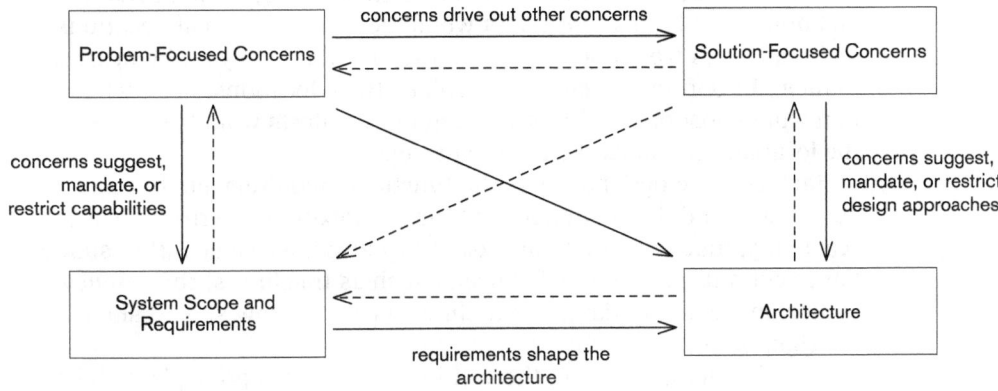

FIGURE 8–2 RELATIONSHIPS BETWEEN CONCERNS, REQUIREMENTS, AND ARCHITECTURE

A useful technique for dealing with such a jumble of cause and effect is to establish some *principles* about the construction of the architecture, and to use these to help drive answers to the important decisions you have to make. Principles are statements of approach or intent that can provide a decision-making framework for the architecture, defining rules that should be followed in its design, and are derived according to the specific needs and priorities of the stakeholders.

EXAMPLE An international organization that monitors weather conditions around the world wants to make this information available to developers of applications for smartphones and other mobile devices. Most data is captured automatically from weather stations, augmented by physical observations by meteorologists. The data will be published over the Internet in real time using standard XML- and HTTP-based protocols. After some initial investigation the architect comes up with several different approaches to managing and distributing the captured data. All solutions meet the functional requirements as expressed by the users but are architecturally very different and make architectural tradeoffs (such as scalability as opposed to consistency) in different ways.

Her first architecture, which she called Option A, has data collected locally and transferred to a single, central database that would manage all of the weather data and respond to all requests. This solution is architecturally simple and cheapest and quickest to implement and run. However, the architect realizes that it has some limitations: It has a single point of failure, for example, and has limited scalability. She therefore comes up with two more candidate architectures.

Option B involves having a copy of all of the data at three different locations around the world: a site in North America, a site in Europe, and one in the Far East. All data would be distributed to all locations, and requesters would be directed to the one that is physically nearest to them. In Option C, there would still be three locations, but each location would host data only for that region. Requests would be routed to the location that holds the data requested.

Each of these options meets the functional requirements but has advantages and disadvantages in terms of flexibility, performance and scalability, time to market, and cost. They also have some rather subtle but important implications for users, such as timeliness, consistency, and completeness of data. The architect is stuck: How should she pick the right one?

After further discussion, the architect agrees on a principle with key stakeholders, which states that data required for processing a user's request should be held as "close" to that user as possible, even if this means it has to be replicated or redistributed. The rationale for this principle is that users might be interested in weather forecasts for anywhere in the world, not just their own area, and that the data needs to be easily available near the point at which it is accessed to achieve a good user experience (by minimizing latency) and to improve availability. This principle rules out Options A and C and also provides a rationale for choosing Option B.

Defining a clear set of principles for your system is one of the ways that you can provide some transparency into the involved process of analyzing, rationalizing, and addressing (or indeed rejecting) the varied concerns of your stakeholders. Some principles might be mandated by the organization—which would also make them constraints—or you might conclude that they are the right thing to do specifically for this architecture (we'll see how you would come to a conclusion like that shortly).

An appropriate use of principles is invaluable in establishing a baseline or framework for architecture definition. Principles expose stakeholders' underlying assumptions and bring them out into the cold light of day—in other words, they make the implicit explicit. They are a great way to kick off an architecture project, especially when motivation or scope is unclear. They are also useful if you suspect that there are significant but unrecognized conflicts among your stakeholders.

You have seen examples of principles throughout Part I and Part II, and we hope that you are beginning to appreciate their usefulness. Let's formally define them now.

 DEFINITION An **architectural principle** is a fundamental statement of belief, approach, or intent that guides the definition of an architecture. It may refer to current circumstances or to a desired future state.

Principles can be a great way of ensuring that concerns are addressed consistently throughout the architecture and explaining why the architecture needs to be built in a certain way. If you search on the Internet, you will quickly discover that there are a great many principles of good architectural design that are available to you "off the shelf." However, you should avoid the temptation to just download a set of best-practice principles and try to blithely apply them to the problem at hand. You must ensure that any principle you select is right for your specific situation and for the needs and priorities of your stakeholders.

EXAMPLE A retailer wants to develop a new contact center system to deal with postal, telephone, and e-mail inquiries from its customers. However, when the hardware-sizing exercise is completed, it is discovered that the cost is way over budget because high-availability technologies such as clustering, hardware replication, and high-speed online backup have been used to provide a very high level of system availability.

Discussion with the sponsor and users reveals that, in fact, different parts of the system are considered to be of varying levels of importance to the business, and this can be taken into account when planning the high-availability design. This is encapsulated in the following principle:

While the availability of the contact center system is of paramount importance to the operation of the business, the parts of the system that support the customer-facing staff should be prioritized over other parts of the system (such as workflow monitoring and management reporting). If tradeoffs need to be made relating to the performance, availability, or resilience of different parts of the system, the parts that support the customer-facing workflow should always take precedence.

This principle is discussed extensively with a range of stakeholders, and as a result, the hardware architecture is considerably simplified by focusing the high-availability technology on the parts of the system that support customer interactions and reducing the amount of such technology used in other parts of the system.

What Makes a Good Principle

A good principle has the following characteristics.

- It is *constructive*. It helps highlight issues, drive architectural decisions, and establish the right architectural framework.
- It is *reasoned*. It is strongly motivated by business drivers, goals, and other principles. (Indeed, we illustrate in the section Using Principles to Link Concerns and Decisions how you can use principles to justify architectural decisions from business drivers.)
- It is *well articulated*. More than for any other artifact, it is important that your principles can be understood by all stakeholders and are not open to misinterpretation (accidental or willful).
- It is *testable*. Principles are (usually) valid over the entire lifetime of the architecture, and it must be possible to determine objectively whether they are being adhered to.
- It is *significant*. A principle that is a truism has little value. A good test of significance is to ask whether the opposite statement could ever be true. If

the statement opposing the principle is still meaningful (although obviously wrong for your circumstances), the principle is probably significant.

Let's look at an example of how a little analysis can turn a poor principle into a more useful one.

EXAMPLE An early workshop for a retailer's online store translated the goal "The online store must be easy to use by customers who have limited experience with computers and e-commerce" pretty much word for word into an architectural principle. However, applying the test for significance, it is clear that the opposite statement, "The online store will be hard to use," is not one that would ever make sense. As it stands, this first attempt at a principle is a truism and not of much value.

Ease of use is clearly important to the stakeholders, and further discussion reveals that this is particularly important for new customers because it is so easy for potential customers to click away to another site if they are having problems. The principle is broken down into several more specific ones, including *"We should minimize the amount of data that is collected from customers, particularly during early interactions such as sign-up for the site. Rationale: This minimizes data protection concerns and avoids slowing down the customer's browsing and product selection experience."* This principle is now more reasoned (because it is supported by the rationale to avoid inconveniencing customers and to avoid data protection concerns around personal data) and more constructive because it highlights the specific need for ease of use in initial customer interactions. It is also more significant because requiring a sign-up process that captures a lot of data might be necessary in some other situations.

However, it is still not particularly testable: How do the stakeholders know whether they have achieved their objectives for ease of use? Some more work produces a final version of the principle: *"We should minimize the amount of data that is collected from customers, particularly during early interactions such as sign-up for the site, aiming to collect less than our competitors' sites. Rationale: This minimizes data protection concerns and avoids slowing down the customer's browsing and product selection experience."* The principle now provides a clearer target for analysts and developers.

Principles are typically expressed in one or a few sentences in the present tense (or sometimes in the future tense if they express a desired state) in plain, jargon-free language.

Defining Your Own Principles

Although there may be some high-level principles you can pick up "off the shelf," you will likely need to develop more specific principles of your own as you explore issues in more depth. You will soon find this to be an invaluable technique in shaping and refining the architectural design.

When you first start to use them, principles may come across to you and your stakeholders as an overblown way to state the obvious, but you will recognize their usefulness the first time you start having trouble reaching consensus over one. Because principles reach right down to core beliefs, disagreement over the wording or meaning of a principle is a sure sign of some fundamental differences among your stakeholders. It is good to get these differences out in the open and resolve them early in the process.

It can take a lot of effort to obtain consensus on your principles, so try to get them right the first time. Revising a principle later consumes valuable time and can lead to a significant amount of architectural rework. Don't make your principles too specific: Your aim at this point is to capture the spirit and motivation of your stakeholders, rather than the details (which you will capture later).

Architects often ask, "How many principles should we define?" There is, of course, no right answer to this question; you should define as many as the stakeholders need. Don't go overboard, though—if you have hundreds of principles, no one will remember them.

ARCHITECTURAL DECISIONS

It has been argued that the architecture of a system is the accumulation of the significant decisions made in its definition—indeed, this forms the basis of the definition of architecture used by IBM's Rational Unified Process ("Software architecture encompasses the set of significant decisions about the organization of a software system"). While we don't go as far as incorporating this in our own definition, there can be no doubt that as an architect you need to make a number of decisions about how the system should be built that will have a fundamental effect on its eventual success.

Getting the big "architectural" decisions right is vitally important because they are usually difficult, expensive, and time-consuming to change later. For example:

- If a system's architecture follows a certain architectural pattern, and this pattern subsequently proves to be inappropriate, refactoring to use another one may require that every element be redesigned.
- If the architecture prioritizes one quality property over another, such as performance over flexibility, it can be very hard, if not impossible,

to redress this balance once a significant amount of software has been written.

- If the system is constructed using a specific programming language or technology platform that subsequently proves to not meet some key stakeholder goals, a complete rewrite may be required.

It's not only the explicit decisions—those that have been discussed, agreed upon, and written down—that you have to worry about. In our experience, many architectural decisions are *implicit*, that is to say, they are not documented anywhere or even discussed. This may happen because the decision is so "obvious" that no one thinks to question it, because it gets lost in the detail, or because you don't have time to think about it. Implicit decisions are even harder to deal with, because you often don't realize that they have been made until it is far too late to change them.

EXAMPLE A government department with offices in every town decides to replace its legacy human resources system because it is inflexible, does not scale, and is implemented using very old technology. The department has strong business drivers for local autonomy and accountability, and this leads to an architecture that has an autonomous instance of the new system in each local office. After lengthy discussions, an architectural decision is made to master the data for each member of staff in the office in which that staff member works. There would be a weekly upload of key data to a central management reporting database, which could be used to give a high-level consolidated view.

Development of the new system begins. After a few months, the department runs a disaster recovery exercise and as part of this gives formal consideration to the new HR system. The exercise explores a disaster scenario of a fire taking place in one of the offices and some staff being unaccounted for.

The project team realizes that the HR data on the missing staff, including their contact details and contact details for their next of kin, could be lost in such a fire. This is unacceptable, since the data would have to be restored from an off-site backup and there would be a delay before concerned relatives could be contacted.

This realization means that a major re-architecting of the system is required, so that updates to key staff data—including next-of-kin information—are replicated from each local office to a central consolidated database. The project suffers significant delays and cost overruns before it is deployed.

Making your architectural decisions explicit is a good way of engaging stakeholders who might not otherwise have the time or inclination to participate in architectural definition. In our HR example, publicizing the key decisions about the information architecture would have led to the realization that it did not meet the department's business continuity concerns.

This open approach ensures that your stakeholders are aware of the decisions that have shaped your architecture and can validate that they are sensible and meet their specific concerns. It also helps to "embed" the fundamentals of the architecture into everyone's thinking, so that decisions are not reversed later without due consideration of the consequences.

As we shall see shortly, it also provides traceability of decisions back to fundamental business drivers, which helps you get stakeholder buy-in to the key features and capabilities of your architecture and gives early visibility of the implications of your decisions so that these can be acted upon.

Architecturally Significant Decisions

Obviously you can't document and review every decision you make about your architecture—indeed, it would make no sense to do this. However, you can apply the idea of *architectural significance*, which we explained in Chapter 2, to help you determine which decisions need wider stakeholder review and oversight.

Architecturally significant decisions usually answer the important "what," "how," and "with what" questions about the architecture and are the decisions that are critical to ensuring that the system achieves its key goals. (The important "why" questions are answered by the concerns, constraints, and principles, of course.)

Architecturally significant "what" decisions help to map out the functional components of the architecture, its data stores, concurrency mechanisms, deployment platforms, and operational tools, and the ways that these elements work together to address stakeholder concerns. "What" decisions often have significant stakeholder impact and therefore need to be made in consultation with key stakeholders and usually require their ratification.

Architecturally significant "how" decisions drive the way that elements of the architecture will be constructed. They often make use of standard patterns or approaches, such as a decision to design a multithreaded server using pools of stateless components, or a reporting database using a star schema database. "How" questions usually have more impact on the solution space than on the problem space.

Architecturally significant "with what" decisions usually define what software (and sometimes hardware) technologies will be used to build the system. These almost always are aimed at the solution space.

EXAMPLE An events-booking service accepts bookings from customers over the Internet. However, concern has been expressed that card authorization could be unacceptably slow, especially at peak times. A "what" architectural decision is therefore made that "the order-processing system will include a service to collect payment after the order has been accepted and will notify the customer at some later point that payment has been successful (or otherwise)." The implications of this decision are that in some cases, a customer who thought her order had been accepted would need to be notified that an alternative means of payment was required.

In this example, a "how" decision might be that "credit card payments will be authorized using the payment authorization service of XYZ Card Services." A "with what" decision might be that "messages will be sent to XYZ Card Services using their standard gateway connected to their servers over a private VPN using their proprietary protocol."

When deciding whether an architectural decision is architecturally significant, and therefore needs stakeholder involvement and ratification, ask yourself the following questions.

- Does it have a significant impact on the system's functionality or quality properties?
- Does it address a significant risk that the project is facing?
- Does it have implications in terms of the time or cost to build the system?
- Is the decision or its rationale or implications complex or unexpected?
- Has a significant amount of time or effort been spent reaching the decision?
- Is the decision contentious or politically important, perhaps relating to an approach, technology, or vendor that is favored (or deprecated) in the organization?

USING PRINCIPLES TO LINK CONCERNS AND DECISIONS

One of the most powerful uses of principles is to provide traceability for your architectural decisions. In other words, you can use principles to help justify and explain particular elements or features of your architecture.

This approach relies on associating two additional pieces of information with each of your principles: its *rationale* (why it is an appropriate and valuable principle for your architecture) and its *implications* (what needs to happen in order for the principle to become reality).

FIGURE 8-3 USING PRINCIPLES TO DEMONSTRATE TRACEABILITY

Traceability comes about by linking principles together using implications and rationales. You do this as follows.

- Start with the *business drivers and goals* for the architecture.
- Use the business drivers to develop a set of *business principles*, many of which have as their rationale one or more business drivers (i.e., the business driver has as an implication for the business principle). A business principle generally focuses on the "why" and "what" questions rather than on how the architecture will be built or deployed.
- Use the business principles in a similar way to develop a set of *technology principles*, many of which have as their rationale one or more business principles. Technology principles usually focus on the "how" and "with what" questions.
- Finally, use the technology principles to develop a set of *architectural decisions*, many of which have as their rationale one or more technology principles.

Following the business drivers through to architectural decisions, via rationales and implications, helps you explain the reasoning behind your architectural decisions, as shown in Figure 8–3.

Let's illustrate this by means of a rather simplistic example.

EXAMPLE Because the retailer described previously has grown by acquisition, it now has a number of separate online catalogs in its portfolio. Each catalog fronts a separate shopping system, with its own ways of ordering goods and managing accounts. This makes life difficult for enthusiastic shoppers, who need to pay separate bills and keep each account up-to-date with changes in personal details.

The company's business strategy therefore includes the following business goal:

G1. To interact with customers in a "joined-up" manner that places them at the heart of the contact process, making it easy and enjoyable for them to browse our entire portfolio and shop with us.

As a result of this, a number of business principles are accepted, including the following.

B1. All customers will gain access to any information, service, or catalog via a single point of entry (the company portal).

B2. Certain customer data items (name, address, e-mail address) are viewed as core information, and it should be necessary for a customer to update these only once for the changes to be immediately visible everywhere.

Each of these principles has goal G1 as a rationale.

After some discussion, these are driven down into the following set of technology principles.

T1. Each item of core customer data will be held only once, updated in real time, and used as the authoritative source of the truth.

T2. Any system that requires access to a core data item will retrieve it from the central data store at the time of use.

T3. Noncore data (i.e., data that applies only to a specific service or catalog) will be managed by the system to which it pertains.

The rationales for these principles are business principles B1 and B2.

An architecture is developed from these principles and includes the following elements:

D1. A central consolidated data store that manages all core customer data

D2. A messaging framework used to synchronously retrieve or update all core data

The rationales for these design decisions are technology principles T1, T2, and T3.

You can see from this simple example that the decision to deploy a central data store can be justified from business goal G1, through business principles B1 and B2, and through technology principles T1, T2, and T3.

CHECKLIST

- Have you consulted all stakeholders who may be able to mandate or suggest important concerns?
- Have you captured and documented the important influencing concerns— the goals and drivers that have caused the key stakeholders to initiate the project?
- Have you captured and documented the important constraining concerns— the standards and policies that may restrict your architectural choices?
- Have you also understood the "real-world" constraints that you need to comply with but may not necessarily want to write down?
- Have you documented all concerns, using simple, clear language that stakeholders can understand?
- Are all principles supported by rationales and implications? Do these ultimately tie back (via rationales) to business goals and forward (via implications) to architectural decisions?
- Have the stakeholders reviewed and ratified your concerns and principles?

SUMMARY

A wide range of factors guide and shape your architecture, including business and IT strategy, goals and drivers, scope and requirements, standards and policies, and real-world constraints such as time or skills. We call these *concerns* and group them into *problem-focused concerns*, which guide the problem that the system is trying to solve, and *solution-focused concerns*, which guide the possible solutions to that problem. You need to understand and document these to make sure that you make the right architectural decisions.

Some concerns have *influence* and drive decision making in a certain direction (for example, a business or technology goal), while others impose *constraints* and therefore restrict the decisions you can make (such as a standard or policy that you have to follow).

Stakeholder concerns may be specific and measurable (in which case we call them requirements) or may be vague and loosely stated but nonetheless important to your stakeholders. We described how to effectively document your stakeholders' concerns.

We defined an *architectural principle* as a fundamental statement of belief, approach, or intent that guides the definition of an architecture. We explained how principles are extremely useful in creating a framework for architecture definition and showed how you can use principles to capture the relationships between your architectural decisions and the concerns that shaped them.

FURTHER READING

One of the reasons that we devote quite a lot of space to these ideas is that while concepts like goals, drivers, principles, and concerns are talked about a lot, few books discuss them in the context of software architecture.

However, one book that places software architecture firmly in the context of business drivers is [BASS03], the early chapters of which describe the relationship by reference to the "Architecture Business Cycle" (ABC). While approaching the subject from an enterprise architecture perspective, another reference that discusses business strategy, goals, and principles and how they relate to technology drivers is [PERK03].

One of the early articles that discusses the importance of capturing architectural decisions is [TYRE05]; and a thorough discussion of architectural decisions, including templates and a decision-making process, can be found in [CLEM10].

You can find out more about Capgemini's IAF methodology in [WOUT10].

9

IDENTIFYING AND ENGAGING STAKEHOLDERS

As we saw in Part I, the people affected by a system are not limited to those who use it. Systems are not just used: They have to be *designed and built*; they have to be *operated*; they may have to be *repaired*; they are usually *enhanced*; and, of course, they have to be *paid for*.

Each of these activities involves a number—possibly a significant number—of people distinct from the users. Each of these groups of people has its own requirements, its own interests, and its own needs from the system. We refer collectively to these people as *stakeholders*. In Part I we defined a stakeholder as follows.

 DEFINITION A **stakeholder** in the architecture of a system is an individual, team, organization, or classes thereof, having an interest in the realization of the system.

Correctly identifying stakeholders and gaining their commitment are among the most important (yet underrated) tasks in software development. The concept of architectural stakeholder is clearly explained in the ISO standard ([ISO11]), and our discussion builds on theirs.

SELECTION OF STAKEHOLDERS

Although a large number of people may have some level of interest in your architecture, you almost certainly do not have time to consider everyone's concerns. Your first challenge, therefore, is to work out whose opinions and priorities it is most important to take into account and focus on them. Your high-priority stakeholders will fall into one or more of the following groups:

- Stakeholders who are most affected by your architectural decisions, for example, those who have to use the system, operate and manage it, or pay for it
- Stakeholders who have influence over the shape and eventual success of the development, for example, those who will have to pay for it
- Stakeholders who have specialist knowledge of the business or technology domain and can provide you with useful advice or even review your architecture
- Stakeholders who need to be included for organizational or political reasons, such as compliance officers, a central architectural governance team, or a respected opinion former within the organization

It is, in our experience, a subjective choice whom you select to populate your community of stakeholders. We have found, however, that casting your net more widely at the beginning is important in the long term (although in the short term, it may make your life more difficult because you will have more potentially conflicting requirements to reconcile). If you don't take stakeholders' concerns into consideration at the beginning of your development project, you can be sure that they will complain at the end, when making changes is much harder—and making architectural changes may be practically impossible.

STRATEGY The selection of stakeholders with whom you will engage is a subjective activity, but in general, the wider the stakeholder community, the better your chances of delivering a successful product or system.

Unfortunately, there are no purely objective criteria for determining whether you have correctly identified your stakeholders. Whom you select depends on a range of factors, including the goals of the system, organizational and political considerations, availability of resources, and cost and timescale constraints.

(We sometimes find, for example, that stakeholders are consulted in a spirit of openness, to demonstrate a desire to reflect a wide range of concerns, rather than an absolute need to take account of their views. There is absolutely nothing wrong with this, as long as it contributes to the success of the architecture.)

Drawing up your list of stakeholders, therefore, is a collaborative activity that sets the tone for the future direction of the project, and it is essential that you get this right. As well as ensuring that your stakeholder list is complete (we explore this issue further in the next section), there are four criteria to help make sure your list is right.

PRINCIPLE A useful stakeholder in an architecture is *informed*, *committed*, *authorized*, and *representative*.

We explain each of these criteria in Table 9–1.

TABLE 9–1 CRITERIA FOR A GOOD STAKEHOLDER

Criterion	Description
Informed	Do your stakeholders have the information, the experience, and the understanding needed to make the right decisions?
Committed	Are your stakeholders willing and able to make themselves available to participate in the process, and are they prepared to make some possibly difficult decisions?
Authorized	Can you be sure that decisions made now by your stakeholders will not be reversed later (at potentially high cost)?
Representative	If a stakeholder is a group rather than a person, have suitable representatives been selected from the group? Do those representatives meet the criteria for individual stakeholders?

CLASSES OF STAKEHOLDERS

In Table 9–2, we classify stakeholders according to their roles and concerns.

TABLE 9–2 STAKEHOLDER ROLES

Stakeholder Class	Description
Acquirers	Oversee the procurement of the system or product
Assessors	Oversee the system's conformance to standards and legal regulation
Communicators	Explain the system to other stakeholders via its documentation and training materials
Developers	Construct and deploy the system from specifications (or lead the teams that do this)
Maintainers	Manage the evolution of the system once it is operational
Production engineers	Design, deploy, and manage the hardware and software environments in which the system will be built, tested, and run

Continued on next page

TABLE 9-2 STAKEHOLDER ROLES *(CONTINUED)*

Stakeholder Class	Description
Suppliers	Build and/or supply the hardware, software, or infrastructure on which the system will run
Support staff	Provide support to users for the product or system when it is running
System administrators	Run the system once it has been deployed
Testers	Test the system to ensure that it is suitable for use
Users	Define the system's functionality and ultimately make use of it

Most system development projects include representatives from most if not all of these stakeholder groups, although their relative importance will obviously vary from project to project. However, if you do not at least consider each class, you will have problems in the future.

Widening your set of stakeholders leads to a tradeoff—the larger the group, the more difficult it will be to reach a consensus. Part of the architect's role is to ensure that large stakeholder communities do not become an obstacle to making progress. This requires you to actively manage the decision-making process and have a clear understanding of the relative importance of the needs of each stakeholder group. Doing this will help you defend your architectural decisions when challenged by stakeholders who feel that their needs have been ignored.

STRATEGY If you have a large stakeholder group, you need to actively manage it to ensure that its size does not impede progress. In particular, you need to balance and prioritize the needs of the different stakeholder groups, so that when conflicts occur, you can make sound, well-reasoned decisions.

It is also worth noting that, although we don't consider the architect's needs explicitly, when acting in that role you are also an architectural stakeholder. (We assume that you can represent yourself adequately to ensure that your views are taken into account!)

PRINCIPLE The architect must ensure that there is adequate stakeholder representation across the board, including nontechnology stakeholders (such as acquirers and users) and technology-focused ones (such as developers, system administrators, and maintainers).

Let's define the stakeholder classes in a little more detail.

Acquirers

Acquirers oversee the procurement of the system or product. Acquirers typically include senior management, which provides or authorizes funding for product or system development, and may also include the purchasing and legal departments, which represent the commercial interests of users in negotiations with third-party suppliers.

In a system development project, acquirers are often referred to as business sponsors, and for product development, acquirers are likely to be senior executives from the sales, marketing, and technology groups. There may also be investor representation in this group if specific external investment is required to fund the project. In seniority terms, acquirers are usually your most important stakeholders.

Acquirers' concerns typically center around issues such as alignment with strategic objectives, return on investment, and the costs, timescales, plans, and resources involved in building and running the system. Their goals are usually value for money and efficient expenditure of resources during delivery and operation.

Assessors

Assessors oversee the system's conformance to standards and legal regulations. Assessors may come from the organization's own internal quality control or conformance departments, or they may be external legal entities.

Assessors' concerns are focused around testing (to demonstrate conformance to requirements) and on formal, demonstrable compliance.

Communicators

Communicators explain the system to other stakeholders. Internal or public trainers provide training for support staff, developers, maintainers, and so on, and technical authors create manuals for the users and administrators of the product or system. In the case of a product, the marketing department needs to communicate its key features, strengths, and benefits to potential customers.

Communicators' interests lie in understanding the rationale behind and the details of the architecture and explaining it to technical and lay audiences.

Developers

Developers construct and deploy the system from specifications; in other words, they take it through the software development lifecycle from design, code, and test to acceptance. Developers need to understand the overall architecture but also have specific concerns that focus on development issues such as build standards, choice of platform, language, and tools as well as other issues such as maintainability, flexibility, and the preservation of knowledge over time.

This category also includes development managers, who plan the development activities and lead the teams that do the work.

Maintainers

Maintainers manage the evolution of the system once it is operational. Maintainers' concerns focus on issues such as development documentation, instrumentation (facilities for operational system monitoring), debug environments, production change control, and the preservation of knowledge over time.

Production Engineers

Production engineers design, deploy, and manage the hardware and software environments in which the system will be built, tested, and run. They are responsible for server and desktop computers; networking infrastructure; special-purpose appliances such as search engines or communications gateways; peripherals such as printers, cell phones, and other handheld devices; and in most cases infrastructure software such as operating systems, systems management, messaging middleware, and relational databases.

Most large organizations run their computing environments in data centers, which provide a safe, secure, and highly available environment with sophisticated features such as redundant power supplies, redundant high-bandwidth data communications, and environmental controls such as air conditioning and fire prevention. As well as the main production environments, data centers usually also house environments for disaster recovery, acceptance testing, and in some cases development. These represent a substantial financial asset, and the production engineers control them carefully and rigorously.

Production engineers have significant input to the deployment architecture of any system, and their approval is usually required before any component is installed into the data center.

Suppliers

Suppliers build and/or supply the hardware, software, or infrastructure on which the system will run, or possibly they provide specialized staff for system development or operation.

Suppliers are a slightly special class of stakeholder: They are not usually involved in building, running, or using the system, but they may impose constraints due to the limitations or requirements of the products they supply.

For example, a software application may mandate a particular version of the operating system to run, or may run only on certain hardware configurations, or may impose limitations on the number of concurrent connections or maximum data size. It is essential that you factor such constraints into the design of the architecture.

Support Staff

Support staff (help desk, technical support, customer service departments, and so on) provide support to users of the product or system when it is running. Support staff concerns revolve around having the information required to solve problems with users who may be communicating via telephone, e-mail, or the Internet—or in person.

System Administrators

System administrators run the system once it has been deployed. In large-scale commercial environments, system administrators play a key role because operation of the system is essential to the continuity of the business. In some scenarios, such as products aimed at the domestic PC market, the system administrators may also be the users.

System administrators may focus on a wide range of concerns, such as system monitoring and management, business continuity, disaster recovery, availability, resilience, and scalability.

Testers

Testers act as the conscience of the system development team. They systematically test the system in order to establish whether or not it is suitable for deployment and use. Although developers also perform testing, testers should be independent and do not have the same sense of ownership of the system's implementation. This, along with their specialist knowledge and experience, means that they can perform a more thorough and objective job of evaluating the system than the other stakeholders can.

Testers may be part of the same team as the developers or may be in a separate organizational unit or even a distinct organization (e.g., independent testing may be subcontracted to a specialist testing company). Wherever they are found organizationally, testers are concerned with establishing requirements, designing tests to prove whether requirements have been met, and building systems on which to run their tests.

Users

Users define the system's functionality and will ultimately make use of it. In the case of internal systems, users are internal staff who may be dealing with customers or performing back-office functions. In the case of a software product, users are the eventual purchasers of the product; here it is necessary for the product manager to represent their interests in some way, for example, by market testing. In some scenarios (e.g., e-commerce or other customer-facing systems), users may be members of the public; again, it is necessary to represent their interests secondhand.

Users' concerns obviously center around scope and functionality; however, they have operational concerns too, such as performance and security, although the architect may need to bring these to the users' attention.

EXAMPLES

We can illustrate the characteristics of these stakeholder classes by means of some examples.

An Off-the-Shelf Deployment Project

An off-the-shelf deployment project involves the selection, tailoring, and implementation of an existing software package and so involves the development of less software than a traditional system development project. However, the role of stakeholders is still vital, and many of the stakeholders from a traditional software development project are still relevant to an off-the-shelf deployment project.

EXAMPLE Company A, a manufacturer of computer hardware, wants an enterprise resource planning (ERP) system to better manage all aspects of its supply chain from ordering through delivery. Management anticipates the system being constructed from a custom off-the-shelf (COTS) package combined with some in-house development for specialized aspects of functionality. The new system must be deployed within one year, in time for a meeting where shareholders will consider future funding for the company.

Acquirers of the system include the business sponsor (senior management), who will authorize funding for the project, along with the purchasing department and representatives of IT, who will evaluate a number of potential ERP packages.

The users of the system cover a wide range of internal staff, including those who work in order entry, purchasing, finance, manufacturing, and distribution.

Developers, system administrators, production engineers, and maintainers are staff members of the internal IT department, and assessors are taken from the internal acceptance test team. Communicators include internal trainers, and support is to be provided by an internal help desk (possibly in conjunction with the COTS supplier).

A Software Product Development Project

A software product is usually developed by a specialist supplier, with the development often partially funded by external investors. The intended users of the product will be in other organizations that, it is hoped, will purchase the product once it is complete. The stakeholders for such projects are often spread across a number of organizations.

EXAMPLE Company B, an educational software supplier, wants to develop a product that will be used by college lecturers to manage their schedules of classes. Company B has formed a partnership with a local college and has obtained some venture capital funding for the product. The system will run on PCs and will be inexpensive and easy to operate.

Acquirers in this case include senior management and product managers at Company B, the educational partner, and representatives from the venture capitalists.

Users of the system are college lecturers and administrative staff; note that these users do not actually exist as such because no one has yet bought the product. User representation will have to be obtained in some other way (e.g., by talking to some potential users of the product).

Developers and maintainers are product development staff from Company B, and assessors are taken from the three partner organizations. There are no real system administrator stakeholders in this example (this needs to be factored into the architecture, for example, by making the system self-managing). Support staff might be provided by Company B and/or colleges that buy the product.

Communicators include technical authors from Company B who write the user guide.

> Production engineers provision the development and test environments for Company B. They also provide and manage the infrastructure for manufacturing product CDs and for distributing software updates to users over the Internet.

A Partnered Development

A partnered development project involves one organization using the services of another to provide systems or services it would normally provide with its own internal resources. These projects result in stakeholders who would typically be found within the acquiring organization actually being found within the external service organization. This can make it more difficult to identify and interact with these stakeholders.

> **EXAMPLE** Company C, an established financial organization, wishes to expand its presence on the Internet with the ability to market a range of financial services to members of the public. These services are aimed at residents of the country where Company C is based, as well as some international customers. Company C plans to contract out the development and operation of the system to an established Web developer.
>
> Acquirers include senior managers who will authorize funding for the project. Users include ordinary members of the public, who will access the public-facing Web site (as in the previous example, these don't exist yet), along with internal administrative staff, who will carry out its back-office functions.
>
> Developers and system administrators are staff from the Web development company. Assessors include Company C's internal accounting and legal staff, as well as external financial regulators from any country in which Company C wants to trade.
>
> Communicators, production engineers, and support staff are provided by Company C and/or the Web development company.

PROXY STAKEHOLDERS

We can see from the examples in the previous section that it may not be possible to identify all stakeholders until the system is developed. While some stakeholders will almost always be identifiable—particularly the acquirers and probably the users—others may not physically exist as a group. In these situations, you must identify *proxy stakeholders*. The proxy is an individual or group who speaks for the concerns of the real stakeholders and ensures that they are given as much weight as other concerns.

For a new product, for example, the user stakeholders are potential customers. Your proxy user stakeholders might be the product managers from the marketing group, armed with the results of market testing, or members of the target user population willing to be involved in the product's inception.

STRATEGY When real stakeholders cannot be identified (e.g., when a user community does not yet exist), or when there are too many to consult individually, the architect should identify proxy stakeholders to represent their interests. As much as possible, the proxy stakeholders should meet the same criteria as their real counterparts.

STAKEHOLDER GROUPS

Another possible complication occurs when a stakeholder actually represents a class of person, such as user or developer, rather than an individual. It may be impossible to capture and reconcile the needs of all members of the class in the time you have available, or you may not have the stakeholders at hand (e.g., in the case of potential users of a new product in development).

A stakeholder can also be a more external group, such as a professional standards body, the company's quality assurance department, or external legal regulators. The same principle applies in this case—you need to select representative stakeholders authorized to stand in for the whole group.

STRATEGY When a stakeholder comprises a group, team, or organization, it is necessary to select and authorize one or more stakeholder representatives to speak for the group.

STAKEHOLDERS' RESPONSIBILITIES

Effective stakeholders fulfill the following responsibilities.

- They ensure that all of their concerns are clearly communicated to the architect.
- Representative or proxy stakeholders clearly convey to the architect all of the concerns of the people they represent.

- They make decisions in a timely and authoritative manner and stick to them.
- If the stakeholders do not have the authority to make a decision, they escalate it appropriately and obtain a decision from someone who has that power.
- They review the AD to ensure that the system meets their concerns and is—as far as they can ascertain—functionally correct.

CHECKLIST

- Have you identified at least one stakeholder of each class? If not, is the omission justified?
- Have you informed the stakeholders of their responsibilities (e.g., as defined in the previous section), and have they agreed to these?
- In particular, does each stakeholder understand the level of commitment involved, in terms of attending meetings, reviewing documents, and making decisions?
- Is each stakeholder aware of the particular role to fulfill (acquirer, user, and so on)?
- For each group of stakeholders, have you identified and engaged a suitable representative? Does this proxy have the knowledge and authority to speak on behalf of the group?
- For each stakeholder group that does not yet exist (e.g., customers for a new software product), have you identified and engaged a suitable proxy?
- If suppliers are to be included as stakeholders, are their responsibilities and (if appropriate) contractual obligations clearly understood by both sides?

SUMMARY

Understanding the role of the stakeholder is fundamental to understanding the role of architecture in the development of a software product or system. In this chapter, we showed how to select good stakeholders—those who are informed, committed, authorized, and representative—and defined a set of stakeholder classes, including the following:

- Acquirers, who oversee the procurement of the system or product
- Assessors, who oversee the system's conformance to standards and legal regulation

- Communicators, who explain the system to other stakeholders
- Developers, who construct and deploy the system from specifications
- Maintainers, who manage the evolution of the system once it is operational
- Production engineers, who design, deploy, and manage the hardware and software environments in which the system will be built, tested, and run
- Suppliers, a special class of stakeholders who may impose constraints on the architecture due to characteristics of their products
- Support staff, who provide support to users for the product or system when it is running
- System administrators, who run the system once it has been deployed
- Testers, who test the system to ensure that it is fit for use
- Users, who define the system's functionality and will ultimately make use of it

We also discussed proxy stakeholders, who represent the interests of temporarily nonexistent stakeholders (such as the users of a new product), and explained the responsibilities of stakeholders in general.

FURTHER READING

As mentioned at the beginning of this chapter, we based our definition of stakeholder on that presented by the IEEE standard *Recommended Practice for Architectural Description* [IEEE00], which defines stakeholders in terms of an architecture definition process.

A number of software architecture books [BASS03, CLEM02, GARL03, TAYL09] have useful discussions of the idea of an architectural stakeholder.

10

IDENTIFYING
AND USING SCENARIOS

The most important goal of your software architecture is that it meets the needs of your stakeholders. In practical terms, this means that the system built based on your architectural design must be able to perform certain tasks while exhibiting specific properties that are important to the stakeholders (such as its performance or security).

Architecture definition is inevitably a process of complex tradeoffs between competing needs. In the midst of this, it is very easy for you to lose sight of a particular system's key priorities and for these tradeoffs to start being driven by personal preferences or imagination, rather than stakeholder needs.

A good way to stay grounded when developing your architecture is to continually consider how the ideas you are developing will actually work in practice. One of the most powerful techniques we have come across is to define and apply *scenarios* to your architecture.

The idea of an architectural scenario is simple but worth defining formally nonetheless.

 DEFINITION An **architectural scenario** is a well-defined description of an interaction betwmeen an external entity and the system. It defines the event that triggers the scenario, the interaction initiated by the external entity, and the response required of the system.

Architectural scenarios can be used to capture a wide range of architectural requirements, such as:

- A particular set of interactions with its users to which the system must be able to respond

- The processing that must happen automatically at a particular point in time, such as month end
- A particular peak load situation that could occur
- A demand that an external regulator might make of a system
- How the system must respond to a particular type of failure
- A change that a maintainer might need to be made to the system
- Any other situation with which the design of the system must be able to cope

TYPES OF SCENARIOS

We can divide the possible scenarios for a system into two groups: those concerned with what the system does and those concerned with how it does it. In other words, just as with requirements, scenarios can be divided into functional scenarios and system quality scenarios.

- *Functional scenarios* are nearly always defined in terms of a sequence of external events (normally derived from a system use case) to which the system must respond in a particular way. Examples include users initiating transactions, data arriving at external interfaces, temporal events (such as the end of the day) occurring, and so on. (These scenarios form the "+1" part of Philippe Kruchten's original "4+1" viewpoint approach on which we based our viewpoint set.)
- In contrast, *system quality scenarios* are defined in terms of how the system should react to a change in its environment in order to exhibit one or more quality properties. There are as many types of system quality scenarios as there are quality properties, but the more important ones tend to include security, performance, availability, and evolution (which, not coincidentally, are also our primary architectural perspectives). Examples of system quality scenarios include the ability of the system to be modified to provide a new function, to cope with a particular type of peak load, to protect critical information even if some of the security infrastructure is compromised, and so on.

Functional scenarios are often documented in the form of *use cases*. This technique was originally formulated by Ivar Jacobson, and the use case diagram subsequently became part of UML. A use case views the system as a "black box," describing what it should do in order to perform a task for a specified actor (external entity in our terminology—see Chapter 16). While they are widely used for capturing functional specifications, capturing system quality scenarios with use cases can be difficult.

USES FOR SCENARIOS

You can use scenarios in a number of ways within the architecture definition process.

- *Providing input to architecture definition*: Inspiration and ideas can come from many places. Scenarios can provide part of this input and keep the process grounded in reality by challenging you to design solutions to the specific problems the scenarios pose.

- *Defining and validating the system scope*: As we discuss in Chapter 16, it is common for scope and requirements to be ill defined in the early stages of systems development projects, and it often falls to the architect to make them more precise. Scenarios can be a useful way of exploring aspects of the scope with your stakeholders and gaining their agreement to what is included and excluded.

- *Evaluating the architecture*: Scenarios are a primary input into almost any process of architectural evaluation, which can range from simple credibility checks you perform in your head to heavyweight reviews using a formal process like the Architecture Tradeoff Analysis Method (ATAM). (We describe ATAM as an evaluation approach later in Chapter 14.) However, irrespective of the degree of formality you employ, scenarios drive the whole process by forcing you to consider how well the system can respond to a specific situation.

- *Communicating with stakeholders*: We have found that the discussion of a scenario, and how the system will respond to the situation described in it, is a very useful vehicle for communicating with all types of stakeholders and is often much more effective than using traditional design documentation, particularly for less technical stakeholders. Indeed, for nontechnical stakeholders, scenarios may be the only way to communicate the implications of the proposed architecture in a way that they really understand.

- *Finding missing requirements*: Another benefit of creating scenarios is that they often reveal what is missing as well as the suitability of what already exists. Considering how the system behaves in one scenario often leads stakeholders to realize that another situation they hadn't previously considered was omitted from the requirements analysis. Finding these missing requirements early can be an invaluable side effect of applying scenarios.

- *Driving the testing process*: Scenarios help highlight the things that are important to your stakeholders, thus providing a tremendously useful guide for where to focus testing activity. After identifying your scenarios, use them to plan the sort of testing you will require, and make sure that the system's testers have a copy of the scenarios as a basis for their initial test plans.

Stakeholders often find the process of actively walking through and analyzing scenarios much more interesting and engaging than reading a design document or attending a presentation. It often helps them to understand the proposed system much more deeply and allows them to analyze the proposal and find flaws in it much more effectively than with other forms of design documentation. This alternative view means that a scenario tends to uncover details that formal requirements and designs have often glossed over, by bringing proposals to life and challenging the stakeholders to think them through more thoroughly.

Reviewing how a system will settle a particular set of financial transactions with a requirements analyst, or how it will behave under a specific peak load condition with a technology specialist, is often much more productive than just asking them to review the requirements or designs (which are often simplified, generalized, and abstracted in order to make them easy to understand).

Identifying and Prioritizing Scenarios

In order to work effectively with scenarios, you need to capture a useful set and prioritize them to know where to focus your efforts for greatest effect. You can derive this information from a number of different sources.

- *Requirements*: Each functional requirement will suggest a functional scenario (that probably needs to be fleshed out with more specific detail), while your system quality requirements are likely to suggest behaviors (such as performance under load) that your system must exhibit.

- *Stakeholders*: Your stakeholders are a rich source of possible scenarios. Depending on the type and number of stakeholders, you could run a workshop to brainstorm possible scenarios, or simply meet with representatives of each stakeholder group to solicit ideas. Some stakeholder groups (such as acquirers, testers, system administrators, and maintainers) are particularly valuable sources of system quality scenarios, which are often harder to derive directly from requirements documents. Eliciting scenarios from stakeholders will also result in their thinking much more deeply about what the system should do and how it will affect its environment, often leading to the discovery of undiscovered requirements, constraints, or goals.

- *Experience*: There is no substitute for experience, and your own experience may well be one of the most valuable sources of possible scenarios. If you have experience in a similar domain, with similar technology, or with systems that share important characteristics with the current one, you know what was difficult and caused problems, and these situations point to useful scenarios.

Having identified a set of scenarios, you need to prioritize them, particularly if you have more than 5 or 10. With a large scenario set, it is easy to lose track of which are the most important ones to focus on. If this happens, the scenarios frequently become a hindrance to decision making because their conflicting demands simply confuse the situation.

There are a number of possible ways to do this. In our experience, the two key criteria for scenario classification are the *importance* that the systems' *stakeholders* attach to the scenario, and the likely *risk* that *you* consider the implementation of the scenario will involve. You need to pay significantly more attention to scenarios that key stakeholders consider crucial and that are also risky to implement than to relatively straightforward scenarios that stakeholders don't feel are that important. Scenarios that have straightforward implementations but are important to stakeholders, or those that are risky to implement but have less stakeholder value, fall somewhere between these two extremes.

Your stakeholders should be involved in scenario prioritization because you are creating the architecture for them and they probably understand the problem that the system is trying to solve better than you do. However, as with requirements, your stakeholders normally have overlapping and conflicting interests and opinions, so the priorities they place on different scenarios will vary. You may be able to gather stakeholder representatives in a meeting to vote on scenario importance, with those getting the most votes being considered the most important. In many cases, though, this won't work, and you will need to balance the views of the different stakeholders yourself, in the same way that you often need to balance the relative priority of different requirements.

You should also consider how risky you think it would be *not* to address some of your scenarios. (You will normally do this yourself, rather than asking stakeholders to do it.) When assessing this, consider whether the overall effectiveness of the system is likely to be significantly affected by the missing scenarios. If the omission of any of your scenarios is likely to cause an appreciable difference in stakeholder satisfaction, ensure that they are prioritized accordingly.

Finally, rank your scenarios in terms of both priority and risk, so that you can focus your efforts on the high-priority, high-risk ones and spend less time worrying about the rest.

CAPTURING SCENARIOS

When capturing the scenarios for a system, we describe the functional and quality-based scenarios slightly differently.

For a functional scenario, you usually need to define five pieces of information:

1. *Overview*: a brief description of what the scenario is meant to illustrate.
2. *System state*: the state of the system before the scenario occurs (if significant). This is usually an explanation of any information that should already be stored in the system for the scenario to be meaningful.
3. *System environment*: any significant observations about the environment that the system is running in, such as the unavailability of external systems, particular infrastructure behavior, time-based constraints, and so on.
4. *External stimulus*: a definition of what causes the scenario to occur, such as data arriving at an interface, user input, the passage of time, or any other event of significance to the system.
5. *Required system response*: an explanation, from an external observer's point of view, of how the system should respond to the scenario.

It is also important to give the scenario a short unique identifier and a concise, unique, and descriptive title.

EXAMPLE A functional scenario for a system that summarizes incoming data might be captured as follows.

Incremental Statistics Update

- *Overview*: How the system deals with a change to some of the existing base data.
- *System state*: Summary statistics already exist for the sales quarter that the incremental statistics refer to. The system's databases have enough space to cope with the processing required for this update.
- *System environment*: The deployment environment is operating normally, without problems.
- *External stimulus*: An update to a subset of the sales transactions for the previous quarter arrives via the *Bulk Data Load* external interface.
- *Required system response*: The incoming data should automatically trigger background statistical processing to update the summary statistics for the affected quarter to reflect the updated sales transaction data. The old summary statistics should stay available until the new ones are ready.

We have found that this stimulus–response approach works less well when trying to capture system quality scenarios. These scenarios try to illustrate characteristics that vary widely; in general, they try to show how the system responds to a change it its environment. Sometimes this change can be seen as a stimulus (e.g., being attacked), whereas in other cases (e.g., an external system slowing down or data volume increasing), we have found that viewing the change as a stimulus is rather artificial.

You usually need to define five pieces of information for a system quality scenario.

1. *Overview*: a brief description of what the scenario is meant to illustrate.

2. *System state*: the state of the system before the scenario occurs, if the behavior specified in the scenario depends on it. For quality scenarios, this may need to define aspects of the system-wide state (such as a level of load across the system) rather than the information stored in the system.

3. *System environment*: any significant observations about the environment that the system is running in, such as the unavailability of external systems, particular infrastructure behavior, time-based situations, and so on.

4. *Environment changes*: an explanation of what has changed in the system's environment that causes the scenario to occur. This could be infrastructure changes or failures, changes in external system behavior, security attacks, required modifications, or any of the other environment changes that require the system to possess a particular quality property in order to deal with them.

5. *Required system behavior*: a definition of how the system must behave in response to the change in its environment (e.g., how the system should respond, from a quantifiable performance point of view, to a defined increase in the number of requests arriving per minute).

As with functional scenarios, a system quality scenario needs a unique identifier and a good name.

EXAMPLE Some system quality scenarios for the system that summarizes incoming data might be captured as follows.

Daily Data Update Trebles in Size
- *Overview*: How the system's end-of-day processing behaves when regular data volumes are suddenly greatly exceeded.

- *System state:* The system has summary statistics in its database for data that has already been processed, and the system's processing elements are lightly loaded at the current rate of system load.

- *System environment:* The deployment environment is working correctly, and data is arriving at a steady rate of 1,000 to 1,500 items per hour.

- *Environment changes:* The data update rate on a particular day suddenly increases to 4,000 items per hour.

- *Required system behavior:* When the end-of-day processing starts, the system should process that day's data set for a period until the processing time exceeds a system-configurable limit. At that point, the system should stop processing the data set, discard work in process, leave the previous set of summary statistics in place, and log a diagnostic message (including cause and action taken) to the operational console monitoring system.

Failure in Summary Database Instance

- *Overview:* How the system behaves when the database it is trying to write to fails.

- *System environment:* The deployment environment is working correctly.

- *Environment changes:* While writing summary statistics to the database, the system receives an exception indicating that the write failed (e.g., the database is full).

- *Required system behavior:* The system should immediately stop processing the statistics set it is working on and leave any work in progress behind. The system should log a fatal message to the operational console monitoring system and shut down.

Additional Summary Dimension Required

- *Overview:* How the system can cope with the need to extend the statistical processing provided.

- *System environment:* The deployment environment is operating normally, as initially delivered.

- *Environment changes:* The need arises to support a new statistical dimension in the summary statistics to summarize sales by type of payment option used.

- *Required system behavior:* The development team should be able to add the required processing to provide the new statistical dimension without making any changes to the overall system structure (i.e., changing any interelement interfaces or interactions) and with a total effort of fewer than 4 person-weeks.

A point worth noting from these examples is that a scenario doesn't always indicate good news, and when you create a scenario you may not have all the answers. The required failure behavior outlined in the examples isn't particularly robust, and this may not be acceptable. However, by writing this scenario, you now have a concrete case to discuss with stakeholders to help you learn what the phrase "must cope with failure conditions" in the requirements document actually means. Similarly, it isn't clear yet how the architecture would cope with the need for a new summary dimension, but you can now discuss the need for different types of evolution in a more concrete way.

WHAT MAKES A GOOD SCENARIO?

We have found scenarios to be a very useful architectural technique that can be used in a wide range of situations, including stakeholder communication, architectural evaluation and analysis, and as specifications for live testing. So assuming we want to create scenarios, what qualities should we aim for? We have found the key ones to be as follows.

- *Credible*: A scenario should describe a realistic situation that could credibly occur, and it should include enough realistic detail for the reader to accept the scenario as a valid situation that the system could encounter.

- *Valuable*: While it seems self-evident, a scenario should be of direct use somewhere in the architectural process, whether that is explaining the architecture to a stakeholder, convincing an assessor that the architecture is sound, or illustrating how the architecture works to a development team. It is easy to get carried away with defining scenarios that don't really address the concerns of any stakeholder, so consider this when creating new scenarios.

- *Specific*: A good scenario is quite specific and describes a particular situation accurately, rather than trying to generalize the system's behavior over a whole class of situations. The danger in trying to generalize scenarios beyond fairly specific situations is that it becomes difficult to describe them succinctly, so they are difficult to use since they address so many different concrete situations, each with its own variations.

- *Precise*: The definition of the scenario should be precise enough for the intended user of the scenario to be quite clear about what situation the scenario is describing and the required response of the system.

- *Comprehensible*: Like all architectural deliverables, scenarios should be comprehensible by those stakeholders who need to use them. This means writing them clearly, using widely understood terms, and avoiding acronyms and jargon that stakeholders are likely to misunderstand or find confusing.

APPLYING SCENARIOS

Having defined the scenarios for your system, you can apply them in a number of ways that vary greatly in their likely cost and also in the benefits you can expect to gain. This section briefly discusses the most common ways in which scenarios are applied.

Paper Models

The simplest and most common way to apply a scenario is to use it to create a paper-based model of how the system responds to the scenario. By "paper-based" we mean models like UML and data flow, whether they're created on paper, on whiteboards, in computer-based drawing tools, or in purpose-built software packages (e.g., modeling tools). The key thing about these models is that they are inert and thus can't be tested as such, only reviewed by one or more stakeholders. Their strength is that they are simple to understand and inexpensive to create, but their weakness is that they are only as reliable as the process used to construct and analyze them. The most common notation used for this sort of work is the UML sequence diagram.

EXAMPLE Figure 10–1 shows how the functional scenario presented earlier might be illustrated with a UML sequence diagram.

You've probably seen and used these diagrams in a number of places in the software development lifecycle. The boxes represent system elements that are interacting, the vertical lines represent the lifetimes of the elements (with time increasing down the page), and the horizontal arrows indicate interelement interactions and (optionally) what is returned from an interaction.

UML sequence diagrams are normally used in conjunction with an object-oriented development approach to indicate interobject interactions. However, this notation can usefully illustrate architectural scenarios for any kind of system—not just those built with object-oriented technology. The only requirement is that you have well-defined elements and interfaces.

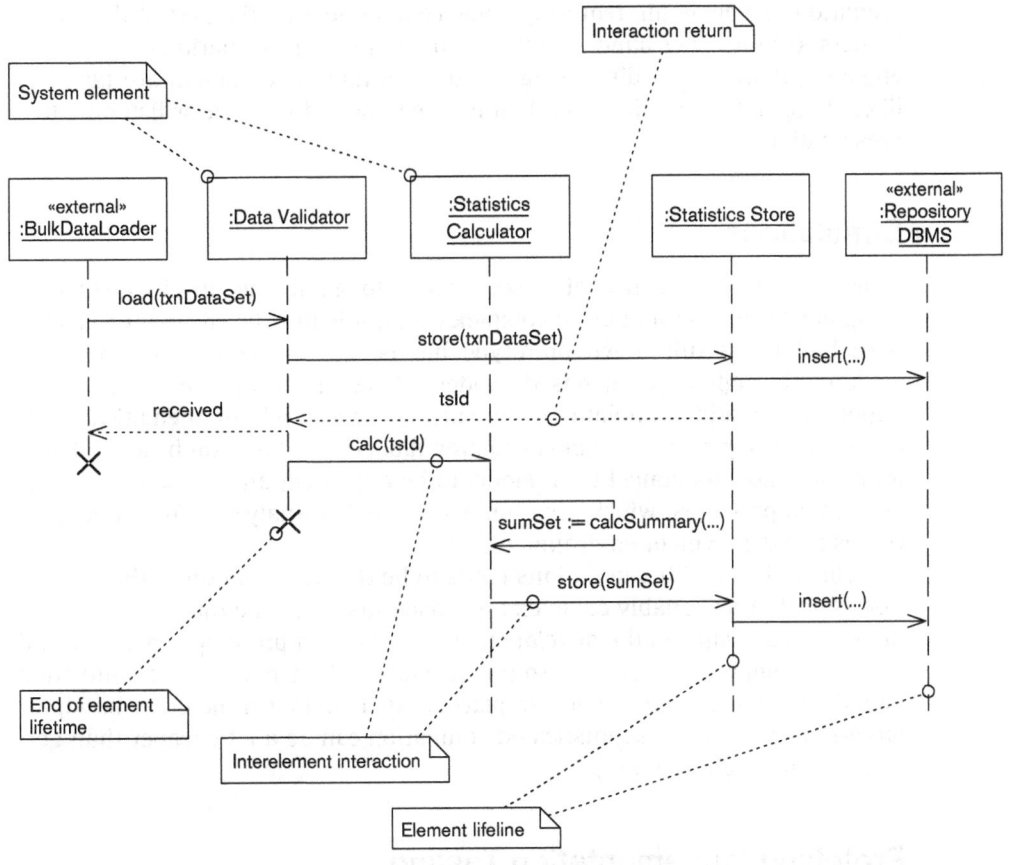

FIGURE 10-1 UML SEQUENCE DIAGRAM FOR THE INCREMENTAL STATISTICS UPDATE SCENARIO

Walkthroughs

An effective way to validate a paper-based model is to review it with a number of stakeholders by using it to bring the system to life with a walkthrough. A walkthrough illustrates how the system responds to one or more scenarios by explaining each step in the process to an interested stakeholder who can ask questions.

This can be a powerful technique because the very process of walking through the system's operation with stakeholders often helps you spot flaws in your design or missing requirements for the system. A problem with this technique can be the need for the audience to understand the system and the scenario in some detail, requiring some commitment on the part of the stakeholders. On the other hand, walking through a system scenario is much more engaging than simply discussing the design, and stakeholders are far more likely to spend time doing this than just reading a document or listening to a presentation.

Simulations

A more sophisticated use of a scenario is to guide the development of a computer-based simulation. In complex cases, this may be cheaper or quicker than building a full-blown prototype but is usually more expensive than walking through a paper-based model. There are a number of technical options for creating simulations: spreadsheets for purely mathematical models (e.g., some performance or calculation models); certain graphical modeling tools that allow a detailed UML model to be animated; and purpose-designed simulation packages, which are often well suited to analyzing functional processes and deployment environments.

The problem with simulations tends to be that the creation of the simulation is itself a reasonably complex and costly task, yet one that often can't be directly reused later in the development process (as a prototype could, even if only as a template). There is also the question of how realistic the simulation is and how much reliance you can place on its results. On the other hand, for large-scale systems, a sophisticated simulation can be a lot cheaper than getting the architecture wrong.

Prototype Implementation Testing

A more involved way to apply a scenario is to use it to guide prototyping work so that you can satisfy yourself that your architecture will be able to meet certain goals. Building a prototype can provide you with a much higher degree of confidence that one or more aspects of your architecture will succeed. However, building prototypes is expensive and time-consuming, so you can afford to do only a limited amount of it. The scenarios you identify can provide a way to focus your prototyping efforts on the high-risk areas of particular importance to stakeholders.

Full-Scale Live Testing

Finally, scenarios can provide a basis for planning real system-level tests. Because the scenarios define situations that the stakeholders have identified as particularly important to them, it often makes sense for the most important scenarios to be used as specifications of the initial system tests. These system tests often provide valuable proof for your key stakeholders that can hugely increase their confidence in the early versions of the system.

An important final point about applying scenarios is that it almost never makes sense to investigate all of your scenarios equally deeply—or at all. You may create paper models for some of them, simulate a few more, and create prototypes to investigate a couple of high-risk ones. Some of your scenarios may never be used except as a personal reality check for you and as a communication vehicle with a stakeholder or two. Focus the majority of your effort on the high-risk scenarios that stakeholders have indicated are particularly important.

EFFECTIVE USE OF SCENARIOS

Scenarios are a straightforward technique, and we are confident that you will be able to apply them without any great difficulty. However, we have found the following general practices helpful in applying scenarios effectively.

Identify a Focused Scenario Set

Although scenarios are very effective, it isn't often useful to end up with dozens and dozens of them. If you consider too many at once, the net result is a lack of focus that prevents them from providing clear guidance for decision making. It is difficult to be prescriptive about the precise number of scenarios you need because it depends very much on the scale and complexity of the system. However, more than 15 or 20 important scenarios is likely to be too many to use effectively for most systems, so work with your stakeholders to prioritize the set you end up with and focus on the riskiest and most important ones to guide decision making.

Use Distinct Scenarios

It is easy to create a number of scenarios that, although they seem different initially, are really very similar in terms of the requirements they place on the system. This leads to a situation where the cost of applying the technique increases (due to the number of scenarios that need to be created and considered) with only a marginal corresponding increase in benefits, thus reducing the effectiveness of the technique. In order to avoid this situation, revisit the scenarios you identify and consider what demands each places on the system. Where you find duplicates using this criterion, remove them; they are unlikely to provide additional significant insights into your architecture.

Use Scenarios Early

Although scenarios can be used throughout the software development lifecycle, they have the most impact when applied early, when the architecture of the system is taking shape. If you don't consider scenarios at an early stage but leave them until, say, they are needed for system testing, much of their potential benefit is likely to be lost. Of course, you may identify additional scenarios as development progresses (perhaps for testing or architectural evaluation), but do not ignore the potential benefits of applying scenarios earlier in the architectural design process. As outlined in the architecture process introduced at the start of Part II, identify the scenarios for your system as early as possible, and use them to help you focus the architecture and design activities on the most important aspects of the system.

Include the Use of System Quality Scenarios

Scenarios are often thought of in terms of *input*, *process*, and *output*, focusing on functional scenarios derived from the use cases in the functional requirements. However, this ignores the potential that scenarios have for investigating, validating, and understanding the quality properties of the system. As you identify the scenarios you are to work with, ensure that all of the system's critical quality properties are reflected in them. You will often need to augment the scenarios obtained from your stakeholders with suitable scenarios reflecting the system's required quality properties.

Include the Use of Failure Scenarios

A common pitfall is that all of the scenarios you identify are positive ones that do not consider problems like missing information, overload situations, security failures, and so on. This has the undesirable effect of focusing attention on situations where everything is working and ignoring cases where things go wrong. This is often particularly dangerous when considering quality properties, where system behavior is particularly critical in failure situations. When identifying your scenarios, ensure that you consider the important failure cases and that corresponding scenarios are identified to address these.

Involve Stakeholders Closely

As the architect for your system, you are in a very good position to identify representative scenarios for the system yourself. This is very tempting to do because it is so much simpler than involving all of your stakeholders who, while providing lots of input, will complicate the process immensely. However, excluding your stakeholders from scenario identification is a dangerous decision. Although you can undoubtedly identify many scenarios yourself, the ones your stakeholders provide and the priorities they place on each may surprise you, revealing aspects of the system of which you were unaware or whose importance you hadn't realized. Make sure that stakeholders are asked to identify candidate scenarios for your system and that they have the final say (as a group) in their prioritization.

CHECKLIST

- Have you defined a wide enough range of system quality scenarios (such as security, performance, availability, and evolution)?
- Have you defined and applied a wide enough range of failure and exception scenarios?
- Have you prioritized your scenarios by stakeholder importance and risk?
- Have you kept the number of scenarios down to a manageably small level, at most 15 to 20?
- Have you reviewed and agreed on the required responses and behaviors with the appropriate stakeholders or subject matter experts?
- Have you included some scenarios that *you* think will be valuable (based on your previous experience) as well as those nominated by your stakeholders?
- Are all of your scenarios cataloged and named?
- If defining a scenario helps indicate a gap or mistake in the requirements, have you made sure that this is addressed?
- If applying a scenario indicates a mismatch between required and actual response or behavior, have you revised the architectural design appropriately?

SUMMARY

Defining and applying scenarios is a powerful way to ensure that your architecture will exhibit the functionality and behavior required of it. It can also help reveal omissions and errors in the requirements and is useful when it comes to testing the system.

We defined two classes of scenarios: *functional scenarios*, which are nearly always defined in terms of a sequence of external events the system must respond to in a particular way; and *system quality scenarios*, which are defined in terms of how the system should react to a change in its environment, as a consequence of one of the quality properties it is meant to exhibit.

Scenarios are normally derived from an inspection of the system's requirements. You should also work with stakeholders to identify others (especially quality scenarios and ones that address failure situations), and you may want to identify some scenarios of your own based on your experience.

The specification of a scenario should include the initial system state and environment, external stimulus or environment changes, and the required system response or behavior.

Applying the scenario is a matter of comparing the actual, or likely, response and behavior with the requirement and addressing any gaps or mismatches. You can do this by using a paper model, a simulation, or a system prototype, or by testing the system, depending on the lifecycle stage you are in.

FURTHER READING

In the architectural context, most architecture books talk about scenarios somewhere, at least as a way to illustrate how the system is meant to work.

Much of our thinking and practice around scenarios has been influenced by a couple of books that clearly explain the idea of using scenarios for architecture work, in particular Clements et al. [CLEM02], where they form a key part of the evaluation approaches explained; Bass et al. [BASS03], where scenarios are used extensively to characterize quality attribute requirements; and Bosch [BOSC00], where scenarios are used to drive the architectural design process. More depth on the ideas and techniques we outlined here can be found in all of these books. Philippe Kruchten's "4+1" approach, where the "+1" refers to use case scenarios, was originally defined in an article in *IEEE Software* [KRUC95], which is still well worth reading today.

Use cases were first described by Ivar Jacobson in [JACO92], and Cockburn [COCK00] contains much useful and practical advice on creating and using them.

A Web search will reveal a number of vendors that can supply simulation tools and UML modeling tools that can animate a UML model, to help you investigate scenarios without building full prototypes.

11

USING STYLES AND PATTERNS

Historically, the software industry hasn't had a very good record of learning from experience. Software designers often ignore existing, proven design solutions and instead develop their own solutions to complex problems. The same can also be said of software architects, who can end up creating new system designs for very familiar challenges.

One of the reasons for this state of affairs used to be the lack of easily accessible, standard solutions for common software architecture and design problems. However, during the 1990s, the design patterns movement emerged with the aim of addressing this problem. Proponents of software patterns, inspired by Christopher Alexander's work on patterns for building architecture, [1] started identifying and cataloging widely used solutions to common design problems. Today, this work has culminated in an ever-growing number of patterns being available for general use.

INTRODUCING DESIGN PATTERNS

The purpose of a design pattern is to share a proven, widely applicable solution to a particular design problem in a standard form that allows it to be easily reused. Many types of patterns have been identified (including organizational and process patterns as well as design patterns), but for our purposes we are interested in three types of design patterns: the *architectural style*, which captures system-level structures; the *software design pattern*, which captures a more detailed software design solution; and the *language idiom*, which provides a solution for a recurring programming-language-specific design problem. These are all types of *design patterns*. Design patterns are usually described using

---

1. *Pattern Language: Towns, Buildings, Construction,* by Christopher Alexander, Sara Ishikawa, and Murray Silverstein (Oxford: Oxford University Press, 1977). Alexander is a building architect, and his books look at building architecture, but his ideas have inspired virtually everyone in the design patterns community.

one of a number of standard forms, but they all aim to provide the following five important pieces of information.

1. *Name*: A pattern needs a memorable and meaningful name to allow us to clearly identify and discuss the pattern and, more important, to use its name as part of our design language when discussing possible solutions to design problems.

2. *Context*: This sets the stage for the pattern, explains its motivation and rationale, and describes the situations in which the pattern may apply.

3. *Problem*: Each pattern is a solution to a particular problem, so part of the pattern's definition must be a clear statement of the problem that the pattern solves and any conditions that need to be met in order for the pattern to be effectively applied. A common way to describe the problem is to describe the design *forces* it aims to resolve, each force being a goal, requirement, or constraint that informs or influences the solution. Examples of forces might be the need to provide a specific sort of flexibility (such as the ability to change the algorithm used for a particular operation) or achieve a particular sort of efficiency that is important in the system (such as minimizing memory usage for a particular data structure).

4. *Solution*: The core of the pattern is a description of the solution to the problem that the pattern is proposing. This is usually some form of design model, explaining the elements of the design and how they work together to solve the problem, along with an example of the pattern's use where possible.

5. *Consequences*: The definition of a software pattern should include a clear statement of the results and tradeoffs that will result from its application, to allow you to decide whether it is a suitable solution to the problem. This should include both positive consequences (benefits) and negative consequences (costs).

Let's look at a simple example of a software design pattern.

EXAMPLE　The widely used *Adapter* pattern is so named because it adapts the interface of a system element to a form needed by one of its clients. An outline definition of the pattern could be as follows.

　The *context* of the Adapter pattern is a number of heterogeneous elements that need to be connected. The pattern solves the *problem* that arises when one system element (the client) wishes to use the services of another system element (the target) but cannot use the interface offered by the target element for some reason. An example could be a system with a .NET client that wishes to access a calculation service offered by a Java-based target. The calculation service is perfectly suitable for the client's requirements, but the client cannot call a Java-based interface and thus cannot use the service.

The *forces* include the following.

- Service interfaces should be decoupled from the underlying physical data structures and implementation algorithms.
- Services should be exposed in a way that is independent of their implementation technology.
- The adapter should provide translation only and should not perform any functional processing (this is the responsibility of the invoked service).
- Use of the adapter must not adversely affect the quality properties of the underlying service (security, resilience, performance, scalability, and so on).

The *solution* to the problem is to introduce a third system element, the adapter, sitting between the client and the target, such that it is called by the client and calls the target. The role of the adapter is simply to interpret the request from the client, transform it into the form required by the target, call the target, and transform the response into the form expected by the client. A real-world example of an adapter is an international power-plug adapter that allows, for example, electrical equipment with French plugs to be used in the United Kingdom with British power sockets.

The *consequences* of using this pattern include the following.

- Decoupling of the client and target implementations allows each implementation to be varied without impacting the other. (+)
- The target can be used by different types of clients simultaneously (possibly via different adapters). (+)
- A reduction in efficiency could result due to the additional level of indirection between the client and target. (−)
- An increase in maintenance overhead could occur if the services provided and used change because the adapter must be changed as well as the client and target. (−)

You can find a much fuller definition of this pattern in the well-known "Gang of Four" book referenced in the Further Reading section at the end of this chapter.

STYLES, PATTERNS, AND IDIOMS

As we said earlier, patterns are generally organized into three groups according to the level of design problem that they address: *architectural styles* that record solutions for system-level organization, *design patterns* that record solutions to detailed software design problems, and *language idioms* that capture useful solutions to language-specific problems. All three types of patterns can be valuable to you as a software architect, although you use them in different places in the lifecycle. However, before considering how to use styles, patterns, or idioms, let's define these three terms more formally. The definitions we present are all based on those defined by Frank Buschmann and his colleagues in their book *Pattern-Oriented Software Architecture*.

Architectural Styles

Architectural styles are probably the type of software pattern that will be of the most interest to you when designing a system because they define system-level structures.

DEFINITION An **architectural style** expresses a fundamental structural organization schema for software systems. It provides a set of predefined element types, specifies their responsibilities, and includes rules and guidelines for organizing the relationships between them.

The key point about an architectural style is that it provides a set of organizational principles for the system as a whole, rather than for the details of one piece of the system. The solution described by an architectural style is usually defined in terms of types of architectural elements and their interfaces, types of connectors, and constraints on how the elements and connectors should be combined.

For example, an architectural style might state that a system will comprise GUI clients, processing servers, and batch jobs and that the clients connect to the servers using messaging and the batch jobs communicate only via the database. If the benefits of the style were attractive for the system you were designing, the style could guide you to design a system with a specific set of processing servers, a specific GUI client, and a specific set of batch jobs. The style has defined the *type* of components to use and how to connect them, while you as the user of the style have defined *specific* components of those types for your system.

Note that the terms *architectural style* and *architectural pattern* are both commonly used, with no widely accepted definition of whether they're the same thing or not. Section P4 at the start of [CLEM10] has a very good discussion of both terms and whether they are the same or different. We haven't found it very useful in practice to separate these possibly different, but rather similar, concepts, and so for our purposes, while we may not be entirely correct, consider the two terms to be synonyms.

Software Design Patterns

A software design pattern is a solution to a much more specific problem related to the structure of one or more specific parts of a system.

> **DEFINITION** A **design pattern** documents a commonly recurring and proven structure of interconnected design elements that solves a general design problem within a particular context.

A design pattern forms an input to the detailed software design of the system and guides a software designer to organize her software design units (such as classes and procedures) appropriately. The solution presented by a design pattern is defined in terms of design-level elements (such as procedures, classes, and data structures) and the structure they form when combined.

Language Idioms

Language idioms are the most specific type of software pattern, applying to situations where a particular programming language is in use.

> **DEFINITION** A **language idiom** is a pattern specific to a programming language. An idiom describes how to implement particular aspects of elements or the relationships between them by using the features of a given language.

A language idiom provides guidance to the programmer when implementing software in a specific language and is normally written to help prevent a common pitfall with the language or to illustrate a unique feature that needs to be learned. The solutions presented by language idioms are defined in terms of programming language constructs.

Using Styles, Patterns, and Idioms

Patterns of all three varieties can play several helpful roles, including the following.

- *A store of knowledge*: Patterns are a store of knowledge about solving a particular type of problem in a particular domain. Documenting this knowledge allows it to be shared among people solving similar problems. People can move between specialist areas more easily and work more effectively within a particular area by sharing knowledge about success and failure.
- *Examples of proven practices*: A set of patterns provides examples of proven design practices. Indeed, a common test for accepting a new design pattern is that it has been used successfully at least three times in different

situations. You can use these design practices directly, but they can also act as a guide and provide inspiration when you're solving somewhat different design problems.

- *A language*: Patterns allow designers to create and share a common language for discussing design problems. This common language helps designers relate ideas to each other easily and analyze alternative solutions to a problem. This allows for more effective communication among participants in the design process.

- *An aid to standardization*: The use of patterns encourages designers to choose standard solutions to recurring problems rather than searching for novel solutions in each case. This has obvious efficiency benefits for the design, build, and support processes, and reliability is also likely to increase because of the reuse that results from the application of an already proven solution.

- *A source of constant improvement*: Because patterns are generally in the public domain, you can quickly learn from a lot of experience that others have had in using them. This allows rapid feedback into the pattern definition and promotes improvement over time, reflecting the experiences of users.

- *Encouragement of generality*: Good patterns are usually generic, flexible, and reusable in a number of situations. Providing flexible and generic solutions to problems is often a goal for architects as well. Using patterns as inputs to the design process and thinking in terms of identifying design patterns within the design process can help you create flexible, generic solutions to the problems within your system.

From our point of view as architects, the real utility of design patterns in software development can be summarized in a single phrase: *reduction of risk*. The use of patterns (and ideally reusable pattern implementations) has the potential to increase productivity, standardization, and quality while reducing risk and repetition.

PATTERNS AND ARCHITECTURAL TACTICS

Having introduced the idea of design patterns and discussed the three types that we're interested in, let's consider the relationship between them and architectural tactics. As we said in Chapter 4, design patterns and architectural tactics are both types of architectural design guidance, but they are quite different. A tactic is much more general and broader than a design pattern. While a tactic provides you with advice on how to address a general issue, a design pattern is a specific solution to a specific problem, in context. Indeed, a tactic could involve the application of one or more design patterns, but it need not, and it could provide much more general advice.

For example, an architectural tactic that is often cited is to "partition and parallelize" in order to split large tasks into independent pieces that can be executed simultaneously. Applying this tactic might involve using the Pipes and Filters architectural style, but that is only one possible way to apply the tactic, and it might be only part of the solution. The way that we like to think of it is that architectural tactics give us a set of *strategies* to use to solve particular general types of problems, while patterns provide us with specific, proven *solutions* for particular constrained design problems.

AN EXAMPLE OF AN ARCHITECTURAL STYLE

Let's consider an example of a specific architectural style.

EXAMPLE   Here is a summary of the Pipes and Filters architectural style. (This is just a summary; you can find a much fuller definition in *Pattern-Oriented Software Architecture* [BUSC96].)

The *context* of the Pipes and Filters style is a system that needs to process data streams.

The style solves the *problem* of implementing a system that must process data in a sequence of steps, where using a single process is not possible and where the requirements for the processing steps may change over time.

The problem has the following primary *forces*.

- Future changes should be possible by changing, reordering, or recombining steps.
- Small processing steps are easier to reuse than large ones.
- Nonadjacent steps in the process do not share information.
- Different possible sources of input data exist.
- Explicit storage of intermediate results should be avoided.
- Multiprocessing between steps should not be ruled out.

The *solution* to this problem is to divide the task into a number of sequential steps and to connect the steps by the system's data flow.

The processing is performed by filter components, which consume and process data incrementally. The input data to the system is provided by a data source while the output flows into a data sink. The data source, data sink, and filter components are connected by pipes. The pipe implements data flow between two adjacent components. The pipe is the only permitted way to connect the components, and it defines a simple, standard format for data that passes through it, allowing filters to be combined without prior knowledge of each other's existence.

The sequence of filters combined by pipes is called a *processing pipeline*. An example of a processing pipeline appears in the informal diagram in Figure 11–1, which shows how the pieces of the Pipes and Filters style are combined. As indicated by the UML-style comments, the boxes represent the filters and the arrows represent unidirectional pipes linking the filters. Each filter performs a single task—for example, the NPV filter calculates the net present value of each of the investments passed to it, writing the result to its output.

The *consequences* of using this style are as follows.

- No intermediate files are necessary, but they are possible. (+)
- Filter implementation can be easily changed without affecting other system elements. (+)
- Filter recombination makes creating new pipelines from existing filters easy. (+)
- Filters can be easily reused in different situations. (+)
- Parallel processing can be supported with multiple filters running concurrently. (+)

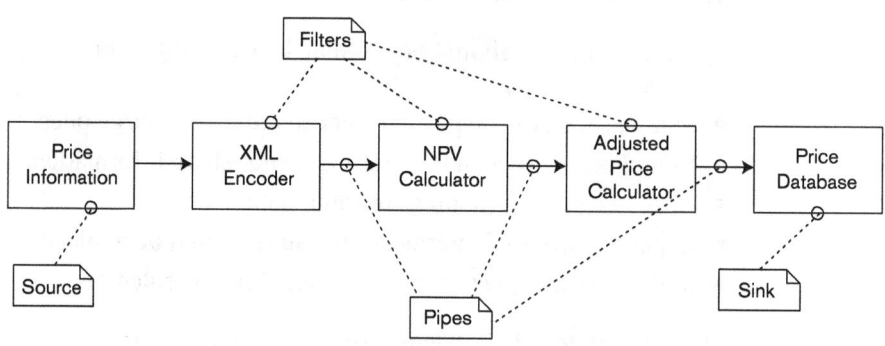

FIGURE 11–1 PROCESSING PIPELINE

- Parallel processing can be supported with multiple filters running concurrently. (+)
- Sharing state information is difficult. (–)
- The data transformation required for a common interfilter data format adds overhead. (–)
- Error handling is difficult and needs to be implemented consistently. (–)

You are almost certainly familiar with this architectural style from the UNIX operating system. However, it has been applied in a lot of other software systems, such as Enterprise Application Integration (EAI) systems, signal- and image-processing applications, and Internet "mashup" systems like Yahoo! Pipes,[2] so it is proving to be a useful system organization for a problem that may occur across a number of application domains.

What conclusions can we draw if we encounter a system based on this architectural style? Some of the important points are listed here.

- The system processes streams of data, rather than transactions.
- The processing can be broken into a series of independent steps.
- There is just one sort of architectural element (the filter) and one type of unidirectional connector (the pipe), and the filters must form a continuous path through the system, connected by pipes, without any cycles.
- The system doesn't need a central persistent data store.
- It should be easy to replace and reuse the system's filter elements.
- It is likely to be difficult to modify the system to address a situation where elements need to maintain or share state.
- The architect of the system will need to define and enforce an error-handling strategy because the style makes this something of a challenge.

An architectural style tells us what sort of structure a system based on it will have, in terms of the types of system elements and the structure they combine to form. The style also explains the design concerns (or forces) that led to its development and the positive and negative implications to be considered when using it.

---

2. See http://pipes.yahoo.com.

THE BENEFITS OF USING ARCHITECTURAL STYLES

Basing your architecture on a recognizable style can have two immediate benefits. First, using a style allows you to select a proven, well-understood solution to your problems and defines the organizing principles for the system. Second, if people know that the architecture is based on a familiar style, it helps them understand its important characteristics.

In our experience, most architects do reuse good ideas they've seen before and do match previously successful solutions to the characteristics of the current problem. It's simply that we do this with varying degrees of formality and may not consider ourselves to be using architectural styles as we do it.

Most of the books documenting architectural styles assume that the styles will be used directly as generic blueprints to guide the design process. However, styles can be used during the architecture definition process in a number of ways.

- *Solution for a system design:* One of the styles you encounter may be a good solution to the particular problems you are trying to solve. In this case, you can simply adopt the style as one of the core structures of your architecture and enjoy the benefits of understanding its likely strengths and weaknesses immediately.

- *Basis for adaptation:* When considering existing styles, you may find that none of them really solve your problem, but they partially address it or address it with some limitations. In these situations, the style forms a starting point for the design process but acts as a base to be adapted to the particular constraints of the current situation. This identifies a candidate variant of the original style.

- *Inspiration for a related solution:* You may also find that none of the styles actually address the problem you are trying to solve. However, simply reading about previously identified styles and the problems they address often helps you understand the current problem in more depth so you can find a solution related in some way to the existing styles. This identifies a related candidate style.

- *Motivation for a new style:* Sometimes you are faced with a problem that does not seem to be addressed by any of the styles you have found. In this case, perhaps you are solving a problem that hasn't been widely solved before, or if it has, its solution hasn't been documented as a style. These situations often act as a spur to solve the problem in a general way and to define a new candidate architectural style capturing the resulting design knowledge.

Having talked about styles individually, we should point out that you rarely use one architectural style in isolation. Like other types of design patterns, most styles focus on solving one particular design problem, but in reality most systems involve solving a number of design problems simultaneously. This means that, in all but the simplest systems, you usually need to combine a number of styles to meet the varied design problems that you face.

EXAMPLE Consider a financial trading system that needs to allow users to perform transactions but also needs to broadcast information (such as news or prices) across the system. At least two architectural styles immediately suggest themselves: the Client/Server style to allow transaction processing via central servers and the Publisher/Subscriber style to allow news and price information to be broadcast throughout the system. Another style may be needed, too, such as Layered Implementation, in order to achieve portability and common use of the underlying platform. In this example, each style is needed for a distinct reason.

- The Client/Server style is present to allow secure, scalable, available transaction processing that performs well.

- The Publisher/Subscriber style is present to allow efficient, flexible, asynchronous distribution of information.

- The Layered Implementation style is present to ensure portability across deployment platforms, to ensure a common approach to the use of underlying technology, and to achieve a good level of development productivity by hiding low-level details of the underlying technology from most of the system developers.

Situations in which we need to combine styles present us with a twofold problem. First, how do we use a number of styles together and retain overall coherence in our architecture? Second, how do we know that the styles will work together and not conflict with each other?

With this problem, as with so many others in software architecture, there really is no substitute for the blend of experience, knowledge, and sound judgment that you bring to the project. Our experience with system architectures has taught us that combining styles can be difficult and needs to be done carefully. We have found that the key to success is to choose one of the styles as the dominant organizing style for the system and to structure the architecture around it, introducing the other styles as subsidiary styles where they are needed to solve particular problems that the primary style cannot address by itself. Such an approach helps retain overall coherence and prompts you to consider the compatibility of the styles as you try to add the elements of the subsidiary styles to the structure imposed by the overall system organization defined by the primary style.

STYLES AND THE ARCHITECTURAL DESCRIPTION

You are likely to adopt a number of specific architectural styles for your system because you want the system to exhibit certain qualities that the styles claim to provide. Once you've chosen the styles to use, it is easy to forge ahead and create an architectural design based on them while forgetting to explain *how* you've used them in the AD. When this happens, the knowledge about the styles used and why they were selected gets lost, so it is likely that, over time, the architecture will diverge from the structure suggested by the style.

In addition, many architectural styles focus on the overall functional structure of the system and will primarily affect the Functional view in the AD. However, in principle, a style could affect any of the architectural views, so explaining the styles you've used can be important to allow readers of the AD to understand the impact a style has had across the different aspects of your architecture. For these reasons, it is useful to explicitly explain the styles you have used in the AD.

We've found that there are a couple of effective ways to do this: textual commentary and model annotation. Textual commentary simply involves adding to the AD document a brief discussion of the styles you've used and why you used them, probably as an early subsection to help set the scene for the reader. Annotating your models takes this a step further and draws the reader's attention to the relationship between the generic style in use and the specific elements in the architecture. If you are using UML as your modeling notation, you can achieve this by using stereotypes to mark model elements as corresponding to particular abstract elements of the style in use. However, you need to avoid cluttering the models with a lot of extra notation, which prevents people from understanding them easily. If this starts to happen, remove the annotation from the model diagrams and just add textual notes in your explanation of the model.

APPLYING DESIGN PATTERNS AND LANGUAGE IDIOMS

Although it's fairly clear how you can use architectural styles because they act as a source of proven architectural design ideas, it's not necessarily as clear how design patterns and language idioms fit into the architectural design process. Given that detailed design and coding aren't your key focus, how do design patterns and language idioms contribute to your main area of work?

The answer is that design patterns and language idioms are a very important communication mechanism between architects and software developers. It's crucial to communicate directly by leading the team and talking face-to-face, but there are also many situations when it's important to get design constraints and guidelines on paper so that everyone can understand and consider them thoroughly. Design patterns and language idioms are perfect mechanisms for communicating design advice and constraints to a development team.

EXAMPLE Here are some typical examples of using design patterns and language idioms.

Examples of Using Design Patterns

- If you are developing a system that requires internationalization, this is an important system-wide design constraint. In order to ensure a common approach across the system's modules, adopt or define a design pattern that illustrates how a module should be internationalized.

- Many database applications need to use specific approaches to locking (e.g., the choice of using optimistic or pessimistic locks depending on data integrity and concurrency needs). The locking approach to use in certain situations may be an important design constraint resulting from the architectural design. When this is the case, use a design pattern to define how database locking must be implemented.

- The evolutionary needs of the system may require that new code can be easily introduced to handle new types of data. In order to guide the design process to achieve the required flexibility, you could suggest the use of relevant design patterns like Chain of Responsibility, Reflection, or Visitor to help developers to understand the type of flexibility you need.

Examples of Using Language Idioms

- Many modern programming languages such as Java, C++, and C# include exception-handling facilities. These facilities can be used in a number of ways, so an important architectural constraint is to define how the programming language's exception-handling facilities should be used and ensure that the idiom is used throughout the system

  To allow a system to be easily instrumented, it can be very useful for each element to be able to return a string containing its state so that this can be written to a debug log. This is possible in most programming languages, but the mechanism available and the best way to use it vary. You can standardize this across your system by defining or adopting an idiom to be used when implementing each system element.

- Many languages have features that need careful use to avoid subtle problems creeping in later (such as the advice to override either both or neither of Java's equals() and hashCode() methods or the

> need to define a copy constructor in C++ to avoid problems when
> using object assignment). You can help to avoid such language-
> specific problems by working with your senior developers to define
> or adopt language idioms to provide guidance where needed.

The identification and definition of patterns and idioms for your system
would normally be part of the activity of creating the Development view. However,
because pattern and idiom documentation can be quite large, it usually makes
sense to create it as part of a development standards document referenced from
the AD, rather than in the Development view itself.

CHECKLIST

- Have you considered existing architectural styles as solutions for your
  architectural design problems?
- Have you clearly indicated in your AD where you have used architectural
  styles?
- Have you reviewed likely sources for possible new styles, patterns, and
  idioms that may be relevant to your system?
- Do you understand the design forces addressed by the patterns you use
  and the strengths and weaknesses of each pattern?
- Have you defined patterns and idioms to document all important design
  constraints for your system?
- Have you considered using design patterns and idioms to provide design
  guidance where relevant?

SUMMARY

Architectural styles, design patterns, and language idioms (collectively known
as *patterns*) are all ways to reuse proven software design knowledge, and all
three are valuable during the architectural design process. Patterns provide a
reusable store of knowledge, help to develop a language for discussing design,
and encourage standardization and generality in the design of your system.

Becoming familiar with a range of architectural styles helps you build your
design vocabulary and provides you with a library of options to consider when
you meet new architectural design problems. Styles can also form the basis for
further refinement and the inspiration for entirely new solutions, as well as
simply being design blueprints. A good selection of relevant architectural styles

for information systems already exists, and part of an architect's training is getting to know these styles and the strengths and weaknesses of each.

Patterns and idioms also help to expand your knowledge of proven design solutions for more detailed problems, but they also are a valuable mechanism for recording the design constraints and guidelines that are important to achieving architectural integrity in the system's implementation.

FURTHER READING

A great deal of literature exists on the subject of design patterns, and we can't provide a thorough overview of it all (for example, at the time of writing, there are about 400 books being sold by Amazon.com with the phrase "design patterns" in their titles). However, there are some important texts and resources for design patterns that are worth being familiar with.

The original book on design patterns is *Design Patterns* [GAMM95], often referred to as the "Gang of Four" or "GoF" book, which is still a definitive source of basic design patterns. A good place to start reading about patterns from the perspective of an architect is Buschmann et al., *Pattern-Oriented Software Architecture* [BUSC96] (generally known as "POSA1"). Our definitions of style, pattern, and idiom come from this book. Shaw and Garlan [SHAW96] is one of the original descriptions of architectural styles.

As its name suggests, POSA1 was the first book in a series of pattern collections, and since it was published, further volumes have appeared on concurrency design [SCHM00], resource management [KIRC04], distributed computing [BUSC07a], and pattern languages [BUSC07b]. All of these books are high-quality collections of proven patterns, authored by well-known figures in the patterns community such as Frank Buschmann, Kevlin Henney, Doug Schmidt, and Michael Stal.

The Pattern Languages of Program Design conference series [PLOP95–99, PLOP06] has produced a large number of design patterns of all sorts during the years it has been running. The books we reference here present some of the notable results of the pattern-writing workshops at the conferences, and they are a rich source of useful design patterns. The Web site www.hillside.net also contains a complete history of the conference series and all of the related conferences (such as the German conference, EuroPLOP). For most of the conferences, all of the submitted pattern papers are available on the Web site, which makes for a comprehensive, if somewhat overwhelming, patterns resource.

The well-known software writer Martin Fowler is the lead author of a book [FOWL03b] containing a large number of patterns found in enterprise information systems that are likely to be of use to most information systems architects. A somewhat related book that contains a valuable set of patterns that focus on the deployment aspects of large information systems is Dyson and Longshaw [DYSO04].

Many technology-specific patterns books have been written, too many for us to list here, and in any case their usefulness obviously depends on which technologies you plan to use in your systems. For the Enterprise Java environment, one of the better-known sets of patterns is [ALUR03]. For .NET, Microsoft has made a similar set of patterns available via the "Patterns and Practices" section of its MSDN Web site (http://msdn.microsoft.com/en-us/practice), and [ESPO08] also contains patterns relevant to .NET application development.

Similarly, there are too many books of language idioms to list here, but one of the originals is Coplien's book of C++ idioms [COPL91], and a well-known set of idioms for Java is presented by Josh Bloch in [BLOC08]; a similar set has been written for C# by Bill Wagner [WAGN10]. There are also books of patterns for other popular technologies such as Ruby, Perl, Python, JavaScript, PHP, and many more. The search function of a good Internet book retailer will provide you with many to choose from.

A fair number of Web sites have appeared that contain design patterns, but the speed of evolution of Web-based information sources makes it futile to attempt to present a list here. Two of the original pattern Web sites are the Hillside Group (www.hillside.net) that we mentioned previously and the patterns area of Ward Cunningham's C2 Wiki site (www.c2.com/cgi-bin/wiki?PatternIndex).

12

PRODUCING ARCHITECTURAL MODELS

As an architect, you face the twin challenges of developing an architectural solution that effectively balances the needs of stakeholders and communicating the important details of that solution to them. Because we can't build the real computer system as part of the architecture definition process—just as a building architect can't construct a real office block while designing the building—we have to find ways to represent and analyze the system's important features so that our different classes of stakeholders can understand them. We call these representations *models*.

 DEFINITION In this context, a **model** is an abstract, simplified, or partial representation of some aspects of an architecture, the purpose of which is to communicate those aspects of the system to one or more stakeholders.

We use models to help us cope with our inherent difficulty in coming to grips with complex concepts or ideas. An effective model, as we shall see, brings out the important aspects of an architecture while hiding less important distractions.

To help us put models in context within the architecture definition process, let's remind ourselves of the relationships between the main elements of the process.

- An architecture is documented in an *architectural description* (AD).
- The AD consists of one or more *views* of the architecture. (It may also include other elements, such as principles, standards, and glossaries,

which lay the architectural foundations.) For example, an AD may include a Functional view, a Concurrency view, and a Deployment view.

- The contents of each view are based on a *viewpoint*. For example, the contents of an Operational view are based on the templates, patterns, and guidelines in the Operational viewpoint.

- Each view consists of one or more *models*. A model is a way to represent some of the salient features of an architecture that pertain to the view. For example, an Information view may include an entity-relationship model, a data ownership model, and a state transition model.

- Applying a *perspective* may lead to changes to existing models or to the creation of one or more secondary architectural models that allow a better understanding of the architecture's ability to exhibit a particular quality property (i.e., models that do not define one of the system's structures). For example, applying the Security perspective usually involves the creation of a threat model in order to understand the security threats the system faces.

We can see from these relationships that models are central to the architecture definition process because they describe the key aspects of the system being designed. With this in mind, let's explore how architects use models during architecture definition.

WHY MODELS ARE IMPORTANT

Although modeling isn't necessarily the most important thing that architects do, the models we create are probably the most important elements of our ADs. There are four primary reasons why we build models as part of the software development process.

1. Models help us *understand* the situations we are modeling. Building a model brings precision to our description and focuses us on the most important elements of the situation.

2. Models act as a medium for *communication*, helping us explain our thinking to others. Models reduce the amount of information the reader needs to understand, and their structure guides the reader through the information.

3. Models help us *analyze* situations by allowing us to isolate key elements and understand their interrelationships. Then we can reason about some aspect of the situation being modeled and draw conclusions about its properties.

4. Models help us *organize* our processes, teams, and deliverables as a result of the structures they reveal in the situation being modeled.

The key skill the model builder uses to achieve these benefits is *abstraction*, the process of suppressing unnecessary detail. By removing such detail from our models, we allow our stakeholders and ourselves to focus on the most important aspects of our architecture. A good model can help stakeholders understand an architecture they might not understand otherwise.

While models are certainly important to software architects, the idea of modeling isn't a new one and in fact has been with us since classical times. The ancient Greek astronomer Ptolemy taught that a central Earth was orbited by the sun, moon, planets, and stars. We now know that Ptolemy's model was wrong, but it was good enough to predict the motion of heavenly bodies to reasonable accuracy. In Renaissance times, the Polish astronomer Copernicus created the more accurate heliocentric model, in which the Earth revolved around the sun. One hundred fifty years later, Sir Isaac Newton set forth his laws of gravity and motion in *Principia Mathematica*. Newtonian mathematics survived unchallenged until Einstein published his general theory of relativity in 1916.

Ptolemy, Copernicus, Newton, and Einstein were all trying to describe the same phenomenon—the apparent motion of the sun, planets, and stars. None of their models were entirely correct, but each of their models could be considered *good enough* for the purposes to which it was put.[1] Indeed, Newtonian mechanics is still adequate for all but the most specialized applications even today. The lesson from these famous attempts at modeling the physical world is that no model is perfect, but even an imperfect model can provide us with useful information about the reality it is modeling. Martin Fowler captures this succinctly in his book *Analysis Patterns* when he says, "Models are not right or wrong, they are more or less useful."[2] We express this principle as follows.

 PRINCIPLE Every architectural model is an approximation of reality, since it abstracts away unnecessary detail in order to focus attention on the most important aspects of the situation being modeled.

The trick with a successful model is to make it *good enough* to achieve the purpose for which you have created it, whether this is communicating important information to your stakeholders, analyzing a system quality, or understanding an architectural structure. This is often difficult to achieve because you often don't have much time to do it—the process of architecture definition is not usually allocated much time in development projects—and the situation you are trying to model may be complex, difficult, or new to you or your stakeholders.

---

1. We'll stick our necks out here and say that someone will eventually successfully challenge Einstein, although probably not in our lifetimes!
2. [FOWL97], p. 2.

However, remember that your models will be refined as part of the specification and design process. A rough-and-ready model that is produced early in the project and becomes established and familiar to the team will be more useful than something considered more fully that appears too late to be used.

STRATEGY Match the complexity and detail of your architectural models to the interests and skill level of your audience, the time you have to produce the models, and (most important) the way in which the models will be used.

As a general rule, simple models are more useful in presentations to nontechnical stakeholders or early in the architectural analysis to bring out some key features, while more sophisticated models are more useful as analysis, communication, and comprehension tools for you and other technical stakeholders, such as software developers.

EXAMPLE An insurance company that has grown by acquisition has, as a consequence, a large number of systems that are connected using a jumble of hard-to-maintain point-to-point interfaces. Although a long-term goal of the company is to replace these systems, budget constraints mean that this may not be done for a number of years. In the meantime, someone has proposed replacing the point-to-point interfaces with a hub-and-spoke messaging infrastructure.

The architect develops some fairly sophisticated architectural models that include technology and application adapters, a message-switching hub, heterogeneous interconnectivity, and data-driven conversion rules. This has allowed her to analyze and understand the necessarily complex candidate architecture; however, she is having a hard time explaining the benefits of the proposed new architecture to the business stakeholders.

The problem is that the mass of technical detail hides the essential simplicity of the concept. The architect develops another model that fits on a single page and illustrates graphically how the current tangle of interfaces will be replaced by an architecture that is cheaper to manage, more easily adapted, and more reliable and is likely to suffer from fewer data quality problems. This model is far more successful with the business stakeholders.

Although producing quick back-of-an-envelope models can be helpful, you shouldn't use this strategy as an excuse for compromising the validity, consistency, and correctness of your important models—particularly ones that will be used later as a basis for the system design. Omitting details from models can lead to the dangerous situation where stakeholders believe that problems have been resolved, but in fact they are just hidden.

STRATEGY Ensure that your audience is aware of any simplifications and approximations in your model and the impact of these on their understanding of the solution.

TYPES OF MODELS

When we think of an architectural model, most of us picture in our minds some sort of diagram supported by definitions of the elements it contains. However, there are many other types of models, and it is useful to broadly classify them as formal *qualitative* or *quantitative* models or informal qualitative models that we term *sketches*.

Qualitative Models

Qualitative models are analogous to the scale models and blueprints produced by building architects and structural engineers to define the structure of a new building and show how it will look in its environment. They aim to present the essence of the thing being modeled—its form and features—rather than to predict its measurable qualities. Qualitative models are extremely important to the architect and are used throughout the system lifecycle, from the early stages of architecture definition while ideas are being crystallized to late in the lifecycle when detailed aspects of the system's design need to be clarified.

DEFINITION Qualitative models illustrate the key structural or behavioral elements, features, or attributes of the architecture being modeled.

Qualitative models form the main content of the views within the AD and are also important outputs of some perspectives (such as the Security perspective mentioned earlier).

In our context, the most common forms of qualitative models are the various sorts of diagrammatic architecture models, such as a functional structure model or an information model, although we group other types under this classification, such as mock-ups, prototypes, and simulations. These all, to some extent, try to show the stakeholders how the system will look when it is built.

Historically, qualitative models tended to be less formal than quantitative ones—in other words, they adhered less strictly to rules of representation and layout—largely because the accepted rules for presenting such models (the *modeling languages*) were on the whole weak or nonexistent. However, this is no longer really the case, as widely used modeling languages, in particular UML, provide a standard way to represent many types of static and dynamic modeling elements. (We'll discuss this further in the Modeling Languages section.)

To get the best out of your models you should aim for rigor, clarity, and consistency. If the modeling language you are using is insufficient for your needs, you should establish your own conventions, such as the standardized use of shape or color to represent different types of architectural element in diagrams; define them clearly; and stick to them faithfully in your models.

STRATEGY   Select a modeling language for your qualitative models, extend it if necessary, and follow it strictly. Make sure to provide a key or other explanation so that your audience understands the notation and conventions you are following.

Some of your models, particularly early or overview models, may be aimed at a mixed audience of business and technology stakeholders. Sometimes models are produced in response to a specific political need within an organization, such as support for a business case, in which case the models will need to fulfill a very specific set of objectives (such as accentuating the financial benefits of a new architecture in the insurance company example presented earlier).

Creating a model for both business and technology stakeholders is probably the hardest situation to deal with. Such mixed models usually need to be less formal and rigorous than the ones aimed at more specialized groups of stakeholders. They may need to use a range of notations or none at all, and they may have to omit details the audience finds confusing—or conversely, drill down into details at certain points to highlight particular features. You can often deal with these situations by using a less formal type of qualitative model, a *sketch*, which we'll discuss shortly.

Quantitative Models

Quantitative models are analogous to the mathematical models of a building produced by structural and building services engineers to establish the physical characteristics of its structure, such as the required thickness of its structural elements or the number of people who will be able to comfortably enter or exit the building at peak times. The output of quantitative models is a set of metrics that predicts the behavior or other characteristics of the system. Quantitative models usually have a mathematical or statistical basis.

DEFINITION Quantitative models make statements about the measurable properties of an architecture, such as performance, resilience, and capacity.

Because they deal with system qualities instead of structures, quantitative models are usually created by applying a perspective, rather than by following the guidance in a viewpoint.

EXAMPLE A mathematical model of the capacity of a system to respond under load would represent the utilization of a hardware component with this formula:

utilization = transaction throughput × busy time per transaction

By analyzing the utilization of hardware components, we can identify potential bottlenecks—heavily used components that slow system response—and see the effect of system changes on performance. (In fact, more sophisticated mathematical models such as queuing theory can often be used to predict system response times to a reasonable degree of accuracy.)

Quantitative analysis such as capacity planning usually requires either sophisticated mathematical ability or the use of mathematical modeling tools. We return to this subject in Chapter 26 when we discuss the Performance and Scalability perspective.

Effective quantitative models are often time-consuming to create and validate, so unless you have the luxury of a lengthy architecture definition phase, your quantitative models, if you produce any at all, may have to be rough approximations. In the worst case, you may not have time to do any more than to establish confidence that your architecture will work and to understand its characteristics at a high level. However, this confidence-building work can be valuable, especially when there is uncertainty or you are breaking new ground, and such models produced early in the lifecycle can provide a useful basis on which to build more complete and accurate models later, if required.

In some cases, of course, critical quality requirements for a system make quantitative models essential. For example, if you are designing some sort of server or service-providing system for which good throughput and scalability are crucial, the creation of a performance model will be a key architectural task. In such cases, the priority of the important quantitative modeling tasks will need to be raised to a level such that sufficient time is allocated for them.

Sketches

A third kind of commonly used architectural model is a sketch, which is an informal qualitative diagrammatic model. Sketches are analogous to the artist's impressions created to help people imagine the impact of a new building without them having to understand all of the details of its structure. Sketches are inherently *informal*, by which we mean that they often incorporate diagramming elements from a range of modeling languages and methodologies—UML, entity-relationship modeling, and so on—while strictly adhering to the rules and conventions of none of them. Sketches often make use of icons, graphics, and pictures to convey their meaning. We separate sketches from formal qualitative models to avoid any confusion between an erroneous or partially completed formal model and a deliberately informal sketch.

DEFINITION A **sketch** is a deliberately informal graphical model, created in order to communicate the most important aspects of an architecture to a nontechnical audience. It may combine elements of a number of modeling notations as well as pictures and icons.

Although they sound rather frivolous, sketches are a useful way to help your stakeholders, particularly nontechnical ones, understand the essence of your architecture. Sketches are often used during the inception phases of a system development project to explain the key features to the wider community. (This process is variously known as evangelizing or socializing the architecture.) You can also use sketches later in the development process to provide accessible, easily comprehensible overview models for less technical stakeholders in situations where the primary architectural models would be difficult for them to understand.

The inherent danger when using sketches is that their informal nature can easily introduce ambiguity into an AD and lead to confusion and misunderstanding. If a primary architectural model starts life as a sketch, you should aim to replace or reinforce it with more formally specified models as soon as you can.

MODELING LANGUAGES

Architecture Description Languages

An architecture description language (ADL) is a special-purpose notation for the sorts of models used to define the architecture of a computer system. The benefit of using an ADL is that it has been specifically designed for the creation of models at an architectural level of detail. By contrast, most general-purpose modeling notations are designed to represent much more detailed programming language structures. The architectural focus of an ADL means that you can use it to explain the architecturally significant aspects of your architecture without getting bogged down in details that are more appropriate to design work.

A number of ADLs have been proposed by groups working in the area, some of the better-known being Acme from Carnegie Mellon University; AADL, which is standardized by the SAE; Rapide from Stanford University; and ArchiMate, which is standardized by the Open Group and is a little different from the others in that it is aimed at enterprise architecture rather than software or systems architecture. However, in practice it is rare to find an ADL in use on an industrial enterprise system development project, and most ADLs are still being experimented with in the research domain rather than used in the mainstream. This means there is a shortage of familiar, functionally rich tools that support the use of ADLs, and your stakeholders are unlikely to understand the notation and the significance of the language elements.

The Unified Modeling Language

An alternative to using an ADL is to use a general-purpose modeling language, adapting and specializing it to suit your needs. Of the many possible notations that can be used in an AD, the most prevalent is probably UML.

As defined in the standard, the goal of UML is to "provide system architects, software engineers, and software developers with tools for analysis, design, and implementation of software based systems as well as for modeling business and similar processes."[3] The language tries to encapsulate proven practices in software design into a standard yet extensible notation. UML provides a number of standard diagramming notations, such as use cases, class diagrams, sequence diagrams, and activity diagrams. In addition, UML has a number of mechanisms, such as stereotypes and profiles, that allow modelers to tailor or extend the language to suit their circumstances.

UML has some specific advantages, including the sophistication of some of its notations and its flexibility and extensibility. It is widely used, and most likely your technical stakeholders will have no trouble understanding it (although some of the more complex notations may be hard for your business stakeholders to follow). Many people are working to apply UML to ADs and to improve its ability to be used as an ADL.

While we have often jokingly referred to UML as "a pretty poor ADL, but the best we've used" (and in fact one of us can be found in print criticizing UML's

---

3. [OMG10a].

abilities as an ADL![4]), we actually use UML extensively for real modeling work and have found it to be a useful tool for architectural description. As you will see later, particularly in our viewpoint definitions, we use it as the primary modeling notation throughout this book, and we wouldn't do this if we had significant reservations about its practical utility.

The qualities that we believe make UML effective for architectural models are its ubiquity, its extensibility, and its strong, consistent underlying semantics. The ubiquity of the language means that many technical stakeholders recognize and understand it and has led to the development of mature and powerful tools to help create, check, and maintain models. The extensibility of UML means that it is quite easy to create a "mini ADL" for the problem at hand, by defining a set of stereotypes to specialize the rather limited and generic set of concepts in the base language (for example, by defining a number of specific component types relevant to your architecture models). Finally, the well-defined semantics mean that it is possible to communicate quite precisely using UML models, and tool support can be quite specific to the type of model being created.

So, in summary, while we still have plenty of criticisms of UML for architecture modeling, we do find that it's a useful tool and the best match we're aware of for the modeling tasks we work on.

Executable Domain-Specific Languages

A limitation of most modeling languages is that they are not directly executable and the model isn't used as part of the system's implementation. This inevitably leads to a gap between the information shown in the model and how the system actually works.

A possible solution to this is to use a domain-specific language (DSL) to define some of your architectural description. A DSL is a computer language that has been designed to solve a specific problem, and there are many existing examples in computing, such as build script languages, CSS, SQL, regular expressions, and so on. Recently, a couple of factors have encouraged more widespread interest in DSLs, including the widespread use of dynamic languages (such as Groovy, Ruby, and Python) and Microsoft's DSL tooling in Visual Studio, added as part of its Software Factories project.

Using a dynamic language (for example, Groovy if you're working in Java) offers the possibility of creating a DSL that allows you to specify parts of your architectural structure in executable form, allowing them to be executed, tested, and even possibly used in the implementation. The drawbacks of an executable DSL for architectural description are the relatively small

---

4. Eoin coauthored an opinion piece with Dave Emery on UML's capabilities for architectural description in the November/December 2010 issue of *IEEE Software*'s "Point-Counterpoint" column.

number of stakeholders who are likely to understand it (probably just the development team), the effort required to define the DSL (which you'll probably have to do yourself), and the fact that such a language is likely to be capable of describing only one narrow aspect of your architecture.

Other Modeling Languages

There are a number of domain-specific modeling languages, such as entity-relationship models for modeling data. We discuss some of these in more detail in Parts III and IV.

GUIDELINES FOR CREATING EFFECTIVE MODELS

Models can be expensive artifacts to produce, and it is easy to spend a great deal of time and effort creating and maintaining them. You need to be sure that your models serve a definite purpose in your AD and are effective for the uses you intend. Some helpful guidelines to follow when creating models are outlined in this section.

Model Purposefully

Make sure that every model you create has a well-defined purpose; if you're not sure what the goals of a particular model are, don't create it. Without a clear purpose for a model, it is unclear what level of detail, completeness, and formality the model should exhibit.

EXAMPLE Let us imagine that you need to consider the possible deployment options for your system. An initial deployment model created to explore deployment candidates is likely to be incomplete and at a relatively shallow level of detail. The goal of the model is simply to allow you and a few key developers to consider the options and tradeoffs involved in running your system across a number of different machines.

In contrast, if the goal is to form a basis for deployment planning and software dependency analysis, your deployment model will need to be much more detailed and reasonably complete in order for it to meet those goals. Otherwise, important aspects of deployment or software platform dependencies are likely to be overlooked. A much more thorough modeling exercise will be required to complete this model compared with the previous one because, although both models are modeling system deployment, they have quite different goals.

As you create and refine a model, continually consider its intended use so that you can create a model that will be effective at meeting its particular goals.

Address an Audience

Because different audiences often need quite different types of models or different presentations of the same model, you must also be clear about who the model's intended audience is. Without a specific audience it is also difficult to know if the effort required to create a model will be worthwhile because you don't know how it will be used.

EXAMPLE The information structure of a system could be represented at two different levels of detail, depending on the audience.

The system's acquirers and assessors will be interested in the information stored and processed by the system, but at a summary level where they are considering types of information rather than individual business entities.

The system's users and developers will be interested in the information stored and processed, but they will also want to know the details of the individual business entities and their attributes. The users want to be sure that the information they need is present, and the software developers need to have this level of information in order to build the system.

If a model is not targeted to a well-defined audience, there is a real danger that it will simply not be reviewed and analyzed because its readers do not feel it is relevant to them. In the example just presented, if you give a detailed data model to acquirers and assessors, they may dismiss it as "irrelevant technical detail," while users and developers may ignore a summary model because they consider it to be "too high-level."

When you have identified your audience, consider the interest they have in the model, the level of detail they are likely to want, and the kinds of notation they are capable of understanding easily. This will help you develop a model that its intended audience will find useful and accessible.

The most challenging situations occur when you need to create models that are of interest to a number of different audiences (such as functional models that often have value for both software developers and the system's acquirers). In these cases, you will need to consider whether it is possible to create a single model that will be of use to all of the members of the potential audience. Often this simply isn't possible, and you will be forced to create a number of different but closely related models in order to address your different audiences (e.g., using sketches of more complex models for less technical audiences). In such cases, clearly define which model is the primary source of information and which one is derived so that you know how to resolve any inconsistencies that may occur.

Abstract Carefully and Precisely

As we described at the beginning of the chapter, abstraction is the technique of selecting only significant concepts for inclusion in a model, while omitting insignificant detail, in order to better communicate its important ideas. A key skill of modelers is achieving an appropriate and effective level of abstraction in their models.

As Ptolemy and the Greek philosophers understood, the real world is extremely complicated, and it is all too easy to be distracted from our analysis by masses of irrelevant detail. However, the Greeks also realized that we can exclude such detail from consideration without significantly affecting the accuracy of our conclusions. Indeed, it is not possible, even with the sophisticated science of the twenty-first century, to include everything in our models of the world around us.

The dictionary definition of *abstraction* is "the act of taking away," which gives us a clear lead for how we should go about doing it. In particular, we should be clear that *abstract* does not mean "woolly" or "vague"—if anything, an abstract model may be more precise and rigorous than a more concrete one, because the reduction in detail allows an increased focus on and fuller definition of the essential elements of the problem.

The key to achieving the right level of abstraction in a model is the ability to spot the essential elements as opposed to irrelevant detail. What is relevant, of course, varies hugely according to circumstances, the purpose of the model, and the needs and abilities of any interested stakeholders, so determining what to include in a model can be a pretty subjective decision.

Focus Your Efforts According to Your Risks

When modeling and analyzing your architectural design, it can be difficult to know where to focus your efforts. Ideally, you would model every aspect of your architecture very thoroughly and think out every detail. However, you never really have time to do this, and in fact, it's a level of architectural design effort that is rarely warranted except on the most critical systems. Given that you can't model every detail of your architecture, how do you decide where to focus your efforts?

Like many other software architecture authors, we advocate a risk-driven approach to deciding where to focus your efforts, working to understand and mitigate your most important risks first. If you don't use risks to prioritize your work, there is always a danger that you'll do the most interesting or the easiest parts of the architecture work first, when in fact these may be the least important, depending on the system.

> **EXAMPLE** If you're a security expert, it seems sensible to use that knowledge and experience to thoroughly analyze and model the system's security early on. After all, this is likely to be useful, you know how to do it, and it allows you to get something significant out of the way immediately.
>
> While on the face of it this seems to be a sensible approach, when you think about it objectively, it's clear that this isn't necessarily the best way to work. If you prioritize your work according to your preferences, rather than thinking explicitly about risk, human nature means that you're likely to choose things that you're interested in or relatively low-risk areas that allow you to deliver "quick wins" to show progress. In actual fact, the highest risks your system is facing could be in different areas such as performance or something relatively obscure and awkward such as regulatory compliance.

Understanding and prioritizing your risks (in terms of impact and likelihood) will allow you to focus your architecture work in the areas where it is most important. We discuss this approach further in Chapter 13.

Choose Descriptive Names

The names of elements in a model can have a significant impact on its effectiveness for communication. Your stakeholders' understanding of a model will be colored by the names of the model elements because of assumptions they make based on particular words. It is also important to choose good names because names tend to be very "sticky": Once a name has been understood and discussed, it becomes part of the common language for a project and so is very difficult to change, even if it isn't a very good name.

When initially creating a model, it is easy to give elements misleading or ambiguous names because you are still trying to understand the role and responsibilities of each element. This makes it important to keep revisiting names as you develop the model to ensure that the element names you finally choose are accurate and meaningful, helping readers of the model to easily grasp its fundamental structure and the role of each element within it.

Define Your Terms

A particular problem with graphical modeling notations is the tendency to draw the diagram that represents the structure of the model and then consider the model complete. Of course, the model isn't complete because none of the symbols on the diagram have really been defined, and the model is wide open to misinterpretation. This problem isn't limited just to models created with graphical notations; it is quite common to encounter quantitative models (e.g., spreadsheet-based performance models) that are very difficult to interpret due to missing definitions of the various elements and relationships captured in the model.

As you develop a model, be sure to spend enough time carefully defining all of its elements so that their meanings, roles, and mappings to the real world are all clear and not open to different interpretations.

Aim for Simplicity

The simpler a model is, the easier it will be to use and the more likely it is that its audience will find it effective. However, if a model is too simple, it will also fail because it no longer represents the essential features that interest the audience. You must aim for a balance somewhere between simplifying a model so far that it is no longer a valid and effective description and overcomplicating it to the point that the model is difficult to use and maintain.

Most models start out being simple and well structured, but as more detail is added and more special cases are considered, their complexity often increases significantly. Increasing a model's complexity quickly reduces its effectiveness for communication and analysis.

As your model develops and becomes more detailed and complex, continually review it yourself and ask others to do the same in order to assess its effectiveness. If a model becomes too complex to use easily, consider replacing it with a number of simpler, related models that contain the same information but in a more accessible form.

Use a Defined Notation

Nearly all models use some form of notation to represent their content, whether it be a graphical notation, a symbolic or mathematical notation, or even program code—you have many choices. Most notations can be used in different ways, yet none of them will match your exact needs, so you will often have to extend them. The result of this is that when your stakeholders read a new model, it can be difficult to be sure what notation it is written in and what the notation means.

Without a clearly defined notation, the readers of your model must rely on their intuition and your explanation and commentary to interpret the model. The difficulty of interpreting the notation can easily become a barrier to understanding.

For every model you create, be sure to define the notation you use carefully, so that stakeholders have no doubts about its meaning and can focus on the content of the model, rather than struggling with its representation. Even with informal models like sketches, define your notation so that the sketch can be interpreted even when you are not available to explain it.

Beware of Implied Semantics

Diagrams provide rich semantics that you can use to impart many shades of meaning to the reader. For example, a layered architecture is usually represented in a diagram with the layers positioned vertically above one another, with the most important layer at the top. We are all familiar with such diagrams, and it is not usually necessary to explain what this notation means.

This is a valuable time-saver, but it also means that any diagram that looks like a set of layers may be interpreted as one, whether the architecture is layered or not. If this is not your intention, this can lead to confusion or worse. In such a case, you should either note somewhere that vertical position does not imply layering, or even better, reorganize your diagram so that your readers do not get the wrong impression.

There are many types of implied semantics that may require you to redraw your diagrams.

- Vertical positioning of similarly sized objects on the page can be misconstrued as implying layering or some other hierarchy.

- Left-to-right positioning may be interpreted as a flow of control or a sequence of events.

- Putting one element inside another may imply ownership or containment.

- The sizes of diagram elements can suggest their relative importance.

- Coloring of diagram elements or text may suggest importance (or otherwise). Similarly colored elements may be assumed to be related in some way.

- Using certain icons for your elements, such as a stick person or a graphic of a computer or a disk, may mislead your readers about the nature of those elements.

These diagrammatic conventions can be very useful, but you should ensure that you use them with care to impart the meaning that you intend.

Validate Models

Models are an approximation of reality. This is what makes them valuable, allowing us to focus on important details to understand, communicate, or analyze, but it is also a potential weakness because you can never be sure whether the approximations you made have rendered the model invalid.

This aspect of models means that it is important that you continually validate your structural models for consistency and practicality and your analytical models for correspondence to the real world. You can do this via expert review, technical prototyping, and checks of your model against the real world. The important point is to validate your models often enough and thoroughly enough to be confident that they will be useful in their intended roles.

Keep Models Alive

Things change during a software development project: Requirements come and go, new constraints emerge, and priorities change. This potential for continual change is something you have to deal with in order to deliver effective systems that meet the real needs of your stakeholders.

The need to absorb changes means that you cannot expect a model developed at the start of a project and left unchanged to still reflect reality by the time the system is delivered. The challenge you face is that if your models stop reflecting reality, they soon stop being used and "die."

In order to avoid the premature demise of your models, it is important to regularly update them so they will continue to be relevant. Although you do not want the maintenance of models to become a major burden that slows the project, you need to get the balance right by investing enough time and effort to keep them current. Scheduling a small amount of routine model maintenance activity into your weekly plans can be a useful aid for achieving this.

Keeping models up-to-date is also much easier if you keep them as simple as possible, by focusing on those core concepts that really need to be modeled to aid analysis and communication. We have often found that the main architectural structures of a system do not change very quickly when compared to the details of the system built upon them. These key structures are also the things you need to model in order to understand the system (it is very difficult to re-create these models from the code later). Keeping such models current is much less difficult than maintaining comprehensive models of every aspect of the system.

Modeling with Agile Teams

With the emergence of agile development as a mainstream approach, it has become a common situation for software architects to be working with agile teams. Common wisdom is that architects and agile teams mix like oil and water because of concerns on the part of the agile team about big up-front design and unnecessary documentation. However, our experience is that working in and with good agile teams isn't difficult, and there's a lot to be gained from it, but it is necessary to be flexible with respect to the approach that the team wants to use.

We've found that working with an agile team involves an intelligent application of many of the points that we've already made in this chapter, in particular:

- *Work iteratively*; rather than trying to produce complete models in one go, deliver incrementally developed and refined ones.

- *Share information via simple tools* rather than assuming that everyone will be happy to use a complicated modeling tool that works well for you (agile developers probably won't).

- *Ensure that there are customers for all of your models* and you know what they'll use them for (even if you're the customer); otherwise you're not modeling with a definite purpose.

- *Create models that are good enough* rather than aiming for perfection, which is both unattainable and probably less useful given the time it will take (although make sure that they are good enough!).

- *Focus on architectural concerns that solve problems* that the team is having or will have to clearly differentiate the architecture work from the core development work (unless, of course, the team is clearly struggling, in which case you'll need to step into the detailed design too).

- *Create executable deliverables* such as prototypes or executable models to help validate ideas, communicate with the development team, and bring your work alive for them.

To help place modeling in context for agile teams, consider introducing them to the ideas of agile modeling (AM), which is a set of values, principles, and practices aimed at ensuring the effectiveness of modeling activities, with particular reference to the values of the agile approach. AM embraces and extends many of the points we've already made in this chapter, being based on the recognition that models are only ever an approximation of reality and as such must always be developed with an explicit aim to be useful in a particular situation.

CHECKLIST

For each model you have produced, ask yourself the following questions.

- Does the model have a clear purpose and audience?
- Is the model going to be understood by its audience (business and technical stakeholders, as appropriate)?

- Is the model complete enough to be useful?
- Is the model as simple as possible while still being detailed enough for its purpose and audience?
- Have you clearly defined the notation(s) used in the model?
- Is the model well formed; that is, does it conform to the rules of the modeling language you are using?
- Do model elements have meaningful names and definitions?
- Is the model internally consistent and consistent with other models?
- Does the model have a level of abstraction appropriate to the problem to be solved and the expertise of the stakeholders?
- Does the model have the right level of detail? Is it sufficiently high-level to bring out the key features of the architecture? Does it present enough detail for a specialist audience?
- Have you provided a definition of the terminology and conventions used in the model?
- Does your model have appropriate scope? Are the boundaries clear?
- Is the model accompanied by an appropriate level of supporting documentation?
- For quantitative models, does the model have sufficient rigor (mathematical basis) and an appropriate degree of complexity?

SUMMARY

The most important parts of any AD—and sometimes the only things that are actually produced—are its models. Models are a way to represent the salient features of the system and to communicate these to stakeholders. A good model can make all the difference when helping stakeholders understand your architecture. The AD consists of a collection of views, and each view consists of a collection of models (plus other elements such as principles, standards, and glossaries).

There are three broad classes of models, two formal and one informal. The two classes of formal models are *qualitative models* (which illustrate the key structural or behavioral elements of the system) and *quantitative models* (which make statements about measurable aspects of the system). Both are useful, although architects typically focus on qualitative models because there often isn't enough detailed information available to do any reliable quantitative analysis. We refer to the informal models as *sketches*, and they are used primarily for communication with less technical stakeholders.

A model is only an approximation of reality, and the architect must always be aware of its simplifications and approximations (and make stakeholders aware of these also).

FURTHER READING

Numerous books cover specific modeling languages, particularly UML, and more general topics such as entity-relationship modeling, object-oriented modeling, security modeling, and performance modeling. We cite several relevant books in Parts III and IV.

You can obtain information on agile modeling from the Agile Modeling Web site (www.agilemodeling.com), in the "Resources" section of the Agile Alliance's site (www.agilealliance.org), and in Scott Ambler's book on the topic [AMBL02].

You can obtain the most up-to-date information on ADLs by searching the Internet. This is largely true of DSLs, too, but a number of DSL books have recently been published, such as [FOWL10] and [GHOS10], both of which cover the topic from a language-independent perspective. There are also quite a number of books explaining how to create DSLs in particular languages, which can be found by searching any major online bookseller.

13

CREATING THE ARCHITECTURAL DESCRIPTION

I f you follow the architecture definition process that we describe in this book, you will end up with a wide collection of material that shapes, informs, and describes your architecture: constraints, principles, decisions, requirements, scenarios, and, most important, a set of architectural views, each comprising one or more architectural models. Some of this material will be vitally important to the proper understanding of your architecture, some of it will provide useful details, and some of it may be more appropriate for other software development documentation such as the requirements definition or design documents.

Your challenge is to gather and organize the relevant material into a coherent, consistent, and complete description of the architecture, its essential features and benefits, and its underlying philosophy in a way your stakeholders can understand and accept. Let's revisit a definition we first presented in Part I.

 DEFINITION An **architectural description (AD)** is a set of products that documents an architecture in a way its stakeholders can understand and demonstrates that the architecture has met their concerns.

The purpose of the AD is to communicate the architecture to all stakeholders, throughout the system's lifetime from conception to decommissioning. The AD establishes a common understanding of the required functionality and quality properties of the entire system and ensures that the right choices are made about aspects such as scope, performance, resilience, and security.

Most important of all, the AD is often a *selling* document. It may have to present, explain, and justify ideas that are unfamiliar to its readership;

convince a skeptical audience that your architectural choices are the correct ones; and persuade stakeholders that the risks your solution brings are outweighed by its benefits.

Given all of the things you have to address in your AD, there is a temptation to bury your stakeholders under a mountain of detail. This is a mistake—the AD must capture the key architectural structures and decisions for your system, which are usually those that need to be widely communicated, or those that address high-risk concerns, or those that will be difficult to change later. The AD should be crisp, concise, and to the point. Otherwise, you will end up with an unwieldy document that doesn't help your stakeholders to understand the rationale behind or the implications of your key architectural decisions.

For example, UML use cases are one way to capture and annotate interactions between a computer system and its environment. Diagrams and text represent the participants (known as *actors*), the functional units, and the interactions among them. Of all the UML notations, use cases are probably the most easily understood by both technical and business stakeholders.

However, use cases are by their nature fairly local or atomic—in other words, they typically address a single interaction or a small group of related interactions. Because many architectures are so complex, an architectural model could comprise hundreds or even thousands of use cases. Although each individual use case is easy to understand, it is not possible to draw an overall picture from such a large number of individual models. Important or fundamental aspects of the system get lost in this mass of detail.

Architecturally, use cases are more effectively used to elaborate specific aspects of the system's functionality or to present a small selection of key interactions, rather than to represent the entire system.

PROPERTIES OF AN EFFECTIVE ARCHITECTURAL DESCRIPTION

An effective AD must balance seven desirable properties: *correctness*, *sufficiency*, *timeliness*, *conciseness*, *clarity*, *currency*, and *precision*. We discuss each of these in the following subsections.

Correctness

The most important quality of your AD is that it be right. *Right* is, of course, a subjective term, but we can define two correctness criteria that your AD must meet.

1. It must correctly represent the *needs and concerns of your stakeholders.* You can do this explicitly, by reflecting some of these needs back to stakeholders in the form of architectural principles, and implicitly, by presenting the features of your chosen solution. (In the latter case, you need to highlight these features in some way so that the stakeholders can recognize them.)
2. It must also correctly *define an architecture that will meet those needs* so that a system can be built, based on the architecture, that will satisfy the stakeholders.

Achieving this objective is, in theory anyway, straightforward—present the AD to your stakeholders and ask them, "Is this what you need?" In practice it is often significantly more difficult than that, and we talk about this in more detail in Chapter 14.

Sufficiency

Your AD must contain enough information to allow your stakeholders to understand the key architectural decisions you have made, which are usually those that mitigate significant risks or those that will be difficult to change once the system has been built. In our experience, this is where most ADs tend to fall short. The structural and functional aspects of the architecture are usually addressed, but other issues may not be considered—at least not explicitly. If you haven't communicated something important about your architecture because "everybody knows that," you do not have a complete AD.

If you don't include enough information in your AD, you are effectively *postponing* architectural decisions until later in the system development lifecycle. While it's important to avoid premature decision making, we also want to avoid architectural decisions being made in an ad hoc and localized way. It is difficult to make good architectural decisions without a system-wide perspective, because people won't have the right information and the decisions (or their impact) won't become apparent until it's too late to do anything about them.

Of all the properties that make an effective AD, sufficiency can be the most difficult to judge. Your challenge is to work out when the AD contains enough information to make a compelling argument that the architecture is going to meet its requirements and the system will be successful, but doesn't try to define every detail of how the system will work. Achieving this balance allows you to focus on making and capturing the architecturally significant decisions, leaving the rest to the skill and judgment of the development teams.

STRATEGY Clearly document your key architectural decisions in the architectural description, and provide the rationale for any decisions that are contentious or had substantial alternatives. For significant decisions this involves capturing the alternatives that you considered, any assumptions you made that underpin your decision, and a brief summary of why you made the choice you did and rejected the others.

If you have worked hard to identify and engage your stakeholders and have captured and agreed with all of their requirements, ensuring sufficiency should be almost automatic. If a stakeholder need is not explicitly or implicitly reflected in some element of the architecture or has not been documented in the AD, you may have a gap.

A good way to ensure sufficiency is to select appropriate viewpoints, create views, and apply appropriate perspectives, as we discuss in Parts III and IV.

Timeliness

Most of us have a tendency to want to complete deliverables "perfectly" before letting other people start to work with them. For many sorts of engineering work products this is a mistake, and this is definitely the case with architectural descriptions.

An architecture definition exists to guide the design and construction of a system and so must be available in time to meet the project's milestones. There is no point in delivering the "perfect" AD a month late when the delivery process has had to move on without it. A minimal and perhaps partial AD that fits in with the time constraints of the project is of much more use than an ideal one delivered too late to be of use. It is also important to deliver drafts of your AD as early as possible in order to get feedback on your architectural ideas and allow them to be socialized, understood, refined, and validated.

The challenge inherent in achieving timeliness is to produce something that is still of value in the inevitably limited time available. While there is no point in delivering an AD too late to be used, there is also little point in delivering one that is so shallow or poorly thought out that it can't be used as an effective guide when building the system. This means that it is important to limit the scope of your architecture work, based on the risks that the project faces, so that you can produce something solid and useful.

All that being said, if you can't do enough architecture work to address the project's risks, it is incumbent on you to point this out to the project's sponsors and key stakeholders. If they decide to press ahead while leaving risks unaddressed, that is their choice. However, if they don't know what risks they face, they can hardly be expected to invest in architecture work to mitigate them. You are in an ideal position to work with the system's stake-holders to help them understand their key risks and what can be done to mitigate them.

STRATEGY In order to deliver a useful AD in a limited time, first focus on the key risks that the project faces, and second, deliver the work incrementally.

Focusing your architecture work on the riskiest aspects of the system will ensure that you spend the limited time you have on the most important concerns and that you maximize the return on your investment. There are many architecturally significant concerns on which you can spend time, so it is important to prioritize your work so that the highest risks that the project faces are understood and mitigated first.

Delivering the AD in an incremental manner has a number of advantages, not least of which is that you are learning about the problem and your solution throughout the development process. Deferring architectural decisions until they are needed allows you to make more informed (and therefore better) decisions. Incremental development of your architecture also allows you to work with the project's milestones and fit more architecture work into the project than you could at the start of the lifecycle. You can create a minimal AD right at the start to guide prototyping or proof-of-concept work, fleshing it out to capture the important architectural structures as decisions are made, and then refining the architecture as the project progresses.

The trick with deferring decisions is knowing when the "last responsible moment" to make a decision (as the agile community puts it) really is. Making uninformed decisions in a panic without any time for investigation, re search, or reflection isn't being agile; it's just being sloppy. It is important that you look far enough ahead in the project to see when decisions will be needed so that you have enough time to formulate good solutions for them as they emerge.

Finally, don't leave things out of your AD just because they are hard. It is tempting to defer decisions until later with the expectation that solving a difficult problem will somehow be easier in the future. You are almost always building up trouble for yourself if you do this, and you may find that a decision ends up being made for you by default. You should defer a decision only when you don't yet need to make it.

Conciseness

To help stakeholders grasp the key features of your architecture, your AD should focus on its important elements—in other words, the things that are *architecturally significant*—and not spend too much time on other details.

Unfortunately, the distinction between what is and isn't architecturally significant can be difficult to judge. For most systems, a single context diagram with a couple of pages of description won't be sufficient; similarly, most systems don't need a 200-page physical data model as part of their architectural description. You need to create an architectural description that is as concise as possible but still has enough detail to capture and communicate the architecturally significant aspects. How much you need to capture will depend on a number of factors.

- *The extent to which you are mandating new or unfamiliar technology*: If you are facing significant technology risk due to the use of unproven technology, you will need to spend more time explaining in your AD what the new technology does, how it works, and how the system will use it.

- *The difficulty or criticality of the problem you are trying to solve*: If you are facing significant functional risk because your system is functionally complex or has very great significance for the organization implementing it, you will need to explain how your architecture will mitigate these risks.

- *The scale of the quality property requirements*: If you are facing significant risk in meeting your system quality property goals because you have demanding or ambitious requirements for qualities such as performance, scalability, or resilience, you may need a comprehensive explanation of how these requirements will be achieved.

- *How much time and resources you have available to produce and gain acceptance for the AD*: If you have 6 months to define and build your system, it is pointless to spend 5 months producing a perfect AD.

If you don't keep your AD concise, by focusing on architecturally significant information, your stakeholders will find it difficult to understand the implications of your decisions, and you risk having them miss something important. A lengthy AD is also much harder to maintain and keep current (see the discussion in the Currency subsection).

STRATEGY Restrict your architectural description to things that are architecturally significant, and tailor the level of detail to the skills and experience of your readership, the complexity of the problem and your solution, and the time you have available to produce the architectural description.

Striking the right balance between conciseness and depth largely comes down to the experience and judgment of the architect. However, one thing is certain—a well-focused document has a better chance of being read and understood than a long, rambling one that contains a lot of information that isn't of interest to your readers (such as a lengthy description of the software development process being used by the software development team).

Clarity

The most challenging quality to achieve in your AD is its ability to be under-stood by all classes of stakeholders. At a minimum, each stakeholder group should be able to understand those parts that are relevant to them.

Remember the dual purposes of the AD: to document the architecture in a way that each stakeholder group can understand and to demonstrate that the architecture has met their concerns. For technical stakeholders such as develop-ment teams, this is fairly straightforward: They understand technology and are probably familiar with the notation (such as UML) you are using to represent it.

However, for nontechnical stakeholders, providing clarity in your AD is more of a challenge. Although most people have a basic, if vague, under-standing of computing, many will not appreciate the subtle ramifications of your architectural decisions without your help.

The good news is that nontechnical stakeholders require less of your AD in terms of depth and detail: just enough to grasp the main functional compo-nents and their high-level interactions. Nontechnical stakeholder concerns, as we have seen, focus more on the user experience and (indirectly) on system qualities such as response and availability.

STRATEGY Always consider your intended readership when writing parts of an architectural description, and tailor its content and presentation toward their skills, their knowledge, and the time they have available to read it.

In practice, you will aim different parts of your AD at different classes of stakeholders (indeed, that's part of what viewpoints are about). Your challenge is to make sure that these parts are all compatible with one another and with the overall design.

The physical presentation of your AD plays a big role in ensuring that stakeholders understand the aspects of the architecture that are relevant to them, grasp the significance of the architectural decisions that have been made, and are won over to its merits.

Different audiences may prefer different types of presentations, and different parts of the AD will be communicated more effectively if presented in different ways. A lot depends on the situation in which you find yourself. We have found that documents, models in modeling tools, code, wiki pages, and slide presentations all have their place in communicating an architecture clearly. Frequently a combination of them will provide the clearest presentation of the architecture to your various stakeholder groups. One word of warning, though: If you do decide to use a number of separate representations for the AD, make sure that they stay consistent with each other and that everything that needs to be captured is captured somewhere, ideally only once.

Finally, it is also important to remember that presentation is never a substitute for content, and some people are suspicious of documentation that comes across as too polished or glossy. However, good layout, clear use of language, and correct spelling and grammar will make your job of imparting architectural knowledge that much easier.

Currency

It is inevitable that your architecture will evolve over time. During development, you will find problems with your design or ways to improve it, or you may need to take on new technologies or provide new features. These may result in changes to the architecture that must be reflected in the AD.

Once the architecture diverges from the AD, the AD starts to become worthless. It is no longer trusted and is no longer used as the definitive source of information about the architecture. However, you can't gauge the important properties and qualities of your architecture by inspecting source code. Your high-level, system-wide view would be lost among the detail.

The architecture will continue to evolve once your system goes live, although usually at a slower pace. The AD, which should be kept up-to-date with these changes as well, can play an important part later in assessing and evaluating proposed changes.

A smaller, more concise AD will, of course, be easier to keep current, so this is another reason to limit your AD to the essential information that it needs to contain. An AD that tries to define every detail of the system will be in a constant state of change, while an AD that defines only the architecturally significant aspects of the system will be easier to keep current and relevant.

STRATEGY Think early in development about how the architectural description will be kept up-to-date throughout the life of the system, and try to ensure that development, operation, and support plans take this need into account.

Also consider whether all of your architectural documentation needs to be kept at the same level of currency, or whether some of it can safely be updated less frequently once some aspects of the architecture have stabilized. If you find that some of it is not regularly referred to, you can allow it to become out-of-date. However, you must make sure that any part of the AD that becomes out-of-date is clearly marked as such, so that people understand the relative currency of the different types of information that the AD contains.

Precision

As we've said already, an AD must contain sufficient information to allow the system's architecture to be understood, but it must also be precise in order to provide a solid basis for analysis, design, and implementation. We have seen many architectural descriptions that attempted to define the right information but the information provided was ambiguous or poorly written, meaning that it was difficult to be sure what the architect intended.

On the other hand, being precise doesn't mean adding a lot of unnecessary information, such as the fine detail of implementation options that aren't architecturally significant. In fact, if you're not careful, precision can become the converse of conciseness: It is easier to concentrate on the precision and quality of a smaller set of key architectural structures than to be precise about a large number of varied concerns. A number of techniques can help you here.

- Make use of abstraction and layering so that you describe things once rather than many times. (Refer to Chapter 12 for a discussion of these concepts.)
- Focus on the system's key architectural structures and decisions, and exclude anything that is not needed to demonstrate that the architecture will address stakeholder concerns.
- Present detailed information in tables or lists rather than in ordinary text.
- Number requirements, principles, and other elements of the AD and refer to them by number.
- If you need to specify lower-level details, put them in appendices or separate documents rather than in the main body of the AD.
- Make plentiful use of diagrams to explain difficult concepts.
- Break down very large documents into several smaller ones by topic or by audience.

If your AD becomes too large, this can be a good reason to divide your document by view—having one physical document for your Functional view, another for your Information view, and so on—or (more likely) by the type of stakeholder who will read it. In this case, you might have the following as parts of your AD:

- The benefits of the architecture extolled in an overview document aimed at the sponsor and senior management
- More functional detail in a document aimed at users
- The bulk of technical detail in one or more documents aimed at development teams and other technical stakeholders

STRATEGY Aim for precision in your architectural description, but when this necessitates a large amount of detail, physically break the document into several smaller ones or put the details into appendices, so that the main document does not become too large.

GLOSSARIES

As an architect, your skills and experience—particularly of the business domain—tend to be, with exceptions, broad rather than deep. This means that you often end up asking your stakeholders what may seem like "obvious" questions: "What is an account?" "How does a bill of materials work?" "Why do you need to clear all your transactions at the end of the day?"

You may sometimes be surprised by the answers, and your stakeholders may find themselves thinking afresh about concepts they have taken for granted for years. You may find it valuable to capture your understanding in a glossary of terms (sometimes called a dictionary) to ensure that everyone is using the same definitions.

STRATEGY Include a glossary in your architectural description if terminology may be unclear or ambiguous to some readers. If possible, base the definitions on standard ones used in your organization or industry.

Glossaries have a more concrete benefit, too. As your analysis proceeds, they will feed directly into your models. Nouns translate easily into classes or entities, and verbs often translate into processes.

THE ISO STANDARD

ISO/IEC Standard 42010, *Systems and Software Engineering—Recommended Practice for Architectural Description of Software-Intensive Systems*, is one of the few formal standards covering the practice of software systems architecture. In its own words, it "addresses the creation, analysis and sustainment of architectures of systems through the use of architecture descriptions."[1]

Clause 5 of the standard defines six recommended practices for documenting an architecture. An AD that conforms to these requirements (which include more detail than we present here) can be considered compliant with Standard 42010.

---

1. [ISO11], Abstract.

1. *Architecture description identification and overview*: The AD must include standard control and context information, such as issue date and version, change history, and scope.

2. *Identification of stakeholders and concerns*: The AD must identify the stakeholders and their concerns (such as purpose, appropriateness, feasibility, and risks).

3. *Selection of architecture viewpoints*: The AD must identify the viewpoints used, explain the rationale for their selection, and define which viewpoint addresses each concern.

4. *Architecture views*: The AD must contain one or more views, each conforming to its corresponding viewpoint, with each view containing one or more models.

5. *Consistency and correspondences among architectural views*: The AD must analyze consistency across views and record known inconsistencies as well as clearly identify required relationships ("correspondences") that should exist between elements of the AD (such as ensuring that each executable in a system has a target runtime machine).

6. *Architectural rationale*: The AD must include the rationale for each view used in the description and can capture key decisions made, the rationale for them, and the alternatives considered.

The aim of the standard is that it "enables the expression, communication and review of architectures of systems and thereby lays a foundation for quality and cost improvements through standardization of conventions for architecture description."[2] If the architecture function in your organization would benefit from formalizing its approach, you should adopt the ideas from ISO Standard 42010—and if you follow the recommendations of this book, that should not be too difficult.

CONTENTS OF THE ARCHITECTURAL DESCRIPTION

Because the experience and concerns of your stakeholders, the type and complexity of the problems you are trying to solve, and the time you have available for architecture definition vary from project to project, no two ADs are ever structured in the same way. It is difficult, therefore, to present a generic template for an AD. The contents listed in this section, while incorporating the documentation elements we discuss in this book and complying

---

2. [ISO11], p. 1.

with ISO Standard 42010, are a superset of what you are likely to produce in practice. Real-world ADs will differ from this template for a number of reasons.

- You may refer to other material (such as scope or requirements definitions) rather than summarizing it in the AD.
- You may not capture all views or apply all perspectives (you probably don't have time to do this even if you'd like to).
- You may choose to document some perspective enhancements and insights, such as more detailed security models, separately from the main document.
- Your AD may be produced by more than one person (especially if the system is large or has some complex features), which may necessitate some changes to the structure presented here.

With these caveats in mind, let's explore the different sections you may include in your ADs.

Document Control

The Document Control section clearly identifies individual versions of the AD. If there is more than one version (which will be the case on all but the simplest systems), effective document control is essential to ensure that everyone is working from the most up-to-date copy.

For the current version of the AD, Document Control normally contains the document version number, the document issue date, the document status, an overview of the changes since the previous version, document authorization, and commentary.

It is also common to include a version history (which summarizes the changes in each version, authorization, and so on) and any details on planned future versions of the AD. It may also be appropriate to include copyright, ownership, and confidentiality statements here.

Table of Contents

You can use the automated capabilities of your word processing software to generate the Table of Contents. You may want to briefly introduce the purpose and content of each main chapter, especially if your stakeholders are not familiar with this type of document.

Introduction and Management Summary

This section (which may also be called Executive Summary, Abstract, and so on) introduces the AD by doing some or all of the following:

- Describing the objectives of the AD
- Summarizing the goals of the system described
- Summarizing the scope and key requirements
- Presenting a high-level overview of the solution
- Highlighting the benefits of the solution, the risks in its implementation, and mitigation strategies
- Identifying the key decisions that have shaped the architecture
- Highlighting any outstanding issues still awaiting resolution

It is good practice to acknowledge your stakeholders and other sources of information here.

Depending on your audience, you may want to give an overview of the process you went through to produce the AD, particularly if there were a number of iterations, and describe the next steps (e.g., formal review of the AD).

Stakeholders

This section of the AD should define the system's stakeholder groups and the primary concerns of each. This allows you to review whether you have the right set of stakeholders, spot any that are missing, consider how the concerns of each group will shape your architecture, and consider the likely interaction of different concerns and how this will affect your work.

General Architectural Principles

In this section, present the architectural principles that inform the architecture but don't fit naturally into any of the views—for example, "We buy and configure off-the-shelf software rather than build our own whenever possible."

Each principle should be numbered and should include rationale and implications. Whenever possible, tie the principles back to business drivers and forward to architectural decisions.

Architectural Design Decisions

One of the most valuable things that you can communicate to those involved in building and evolving the system is an explanation of its key architectural decisions. They need to know what decisions were made, their rationale, the alternatives you considered, and why they were rejected. Documenting the decisions as they are made also helps to ensure that they are captured accurately and provides context and background for the system's stakeholders as they try to understand the architecture.

In this section, describe the key decisions that have shaped the architecture and that someone will need to understand in order to grasp the design of the system as a whole. If there are architectural decisions that are very specific to a particular view, consider documenting them in that view, as they will make more sense to the reader in that context.

This section of the AD has the potential to grow quite large, depending on the number of decisions that you think are important and the level of detail needed to clearly explain each one. Therefore, it may be better to limit this section to a short summary of the more important decisions and to defer a full explanation of the decisions made and the alternatives rejected to an appendix.

Viewpoints

Users of the AD need to understand the views you have selected, the scope of each, and how they fit together to document the architecture, so it is important to define the viewpoints that the views are based upon. You should be able to do this by reference to an external set of viewpoint definitions, but it can still be useful to include a short recap of the role and content of each viewpoint here.

Views

Your AD can include sections on each of the views associated with the seven viewpoints we describe in Part III. For example, the section on the Functional view could contain the following information.

- *View-specific architectural principles*: Present the architectural principles that inform the models in this view. Each principle should be numbered and should include rationale and implications, and wherever possible the principle should be tied back to business drivers and forward to architectural decisions.

- *View model(s)*: Present the models that make up the view. This includes enhanced and new models created as a result of applying perspectives. Models should be named and a brief description given of the notation and documentation conventions used (especially if these are nonstandard or extended).

- *Perspective improvements*: It may be appropriate to highlight some of the outcomes of applying perspectives to the view, namely:

- Enhancements to view models (including new models created as a result of applying the perspective)
- Perspective insights demonstrating that the architecture will meet its quality properties

    Alternatively, you may refer readers to an appendix for some or all of this information.

- *Application of scenarios*: Document the key scenarios that have informed the view models, here or in an appendix.
- *View-specific architectural decisions*: If architectural decisions have been made that are specific to this view, capture them here if they have not already been described elsewhere. Describe the decisions made, their rationale, any alternatives considered, and why they were rejected.
- *Commentary*: Include here any other general commentary appropriate to the view (e.g., advice and guidance to development teams).

If included in the AD, sections for the Context view, the Information view, the Concurrency view, the Development view, the Deployment view, and the Operational view would contain the same type of content as described here for the Functional view.

Quality Property Summary

As we described in Part I, applying a perspective leads to insights, improvements, and artifacts. Improvements (changes to view models) are documented in the section for the appropriate view. Include in this section the following:

- General insights that provide a better understanding of the system's ability to meet a required quality property
- Non-view-specific artifacts, that is, models and analyses that may be of lasting interest

It may be appropriate to provide an overview here and refer readers to an appendix for more details.

Important Scenarios

For each important scenario, record the initial system state and environment, the external stimulus, and the required and actual system behavior. Again, it may be appropriate to provide an overview here and refer readers to an appendix for more details.

Issues Awaiting Resolution

We often find it is useful to publish early versions of the AD to share knowledge, assumptions, and decisions made and to obtain early informal feedback. It will aid understanding in this case to list any issues or questions that have not yet been resolved—for example, there may not yet be consensus on the purpose or functionality of a particular component, or the choice of implementation technology may not have been finalized. Doing this will highlight the fact that more work is required in these areas and ideally prevent you from being bombarded with questions you are not yet able to answer.

In some cases you may even need to include this section in the final version of the AD. While it is clearly undesirable—and possibly even fatal—to have unresolved architectural issues when you start work on detailed design and build, this is sometimes unavoidable. For example, there might be a subsystem or component that is going to be further defined (and built) in a subsequent project phase.

If you do have unresolved issues, it is essential that you highlight them to management for action and resolution. You can do this in the Management Summary section of the AD and also feed them into your development project's risk and issue register.

Appendices

It is generally preferable to move detailed content into an appendix, which may be part of the main AD or even a separate document. This makes the important parts of the AD easier to digest but ensures that the details are not forgotten.

Almost anything can go into an appendix; here are some of the topics you may want to cover:

- References to other documents or sources of information
- A glossary of terms and abbreviations
- A stakeholder map (defining the key stakeholders, their areas of interest, key concerns, and so on)
- More detailed specification of scope, functional requirements, or quality properties
- A map between requirements and architectural features
- A description of architectural design decisions that you have made, if they are not captured elsewhere in the document, along with their rationale, any alternatives considered, and why they were rejected
- Explanation of any architectural styles, design patterns, and so on that you have used

- More detailed view models
- More detailed perspective models and insights
- More details on the application of scenarios
- Policies, standards, and guidelines
- Output from formal reviews of the AD
- Output from consistency checks between views (see Chapter 23)
- Other supporting documentation

Consider the needs of your readership when writing the appendices. As with the rest of the AD, don't overburden them with a mass of detail that may be of little value.

PRESENTING THE ARCHITECTURAL DESCRIPTION

A common problem that we all face as software architects is how best to present the AD to stakeholders. Given the breadth of information that an AD may contain, and the different styles of presentation that may be needed for different stakeholder groups, it often isn't clear how best to do this. As we said earlier, over the years we have used documents, spreadsheets, drawing tools, code, wikis, UML modeling tools, presentations, and more to capture and present our architectural descriptions.

In short, we would suggest that each of these approaches has its place, and a lot depends on the situation in which you find yourself, the scale of the architectural description, the stakeholders who are interested in it, and the skills and resources you have available to you.

- *Formal documents* are useful when the architecture forms part of a formal agreement, such as a supplier contract; when the AD is to be distributed for review; or when stakeholders want a holistic view of the architecture in a single place. Formal documents are also the best option when the AD is very complicated and there is a lot of information to present (although it needs to be presented carefully—possibly as a number of related documents—in order to avoid overwhelming people with its sheer size). Formal documents are harder to put together when information changes frequently, or when more than a few people want to collaborate in the development and maintenance of the AD.

- *Wiki documents* excel when you wish to make the information in the AD very accessible, you want to change it frequently, or you want other people to be able to collaborate in developing and maintaining it. Where wikis are less strong are situations requiring complicated formatting, a large number of diagrams, or very large documents, which can become confusing forests of pages that are difficult to navigate around clearly.

- *Presentations* are probably one of the most widely used approaches to architectural description and do have the benefit of being accessible and ubiquitous. On the other hand, frankly, we've rarely seen a good AD presented solely in slide form, and the format of a presentation encour-ages rather sketchy and incomplete definitions of the architecture. Of course, presentations do have their place as communication tools, but we shudder when we encounter them being used as definitive architec-tural documentation.

- *UML models*, as we explain in our viewpoints, are a good way to repre-sent many kinds of architectural structure, although the base notation often needs to be tailored and extended in order to support the key ele-ments of architectural models. As we said in Chapter 12, UML's ubiquity has made it a de facto as well as a de jure standard for creating software models. With the right approach and right tool for the situation (be that a whiteboard or a sophisticated modeling tool), we have found it to be a useful part of our architectural definition process. Where UML is of less value is in situations where a lot of communication is with nontechnical stakeholders who find the notation offputting, or simply in situations where for some reason precise graphical models are not perceived as valuable (wrongly in our view).

- *Drawing tools* are also very popular for architectural description in prac-tice, with the widely used Visio tool probably being the most common. Many drawing tools are very powerful and allow clear diagrams to be created and maintained easily. The problem we observe is usually what the tools are used to draw rather than the tools themselves. If they are used to draw diagrams using a well-defined notation (perhaps using a UML stencil or a homegrown architectural definition notation), they can be useful, efficient, lightweight modeling tools (provided that the model elements are defined somewhere else). However, if no defined notation is used, then as we said in Chapter 12, the result is usually a pretty confusing diagram.

- *Code* can be useful for certain aspects of the AD, particularly those aimed at software developers. A skeleton system is in effect an executable architectural description, and the definition of some aspects of the archi-tecture, such as interelement interfaces, is often best done directly using code rather than some woolly intermediate notation such as pseudo-code that leaves everyone guessing what it really means. We have also found that documenting key architectural patterns and conventions as executable examples is a very effective way of communicating them to software development teams.

- *Spreadsheets* are very useful when creating quantitative models (such as those used to predict performance and scalability characteristics of a system) and can also be useful lightweight databases for the tabular data that many projects need to manage (for example, lists of inbound and outbound system data feed characteristics).

In short, our advice is to consider what you need to represent, who needs to work on it, and who needs to access it when deciding how to capture and present your AD. You will usually use some combination of the technologies we have listed and frequently more besides.

CHECKLIST

- Are all key architectural decisions documented in the AD?
- Are there any key architectural decisions that you feel have yet to be made, and if so, what is your strategy for dealing with these?
- Does the AD strike an appropriate balance between conciseness and the other desirable properties (correctness, sufficiency, timeliness, clarity, currency, and precision), especially given the skills and experience of your stakeholders?
- Do the sections of the AD aimed at a nontechnical audience (acquirers, users, and so on) avoid the overuse of technical jargon and define it wherever it appears?
- Do you know how the AD will be maintained once it has been accepted (during the development process and into live operation)?
- Have you reviewed the AD content suggested in this chapter (Table of Contents, Introduction and Management Summary, and so on) and included all of it that is appropriate?
- Does the presentation of the document conform to your corporate standards (if any) for such documents?
- Have you provided an accurate glossary of business or technical terms that may be unfamiliar to your readers?
- If there are any issues requiring management attention or resolution, have you clearly highlighted these in the AD and in the project's risk and issue register?
- Have you considered following the recommendations of ISO Standard 42010 on your project or in your organization?
- Have you presented your architecture description using formats and tools that are appropriate to your audience and to the information you want to communicate to them?

SUMMARY

Although every system has an architecture, not every system has an AD that effectively communicates the essence of the architecture to all of its stakeholders. A good AD will lay a solid foundation for the remaining system development work, while a poor AD may fail to address key concerns or may be ignored altogether. In this chapter, we described how you can ensure that your AD meets its goals.

An effective AD has seven desirable properties: correctness, sufficiency, timeliness, conciseness, clarity, currency, and precision. These properties can sometimes conflict with one another, so (as always) you have to achieve an effective balance.

Producing an AD that all stakeholders can understand is one of the greatest challenges you face. We reminded you to always consider the needs and capabilities of your readership when writing the AD. Glossaries are useful as aids for understanding and as input to more detailed modeling.

We presented a generic template for an AD that is a superset of what you are likely to produce in practice. Whichever sections you decide to include in your AD, it's important to keep the AD up-to-date during its lifetime.

Finally, in this chapter we explained the key features of ISO Standard 42010, *Systems and Software Engineering—Recommended Practice for Architectural Description of Software-Intensive Systems*, and outlined its benefits.

FURTHER READING

Documenting Software Architectures [CLEM10], written by a team from the SEI and now in its second edition, is a practitioner-oriented book that provides a great deal of well-presented, useful information on writing ADs.

When considering how to document architectural design decisions, and indeed why this is important, start with [TYRE05], which is an article written by two practicing software architects that explains this very clearly.

14

EVALUATING
THE ARCHITECTURE

There is always a great sense of achievement as your architectural ideas start to gel into a coherent design for your system. Getting to the point where you have made most of your key architectural decisions means that you have identified possible solutions to most of the major challenges your system faces and that you have designed the key architectural structures for your system. However, at this point you don't actually know whether or not you have a workable architecture. Just as you don't know whether your software works correctly just because it compiles cleanly, you don't know whether your candidate architecture is sound until it has been tested, too. We term the process of testing possible architectures for a system *architectural evaluation*.

In the architectural evaluation process, you check whether you made the right architectural decisions during architecture definition and, in particular, whether you made appropriate tradeoffs between competing needs. The evaluation process should begin as soon as architectural decisions start to be made, and it doesn't end until a system that the stakeholders deem to be acceptable is delivered (which is the final, ultimate validation of the architecture).

Of course, conventional ADs aren't executable (in the way that a program is) and so can't be directly tested like a piece of software. However, there are a number of other useful techniques for "testing" an architecture that vary in cost, complexity, and formality, and each has its place and is appropriate in different situations and during different lifecycle stages. You will nearly always need to use a number of techniques during the system lifecycle in order to evaluate your architecture effectively.

Remember that although your opinion is important, you aren't the ultimate arbiter of whether or not the architecture is right. You have created the architecture to meet the needs of your stakeholders, and it is their endorsement you need. Also keep in mind as you read this chapter that architectural evaluation isn't a one-shot activity to be done at any one point in the lifecycle; it should be approached as a continual process.

WHY EVALUATE THE ARCHITECTURE?

Let's start by considering in a little more detail why we should evaluate a candidate architecture as we create it. First, architectural evaluation is valuable because of the inevitable limitations of an AD.

- *Validating abstractions*: An AD (of the sort we talk about in this book) is an *abstraction of reality*. Many details aren't captured in the AD; if this weren't the case, the AD would lose the characteristics of conciseness and minimalism that we try hard to achieve. Evaluation will make sure that the abstractions you have made are reasonable and appropriate.
- *Checking technical correctness*: An AD is also *static* and can't be directly executed by a computer—it can't be tested in the same way that a piece of software can. As Bertrand Meyer has dryly noted, "Bubbles don't crash," meaning that it is easy to create models of software that look perfectly credible until someone tries to implement and test them. Only then may errors and inconsistencies become obvious, when the software fails.

Evaluation is also a useful process from a communication point of view.

- *Selling the architecture*: An architectural evaluation process can help sell your architecture to key stakeholders by showing them how it will meet their needs. Involving the stakeholders in the evaluation process can also help them understand the main tradeoffs that need to be made to meet the requirements and satisfy themselves that the right tradeoffs were chosen. For more technical stakeholders (such as system administrators, testers, and developers), the evaluation process can act as a valuable communication vehicle, allowing them to thoroughly understand the architecture and feel some ownership of its development.
- *Explaining the architecture*: An interactive architectural evaluation process can often be the most effective way to engage many of the less technical system stakeholders, who may not want to read detailed ADs but need to have the key features of the architecture explained to them.

Finally, the software development process also benefits from architectural evaluation in a number of ways.

- *Validating assumptions*: The architectural design process involves making a lot of assumptions about a wide variety of subjects (such as priorities, speeds, space, the system's external environment, and so on). Each of the perspectives that guides design for a particular quality property aims to validate key assumptions as part of its process, but some assumptions may slip through the net. Architectural evaluation can guide this process and help ensure that key assumptions are tested before it is too late to change the resulting decisions.

- *Providing management decision points*: From a project management perspective, architectural evaluation can provide a natural framework for the key go/no-go decision points in the system development lifecycle, allowing important decisions about the system's viability to be made before too much money is spent. These project management decision points form a management decision framework that complements the technical design decision framework that results from using viewpoints and perspectives to guide architectural design.

- *Offering a basis for formal agreement*: Architectural evaluation can also provide the basis for formal agreement about the form of the system to be built. Using an evaluated AD as the basis for, say, a contract to create the software may be more effective than trying to use an initial requirements document for this purpose, because of the deeper level of understanding that architecture definition and evaluation require.

- *Ensuring technical integrity*: Part of the architectural evaluation process involves ensuring compliance between the system that is built and the AD. This is an important check of the system's technical integrity and helps make sure that the right system is delivered.

In summary, architectural evaluation can be a valuable addition to the software development process right through the lifecycle, and in particular it can provide early insights into the strengths and weaknesses of various architectural options. Let's continue by considering the different types of techniques we can use for architectural evaluation.

EVALUATION TECHNIQUES

A number of approaches exist for evaluating a software architecture. They differ significantly in the cost, depth, and complexity of the evaluation performed, so it is important to choose the correct techniques for your particular situation.

Presentations

The simplest form of architectural evaluation is to present an informal explanation of the proposed architecture to stakeholders. However, simply presenting a candidate architecture to a group of stakeholders doesn't actually achieve any evaluation. For any degree of evaluation to occur, the people to whom you are presenting must be really engaged and be thinking critically about the options and decisions that you are describing. This requires you to structure the presentation carefully so that it engages the audience throughout and forces them to think deeply about the implications of what you are explaining.

In practice, we have never really seen a presentation act as an effective architectural evaluation exercise. At best, presentations can act as a useful communication and selling aid for the architecture and, at the same time, start the stakeholders thinking about the important issues. Early on in the architecture definition process they can be useful to help validate some of your fundamental assumptions. However, given the limited amount of analysis that a presentation usually allows, you should ensure that as your architecture takes shape, you use them in conjunction with more sophisticated, rigorous techniques to achieve an effective evaluation.

ADVANTAGES

- Presentations are fairly quick to create and can be easily tailored to different audiences.
- A presentation is cheap and easy to do, with little or no attendee preparation required.
- You can gather feedback immediately from audience reaction and questions.

LIMITATIONS

- You get a shallow level of analysis at best during a presentation meeting. In fact, our experience is that you usually get little or no real evaluation and the best the presentation can be is a communication vehicle.
- The effectiveness of the approach relies heavily on the engagement and commitment of the attendees, and this is affected by the quality of the presentation materials. It is easy to gain a false sense of security from a presentation that simply didn't engage the audience and make them analyze what they were hearing.
- The lack of attendee preparation usually results in a lack of time to reflect on the architecture and its strengths and weaknesses, which may result in the loss of valuable insights.

Formal Reviews and Structured Walkthroughs

Formal reviews can be an effective way to evaluate your AD with stakeholders, thus confirming that your understanding of their concerns is correct and allowing you to improve the design or the documentation based on their input.

The formal review involves gathering a group of people to go through a document page by page, raise comments about it, discuss the concerns as a group, and agree on what actions need to be taken, if any. Formal reviews can be used for specifications or other written documents, as well as source code and other such material.

You should give each of the attendees a role before the review meeting.

- The *moderator* runs the meeting, records the actions accepted by the group, and arbitrates any disputes or disagreements.

- The *presenter*, usually the author of the work being reviewed, presents and explains it to the group. If possible, the presenter and the moderator should be different people.

- The *reviewers* provide comments on the work being reviewed. Reviewers are sometimes given specific areas to consider, especially when the item under review is large or complex.

Send the item being reviewed to the reviewers a few days before the meeting, together with pointers to any background reading and instructions for the review. The moderator captures brief comments in a review record that is passed to the author after the review. The author makes the appropriate changes and returns the document to the moderator, who checks it, decides whether a second review is necessary, and signs off the review comments as having been implemented.

Minor comments (such as spelling or typographical errors) can usually be captured separately (e.g., on a marked-up copy of the document).

Structured walkthroughs are another way for a group of people to assess in detail a specification, design, or piece of code for correctness and conformance to requirements. As with formal reviews, this technique is an extremely useful method for validating a design and exposing potential weaknesses or gaps. A walkthrough usually involves stepping through one or more scenarios, exploring system behavior, and confirming that this behavior is as expected. When problems are discovered, possible solutions can be explored by the group or put to one side for later discussion.

ADVANTAGES

- A formal review or walkthrough involves the participants much more deeply than a presentation and is likely to result in much more valuable insights.

LIMITATIONS

- A formal review or walkthrough requires a significant amount of preparation before the meeting. This preparation is essential because the results of the exercise are highly dependent on the quality of the preparation.

- For the meeting to be effective, preparation for a review or walkthrough must be undertaken by both the leader or presenter and the participants, and it can be difficult to get people to commit the time required to prepare thoroughly.

Evaluation by Using Scenarios

Scenario-based architectural evaluation is a structured approach to evaluating how well an architecture meets stakeholder needs, in terms of the attributes (or qualities) that the architecture exhibits. The best-known scenario-based evaluation method is probably the Architecture Tradeoff Analysis Method (ATAM), developed by the Software Engineering Institute (SEI). We describe ATAM in more detail later in this chapter.

The key concept underpinning these methods is a set of scenarios (i.e., particular situations that the system is likely to face during operation) that are important to the system's stakeholders and allow the system's properties to be estimated. Scenario-based approaches to evaluation contain five fundamental steps.

1. *Understand the requirements*: Review the requirements of the system, if you have them, or gather some key requirements if you don't, to make sure that they are well understood. Evaluation needs to be performed against the stakeholder requirements, and because people from outside the project usually perform an evaluation, it is important that they understand the key requirements thoroughly.

2. *Understand the proposed architecture*: As well as understanding the requirements, the evaluators need to understand the proposed architecture in enough detail to evaluate it thoroughly. They normally gain this knowledge by reading the AD and having the architecture presented to them by the architect responsible for the project.

3. *Identify prioritized scenarios*: A scenario-based evaluation method works by considering how well an architecture meets the needs of a particular scenario. Some scenarios are functional (such as "Web-site customer wishes to obtain duplicate receipt for transaction more than 6 months ago"), while others focus on a system quality (such as "During weekly consolidation processing, 400 online transactions per minute are received"). In order to ensure that the evaluation process is valid, the scenarios must reflect the interests and priorities of the stakeholders (rather than the interests of the evaluators), so the set should normally be developed in direct consultation with stakeholder representatives. The scenarios are usually prioritized (e.g., as high, medium, or low priority) to help focus attention on the more important ones during evaluation.

4. *Analyze the architecture*: The core of a scenario-based technique is the consideration of each high-priority scenario in turn, analyzing how well the architecture meets the needs of that particular situation. Doing this usually reveals possible weaknesses in the architecture, where the needs of important scenarios can't be met, and also tends to highlight places where there is conflict between different scenarios that could be comfortably met in isolation but cause problems when both need to be handled by the same system.

5. *Draw conclusions*: Having analyzed the architecture against the set of scenarios, the evaluators capture the results of the exercise in a report and draw some specific conclusions about the suitability of the architecture. If the proposed architecture cannot deal with particular scenarios or groups of scenarios, you must draw up a plan of action to address the problems.

Scenario-based techniques are not particularly difficult to apply, and provided that the system is not too large or complex, the overall approach can be used effectively in an informal way. However, in more complex situations, you should use a more structured approach to keep control of the process and to ensure that the results are valid. Methods such as ATAM and SAAM (Software Architecture Assessment Method) are very valuable in these situations because they are based on a lot of existing experience and contain a lot of advice on managing the process.

ADVANTAGES

- Scenario-based approaches can provide a deep, sophisticated analysis of the strengths and weaknesses of a particular architectural approach.

- These methods lead to a more explicit understanding of the tradeoffs made in the architecture and can help explain the rationale to stakeholders.

- Scenario-based techniques help architecture teams understand the decisions they have made, why they made them, and their implications.

LIMITATIONS

- These approaches are considerably more complex and expensive to apply than simple reviews or walkthroughs.

- Because the approaches are reasonably sophisticated, training or significant preparation is required for those leading them.

- Approaches like ATAM assume that all stakeholders will be prepared to participate reasonably deeply in order to (at least) identify, understand, validate, and prioritize the scenarios to be used for the evaluation exercise. If this isn't the case, the process may be of relatively little benefit.

Prototypes and Proof-of-Concept Systems

Prototypes and proofs-of-concept are most often used to mitigate technical risk (when a new or unfamiliar technology is under consideration) or to help design the user interface. For our purposes, we define a *prototype* as a temporary implementation of some functional subset of the system, often presented to users for feedback and validation, which is then discarded when the validation exercise is complete. We define a *proof-of-concept* as some code designed to prove that a risky element of the proposed architecture is feasible and to highlight any problems and pitfalls. A proof-of-concept is also a temporary implementation, which is discarded when it has served its purpose and the risk under investigation is understood. (Some people also talk about "evolutionary prototypes," but we have found that there is a great danger of confusion about the future plans for a prototype if this term is used. We refer to such evolving partial implementations as "skeleton systems"; see the following section.)

One problem with prototyping is that the risks that need to be mitigated can be quite complex. For example, a prototype may be suggested to demonstrate that an architecture can handle a large volume of transactions. In order to do this, you may have to set up a large amount of dummy data and a sophisticated simulation environment that can apply large numbers of transactions to the prototype and monitor performance. In addition, the prototype needs to be fairly sophisticated in its ability to scale in order for its results to be meaningful.

Prototyping is therefore the most expensive and time-consuming way to assess an architecture and needs careful justification. However, proving that something works by actually building it is a powerful risk-reduction mechanism.

The downstream risk with building a prototype is that the stakeholders view it as a finished system. A prototype typically has limited functionality, particularly related to error and exception handling as well as resilience, and you should normally discard it after it has served its purpose. You must clearly manage your stakeholders' expectations in this area.

ADVANTAGES

- Prototypes and proofs-of-concept can provide concrete evaluation of technical decisions at the point in the lifecycle when they can still be changed easily.

- Building a prototype or proof-of-concept provides an opportunity to learn about and understand the system's implementation technology, in a safe environment, before you need to use it to implement the system.

- Prototypes and proofs-of-concept can provide useful demonstrations to stakeholders to increase their confidence in the people, technology, and processes in use.

LIMITATIONS

- Prototypes and proofs-of-concept can be quite expensive and time-consuming to create, so you should use them only if a decision is important enough to justify the cost.

- Prototypes and proofs-of-concept all too often end up being hijacked and evolved to be the production system. However, they are usually (and quite correctly) built in a very "quick and dirty" manner and are a very poor basis for a real system. If you build a prototype, discard it once it has served its purpose. If you want something to evolve into a production system, use a skeleton system.

Skeleton System

The ultimate form of architectural evaluation is to build the system. The architectural form of this is to create a first version of the system, known as a *skeleton*, that implements the system's main architectural structures but contains only a minimal subset of the system's functionality. The minimal subset of functionality chosen should allow a small amount of end-to-end processing to occur, so it can prove that the system's overall structure is sound.

Unlike a prototype or proof-of-concept, a skeleton system is retained rather than discarded and becomes the basis for the construction phase, which fleshes out the skeleton with the implementation of all the required functions.

ADVANTAGES

- Skeleton systems are often the most thorough and convincing type of architectural evaluation possible.

- The delivery of a successful skeleton system is a major morale boost for the system development team.

- The skeleton system created is a tangible deliverable that can be used beyond the evaluation activity.

LIMITATIONS

- Skeleton systems are probably the most expensive form of architectural evaluation.

- The skeleton system needs to be created with the same software engineering discipline as your production system—after all, it is the first version of it. This is a much more time-consuming and involved exercise than producing a quick prototype, requiring different skills.

SCENARIO-BASED EVALUATION METHODS

SAAM and ATAM are well-known examples of scenario-based architectural evaluation methods. Both of these methods were created at the SEI; SAAM is the original, simpler method, while ATAM is a more sophisticated approach developed later.

The key concept underpinning both of these methods is a set of system usage scenarios that are of importance to the system's stakeholders and allow assessment of the system's properties. SAAM uses functional scenarios to evaluate how well a system will provide its key functionality and how easily it could be modified to meet likely changes. ATAM broadens this focus by using a set of quality property scenarios to test the ability of the system to exhibit its important quality properties (performance, security, availability, and so on).

We don't have space here to describe these methods in detail (although references mentioned in the Further Reading section at the end of this chapter do provide more information). Here we will briefly describe ATAM to give you an overview of the approach.

The UML activity diagram in Figure 14–1 illustrates the main steps in an ATAM architecture evaluation process. ATAM recognizes that there are two important but distinct aspects to architectural evaluation:

1. *Architecture-centric evaluation*, performed by the key project decision makers (those who created and own the architecture as well as key customer representatives—acquirers and user stakeholders, in our terminology)

2. *Stakeholder-centric evaluation*, performed by representatives from the wider stakeholder community (all those affected by the architecture)

The first half of the ATAM process (shown on the left in Figure 14–1) focuses on understanding the architecture and the decisions made to define it, while the second half (shown on the right) tests the results of the first part by directly involving representatives of the entire stakeholder community.

Architecture-Centric Activities

The steps in the architecture-centric half of the process are as follows.

- *Present the business drivers*: The members of the architecture review team (probably made up of architects, lead designers, key customer representatives, and possibly external consultants) examine the business drivers that underlie the system's existence and make sure they understand them. This step normally consists of a business expert (perhaps the project sponsor or a business analyst) presenting the context for the system and the key business drivers to the group. Ideally this will be a process of confirming your knowledge of the business drivers, but it may result in new insights gained from the presenter.

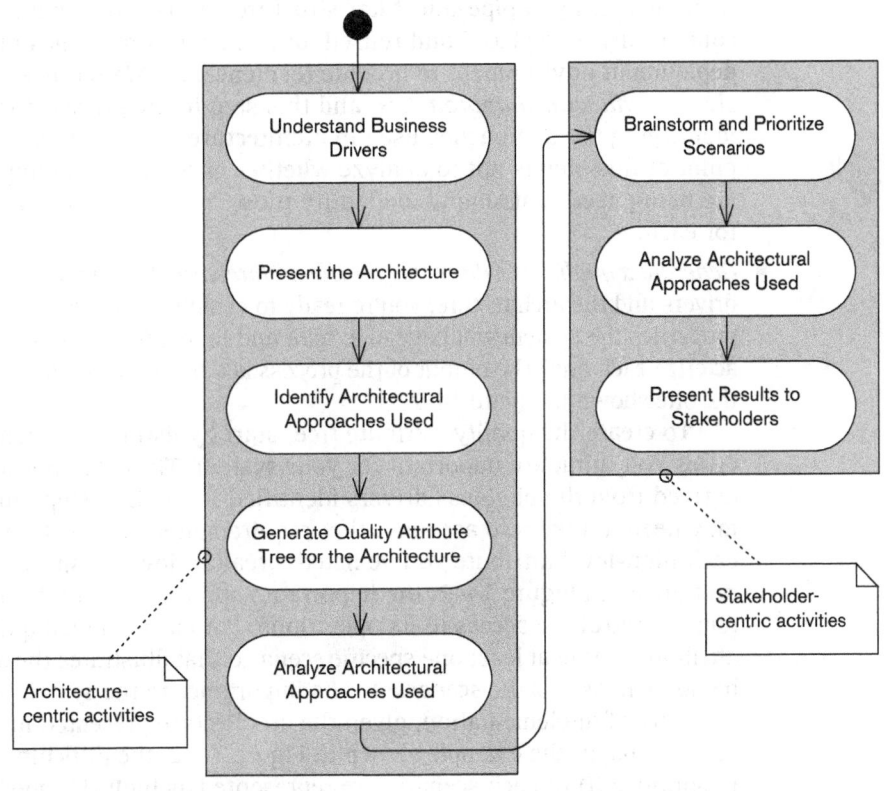

FIGURE 14-1 THE ATAM PROCESS

- *Present the architecture*: The owner of the architecture (probably you) should now present the architecture to the rest of the group. The form of the presentation varies between assessments; the key is to communicate the entire architecture to the group evaluating it, in a way that they can understand it, in sufficient detail for them to analyze it. Due to specialization of roles, this is often the first time that many of those involved in developing the architecture will actually see and try to understand all of it. The focus of this step should be communicating and understanding, rather than analyzing and evaluating, which will come later.

- *Identify the architectural approaches used*: When developing any software architecture, you make a number of architectural decisions to ensure that the architecture meets certain critical goals. For example, perhaps you chose a client/server structure to allow hardware to be upgraded easily, a pipe-and-filter structure so that processing steps could easily be replaced and reused, or a cluster of machines in the deployment environment to provide resilience. ATAM terms such decisions *architectural approaches*, and this step in the process focuses on identifying the approaches used in architecture definition. Again, the point of this step is not to analyze whether or not the right approaches are being used, but simply to identify those in use and the reasons for each.

- *Generate a quality attribute tree for the architecture*: Having understood the drivers and the architecture, you're ready to establish the critical quality properties the system will have to exhibit and to identify scenarios to characterize each one. The output of the process is a tree of attributes, similar to the one shown in Figure 14–2.

    To create the quality attribute tree, start by listing the quality properties you think are important for your system. These are normally derived from the business drivers identified in the first step, but you may need to take into account other requirements as well. Then, for each high-level attribute you've listed, break it down to specific important areas. In Figure 14–2, the important aspect of security for this system is controlling access to its operations. For each detailed quality attribute, define at least one specific scenario that illustrates the attribute being met. Assess the scenario for its importance to the system and its difficulty of implementation, given the architecture presented in the previous steps. In the example shown in Figure 14–2, the difficulty (D) and importance (I) of each scenario are represented as high (H), medium (M), or low (L).

FIGURE 14–2 QUALITY ATTRIBUTE TREE

The result of this process is a quality attribute tree that provides a set of scenarios with which to evaluate the architecture. The importance rating of each scenario helps focus attention on the most important aspects of the system, while the difficulty rating helps draw attention to areas where the architecture may need modification and improvement. Obviously, the high-importance, high-difficulty scenarios need the most attention during the rest of the evaluation process, while the low-importance, low-difficulty scenarios need the least.

▪ *Analyze the architectural approaches used*: In this step, the review team analyzes the architecture in more detail, in light of the quality goals, in order to establish how well it supports its required quality properties. The analysis can take a number of forms, and the authors of the ATAM process provide a fairly detailed process description for this step. Whatever approach you use, it needs to work systematically through the quality property scenarios and help you understand *how* the architecture supports the scenario and *which* architectural decisions are important to achieving it. While you do this, take special care to identify critical architectural decisions of the following types:

  ● Decisions that are critical to meeting a particular quality property (termed *sensitivity points* in ATAM), such as a decision to use clustered servers to meet high-availability targets

  ● Decisions that require a tradeoff between the needs of two competing quality properties (termed *tradeoff points* in ATAM), such as a decision to denormalize a database to achieve acceptable performance at the cost of more complex evolution

  This process should result in a thorough understanding (with reasoning) as to how the architecture supports (or does not support) each quality attribute scenario. This allows the creation of a list of the sensitivity and tradeoff points in the current architecture and for the risks where the architecture does not support particular quality attribute scenarios (and the nonrisks where it does) to be understood and recorded.

Stakeholder-Centric Activities

This first half of the evaluation process has, in fact, performed an architectural evaluation, and the architects should now understand their architecture better and feel confident that it suits its intended purpose. However, in order to test the results of this evaluation, it is important to ensure that the criteria match the priorities of the stakeholders. The second half of the ATAM process does this by using stakeholder scenarios to test the architecture. The steps in this half of the process are as follows.

▪ *Brainstorm and prioritize scenarios*: Having gathered representatives of the interested stakeholder groups, explained ATAM, and summarized the steps performed so far, you can now work with the stakeholders to create a list of scenarios that *they* believe are important, both immediately and in the longer term. Have the stakeholders prioritize the scenarios to focus attention on the more important ones (a vote is often the most effective way to do this). Once the scenarios have been identified and prioritized, you can merge them into the quality attribute tree.

- *Analyze the architectural approaches used*: This step is analogous to the same step on the architecture-centric side but considers how the architectural approaches support (or don't support) the *new* scenarios the stakeholders have identified. Ideally, these new scenarios will be similar to the set identified by the architecture team, and this step will simply be a confirmation of the previous analysis. In reality, this step quite often sets "a cat among the pigeons" as the architecture team realizes that the architecture won't be able to meet some scenarios that are important to stakeholders. As in the corresponding architecture-centric step, you should identify sensitivity and tradeoff points.

- *Present the results to the stakeholders*: Finally, you present the results of the evaluation back to the stakeholders so that they understand how the architecture is going to support their scenarios. Your presentation should also highlight sensitivity and tradeoff points to help stakeholders understand how important, say, the new clustered server environment is in meeting *their* scenarios and, similarly, why meeting, say, a security requirement means that a usability requirement will have to be compromised. This step is an important communication and selling activity, helping the stakeholders feel ownership of *their* architecture and ideally gaining their confidence in and support for the architecture team's work.

Although this is no more than a thumbnail sketch of the ATAM process, we hope it is enough to give you a flavor of what it is and how it works.

EVALUATION DURING THE SOFTWARE LIFECYCLE

Evaluation shouldn't be thought of as a single activity, performed at a particular point in the development lifecycle, but should be treated as an ongoing task that continually assesses the system's architecture as it is being developed. Having said this, not all evaluation activities work equally well at each lifecycle stage, so you need to choose carefully the approaches used. Figure 14–3 illustrates where the different evaluation approaches typically fit into the software lifecycle.

When you are defining scope and exploring options for the architecture, the emphasis is on the following evaluation techniques, which help you make sound architectural decisions.

FIGURE 14-3 EVALUATION APPROACHES AT DIFFERENT POINTS OF THE LIFECYCLE

- *Presentations*: The proposed architecture should be widely presented as early as possible. Presenting the architecture to different stakeholders is cheap and easy to do and helps you validate the fundamental assumptions you're making about the role and nature of the system. However, as we've already said, don't expect much real evaluation from this stage in the process, as presentations are more successful at sharing ideas than analyzing them.

- *Reviews and walkthroughs*: As the architecture starts to emerge, organize more formal reviews of parts of it with stakeholders particularly affected by the decisions being made. For example, as soon as the system's deployment platform is designed, have a formal review of it with the groups in the organization that are responsible for providing the IT infrastructure on which you plan to rely. As soon as the system structure starts to emerge, review it with the testers to make sure that they understand the scale and scope of testing required and that the proposed architecture actually is testable. The key point here is to start holding reviews as soon as there is anything to review, rather than waiting until the complete "perfect" AD has been completed. It's best to get the bad news as early as possible, and formal reviews can provide some confidence that the major decisions you're making are valid.

- *Prototypes*: Build prototypes of parts of the system in order to support technical decision making and to better understand the technologies included in the architecture.

During the detailed architecture definition process, the focus of evaluation moves to understanding the strengths and weaknesses of the proposed architecture and ensuring that it is suitable for the system being built. The techniques used in this phase include the following.

- *Reviews and walkthroughs*: From the point when you start to have some of the AD available, you can perform formal reviews and walkthroughs to gain general consensus that the architecture is feasible, suitable for the proposed system, and free of major problems (as far as people can tell). The completion of these reviews is a suitable point to get formal agreement (possibly in the form of a sign-off) that the architecture is acceptable to the system's important stakeholders.

- *Prototypes*: Build prototypes in order to resolve technical concerns that emerge during the architecture definition process and to evaluate particular architectural decisions.

- *Scenario-based evaluation*: In order to provide a deeper understanding of the system's attributes (such as performance, security, maintainability, and functionality), you can apply a scenario-based evaluation technique once your architecture is taking shape. Such an evaluation allows a more sophisticated level of analysis than a simple review or walkthrough, while still being achievable within a short time frame and at a reasonable cost.

- *Skeleton system*: When your key architectural decisions have been made, the architecture team, working with the lead designers, can create a skeleton implementation of the system to demonstrate how it will work and also to provide a development environment in which the full development of the system can take place. A skeleton system implementation can be a powerful proof point for many stakeholders, proving that the architecture really can provide the facilities needed, as well as demonstrating some directly useful deliverables as early as possible.

Another good point for evaluation comes later in the development lifecycle, when most of the important parts of the system are being or have been developed, with the focus now on the consistency of the AD and the architecture as realized in the system. The techniques of most use during system construction are as follows.

- *Reviews and walkthroughs*: Work closely with the development team to review the implementation as it is taking shape, acting as consultant and mentor and advising how best the architecture should be interpreted. Ideally, you will be able to work as part of the development team, but you might work externally to it. In either case, it is important to perform continual reviews so that the implementation actually reflects the architecture. Then when problems are found, you can modify the architecture to address them, rather than just letting the implementation drift away from the architecture described in the AD.

- *Skeleton system*: As development progresses, the skeleton system will be fleshed out with the implementation of the system and so over time become a full implementation. Ensure that every development iteration adds working, useful functionality to the system.

VALIDATING THE ARCHITECTURE OF AN EXISTING SYSTEM

Another situation in which we have often found ourselves is when a system exists already and you are asked for your opinion of the "quality" of its design (with the definition of *quality* usually being left open). In principle in such situations, you can use the techniques we have outlined to assess the architectural qualities that the system exhibits, maybe with some practical testing to evaluate that your assessment reflects the reality of the system in production. However, our experience is that if you try to apply something like ATAM in these situations, you will not get very far, because the commitment of time and resources needed is too high and people do not understand what the investment will buy them. What is needed in these situations is a simple, lightweight approach that you can perform yourself, without a large team, in days rather than weeks. We call our approach the Tiny Architectural Review Approach, or TARA.

The essence of TARA is a lightweight, flexible approach that does not make any assumptions about existing design documentation, needs relatively few resources in order to use it, can be performed largely by the architect herself, and produces a set of deliverables that are easily comprehensible. The tradeoff is that a TARA review is nowhere near as thorough as one performed with an approach like ATAM, and it is much more vulnerable to the biases and strengths and weaknesses of the person performing it.

We have probably never used TARA in quite the same way twice, so in this section we outline our general approach in the hope that you will find it useful. The general steps that we include in a TARA-style architectural review of a system are as follows.

- *Goals and target audience*: The first step is always to understand the context of the review being requested. Who is requesting it? Why are they requesting it? Who is the output for? What will be done with the output? Answering these questions helps to scope and focus the whole exercise and is key to making sure that the effort you put into the review is well spent and you know what a successful outcome from the requestors' point of view is likely to look like. It is often at this stage that you may realize that there are a number of vested interests at play; people do not always request system reviews for entirely positive reasons, and it is useful to understand up front what the underlying motivation for the request is!

- *Context diagram and requirements summary*: It is possible that the system you have been asked to review has good documentation associated with it, in the form of documents, models, requirements scenarios, checklists, and so on. If so, that's great. However, in our experience we are rarely asked to review those systems; we usually get asked to review the ones that got off to a bad start because their scope was not clearly defined and their requirements were not understood. So for you to perform a meaningful review, you will need to do enough investigation to understand the system's scope, context, and key requirements. You can then present a summary of these in the review report, and they will form a useful record of the assumptions that you made. The idea here is not to go into a lot of detail, but rather to be able to understand the main external systems and other actors with which the system interacts, the types of interactions that take place, and the key functional and nonfunctional requirements that the system is meant to provide. This sets the scene for the remainder of the review and provides you with something against which to review the system.

- *Functional and Deployment view sketches*: Again, if there is good architectural design documentation, you can use it as the basis of your assessment. However, you may well need to do enough design recovery to be able to draw up the main structures of the system for yourself in order to review and understand them. We have found that a Functional view (the main components, interfaces, connectors, and interactions) and a Deployment view (showing the overall deployment structure used to run the system) usually suffice if there is not enough time to do more. For some sorts of systems (e.g., data warehouses or ETL systems) you might alternatively choose to create an Information view and a Deployment view if the functional structure is very simple. Again, if you are creating these views for yourself, the aim is to produce accurate but abstract descriptions that provide useful sketches of the architecture, rather than trying to capture every detail. The goal is to have something to review, analyze, and assess, rather than to define the level of detail needed to build the system.

- *System implementation quality*: The great advantage of an existing system is that the code is available to you, so as well as reviewing the Development view, you can analyze the code to find out whether it is well structured, clearly supports the main architectural structures, has been developed with a good level of basic craftsmanship, and other qualities. At this stage we review the structure of the codeline in the source control system; use static analysis tools to derive the structure, dependencies, key metrics, and so on; and then perform detailed reviews of a few code modules from different parts of the system. If the system is well structured, you will be able to generate module and layer diagrams fairly automatically and include these in your report. This is also the stage where we look at the software engineering approaches used, looking for version control, automated build, continuous integration, good automated tests, use of static analysis tools, sensible use of third-party technologies, and so on.

■ *Requirements fit*: You now have to get to the most important assessment criterion, which is whether this system is fit for the purpose for which it has been designed. This involves understanding whether the functions provided by the system provide good functional coverage and assessing whether the key qualities of the system are acceptable for its intended use. Given that these lightweight review exercises are usually carried out under time pressure, with few resources, it is often difficult to perform a thorough evaluation of the system against its requirements. It is normally necessary to involve the expert judgment of others, focus on the most important areas, and perform the evaluation at a relatively high level, rather than investigating every detail. Some of the techniques we have found useful for this include:

  ● Sitting with expert users of the system to watch them work, asking their opinions of the system and what they would improve or change, as well as seeing whether they ever have to work "outside" the system (on paper, in spreadsheets, copying information to other systems, and so on)

  ● Talking to the IT administration and operations groups to obtain impressions, or better data, on the system's reliability, performance, and reputation in its production environment

  ● Comparing the functions that the system provides to other systems or packaged solutions that you have seen in the same or similar domains

  ● Talking to the system's development and support team frankly about the system's strengths and weaknesses

■ *Recommendations*: Once you have reviewed the system and its implementation, you will have gathered and analyzed quite a lot of information. We have found it very valuable to deliver a report at the end of an architecture review that contains all of the information gathered. This forms a useful deliverable in its own right, particularly if the system is short of good documentation. The rest of the review report will then be the findings of your analysis and recommendations for improvement, if you have some and they were requested as part of the exercise.

We should stress that these steps and deliverables are just a representative example of how we approach a TARA review. We do alter the approach if the situation requires it, and in particular we find that the presentation of the results often requires significant tailoring to the needs, sensitivities, and desires of the target audience. You should always bear in mind that when you are assessing someone else's system, you are in constant danger of "calling their baby ugly."

In order to be effective, the results of the exercise usually have to be presented carefully and tactfully, even if in essence they are quite critical. We have found clarity, conciseness, and tact to be three key attributes of good recommendations!

RECORDING THE RESULTS OF EVALUATION

It's important to clearly and formally record the evaluation results to avoid misunderstandings about the problems found and the resulting decisions or changes. Failing to do this can lead to useful architectural improvements being ignored or getting lost, and in turn, this can often lead to a significant reduction of the stakeholders' confidence in the architecture and the architect.

There are many ways to record evaluation results, each with advantages and limitations. We find the following approaches useful.

- *Meeting minutes*: Recording the progress of meetings is a standard business technique that, if done accurately, can provide a definitive record of discussions and their results. The problem with meeting minutes is that they are hard to take properly, and often the important points are swamped by details that are not that significant. The difficulty in taking good minutes can also lead to different groups of people writing a number of subtly different sets of minutes, which people use later as ammunition to win arguments. Given these problems, it's not very surprising that many people view meeting minutes with a certain amount of suspicion.

- *Decision logs*: A more focused approach to recording evaluation results is to use a decision log, which records decisions as they are made, along with their rationale and an identification of who made and agreed on them. A decision log can be kept in a spreadsheet, a word processor document, a collaborative Web site, or even a purpose-built software tool. Their great advantage is simplicity, although they do need to be carefully maintained and can suffer from a lack of context, which is often important later when you're trying to remember why a particular decision was made.

- *Review records*: Using a well-defined approach to reviews or walk-throughs should result in problems and possible resolutions being documented in a reasonably standard form.

- *Evaluation reports*: Evaluation reports document the outcomes of architectural evaluation exercises in a standard, structured way to make them useful to the architect and stakeholders. This ensures that you won't lose the benefits of the exercises and lessons learned.

- *Document sign-off*: The normal way to record agreement with a particular decision or architecture is to gain a formal sign-off of a document, recording the agreement with its content. This can often be necessary if there is some form of contractual agreement required or if the agreement of certain key stakeholders is needed to progress past a particular project checkpoint. For you as the architect, it can also be quite reassuring to have a signature to approve a particular course of action. However, bear in mind the limitations of relying on document sign-off to prove stakeholder satisfaction—it really doesn't prove that the signer understood the content and is unlikely to guarantee that building the system will result in happy stakeholders.

CHOOSING AN EVALUATION APPROACH

In this chapter we have introduced a number of approaches for evaluating the suitability of a software architecture, from very informal approaches like presentations to very involved techniques like building skeleton systems. Given this range of possible approaches, the question is often how to choose among them. In Table 14–1 we summarize our advice on choosing among these techniques in different situations.

TABLE 14–1 CHOOSING AN EVALUATION APPROACH

Project Environments	Suggested Evaluation Approaches
Small-scale, low-risk system	• Structured walkthrough with key stakeholders • Skeleton system that evolves into production
Large-scale, low-risk system	• Presentations to key stakeholders to gain buy-in • Scenario-based evaluation to ensure soundness of architecture • Skeleton system that evolves into production
Small-scale, high-risk system	• Scenario-based evaluation to ensure that key scenarios can be achieved • Proofs-of-concept to address specific technical risks (or prototypes to address functional or scope risks) • Skeleton system that evolves into production
Large-scale, high-risk system	• Presentation to key stakeholders to explain scope, risks, and benefits and obtain buy-in • Scenario-based evaluation to ensure suitability of architecture for the scale and challenges of the system • Proofs-of-concept to address specific technical risks and prototypes to address functional scope and risk • Skeleton system that evolves into production

Continued on next page

TABLE 14-1 CHOOSING AN EVALUATION APPROACH (CONTINUED)

Project Environments	Suggested Evaluation Approaches
Package implementation	• Presentation to key stakeholders to explain approach and gain buy-in • Scenario-based evaluation to ensure the suitability of the proposed product and deployment • Proof-of-concept deployments to test assumptions about the product and planned deployment
Assessment of small existing system	• TARA-style lightweight architectural assessment
Assessment of large existing system	• Scenario-based evaluation to assess the suitability of the system's existing architecture for the key scenarios it must face now and in the future

CHECKLIST

- Have you planned how your software architecture will be evaluated throughout its development?

- Have you identified suitable evaluation techniques for use at each stage of the lifecycle? Do you know when you will use each?

- Have you allocated time and resources for evaluation and rework?

- Are the system's stakeholders ready and willing to engage in the evaluation process? If not, have you started to try to persuade them to participate?

- Are the architects suitably trained to perform architectural evaluation (e.g., presentation skills; soft skills for stakeholder interaction; specific technique skills such as inspections, ATAM, or SAAM)?

- Have you considered using experts from outside the immediate project team (perhaps other architects elsewhere in your organization) to provide independent evaluation?

- Have you defined a mechanism whereby decisions arising from reviews can be tracked and monitored to ensure that the appropriate changes are made to the architecture?

SUMMARY

Software architecture can't be executed like a piece of software, so we need to find other ways to test it. Architectural evaluation is the process of testing a software architecture for its fitness for purpose and for the presence of possible defects. This evaluation uses different techniques to test different aspects of the architecture at different stages during the lifecycle.

Some of the more important techniques for architectural evaluation include presenting the architecture to stakeholders, performing reviews and walk-throughs, using more formal scenario-based architectural evaluation techniques, building throwaway prototypes and proofs-of-concept, and creating early skeleton versions of the real system. Each of these techniques applies to different stages of the lifecycle, and they all come with different advantages and limitations.

You should treat the activity as a continual process of evaluation and improvement, running alongside architectural design, rather than as a one-shot review that the architecture must pass.

FURTHER READING

Not many books or articles about architectural evaluation are aimed at practitioners. A couple of notable exceptions are Clements et al. [CLEM02], which is a thorough and practical guide to applying the SEI's scenario-based techniques, particularly ATAM; and Gilb and Graham [GILB93], which is a comprehensive guide to running formal reviews ("inspections"). The practitioner-oriented TARA approach that we describe in this chapter is described more thoroughly in a paper from the WICSA 2011 conference [WOOD11].

Another useful practitioner-oriented resource is the "Software Architecture Review and Assessment Report," published by the SARA Industry Working Group [SARA02]. This is a short technical report written by a number of practitioners and experienced researchers that provides a very practical and accessible introduction to architectural review processes and a lot of information on how to go about performing architectural reviews. Another useful technical report, which is available from SEI, discusses how to perform structured reviews of architecture documentation [NORD09].

Two useful academic articles on architectural evaluation are Dobrica and Niemela [DOBR02] and Babar and Gorton [BABA04], both of which review a number of approaches to architectural evaluation and analysis (including SAAM and ATAM), explaining the similarities and differences between them.

PART III

A VIEWPOINT CATALOG

15

INTRODUCTION TO THE VIEWPOINT CATALOG

Part III is a catalog of our seven core viewpoints: Context, Functional, Information, Concurrency, Development, Deployment, and Operational. There are many options for structuring an architectural description, but we believe that this set of viewpoints does a good job of partitioning the AD into a manageable number of sections, while ensuring widespread coverage of concerns.

Figure 15–1 shows the relationships between views created using these viewpoints.

FIGURE 15–1 VIEW RELATIONSHIPS

For convenience, in Table 15–1 we reiterate the viewpoint taxonomy we presented originally in Part I.

For each viewpoint, we present the following details:

- The most important *concerns* addressed by the viewpoint, with an identification of the stakeholders who are most likely to be interested in its views
- The most important *models* you might build to present the views, together with the notations used and the activities for building them
- Some *problems and pitfalls* to be aware of and risk-reduction techniques for mitigating these
- A *checklist* of things to consider when developing the viewpoint and when reviewing it to help ensure correctness, completeness, and accuracy

Because of space limitations, we can present only an overview of some complex and detailed topics. Most of the chapters in Part III could easily expand into entire books in their own right. Our objective is to get you started, and to that end, each viewpoint chapter includes a number of references to sources of further information.

TABLE 15–1 VIEWPOINT CATALOG

Viewpoint	Definition
Context	Describes the relationships, dependencies, and interactions between the system and its environment (the people, systems, and external entities with which it interacts). The Context view will be of interest to many of the system's stakeholders and plays an important role in helping them to understand its responsibilities and how it relates to their organization.
Functional	Describes the system's runtime functional elements, their responsibilities, interfaces, and primary interactions. A Functional view is the cornerstone of most ADs and is often the first part of the description that stakeholders try to read. It drives the shape of other system structures such as the information structure, concurrency structure, deployment structure, and so on. It also has a significant impact on the system's quality properties such as its ability to change, its ability to be secured, and its runtime performance.
Information	Describes the way that the architecture stores, manipulates, manages, and distributes information. The ultimate purpose of virtually any computer system is to manipulate information in some form, and this viewpoint develops a complete but high-level view of static data structure and information flow. The objective of this analysis is to answer the big questions around content, structure, ownership, latency, references, and data migration.

TABLE 15-1 VIEWPOINT CATALOG *(CONTINUED)*

Viewpoint	Definition
Concurrency	Describes the concurrency structure of the system and maps functional elements to concurrency units to clearly identify the parts of the system that can execute concurrently and how this is coordinated and controlled. This entails the creation of models that show the process and thread structures that the system will use and the interprocess communication mechanisms used to coordinate their operation.
Development	Describes the architecture that supports the software development process. Development views communicate the aspects of the architecture of interest to those stakeholders involved in building, testing, maintaining, and enhancing the system.
Deployment	Describes the environment into which the system will be deployed and the dependencies that the system has on elements of it. This view captures the hardware environment that your system needs (primarily the processing nodes, network interconnections, and disk storage facilities required), the technical environment requirements for each element, and the mapping of the software elements to the runtime environment that will execute them.
Operational	Describes how the system will be operated, administered, and supported when it is running in its production environment. For all but the simplest systems, installing, managing, and operating the system is a significant task that must be considered and planned at design time. The aim of the Operational viewpoint is to identify system-wide strategies for addressing the operational concerns of the system's stakeholders and to identify solutions that address these.

16

THE CONTEXT VIEWPOINT

Definition	Describes the relationships, dependencies, and interactions between the system and its environment (the people, systems, and external entities with which it interacts)
Concerns	System scope and responsibilities, identity of external entities and services and data used, nature and characteristics of external entities, identity and responsibilities of external interfaces, nature and characteristics of external interfaces, other external interdependencies, impact of the system on its environment, and overall completeness, consistency, and coherence
Models	Context model, interaction scenarios
Problems and Pitfalls	Missing or incorrect external entities, missing implicit dependencies, loose or inaccurate interface descriptions, inappropriate level of detail, scope creep, implicit or assumed context or scope, overcomplicated interactions, overuse of jargon
Stakeholders	All stakeholders, but especially acquirers, users, and developers
Applicability	All systems

Many architecture descriptions we've seen focus on views that model the system's internal structures, data elements, interactions, and operation. Architects tend to assume that the "outward-facing" information—the system's runtime context, its scope and requirements, and so forth—is clearly and unambiguously defined elsewhere. In fact, in the first edition of this book, we didn't have a viewpoint for the system's context for this very reason. However, we have decided that we were wrong! In practice, it often isn't realistic to delegate all of these concerns elsewhere, and you frequently need to include a definition of the system's context as part of your architectural description. This can be for a number of reasons, including the following.

- The system context is often implicit rather than being explicitly defined as part of project initiation or requirements capture.
- The system context may be loosely defined during requirements analysis, but at a level of detail that means that you need to add significantly to it.
- You need to refer to elements of the system context elsewhere in your architectural description, which makes it desirable for this information to be part of the architectural description and so under your control.

In practice, most of the architectural descriptions we have created have included a "context diagram," which is essentially a view but without an associated viewpoint definition to guide its structure and content. We therefore decided that we should formalize the definition of context as we have for the other views.

The Context view of a system defines the relationships, dependencies, and interactions between the system and its environment—the people, systems, and external entities with which it interacts. It defines what the system does and does not do; where the boundaries are between it and the outside world; and how the system interacts with other systems, organizations, and people across these boundaries.

The Context view focuses on the outside world and usually represents the system itself as a "black box," hiding all details of its functional elements, data, implementation, and so forth, since these are documented in one of the other views.

CONCERNS

System Scope and Responsibilities

This concern considers the main responsibilities of the system, that is, what, in broad terms, it is required to do. For clarity, it may also identify some specific exclusions, although by definition, anything not listed here is excluded.

Note that this concern does not extend to a complete definition of the system's requirements, which is the responsibility of requirements analysis. Scope definition should be brief, succinct, and easily understood by all stakeholders without going into a lot of detail. It is usually defined in the form of a high-level list of the system's key capabilities or requirements, and it may also be useful to highlight some functional exclusions explicitly for the avoidance of doubt.

Clear definition and agreement of scope are vital early milestones of any system development project. Ideally the scope has already been defined for you, in which case you may limit yourself to summarizing it in the Context view and ratifying it with stakeholders as the AD develops. If the scope is not defined, you may need to do this yourself, again based on input from your stakeholders.

EXAMPLE The scope definition for a simple online retailer might include the following capabilities.

- Present the retailer's catalog to the user, including pictures and product specifications
- Provide a flexible search facility (search on product name, type, keyword, size, and so on)
- Accept orders for goods
- Accept payment by credit card (with asynchronous approval and notification to the customer)
- Provide automated interfaces into back-end systems for fulfillment

The exclusions for the first version of such a system might be:

- The ability to amend or cancel orders (this will need to be done over the telephone but is planned to be automated in a subsequent release)
- The ability to make payments by means other than credit card
- Display of live stock levels and the ability to reserve out-of-stock items

Identity of External Entities and Services and Data Used

An *external entity* is any system, organization, or person with which this system interacts in some way, for example:

- Another system that runs in the same organization as the system being modeled (we refer to these as "internal systems")
- Another system that runs in another organization (we refer to these as "external systems")
- A gateway or other implementation component that has the effect of hiding other systems (which may themselves be internal or external)
- A data store that is external to the system (for example, a shared database or data warehouse)
- A peripheral or other physical device that is external to the system (such as a shared messaging appliance or enterprise search engine)
- A user, a class of user, or some other person or role, such as operational or support staff

Each external entity will implement and offer some services, and manage and provide some data, that are used by this system. Similarly, each external entity will use some services and/or data offered by this one. External entities that do none of these things are not normally of interest.

Note that in this chapter we use the term *services* to refer to functionality that systems provide for each other. This important concept is relevant whether it is implemented by a formal service-oriented architecture (SOA), or some other, more traditional means such as messaging or file transfer.

Nature and Characteristics of External Entities

The quality properties of external entities, such as system stability and availability, performance and throughput capabilities, physical location, or data quality, may significantly affect the architecture of the system.

EXAMPLE A travel booking system exchanges information with many other systems located around the world. Some of these systems in more exotic locations may be only intermittently available, because of time zone differences or because they are more liable to failure. However, a failed communication with such a system might result in a customer's booking being lost, which is highly undesirable.

The travel system's interfaces with external systems will therefore need to be carefully designed. All failed interactions should be automatically re-tried a configurable number of times, and these retry attempts should be logged to a database so that operational staff can monitor trends. Interactions will need to be designed so that they can potentially be submitted multiple times without error (this is known as "idempotence"). It should be possible to restart very large transfers that fail partway through from the point of failure rather than having to retransmit the whole file.

The quality properties to be considered are exactly those properties that are defined in Part IV of the book, The Perspective Catalog.

However, it is only the "externally visible" properties that need to be considered—it is not normally necessary to consider the internal properties of external systems. For example, an external system may have some unreliable internal components but mask this to the outside world using load distribution techniques to give a high level of external availability. Similarly, you need only consider those interfaces that you will need to use—it is not necessary to understand or document every interface of each of your external entities.

It may be necessary to consider the "nature" of external entities that are not systems. For example, a user may not speak the primary language of the system, or a peripheral such as a shared fax gateway may have performance characteristics that need to be taken into consideration.

Identity and Responsibilities of External Interfaces

For each external entity, the nature of all interfaces between it and this system should be identified. Such an interface may serve one of the following purposes.

- *Data provider or consumer*: The external system supplies data directly to this system or receives data directly from it.
- *Service provider or consumer*: The external system is requested to perform some action by this system or requests some action of this system (e.g., a service call), and the service may return data and/or status information in response to the request.
- *Event provider or consumer*: The external system publishes events that this system wishes to be notified of, or this system publishes events that the external system wishes to be notified of.

For data provider and consumer interfaces, the concern identifies the content, scope, and meaning of the data to be transferred.

For service interactions, the concern identifies the semantics of the request (the nature of what is being requested and any parameters); the actions to be taken by the system fulfilling the request; any data to be returned; any acknowledgment, status, or error information that may be returned; and any exception actions to be taken by either side.

For event provider and consumer interfaces, the concern identifies the events of interest, their meaning and content, and the volume and likely timing of their occurrence.

It may be appropriate to go into more detail for more complex interactions between this system and external entities, such as a payment authorization which must be followed by a payment request.

Nature and Characteristics of External Interfaces

The quality properties of external interfaces may differ significantly from the quality properties of the systems at the other end. For example, there may be a low-bandwidth, relatively unreliable data link to a highly resilient system in another country. The interface is the constraining factor in this case and again will have a significant effect on the architecture of the system.

System characteristics include the following:

- The expected volumes—number of requests or transfers, size of data, seasonal fluctuations, and expected growth over time
- Whether interactions are scheduled (occurring at predefined times), occur in response to events, or are ad hoc

- Whether interactions are completely automated, completely manual (e.g., a user saves a file or sends an e-mail), or somewhere in between
- Whether interactions are transactional—that is, they are required to complete fully or not at all
- Criticality and timeliness—for example, a particular interaction that may be required to complete before the end of the business day in order to be captured by an auditing or accounting system
- Whether interactions are batch (large data sets transferred as a "unit"), message-based, or streaming in nature
- What level of security is required (authentication, authorization, confidentiality, and so on)
- The service level that can be expected of the interface (in terms of response time, latency, scalability, availability, and so on)
- The technical nature of the interface and what protocols are used (open standards or proprietary)
- Data and file formats

Again, you can use the material in Part IV (The Perspective Catalog) to frame your analysis.

Other External Interdependencies

There may be interdependencies between this system and external entities other than data flows or function invocations. These interdependencies may act in either direction—the system may be dependent on an external entity or vice versa. Such dependencies can be subtle and are sometimes hard to find.

This concern identifies the nature of the dependency and may also articulate its architectural impact—that is, what capabilities or features need to be built into the architecture in order for the dependency to be observed.

EXAMPLE An online retailer accepts orders for goods over the Internet through its main e-commerce system. However, to fulfill an order, this system has to interact with a separate payment system to collect payments, a customer account details system to make any updates to the customer's account (such as shipping addresses), and a fulfillment system that dispatches the goods.

From the perspective of the e-Commerce System, it is dealing with three separate independent systems and can treat them as such. However, as can be seen in Figure 16–1 there is a data dependency between two of them that in certain situations must be taken into account. The Fulfillment system

FIGURE 16–1 ONLINE RETAIL SYSTEM DEPENDENCIES

in this organization contains its own list of verified dispatch addresses for each customer, and it will reject orders that are not being sent to these addresses. However, this list is maintained by data replication from the Customer Accounts System. When the workflow for a customer order involves updating dispatch addresses, the e-Commerce System must take this dependency, and the latency of the replication, into account. Otherwise, orders may be rejected by the Fulfillment System because their dispatch addresses are not listed in its database.

The architectural impact in the case of this system might be to allow for resubmission to the Fulfillment System after a delay if a fulfillment request is rejected or to delay orders that have associated address updates to allow data replication to occur. (Interestingly, having talked about the need to understand the details of external interfaces, this is an example that bears this out: The tactic of resubmitting failed orders can be made much more efficient if the interface to the Fulfillment System allows the reason for failure to be reliably discerned from the dispatch status returned by that system.)

Impact of the System on Its Environment

This concern addresses the impact of the system's deployment on its environment, both within the organization in which it is deployed and externally. This includes the following:

- Any systems that are dependencies and so may require functional changes, interface changes, or performance or security improvements
- Any systems that will be decommissioned (switched off) as a result of this system's deployment
- Any data that will be migrated into this system

Although these changes may be someone else's responsibility, they should still be itemized to ensure that they are being addressed by someone and their progress tracked. (We return to this issue in our discussion of functional migration and data migration in Chapter 21.)

Overall Completeness, Consistency, and Coherence

In most cases this system will be part of something much larger: the overall "application landscape." This may even extend to systems distributed across multiple organizations and linked together over private or public networks. Such application landscapes can be very complex and are often poorly understood.

A key concern of your stakeholders (particular users) is that the overall end-to-end solution provides them with the functionality that they need in a sensible way, irrespective of which system provides a specific piece of functionality or manages a specific piece of data.

EXAMPLE In the early days of Internet shopping, retailers worked hard to get their catalogs onto the Internet in a pleasing and visually compelling way. The overriding concern was to get shoppers to visit their site rather than a competitor's. However, many of these retailers did not put nearly as much effort into the behind-the-scenes processes for accepting payment, fulfilling orders, or dealing with exceptions. As a result, they lost customer goodwill and gained a reputation for poor customer service, and in the most extreme cases they went out of business.

TABLE 16–1 STAKEHOLDER CONCERNS FOR THE CONTEXT VIEWPOINT

Stakeholder Class	Concerns
Acquirers	System scope and responsibilities, identity of external entities and services and data used, impact of the system on its environment
Assessors	All concerns
Communicators	System scope and responsibilities, identity and responsibilities of external entities, identity and responsibilities of external interfaces

TABLE 16-1 STAKEHOLDER CONCERNS FOR THE CONTEXT VIEWPOINT *(CONTINUED)*

Stakeholder Class	Concerns
Developers	All concerns
Production engineers	Nature and characteristics of external interfaces, impact of the system on its environment
System administrators	All concerns
Testers	All concerns
Users	System scope and responsibilities; identity of external entities and services and data used; overall completeness, consistency, and coherence

While this concern is more the responsibility of the enterprise architect than of the application architect (see Chapter 5), giving it some consideration will improve your likelihood of success, possibly significantly. An overall solution that hangs together in a consistent and coherent way is much more likely to delight your users than one that is fragmented and misaligned.

At a minimum you should ensure that the main business processes appear to have adequate coverage, with either systems or defined manual processes. Similarly, all of the data required for these processes should be stored somewhere (in this system or externally) and be accessible by those systems that need it.

Stakeholder Concerns

Typical stakeholder concerns for the Context viewpoint include those listed in Table 16–1.

MODELS

Context Model

The context model is the main architectural model within the Context view and often the only one produced. It places the system clearly in its environment and relates it to the external entities with which it interacts, via explicit relationships that represent the interfaces to and from it.

The purpose of the context model is to explain what the system does and does not do, to present an overall picture of the system's interactions with the outside world, and to summarize the roles and responsibilities of the participants in these interactions. This understanding is essential in order to make sure that all who are involved in the development of the system (and in making any necessary changes outside of it) know what they are responsible for and exactly where the boundaries are. This avoids potential duplication of development effort or, even worse, gaps or inconsistencies in the solution.

The context model has a wide audience, being of significant interest to all of the system's stakeholders. For this reason it should use simple, familiar terms, avoid business or technology jargon, and aim for simplicity without abstracting away so much information as to be worthless. It often uses business language to name and describe the elements within it and typically focuses on overall functionality and information flow, rather than the technologies used to implement them.

The context model is usually fairly high-level and abstract, answering the important "why" and "what" questions about the architecture. It does not specify in any detail how the system or its interfaces will be built; these questions are answered in the other architectural views.

The context model presents an overall picture of the system in its environment and typically includes the following types of elements:

- The *system* itself, represented as a black box, with its internal structure hidden, since the Context view is not concerned with how the system is built.

- The *external entities*, represented as black boxes for the same reason. (Indeed, it is likely that the internal details of external entities are not visible or known.) For each external entity, it is important to capture some key information, namely, the *name* of the entity, the *nature* of the entity (e.g., system, data store, person, group), the *owner* of the entity, and the *responsibilities* of the entity from the perspective of this system (the services, functions, and data upon which this system relies).

- The *interfaces* between the system and the external entities, presented at a summary level, highlighting the key data items or function invocations across the interface. Often all of the individual interfaces between the system and each external entity are "rolled up" into a single interface, to make the diagram easier to follow. For each external interface it is important to capture an overview of the *interactions* expected over the interface, the *semantics* of the interface (i.e., the data exchanged and its meaning), the *exception processing* approach that will be used when unexpected things happen, and the key *quality properties* of the interface upon which this system is relying. In many cases, you will just capture a short summary of this information in the context model and reference external sources of information for fuller descriptions.

The context model is a vital communication tool with a wide range of stakeholders from business and technology. It is often used to summarize "what the project is about," identify who the external partners are, and explain the interactions with them. Since it has a wide audience of varying degrees of business and technical expertise, it should be kept relatively simple, and the context diagram should fit on a single page if possible.

FIGURE 16-2 UML CONTEXT DIAGRAM

NOTATION The two notations that we commonly see used for context models are UML and "boxes–and–lines."

Unfortunately, the UML standard doesn't define a context diagram. The assumption seems to be that the context of the system will be captured using a "use case" diagram, with the boundary of the system being represented by a classifier (class, component, or package) that contains the use cases, or simply by a diagrammatic annotation such as a rectangle drawn around the use cases. However, there are a number of practical difficulties with this approach, including the complexity of the resulting diagram, the fact that the use case list may not be available when the context diagram is created, and the convention that the external interfaces are made to specific use cases. In the context diagram, we really want to abstract this detail away and treat the system as a black box.

The solution to these difficulties is to create a UML diagram of the form shown in Figure 16–2.

This sort of UML diagram can be created using the "use case" or "class diagram" diagram editors of many mainstream UML modeling tools, although in fact it doesn't share a lot of similarity with either standard diagram. The key points about it are as follows:

- The system is represented as a UML component, stereotyped as a subsystem, a stereotype found in the UML standard profile, or with a more specific stereotype that you create yourself.

- External entities that cause human interactions with the system are represented as UML actors.

- External entities that are systems are represented as either further subsystem components or actors, possibly with their icons changed via stereotyping to be more representative of the entities that they represent (as suggested by the UML standard).

- Interfaces between the external entities and the system being designed can be represented as UML information flows, UML dependencies, or UML associations, optionally augmented with UML "conveyed information" icons that define the information flowing over the interface (which we don't show in the example but would be represented as small black arrowheads on the associations).[1]

While UML can be used to create a context diagram, it would be fair to say that the language does not provide particularly strong support for this type of model. For this reason, we often use informal boxes–and–lines notation instead, drawing something more akin to a "rich picture" of the system's context using a simple, ad hoc notation (and it's obviously important to define the notation clearly). Figure 16–3 shows the same system represented in boxes-and-lines notation.

The advantage of this style of diagram is that it can be much more expressive than plain UML, and it's probably easier for most people to create and understand than one created in strict accordance with UML. One of the major disadvantages, apart from your having to design and explain the notation, is that this model (or picture) is separate from the rest of your architectural models, assuming they're in UML. However, a number of UML modeling tools can now draw this sort of informal picture, which largely addresses this concern.

ACTIVITIES Definition of context takes place very early in the project lifecycle and is often rather ad hoc and unstructured as a result. It is also rarely under the control of the architect—you will be a participant and will provide input and feedback, but key decisions will probably be made by the senior stakeholders (typically the acquirer and some senior users).

It is possible to put some level of formality in place, however. At a minimum, a single document should be maintained and lodged in a place where everyone who needs access has it. It may be necessary to restrict access to the

---

1. Information flows and conveyed information annotations were introduced as part of UML
2. They are supported at differing levels of fidelity by different modeling tools, but they are a valid part of the metamodel, defined in the "Superstructure" specification [OMG10b].

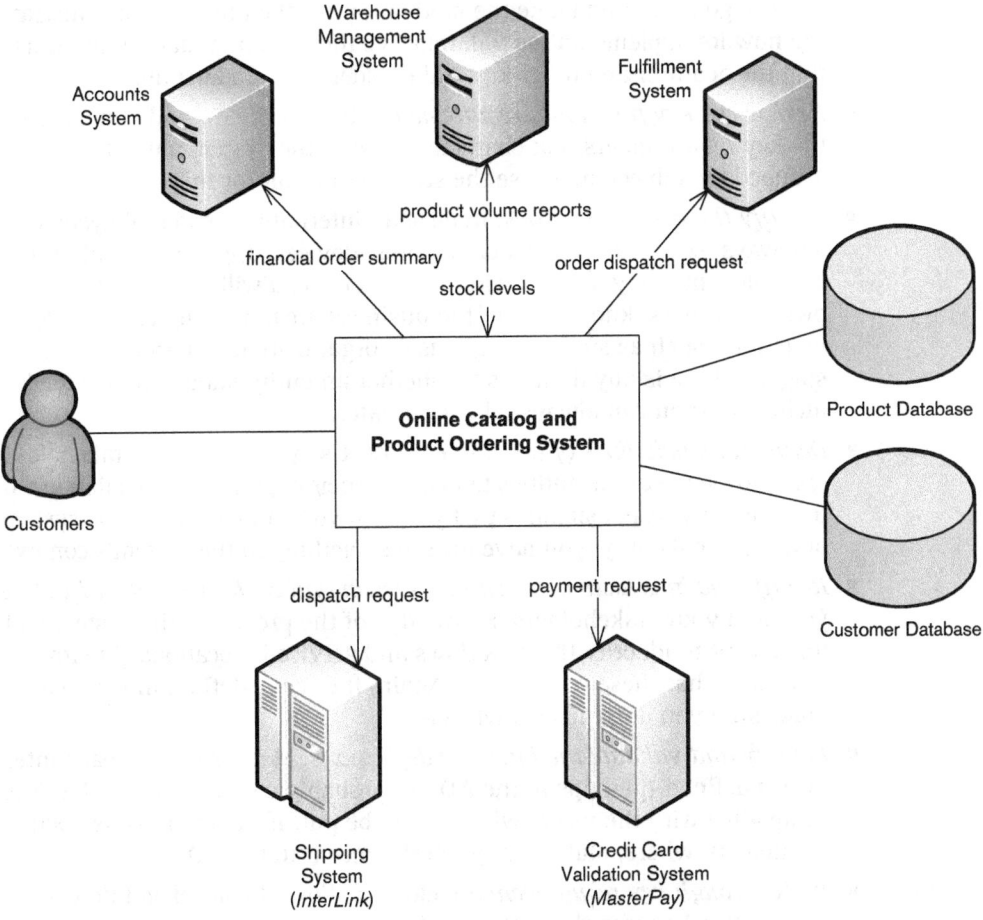

FIGURE 16-3 INFORMAL CONTEXT DIAGRAM

document to key personnel if the project is sensitive (for example, if it will lead to the retirement of existing systems or has contractual implications with suppliers). If possible, historical versions of the document should be retained along with a log of who changed what.

You will typically go through the following steps when preparing a context model.

- *Review the goals of the system*: Briefly review and capture the business and technology goals of the system—for example, "Reduce cost per transaction by 15%," "Streamline the ordering and fulfillment process, enabling better customer service," "Replace the current architecture with one that is more performant, resilient, and amenable to change," and so on. The goals should make the motivation for the project clear, illustrating how its implementation will improve the current situation, in terms that the acquirer and other key stakeholders can understand.

- *Review the key functional requirements*: Briefly review and summarize the key requirements that characterize what the system must do, grouped by subject area. Use the scope definition for this.

- *Identify the external entities*: Itemize all internal and external systems, gateways, services, external data stores, devices, appliances, and users and roles that may interact with the system. You will need to use your own and others' knowledge of the business area, and any existing documentation such as system diagrams or organizational charts. At this stage, if there is any doubt as to whether an entity should be included, include it—you can always take it out later.

- *Define responsibilities of external entities*: Use your and your stakeholders' knowledge of the entities to map out their expected responsibilities. If there are any responsibilities that you find you can't assign to the system or an external entity, you have missed something in the system's context.

- *Identify the interfaces between this system and each external entity*: Use your and your stakeholders' knowledge of the processes the system will implement to identify the data flows and service invocations (in either direction) that these will require. Again, the scope definition will help make sure you don't miss anything.

- *Identify and validate the interface definitions*: Make sure that each interface is defined (perhaps in the AD but probably elsewhere) and that it is compatible with the use to which it will be put. If the interface is documented elsewhere, make sure you reference it in the AD.

- *Walk through key requirements*: Follow the flow of control and flow of information between the system and the external entities. As you do this, add all the external interfaces that are needed to implement these flows.

- *Walk through scenarios or use cases*: If you have more detailed scenario definitions or use cases, walk through these to validate the model. Add or update any external entities or interfaces required.

Interaction Scenarios

It is often useful to model some of the expected interactions between your system and the external entities in more detail than is provided in a context diagram. This sort of model helps to uncover implicit requirements and constraints (such as ordering, volume, or timing constraints) and helps to provide a further, more detailed level of validation. While you are unlikely to have time to model all the scenarios in which your system will participate, it can be useful to model some of the more complicated, contentious, or less well-understood ones, especially when system usage is unclear or there is disagreement among your stakeholders.

An interaction scenario represents two or more *participants* (usually the system and one or more external entities), and a sequence of *interactions* between them, where an interaction is a flow of information and/or a request to perform an action. The interactions should collectively serve a specific purpose or implement a specific function. Refer to Chapter 10 (Identifying and Using Scenarios) for more detail.

NOTATION   Interaction scenarios are usually captured using simple textual interaction lists (rather like those used for use case definitions) or UML sequence diagrams that illustrate the interactions via a graphical notation. More detail is given in Chapter 10.

ACTIVITIES Refer to the discussion of scenarios in Chapter 10.

PROBLEMS AND PITFALLS

Missing or Incorrect External Entities

Most systems development projects tend to be relatively chaotic in their early stages (their teams are in their "forming" or "storming" stages in Tuckman's model of group development). Roles, even senior roles, may not be formally defined, and as a result context is often unclear and subject to frequent change. It is therefore easier than you might think to accidentally leave something out of the context model, include something that is not needed, or put the system boundaries in the wrong place.

Getting the context wrong can have a huge impact later on: Either the project will have to undergo significant change at a late point in the lifecycle, which adds considerably to its cost, duration, and complexity; or the delivered system will be incomplete or provide unnecessary functionality.

RISK REDUCTION

- Work with a wide range of stakeholders to ensure that their concerns are adequately reflected in the context model and interaction scenarios. For example, you should ensure that any functionality they require either is part of the system scope, is provided by an external entity, or is excluded entirely with the agreement of the people who need it.
- Involve a domain expert in this analysis as early as you can, and make sure that person is involved in review and sign-off of this part of the AD.
- Ensure that once the context model has stabilized, it is change-managed and subsequent changes to it are reviewed and agreed upon.

Missing Implicit Dependencies

It is easy to miss the subtle dependencies between external entities. For example, you may assume that a particular business entity or data item is instantaneously available in two external systems, when there is actually a significant latency due to the mechanics of data transfer. Or you could assume that the availability of an external system will affect only one part of your system, whereas in fact other systems you rely on are also dependent on it, making its nonavailability much more important to you. Such implicit dependencies can be hard to understand yet may have significant implications for the architecture. They should therefore be captured early and documented clearly.

RISK REDUCTION

- Assume nothing, work with your stakeholders to uncover and understand implicit dependencies, and ensure that they are documented in the Context view.

Loose or Inaccurate Interface Descriptions

It's tempting to get the basic idea of an external interface and leave it at that, hoping that the design process will elicit the details. In fact, you always have to do this to some extent as you can't understand every detail of every interface. However, it is important that you capture enough detail so that the architectural implications can be understood.

RISK REDUCTION

- Ensure that you understand your external interfaces in sufficient detail to use them confidently, and capture enough information about them in the Context view to characterize the effect they have on your architecture.

- Avoid the temptation to gloss over things that are complex in the expectation that problems will be resolved later.

Inappropriate Level of Detail

Getting the level of detail right is a challenge everywhere in the AD but is especially important in the Context view. If you provide too much detail, stakeholders, especially senior stakeholders like the acquirer, may become overwhelmed and fail to understand the big picture. Conversely, if you gloss over some aspects of the context or scope, expecting them to be fleshed out later, you may miss something important, mislead your stakeholders, or allow incorrect assumptions to be made.

RISK REDUCTION

- Look out for scope or requirements that appear vague because nobody understands what they mean (or people assume different meanings) and explore them further in order to ensure that they are understood.

- If the Context view becomes too detailed, move some of the information either into appendices in the document or into another view in the AD (typically the Functional or Information view).

- Consider applying some rules of thumb to determine whether your Context view is becoming too detailed. Although every situation varies, we have found the following rules to be useful in practice:
  - A context diagram should usually fit on a single sheet of paper.
  - A scope definition should not usually be more than 2 to 3 pages.
  - If there are a lot of requirements, they should be grouped by functional area, organizational responsibility, or some other logical category.
  - If there are more than, say, 10 to 20 external entities, consider whether they can be grouped by type (for example, a large number of suppliers of the same type of goods), or whether you really have a single system at all, rather than a collection of systems.

Scope Creep

Scope creep is the phenomenon of uncontrolled changes to system scope, which often occur gradually without being particularly visible to stakeholders. These changes usually have the effect of increasing what the system is expected to do, often without due consideration of whether this is sensible or achievable. For example, when interviewing users about required functionality, it is easy for each user to add a few more requirements to the mix that really are "nice-to-haves" rather than truly essential. By the time this process is completed, the system is significantly larger and more ambitious, possibly fatally so.

Scope creep can also occur once the scope has stabilized if it is not subject to well-managed change control.

RISK REDUCTION

- Challenge additions or changes to scope to confirm that they really are necessary and make sure their implications are understood.

- Work to help stakeholders understand the consequences of adding requirements, such as increased time to market, development and operational cost, or system complexity and stability.

- Ensure that scope changes are change-managed once the scope has stabilized.

Implicit or Assumed Context or Scope

More than in any other part of the AD, the scope definition is where you should state the obvious when there is any chance of misunderstanding. Don't be tempted to leave things out because "everybody knows that"—the odds are that there are some stakeholders who don't, or that some of these nuggets of information will get lost along the way.

RISK REDUCTION

▪ Don't be afraid to state the obvious in the Context view. You will be glad you did later on!

Overcomplicated Interactions

Interactions with some external entities (particularly older systems) can be a lot more complicated than expected, so it's easy to end up with unexpected problems when you come to build the interfaces. For example, some of the problems we have encountered when dealing with interfaces to long-established systems have included the need for unusual data encodings, poorly understood (yet complicated) conversational protocols, and complex and proprietary interface technologies that can cause difficulties for development, testing, and operational activities.

RISK REDUCTION

▪ Take the time to understand interfaces to external systems early in the architectural design process, and don't assume that they're necessarily the same as the interfaces you've met before.

▪ Find expertise in the interfaces that you need to use, prototype interactions with them, and test them thoroughly in order to understand how they behave in different situations.

Overuse of Jargon

Inputs to the Context view come from a wide variety of sources. It is easy, therefore, to make careless use of business and technology terminology that may not be well understood by the majority of your stakeholders. Since people are often reluctant to question things they do not understand, you risk confusion and misunderstanding.

RISK REDUCTION

▪ Try to avoid any terminology that is not widely understood. If you need to use jargon and there is any risk of confusion, provide a glossary.

Checklist

- Have you consulted with all of the stakeholders who are interested in the Context view (which is probably all of them)?
- Have you identified all of the external entities with which the system needs to interact and their relevant responsibilities?
- Do you have a good understanding of the nature of every interface with each external entity, and is this documented to an appropriate level of detail?
- Have you considered possible dependencies between the external entities with which you have to interact? Are these implicit dependencies documented in the AD?
- Does the context diagram adequately illustrate all of the interfaces from the system to its environment, with sufficient definition underpinning the diagram?
- Have all key stakeholders formally agreed to the content of the context model? Is this documented somewhere?
- Has the context model been placed under formal change control?
- Is the change control process being followed? Are stakeholders being consulted on changes and their consent obtained?
- Is the context model placed somewhere where everyone can easily find it, such as a public shared folder or wiki page?
- Have you identified all of the key capabilities or requirements of the system, and are they documented to an appropriate level of detail?
- Is the scope definition internally consistent?
- Does the scope identify any important technology constraints, such as mandated platforms?
- Is the scope specified at an appropriate level of detail, balancing brevity with clarity and completeness?
- Have you explored a set of realistic scenarios for external interactions between your system and external actors?
- Are other teams with which you interact clear on the context and scope and any implications for them?
- Have you checked the context model to see if there are any "obvious" statements that should be explicitly stated but have been omitted?
- Do the main business processes appear to have adequate coverage, by either systems or defined manual processes?
- Does all the data needed to support the main business processes appear to be stored somewhere, on-site or externally?
- Does the overall solution hang together in a coherent way?

FURTHER READING

Many software architecture books discuss the process of setting the context of the system; examples include Garland and Anthony [GARL03], which describes a Context viewpoint, and Bosch [BOSC00], which describes how to define the system context at the start of the architectural design process.

A number of requirements engineering books also discuss scoping systems. A particularly good example is Sommerville and Sawyer [SOMM97], which presents a clear set of guidelines around requirements capture, presentation, and ratification. Each guideline is accompanied by a cost/benefit analysis and practical suggestions for how it can be implemented.

Information on Tuckman's model of group development can be found in [TUCK65] and elsewhere.

17

THE FUNCTIONAL VIEWPOINT

Definition	Describes the system's runtime functional elements and their responsibilities, interfaces, and primary interactions
Concerns	Functional capabilities, external interfaces, internal structure, and functional design philosophy
Models	Functional structure model
Problems and Pitfalls	Poorly defined interfaces, poorly understood responsibilities, infrastructure modeled as functional elements, overloaded view, diagrams without element definitions, difficulty in reconciling the needs of multiple stakeholders, wrong level of detail, "God elements," and too many dependencies
Stakeholders	All stakeholders
Applicability	All systems

The Functional view of a system defines the architectural elements that deliver the functions of the system being described. This view documents the system's functional structure—including the key functional elements, their responsibilities, the interfaces they expose, and the interactions between them. Taken together, this demonstrates how the system will perform the functions required of it.

The Functional view is the cornerstone of most ADs and is often the first part of the description that stakeholders try to read. (Too often, it is also the only view of the architecture produced.) It is probably the easiest view for stakeholders to understand. The Functional view usually drives the definition of many of the other architectural views (particularly Information, Concurrency, Development, and Deployment). You will almost always create a Functional view and will often spend a lot of time refining the functional structure that it defines.

A major challenge when defining the Functional view is to include an appropriate level of detail. Focus on what is architecturally significant—in other words, what has a visible impact on stakeholders—and leave the rest to your designers. Avoid documenting physical implementation details such as servers or infrastructure in your Functional view, as this will overcomplicate your models and confuse your stakeholders. (You will document these elements in your Deployment view.)

CONCERNS

Functional Capabilities

Functional capabilities define what the system is required to do—and, explicitly or implicitly, what it is not required to do (either because this functionality is outside the scope of consideration or because it is provided elsewhere).

On some projects, you will have an agreed-upon set of requirements at the start of architecture definition, and you can focus in the Functional view on showing how your architectural elements work together to provide this functionality. However, in many projects this isn't the case, and as we discussed in Chapter 8 and Chapter 16, the onus will be on you in this case to ensure that there is a clear definition of what the system will (and won't) be required to do.

External Interfaces

External interfaces are the data, event, and control flows between your system and others.

Data can flow inward (usually resulting in an internal change of system state) and/or outward (usually as a result of internal changes of system state). Events can be consumed by your system (notifying your system that something has occurred) or may be emitted by your system (acting as notifications for other systems). A control flow may be inbound (a request by an external system to yours to perform a task) or outbound (a request by your system to another to perform a task).

Interface definitions need to consider both the interface syntax (the structure of the data or request) and semantics (its meaning or effect).

Internal Structure

In most cases, you can design a system in a number of different ways to meet its requirements. It can be built as a single monolithic entity or a collection of loosely coupled components; it can be constructed from a number of standard packages, linked together using commodity middleware, or written from scratch; or its functional needs can be met by using network-accessible services provided by systems external to this one or even to the organization. Your challenge is to choose among these many options in order to create an architecture that meets the requirements, exhibits the required quality properties, and is fit for purpose.

The internal structure of the system is defined by its internal elements, what they do (i.e., how they map onto the requirements), and how they interact with each other. This internal organization can have a big impact on the system's quality properties, such as its availability, resilience, ability to scale, and security (e.g., a complex system that crosses organizational boundaries is generally harder to secure than a simple one running on a couple of collocated machines).

Functional Design Philosophy

Many of your stakeholders will be interested only in what the system does and the interfaces it presents to users and to other systems. However, some stakeholders will be interested in how well the architecture adheres to established principles of sound design. Technical stakeholders, in particular the development and test teams, want a sound architecture, because a well-designed system is easier to build, test, operate, and enhance. Other stakeholders—particularly acquirers—implicitly want a well-designed system because it is faster, cheaper, and easier to get such a system into production.

The design philosophy will be underpinned by a number of design characteristics such as the examples listed in Table 17–1.

TABLE 17–1 DESIGN CHARACTERISTICS

Design Characteristic	Description	Significance
Coherence	Does the architecture have a logical structure, with the elements working together to form a whole?	If the architecture doesn't look coherent, this may indicate that the element decomposition is wrong, and it may make it hard for stakeholders to understand.
Cohesion	To what extent are the functions provided by an element strongly related to each other?	In a highly cohesive system, related functions are grouped together, resulting in simpler, less error-prone designs.
Consistency	Are mechanisms and design decisions applied consistently throughout the architecture?	A consistently designed and implemented system is much easier to build, test, operate, and evolve than one with a lot of accidental inconsistency.

Continued on next page

TABLE 17-1 DESIGN CHARACTERISTICS *(CONTINUED)*

Design Characteristic	Description	Significance
Coupling	How strong are the element interrelationships To what extent do changes in one module affect others?	Loosely coupled systems are often easier to build, support, and enhance but may suffer from poor efficiency compared with a monolithic approach.
Extensibility	Will the architecture be easy to extend to allow the system to perform new functions in the future?	Extensibility is often the result of other properties such as coherence, low coupling, simplicity, and consistency, but it is worth bearing in mind explicitly when considering your designs.
Functional flexibility	How amenable is the system to supporting changes to the functions already provided?	Systems that are designed to be easy to change are usually harder to build and typically are less efficient than systems that are less adaptable.
Generality	Are the mechanisms and decisions in the architecture as general as is practicable?	If the solutions embodied in the architecture are generic, the architecture will be amenable to extension and change. However, this must be balanced against any resulting increase in cost and complexity.
Interdependency	What proportion of processing steps involves interactions between elements as opposed to within an element?	Communicating between certain types of elements can be an order of magnitude more expensive (in terms of processing time and elapsed time), and significantly less reliable, than performing an operation within a functional element.
Separation of concerns	To what extent is each internal element responsible for a distinct part of the system's operation? To what extent is common processing performed in only one place?	High separation results in a system that is easier to build, support, and enhance but may adversely impact performance and scalability compared with a monolithic approach.
Simplicity	Are the design solutions used within the system the simplest ones that would be suitable?	Complexity makes systems difficult and expensive to build, comprehend, operate, and evolve, but a *simplistic* approach may well not meet the requirements of a sophisticated system.

In general, these design characteristics have a positive effect on a number of system qualities, particularly those relating to evolution, such as flexibility and maintainability. They also usually have a positive effect on other system qualities such as performance and security (e.g., separation of concerns and simplicity can make security easier to achieve, while consistency is likely to make performance

TABLE 17-2 STAKEHOLDER CONCERNS FOR THE FUNCTIONAL VIEWPOINT

Stakeholder Class	Concerns
Acquirers	Primarily functional capabilities and external interfaces
Assessors	All concerns
Communicators	Potentially all concerns, to some extent, depending on context
Developers	Primarily design quality and internal structure, but also functional capabilities and external interfaces
System administrators	Primarily functional design philosophy, external interfaces, and possibly internal structure
Testers	Primarily design quality and internal structure, but also functional capabilities and external interfaces
Users	Primarily functional capabilities and external interfaces

and scalability easier to achieve). In some cases, though, you need to consider the possibility of a negative relationship between "good" design and other system qualities (e.g., very loosely coupled systems can be less performant than more tightly coupled ones); in some cases this can mean the need to compromise over the design characteristics that can be achieved (we note the need for occasional design compromises in some of the perspectives in Part IV).

Principles and patterns are good techniques for defining how you want the design of the system to embody these design characteristics, as they can guide the system's designers to make design decisions that support the characteristics that you are most interested in achieving. We discuss this further in Chapter 8.

Stakeholder Concerns

Typical stakeholder concerns for the Functional viewpoint include those listed in Table 17–2.

MODELS

Functional Structure Model

The functional structure model typically contains the following elements.

- *Functional elements*: A functional element is a well-defined runtime (as opposed to design-time) part of the system that has particular responsibilities and exposes well-defined interfaces that allow it to be connected to other elements. At its simplest level, an element is a software code module, but in other contexts it could be an application package, a data store, or even a complete system.

- *Interfaces*: An interface is a well-defined mechanism by which the functions of an element can be accessed by other elements. An interface is defined by the inputs, outputs, and semantics of each operation offered and the nature of the interaction needed to invoke the operation. Common types of interfaces found in information systems are remote procedure calls (RPCs) of various types, messaging, events, and in some cases interrupts.

- *Connectors*: Connectors are the pieces of your architecture that link the elements together to allow them to interact. A connector defines the interaction between the elements that use it and allows the nature of the interaction to be considered separately from the semantics of the operation being invoked. The nature of the interactions between elements can be intimately bound up in how they are connected.

  The amount of consideration you need to give connectors depends on your circumstances. At one extreme—for example, when one element calls another via a simple procedure call—you can just note that one element connects to another. At the other extreme, such as a message-based interface, a connector can be defined as a type of element in its own right as it provides capabilities to the interactions that occur across it. As always, the focus needs to be on what is architecturally significant in the context in which you are working.

- *External entities*: As we defined in Chapter 16, external entities are other systems, software programs, hardware devices, or any other entity with which your system interacts. They are obtained from your system's Context view, and each appears in the functional model at the far end of an interface, external to your system.

The functional structure model does not define how code is packaged and executed in processes and on threads, so this view doesn't constrain element packaging or deployment—this is the domain of the Concurrency and Deployment views.

Similarly, it is generally not a good idea to model underlying infrastructure as functional elements, unless that infrastructure performs a functionally significant task, independent of the other functional elements, without which the view doesn't make sense. Infrastructure that simply supports the operation of the functional elements should normally not be shown in the Functional view; it is best considered in the Deployment view.

For example, you might well want to show message queues, as they are important interelement connectors and so the view doesn't make sense without them, but you probably don't need to show the message broker that provides the queues, which doesn't add anything in this context. The message broker would be shown in the Deployment view.

NOTATION You can use a number of techniques to represent the Functional view in a model.

- *UML component diagrams*: Using UML for a Functional view has a number of advantages, including its widespread comprehension and its flexibility. The main UML diagram you will use for the Functional view is a component diagram, which shows a system's elements, interfaces, and interelement connections.

EXAMPLE Figure 17–1 shows the typical elements in a UML component diagram. The system consists of two internal elements, Variable Capture and Alarm Initiator, interacting with one external element, Temperature Monitor. Variable Capture exposes one interface, VariableReporting, which is invoked by Temperature Monitor, and Alarm Initiator exposes one interface, LimitCondition, which is invoked by Variable Capture. VariableReporting is tagged with information that tells us it is an XML remote procedure call, over the HTTP protocol, and that, at most, 10 concurrent invocations can exist at one time.

You represent each of the system's elements and external entities with a UML component icon, annotated with its name and any stereotype needed to make the nature of the element clear. (Stereotypes allow you to extend the semantics of standard UML in a logical and consistent way to meet your individual circumstances.) One particularly useful stereotype is <<external>>, which indicates that the icon refers to an external entity, rather than a system element. Another is <<infrastructure>>,

FIGURE 17–1 EXAMPLE OF A FUNCTIONAL STRUCTURE IN UML

which indicates an infrastructure element of the system that has a distinct functional role.

UML interface icons attached to a system element represent the interfaces it exposes. We have found that the small "lollipop" interface icon is more effective in the Functional view than the larger stereotyped class icon. In order to differentiate between types of interfaces, stereotypes may be defined with associated sets of tagged values that allow the characteristics of particular interfaces to be captured (such as "transport"). Using tagged values to capture the type of interface, the protocol used to access it (if any), and the number of concurrent users or connections allowed provides a good basis for interface classification.

Once you have identified elements and interfaces, you can show the connectors between the interfaces with UML dependencies and information flows, as described in the following example.

EXAMPLE The UML component diagram shown in Figure 17–2 is an example of using UML to document the functional structure of a simple system. The system under consideration provides a Web storefront (called the Web Shop) for customers to use when purchasing items from an online catalog that fits into an existing enterprise software environment. (To save space, we have omitted the detailed descriptions of the system components and their interfaces, but obviously these would be crucial information for a real model.)

The model shows that the system communicates with four external entities: the Web browsers of the three main user types (customers, customer care representatives, and catalog administrators) and an external system (the order fulfillment system). Our system is composed of five main functional components linked via a number of connector types (including HTML over HTTP and publish/subscribe messaging, with an LU 6.2 external interface).

Customers order from the Web Shop, which interacts with the Product Catalog, the Order Processor, and the Customer Information System. The catalog administrators maintain the product catalog via their Web-based interface, and the customer care representatives maintain the customer information via a dedicated interface client program (the Customer Care Interface). When the stock level of a particular item in the catalog is needed, the Product Catalog accesses this information from the Stock Inventory (which already exists).

We also have some insights into the nature of the intercomponent interactions. We know that up to 1,000 customers, 80 customer care representatives, and 15 catalog administrators may access the system simultaneously. We also note that the interaction between the Product Catalog and the Stock Inventory components takes place using a specific protocol (presumably due to preexisting technology). We can assume for this example that the unadorned intercomponent communication takes place via some form of standard remote procedure call (which we will assume has been clearly defined elsewhere).

Having said this, one of the interesting points to note about this model is how much is *not* obvious from the diagram. The responsibilities of the components aren't clear, the details of their interfaces aren't clear, and the details of how the components interact aren't clear. This impresses on us the need to complete the textual descriptions that underpin the diagram and the need to understand the system via a number of models rather than just one (e.g., intercomponent interactions can be shown via system scenario modeling, as we described in Chapter 10).

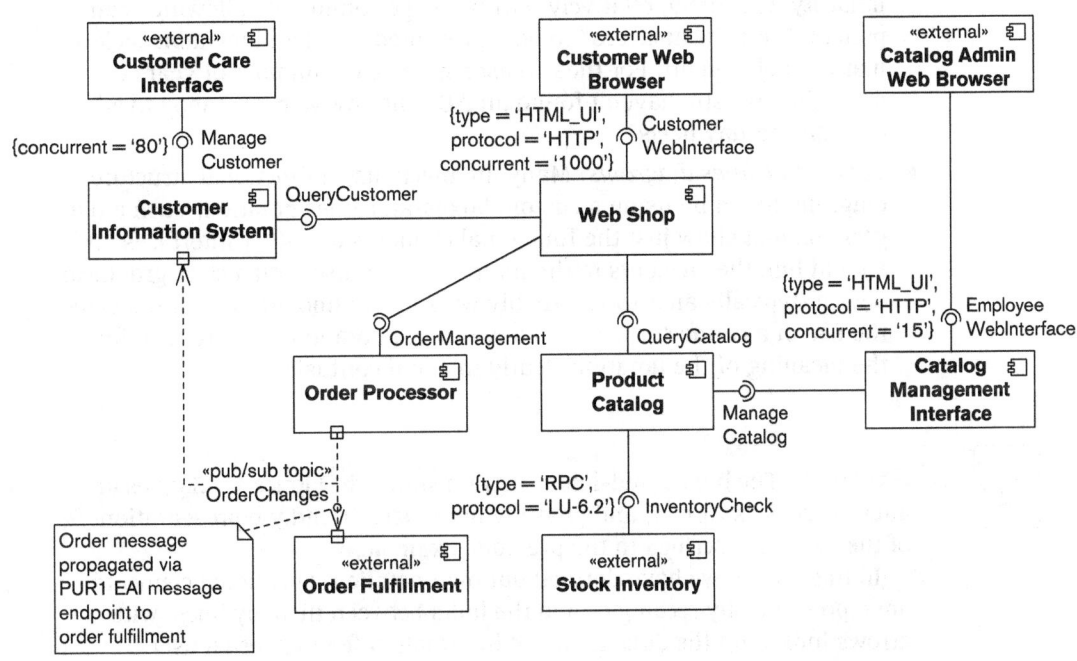

FIGURE 17-2 EXAMPLE OF A UML COMPONENT DIAGRAM

- *Other formal design notations*: UML is not the only well-defined design notation suitable for software development. A number of older structured notations (such as Yourdon, Jackson System Development, and the Object Modeling Technique of James Rumbaugh) have been successfully applied to software development problems for many years. The problem with using any of the notations developed for software design is that they tend to be fairly weak at describing the concepts (such as large-scale elements, interfaces, deployment options, and so on) that are important to architects. The older methods also aren't widely taught or used today, and so tool support may be difficult to come by, and they lack the general familiarity of UML for most people.

- *Architecture description languages (ADLs)*: Languages that do directly support the concepts that software architects are concerned with are generally known as ADLs. A large number of ADLs have been created (including Unicon, Wright, xADL, Darwin, C2, and AADL). The great attraction of ADLs is that they provide native support for some of the things that we need to capture and reason about in our architectural designs (such as components and connectors). However, nearly all ADLs have been developed in the research environment and tend to suffer from a number of practical drawbacks, including lack of stakeholder familiarity with them, relatively narrow scope (often only allowing "components" and "connectors" to be represented), and an inevitable lack of mature tool support. For these reasons, despite a number of years of searching, we still haven't found an ADL that we've been happy to adopt on a day-to-day basis.

- *Boxes-and-lines diagrams*: Many architects use a functional structure diagram drawn by using a custom boxes-and-lines notation. Such a diagram should show just the functional elements and their interfaces and should link the elements to the interfaces they use with a clear graphical device (typically an arrow, possibly with some annotation) that indicates the use of a connector. As with any custom notation, be sure to define the meaning of the notation clearly to avoid confusion.

EXAMPLE The boxes-and-lines diagram shown in Figure 17–3 gives an alternative, less formal, and possibly more user-friendly representation of the system described in the previous example.

In this model, we have defined our own notation. Functional elements are represented by rectangles and the links between them by lines, with arrows indicating the direction(s) of information flow. External user-facing interfaces are represented by an icon meant to look like a computer monitor, and external back-end systems are represented by rectangles with rounded corners. Data stores are represented by an icon that looks like a disk drum, and functional interfaces (the Internet, the message bus) are represented by a cloud icon. The scope of the system is those elements within the dotted rectangle.

The benefit of the boxes-and-lines diagram is that nontechnical stakeholders, particularly business users and sponsors, may find it easier to understand. Such a model can be an invaluable tool in selling the features and benefits of the system to these stakeholders without getting bogged down in technical detail. Often you may use the boxes-and-lines diagram as a front for more detailed, rigorous UML models.

Although the boxes-and-lines diagram can be used less formally than a UML model, you shouldn't use this as an excuse for being less rigorous. In particular, early in architecture definition, you should define a standard notation for your diagrams—and make sure you stick to it. Try to develop icons that give an indication of the underlying purpose of the elements modeled (e.g., the disk-drum icon shown in Figure 17–3 is often used to model data stores).

You should always support any such model with a definition of its elements and the interfaces between them, presented in a standardized way.

▪ *Sketches*: You can create a less formal feel for the view by using a sketch, that is, by introducing an ad hoc notation as required to represent each of the aspects of the view that are significant for your system. The use of a sketch is often required to effectively communicate essential aspects of the view to nontechnical stakeholders. The problem with this approach is that it can lead to a poorly defined view and confusion among stakeholders. As with the boxes-and-lines diagram, you can get around this by using a sketch to augment a more formal view notation (such as UML) and using different notations for different stakeholder groups.

Representing procedure-oriented element interactions is relatively straightforward, but modeling message-oriented interactions (such as those found where elements are connected via publish/subscribe messaging systems) can be significantly harder.

We used to model message-oriented interfaces by showing the message distribution mechanism (typically a piece of message-oriented middleware) as a functional element and connecting the various message source and destination elements to it. This does get the point across, but it's difficult to discern the overall message flow in the system. A better approach, originally suggested by Garland and Anthony [GARL03], is to use ports and information flows to model message-oriented interactions between system elements.

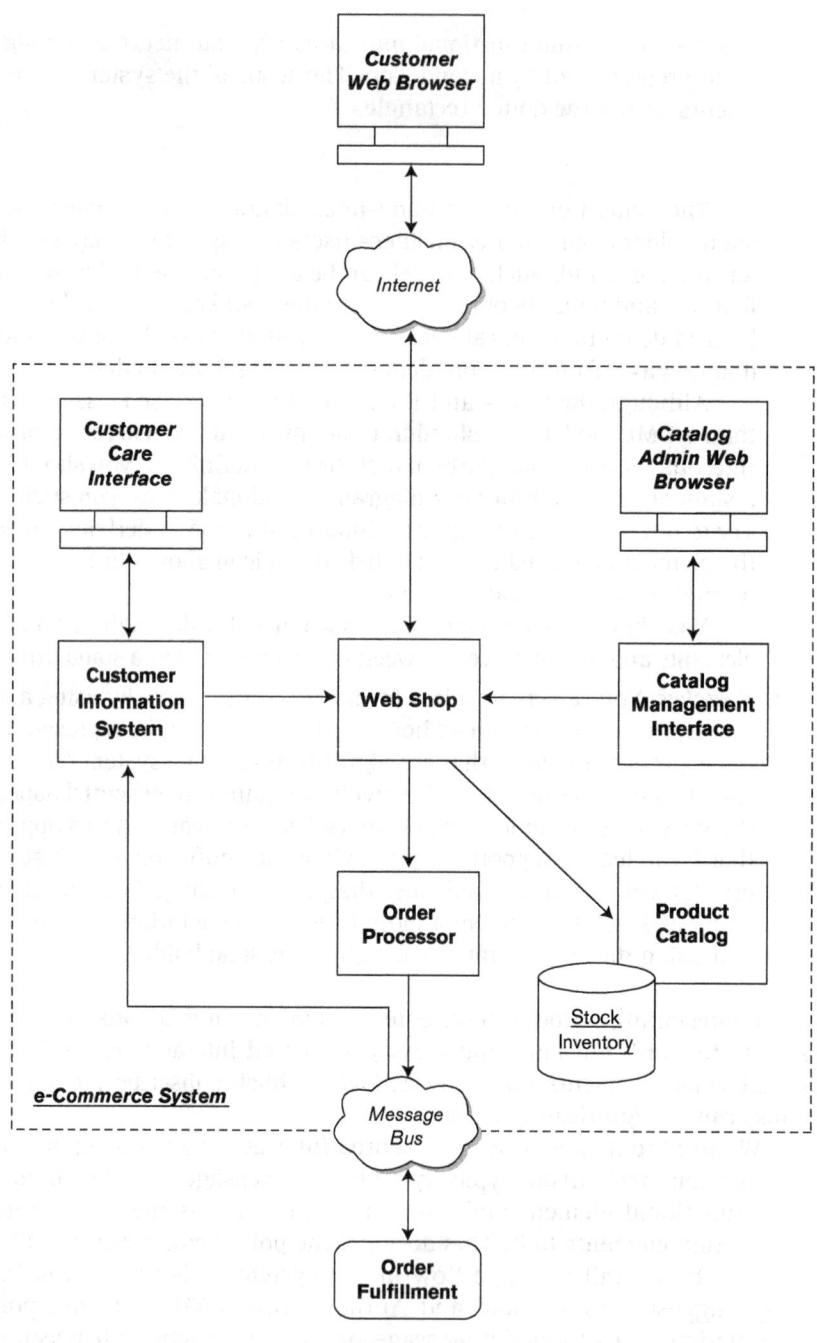

FIGURE 17–3 EXAMPLE OF A BOXES-AND-LINES DIAGRAM

The notion of ports comes originally from the real-time systems community, where a port is an abstract representation of the source or destination of messages. A more general notion of ports was integrated into version 2 of UML, and one of their uses can be to clearly show the messaging within a system.

EXAMPLE An example of using ports and information flows for messaging is shown in the UML model in Figure 17–4.

This diagram illustrates part of a notional system in a financial institution where prices are calculated by one system element (the Price Calculator) and distributed to the other system elements via asynchronous messages. The small boxes attached to the system elements represent ports. The one attached to the Price Calculator is an output port (it creates messages), and the ones attached to the other elements are input ports (they receive messages). A UML 2 information flow connector is used to indicate the message flow between elements, with a stereotype to indicate the type of messaging in use and the "information conveyed" annotation capturing the message type (publish/subscribe messaging and "Prices" in the example).

When the message-oriented interactions are illustrated by using a separate notation, they can be combined with procedure-oriented element interactions on a single diagram without fear of confusion. You can also use such a technique to model higher-level messaging systems, such as those that implement EAI architectures.

Remember that as we said earlier, a Functional view should describe only the system's functional elements. If you need notational items to represent deployment, concurrency, or other aspects of the system, your Functional view has become overloaded.

Note: When talking about system design notations, it's also worth mentioning the existence of SysML, a design language for systems engineering, which is based on UML 2 (SysML is actually defined as a UML 2 profile). We've been following the development of SysML over a number of years, and while it's undoubtedly a useful tool for people working in systems engineering, we haven't found it to be a better alternative to UML 2 for information systems design. SysML is aimed at situations where systems engineers need to integrate hardware, software, personnel, facilities, and other varied aspects of very large systems, rather than the more focused problem of the design of an information system. The sysml.org, omgsysml.org, and sysmlforum.com Web sites are good places to find out more about SysML and to track its evolution.

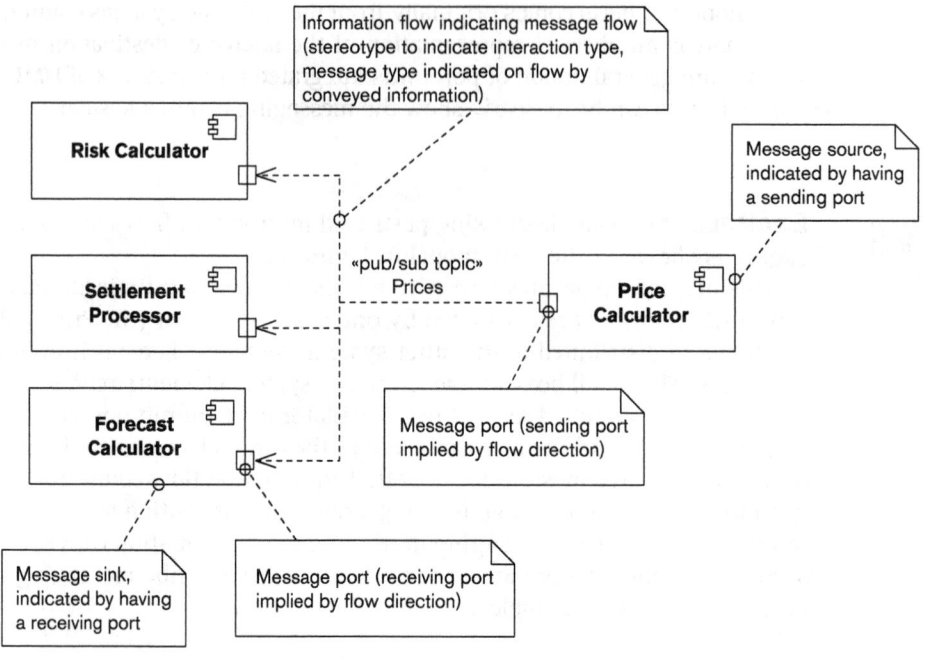

FIGURE 17–4 EXAMPLE OF A MODEL FOR MESSAGING INTERACTIONS

ACTIVITIES

Identify the Elements. You can identify the functional elements by following these steps.

1. Work through the functional requirements, deriving key system-level responsibilities.
2. Identify the functional elements that will perform those responsibilities.
3. Assess the identified set against the desirable design criteria.
4. Iterate back to refine the functional structure until you judge it to be sound.

Of course, some elements may be defined for you already (e.g., software libraries, software packages, preexisting systems or subsystems), in which case the process for these elements is one of understanding rather than identifying and designing.

Refining the set of functional elements involves applying one or more refinements to the functional structure.

- *Generalization*: identifying some common responsibilities across a number of elements and introducing a number of more general elements that can be reused across the system to perform these tasks. Generalization is particularly important as part of a larger enterprise or product-line architecture to allow reuse of software assets across a number of similar products or systems.

- *Decomposition*: breaking a large, complex element into a number of smaller subelements. For large systems, you will often need to break the top-level functional elements into more manageable subsystem-level elements to allow them to be designed and built.

- *Amalgamation*: replacing a number of small functional elements with a larger element that includes all of the functions of the smaller ones. Amalgamation is typically used when a large number of small but similar functional elements have been identified. In such cases, it often makes sense from an architectural perspective to replace the smaller elements with a single large element that can factor out the commonality between the smaller ones and reduce the amount of interactions the system requires.

- *Replication*: replicating either a system element or a piece of processing. An example is data validation, where you identify a validation element for incoming data and then replicate it across a number of the system's external interfaces. Replication can bring performance benefits, but care must be taken to keep the replicated components consistent.

If you are using an architectural style to guide your design process, the process is slightly different because it will involve creating an instantiation of the style such that the system-level responsibilities are assigned to elements of the style. This activity is closely related to the next step—assigning responsibilities to the elements.

We don't talk about the element identification process in a lot of detail in this book because there are many ways to do it, and the correct method to use depends on the type of system and the software development approach you are using. (Procedural, object-oriented, and component-based approaches all influence component identification in different ways.) See the Further Reading section at the end of this chapter for some sources that discuss element identification.

Assign Responsibilities to the Elements. Once you have identified candidate elements, your next activity is to assign clear responsibilities to them—that is, the information managed by the element, the services it offers to other parts of the system, and the activities it initiates. You may have done this in the previous step; if not, complete it here.

EXAMPLE Table 17–3 shows the responsibilities assigned to two of the elements for the e-commerce system described in earlier examples.

TABLE 17–3 EXAMPLES OF ELEMENT RESPONSIBILITIES

Element Class	Responsibilities
Web Shop	• Present customers with an HTML-based user interface they can access with a Web browser. • Manage all state related to the customer interface session. • Interact with other parts of the system to allow customers to view the catalog and stock levels, buy goods, and view their customer information.
Customer Information System	• Manage all persistent information about customers of the system. • Provide a query-only interface that can be used to retrieve information held on a particular customer that should be visible to that customer. • Provide an information management programmatic interface that can be used to create customer information management applications. • Provide an event-driven message-handling interface to accept details of orders placed by customers and the state changes of those orders.

Design the Interfaces. The services offered by your elements need to be accessed via well-defined interfaces. The definition of an interface must include the operations that the interface offers; the input, outputs, preconditions, and effects of each operation; and the nature of the interface (messaging, remote procedure call, Web service, and so on).

A good approach to consider when developing element interfaces is Design by Contract, an interface design method originally created by Bertrand Meyer for developing interfaces in object-oriented systems. This approach involves defining interfaces via "contracts" that use preconditions, postconditions, and invariants to precisely define operation behavior and relationships.

The appropriate notation for interface definition depends on the type of interface and who needs to understand this information (considering factors such as the likely implementation technology, the background of the development team, and the kinds of interfaces that need to be described). The following are some common interface definition notations.

- *Programming languages*: Interfaces can be defined directly by using a programming language to define the operation signatures along with text and/or language assertions to define the operation semantics. This approach is simple but ties you to the style, assumptions, and limitations of the particular programming language. This may not be ideal, particularly if you're using multiple technologies. This approach works particularly well for programming libraries or in other situations where the system is really a single, large programming artifact or where a single programming language is used to implement the entire system.

▪ *Interface definition languages (IDLs)*: Specialist IDLs have been developed to support mixed-language distributed systems technology (so there is an IDL for CORBA, an IDL for .NET, WSDL for Web services, and so on). These languages are independent of implementation technology and tend to offer simpler facilities than programming languages do, more suitable for defining architectural interfaces. Provided that your interested stakeholders can read (or be taught to read) them, these languages offer a good option for defining operation signatures.

▪ *Data-oriented approaches*: Interfaces can also be described purely in terms of messages that are exchanged. Examples of this type of interface definition include interfaces accessed via messaging systems and interfaces defined in terms of structured document exchange (e.g., document-oriented, Web-service-based interfaces with messages defined using XML Schema). This approach works particularly well for event-based interfaces that are defined in terms of the exchange of business events rather than the invocation of operations.

Whatever notation you use to describe interfaces, remember that an interface is significantly more than just a simple definition of how you call the operations. Unfortunately, none of the approaches we have described offer facilities for defining interface semantics, and so a clear definition of an interface will involve the use of natural language or specialist languages like Object Constraint Language (OCL) to achieve this. An interface definition must accurately communicate the pre- and postconditions of each operation and how the operations should be combined in order to perform a useful function (preferably with examples). Anything less than this is likely to cause significant problems when the interfaces come to be used.

Design the Connectors. The elements of your system need to communicate in order to achieve the system's goals, and as you identified your element responsibilities, you probably noted the need for elements to interact in order to implement their responsibilities. The interactions take place across *connectors* of some sort that link delegating elements to the interfaces offered by the elements to which they wish to delegate. Sometimes the type of connector required is self-evident (such as a simple procedure call), whereas in other cases you'll need to think carefully about whether you need synchronous or asynchronous communication, the resiliency required of the connector, the acceptable latency of interactions across it, and so on. For each required interelement communication path in your architecture, add a connector to the model to support it (be that RPC, messaging, file transfer, or other mechanisms).

Check the Functional Traceability. The requirements documentation for your system will have defined a number of functions that the system has to offer. You should carry out a traceability check to ensure that all functional requirements have been met by the proposed functional structure. Such an analysis often reveals missing or incomplete functions in the functional structure model. If it needs to be captured formally, the traceability analysis is usually presented as a table of functional requirements cross-referenced against the functional model elements with responsibilities relating to those requirements.

Walk through Common Scenarios. It can be extremely valuable and illuminating to walk through common system usage scenarios with your stakeholders, using the Functional view to illustrate how the system will behave in each case; doing this with the testers, the development team, and the system administrators can be particularly useful. In such a walkthrough, you should explain how the system's elements would interact in order to implement the scenario. Often, architectural weaknesses or misunderstandings as well as missing elements are identified as part of such a process. Such a walkthrough can form part of a larger architectural assessment exercise such as that introduced in Chapter 14.

Analyze the Interactions. Given the impact that excessive interelement interactions can have, it is useful to analyze the chosen structure from the point of view of the number of interelement interactions taken during common processing scenarios. Refining the functional structure to reduce interelement interactions to a minimum set without distorting the coherence of the functional components usually results in a well-structured system with cohesive, loosely coupled elements. It is typically an important step toward an efficient and reliable system. When performing interaction analysis, you need to make tradeoffs to ensure that reducing interelement interactions does not result in a distorted system structure with undesirable redundancy or inappropriate element partitioning.

Analyze for Flexibility. Successful systems are always under pressure to change. Given this reality, you should consider how flexible your architecture is in the face of change, as early in the project as you can. The functional structure of a system is often one of the primary factors affecting the flexibility of information systems. It's useful to work through some "what if" scenarios that reveal the impact of possible future changes on your system. A common problem at this point is that the changes implied by the change analysis conflict with those suggested by the interaction analysis. Therefore, it is important that you trade off these two factors during architectural evaluation in order to find the right balance for your system, and that you avoid burdening your design with complexity that will never be used. Again, assessing this can be part of your architectural evaluation activities; we talk more about this aspect of design in Chapter 28.

PROBLEMS AND PITFALLS

Poorly Defined Interfaces

Many architects define their elements, responsibilities, and interelement relationships well, yet totally neglect their connectors and interface definitions. Defining interelement interfaces clearly can often be something of a chore. However, it is one of the most important tasks you can perform for the system. Without good interface definitions, major misunderstandings will occur between subsystem development teams, leading to a range of problems from build errors to obviously incorrect behavior to subtle, occasional system unreliability.

RISK REDUCTION

- Define your interfaces and interelement connectors clearly and as early as possible.
- Review interfaces and connectors frequently to ensure that they are clearly understood.
- Do not consider element definition complete until interfaces have been designed.
- Make sure that interface definitions include the operations, their semantics, and examples where possible.

Poorly Understood Responsibilities

It is easy to become very focused on a couple of key scenarios and to consider the functional elements only in this context. If you don't define all of the responsibilities of the elements (and don't perform traceability analysis), a lot of confusion can remain over *exactly* what each functional element is meant to do. This often leads to problems later: Either functionality is missing because it fell between the gaps, or functionality is duplicated because two subsystem development teams both thought that a piece of functionality was their responsibility.

RISK REDUCTION

- Ensure that element responsibilities are formally defined as early as possible.
- Do not allow the development process to drift into element design without element responsibilities being formally defined and agreed upon.
- Make sure that all implementers understand where their boundaries are (and why they are there).
- Make sure that all requirements have been mapped to the elements that implement them.

Infrastructure Modeled as Functional Elements

In general, you should not model underlying infrastructure as functional elements. Adding infrastructure elements to the Functional view simply makes it more confusing without adding useful information. Infrastructure can normally be hidden inside the functional elements; the Deployment view defines the infrastructure in more detail. Include infrastructure elements only if their role is important to understanding how the Functional view works (e.g., you might want to include a messaging gateway that performs some functional processing for you, but it's very rarely the case that including the application server you are using adds anything).

RISK REDUCTION

- Avoid modeling underlying infrastructure elements as you develop your initial element model. Focus on functional elements that solve part of the problem the system is going to address.

- Question the need for any elements that do not have names related to the domain of the problem being addressed.

- Address specific infrastructure concerns in another view (typically, a Deployment view).

Overloaded View

The Functional view is the cornerstone of the AD and is often the primary structuring device. However, beware of letting it become *all of* the views rather than just the central view. It is often tempting to overload the Functional view with the intent to make things clearer by adding deployment or concurrency information or other aspects of the architecture to this view. If you decide to use a compound view, make this an explicit decision. Don't allow the Functional view to simply creep into being an overloaded description of many aspects of the system. Such a description is very unlikely to be easy to understand and therefore is of limited use.

EXAMPLE Figure 17–5 shows an example of what we mean by view overloading.

This model has a number of problems (even assuming that good textual descriptions are used to back up the diagram to form a complete model). It's obviously related to UML 2, but various bits and pieces of ad hoc notation have been added: the dashed line from the Socket Library box to the Web Server box, the dashed lines within the Server Node(s) box, and so on. This means that we don't really know what the diagram means and will have to ask the architect who drew it. We can probably discern enough for ourselves to continue, although some problems remain.

- The system provides a salesperson with an interface to allow something (perhaps a holiday or flight) to be booked.
- A number of server-side components (presumably Enterprise Java Beans, given the name used) implement something on a server computer. However, we don't know what components exist, just that (presumably) there is a group of them.
- The server components appear to be implemented by using a utility library that in turn uses a calendar library (presumably for specialist calendar processing for dates). This implies that a layered model is planned for the component design.
- A number of processes run on the server computers: one for the Web server, one for the application server, and one for the Oracle database management server. (We're interpreting the dashed lines as operating system processes.)

We can discern this sort of information from the model (and presumably could untangle the notation if we could talk with the architect); the real problem is the overloading of the diagram. Even in our initial understanding of it, we need to consider functional structure, deployment across machines, concurrency, software design constraints, and so on. These are separate concerns, at different abstraction levels, of interest to different stakeholders. The result is that none of the concerns are addressed very clearly, and this model probably can't be used with any of our stakeholders apart from developers and testers (and even they will probably need more detail about each of their concerns).

The overloading of the model is probably also one of the reasons that the notation is confusing. It is very hard to overload a diagram's function and not end up with notational confusion because of the need to represent a number of unrelated concepts together on one diagram.

RISK REDUCTION

- Remove everything from your Functional view except for items related to the functional elements and their interfaces and connectors.
- Create other views, based on the other viewpoints we define in this book, to describe the other aspects of your architecture.
- Develop the other views in parallel and cross-reference between views to illustrate other aspects of the architecture. (We talk about this in Chapter 23.)

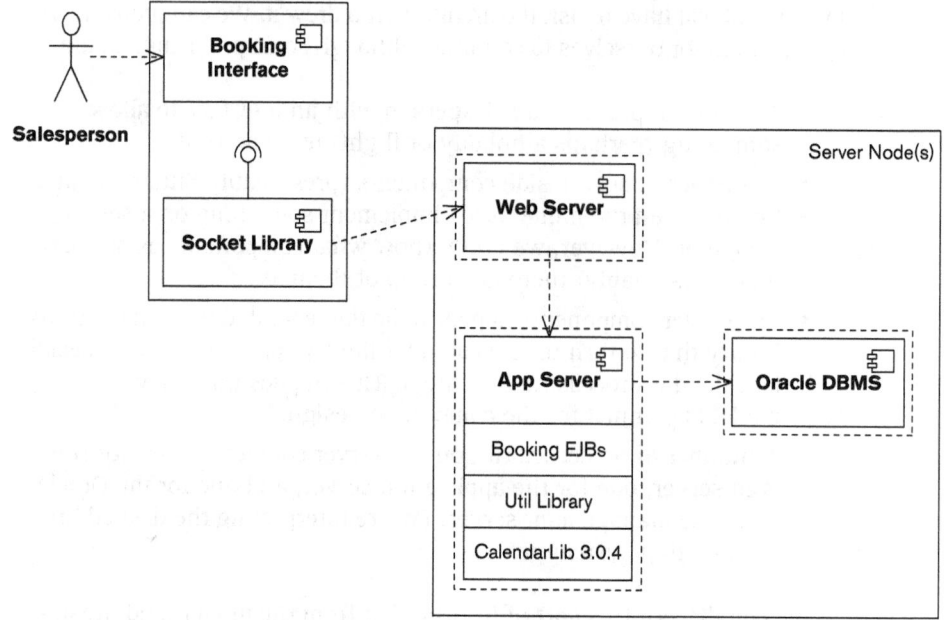

FIGURE 17–5 VIEW OVERLOADING

Diagrams without Element Definitions

When developing models that are inherently structural in nature (such as the functional structure model), there is a tendency to draw the diagram representing the model's structure and then to move on to something else without really defining the entities shown in the model. Defining each of the model elements carefully can be a tedious process, but unless this is done well, the model is meaningless.

RISK REDUCTION

- Define each element as it is added to the model, and review the definitions with your stakeholders to check that the definitions are clear and accurate.
- Do not consider the model complete until every element has a good definition.

Difficulty in Reconciling the Needs of Multiple Stakeholders

The central role of the Functional view means that most stakeholders are interested in it. This can cause you significant problems when formulating the view—how do you create a view description that means something to all of these different types of stakeholders? End users, developers, system administrators, and all of the other groups have specific interests and needs, and you often need to communicate with each in a different way. It is often difficult to identify a single model or notation suitable for use with all of these parties.

RISK REDUCTION

- Use different modeling languages with different stakeholders. In general, stakeholders break into two major groups—technical stakeholders and nontechnical (business) stakeholders.

- You can communicate effectively with the technical stakeholders by using your primary architectural models (such as the functional structure model). Some explanation of notation may be required, but on the whole a technical stakeholder will understand these models.

- The nontechnical stakeholders are unlikely to understand your primary architectural models, so you'll need to create simplified models for them, derived from the primary models. We have found that a less technical notation (such as the sketches we described in Chapter 12) with brief textual annotation is often a more effective communication medium here.

Wrong Level of Detail

A common question when creating the Functional view is when to stop. If the process of functional analysis becomes too detailed and ends up defining too many layers of elements, you are starting to design all of the software, rather than just the architecturally significant parts. This can cause real problems, not least of which is the lack of input from the development team. Conversely, if you don't include enough detail, there is a risk that people will misinterpret your ideas and the system won't be able to deliver the qualities that you need it to. Obviously, there is no simple solution to this problem—it depends on the context.

RISK REDUCTION

- Our experience suggests that if you have to define more than two or three levels of elements, assuming a limit of about eight to ten functional elements at the top level, you may have a problem. So, if possible, keep your level of detail below this limit.

- Another danger sign can be the inclusion in the Functional view's models of details about the workings or internal structure of functional elements. If your system is very large, modeling it as a group of systems rather than working down into the elements would make the problem tractable.

"God Elements"

Software designers often see object-oriented designs that have a single huge object in the center, with lots of small objects attached to it. This situation is often dubbed the "God object" problem. The underlying problem in such cases is usually an inappropriate partitioning of responsibilities among design elements—the large object (often called "Manager") is really the entire program, and the small objects are often just data structures that this object uses. A very similar problem can exist in ADs, particularly if you consolidate too zealously (perhaps as a result of interaction analysis).

This problem leads to a situation where the system is hard to maintain because the God element is terribly complex and difficult to understand. It also results in this one component's characteristics dominating the quality properties that the system exhibits. It becomes difficult to solve related problems like performance, reliability, or scalability because they all involve changing this one system element.

EXAMPLE   The UML element diagram in Figure 17–6 illustrates the sort of structure that often suggests the presence of a God element in your system.

In this situation, the Customer Management system element appears to exhibit the major characteristic of a God element, namely, nearly all interelement interactions involve it. From this structure, it is likely that the Customer Management element contains too much of the system's functionality and has dependencies with too many of the system's elements. Repartitioning the system into a set of elements with more evenly distributed functionality would make sense.

RISK REDUCTION

▪ Aim for a broadly even distribution of system-level responsibilities among your major elements. As a guideline, if you find more than 50% of your system's responsibilities concentrated in less than 25% of your functional elements, you may be heading toward a number of large elements and your system will lack cohesion, be difficult to develop, and be resistant to change.

Too Many Dependencies

The converse to the God object problem is static object diagrams that look like a number of spiders fighting for control. Complex interactions between elements

FIGURE 17-6 A GOD ELEMENT

make the system harder to design and build and may lead to a solution that is hard to change and performs poorly.

RISK REDUCTION

- This problem can often be the symptom of too many small elements in the system; practicing some judicious compression may help you resolve it.

- In general, a system element should need to be aware of the existence of only a couple of other elements in order to perform its functions. If any of your elements need to use services from more than 50% of the other elements in the system, consider revising your functional structure.

CHECKLIST

- Do you have fewer than 15 to 20 top-level elements?
- Do all elements have a name, clear responsibilities, and clearly defined interfaces?
- Do all element interactions take place via well-defined interfaces and connectors that link the interfaces?
- Do your elements exhibit an appropriate level of cohesion?
- Do your elements exhibit an appropriate level of coupling?
- Have you identified the important usage scenarios and used these to validate the system's functional structure?

- Have you checked the functional coverage of your architecture to ensure that it meets its functional requirements?
- Have you defined and documented an appropriate set of architectural design principles, and does your architecture comply with these principles?
- Have you considered how the architecture is likely to cope with possible change scenarios in the future?
- Does the presentation of the view take into account the concerns and capabilities of all interested stakeholder groups? Will the view act as an effective communication vehicle for all of these groups?

FURTHER READING

Many software architecture books focus on the functional aspects of architecture, and the subject is (rightly) central to those that take a broader view. In addition to the many books we mentioned in Parts I and II, the following are relevant to the concepts we introduced in this chapter.

Clements et al. [CLEM03] is a detailed, thorough, and practical guide to documenting various architectural styles. In the context of this chapter, the discussions of overloading views and documenting the various styles of interfaces are particularly pertinent. Garland and Anthony [GARL03] describes how to go about designing the software architecture for large-scale information systems; the approach we suggest for modeling message-oriented element interactions comes from this book. The techniques we outline for element identification are based on the architectural "unit operations" described in Bass et al. [BASS03], where they are described more fully.

Many good books explain UML in a tutorial style [FOWL03a, MILE06], and there are a number that focus on how to use it to produce rigorous architectural descriptions [CHEE01, DSOU99]. Another timeless book that explains how to produce rigorous models is [COOK94], now out of print but freely available in PDF form (www.syntropy.co.uk/syntropy). Checkland [CHEC99] presents an approach to understanding real user requirements, using an informal diagrammatic approach called the "rich picture" (analogous to our description of sketches) to help communicate with end users.

Meyer [MEYE00] is the definitive reference on Design by Contract (and much more related to object orientation), and Mitchell and McKim [MITC02] provides a nice, concise, practitioner-oriented introduction to the approach. Wirfs-Brock et al. [WIRF90] is one of the original books on responsibility-driven design, and a refinement to the approach by the same lead author can be found in [WIRF02]. Finally, Shaw [SHAW94] is one of the first written attempts to explain why connectors between elements are just as important to models as the elements themselves.

18

THE INFORMATION VIEWPOINT

Definition	Describes the way that the system stores, manipulates, manages, and distributes information
Concerns	Information structure and content; information purpose and usage; information ownership; enterprise-owned information; identifiers and mappings; volatility of information semantics; information storage models; information flow; information consistency; information quality; timeliness, latency, and age; and archiving and information retention
Models	Static information structure models, information flow models, information lifecycle models, information ownership models, information quality analysis, metadata models, and volumetric models
Problems and Pitfalls	Representation incompatibilities, unavoidable multiple updaters, key-matching deficiencies, interface complexity, overloaded central database, inconsistent distributed databases, poor information quality, excessive information latency, and inadequate volumetrics
Stakeholders	Primarily users, acquirers, developers, testers, and maintainers, but most stakeholders have some level of interest
Applicability	Any system that has more than trivial information management needs

The ultimate purpose of any information system is to manipulate data in some form. This data may be stored persistently in a database management system, in ordinary files, or in some other storage medium such as flash memory; or it may be transiently manipulated in memory while a program executes.

Nowadays, many organizations possess massive amounts of information on their customers, their products or services, their own internal processes, and their competitors. Although some of this information may be hard to access, inconsistent, and inaccurate, it still represents a substantial asset—one that, if correctly used, can bring substantial benefits. We see this often in large systems integration projects that attempt to bring together information from a variety of sources to produce a consolidated customer view, an integrated view of the supply chain, or an accurate financial picture.

Formal data modeling and design can be a long and complex process. As an architect, you can do data modeling only at an architecturally significant level of detail. You need to focus on those aspects of the data model where getting it wrong would affect the system as a whole rather than just a part of it. Your task is to develop a summary view of static information structure and dynamic information flow, with the objective of answering the architecturally significant questions around ownership, latency, relationships and identifiers, and so forth.

You use the Information view to answer, at an architectural level, questions about how your system will store, manipulate, manage, and distribute information.

CONCERNS

Information Structure and Content

The structure and content of the information that your system manages are clearly significant concerns. Your challenge as an architect is to focus on the most important aspects of information structure, those that have system-wide impact, and to leave most of the modeling and decision making to the data modelers and data designers.

You should focus on a relatively small number of data items (entities, classes, and so on) and the relationships among them. Deciding which data items are important depends on the problems you are trying to solve and the concerns of your stakeholders. However, you should bear the following in mind when selecting the data items of interest.

- Focus on a small number of data items that are core to the primary responsibilities of your system or that your stakeholders view as particularly significant or meaningful. When considering the interests of the stakeholders, primarily consider your users, but also take into account the concerns of other stakeholder types such as maintainers.
- Focus on information-rich data items, rather than ones that have few attributes (e.g., type entities are typically less important in architectural information models). Choose data items that:
  - Are fundamental to the nature of the concerns being addressed
  - Are significant to the users or other stakeholders

- Have a complex or poorly understood internal structure
- Can have a significant impact on the system's quality properties, depending on how they are represented
- Are heavily used or volatile (the contents are expected to change frequently)

- In the early stages of developing your models, try to focus on abstract rather than physical information, and keep the models simple. Don't worry too much about formal modeling techniques such as relational normalization at this point.

- Your early models should typically align with and be driven by your system's functionality, and you should be concerned less with physical considerations such as location or ownership (although we address these issues and others in this chapter).

Information Purpose and Usage

Information can be used in different ways—to support operational processes, such as taking an order or making a payment; to present current operational status, such as stock levels or production rates; or to analyze historical information and uncover trends and patterns. While it is the same information in each case, the distinction is important in the design of information systems, since the different usage patterns often have significantly different information ownership rules and may require significantly different architectural solutions.

- Most information systems have at their heart a *transaction store* or online transactional processing (OLTP) database. The transaction store manages the information required to support day-to-day operational business processes. This information is highly volatile, and the system needs to be able to process a large number of concurrent read and write operations with short latency and high reliability.

- If the system has significant reporting requirements, this can put a severe strain on the transaction store. A long-running or complex query can disrupt access by operational users, leading to increased response times and lower throughput. For this reason, some systems implement a separate *reporting database* to service these large queries, which is fed in batch or real time from the transaction store. The reporting database is essentially read-only (apart from the incoming information feeds) and is optimized for complex ad hoc queries rather than updates, with many indexes and significant denormalization.

- The transaction store and reporting database usually store only information related to current activity, such as open orders, current stock levels, or today's prices. Some users require access to historical information, to look at individual transactions or to analyze and summarize the information in different ways. Historical information is usually managed in a separate *data warehouse*, sometimes called an online analytical processing (OLAP) data store. The data warehouse may in turn feed into more specialized *data marts*, which manage information from a specific domain or time period. The data warehouse holds a record of all activity going back many years and can be used to retrieve specific historical information or to analyze trends over time.

▪ Most systems rely heavily on *reference data* (sometimes known as *static*, *master*, or *lookup data*), which is the information on people, places, and things that categorizes or classifies the system's transactional information. It includes a wide range of business entities, such as calendars, customers, products, parts and supplies, prices, locations, employees, and external organizations. It also includes the "type" information (such as product type or employee role) that characterizes other information. Every organization has its own definition of what it classes as reference data, but it is almost always fairly static, changing relatively infrequently, and there is usually much less of it compared with transactional and operational information. As we will see shortly, reference data may not be owned by your system, which can be a significant architectural challenge.

While the distinction here may not be important in the early days of an information system, over time the system will amass larger and larger volumes of data. It will be much easier to hive off a separate reporting database, data warehouse, or enterprise data store in the future if the initial architectural design has taken this possibility into account and allowed for the impact of partitioning, speeds of different stores, data duplication between stores, and so on.

Information Ownership

In many architectures, particularly those that involve the integration of new and/or existing systems, information is physically distributed across multiple data stores and accessed in different ways. This situation, while often unavoidable, creates all sorts of problems.

▪ Which copy of a particular data item is the most up-to-date one?

▪ How do you keep synchronized any information held in multiple places?

▪ How do you deal with information that is derived from information managed and owned elsewhere, such as account balances derived from account activity?

▪ What validation and business logic should be applied to the modification of data items, and what assumptions can be made about data items that have been validated elsewhere?

▪ If the same data item can be modified in several places, how are conflicts reconciled?

EXAMPLE An insurance company employs a large number of workers who visit customers at home to sell them financial products. The company maintains a central database of customers and prospects, an extract of which is downloaded to each salesperson's laptop when visiting the office. Whenever a sale is closed at a customer's home, the information is stored in a holding area on that laptop until it can be uploaded to the central database later.

The company opens a call center that allows customers to update their details and also offers limited capabilities to sell products. This leads to an increase in the number of complaints for various reasons. Sometimes, details stored on laptops overwrite more recent data on the central database, and vice versa. In other cases, updates to the central database are rejected because they fail the central system's more stringent validation.

In order to address these problems, the architect first has to agree with the business stakeholders on some general rules about how to deal with update conflicts and failures (e.g., recent updates always override older ones). These rules are then coded into the central system and laptop applications.

A useful way to analyze these problems and develop architectural strategies to handle them is to develop a model of *information ownership*. The information owner (or master) of a data item is the system or data store that contains the definitive, up-to-date, validated value of that data item. The information owner always has the correct value for that information and can act as the final arbiter when any disputes over accuracy occur.

By defining the owner of each data item, you can ensure that your information consumers are always working with the right information and that your information producers write it only to the correct place. When this is not possible in practice, you can analyze potential conflicts and inconsistencies and then develop strategies to deal with them.

EXAMPLE A national system for registering motor vehicles operates from a number of semiautonomous regional centers. Each center is responsible for registering vehicles purchased in that region. Each vehicle must be allocated a unique number, but conflicts could arise because there is no real-time communication between the regional centers. (In information ownership terms, each center is a creator of the vehicle registration number data item.)

> The problem is resolved by partitioning the information ownership, that is, by allocating to each center a separate, distinct range of numbers to assign to vehicles purchased in its area. Care must be taken to ensure that the ranges will never overlap. This is done by making each range far larger than the anticipated number of cars to be registered: The North center is given the range 1 to 100 million, the West center 101 million to 200 million, and so on.

A by-product, incidentally, of your information ownership analysis will be a high-level definition of some of your system's interfaces. Where one system is an information owner and another is an information consumer (or maintains a copy of that information), some sort of interface is required between them. You can use the interface definitions to cross-check the models in your Information view against the models in your Functional view. Any interface derived from information ownership rules should also exist as a process flow between the two participants.

Enterprise-Owned Information

Nowadays many large organizations maintain "enterprise" sources of important information, and you are usually required to use them rather than owning and managing such information yourself. Enterprise information is usually highly valuable to the organization, and the consequences (to you, and to the organization as a whole) of it being incorrect or out-of-date are severe.

The most common form of enterprise information is enterprise reference data. (As we described earlier, reference data is the information on people, places, and things that categorizes or classifies your system's transactional information.) This may be general-purpose information, such as country codes or currencies, or it may be specific to your organization, such as products, suppliers, or customers. You may also need to make use of more volatile enterprise information, such as end-of-day stock levels or account balances.

Your system may be expected to access enterprise information directly from the source system when it needs it, or it may be required to maintain its own copy that is refreshed regularly in real time or batch. In some cases your system may also need to update the enterprise information itself, using standard mechanisms and business processes defined by the information owner.

In any case, the enterprise information your system uses must be accurate, up-to-date, consistent, and complete. There are several ways this can be achieved, each of which has implications for users as well as for the architecture.

> **EXAMPLE** A travel agency has branches across the country and also sells directly to customers over the Internet and from a call center. The travel agency has started a customer affinity program and wants to build a system to make holiday recommendations to select customers based on their preferences, budgets, and travel history. The system will make use of various types of enterprise reference information, including details of holiday destinations, tour operators, airlines, and hotels. In addition, it will use more volatile enterprise information on standard pricing plans and special offers.
>
> All of this enterprise reference information is held in central data repositories but needs to be managed in different ways. Information on holiday destinations, airlines, and tour operators changes rarely, and a copy can be downloaded to the system's own database weekly. Hotel information and list prices are more volatile, and an overnight extract is required. Special offers arise at short notice, and a "semi-real-time" feed of these is needed (in reality, a small batch extract that runs at regular intervals during the day).
>
> Affinity customers sometimes like to suggest hotels they have used in the past but are not on the travel agency's database. In this case the system needs to be able to upload the hotel details to the enterprise store, and after some validation these should be added so that they are available for other systems to use.

As discussed elsewhere in this chapter, each of these different access models has its advantages but also may lead to problems. Data that is refreshed on an overnight batch schedule may be out-of-date when it is used. Obtaining data in real time mitigates this problem but is more complicated to implement and manage. Accessing a single central repository ensures that data is always up-to-date, but the repository becomes a bottleneck and a single point of failure, and it may not be feasible to do this for systems that are geographically dispersed.

We address some of these concerns further in our discussion of the Location perspective in Chapter 29.

Identifiers and Mappings

Whether information is managed by using relational entities or objects and classes, each data item needs a unique identifier or key that distinguishes it from others of similar type (e.g., customer number, machine serial number, or ISBN). In relational database terminology, this is called a *primary key*; in object-oriented programming, the term *object ID* is often used; a more useful general term (which does not assume any underlying information model) is *identifier*.

When information is spread over multiple repositories, identifiers often become an issue. Different systems may use different mechanisms to identify the same data item, and these mechanisms will need to be reconciled at points where data exchanges occur. Because key assignment can be a volatile activity (consider a sales system where many new orders are created per second), you will need to keep this reconciliation process up-to-date with new information as it arrives.

EXAMPLE A newspaper captures sports information submitted by journalists along with results and scores that arrive electronically. The paper collates the information and publishes daily league tables for individual competitors and teams. Although the paper's own central database allocates identifiers to each competitor and team, most of the information sources refer to them only by name—and in the case of foreign competitors, these names are not always spelled correctly.

The database is suffering some significant information quality issues. Scores and results are sometimes allocated to the wrong player or team, phantom teams with spellings similar to real ones are created regularly, siblings' results are often allocated to the wrong person, and some results fail to be loaded at all.

Problems like these can often be only partially addressed by architectural capabilities and features. Defining standard identifiers for teams and players in this example will help, but business process changes will also be required to ensure that users of the system carefully map names to their correct identifier—perhaps by being required to pick names from a drop-down list rather than type them in directly. However, imposing rules like these can make a system awkward to use, and you should collaborate carefully with your business stakeholders to come up with a solution that is both usable and effective (perhaps using an exception workflow to confirm the correctness of automatically matched identifiers, allowing partial automation with manual input to ensure data quality).

There are many other architectural challenges associated with the use of identifiers. For example, identifiers are normally *invariant*, that is, they never change over the lifetime of the data entity that they identify. However, it is not always possible to enforce this rule. In such cases, the mechanisms (and business processes) for creating and changing identifiers must be very carefully specified and designed.

There can also be some subtleties around the question of whether two data entities actually represent the same thing and should therefore have the same identifier. For example, every book is allocated an ISBN (International Standard Book Number) when it is published. A second edition of the book

> **EXAMPLE** *Derivatives* are financial products whose value is derived from the value of some other underlying asset. For example, a *share option* gives the purchaser the right, but not the obligation, to buy an agreed-upon number of shares at an agreed-upon price at an agreed-upon date in the future. The derivatives market is constantly changing, with new and more complex products being introduced all the time.
>
> When a new derivative product is created, it goes through an approval process to ensure that it is sound, that it is compliant with regulations, and that its financial parameters are clear. This process can take a relatively long time, and in the interim it is common for the product to be allocated a temporary identifier so that a provisional price can be quoted and measures of value and risk can be calculated. Once the product is formally approved, it is given a permanent identifier, which may be different from the temporary one since it is allocated by a different part of the organization.
>
> A link must be established between the two identifiers, so that the provisional quote can be turned into a firm quote and a sale made with a clear audit trail.

may contain only minor revisions and corrections, or may be substantially different, with a new structure and a substantial amount of new content. Should such a major revision be allocated a new ISBN? If so, how can it be linked to the ISBN of the first edition? If not, how are the two editions distinguished from one another? In this example, there are agreed-upon rules about allocating ISBNs, but in many cases it will be down to the architect to decide (or at least capture and agree on the requirements from users).

Another important consideration is whether your identifiers are going to be *user-visible* or not. For example, every debit and credit card has a unique 16-digit card number that the cardholder uses when making a purchase online or over the telephone. On the other hand, although each individual purchase on a credit card statement has its own identifier, this is not usually printed. If a transaction needs to be queried or confirmed, it is identified by the transaction date, the merchant name, and the amount (which is usually unique enough for this purpose).

Volatility of Information Semantics

It is common nowadays for the syntax, semantics, and interrelationships of business information to undergo frequent and unpredictable change. New fields may need to be added to existing entities, new constraints and relationships may arise, or new types of entities may be needed to meet changing business needs.

Although there are mitigation strategies to make such changes less painful (including abstract database access libraries, tools for impact analysis, and designing interfaces to allow for variation and change), even small changes to an information model can have wide-ranging implications for the systems that use that information. For example, if a new mandatory field is added to a database table, every process that creates or updates rows in that table needs to be changed so that it can provide a value for that field. This process needs some form of control, traditionally managed through a formal process of *data model change control*: The impact of a change on every module in the system is assessed, and only when all parties have implemented the required functional changes is the database change rolled out.

This approach is established and effective, but it drastically slows down the rate at which systems can be changed, and in practice change control often ends up being subverted or bypassed altogether. An alternative approach, which is more flexible while still retaining a level of control, is to decouple the information semantics from the physical structures used to store it. A common way of doing this is to store complex information structures in structured text forms such as XML, JSON, or YAML, either within a database or in external data files. With a disciplined approach, and the possibilities that exist today for automation, you can also take a more dynamic and flexible approach to changing a database schema, as proposed by the Evolutionary Database Design technique (see Further Reading for more details).

The XML family of data management standards includes mature mechanisms for defining the schemas of XML documents and accessing their contents. While changes to the schema still need management and oversight, they can often be implemented more quickly with less effort. The downside of this approach is that XML-based systems tend to be less performant and scalable, due to the XML management overhead and the fact that most database optimizers don't work very well with XML data.

Information Storage Models

The third-normal-form relational database is so dominant in enterprise information systems that it can be easy to forget that there are other approaches available for storing information. The following four major types of information stores are all in wide use today.

- *Relational databases* dominate the enterprise information systems landscape and need little introduction. A typical relational database contains a largely third-normal-form schema and is usually used as some form of transactional or operational data store. Relational databases are usually implemented using a third-party database management system and allow data retrieval and manipulation operations to be expressed in a declarative form using the SQL language. They typically enforce data integrity via an ACID transaction model (meaning that database transactions are used to ensure that updates are Atomic, Consistent, Isolated, and Durable—hence

ACID). Well-designed relational databases avoid data duplication (via normalization), are flexible (due to the ability to write queries in an unconstrained manner across the data model), can provide good performance and scalability characteristics, and are relatively easy to use for small and midsize problems. The limitations of a relational database tend to be the difficulty of scaling them to very large problems and the complexity of the schema and queries that often results when implementing a large enterprise application.

- *Dimensional databases* are another storage model based on the relational storage model and can be implemented using standard relational database engines, although specialized column-based or dimensional stores are often used instead. Rather than using a third-normal-form schema, a dimensional store is based around a multidimensional (or "star") schema model, with large "fact" tables containing the primary data in the database, linked to small "dimension" tables that contain classification data that can be used to group and summarize the fact data. (We describe multidimensional schemas in the Static Information Structure Models section later in this chapter). Dimensional databases are particularly well suited for complicated reporting problems, and so this storage model is often used for reporting databases rather than transactional databases. The major limitation of a dimensional model is the relative difficulty of updating information after it has been added to the database.

- *NoSQL databases* are a relatively recent development and at the time of writing are still fairly rare in mainstream enterprise systems, but they have proved their usefulness in many very large-scale Internet services for e-commerce, Internet search, and social networking.[1] There are many data storage technologies that classify themselves as "NoSQL" products, and each one has its own unique characteristics, strengths, and weaknesses. What is common among the NoSQL products is the fundamental tradeoff they have made, which is to abandon the traditional RDBMS characteristics of strict tabular data storage and SQL-query-based data access (and in some cases ACID transaction semantics) in order to achieve simplicity and very high scalability and performance. Most of these databases are accessed via a simple "map"-based interface that allows records to be stored and retrieved by key, sometimes also offering simple query facilities based on the attributes of the records being

---

1. In fact, the very first commercial database management systems were network and hierarchical databases, which also didn't use SQL. Since then, object-oriented databases, which also don't use SQL, have come and gone too. Here we're referring to the more recent database technologies aimed at solving very large, distributed data management problems that have been developed primarily to meet the demands of Internet-scale systems.

retrieved. This simpler model of data storage allows the database engine to be distributed across a very large number of servers, a configuration that provides good performance and a high degree of scalability. Of course, if you decide that you need a rich strongly typed database, or a powerful query-processing engine, these technologies are less suitable.

- *File-based stores* shouldn't be forgotten either, and even today, a surprising amount of enterprise data can usually be found stored in flat files. Files have the benefits of simplicity and ubiquity and, for some situations, the best performance too. They are particularly well suited to "write-once" requirements such as logging and auditing. Nearly every technology can read and write files directly, and there are a number of simple query engines that can be used with flat files to simulate a database. Of course, the simplicity of flat files can also make them unsuitable for many demanding tasks, where complicated queries, reliable transactional updates, or complicated data structures make the use of files difficult.

As an architect, you need a good awareness of the different information storage models available to you, and you should carefully consider the needs of your system so that you can match the right sort of storage model to your data storage requirements.

Information Flow

Just as important as the static information structure is the way that information moves around the system and is accessed and modified by its elements. The important questions here include the following.

- Where is data created and destroyed?
- Where is data accessed, modified, and enriched?
- How do individual data items change as they move around the system?

As with information structure, it is usually necessary to consider only the most important information flows as part of architecture definition, that is, those that are crucial to the system's primary responsibilities or those that will have a material impact on its quality properties. In any case, because you will have only a high-level data model to work with, you won't be able to drill down into too much detail here.

Because the main purpose of most systems is to process information, information flow is often analyzed within Functional rather than Information views. This works well as long as you don't end up with a small number of complex, overloaded models that are hard to understand—and as long as you make sure that the data-specific concerns discussed in this chapter are also addressed.

Information Consistency

Information consistency means that information held in different parts of the system, or in different but related data items, should be compatible, congruent, and not in conflict. This may be as simple as a referential integrity constraint (e.g., if a customer is recorded as owning several products of specific types, these products should all exist) or may be more subtle and complex (e.g., a summary financial position should always match the underlying data used to calculate it). Most businesses have sophisticated rules for information consistency, although it is rare in our experience for these to be written down anywhere.

Information consistency is so fundamental to the operation of modern relational databases that its significance in the architectural context can easily be forgotten. A classic example, which we repeat here, illustrates its importance.

EXAMPLE A bank customer uses an automated teller machine to transfer $500 from her checking account to her savings account.

The bank uses two data stores, CHECKING and DEPOSIT, to manage these two different types of accounts. The transfer is implemented as two updates: a withdrawal of $500 from CHECKING, and a corresponding deposit of $500 into DEPOSIT, as shown in Figure 18–1.

It's essential that either both of these updates complete successfully or neither of them do. For example, the transaction might not go ahead if the customer doesn't have sufficient funds in her checking account. If only one of the transactions completes, either the customer or the bank would lose money.

FIGURE 18–1 TRANSACTION MANAGEMENT FOR FUNDS TRANSFER

A *transaction* is a sequence of data updates that occur as an atomic unit—that is, either all updates are accepted and written to permanent storage or none of them are. Transaction management ensures the right outcome by *committing* updates (writing them permanently to disk) only if all updates can be successfully applied. Transaction management will *roll back* (undo) all of the updates if one of them fails.

Transaction management features are provided by all modern relational database systems, and their use is nowadays almost automatic (although care must be taken to avoid pitfalls such as heavy contention or deadlocking). Transaction management across multiple systems is much more complicated to design, build, and operate, requiring complex techniques such as two-phase commit. Such techniques can impose a heavy burden on processing power, leading to increasing latency and response time, and you should use them only when absolutely necessary.

An alternative approach that avoids some of the difficulties with distributed transactions is to use *compensating transactions* to maintain data integrity. In this model, each data update is committed individually, and if a later update fails, each committed update is reversed by a transaction with an equal and opposite effect to the original one. In the preceding example, if the withdrawal was successful but the deposit failed, a compensating deposit of $500 to the checking account could be applied to bring everything back to a consistent state.

Compensating transactions often work better in practice than two-phase commit since they do not require database locks to be held over separate data stores at the same time. However, they have problems of their own, particularly if changes cannot easily be reversed or if a compensating transaction itself fails.

Another approach is known as *eventual consistency*. In this model, distributed applications favor high availability over consistency and are designed to be able to cope with data that is out of synch for a period of time. Such a system guarantees that after an update, all instances of the same data will eventually be updated to this value, without guaranteeing how long this will take.

Eventual consistency is used for infrastructure software such as DNS (the Internet's Domain Name Service) and for some Internet-scale applications such as global search engines, e-commerce sites, and social networking sites, but the principles may also be useful to smaller-scale applications. The model is sometimes referred to as following BASE principles (Basically Available, Soft state, Eventual consistency) in contrast to traditional transaction management, which is referred to as ACID (because, as we noted previously, the transactions are Atomic, Durable, Isolated, and ensure that data is Consistent).

We also discuss the application of this technique as a way of scaling to very large data volumes in Chapter 26 and its relevance to achieving high system availability in Chapter 27.

Information Quality

The quality of a particular data item is the extent to which the current value of that data item agrees with the correct value in the real world. Poor-quality information can have a significant impact on an organization's ability to carry out its operations. If you don't have accurate information about your customers, for example, you risk annoying them, losing them, or even being sued by them. (Given all this, it is still a surprise how many systems manage to survive on information that is incomplete, incorrect, or outdated, proving the old adage that something is often better than nothing, even if it is imperfect.)

EXAMPLE A mail-order furniture company has created a marketing database from customer orders and requests for brochures or quotations. It uses this customer database to phone customers about special offers and to try to persuade them to buy more of the company's products.

Unfortunately, the data in the marketing database has been cobbled together from a number of sources and is therefore outdated and inaccurate. Moreover, a number of customers have asked not to be cold-called, but these requests have not always been transferred from the spreadsheet where they're managed into the marketing database.

As a result, many customers receive cold calls who do not want them, or are offered products they already own, or are offered unsuitable products (e.g., those that are too expensive). This creates a significant amount of dissatisfaction among existing and potential customers, leading to bad publicity and possibly to lost sales.

Information quality becomes an issue for you as an architect in cases where the system makes use of information from a variety of sources, particularly when some of these are external to your sphere of influence. If your information quality is variable, you must consider such issues as the following.

- How will information quality be assessed and monitored (especially when information is frequently updated)?
- What minimum information quality criteria must be met?
- How will these criteria be enforced?
- How will poor-quality information be improved? Will this be done in an automated way, or will it require manual intervention?

- Can good-quality information be corrupted by information of lesser quality? (For example, a customer address is updated, but the postal code is omitted.) If so, should this be prevented or checked?
- Is it possible for information quality to degrade as it flows around the system?

The answers to these questions are likely to have implications for your architecture. For example, it may be necessary to develop or deploy automated tools for monitoring or assessing information quality or for repairing poor-quality data. If repairing data needs some human intervention, you may have to set up a holding area where data can sit until it has been manually repaired.

It is becoming more common to use *workflow* to address information quality problems when repair processes cannot easily be automated. In this model, a list of tasks, such as correcting a customer's name or address or dealing with a suspect transaction, is managed in a central database. Tasks are assigned to users and the system tracks their status to completion. Tasks can either be standardized (defined at design time) or, in the most sophisticated workflow systems, ad hoc (created by someone at runtime). Service levels may be defined that commit the company to fixing problems within a certain time or at a certain rate.

If well designed, this approach can be an effective way of improving information quality and customer satisfaction.

Timeliness, Latency, and Age

If your information is held in a single data store and always accessed synchronously in real time, timeliness, latency, and age may not be significant issues. Unfortunately, many systems do not work this way, and it is inevitable that some scenarios involve information that is old or out-of-date, if only by a few minutes.

EXAMPLE   A commodity brokerage accepts a number of feeds from information sources that provide up-to-date pricing and volume information, as well as news stories relevant to the commodities being traded. The feeds are all channeled through a single gateway application that sorts, filters, and distributes the information to appropriate subscribers.

A catastrophic hardware failure renders the gateway unavailable for several days. When it comes back online, the subscribers are flooded with several thousand cached price messages that, because they are several days old, are of no interest to the recipients.

> The gateway is modified so that after a failure, it discards cached price messages that are older than a certain configurable age. Another failure occurs (a change of hardware supplier is called for), and recovery is much faster.

In this example we have separate *information providers* (the external systems that provide pricing and volume information) and *information consumers* (the internal users who make use of it). Because the process of information transfer from provider to consumer takes a finite (and possibly long) time, discrepancies can occur. If the time lag cannot be reduced to close to zero, you need to work with stakeholders to develop solutions to the problems that may arise from inconsistent information.

The time lag between the visibility of information to providers and to consumers is expressed by means of *latency*, the length of time between a data item being updated at the data source and the updated value being available to all parts of the system.

You may also need to take into account the age of some data items (the time since the data item was last updated by its data source). A system that disseminates information on volatile stock prices, or the physical location of trucks, for example, may not be interested in information that is hours or even minutes old. You may be able to discard this information because it is no longer needed.

You should identify key points where time-based inconsistencies can arise and, with the help of your stakeholders, develop strategies to handle them, such as the following.

- Tag important data items with a "last updated" date and time.
- Define "currency windows" for significant data items.
- Warn users when information may be outdated.
- Hide or discard information that may be too old.
- Reduce latency by means of faster interfaces or direct access to data sources.

Archiving and Information Retention

In many systems, it is becoming rare for information to be deleted; it may be kept for legal reasons or for historical analysis. Although disk storage is now relatively inexpensive, managing large databases is a complex process and even enterprise disk architectures cannot expand indefinitely, so sooner or later your information will grow to a point where it is not desirable to keep it all online. Then you will need to archive older, less useful information to some other storage medium such as high-capacity offline storage.

You must define carefully the scope of information to archive. It obviously can't be information that is still needed to support any production activities, nor should it be information that is likely to be useful for regular analysis. Information is usually selected on the basis of age combined with business rules to determine its usefulness.

Your archiving strategy can have a significant impact on your architecture.

- Archiving large volumes of information may make some systems fully or partly unavailable for significant periods of time.

- Your physical disk sizing needs to take into account the length of time that information will be retained.

- You may need to define the processes that move production information to archive media.

- You may need to take special actions to ensure the integrity and consistency of the production and archive storage.

- There may be an impact on the network infrastructure if archive storage is remote.

Don't try to add archival capabilities as an afterthought. Design your architecture from the beginning in such a way that archiving is a natural part of the information lifecycle.

Stakeholder Concerns

Typical stakeholder concerns for the Information viewpoint include those listed in Table 18–1.

TABLE 18–1 STAKEHOLDER CONCERNS FOR THE INFORMATION VIEWPOINT

Stakeholder Class	Concerns
Acquirers	Concerned with preserving and safeguarding the value of the organization's information assets, so the following are key (although not always recognized as such): • Information quality and archiving • Reference data • Information retention
Assessors	Interested in all aspects, with a focus on information structure and flow, identifiers and mappings, and information quality
Communicators	Rarely focus on detail on the information architecture, but may find a background understanding of the key principles and strategies helpful

TABLE 18-1 STAKEHOLDER CONCERNS FOR THE INFORMATION VIEWPOINT *(CONTINUED)*

Stakeholder Class	Concerns
Developers and maintainers	Interested in how the architect's models will translate into real databases and (real-time, batch) information interfaces, and implementation details such as how the data structures will support the required processing and how consistency will be guaranteed
System administrators	Interested in how these real-world system components will be managed and supported
Testers	Interested in the main database structures, how they are affected by the operation of the system, the data flow through the system, and how to create realistic test data sets
Users	Concerned with functional aspects of the information architecture (e.g., information ownership and regulation) and user-visible qualities such as timeliness, latency, and age; and information quality

MODELS

Data modeling is probably the best-served area of information systems in terms of established, rigorous, and generally understood analysis and modeling techniques. The three most important types of models are the following:

1. *Static information structure models*, which analyze the static structure of the information
2. *Information flow models*, which analyze the dynamic movement of information between elements of the system and the outside world
3. *Information lifecycle models*, which analyze the way information changes over time

We discuss these models in this section—particularly how they are used in the architectural context—and briefly describe some other types of models you may find useful, such as information ownership models, information quality analyses, metadata models, and volumetrics models.

Static Information Structure Models

Static information structure models analyze the static structure of the information: the important data elements and the relationships among them.

Entity-relationship modeling is an established technique of data analysis that is based on a solid underlying mathematical model. Data items of interest are referred to as *entities*, and their constituent parts are called *attributes*. The information semantics defines the static *relationships* among entities. Each relationship has a *cardinality*, which defines how many instances of one of the entities can be related to an instance of the other.

EXAMPLE A library stores a number of *books* for its *members*. Members *check out* books for a period of time, after which they are renewed or returned. Each book has one or more *authors*, who receive a fee each time a book is checked out. The fee is paid to the author via the book's *publisher*.

Each of the italicized terms in this description is represented as an entity in the entity-relationship model. Attributes of the model include book title, author name, ISBN number, and publisher name and address.

Class models perform a role similar to that of entity-relationship models but for the object-oriented world. They model data items (*classes*), their constituent data parts (*attributes*), and the static relationships among them (*associations*). It is possible to use class model notation to model relational entities by omitting the behavioral aspects from the model and limiting the association types (e.g., no generalization or composition).

Class models can also document the behavioral aspects of a system, such as interfaces and methods, and features specific to object-oriented analysis, such as inheritance.

EXAMPLE In the previous example, classes would be modeled for *books*, *members*, *authors*, and *publishers*. Methods would provide the necessary functionality for *checking out* books.

NOTATION There are a number of similar notation styles for documenting entity-relationship models. Figure 18–2 shows an entity-relationship diagram in the crow's foot style for the library example.

A UML class model for the same example would look something like Figure 18–3.

Data warehouses and data marts are usually modeled using more specialized semantics called a *star schema* (also known as a *multidimensional schema* or *cube*). A star schema consists of *fact tables*, which contain numerical data or other "facts" aggregated at many different levels and have large compound keys. Clustered around each fact table are a number of *dimension tables*, which model the different levels at which information can be aggregated. The chief advantage of using a star schema is that an aggre-

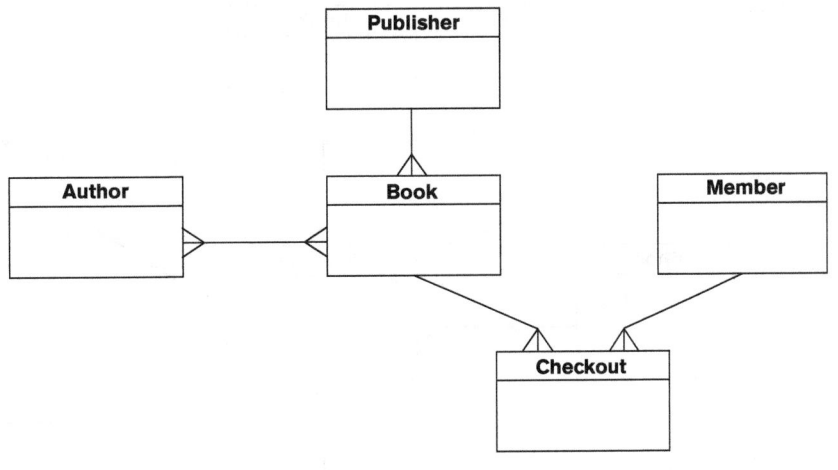

FIGURE 18-2 ENTITY-RELATIONSHIP DIAGRAM FOR THE LIBRARY EXAMPLE

gated value can be retrieved in a single database read, rather than querying and summing all the underlying transactions. A snowflake schema extends this model by normalizing the dimension tables into a hierarchical structure.

An example star schema for the library system is given in Figure 18–4 (although in practice a library management system is unlikely to need to manage the sort of volumes that would necessitate a data warehouse).

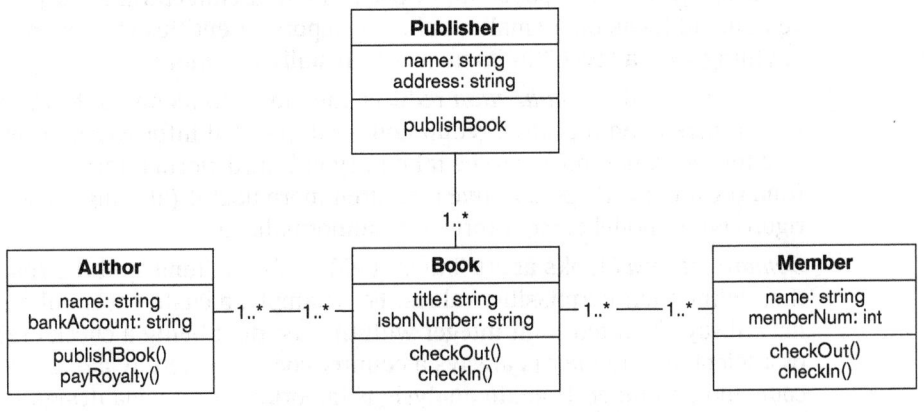

FIGURE 18-3 UML CLASS MODEL FOR THE LIBRARY EXAMPLE

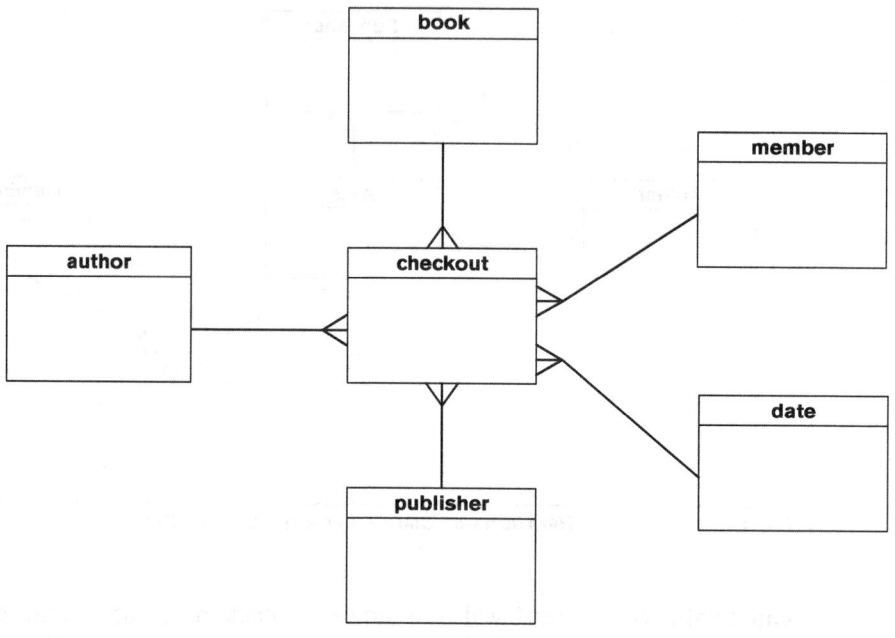

FIGURE 18–4 STAR SCHEMA ENTITY-RELATIONSHIP DIAGRAM FOR THE LIBRARY EXAMPLE

ACTIVITIES Formal information modeling includes a wide range of activities.

- The first step is to identify the important *data entities*. This is usually done by inspecting the business processes and use cases for nouns such as customer, product, payment, or event. In an architectural description, you should focus on a small number of important entities (for example, anything with a "type" in its name can usually be ignored).

- A process called *normalization* reduces the model to its purest form, in which there is no repeated, redundant, or duplicated information. It is rare for relational models to be taken beyond third-normal form, and from the architect's perspective it is often more useful (although less rigorous) to model some information unnormalized.

- *Domain analysis* looks at attributes (fields) of data items and the rules that define their permissible values. For example, a customer number may always be a ten-digit integer with the last digit being a check digit, or a telephone number is always a country code followed by a dialing code and a number. Domain analysis is important in schema design but is usually too detailed for an AD.

- Techniques such as *structural decomposition* or *aggregation* are used to derive class models. Structural decomposition involves breaking an element into smaller coherent pieces, while aggregation is the reverse process—creating a new element by combining other, similar elements.

Unfortunately, static information structure models are not easily decomposed into levels of detail—for entity-relationship diagrams in particular, it is, in theory, "all or nothing." In practice, you do not have time to produce a hundred- or maybe thousand-entity information model as part of your architecture. The way to approach this is to focus on a small number of the most important entities/ classes and the relationships among them.

You can usually omit from your model detail such as intersection entities (replace these with nonnormalized, many-to-many relationships, as we did in the entity-relationship diagram shown in Figure 18–3 between author and book) and type entities (such as product type).

As a very general guideline, if you have more than about 20 to 30 entities, or if your entity-relationship diagram won't easily fit on a single page, you have probably presented too much detail. In this case, you need to either remove some less important entities from the model or use partitioning and/or decomposition to simplify the overall picture.

Information Flow Models

Information flow models analyze dynamic movement of information between elements of the system and the outside world.

These models identify the main architectural elements and the information flows between them. Each flow represents some information transferred from one component to another—in other words, an information interface. Associated with each flow is a direction, the scope of the information transferred, volumetric information, and (in a physical model) the means whereby information is exchanged, whether it is a transfer of flat files or a real-time exchange of XML messages.

EXAMPLE A publisher supplies *lists of newly published books* to libraries in a PDF document that is mailed to librarians monthly. When a library receives a book, it is accompanied by an *electronic delivery note* in the form of an XML file, which is imported directly into the library's book management system. When books are checked out and back in, the *new state* is recorded by means of bar-code readers. When a book is disposed of, it is manually *marked as deleted* in the system by a PC application that accesses the database directly.

Each italicized term represents an information flow into, out of, or around the system.

As with static information modeling, you should aim to keep your information flow models high-level and simple. It is not necessary to provide much detail at the architectural stage. Fortunately, most notations support this naturally through decomposition.

Information flow modeling is most useful for data-intensive systems, and it complements the modeling of interfaces and function invocations in the Functional view (see Chapter 17), which is often more appropriate to processing-intensive systems. In practice, you usually do only one or the other, depending on the nature of the system, the skills of the architect, and the interests of the key stakeholders.

NOTATIONThere are a number of information flow notations from classic systems analysis, such as Gane and Sarson or SSADM data flow diagrams, although these are as much about process as about information flow. Figure 18–5 shows an example of a data flow diagram.

The following notation is used in the diagram.

- Large rectangles represent processes that manipulate information.
- Narrow open rectangles represent data stores (logical or physical collections of information).
- Arrows represent information flows.

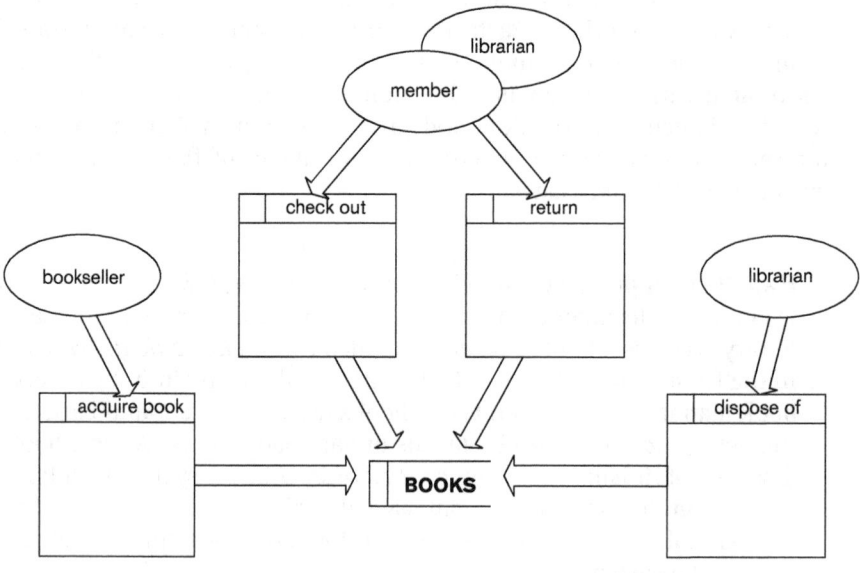

FIGURE 18-5 DATA FLOW DIAGRAM FOR THE LIBRARY EXAMPLE

- Ellipses represent external entities (people or other systems that interact with this system).

The diagram conveys several pieces of information.

- Members and the librarian provide information to the checkout and return processes.
- A bookseller provides information to the acquire book process.
- The librarian provides information to the dispose of process.
- All this information is written to the BOOKS data store.

Information flow is usually represented in UML using activity diagrams, which include the same sort of elements as shown in Figure 18–5.

ACTIVITIES Information flow models are typically created through a process of stepwise refinement, with the most important flows being considered first and then broken into further detail where necessary.

You can use your information ownership model, if you have one, to cross-check against the information flows required to maintain information integrity where ownership is distributed (as discussed earlier).

Information Lifecycle Models

Lifecycle models analyze the way information values change over time.

Entity life histories model the transitions that data items undergo in response to external events, from creation through one or more updates to final deletion. A life history can be a useful cross-check to ensure that there is processing to deal with all of the life events associated with an entity. In particular, it can help you ensure that entities are created in a controlled manner and that all entities have a means of deletion.

EXAMPLE A book is created when it is *published* (as far as the library system is concerned, anyway). The book is then *acquired* by the library and repeatedly *checked out* and *returned* until it is finally *disposed of*.

Each italicized verb in this description is an event in an entity life history for a book.

State transition models (or *statecharts* in UML terminology) model the overall changes in a system element's state in response to external stimuli. This is a useful way to model systems whose interactions with the outside world cause their internal state to go through many transitions in seemingly unpredictable ways. A statechart models a system element as a finite state machine (FSM). An FSM always has a current state, which is the sum total of the information it holds. When an external event occurs, the FSM changes deterministically to another state and may also instigate some special processing as a result of the change.

EXAMPLE A book is initially *published*; it is then *acquired* by the library, and once on the shelves it alternates between being *available for loan* and *checked out*, until it is *disposed of*.

Each italicized term represents a state of a book.

NOTATION An entity life history is usually represented by using some sort of tree structure, with nodes for each event and branches to represent iteration, selection, and so forth, as shown in Figure 18–6.

A UML state diagram uses railroad tracks to represent the possible state transitions of a book, as shown in Figure 18–7.

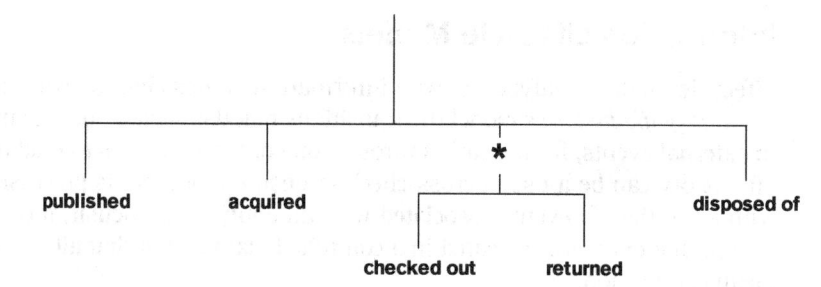

FIGURE 18–6 ENTITY LIFE HISTORY FOR THE LIBRARY EXAMPLE

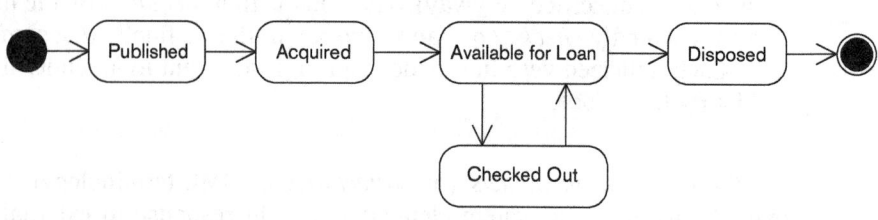

FIGURE 18–7 UML STATE DIAGRAM FOR A BOOK IN THE LIBRARY EXAMPLE

ACTIVITIES Lifecycle models are derived through an understanding of the system's functional requirements, by identifying all of the significant events and understanding the information impact of each.

Other Types of Information Models

INFORMATION OWNERSHIP MODELS Information ownership models define the owner for each data item in the architecture. In this context, "data item" typically means entity (table) or, occasionally, attribute (field), although more complex partitions can be modeled. Of course, in practice, life is never this simple, and you may have to model a number of different classes of information ownership, such as:

- Owner or master, which holds the definitive value for that data item
- Creator, which creates new instances of that data item
- Updater, which modifies existing instances of that data item
- Deleter, which deletes existing instances of that data item
- Reader, which can read but not change instances of that data item
- Copy, which holds a read-only copy of that data item
- Validater, which performs validation on the data item to ensure that it meets business rules
- A combination of these

At its simplest level, information ownership can be modeled by using a grid, with systems and data stores along one axis and data items along the other. Each cell in the grid defines the ownership class of that data item, as shown in Table 18–2.

It may be useful to develop a *trust and permissions model* to define which systems, under which circumstances, are allowed to modify which data items. For example, an external system that provides data updates in a weekly batch might be trusted less than one managed and monitored internally, might require further validation before updates are accepted, or might be constrained to updat-

TABLE 18–2 EXAMPLE OF AN INFORMATION OWNERSHIP GRID

System	Customer	Product	Order	Fulfillment
Catalog	None	Owner	None	None
Purchasing	Reader	Updater	Owner	Creator
Delivery	Copy	Reader	Reader	Updater
Customer	Owner	Reader	Reader	Reader

ing only noncritical data values. As well as being useful here, the definition of information ownership will be an important input to the process of securing the system, as explained with regard to the Security perspective in Chapter 25.

In practice, you may not be able to avoid having more than one creator/ updater/deleter for a data item (although it is useful to try to define a single information owner). This particularly occurs when valuable information is held in legacy systems. When two systems can modify the same piece of data, you need to develop *conflict resolution strategies*, such as the following, to ensure that business rules are followed and that information is left in a consistent state.

- Always accept the latest update.
- Maintain multiple copies of the same data item, tagged with their sources.
- Maintain a history of data changes rather than just the latest version of the data.
- Trust one system more than another, so that system's updates take priority.
- Create more complex rules depending on the data changed and the nature of the change.
- Record multiple values and require manual intervention to fix the conflict.
- Reject conflicting updates altogether.
- Use a combination of these strategies.

With multiple updaters a particular problem is detecting that a conflict has occurred. This can be addressed by stamping each record with an incrementing version number and the date and time that the record was last updated.

Although you are unlikely to define detailed rules as part of your AD, it is important to provide sufficient advice and guidance for your designers.

INFORMATION QUALITY ANALYSIS From the architectural perspective, your information quality analysis will focus on defining *sources* of poor-quality information and *principles and strategies* for dealing with this information. Possible strategies include the following.

- *Accept poor-quality information*: This approach is suitable when poor-quality information is not an issue or when the cost of repairing information far outweighs the benefit of improving it.

EXAMPLE An Internet search engine manages a database of many hundreds of millions of URLs. At any one time, a small proportion of these will no longer be valid because pages have been renamed or Web sites removed. However, it is not cost-effective for the search engine to regularly clean up its database to remove these links.

- *Automatically fix poor-quality information*: There are a number of tools available to do this, depending on the type of information.

> **EXAMPLE** You can use tools that will repair or complete addresses or telephone numbers, based on databases of postal codes or telephone dialing rules.

- *Discard poor-quality information*: This may be the best approach when the cost of bad information far outweighs the cost of not having the information at all.

> **EXAMPLE** A company receives bulk mailing lists of variable quality from an external supplier, which it uses to send out marketing material to potential customers. For about 10% of the data, postal codes are missing, invalid, or do not correspond to the mailing address. Such records are discarded because the company is penalized by the postal service if too much of its outgoing mail is incorrectly or incompletely addressed, and material sent to these addresses is unlikely to arrive anyway.

- *Repair poor-quality information manually* (in other words, get users to fix it): This is a very costly approach, however, and you must consider how poor-quality information will be identified and how it will be forwarded to users for correction.

Be aware that there may be legislative requirements for information quality (e.g., some countries charge penalties for maintaining or using incorrect information on members of the public). We consider this point further in our discussion of the Regulation perspective in Chapter 29.

METADATA MODELS *Metadata* is "data about data." Metadata consists of rules that describe and prescribe data items of interest—entities, attributes, relationships, and so forth. Metadata originated in the study of geospatial data and has had an increased profile in recent years following the growth of the World Wide Web and various initiatives around business-to-business communication.

ISO Standard 11197-3 defines metadata as "the information and documentation which makes data sets understandable and sharable for users."[2] Metadata may address a number of aspects of the information it describes, such as:

---

2. [ISO96], p. vii.

- Data format (syntax)
- Data meaning (semantics)
- Data structure
- Data context (the relationships among data items)
- Data quality

Many organizations are beginning to develop enterprise-wide metadata models; if these are available to you, they can form an extremely valuable input to your Information view. In addition, a number of cross-industry metadata models are being developed under the auspices of groups like the Dublin Core Metadata Initiative.

Metadata models are closely allied to the other types of information models we have described, particularly information structure models that include some elements of metadata (field attributes, relationships, and so on). Most metadata models take the form of structured (or unstructured) text, but some more formal notations are available, in particular those based around XML.

Some automated tools can extract metadata from large databases. Although these are to some extent in their infancy, they can be extremely useful, especially when dealing with legacy systems whose data internals may not be well understood.

There are some industry standard data models that may be of use in your metadata analysis, such as the ARTS Standard Relational Data Model for retail, or the ISO 20022 standard for financial services messaging.

VOLUMETRIC MODELS Volumetric models look at current and predicted data volumes. These can range from a few simple calculations on a scrap of paper to sophisticated statistical models to complete online simulations of systems. At the architectural level, they are usually kept fairly simple because the execution details of the system aren't yet known to any degree of accuracy.

PROBLEMS AND PITFALLS

Representation Incompatibilities

At their simplest, data incompatibilities arise because different systems represent field-level information in different ways, either by using different models for the information (e.g., polar versus Cartesian coordinates) or simply different encoding schemes (e.g., metric or imperial lengths). For example:

- One system may use Y and N for Boolean values, while another uses 1 and 0, or hex FF and 00.

- One system may use standard ISO abbreviations such as FR or DE for countries, while another has its own numeric encoding.
- One system may record monetary amounts in euros, while another uses the local currency in which the transaction took place.
- One system may record amounts by volume, another by weight.
- One system might keep running totals, and another system might just deal in deltas.

These sorts of problems are usually fairly easy to resolve. Much more problematic, however, are incompatibilities between business models.

EXAMPLE An architecture is required to integrate a telephone billing system with another system used to manage prospects, sales, and marketing promotions. A telephone customer may have several phone lines or may charge calls on a single line to different charge codes; for this reason, the billing system is based on the concept of a telephone account. Even worse, some accounts may be held jointly by several customers (especially business accounts), and some others (such as public emergency phone lines) have no real customer at all.

The sales system is concerned solely with customers (and, more important, prospective customers). However, the system needs to know about these customers' existing accounts, as well as other details such as payment history and usage, in order to avoid trying to sell customers something they already have.

The business models for these systems are fundamentally incompatible, and a lot of work is going to be needed to develop an architecture that successfully brings them together.

Incompatible business models can usually be reconciled only by using what may turn out to be fairly complex processing. In the example, you would probably have to develop a subsystem or service that was responsible for maintaining the links between customers and their accounts. This service would have to be updated (possibly in real time) when customers or accounts were created, deleted, or updated, or when the links between them were changed. It would own and manage the information itself and provide that data on demand to any other architectural element that required it.

Such a service would sit at the core of the architecture, being accessed by many other architectural elements, with ambitious targets for performance, scalability, and availability. This service would need to be very carefully designed, built, and tested.

RISK REDUCTION

- Develop a common, high-level model of the data structure, the key data attributes, and their domains, and validate it against all parts of the system (internal and external).

- Review your model with the business to ensure that it reflects reality.

- Focus on a small number of critically important attributes, rather than trying to model everything.

- Don't forget to include external entities in your model (e.g., if you exchange data with other organizations).

- Consider developing a data abstraction layer on top of data sources to hide the incompatibilities from other parts of the architecture.

Unavoidable Multiple Updaters

When creating distributed architectures, we all strive to achieve models whereby each data item is updated in one place and one place only. Unfortunately, in the real world this ambition cannot always be realized, for a number of reasons: Legacy systems cannot easily be changed, information may be sourced from outside the organization, or there may be limitations imposed by geography or politics.

As we have seen, multiple creators or updaters can have a significant impact on the architecture, and resolving such problems is not always easy. From the architectural perspective, you need to be aware of where this can happen so that you can take suitable measures to mitigate the risks.

RISK REDUCTION

- Ensure that your information ownership model is complete and accurate and that all data items with multiple updaters are identified.

- Determine with your stakeholders (primarily your users) which of these multiple updaters are important, and focus on these.

- Understand where inconsistencies through multiple updaters can arise and locate the crunch points where incompatible data items meet.

- Develop strategies for resolving these, such as always overriding old updates with newer ones, or maintaining two copies of data and resolving problems manually.

Key-Matching Deficiencies

When you are bringing together information from multiple systems, key-matching problems almost inevitably arise, as we saw earlier. These may not become apparent until you get into detailed design—by which time it is very expensive to change the architecture—or, even worse, once the system is running.

RISK REDUCTION

- Make sure that you have identified keys for all entities, and satisfy yourself that these keys are compatible across the architecture.

- At all points where information from different systems comes together, ensure that you have the means to map keys from one system to the other.

- Sample real data and run consistency checks on it.

- Whenever possible, go for common keys and standardized ways of modeling information.

Interface Complexity

If two systems need to transfer information between themselves, one bidirectional interface needs to be built. For three systems, three interfaces are needed; for four systems, six. In the worst-case situation, if your architecture comprises n systems, each of which needs to exchange information with every other, you need to build $n(n - 1)/2$ interfaces, as shown in Figure 18–8.

Even though it is unlikely that every system in your architecture needs to exchange information with every other, once you have more than a handful of systems, the number of interfaces required becomes unmanageable. Change the interface definition for any one of your n systems, and $n - 1$ interfaces need to be redesigned, recoded, tested, and deployed. This represents a significant burden for developers and often acts as a barrier to change.

FIGURE 18-8 INTERFACE COMPLEXITY

FIGURE 18-9 EXAMPLE OF AN INTEGRATION HUB

RISK REDUCTION

▪ When interface requirements are complex, consider applying an architectural style called the *integration hub*. In this model, all systems are linked once via a specialized adapter to one central integration hub. The adapter performs system-specific translation, and the hub handles message routing, resilience, and more specialized functions such as publish and subscribe, acknowledgment, and guaranteed delivery. An example is shown in Figure 18–9.

The advantage of this approach is that if a system changes, often only the adapter for that system needs to be modified. Furthermore, specialized code for routing, resilience, and so forth has to be implemented only once, in the central hub. (Of course, central hubs also have disadvantages in that they are often a single point of failure, can be a scalability bottleneck, and ironically can slow down change due to the difficulty of scheduling and prioritizing changes to such a critical shared component.) A third-party product is typically used to implement an integration hub. A large number of such off-the-shelf, highly configurable integration hubs are available as both commercial and open source products.

Integration hubs and similar architectures (such as a message bus) form part of the wider topic of Enterprise Application Integration, a full consideration of which is outside the scope of this book. We provide some references on this subject in the Further Reading section at the end of this chapter.

Overloaded Central Database

Many of the problems described in this chapter can be eliminated by storing all information in a single central database. This approach is much simpler and cleaner, since there is no need for key mappings, update reconciliation, or complex interfaces, and all data is immediately available.

However, a single central database is a single point of failure and will eventually become a performance bottleneck. For geographically distributed systems, a central database will give poor latency for remote users, and they may find that system availability is constrained due to limitations of the global network. Managing all data in a single central database can cause the data model to become overloaded or unworkable and can cause design-time and runtime contention. For these reasons, care must be taken when designing a system based on a single central database.

RISK REDUCTION

- Carefully consider the likely growth of your system in terms of data volumes, numbers of users, and their locations. (We discuss this issue in Chapter 28 on the Evolution perspective.)

- Consider the deployment (now or in the future) of a reporting database, separate from the main operational data store, and design your architecture with this possibility in mind.

- Be aware of the need to partition data in the future and design a strategy for it now (even if it is not yet implemented).

- If you do opt for a single central database, make sure that there are some scalability options available in case the system is more successful than expected.

- Look into the use of database clustering technologies and other mechanisms for improving availability and performance.

Inconsistent Distributed Databases

Conversely, some of the problems described in this chapter can be eliminated by replicating information between multiple databases in different locations or even geographical regions. This approach brings data near to where it is needed, with a consequent reduction in latency and improvement in availability.

However, distributed information architectures are harder to design and build and often lead to information inconsistency due to the replication delay. Furthermore, updates are harder to manage in cases where replicate copies are not read-only. While these problems are not insurmountable, they require careful design and a solid implementation.

RISK REDUCTION

- Carefully consider the need for a distributed information architecture, balancing the benefits this brings against the cost in complexity and data inconsistency.

- If you adopt a distributed model, ensure that you have effective strategies in place for dealing with inconsistency and that these are agreed upon with your key stakeholders, especially users.

- Ensure that there are effective operational tools and processes in place for detecting and dealing with problems that can't be dealt with automatically.

Poor Information Quality

If the actual data is inconsistent, inaccurate, or incomplete, it doesn't matter how good your information model is—you will face big problems when your system goes into operation.

In fact, the real problem is not necessarily poor information quality but *unexpectedly* poor information quality. If you know that some information will be inadequate, you can develop strategies early to deal with it and successfully manage the expectations of your stakeholders in this area.

RISK REDUCTION

- Validate your key assumptions about information quality early (e.g., "All products can be uniquely identified globally by using an immutable common key").

- Make sure that you understand what information is important and what is less important (your stakeholders, primarily users, can tell you this), then focus on the important information.

- Make use of commercially available information quality tools to analyze the quality of existing information.

- Identify the places where poor-quality information can appear, and develop strategies for dealing with it, such as rejecting poor-quality information, marking it as suspect, or attempting to fix it.

Excessive Information Latency

Excessive latency typically arises from overly complex architectures or architectures that are not designed to handle the volumes of information they are presented with. You may also have latency issues that are outside your control. For example, information may arrive from an external source only once a week, or updates may need to be applied in batches overnight because of the limitations of a legacy system.

As with information quality, poor latency becomes an issue only if it is *unexpectedly* poor. By identifying expected latency early, you can identify problem areas and develop strategies to deal with them.

RISK REDUCTION

- When there is distance or complexity between information providers and information consumers, ensure that you predict, as best you can, what the information latency will be.

- When latency is significant, review this with your stakeholders to determine whether it is a concern.

- Better still, obtain agreement on realistic latency requirements for all data items up front, and validate your model against these.

Inadequate Volumetrics

A system designed to handle a thousand updates per day is unlikely to cope well when faced with a million updates per day. Unless you are clear about the volumes of information the system is expected to handle, you have little chance of designing an appropriate architecture. (We address the issue of volumetrics in more detail in Chapter 26.)

RISK REDUCTION

- Make sure that data volumes are captured, reviewed, and approved by your stakeholders. You may want to separately capture "business" volumes (such as numbers of orders) from acquirers and users, and "technical" volumes (such as numbers of database updates) from technical stakeholders.

- Make sure that volumes are realistic. If the stakeholders convey doubt or vagueness about this, pursue the issue, and if in doubt, increase them to allow for the margin of error.

- Make sure that your data volumes cover all scenarios—not just the online day, for example, but also the overnight processing and peak periods such as the end of the year or holiday processing.

- Make sure that there is an effective translation of business volumes into physical ones. For example, a single business transaction, such as placing an order, may result in several physical transactions, such as decrementing stock levels, posting account records, assigning compensation to sales staff, and arranging delivery of the ordered item.

- Make sure that your volumes take future expansion into account.

- Prototype your data stores and the access to them for the expected volumes you do have.

CHECKLIST

- Do you have an appropriate level of detail in your data models (e.g., no more than about 20–30 entities)?
- Does the data model support the processing requirements now and those likely in the future?
- Are keys clearly identified for all important entities?
- When an entity is distributed across multiple systems or locations with different keys, are the mappings between these keys defined? Do you have processes for maintaining these mappings when data items are created?
- Have you taken account of data in one place that is derived from data managed and owned elsewhere, such as account balances derived from account activity?
- Have you defined strategies for resolving data ownership conflicts, particularly when there are multiple creators or updaters?
- Are latency requirements clearly identified, and are mechanisms in place to ensure that these are achieved?
- Do you have clear strategies for transactional consistency across distributed data stores, and do these balance this need with the cost in terms of performance and complexity?
- Have you considered which data storage models to use for the various data stores in your system, taking into account the strengths and weaknesses of each?
- Do you have mechanisms in place for validating migrated data and dealing appropriately with errors?
- Do you have the right sort of data stores (operational data store, reporting databases, data warehouses, and data marts) for the expected volumes and performance requirements?
- Have you defined sufficient storage and processing capacity for archiving? For restoring archived data?
- Has a data quality assessment been done? Have you created strategies for dealing with poor-quality data?
- Have you confirmed which entities in your information model should be obtained from shared enterprise sources, and if so, does your architecture make use of these appropriately?

FURTHER READING

The literature on information architecture per se (as opposed to data design techniques or specific data management technologies) is sparse.

Fortunately, data modeling, and particularly relational modeling, which underpins much that we do, has a strong theoretical grounding, so there is a plethora of books on the subject. The classic of the genre, which is still being updated, is probably Date [DATE03]. Other good general books include Elmasri and Navathe [ELMA99] and Kroenke [KROE02].

Kim [KIMW99] looks at some of the newer techniques such as object-oriented databases. Redman [REDM97] provides a detailed discussion of the issues around data quality and how to develop strategies for data quality analysis and improvement.

Enterprise Application Integration architectures are covered in a large number of books, such as Linthicum [LINT03] and Ruh et al. [RUHW00].

You can find further information on metadata modeling in ISO Standard 11197-3 [ISO96] and books such as [MARC00]. Information on specific metadata models such as the ARTS Standard Relational Data Model or the ISO 20022 standard for financial services messaging can be found on the Web sites for those organizations.

If you are interested in ideas on how to flexibly evolve a database schema as part of the software development process, Scott Ambler and Pramod Sadalage's book on database refactoring [AMBL06], which introduces the Evolutionary Database Design technique, will be of interest.

There are many books on data warehousing, from the two pioneers of this approach, William Inmon (e.g., [INMO05]) and Ralph Kimball (e.g., [KIMB02]), and many others.

Alec Sharp and Patrick McDermott's book [SHAR08] provides a good description of the subject and the techniques used. A vast number of books (too numerous to mention here) cover specific relational database products (e.g., Oracle, SQL Server, DB2, Sybase, MySQL) and tools and technologies for application development, systems management, and integration.

The best place to obtain information on nonrelational database technologies, such as the NoSQL movement, is the Internet.

The Data Management Association (DAMA) has much useful information, runs conferences and seminars, provides training and certification, and has chapters worldwide. They can be found at www.dama.org.

19

THE CONCURRENCY
VIEWPOINT

Definition	Describes the concurrency structure of the system and maps functional elements to concurrency units to clearly identify the parts of the system that can execute concurrently and how this is coordinated and controlled
Concerns	Task structure, mapping of functional elements to tasks, interprocess communication, state management, synchronization and integrity, supporting scalability, startup and shutdown, task failure, and reentrancy
Models	System-level concurrency models and state models
Problems and Pitfalls	Modeling the wrong concurrency, modeling the concurrency wrongly, excessive complexity, resource contention, deadlock, and race conditions
Stakeholders	Communicators, developers, testers, and some administrators
Applicability	All information systems with a number of concurrent threads of execution

Historically, information systems were designed to operate with little or no concurrency, running via batch mode on large central computers. However, a number of factors (including distributed systems, increasing workloads, and cheap multiprocessor hardware) have combined so that today's information systems often have little or no batch processing and are inherently concurrent.

In contrast, control systems have always been inherently concurrent and event-driven, given their need to react to external events in order to perform control operations. It is natural, then, that as information systems become more concurrent and event-driven, they start to take on a number of characteristics traditionally associated with control systems. In order to deal with this concurrency, the information systems community has naturally adopted and adapted proven techniques from the control systems community. Many of these techniques form the basis of the Concurrency viewpoint.

The Concurrency view is used to describe the system's concurrency and state-related structure and constraints. This involves defining the parts of the system that execute at the same time and how this is controlled (e.g., defining how the system's functional elements are packaged into operating system processes and how the processes coordinate their execution). To do this, you need to create a process model and a state model: The process model shows the planned process, thread, and interprocess communication structure; the state model describes the set of states that runtime elements can be in and the valid transitions between those states.

Once you have created process and state models, you can use a number of analysis techniques to ensure that the planned concurrency scheme is sound. The use of such techniques is typically part of creating a Concurrency view, too.

It's worth noting that not all information-based systems really benefit from a Concurrency view. Some information systems have little concurrency. Others, while exhibiting concurrent behavior, use the facilities of underlying frameworks and containers (e.g., application servers and databases) to hide the concurrency model in use.

EXAMPLE Data warehouse systems tend to be batch-loaded overnight and accessed from a number of desktop machines. These systems do exhibit concurrent behavior—multiple clients can request information from the data warehouse concurrently. However, such a system will typically rely on the underlying database management system to handle all of the concurrency for it (in any way it chooses). Therefore, the process model used is of little architectural significance, and you have little or no control over it. The interesting aspects of concurrency relate much more to the design of the physical data model and should be handled there.

In contrast, however, many of today's information systems are inherently event-driven, reactive, concurrent systems. This is particularly the case when considering infrastructure such as middleware products. Systems of this type typically sit idle until an external event occurs and then process the event. Given that many external events can occur simultaneously and that the interarrival time of such events may be lower than the time taken to process them, this kind of information-based system is inherently concurrent, with many operations being executed at once.

> **EXAMPLE** Consider an e-commerce system that uses a message-based approach to processing transaction requests. In such a system, when a request arrives, it is translated into a message that is queued for the appropriate functional element that can process it. In order to prevent message queues from growing too long and to make efficient use of processing resources, the processing element will need to process a number of messages concurrently. In this case, there may be a large number of concurrent operations within the functional element, each one needing access to shared resources.

The Concurrency viewpoint is extremely relevant to systems that exhibit this kind of behavior. Creating a Concurrency view allows the concurrency design of such systems to be made explicit and helps interested stakeholders understand concurrency constraints and requirements. It also allows you to analyze the system to avoid common concurrency problems such as deadlocks or bottlenecks.

CONCERNS

Task Structure

The most important aspect of creating a Concurrency view is establishing the system's process structure, which identifies the overall strategy for using concurrency in the system. It defines the set of processes across which the system's workload is partitioned and how the functions of the system are distributed across them. It is also usually necessary to consider the use of operating system threads within processes or to abstract away from individual processes and consider groups of similar processes instead.

Note: Throughout this chapter, we use the word *task* as a generic term to describe a processing thread—whether it is a single operating system process, one thread within a multithreaded process, or some other software execution unit. When the difference is significant, we specifically use the terms *process* or *thread* as appropriate.

The aspects of the system's task structure that this view needs to address depend very much on the kind of system you are dealing with.

> **EXAMPLE** A complex, small-footprint system may have only one or two operating system tasks but may need to use a very complex thread model to meet its efficiency and responsiveness goals. In this case, the focus of the task structure activity needs to be at the thread level.
>
> A large enterprise system may be composed of literally hundreds of concurrent processes, many containing dozens of threads. In this sort of system, the task structure activity needs to be at the level of groups of similar processes in order to focus on the architecturally significant aspects of the concurrency.

Mapping of Functional Elements to Tasks

The mapping of functional elements to tasks can have a significant effect on the performance, efficiency, resilience, reliability, and flexibility of your architecture, so this needs careful consideration. The key question to address is which functional elements need to be isolated from each other (and so placed in separate processes) and which need to cooperate closely (and so need to run within the same process).

Interprocess Communication

When functional elements reside within a single operating system process, communication among them is relatively simple because of their shared address space. While some coordination may be required (see the Synchronization and Integrity concern), you can use any number of data structures to pass information among them. Similarly, a number of easily used control mechanisms (such as the procedure call and variants of it) can transfer control among elements as needed.

In contrast, when elements reside in different operating system processes, communication among them becomes more complex. This complexity increases if the processes also reside on different physical machines.

A number of interprocess communication mechanisms can be used to link elements in different processes, including remote procedure calls, messaging, shared memory, pipes, queues, and so on. Each has its own strengths, weaknesses, and constraints, and inappropriate use of these mechanisms can cause problems at the system level (e.g., message queue latency between processes causing scalability or throughput problems). In order to deliver a system with an acceptable set of quality properties, the Concurrency view needs to consider and identify the set of interprocess communication mechanisms that will be used to provide the interelement communication required by the system's functional structure.

State Management

In many systems, the runtime state of system elements is important to the correct operation of the system. This is particularly the case for event-driven systems that exhibit a high degree of concurrency, where business operations tend to be processed via state machine implementations.

In such systems, a concern of the Concurrency view is to clearly define the set of states that each functional element of the system can be in at runtime, the set of valid transitions between those states, and the causes and effects of the interstate transitions. Such careful state management is a major factor in ensuring reliability and correct behavior for most concurrent systems. Again, if you are using a formal architectural style, it may define how the system's runtime state should be handled.

Note that this concern refers to the state of the runtime elements of the system (which could be termed the *technical state* of the system). Another type of state management important to many information systems is the set of valid states and transitions for their core persistent information (business objects—the *business state* of the system). However, this is a distinct concept of state, and we refer to persistent object state models as *lifecycles* to avoid any confusion between the two. Object lifecycles are discussed in Chapter 18 as part of the Information viewpoint.

Having said this, it is also quite reasonable to consider state management in the Functional view—after all, the state of functional elements is what we're considering. However, our experience is that the design of the system's state management usually fits better in the Concurrency view. Those systems where state is important are usually those where concurrency is important too, and considering system-level state usually involves the consideration of the concurrency around it as well.

Synchronization and Integrity

As soon as more than one thread of control exists in the system, it is important to ensure that concurrent execution cannot result in corruption of information within the system. This concern applies at a number of levels in the system, from a shared variable within a multithreaded module at one end of the scale to critical corporate transaction data in shared data stores at the other.

An important concern for the Concurrency view to address is how concurrent activity will be coordinated so that the system operates correctly and maintains the integrity of the data within it.

Supporting Scalability

In any highly concurrent system, the approach taken to concurrency, synchronization, and state management can have a profound effect on the scalability that the system can achieve. Too much or too little concurrency can slow a system down and prevent it from handling heavy workloads efficiently, while excessive or simply naïve synchronization can result in a system that performs very well for light workloads but grinds to a halt when heavy workloads are applied. The problem is that designing high-performance, highly concurrent systems is difficult and can be an error-prone process. An important concern for this view to address is how the concurrency approach used will support the performance and scalability required while being simple enough to implement cost-effectively and reliably. We discuss an approach to achieving this in Chapter 26 on the Performance and Scalability perspective.

Startup and Shutdown

When you have more than one operating system process in your system, startup and shutdown of the system can become more complicated to manage. Intertask dependencies may mean that tasks need to be started and stopped in very specific orders so that if some tasks fail to start, others will not be started. The system startup and shutdown dependencies are an important part of your concurrency design and need to be clearly understood by developers, testers, and administrators.

Task Failure

When functional elements reside in different processes or run on different threads, dealing with element failure can be complex. This is because an element in one task cannot rely on another task being available when it needs to communicate with it, whereas when an element calls another one in the same task, it knows it will be there. Your concurrency design needs to take into account this added possibility of failure and ensure that the failure of one task doesn't bring the entire system to a halt. In order to address this concern, you need a system-wide strategy for recognizing and recovering from task failure.

Reentrancy

Reentrancy refers to the ability of a software element to operate correctly when used concurrently by more than one processing thread. This is primarily a concern for software developers when designing their software elements. From an architectural perspective, reentrancy is an important constraint for certain elements, so the architecture must clearly define which modules need to be reentrant and which do not.

> **EXAMPLE** If you are developing an e-mail server, the ability to support a great deal of concurrency is likely to be a key concern. Without this, it will be hard to use the e-mail server for large user populations who will want to send and receive e-mail simultaneously. You can take a number of approaches to achieve such concurrency, but for the sake of argument, let's assume that you have decided to implement the server by using a single operating system process and many (perhaps hundreds of) concurrent operating system threads running within it: some sending e-mail, some receiving e-mail, and some managing the server's internal state.
>
> In this sort of environment, it is crucial to decide which of the elements of your system have to be reentrant and which do not. Any element involved in sending and receiving e-mail (e.g., a name resolution library that translates e-mail domains to network addresses) will need to be reentrant to ensure that it can be used simultaneously by many sending and receiving threads. Without such a guarantee, the name resolution library could be the source of many subtle problems later if its internal state could be corrupted by concurrent access.

The reentrancy needs of your architecture can also affect which third-party software elements you can use within the system and where you can use them.

Stakeholder Concerns

Typical stakeholder concerns for the Concurrency viewpoint include those shown in Table 19–1.

TABLE 19–1 STAKEHOLDER CONCERNS FOR THE CONCURRENCY VIEWPOINT

Stakeholder Class	Concerns
Administrators	Task structure, startup and shutdown, and task failure
Communicators	Task structure, startup and shutdown, and task failure
Developers	All concerns
Testers	Task structure, mapping of functional elements to tasks, startup and shutdown, task failure, and reentrancy

MODELS

System-Level Concurrency Models

The Concurrency view maps the functional elements onto runtime execution entities via a concurrency model. The concurrency model typically contains the following items.

- *Processes*: In this context, the term *process* refers to an operating system process, that is, an address space that provides an execution environment for one or more independent threads of execution. The process is the basic unit of concurrency in the design of the system. At the architecture level, the processes are normally assumed to be isolated from each other so that if one process wants to affect the execution of another, it must use an interprocess communication mechanism.

- *Process groups*: At the architecture level, it can often be useful to group individual processes so that a collection of closely related processes can be considered as a single entity at the system level. This can provide a useful abstraction that allows less important concurrency concerns to be deferred until subsystem design. An example is a database management system (DBMS). The important point from the system level is that the DBMS is a functional unit, accessed via well-defined interfaces, that runs in its own process or group of processes. However, the details of the exact number of processes it uses (e.g., how many logging processes run within the DBMS) and the function of each are almost certainly irrelevant to the architecture—indeed, this will probably be decided by a technical specialist later in the design process. Using a process group in this situation makes it clear that a group of related processes will be used but defers the details of the set until later. The other common use for process groups is simply as a hierarchical structuring technique for large or complex systems that contain many processes. All of the processes may need description, but the use of process groups can make the process model easier to comprehend.

- *Threads*: In this context, the term *thread* refers to an operating system thread, that is, a thread of execution that can be independently scheduled within an operating system process. Threads are known as *lightweight processes* by some operating systems. At the level of system architecture, threads can often be ignored, with the details of their use being the responsibility of subsystem designers (perhaps with you guiding their use via design patterns in the Development view). However, for some systems you do want to model the use of threads in at least some parts of the system. Threads are normally represented in process models via a decomposition of a process.

- *Interprocess communication*: When processes are running, they are assumed to be isolated from each other so that one process cannot change anything in another process. However, in most concurrent systems, processes do need to interact in order to coordinate their execution, request services from each other, and pass information among themselves. They achieve these interactions via a number of interprocess communication mechanisms ("IPC mechanisms"), which are the connectors in the system's runtime architecture.

  The mechanisms available vary depending on the underlying technology platforms in use. However, interprocess communication mechanisms generally fall into one of these groups.

  - *Procedure call mechanisms* are all some variation on an interprocess function call and are usually based on some form of remote procedure call or some sort of message-passing operation.
  - *Execution coordination mechanisms* allow two or more processes (or threads) to signal to each other when certain events occur. Coordination mechanisms include semaphores and mutexes and are typically limited to coordination between processes or threads running on the same physical machine.
  - *Data-sharing mechanisms* allow a number of processes to share one or more data structures and access them concurrently (possibly coordinating this access via coordination mechanisms). Data-sharing mechanisms include shared memory, distributed tuple spaces (such as Linda and more recent implementations such as GigaSpaces), and simple, traditional mechanisms such as client/server databases and shared file storage.
  - *Messaging mechanisms* are related to data-sharing mechanisms, but rather than placing data structures in a shared space for concurrent access, they transmit data structures from one task to another. Messaging systems normally implement one or both of two well-defined messaging models: queuing and publish/subscribe. Queuing introduces a "first in, first out" queue structure between producers and consumers where consumers destructively read messages from the queue (i.e., a message is delivered to only one consumer). Publish/subscribe introduces a "topic" or "bus" between producers and consumers where the consumers indicate the types of messages that they are interested in and a message is consumed by all consumers interested in it.

As the architect, you need to choose the interprocess communication mechanisms carefully because of the impact that they can have on the quality properties that the system exhibits (such as its performance, scalability, and reliability). The IPC mechanisms also impose significant constraints on the functional elements that use them, and so it is important to choose them early so that these constraints can be taken into account.

NOTATION You can represent the Concurrency view in a number of ways. Some of the more common notational approaches include UML and other formal notations, along with less formal notations, which we describe briefly here.

- *UML*: UML's concurrency modeling facilities are rather simple but do include the notion of an active object (i.e., an object with a thread of control). There are a number of ways that concurrency structures can be represented in UML, including stereotyped packages, components, and classes, but unfortunately no approach has become a standard. We have used a number of conventions in our models and have found that stereotyped active components are a good place to start when modeling processes and threads. We sometimes also add a process group stereotype to represent a group of related processes (such as a database engine) if this is a useful abstraction for the system we are working on.

  Simple examples of interprocess communication, like remote procedure calls, can be represented by using standard UML intercomponent associations, with arrowheads indicating the direction of communication (and possibly using tagged values on the association to make the communication mechanism clear). More complex forms of interprocess communication (shared memory, semaphores, and so on) can be represented quite effectively by introducing further stereotypes and showing associations between the components in the tasks and the interprocess communication mechanisms they use.

  Figure 19–1 shows an example of UML being used for a concurrency model.

  This model shows how the system is implemented by using three processes (a client, a statistics service, and a statistics calculator) along with a process group to implement the Oracle DBMS instance. The concurrent activity between the Statistics Accessor and Statistics Calculator components needs to be coordinated because they are in different processes; a mutex is used to achieve this. The illustrated scenario is very simple, and there is little or no architecturally significant thread design in this model. Figure 19–2 shows a more involved model with more architecturally significant threading.

  The concurrency model shown in Figure 19–2 illustrates a case where the process structure is very simple, namely, two processes that communicate via a socket stream. However, the thread structure in the DBMS Process instance is architecturally significant, and its structure and interthread coordination strategy need to be documented and explained. The model shows that there is a single thread containing the Network Listener component, which communicates with between 1 and 40 threads that contain the four main query-processing components via an interprocess communication queue. The Disk I/O Manager component

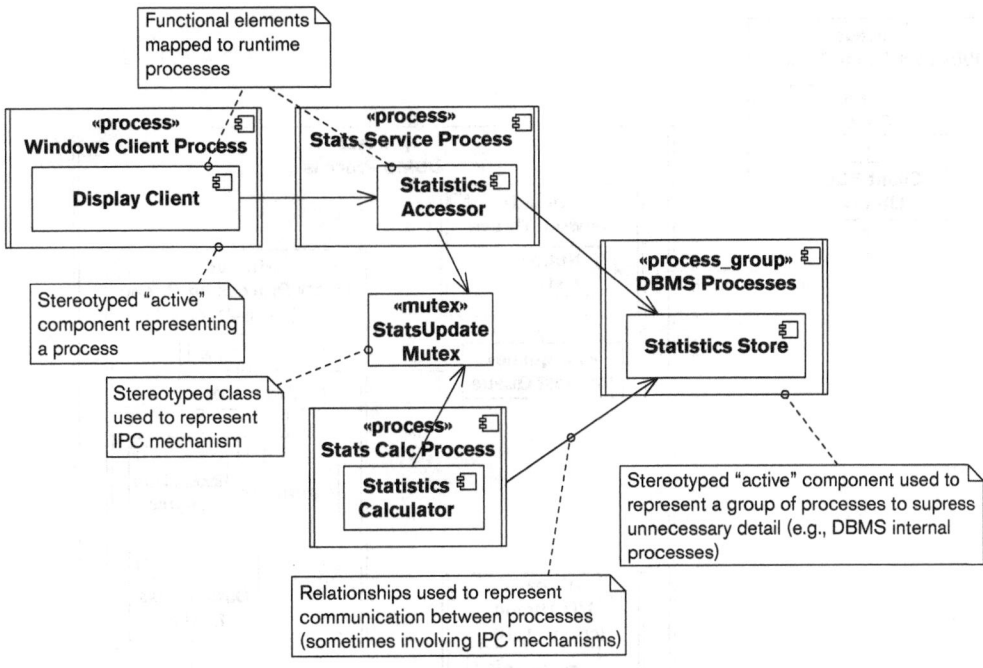

FIGURE 19-1 CONCURRENCY MODEL DOCUMENTED BY USING UML

is hosted on its own thread, and there may be up to 10 instances of this running. The Data Access Engine component communicates with the Disk I/O Manager instances via the shared memory mechanism.

- *Formal notations*: The real-time and control systems research community has created a number of concurrency modeling languages that allow the creation and analysis of process models. A number of these languages, such as LOTOS, Communicating Sequential Processes (CSP), and the Calculus of Communicating Systems (CCS), are formal and represented textually. Most of these languages are mathematical and fairly abstract, and they aren't widely used in information systems development. While this doesn't mean they can't be useful, we have yet to come across a large-scale industrial application of them to information systems. The problem with using these languages in practice is often the need to teach them to the interested stakeholders, and there is always a need to ensure that the representation and analysis that they allow will be useful for the specific situation to which you are trying to apply them.

- *Informal notations*: In our experience, by far the most common notation used to represent process models is an informal one, created by the author of the model. Given the relatively small number of object types in a process model, an informal notation invented for the problem at hand

FIGURE 19-2 THREAD-BASED CONCURRENCY MODEL

often works very effectively as a communication tool as long as it is explained clearly. The notation needs to capture processes, process groups, threads, and the interprocess communication mechanisms in use. As long as the notation to represent each of these concepts is well defined, an informal notation often has much to recommend it. In particular, the notation can be kept simple and avoids the potentially awkward process of bending a general-purpose notation like UML to represent the model being described. The risk with informal notations is that they are never clearly defined and so lead to ambiguous descriptions.

ACTIVITIES

Map the Elements to the Tasks. The first step when creating your process model is to work out how many processes you need and to decide which functional elements will run in which processes. In some cases, this is a straightforward job—each functional element ends up being a process (or perhaps a process group), or all of the elements end up in a single process. In other cases, there is a complex N:M mapping between functional elements and processes, with some elements partitioned between processes and other elements running in shared processes. The important point about this mapping is that you should introduce concurrency only where it is actually required. Concurrency adds complexity to the system and adds significant overhead to interelement communication when it must cross process boundaries. Therefore, add more processes to your system only if you need them for distribution, scalability, isolation, or other reasons guided by the requirements for your system.

Determine the Threading Design. The term *threading design* refers to the process of deciding on the number of threads to include in each system process and how those threads are to be allocated and used. In most cases, threading design is not something that the architect needs to get directly involved in—this is usually the job of the subsystem designers. However, you may get involved in designing and specifying general threading approaches or patterns that should be used at various points in the system in order to meet the system's required quality properties or to ensure consistency across the implementation.

Define Mechanisms for Resource Sharing. As soon as concurrency is introduced into the system, you must carefully consider how to share resources between concurrent threads of execution. Resource sharing is considered in some other parts of the architecture, too (notably, the Information view), and the two activities might be best tackled as a single task. This isn't a book on concurrent computing, so we don't have space to discuss all of the options and potential pitfalls to consider when sharing resources. The simplistic advice is simply that whenever a resource (such as a piece of data in memory, a file, a database object, or a piece of shared memory) is shared among two or more concurrent threads of execution, it must be protected from corruption. This is usually achieved with some form of locking protocol. As with threading design, the details of resource sharing are rarely architecturally significant. Your role in relation to this is to ensure that suitable resource-sharing approaches are used where necessary and that the approach used is suitable in the overall context of the system and does not produce unacceptable side effects for the system as a whole.

Define the IPC Mechanisms to Use. In most concurrent systems the tasks need to communicate frequently, and so, along with deciding how to share resources between tasks, you will need to consider what communication is needed between them and which interprocess communication mechanisms you will use to enable it. Again, we don't have space here to discuss all of the options and the tradeoffs that they imply, but as is usually the case, a simple and regular scheme that minimizes the amount of intertask communication is likely to be the best choice. Better still is using a library or framework (such as an implementation of the Actor pattern) to avoid having to deal with a lot of this complexity yourself. While this sounds like simplistic advice, implementing complex intertask communication correctly is a very difficult job best left to specialists. As with other architectural concerns, your focus needs to be on defining a common system-wide approach and on reducing the risk involved in its implementation.

Assign Priorities to Threads and Processes. Some tasks in your system may be more important than others. If you have tasks of different importance running on one machine, you need to control their execution so that the more important work gets done before the less important work. The normal method for achieving this is to use the facilities of the underlying operating system to assign priority levels to the different threads and processes. All modern operating systems provide this feature in roughly the same way. Tasks are explicitly or implicitly given runtime priorities. When the operating system's thread scheduler is choosing tasks to run, it considers the higher-priority tasks before the lower-priority ones, thus getting the important work done first. If you can avoid assigning explicit priorities to threads, in general do so—processing priorities can add a lot of complexity to your process model and can introduce subtle but serious problems such as priority inversion. However, sometimes you can't avoid it. In these cases, keep the assignment of priorities as simple and as regular as possible, and analyze and prototype your approach to make sure that you aren't introducing problems worse than the one you're trying to solve.

Analyze Deadlocks. Having introduced concurrency into the system, you have also introduced the risk of the entire system grinding to a halt in unexpected ways. Whenever you have concurrency in the presence of shared resources, you always have the possibility of deadlock. You can use a number of modeling and analysis techniques to try to spot potential deadlocks. An example of such a technique is Petri Net Analysis, which allows you to create a model of your processing threads and shared resources and then analyze the model to catch potential deadlock situations. With experience, it is also usually possible to perform effective deadlock analysis through careful, informal consideration of your concurrency model.

Analyze Contention. Whenever you have a number of tasks and shared resources, you almost always find contention. Contention occurs between tasks when more than one task requires a shared resource concurrently. The introduction of coordination mechanisms (such as mutexes) inevitably introduces contention when workloads are high. If contention rises beyond a certain point, the system will slow dramatically, and little useful work will get done. In order to avoid this during normal operation, you need to analyze your shared resources from this point of view. The basis of the technique is to identify each of your possible contention points. Then, for each, estimate the likely number of concurrent tasks contending for the resource and for how long each will need the resource. This allows you to establish the likely wait times that each task experiences at each point and then to estimate how such contention will affect your processing times and throughput. Repeating the exercise for different workloads allows you to estimate the maximum theoretical workloads your system can possibly support. Once you understand the potential for the system becoming overloaded, you can design mechanisms into your software to handle such conditions gracefully (such as implementing the Circuit Breaker pattern).

State Models

A state model is used to describe the set of states that a system's runtime elements can be in and the valid transitions between the states. The set of states and transitions for one runtime element is known as a *state machine*, and the collection of all of the interesting state machines for your system forms the overall state model.

Usually, you will find that each system task identified in the concurrency model will have one or at most a few functional units mapped to it that are effectively in control of the task. These functional units normally have the system's interesting state models associated with them. If you create a state model, be sure to focus on these system elements so that the state model describes only architecturally significant information. You don't need to capture all of the state machines inside all of the system's elements; the AD needs to describe only state that is visible at the system level, not state that is hidden inside the system's elements.

An important decision to make before you start creating the state model is the set of semantics you want to use in your state machines. Modern state modeling notations (in particular, UML's statechart, discussed later) allow you to introduce a mind-boggling degree of complexity. You need to use such notations carefully if you want to produce a comprehensible model.

A basic state machine in the state model would normally contain the following types of entities.

- *State*: A state is an identifiable, named, stable condition during a runtime functional element's lifetime. States are normally associated with waiting for something (an event) to occur or performing some sort of operation.

- *Transition*: A state transition defines an allowable change in state, from one state to another, following the occurrence of an event. From a modeling point of view, transitions are normally considered to occur in zero time and so cannot be interrupted.

- *Event*: An event is an indication that something of interest has happened in the system (and is normally recognized by an operation being invoked on an element or a time period ending). Events are the triggers that cause transitions between states to occur.

- *Actions*: Actions are atomic (noninterruptible) pieces of processing that can be associated with a transition (so an event causes the transition to occur, and then an action is executed as part of the state transition).

More sophisticated state modeling notations allow additional modeling elements such as *guards* (Boolean conditions governing state transitions), *activities* (long, interruptible items of processing that can be associated with states), and *hierarchical states*.

NOTATION State models are typically represented by a graphical notation derived in some way from the classic state transition diagram. The most popular variant in use today is probably the UML notation for representing state, the *statechart*. At the end of this subsection we briefly discuss other graphical notations as well as some nongraphical ones, but first we focus on UML's statechart.

- *UML*: A statechart is a flexible notation that can be used in a number of different ways at differing levels of sophistication. Deciding which parts of the notation to use is an important step before getting too far into the modeling process. Figure 19–3 shows a UML statechart that represents the state model for a calculation engine.

  This statechart shows much of the important notation for a UML statechart, with a composite primary state, concurrent state management, and the use of start and end pseudo states to indicate how the element's lifecycle begins and ends. The single top-level state (Running) is entered when the element is started and exited when a shutdown event is received (the `reset()` action is performed as part of that transition).

  The Running state has been decomposed into four substates that comprise the business of running this element: Waiting for Data, Calibrating Metrics, Calculating, and Distributing Results. The transition arrows indicate the possible transitions between states (along with the events that cause the transitions and the actions that will be executed).

  The Calculating state is interesting because it is a concurrent state, as you can see from the dashed line that bisects it. This means that while in the Calculating state, the element is actually in two concurrent substates (Calculating Values and Calculating Risk). When the activity associated with these states completes, the transition from the states is taken, and when both are complete, the element can leave the Calculating state.

  There are two architecturally significant aspects to this state machine.

  - If new input data becomes ready when the element is in the Calculation state, in-progress results are discarded (by executing the `reset()` action), and calculation starts again. In contrast, if this occurs while results are being distributed, the distribution process is not interrupted.

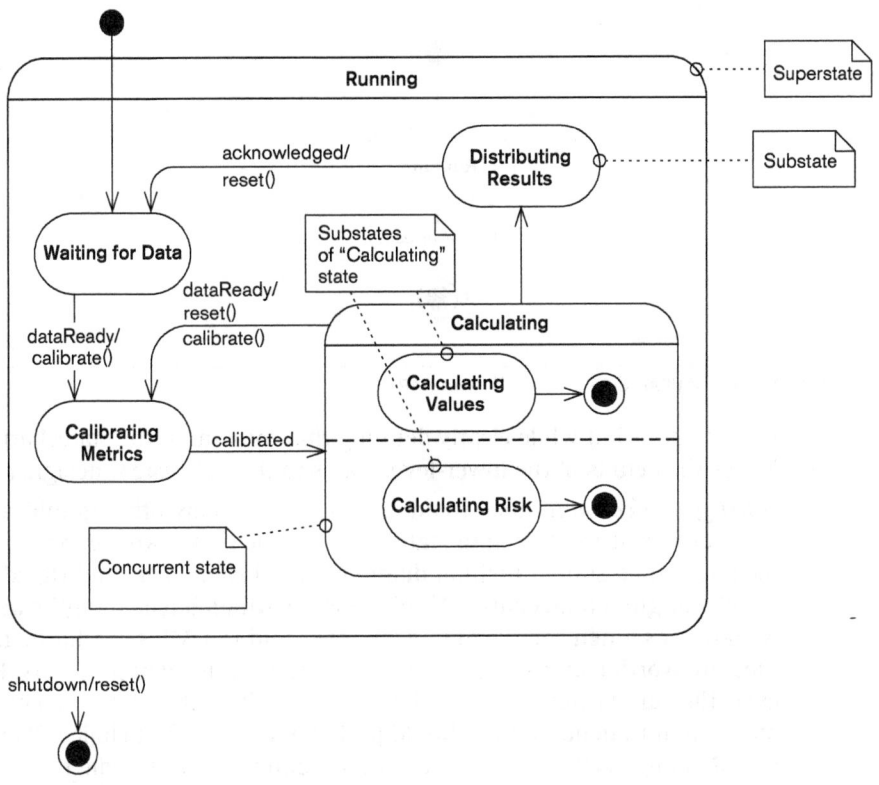

FIGURE 19-3 EXAMPLE STATECHART FOR A CALCULATION ENGINE

- No matter the state of the element, if a shutdown event is received, all processing immediately stops, the state is reset, and the element exits.

Of course, whether or not these facts are architecturally significant depends on the situation. However, we can make a reasonable argument that these facts are visible at the system level and thus can affect or be relied on by other system elements, and therefore, these facts need to be captured as part of the architecture.

An interesting point to note about the UML statechart is that its ability to show hierarchical state composition allows you to express architectural constraints on state models without needing to define the entire model. The statechart in Figure 19–4 illustrates this point.

This statechart distills one of the architecturally significant features from the statechart in Figure 19–3, namely, that a shutdown event must be immediately responded to in any running state and a reset of the element performed as part of shutdown. In effect, this documents an architectural constraint that the designer of the corresponding part of the system

FIGURE 19-4 ARCHITECTURAL CONSTRAINT STATECHART

must respect; but while clearly defining this constraint, the statechart leaves the details of the lower-level states to the subsystem designer.

- *Other graphical notations*: In addition to UML, many other graphical notations exist for modeling state. Some of the better-known ones include simple state transition diagrams, Petri Nets, SDL, and David Harel's original Statecharts. All of these notations have strengths and weaknesses when compared to each other and to UML statecharts, and they are worth considering if UML statecharts cause you problems. However, the standardization of and wide familiarity with UML statecharts means that in general they should probably be your first choice. The Further Reading section at the end of this chapter contains some references to information about these alternative notations.

- *Nongraphical notations*: In principle, all of the graphical notations can be represented in a textual form (and indeed many graphical state modeling notations do define an equivalent textual form). Similarly, a number of primarily textual formalisms for modeling and analyzing state can be represented in a graphical form (for an accessible example, look at the Finite State Processes language). A textual state model can be useful when the model needs to be processed in some way by machine, but for human readers it is almost always better to use a graphical notation where possible.

ACTIVITIES

Define the Notation. Before starting to create your state model, spend some time working out your needs for the modeling notation and defining how you will use it.

Identify the States. The primary activity when creating a state model is to work out what states your system elements can be in and the processing (if any) associated with each state. Beware of accidentally modeling activities as states; this is a common modeling mistake. If in doubt, try considering your state machine as a UML activity diagram. If you can do this, you have probably modeled activities rather than states. When performing state identification at the architectural level, focus on the states that are visible from outside the element and thus have a system-wide effect.

Design the State Transitions. Once you know what states your elements can be in, design a set of transitions that allows them to move between the states correctly. For each transition, clearly identify how the transition is triggered and any (atomic) actions that must be performed as a side effect of traversing it. Make sure that the events and actions you identify can be supported by the operations and state of the element for which you are designing a state machine.

PROBLEMS AND PITFALLS

Modeling the Wrong Concurrency

When considering the concurrency design of a system, it is easy to get bogged down in the details of the internal concurrency and state design of each element. It's not part of your job as an architect to design detailed thread models that define how individual threads in a server will be allocated, used, and freed, along with all of the coordination between them. Remember that your role is to concentrate on the system as a whole rather than all of the details of each element. The concurrency with which you should be concerned is the architecturally significant concurrency, that is, the overall concurrency structure, the mapping of functional elements to that structure, and the system-level state model. You may also be involved in specifying common approaches such as design patterns that need to be used for the concurrency within elements, but in general you should not need to design all of the details—this will only distract you from the system-level problems (which are often quite enough to worry about).

RISK REDUCTION
- Focus on architecturally significant aspects of concurrency.
- Involve the lead software developers as early as possible so they can work on the more detailed aspects of this problem.

Modeling the Concurrency Wrongly

Meaningful concurrency models can be quite difficult to create, so it is important to spend the time and effort required to create a good model. To be useful, the models you create should use your notation correctly and be a valid representation of the situation you are representing. The following are some of the common modeling mistakes to be aware of.

- Modeling activities from your system as states in your state model and so accidentally creating an activity diagram rather than a state model. This is a common confusion when people are new to state modeling.

- Having a model with nonterminal states that can't be exited because the required events will never occur. This indicates that some conditions haven't been thought through.

- Having transitions that cannot be traversed due to an invalid combination of events and conditions. This can indicate a misunderstanding or that something is missing.

- The existence of a large number of transitions with just trigger events or just actions. Such transitions are sometimes required, but having a large number of them often indicates that there are too many states in the state model.

RISK REDUCTION

- Before you start, take the time to understand your concurrency modeling notation (and the way that your tool implements the notation, if you're using a modeling tool).

- Watch out for states, transitions, or actions that are difficult to name or that seem to need the wrong sort of name (such as a verb for a state). These suggest that there is something wrong with the model.

- Walk through your models, "playing computer" in order to validate them and check for missing or incorrect elements. If your tool offers model animation facilities, these are a more reliable way of achieving this.

Excessive Complexity

Simplicity should always be an aim when designing a system. Simple designs are easier to create, analyze, build, deliver, and support. However, this is particularly important when considering concurrency because it is fundamentally difficult to understand. As we have seen, the price of complex concurrency can be very high at design time, implementation time, and beyond. More software engineering hours have probably been wasted on reworking problematic concurrency than on almost anything else. Simplicity in your concurrency approach will have a major positive impact on the amount of effort required to deliver and support your system.

RISK REDUCTION

- Be sure that all of the concurrency you introduce is justified in terms of stakeholder benefits.
- When designing state models, use the simplest subset of notation possible to capture your state machines in order to encourage a simple state model.

Resource Contention

Resource contention usually manifests itself as long wait times for shared resources or excessive activity in small, specific parts of the system (colloquially known as *hot spots*). Careful and early analysis of the concurrency model for potential contention can help you avoid such problems, but in reality, as soon as one resource contention point is eliminated, the next one will emerge. Therefore, tackling resource contention is normally a process of reducing the contention to an acceptable level.

RISK REDUCTION

- Analyze your system as it is being designed to spot resource contention as early as possible, and design around it. Use your usage scenarios to predict which parts of the system are likely to encounter high levels of concurrency, and focus your attention in these regions.
- Reduce contention by decomposing locks on large resources into a number of finer-grained locks, thus reducing the amount of time locks are held.
- Consider alternative locking techniques such as optimistic locking that reduce the time locks are held.
- Eliminate shared resources where you can, or consider making them immutable to avoid the need to lock them when accessed by multiple tasks.
- If possible, reduce the amount of concurrency you need around problematic contention points.
- Consider whether it is possible to avoid locking by using approximately correct results that may be in the process of being updated or whether it would be possible to allow copies of data to be loosely rather than tightly consistent, to avoid locking them all simultaneously during the update process.

Deadlock

Deadlock occurs when one task, A, requires access to a resource that has already been locked by another task, B, and task B is also waiting for access to a resource that has been locked by task A. We describe these two tasks as "deadlocked," and neither of them will make progress until the deadlock is broken by one of the tasks releasing one of the locks (possibly by the task being terminated by a supervisor task). As with resource contention, you can often avoid deadlock through early and thorough analysis of the system. Danger points are those parts of the system where different types of processing tasks need access to a number of the same resources. When you find potential deadlock points, you will probably need to redesign the system to avoid the problem.

RISK REDUCTION

- Where possible, ensure that resources are always allocated to tasks and locked in a fixed order.

- Attempt to isolate parallel tasks in such a way that deadlock between them is impossible.

- Reduce the number, scope, and duration of locks held where possible (or even use immutable data structures if possible, to completely avoid locking).

- Certain commercial products that use locks (such as database management systems) provide significant assistance with handling deadlock—in most cases, recognizing it and breaking it by terminating one or more of the problematic transactions. These technologies can be very useful when dealing with deadlock, but their use often needs to be carefully designed into the system so that such deadlock recovery actions are handled correctly.

Race Conditions

A race condition is problematic behavior that results from unexpected dependence on the relative timing of events. It usually occurs when two or more tasks are attempting to perform the same action concurrently. The tasks race for the resource, and the first one to reach the appropriate point in the program code wins and performs the action.

Race conditions are problematic only when they are unplanned because the system has not been designed to cope with more than one task performing the action concurrently. In these cases, information can be corrupted or lost, and the system can behave in unpredictable ways. A classic example is a system-wide data structure in an operating system process that a number of threads can update. If multiple tasks try to update the data structure concurrently (e.g., to increment a counter indicating the number of requests accepted), the resulting value will be undefined and very likely incorrect.

RISK REDUCTION

- Ensure that there are no unprotected, shared system-level resources that can cause race conditions.
- Use immutable data structures where possible to avoid the possibility of race conditions.
- Automatically introduce protection mechanisms for all potentially shared resources.
- Ensure that the definition of each element interface clearly states whether or not the interface is reentrant.

CHECKLIST

- Is there a clear system-level concurrency model?
- Are your models at the right level of abstraction? Have you focused on the architecturally significant aspects?
- Can you simplify your concurrency design?
- Do all interested parties understand the overall concurrency strategy?
- Have you mapped all functional elements to a process (and thread if necessary)?
- Do you have a state model for at least one functional element in each process and thread? If not, are you sure the processes and threads will interact safely?
- Have you defined a suitable set of interprocess communication mechanisms to support the interelement interactions defined in the Functional view?
- Are all shared resources protected from corruption?
- Have you minimized the intertask communication and synchronization required?
- Do you have any resource hot spots in your system? If so, have you estimated the likely throughput, and is it high enough? Do you know how you would reduce contention at these points if forced to later?
- Can the system possibly deadlock? If so, do you have a strategy for recognizing and dealing with this when it occurs?

FURTHER READING

The area of concurrency has been studied and written about widely, although not many books consider it from an architect's perspective.

A good overview of concurrency (albeit with a Java-specific slant) and a good introduction to (fairly formal) modeling and analysis appear in Magee and Kramer [MAGE06]; this book also introduces the Finite State Processes language mentioned earlier. Unfortunately, Cook and Daniels [COOK94] is out of print; however, it has recently made a welcome reappearance as a freely available online book at www.syntropy.co.uk/syntropy, as it contains a lot of good advice on modeling and a particularly good discussion of using state-charts to model object state. You can find a lot of good UML-specific advice about state modeling in Rumbaugh et al. [RUMB99], which is organized as a reference so it's easy to find definitions of the various UML elements involved.

Each of the visual formalisms has its own following and literature. Girauld and Valk [GIRA02] is a relatively academic text that explains how to apply Petri Nets to the analysis of concurrency characteristics, while the SDL Forum Society Web site [SDL02] is a good starting point for finding out more about SDL. A fairly recent reference on CSP is Roscoe [ROSC97]; the definitive book on CCS is still Milner [MILN89]; and the original reference for state-charts was Harel's paper [HARE87].

We reference it elsewhere too, but Michael Nygard's book [NYGA07] has much to say on the topic of safely introducing concurrency into systems. A rich collection of design patterns for creating concurrent systems is documented in [SCHM00], and a thorough programming-level "nuts and bolts" introduction to concurrency practice can be found in [BRES09]

20

THE DEVELOPMENT
VIEWPOINT

Definition	Describes the architecture that supports the software development process
Concerns	Module organization, common processing, standardization of design, standardization of testing, instrumentation, and codeline organization
Models	Module structure models, common design models, and codeline models
Problems and Pitfalls	Too much detail, overburdened architectural description, uneven focus, lack of developer focus, lack of precision, and problems with the specified environment
Stakeholders	Production engineers, software developers and testers
Applicability	All systems with significant software development involved in their creation

A considerable amount of planning and design of the software development environment is often required to support the design, build, and testing of software for complex systems. Things to think about include code structure and dependencies, build and configuration management of deliverables, system-wide design constraints, and system-wide standards to ensure technical integrity. It is the role of the Development view to address these aspects of the system development process, as it is this view that addresses the specific concerns of the software developers and testers.

This viewpoint is relevant to nearly all large information system projects because almost all of them have some element of software development, whether it is configuring and scripting off-the-shelf software, writing a system from scratch, or something between these extremes. The importance of this view depends on the complexity of the system being built, the expertise of the software developers, the maturity of the technologies used, and the familiarity that the whole team has with these technologies.

In this view you need to focus on concerns that are architecturally significant. You should view your work as providing a stable environment for the more detailed design work that will be performed as part of the software development activity.

CONCERNS

Module Organization

The large systems you are likely to encounter as an architect may be built from hundreds of thousands of lines of source code spread over thousands of files. Source files are normally organized into larger units called *modules* that contain related code (such as the code to implement a library or a functional element). Arranging code in a logical structure like this helps to manage dependencies and helps developers to understand it and work on it without affecting other modules in unexpected ways.

When working with a complex module structure, you need to identify and thoroughly understand and manage the dependencies between the modules to avoid ending up with a system that is difficult and error-prone to maintain, build, and release.

Common Processing

Any large system will benefit from identifying and isolating common processing into separate code modules. For example, standardizing how the system logs messages and handles configuration parameters can significantly simplify its administration.

The Development view helps ensure that the areas of common processing are identified and clearly specified. You will typically do this only in outline form, adding further refinement and detail as development progresses.

Standardization of Design

Most systems are developed by teams of software developers rather than individuals. Standardizing key aspects of design provides critical benefits to the maintainability, reliability, and technical cohesion of the system (and saves time, too). You can achieve design standardization by using design patterns and off-the-shelf software elements.

Standardization of Testing

Standardization of test approaches, technologies, and conventions helps ensure a consistent approach to testing and speeds up the testing process. Key concerns include test tools and infrastructure, standard test data, standard test approaches, and test automation.

Instrumentation

Instrumentation is the practice of inserting special code for logging information about step execution, system state, resource usage, and so on that is used to aid monitoring and debugging. Because instrumentation can have an adverse impact on performance, it should be possible to switch off this capability, alter the level of detail at which messages are logged, and possibly even use build tools to remove the instrumentation code altogether.

System messages can be logged to a system console, a file, or a message service, and metrics on system usage can be logged to a file or a database for later analysis.

Codeline Organization

The system's source code needs to be stored in a directory structure, managed via a configuration management system, built and tested regularly (ideally every time the software changes—"continuous integration"), and released as tested binaries for further testing and use. The way that all of this is achieved is normally termed the *codeline organization* for a system. The *codeline* is a particular version of a set of source code files with a well-defined organizational structure, usually with an associated automated system to build, test, and release a specified version or variant of the system.

Ensuring that the system's code can be managed, built, tested, and released is crucial to achieving a reliable system—particularly when you're using iterative development and many releases are necessary. As an architect, you may wish to specify, in outline form at least, how this is to be done, or better still, work with the development team to define the approach and design its implementation.

Stakeholder Concerns

Typical stakeholder concerns for the Development viewpoint include those shown in Table 20–1.

TABLE 20-1 STAKEHOLDER CONCERNS FOR THE DEVELOPMENT VIEWPOINT

Stakeholder Class	Concerns
Developers	All concerns
Production engineers	May be involved in or have responsibility for provisioning development and test environments, and mechanisms and controls over the system's transition into production
Testers	Common processing, instrumentation, test standardization, and possibly codeline organization

MODELS

Module Structure Models

The module structure model defines the organization of the system's source code, in terms of the modules into which the individual source files are collected and the dependencies among these modules. It is also common to impose some degree of higher-level organization on the modules themselves to avoid having to enumerate many individual dependencies.

Once you have identified a set of modules into which you can organize the source files, you can use the common architectural approach of grouping modules at similar abstraction levels into layers. You can then organize these layers into a dependency stack from the most abstract or highly functional (conceptually at the top) down to the least (at the bottom). You can then define interlayer dependency rules to avoid unwanted dependencies between modules at very different abstraction levels. Typically, software in a module communicates only with other modules at the same layer or in the layers directly above and below it (although there are often exceptions to this rule for performance or efficiency reasons).

In some situations (e.g., when separate module structures are needed for client and server elements), you may need a number of such models. In other cases (e.g., when developing an extension to a monolithic application package), a module structure model is less useful.

NOTATIONA module structure model is often represented as a UML component diagram, using the package icon to represent a code module and dependency arrows to show intermodule dependencies. If you require higher-level module organization, you can show module grouping by enclosing packages annotated with suitable stereotypes.

Another common alternative is a simple boxes-and-lines diagram that shows the layers, their relative ordering, and the components within them.

EXAMPLE Figure 20–1 shows an example of using UML to document a module structure model.

This layer model shows a module organization with three layers, each layer being represented by a stereotyped package. The system's modules are shown as UML packages within the layers.

The model shows that the domain layer depends on the utility layer, which in turn depends on the platform layer (i.e., the domain-layer components can access only the utility-layer components, and so on).

However, you can also see that nonstrict layering has been used in this system because all of the domain-layer components depend on facilities provided by the Java Standard Library component rather than accessing its facilities via intermediate utility components. (In contrast, the domain-level components cannot access the JDBC Driver component.)

«layer»
domain

A software module residing within a layer

Stereotyped package used to represent a layer within the software module structure

Date Scheduler   **Quote Pricer**

Interlayer dependency relationships showing allowed dependencies between modules in the layers

«layer»
utility

Servlet Container   **Logging Library**   **Message Handling Library**   **DB Access Library**

«layer»
platform

Java Standard Library   **JDBC Driver**

Explicit intermodule dependency showing allowable dependency between two specific modules

FIGURE 20–1 EXAMPLE OF A UML MODULE STRUCTURE MODEL

Identify and Classify the Modules. Group the source code for the system into a set of modules, and (optionally) classify them—by abstraction or other criteria—into a higher-level organization.

Identify the Module Dependencies. Identify a clear set of dependencies between the modules (or the higher-level groups) so that everyone involved in the design and construction of the system can understand the impact of making changes.

Identify the Layering Rules. If a layered approach is to be used, you need to design a set of rules to be followed with respect to the layers. Can modules call modules only in their own layer and the one above or below, or do you want a less rigid rule in order to meet system quality properties such as performance and flexibility?

Common Design Models

To maximize commonality across element implementations, it is desirable to define a set of design constraints that apply when designing the system's software elements. Such design constraints are valuable for two principal reasons.

- You can reduce risk and duplication of effort by identifying standard approaches to be used when solving certain types of problems.
- Commonality among system elements helps increase the system's overall technical coherence and makes it easier to understand, operate, and maintain.

A common design model has the following three important pieces.

1. A definition of the *common processing* required across elements, such as:
   - Initialization and recovery
   - Termination and restart of operation
   - Message logging and instrumentation
   - Internationalization
   - Use of third-party libraries
   - Processing configuration parameters (at startup or while running)
   - Security (e.g., authentication or encryption)
   - Transaction management
   - Database interaction
   - Internal and external interfacing

   These aspects of your software element designs can benefit greatly from using a standard approach across all system elements. Identifying and defining common processing is a key architectural task that directly contributes to the overall technical coherence of the system.

2. A definition of *standard design approaches* that should be used when designing the system's elements. These start to emerge when (having defined the functional structure) you think ahead a little about how the subsystems might be implemented. When you see situations where the same sort of processing is performed by different elements, or where you know that the implementation of a certain aspect of an element will have a system-wide impact, you should consider whether you need a standard design approach. When identifying such an approach, you must define what the approach is, where it should be used, and why it should be used. In other words, it is a special sort of design pattern.

3. A definition of what *common software* should be used and how it should be used. This may be the result of making other higher-level decisions (e.g., selecting an access library for your chosen database) or identifying a reusable component (e.g., a third-party message-logging library or a locally developed graphical user interface element) that can save you development time and reduce risk. In either case, your common design model needs to clearly identify what common elements should be used, where they should be used, and how they should be used.

As with the module structure model, you may need to define different design constraints for different parts of the system. In any case, as an architect, you are only starting a task that will continue throughout the design and build.

NOTATION The common design model is a partial design document, and as such, the notations it uses are those of software design—usually a combination of text and more formal notation such as UML.

The following example shows some possible design constraints from a common design model.

EXAMPLE Here is an example of a common design model.

Common Processing Required

1. Message logging

   - All components must log human-readable messages that clearly state what has occurred and any corrective action that is expected in response.

- Messages must be logged at one of the following levels: Fatal, Error, Warning, Information, Debug. Fatal should be used to indicate an unrecoverable error, where the component will stop immediately; Error indicates an unrecoverable error, where the component can reset itself and continue execution; Warning indicates a possible error or unexpected condition that may need operator intervention to review and address; Information is used to report conditions that occur during normal operation and require no operator intervention; Debug should be used to indicate internal details of the component's operation.
- Components should log messages at all five possible logging levels.
- Logging should be achieved via a standard library (as defined later) to standardize destination, format, configuration, and so on.

[. . .]

2. Internationalization

- All user- and administrator-visible strings must be stored in message catalogs so that hard-coded strings are not present in source code.
- Parameters must be inserted into internationalized strings using position-independent placeholders to avoid problems with ordering across languages.
- Locale-sensitive information (dates, times, currency strings, and so on) must be formatted according to the current locale in force, and default formats should not be used.
- Strings logged at Debug level or for other purely internal use should not be internationalized but should be hard-coded in the source code.

[. . .]

Standard Design

1. Internationalization

- For internationalization of locale-sensitive resources (primarily strings), use an external resource catalog to store resources outside the source code files. This means that all strings must be extracted from a message catalog before they can be used in a program (e.g., to write a log message).
- As the server software is being written entirely in Java, the internationalization implementation will use the Java Platform's native internationalization facilities: the resource bundle, the formatting classes in the `java.text` package, and the `Locale` class.

- The relationships between these different elements of the internationalization technology are as follows. [. . .]
- *[You would place a definition of a design pattern for using the Java internationalization facilities here.]*

[. . .]

Standard Software Components

1. Message logging

- All message logging must be performed using the standard `CCJLog` package, which is part of the standard build environment.
- The `CCJLog` package must be used in a standard way, which is documented as a code sample in the `src/server/sample/logging/CCJLog` source directory.

[. . .]

ACTIVITIES

Identify Common Processing. Identify *what* common processing is required, *where* the processing is required (in all elements or just some?), and *how* the common processing should be performed.

Identify the Required Design Constraints. Establish whether any common processing should be standardized and whether critical aspects of subsystem design will have a negative system-wide impact if not designed in a certain way. If you find such situations, consider whether you can impose a design constraint that will resolve the problem, and, if so, add it to the list.

Identify and Define the Design Patterns. Document a set of mini design patterns that clearly define the constraints. The constraints are defined in terms of the software design that needs to be followed, the applicability of the constraint (i.e., where to use it), and the rationale for the constraint (to allow those following it to understand its role).

Define the Role of Standard Elements. Consider whether you have any standard software elements that can be shared among subsystems. You will often identify such standard elements when considering the system's common processing. If you find standard elements, clearly define their roles and how they should be used.

Codeline Models

Although you certainly don't want to be dictating the minutiae of the software developers' lives, you do need to ensure that there is order rather than chaos when it comes to the organization of the system's code.

The key things to define are the overall structure of the codeline; how the code is controlled (usually via configuration management); where different types of source code live in that structure; how it should be maintained and extended over time (in particular, how any concurrent development of different releases should work); and the automated tools that will be used to build, test, release, and deploy the software. A codeline model normally needs to capture the following essential facts:

- How code will be organized into source files
- How the files will be grouped into modules
- What directory structure will be used to hold the files
- How the source will be automatically built and tested to form candidate releasable binaries
- What type and scope of tests will need to be run regularly and when they should be run
- How the binaries will be released into a test or production environment for testing and use, again ideally via an automated process
- How the source will be controlled using configuration management (including any use of branching, change sets, and so on) to coordinate multiple developers working on it concurrently
- What automated tools will be used for the build, test, and release process and how they will work together in order to form a complete continuous integration and delivery system

Defining these aspects of the development environment is an important part of achieving reliable, repeatable build and release processes. The information you provide through your model will help prevent confusion and frustration as developers work together.

In situations where development of the system will be distributed among different teams or among members of teams working at different locations, addressing this concern becomes even more important. You may have to take into account factors such as different time zones or even the different languages spoken by development staff.

Depending on the skill and experience of the developers, you may be comfortable leaving the majority of this work to your design team; at the other extreme, you may want to specify this in some detail.

NOTATION In principle, you can represent the codeline model by using structured notations such as UML. However, our experience of trying this suggests that it often isn't worth the bother. A simple approach based on text and tables with a few clear diagrams to explain the conventions used should suffice.

ACTIVITIES

Design the Source Code Structure. Design the overall structure of the directory hierarchy to be used to store your system's source code. This must be flexible enough to provide easy maintenance but simple enough that developers know where their source files should live.

Define the Build, Integration, and Test Approach. To achieve a reliable system build process, you need to mandate a common approach across the system. A build and release specialist may do this for you, but the approach used for automating the build, integration, and testing does need careful design. Whatever approach you use, it must make it possible to easily build the system automatically and also allow developers to use central or local copies of the latest build.

Define the Release Process. Having completed a clean build of the system, you need to release the resulting work products (binaries, libraries, generated documentation, and so on) for testing and use. To ensure that this process is reliable and repeatable, you must design a clear process, again preferably automated. As before, specialists may do the design for you, or you may need to do it yourself. It is particularly important to be clear about the build validation (such as automated test suite execution) that needs completion before release. This process will need to use any deployment tools that are required in your environment, whether internal to your organization or supplied by a third party if you are deploying software to an external hosting environment, such as externally hosted servers or a public cloud computing service.

Define the Configuration Management. To ensure repeatability and technical integrity, you must use a common approach to configuration management. Its definition should encompass the tools to be used, the configuration structures (such as variants, branches, and labels) to be used, and the process for managing the deliverables under configuration control.

PROBLEMS AND PITFALLS

Too Much Detail

Most software architects are experienced software designers, which means that you probably have a lot of background knowledge related to the process of software design and implementation. The danger that stems from this is the temptation to use the Development view to define low-level details about the system's implementation that are really the concern of the designers and implementers.

RISK REDUCTION

- Minimize the number of design constraints you identify. Identifying too many is often counterproductive and causes problems as developers try to shoehorn their elements into the space left by a number of different constraints (or simply ignore them).

- Carefully review everything you describe in the Development view, and question whether it is architecturally significant. If not, eliminate that detail from the Development view.

Overburdened Architectural Description

A problem related to having too much detail is the question of where to put the contents of the Development view (particularly in the common design model). For a complex system, the common design model can require a significant amount of text, and given that it is aimed at a specialized group of stakeholders, it can seem out of place in the main AD document.

RISK REDUCTION

- Capture the details of the system-wide design constraints in a separate document specifically aimed at the software developers, and then summarize the constraints required and their rationale in a short section of the AD. This allows interested stakeholders to satisfy themselves that the design constraints have been considered, without needing to understand the details of these constraints.

Uneven Focus

We all have a tendency to focus on things that we understand and find interesting. This can lead to a situation where, for example, the design patterns to be used for network request handling are discussed in minute detail, but the initialization processing required of each element is hardly considered at all.

RISK REDUCTION

- Try to step back from the system and consider all of the aspects of software development that need to be defined at an architectural level.

- Find specialist expertise to advise you in areas you aren't familiar with.

Lack of Developer Focus

Always remember that the primary (and often only) customers of the Development view are the software developers and testers working on your project.

The Development view must answer their questions and be relevant to their concerns. If it isn't, it will almost certainly be ignored.

RISK REDUCTION

- Involve the developers and testers in defining the Development view.
- Delegate aspects of the view's development to senior software developers when possible, to give the software development team ownership of the aspects of the architecture that affect them.

Lack of Precision

Because the Development view has to cover many aspects of the software development, and because you are unlikely to have expertise in all of them, lack of precision is a risk. Developers might misinterpret imprecise descriptions or, if they cannot understand the descriptions, might ignore them altogether.

RISK REDUCTION

- This problem often occurs when an architect knows that it is important to define some aspect of the system but knows little about it and thus simply states that it needs to be performed. When defining the Development view, make sure to review its contents early with the software developers and testers to check that the view's definitions are precise enough.
- Do not be afraid to make use of the knowledge of subject matter experts where your experience is limited—you are not expected to be an expert in everything!

Problems with the Specified Environment

Keeping up-to-date with new and emerging technologies takes a lot of time. It is particularly hard to get reliable information on how mature those technologies are and how appropriate they might be for your architecture.

This imposes the risk of specifying aspects of the Development view based on out-of-date (or perhaps just incorrect) knowledge and assumptions, which can lead to later problems in development or live operation and damage your credibility with developers.

The other related mistake that is easy to make is to try to impose approaches that have worked well before but that are simply wrong for the project teams in the environment in which you're currently working. Short-lived stand-alone systems require a different development environment from huge long-lived product lines that will be used for many years by external customers. Make sure you understand the needs and constraints of the project environment before trying to define the Development view.

RISK REDUCTION

- Make sure you specify technology and techniques you really know about, or get trusted, expert advice from subject matter experts to help make the relevant decisions.

- Understand what is needed in the current project environment and make sure that your Development view reflects these needs and doesn't over-complicate or oversimplify the development environment.

- Delegating the research and design of aspects of the Development view to members of the software development team can help alleviate this problem while having other positive side effects, such as giving the software developers a heightened sense of ownership of the system.

CHECKLIST

- Have you defined a clear strategy for organizing the source code modules in your system?

- Have you defined a general set of rules governing the dependencies that can exist between code modules at different abstraction levels?

- Have you identified all of the aspects of element implementation that need to be standardized across the system?

- Have you clearly defined how any standard processing should be performed?

- Have you identified any standard approaches to design that you need all element designers and implementers to follow? If so, do your software developers accept and understand these approaches?

- Will a clear set of standard third-party software elements be used across all element implementations? Have you defined the way they should be used?

- Will the development and test environments that have been defined work reliably and be usable and efficient for developers and testers to work in?

- Have you or someone else defined a suitable set of tools to reliably auto-mate the end-to-end build, integration, test, and release processes? Does the set of tools include any internal or third-party tools that you require to deploy to the internal or external test and production environments that you are using?

- Is this view as minimal as possible?

- Is the presentation of this view in the AD appropriate?

FURTHER READING

Many books discuss the use of design patterns in software development, the original book being, of course, Gamma et al. [GAMM95]. This topic is explored further in Coplien et al. [PLOP05–99, PLOP06].

There are a number of good books covering relevant topics such as configuration management, continuous integration, automated testing, release processes, and so forth. [AIEL10] is a fairly high-level overview of the entire area, focusing on configuration management and release control, and [BERC03] is a very thorough guide to software configuration management, illustrated using a set of patterns. [DUVA07] is a thorough and practical guide to continuous integration, and [HUMB10] is a detailed guide to automating the processes involved in building, testing, and releasing software. Finally, there are a large number of books on automated testing, but we particularly like [FREE09], which provides lots of practical advice on automation but also gets behind the mechanisms to show how and why to put automated testing at the heart of the development process.

21

THE DEPLOYMENT
VIEWPOINT

Definition	Describes the environment into which the system will be deployed and the dependencies that the system has on elements of it
Concerns	Runtime platform required, specification and quantity of hardware or hosting required, third-party software requirements, technology compatibility, network requirements, network capacity required, and physical constraints
Models	Runtime platform models, network models, technology dependency models, and intermodel relationships.
Problems and Pitfalls	Unclear or inaccurate dependencies, unproven technology, unsuitable or missing service-level agreements, lack of specialist technical knowledge, late consideration of the deployment environment, ignoring intersite complexities, inappropriate headroom provision, and not specifying a disaster recovery environment
Stakeholders	System administrators, developers, testers, communicators, and assessors
Applicability	Systems with complex or unfamiliar deployment environments

The Deployment view focuses on aspects of the system that are important after the system has been built and needs to be validation tested and transitioned to live operation. This view defines the physical environment in which the system is intended to run, including the hardware or hosting environment (e.g., processing nodes, network interconnections, and disk storage facilities), the technical environment requirements for each type of processing node in the system, and the mapping of your software elements to the runtime environment that will execute them.

A Deployment view is useful for any information system with a required deployment environment that is not immediately obvious to all of the interested stakeholders. This includes the following situations:

- Systems with complex runtime dependencies (e.g., specific third-party software packages or particular network services are needed to support the system)
- Systems with complex runtime environments (e.g., elements are distributed over a large number of machines)
- Systems hosted in third-party environments, such as hosting services or public clouds, in order to allow a clear definition of the environment required and how the system will deploy into it
- Situations where the system may be deployed into a number of different environments and the essential characteristics of the required environments need to be clearly illustrated (which is typically the case with packaged software products)
- Systems that need specialist or unfamiliar hardware or software in order to run

In our experience, most large information systems fall into one of these groups, so you will almost always need to create a Deployment view.

CONCERNS

Runtime Platform Required

The Deployment view must clearly identify the type of runtime platform that the system needs and the role that each part of it plays. This includes general-purpose compute nodes to host servers and computational logic, special-purpose compute nodes to host database engines, storage for databases and file systems, devices that allow users to access the system or print information, network services required to meet certain quality properties (such as firewalls for security), specialist hardware (such as cryptographic accelerators), and so on. The manner in which the platform is provided, whether it be physical hardware commissioned in-house, virtual servers and storage provided by a third-party hosting company, the use of a public cloud computing environment, or some other option, needs to be clearly defined too, as does the location of each part of the platform.

Defining the runtime platform involves identifying the general types of processing elements required (such as compute server node, application server node, storage array, and so on), defining the dependencies between them, and mapping each of your functional elements to one of these types. In effect, this is a logical model of the runtime platform that your system requires. Then, when you have defined what each piece of the platform is used for, you can think about the details of exactly what hardware elements you need to provide it.

Specification and Quantity of Hardware or Hosting Required

This concern, which follows from the previous one, addresses the specific details of the hardware that will need to be procured and commissioned in order to deploy the system—in effect, a physical model of the hardware your system needs. This hardware may need to be ordered and commissioned in-house or via a third party or may be specifications for a virtual computing environment, such as ordering capacity from a cloud computing supplier.

This is a separate concern from the previous one because it is much more specific and of interest to different stakeholders. For example, developers are interested in whether the deployment platform will use Intel or Sun SPARC servers; whether the servers will run Linux, HP-UX, or Windows; and what general processing resources will be available to them. However, system administrators are interested in the detailed specification and quantity of the hardware elements or specification of the hosting environment that needs to be acquired to create your runtime environment. The service-level agreements (SLAs) for each part of the runtime environment will also need to be agreed to and validated as acceptable for the level of service your system needs to provide.

Be specific when considering the specification, quantity, and service level of the hardware and services that you need. If specific models of equipment or specifications of hosted environment services are required, you need to clearly identify and record them for easy reference. If specific models or services aren't required, you should still be precise where needed.

Third-Party Software Requirements

All information systems make use of third-party software as part of their deployment environment—even if only an operating system. Many information systems make use of dozens of third-party software products, including operating systems, programming libraries, messaging systems, application servers, databases, data movement products, Web servers, and so on. If you are deploying your system to a platform-as-a-service environment, there is probably a specific set of platform services and options that you need in order for your system to run successfully.

Your Deployment view should make clear all of the dependencies between your system and any third-party software products. This ensures that the developers know what software will be available for them to use and that the system administrators know exactly what needs to be installed and managed on each piece of hardware. It also helps you to spot any gaps in your analysis as early as possible.

Technology Compatibility

Each software and hardware element in your system may impose requirements on other technology elements. For example, a database interface library may require a particular operating system network library in order to function correctly, or a disk array may require a particular type of interface in the machines that will access it.

Furthermore, if you use a number of pieces of third-party technology together, there is always the danger of uncovering incompatible requirements. For example, your database interface library may require a certain version of the operating system, but a graphics library you want to use isn't supported on that version. Such incompatibilities have a habit of emerging late in the testing cycle and causing a lot of disruption—so if you consider them early, you will avoid problems later.

Network Requirements

Your Functional and Concurrency views define the functional structure of your architecture and make it clear how its elements interact. Part of the process of creating the Deployment view is to decide which hardware elements host each of these functional elements. Because elements that need to communicate often end up on different machines, some of the interelement interactions can be identified as network interactions.

One of the concerns the Deployment view addresses is the set of services that the system requires of its underlying network as a result of these network interactions. This view needs to clearly identify the required links between machines; the required capacity, latency, and reliability of the links; the communications protocols used; and any special network functions the system requires (load balancing, firewalls, encryption, and so on).

Network Capacity Required

In our experience, software architects need to get less involved in specifying network configuration than in identifying the processing and storage hardware because the network is normally provided by a group of specialists who design, implement, and operate the network for an entire organization.

However, this group needs to know how much network capacity your system requires and the type of traffic you need to carry over the network. In order to provide this information, you must estimate and record the amount and type of network traffic that needs to be carried over each intermachine link in the proposed network topology.

Physical Constraints

As software engineers we are lucky when compared to our colleagues working in other engineering disciplines. Normally, we don't have to worry that much about physical constraints because software has no weight, has no physical size, and occupies no physical space. However, when taking a system-level view, physical constraints suddenly become important again.

Considerations such as desk space for client workstations, floor space for servers, power, temperature control, cabling distances, and so on may seem relatively mundane. However, if someone doesn't consider them, your system simply won't be deployed. There is no point in specifying four monitors for each workstation if your users have desk space for only two. Similarly, if there isn't enough floor space in your data center for your servers, they won't be installed.

Stakeholder Concerns

Typical stakeholder concerns for the Deployment viewpoint include those shown in Table 21–1.

TABLE 21–1 STAKEHOLDER CONCERNS FOR THE DEPLOYMENT VIEWPOINT

Stakeholder Class	Concerns
Assessors	Types of hardware or hosting required, technology compatibility, and network requirements
Communicators	Types and specification of hardware or hosting required, third-party software requirements, and network requirements (particularly topology)
Developers	Types and (general) specification of hardware or hosting required, third-party software requirements, technology compatibility, and network requirements (particularly topology)
System administrators	Types, specification, and quantity of hardware or hosting required; third-party software requirements; technology compatibility; network requirements; network capacity required; and physical constraints
Testers	Types, specification, and quantity of hardware or hosting required; third-party software requirements; and network requirements

MODELS

Runtime Platform Models

The runtime platform model is the core of this view. This description defines the set of hardware nodes that are required, which nodes need to be connected to which other nodes via network (or other) interfaces, and which software elements are hosted on which hardware nodes.

A runtime platform model has the following main elements.

- *Processing nodes*: Each computer in your system is represented by one processing node in the runtime platform model. This allows you and other stakeholders to see what processing resources are required for the system. For situations where many similar machines are required (e.g., Web server farms), you can use a summary notation (such as UML's shadow notation) to simplify the diagram, but make sure that the number of nodes required is still clear.

- *Client nodes*: You also need to represent client hardware, but probably in less detail than the main processing hardware. You may have less control over client hardware than server hardware, and if this is the case, you need only represent the types and quantities of client machines required rather than the precise details of each. If you have special needs for presentation or user interaction hardware (e.g., touch screens, printers), this is specified as part of the client hardware.

- *Runtime containers*: Client and server nodes may need to provide a runtime container (such as a software application server or a client virtual machine) to provide a suitable runtime environment for the functional elements deployed onto them.

- *Online storage hardware*: This defines how much storage is needed, of what type, how it is partitioned, what it is used for, the assumptions you are making about its reliability and speed, and whether or not processing takes place close to its associated stored data. The storage hardware could be disk devices within a processing node or dedicated storage nodes such as disk arrays. Make the distinction between the two types clear so that the physical impact of separate storage nodes on the deployment environment is understood. You need to include the capacity (and possibly speed) of each type of storage hardware in the model.

- *Offline storage hardware*: Despite the ever-growing capacity of online storage hardware, many systems that deal with a lot of information still require offline storage (archives) as well. Somehow the problems always grow faster than the hardware capacity. Offline storage will also probably be required to allow backup of information held online. You need to ensure that there is sufficient capacity, that the hardware is fast enough to complete archive and retrieval in an acceptable time, and that there is sufficient network bandwidth between it and the online storage. The requirements for the type, capacity, speed, and location of your offline storage hardware all need to be defined here.

■ *Network links*: Your model needs to capture the essential connections required by your system (rather than your ideas on how the network will be built from specific network elements). It is sufficient at this point to show the links between your hardware nodes; you'll capture more details about the network, such as internode bandwidth requirements, in the network model (described next in this chapter).

■ *Other hardware components*: You may need to consider specialist hardware for network security, user authentication, special interfacing to other systems, or specialist processing (e.g., for automated teller machines).

■ *Runtime element-to-node mapping*: The final element of this model is a mapping of the system's functional elements to the processing nodes where they execute. How to go about defining this mapping depends on how complex your concurrency structure is. If you have a Concurrency view, you can map the operating system processes identified in that view to the processing nodes. If you don't have a Concurrency view, you can map functional elements from the Functional view directly to processing nodes (and in this case, presumably the details of the operating system processes in use aren't architecturally significant).

This runtime platform model is typically captured as a network node diagram that shows nodes, storage, the interconnections required between the nodes, and the allocation of the software elements between the nodes.

NOTATION Common notations used for capturing the runtime platform model include the use of UML, traditional boxes-and-lines diagrams, and textual notations. Each of these options is outlined in this subsection.

■ *UML deployment diagram*: You can use a UML deployment diagram to document a runtime platform model. This diagram shows computing "nodes," and optionally "execution environments" (such as runtime containers), with "artifacts" representing the software elements deployed to them and the "communication paths" between the nodes (the communication path being a specialization of a UML association). Interelement dependencies can also be indicated on the diagram using regular or stereotyped UML dependencies. Figure 21–1 shows an example of using a UML deployment diagram as a simple runtime platform model that maps functional elements to processing nodes, in some cases with execution environments.

When using the UML "artifact" to represent the software being deployed, it may be useful to show the actual binary files that are deployed. Artifacts can

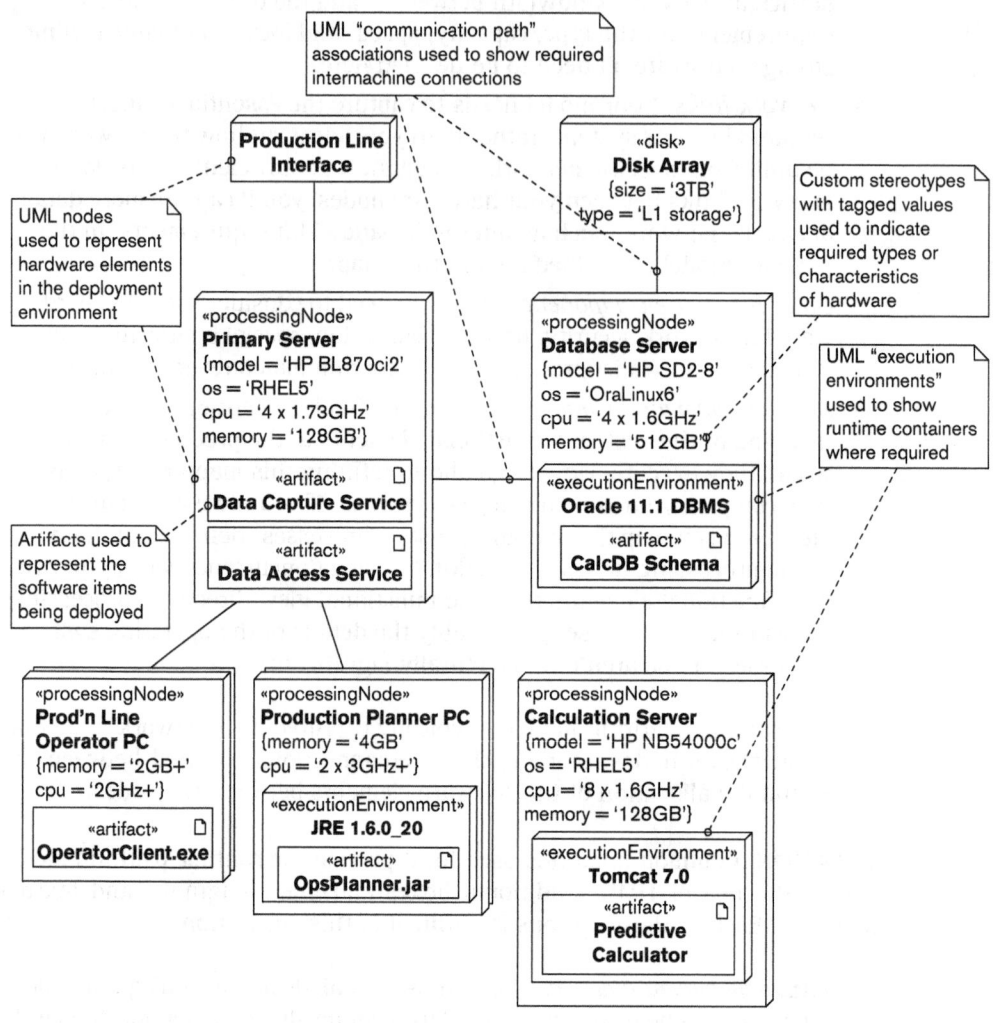

FIGURE 21-1 EXAMPLE OF A RUNTIME PLATFORM MODEL

also be used to represent entire system elements from the Functional view, which can be clearer and simpler. We show both styles of artifact in the diagram (e.g., the "OpsPlanner.jar" artifact is a deployed binary file, whereas the "Data Capture Service" is a system element, which is probably composed of a number of files). If you are using a UML tool to create your models, and the relationships between system elements and deployed artifacts aren't obvious, you may wish to use the «deploy» dependency to record these relationships.

UML does not provide very specific semantics for the nodes and communication paths and does not provide a library of predefined types to choose from. Therefore, effective use of this diagram type usually relies on the use of stereotypes, tagged values, and comments in order to distinguish between different types of nodes and links. A runtime platform model also needs to be augmented by plain-text descriptions of the major elements, clearly defining the role and important characteristics of each.

- *Boxes-and-lines diagram*: Given the basic nature of the UML deployment diagram, many architects choose a simple boxes-and-lines notation for Deployment views. Boxes are used to represent nodes and elements, with arrows for interconnection; the diagram is annotated as required in order to make the meaning of each diagram element clear. With such an approach, you need to carefully define the diagrammatic elements used to avoid causing any confusion for the reader. This notation is easier to draw with drawing tools that don't support UML, and it may be more comprehensible to nontechnical stakeholders.

- *Text and tables*: Reference information such as required hardware specifications is best represented by text that is organized into tables for easy, unambiguous reference.

ACTIVITIES

Design the Deployment Environment. You typically start by identifying the key servers in the system, any important client hardware requirements, and the network links necessary between the nodes. With this done, you have the backbone of your deployment environment. The rest of the process is normally elaboration, adding any special-purpose hardware required (e.g., cryptographic accelerators, or nodes for redundant capacity) and specifying the hardware and software configurations for each node along with any interconnections.

Map the Elements to the Hardware. Once you have a proposed deployment environment, you need to find a home in it for each of your functional (software) elements. In reality, this is an iterative process where mapping the software elements to hardware resources may suggest changes in the deployment environment design (or newly identified deployment environment options may suggest new alternatives for software element locations). The main challenges here relate to managing dependencies, ensuring that enough machine capacity is available, and trading off the advantages of separated versus colocated elements (e.g., security versus performance). Refer to Chapters 25 and 26 for more depth on these topics.

Estimate the Hardware Requirements. This activity normally starts with some initial estimation before initial deployment environment design, followed by an iterative process of refinement as architecture and design progress. The resources you need to estimate include processing power, memory, disk space, and I/O bandwidth for each processing node.

Conduct a Technical Evaluation. In order to design and estimate the deployment environment, you may need to perform a number of technical evaluation exercises such as prototype element development, benchmarks, and compatibility tests. For example, you may wish to create a representative prototype system to ensure that your application server, object persistence library, and database all work smoothly together and to check the transaction throughput you can achieve.

To ensure a representative test, identify the key attributes of your application (size, type of processing, and so on) and make sure you include all of this in your technical evaluation. Involve experts in the test to gain the benefit of their experience and ensure that you do not overlook anything important.

Obtaining time and resources for technical evaluation is often a problem. We have found that arguing for evaluation resources in terms of risk management is often the most effective way to deal with this.

Assess the Constraints. It is rare for architects to be left to define a Deployment view without any external constraints. The constraints you encounter may be formal standards, informal guidelines, or simply implicit constraints that you know exist. However the constraints are expressed, you need to review your proposed deployment environment design to ensure that they are met.

Network Models

In the interests of simplicity, the runtime platform description does not usually define the network in any detail. If the underlying network is complex, it is usually described in a separate network model.

In our experience, the network is usually designed and implemented by networking specialists rather than the software architect. However, it is important that you provide the networking specialists with a clear specification of the capabilities of the network you are expecting. This description must indicate which nodes need to be connected, any specific network services that you require (such as firewalls or compression), and the bandwidth requirements and quality properties required from each part of the network. This model is normally a logical or service-based view of what you require of the network, rather than a physical view that specifies its individual elements. In the case of software product development, such a model is a valuable specification for customers planning the deployment of your software.

The primary elements of a network model are as follows.

- *Processing nodes*: The processing nodes represent your system elements that use the network to transport data. This set of nodes should match the set from the runtime platform model, but here they are abstracted to simple elements with network interfaces.

- *Network nodes*: Additional network nodes can be added to represent network services that you expect to be available (such as firewall security, load balancing, or encryption).

- *Network connections*: The network connections are the links between the network and processing nodes. They are elaborated to include the characteristics of the service you expect the link to provide (most typically bandwidth and latency, but perhaps also quality of service, reliability, or other network qualities).

This description is typically represented as an annotated network diagram, which is really a network-oriented specialization of the runtime environment diagram. In cases where your network requirements are very simple, you can describe the network sufficiently by elaborating the runtime platform model, rather than creating a separate network model. However, given the critical dependency that most of today's systems have on the underlying network, a separate network model is a useful tool to focus attention on this aspect of the system.

Figure 21–2 shows a simple example of a network model for the runtime platform we depicted earlier in Figure 21–1. This diagram would be augmented with textual descriptions for each of the major elements.

FIGURE 21–2 EXAMPLE OF A NETWORK MODEL

NOTATION Common notations used for capturing the network model include the use of UML and traditional boxes-and-lines diagrams.

- *UML deployment diagram*: UML's deployment diagram is a useful base notation for a network model. However, as with the runtime platform description, you will probably need to annotate it with stereotypes, tagged values, and comments in order to make your intentions clear.
- *Boxes-and-lines diagram*: For reasons similar to those discussed earlier, the network model is often drawn using an informal notation.

ACTIVITIES

Design the Network. The network design is typically handled separately from that of the computer hardware because different specialists are involved. From your point of view, this is a process of sketching what you need from the network (in terms of connections, capacity, quality of service, and security). This results in what is effectively a logical rather than a physical network design, which then becomes a specification for a specialist network designer to take further.

Estimate the Capacity and Latency. Part of designing your logical network is to estimate the capacity and latency that you are expecting between each node. Precision isn't that important at this stage, but a realistic estimation of the magnitude of the traffic to be carried and expected round-trip time is important. You can estimate the capacity figures by combining peak transaction throughput and a rough approximation of the size of messages required to carry the transaction's information. The latency is normally estimated using a combination of standard metrics for the type of network in use (combined with the distance between nodes) and some measurement of the existing network. Both results are normally combined with judicious scaling factors to allow for inevitable overheads and prediction inaccuracies.

Technology Dependency Models

In some cases, you can manage the dependencies within your development or test environment by bundling your software and its dependencies into one deployment unit. However, in many cases this simply won't be possible for reasons such as efficiency, cost, licensing, or flexibility. If this is the case, you need to manage the dependencies in your deployment environment.

Technology dependencies are usually captured on a node-by-node basis in simple tabular form. The software dependencies are typically derived from the Development view, where you define the environment used by the software developers. You can also derive hardware dependencies from test or development environments, but in many cases you have to rely on manufacturer specifications and some judicious testing to confirm them.

TABLE 21–2 SOFTWARE DEPENDENCIES FOR THE PRIMARY SERVER NODE

Component	Requires
Data Access Service	HP-UX 64-bit 11.23 + patch bundle B.11.23.0703 HP aCC C++ runtime A.03.73
Data Capture Service	HP-UX 64-bit 11.23 + patch bundle B.11.23.0703
	HP aCC C++ runtime A.03.73
	Oracle OCI libraries 11.1.0.7
HP aCC C++ Compiler & Runtime	HP patch PHSS_35102
	HP patch PHSS_35103
Oracle OCI 11.1.0.7	HP-UX optional package X11MotifDevKit.MOTIF21
	HP-UX patch PHSS_37958

EXAMPLE Table 21–2 shows an example of software dependencies for the Primary Server node in our example from Figure 21–1.

From this table it is possible to see that this node in the system needs a particular version of HP-UX with a patch bundle, a couple of specific operating system patches, a set of C++ libraries, and one optional module installed, as well as a particular version of an Oracle product.

In simple cases, it may be possible to use the Development view contents rather than list dependencies in this view. However, in more complex cases, it is unlikely that the Development view contains the detail required to fully define the software dependencies for each node type in the system.

NOTATION A technology dependency model is often best captured by using a simple text-based approach, but it can sometimes benefit from the use of some simple graphical notations.

- *Graphical notations*: One way to capture software dependencies is to extend your runtime platform model to add an indication of the software stack required on each machine to support the system elements executing there. In simple cases, this can be a useful elaboration of the runtime platform model. The problem with this is that complete and accurate software dependency stacks on each node can clutter the runtime platform model to the point where it is no longer usable—in this case, you should record this information separately.

▪ *Text and tables*: Dependencies are almost always captured as simple text tables. It is important to capture the exact requirements for third-party software (e.g., detailed version numbers, option names, and patch levels).

ACTIVITIES

Analyze the Runtime Dependency. This is usually a manual exercise to work through your system elements, identifying the dependencies they have and then repeating this process for each of the third-party elements. You normally derive the runtime dependencies from documentation supplied with each piece of third-party technology you are using and your own build and test environment requirements. With this done, you can clearly define the third-party elements you need for each processing node in the system.

Conduct a Technical Evaluation. In order to correctly document dependencies, you may need to do some prototyping or technical investigation.

Intermodel Relationships

For complex systems, a Deployment view contains two or three closely related models rather than a single model. We have found that the three models described earlier tend to be used by different stakeholders at different times. People in the groups responsible for deployment refer to the runtime platform model early in the project, a specialist networking group consults the network model, and system administrators use the technology dependency model during more detailed installation planning close to deployment. For this reason, we've found it valuable to present each separately.

A good way to think about these models is as a set of informal layers, with the core of the view being the runtime platform model. You can think of the network model as a lower layer supporting the runtime platform by defining details of the network required. The technology dependency model can be thought of as a more detailed layer on top of the runtime platform that defines the software and hardware installation requirements on each machine in the deployment environment.

In an ideal world, a software architecture tool would allow you to create a single model for yourself and then extract different aspects of it automatically as required. However, we aren't aware of the existence of any such tool today, and so you'll probably have to work with separate models for the foreseeable future.

Figure 21-3 illustrates this relationship between the models within the Deployment view. The runtime platform model is the core of the view, with the network model providing more details of the network underpinning the system and the technology dependency model providing more detail about the hardware and software installed on each node to provide the runtime environment.

EF5 0.4
FRT 4.0
ABC 3.1
XYZ 8.1

AFF 3.1
XYZ 8.1

AFF 3.1
XYZ 8.1

AFF 3.1
XYZ 8.1

Technology
Dependency

Runtime Platform

Network

FIGURE 21–3 MODELS IN DEPLOYMENT VIEW

PROBLEMS AND PITFALLS

Unclear or Inaccurate Dependencies

Large-scale computing technology tends to be fairly complex, and it often has many explicit and implicit dependencies on its runtime environment that will cause problems if not satisfied. This difficulty is compounded by the fact that most of these dependencies are invisible and can't be checked easily—you may not discover that you have the wrong version of a utility library until your database server fails to start.

"You need Oracle and Linux" or "It uses Intel hardware" are pretty common dependency statements. For all but the smallest systems, these are too vague to allow safe deployment of the system. You should specify which versions are required, whether any optional parts of the products are needed, whether any patches are required, and so on. With the complexity and flexibility of enterprise software products today, you need to be very clear about what is required and what isn't.

RISK REDUCTION
- Capture clear, accurate, detailed dependencies between your software elements and the runtime environment in the Deployment view.
- Capture dependencies between third-party software and the runtime environment it needs.

- Perform compatibility testing to ensure that the dependencies between the elements are correct.

- Use existing, proven combinations of technologies where the dependencies are well understood.

Unproven Technology

Everyone wants to use the newest and coolest technology—and understandably so, as it often has the potential to bring great benefits. However, because its characteristics are unknown, using technology with which you don't have experience brings significant risks: functional shortcomings, for example, or inadequate performance, availability, or security.

RISK REDUCTION

- As much as possible, use existing software and hardware that you can test before committing to its use.

- When you must use new technology (or technology new to you), get advice from people who have used the technology before, or if this is not possible, test it thoroughly.

- Create realistic, practical prototypes and benchmarks to make sure that technologies work as advertised.

- Perform compatibility testing to ensure that new technologies work well with existing technologies.

Unsuitable or Missing Service-Level Agreements

The runtime environment for your system is usually provided by other people, whether they are a separate part of your organization or are a completely separate organization. When providing services such as hardware, data storage, networking, and so on, it is usual to specify an SLA to define the service that you can expect from the provider. This will cover aspects of the service such as cost, expected performance and reliability, recovery time guarantees in case of failure, data backup service, and so on. You need to check the SLAs carefully to make sure that the guarantees that they provide will allow you to meet the goals of your system.

RISK REDUCTION

- Obtain a reliable SLA for the runtime environment elements that are provided by third parties (and estimate your own SLA if providing elements yourself).

- Attempt to test the guarantees that the SLAs provide.

- Analyze the SLAs to understand how they combine and the implications of their combination.

Lack of Specialist Technical Knowledge

Designing a large information system is a complex undertaking that requires a huge amount of specialist knowledge about many different subjects. No one person can possibly be an expert on all of the technologies you may need to use. This is why we use teams of people to develop systems and why some people specialize in particular technologies, allowing them to advise others.

Given the number of technologies used in many systems, it can be difficult to assemble a project team with expertise in all of the technologies required. This can lead to a situation where you end up relying on vendor claims for products rather than proven knowledge and experience.

RISK REDUCTION

- Bring specialist knowledge into your team so that you have mastery of all of the key technologies you need to use to deliver your system. If you don't need the knowledge full-time, hire trusted and experienced part-time experts.

- Obtain external expert review of your architecture to validate your assumptions and decisions.

- Obtain binding contractual commitments from your technology suppliers when possible.

Late Consideration of the Deployment Environment

The deployment environment is where your system hits reality. We've seen problems in some projects when the system is designed from a purely software-oriented perspective and the deployment environment is considered only when the software is complete. Remember that an inappropriate deployment environment can make an otherwise good system totally unusable.

The deployment environment also often affects how the software is designed and implemented, and this can be expensive to change. For example, if plans change and you need to use a group of small machines rather than a single large machine to host your server elements, this could have a significant impact on the architecture of your server software, a change that would be expensive to make late in a project.

Risk Reduction

- Design your deployment environment as part of architecture definition rather than as part of a separate exercise performed after the system has been developed.

- Obtain external expert review of your architecture to get early feedback before you spend too much time or money.

Ignoring Intersite Complexities

Many systems are deployed to an environment involving more than one physical site, and this is becoming ever more prevalent as organizations move to use third-party hosting providers and cloud computing environments to augment their own data centers. Even when the entire environment is hosted in-house, concerns such as resiliency, disaster recovery, geographical location of the business, and data movement restrictions can result in systems being hosted across a number of geographically distant sites.

If you do have a multisite deployment environment, it is important to consider the impact of this quite early in your architectural design work as it can have a major impact on the quality properties of the system, particularly its security, performance, and scalability. Network latency between sites is the most obvious problem (meaning that interelement interactions across these links need to be considered carefully), but the need to keep the system secure across multiple sites and the possible scalability limitations of needing to synchronize information across sites are some of the other areas of concern that need to be addressed.

Risk Reduction

- Understand any requirements for multisite deployment as early as possible in your design work, and if it looks likely that multisite deployment is going to be required, consider its impact on all of your system qualities.

- Work with your infrastructure teams to understand the implications of distributing your system to multiple sites and the restrictions that the infrastructure may impose on this.

- Try to test various representative aspects of multisite deployment as soon as you can so that you are confident that you understand its implications.

Inappropriate Headroom Provision

Headroom is additional capacity (CPU power, memory, disk space, network bandwidth, and so on) that you include in your hardware specifications to accommodate spikes in demand or future growth in volumes. You usually add some headroom to your sizing estimates so that your system can cope with additional demand without incurring hardware upgrade costs.

Specifying headroom involves a delicate balance between optimism about future growth and spending restraint. If you get it wrong, you end up deploying either expensive hardware that is insufficiently used or a system that fails to meet its performance requirements. We discuss this further in Chapter 26.

RISK REDUCTION

▪ Make sure your hardware specifications include an appropriate amount of headroom. Refer to the Performance and Scalability perspective, discussed in Chapter 26, for a discussion of how to model this effectively.

Not Specifying a Disaster Recovery Environment

Disaster recovery is the means whereby systems can be kept operational in the event of a significant failure, such as loss of electric power, widespread storage failure, or a natural disaster such as fire or flood.

Many disaster recovery strategies require the deployment of a separate operational environment at a different location (for example, a standby or alternate data center). To keep costs down, the standby environment may have a lower specification than the production environment. In any case, as it is usually the responsibility of a development project to specify, implement, and pay for the standby hardware, this must form part of your architectural description.

We discuss this further in Chapter 27.

RISK REDUCTION

▪ Make sure your Deployment view includes a specification of any disaster recovery hardware required.

CHECKLIST

▪ Have you mapped all of the system's functional elements to a type of element in your runtime platform? Have you mapped them to specific hardware devices if appropriate?

▪ Is the role of each piece of your runtime platform fully understood? Is the specified hardware or service suitable for the role?

▪ Have you established detailed specifications for the system's hardware devices or the hosted services that you require? Do you know exactly how many of each device or how much of each service is required?

▪ Do you have service-level agreements for the elements of the runtime environment that are supplied by third parties? Are the guarantees in the agreements suitable for your system? Can you test whether the guarantees are credible or not?

- Have you identified all required third-party software and documented all the dependencies between system elements and third-party software?
- Are the network topology and services required by the system understood and documented?
- Have you estimated and validated the required network capacity? Can the proposed network topology be built to support this capacity?
- Have network specialists validated that the required network can be built?
- Have you performed compatibility testing when evaluating your architectural options to ensure that the elements of the proposed deployment environment can be combined as desired?
- Have you used enough prototypes, benchmarks, and other practical tests when evaluating your architectural options to validate the critical aspects of the proposed deployment environment?
- Can you create a realistic test environment that is representative of the proposed deployment environment?
- Are you confident that the deployment environment will work as designed? Have you obtained external review to validate this opinion?
- Are the assessors satisfied that the deployment environment meets their requirements in terms of standards, risks, and costs?
- Have you checked that the physical constraints (such as floor space, power, cooling, and so on) implied by your required deployment environment can be met?
- Do your hardware and service specifications include an appropriate amount of headroom?
- Does your Deployment view include a specification of a disaster recovery environment, if required?

FURTHER READING

A great deal of literature describes specific deployment technologies; unfortunately, little of it discusses how to design an entire realistic and reliable system deployment environment. Some other software architecture books [CLEM10, GARL03, HOFM00] contain useful explanations of how to document deployment views. Dyson and Longshaw's book on designing large-scale applications [DYSO04] includes a number of patterns relating to the Deployment view. Some of the further reading we recommend in the perspectives in Part IV also contains principles and patterns relevant to the design of a deployment environment.

22

THE OPERATIONAL
VIEWPOINT

Definition	Describes how the system will be operated, administered, and supported when it is running in its production environment
Concerns	Installation and upgrade, functional migration, data migration, operational monitoring and control, alerting, configuration management, performance monitoring, support, backup and restore, and operation in third-party environments
Models	Installation models, migration models, configuration management models, administration models, and support models
Problems and Pitfalls	Lack of engagement with the operational staff, lack of backout planning, lack of migration planning, insufficient migration window, missing management tools, production environment constraints, lack of integration into the production environment, inadequate backup models, and unsuitable alerting
Stakeholders	System administrators, production engineers, developers, testers, communicators, and assessors
Applicability	Any system being deployed into a complex or critical operational environment

Considerable effort is spent defining the architecture and design of today's large systems. However, it is rare in our experience to find a system for which comparable consideration is given to how the system will be controlled, managed, and monitored. The aim of the Operational viewpoint is to identify a system-wide strategy for addressing the operational concerns of the system's stakeholders and to identify solutions that address these.

For a large information system, the Operational view focuses on concerns that help ensure that the system is a reliable and effective part of the commissioning enterprise's information technology environment, whether it is hosted within the organization or externally by a third-party provider. For a product development project, the Operational view is more generic and illustrates the *types* of operational concerns that customers of the product are likely to encounter, rather than the concerns of a specific site. This view also identifies the solutions to be applied throughout the product implementation to resolve these concerns.

Of all of the views you create for your AD, the Operational view is often the one that is least well defined and needs the most refinement and elaboration during the system's construction. This is simply because many of the details that the Operational view considers are not fully defined until design and construction are well under way. However, considering the issues described in this chapter as early as possible will save you a lot of time and effort later.

CONCERNS

Installation and Upgrade

Installation and upgrade can range from the development team installing and configuring software elements on customer-specific hardware; to the ultimate users of the system obtaining hardware and software from a number of sources and performing installation, integration, and configuration themselves; to allocating resources in a public cloud computing environment and uploading software to it. In many organizations, software installation is performed by a separate team whose members are specially authorized to make changes to the production environment. This team may well expect that the installation process has been carefully preplanned and is largely automated.

The other major area of variability is whether this is a pure installation or whether a previous version of your system is already installed, making the installation of the current version actually an upgrade. Upgrade can be significantly more complex than installation, due to the need to respect existing data, configuration settings, the state of running elements, and so on, and in some cases to keep the system in operation during the upgrade. However, the use of iterative development approaches means that upgrade, rather than installation, is the norm, so you need to master it.

As an architectural concern, installation is less about the design of detailed procedures and plans and more about ensuring that the system can be installed or upgraded in a way that is acceptable to stakeholders. This involves working with technical specialists to understand the installation processes, software developers to ensure that their elements can be easily and reliably installed, and production engineers to assure a practical, low-risk installation approach.

Functional Migration

Functional migration is the process of replacing existing capabilities with the ones provided by your system. This usually means migrating users of an older system to use your new system. Your migration approach may comprise one or more of the following:

- A *big bang* where the migration occurs in a single step at a single point in time (often over a weekend)
- A *parallel run* where new and old versions of a system are used side by side until confidence in the new system is high enough to allow switching off the old one
- A *staged migration* where parts of a process or an organization are moved to a new system, one by one, to manage the risk and cost of the migration activity

Like many architectural concerns, migration is centered on two issues—*risk* and *cost*. The big bang approach, for example, can be the cheapest because it requires no replication of resources, but it can be extremely risky because there is no easy recovery route if the migration goes wrong. Other approaches can be much more expensive (because they require duplication of resources and the implementation of costly processes to ensure that systems run together in lockstep) but reduce risk.

Data Migration

Most if not all system development involves some element of data migration—that is, loading data from existing systems into the new one(s). A goal of a data migration exercise is almost always to automate as much as possible, particularly when large volumes of data are involved. When migrated data is very old, of variable quality, or poorly modeled, data migration may be extremely complex. If you need to migrate data between geographical locations (for example, into a data center in a different region of the world, or into an externally hosted location), additional security and performance concerns can complicate things further.

Data migration software is typically viewed as utility software with a limited life, rather than as a system requiring long-term support. This does not mean that it is of any lesser quality, but it may consist of a collection of automated software, semiautomated procedures, and manual intervention to deal with exceptions (such as missing data or data in unexpected formats). This also adds to the complexity of the process.

Nowadays, systems that manage hundreds of gigabytes or terabytes of data are not uncommon, and this presents its own migration challenges.

Massive data stores are far more likely to include data that does not conform to business rules and therefore requires exceptional processing (possibly manual intervention). It can take days or weeks to extract data from or load data into massive data stores, and it is important that you do not underestimate the time required to reorganize databases, create indexes, and so on.

Fortunately, you can also make use of a wide range of Extraction, Transformation, and Load (ETL) tools that will help you automate this process. Many ETL tools allow you to define transformation rules visually and provide facilities for accessing a wide range of different physical formats, performing standard transformations, and monitoring and analyzing the results. Database replication facilities can also be used for data migration and are useful in situations where you need to keep a number of databases synchronized for a period of time.

Another frequently overlooked problem occurs when you are migrating data from a live system that is continuing to be updated while you migrate from it, as discussed in this example.

EXAMPLE A government tax office has a very large database of taxpayers that it is migrating into a new system. The database is updated through end-user screens in tax offices throughout the country.

The architect predicts that extracting all of the data from the database will take between three and five days. The data must be sorted, which will take another day, and will then be loaded into the new system, which will take ten days. Finally, indexes must be created on the new system, which will take another day. The overall elapsed time to migrate is over two weeks, during which time the original system is estimated to have received 100,000 updates, as shown in Figure 22–1.

It will not be possible to halt the country's tax-collection activities for two weeks while the data is migrated. Special code therefore has to be written to capture these updates as they occur and to apply them to the new system once the bulk of the data has been migrated into it, so that the extract is complete.

In short, data migration may be a significant piece of work in its own right, and you should manage it the same way as any other development project, with requirements, design, build and test, and acceptance—and, of course, architecture. Many of the architectural principles described in this book apply equally well to such a migration subproject, although the success criteria are different. In a migration project, it is the successfully migrated data that has to be accepted, rather than the migration software, which will be discarded once migration is complete.

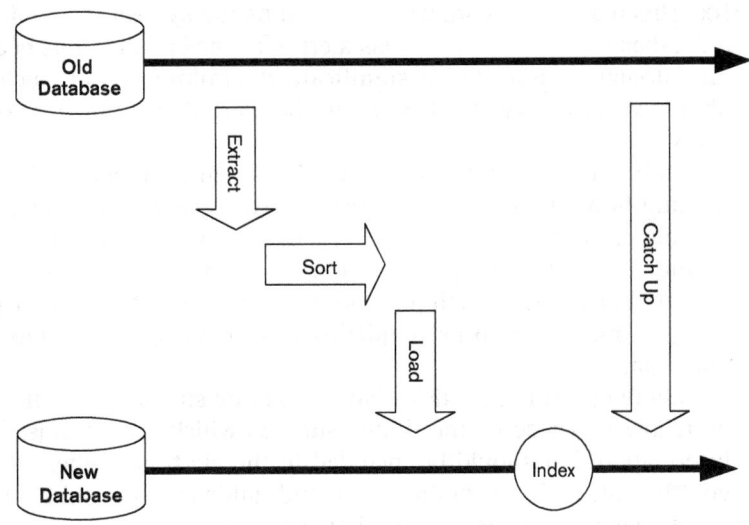

FIGURE 22-1 DATA MIGRATION FROM A LIVE SYSTEM

Operational Monitoring and Control

Once a system is running in its production environment, it will require some amount of routine monitoring, to ensure that it is working correctly, and some routine control operations, to keep it working that way (startup, shutdown, transaction resubmission, and so on).

Some systems need little monitoring or control—for example, a file server that needs only direct operational control when it fails or fills up. Others may need quite a lot—for example, a large financial reconciliation system that accepts data feeds from a variety of sources and may need routine monitoring and control to identify and rectify communication link and data reconciliation failures.

The amount of monitoring and control needed depends on the likely number and variety of unexpected operational conditions the system is likely to encounter in production. However, the development and integration of monitoring and control facilities can be a major effort in itself, so you may have to balance stakeholder needs in this area against cost and time. You also need to consider the system's deployment environment to make sure that the solutions you identify are appropriate.

Alerting

An alert is a notification from the system that an event has occurred, usually that something has gone wrong that requires human intervention in order to fix. This may be a technical alert, such as the system is unable to connect to a database server, or a business alert, such as bad data has been received on an automated input. Some significant nonfailure events, such as startup or shutdown of a service, also should be alerted (for information rather than action).

Unlike operational monitoring (in which systems are largely passive), alerting is an active system function. The system sends alerts to a central console or alert management tool, where they are displayed to support staff so they can take appropriate action. For example, a server may need to be restarted or reset, a batch job may need to be resubmitted, or in some cases the alert may need to be handed over to development teams for diagnosis and repair.

Many large organizations have corporate standards for alerting that must be followed. These define things such as which events must be alerted, the information that should be included in the alert, and where the alert should go. They also often contain advice and guidance to avoid alert flooding (see the Pitfalls section later in this chapter). If your system is deployed to a third-party hosting environment, the hosting provider will almost certainly provide its own proprietary mechanisms for raising and monitoring alerts, and you will need to consider how to use and integrate into them.

Configuration Management

Many of the elements that make up your deployment environment will have their own configuration parameters. Databases, operating systems, middleware products, and of course your own software elements may all require detailed, specific configuration for the system to operate correctly. You may also need to make coordinated sets of changes to these configurations on a regular basis (the canonical example being a switch from online to batch mode and back again every 24 hours). Managing a number of separate element configurations can rapidly become complex enough to be a major source of operational risk for the system.

The discipline of configuration management aims to address this problem. Configuration management encompasses the processes and technologies to group, modify, and track element configuration parameters in a reliable and predictable manner.

The process of operational configuration management tends to be a fairly specialized job, handled by the system administration and production engineering groups that run the production systems. From the architectural perspective, addressing this concern involves understanding the operational configuration your system requires and ensuring that it is possible to achieve it in a way that will be accepted by the interested stakeholders.

Performance Monitoring

The process of understanding and improving system performance is known as *performance engineering*, which we discuss in Chapter 26. However, the basis of all performance engineering work is *measurement*, so performance monitoring is an important concern for most systems. Your system needs to be able to capture, present, and store accurate quantitative performance information.

Production system administrators are often the first people who need to recognize and respond to a performance problem. You need to involve them in this process as early as possible to make sure they can work with the proposed solution.

In Chapter 26, we discuss in more detail the kinds of metrics needed for performance engineering and how you can capture and report them.

Support

End users, support staff, and maintainers have an interest in the type and level of support needed, who will provide that support, and the channels through which it will be delivered. As well as the system itself, support may be needed for the associated hardware infrastructure (computers, printers, and the network).

Backup and Restore

As we saw in our description of the Information viewpoint in Chapter 18, data is an extremely valuable asset to any organization and should be protected and "insured" the same way that its other assets are. Processes to do this should be carefully designed, built, and executed and should also be regularly tested to ensure that they are still working correctly.

> **EXAMPLE** One of us visited a trade organization many years ago that ran its membership database on a stand-alone UNIX system. The system administrator faithfully backed up the database to tape every night, but unfortunately, because the output of the process was not captured to a log file, nobody realized that the tape drive was broken and no data was being written. Only when the inevitable happened and a disk failed did the soon-to-be-unemployed system administrator realize that he had a shelf full of blank tapes. The organization had to re-create its membership database from paper records, which was a slow, painful, and costly process.

You shouldn't forget the restore side of the equation, either. At a minimum, restoring data should leave it in a transactionally consistent state (i.e., with all updates entirely committed to the restored database or not recovered at all). You will need to consider the amount of data lost as a result of the restore; at a minimum, this will be any transactions that are active at the time of failure but may include a lot more, particularly if backups can be done only when the system is offline.

If your data is distributed, this problem becomes much harder to solve. Although a failure in any one program will affect only that program's data, the data may then become inconsistent with the rest of the system; you need to develop strategies to deal with this. Typically, the solution involves recovering or re-creating the lost data, either manually or (preferably) automatically. In some cases, it may be more appropriate to revert the rest of the system to the older state.

A significant complication for backup and restore planning is the fact that, in many situations, transactional consistency must extend across a system's entire distributed data set, as shown in the next example.

EXAMPLE A university maintains academic records for all of its students in a number of databases. The main database stores results for each exam taken by each student, and a consolidated database turns these into an overall score for each student based on exam success, as shown in Figure 22–2.

A database corruption means that the Exam Results Database has to be restored from its latest clean backup, which is almost three months old, and the results for the last three months rekeyed into it. Although the Student Scores Database is unaffected by the corruption, special actions must be taken to prevent this manually recovered data from filtering into the Student Scores Database and corrupting its data. As a result, it could take several weeks to repair the damage due to the corruption of one database.

FIGURE 22-2 EXAMPLE OF BACKUP AND RECOVERY

If your system contains data distributed over a number of data stores, you must ensure that your Operational view takes this into account when considering backup and recovery.

Operation in Third-Party Environments

An increasingly popular option for application hosting is to use external hosting facilities such as external server hosting or cloud computing environments. External hosting can be a simpler, more flexible, and more cost-effective option than traditional internal hosting for some types of organizations and applications, and it seems to be a trend that is likely to increase.

If external hosting is a likely option for some or all of your application, it is important to start considering how you would operate your system in such an environment well before you need to do so. Any external hosting option will bring operational complications, so it is important to understand the particular facilities and constraints of the service to which your application may be deployed.

Some of the aspects of the operational environment that can be affected by the use of third-party hosting environments include the need to integrate into whatever monitoring, alerting, and management tools the service provides; the need to migrate data into the environment in order to support processing there; the need to work with the provider's support channels for problem escalation; and the need to understand and test the backup and restore facilities provided. You are unlikely to be able to gain physical access to your servers in any circumstances—indeed, you may not even know where they are located—and therefore need to be able to perform all operational actions remotely.

Stakeholder Concerns

Typical stakeholder concerns for the Operational viewpoint include those listed in Table 22–1.

TABLE 22–1 STAKEHOLDER CONCERNS FOR THE OPERATIONAL VIEWPOINT

Stakeholder Class	Concerns
Assessors	Functional migration, data migration, support, and operation in third-party environments
Communicators	Installation and upgrade, functional migration, operational monitoring and control, and operation in third-party environments
Developers	Operational monitoring and control, performance monitoring, and operation in third-party environments

Continued on next page

TABLE 22-1 STAKEHOLDER CONCERNS FOR THE OPERATIONAL VIEWPOINT *(CONTINUED)*

Stakeholder Class	Concerns
Production engineers	Installation and upgrade, operational monitoring and control, configuration management, performance monitoring, and operation in third-party environments
Support staff	Functional migration, data migration, alerting, support, and operation in third-party environments
System administrators	All concerns
Testers	Installation and upgrade, functional migration, data migration, monitoring and control, performance monitoring, and operation in third-party environments
Users	Support

MODELS

The Operational view consists of models that illustrate how the system will be put into production and kept running effectively once it is there.

Bear in mind that for most enterprise systems, each of these models can be quite large and involved. When this is the case, it is sensible to summarize the model in the AD and reference a fuller model in another document, to avoid making the AD too large and unwieldy.

Installation Models

Moving a system from its development environment to its production environment is a critical part of the system's lifecycle. Your AD needs to demonstrate that it is possible for a system built using this architecture to be installed (and upgraded) in a practical way.

The installation model should discuss installation and/or upgrade as needed for your system. This model needs to help the reader understand:

- What needs to be installed or upgraded to move the system into production
- What dependencies exist between the various groups of items to be installed and upgraded
- What constraints exist on the process to perform the installation and/or upgrade for the system
- What would need to be done to abandon and undo the installation and/or upgrade if something goes seriously wrong

The AD doesn't need to include a complete installation and upgrade plan—that information goes into a different document produced when needed. Instead, the installation model provides your view of the requirements and constraints the architecture imposes on installation and upgrade. The installation model in your initial AD is likely to contain only an overview of your installation strategy (because the details of what needs to be installed aren't fully known at that time), but you will be able to elaborate and refine this model as construction of the system progresses.

NOTATION The best notation to use for an installation model really depends on the situation and what the primary stakeholders (the system administrators) are familiar with. In our experience, an approach using text and tables is often the best way to communicate this information.

Simple lists work well for laying out and defining the elements of the installation problem. In simple cases, cross-reference tables can describe dependencies, while more involved dependencies are usually effectively addressed with the use of dependency diagrams.

ACTIVITIES

Identify the Installation Groups. Start by considering what elements of your architecture need to be installed and/or upgraded, and identify groups of them that can be handled together. For each group, define which elements it contains and the approach that will be used to install or upgrade that group.

Identify Any Dependencies. Technical dependencies often exist between different parts of a complex system during installation, so that the installation process has to proceed in a specific order. Identify the dependencies that exist between your installation groups to reveal these constraints.

Identify Any Constraints. Consider the overall installation process and the different ways it could be achieved. Other than the ordering dependencies you considered in the previous activity, does your architecture or deployment environment impose any further constraints on the process? (For example, do you need to start one element after it is installed so it can generate code or data needed to install the next one? Do you need to follow any particular environment-specific procedure when installing particular elements of the system? Do you need to restart one of the machines during installation?)

Design the Backout Approach. Consider what would need to be done to undo any of the installation tasks you have identified. In particular, identify anything that would be complex or time-consuming to undo.

EXAMPLE This example shows an installation model for a rental-tracking system, based on the results of the activities just described.

Installation Groups

- *Windows Desktop Client*: contains all of the software in the WIN-CLIENT component. Installation shall be via InstallShield automatic installer, remotely executed via the management tool.

- *Database Schema*: contains all DBMS schema definitions and data abstraction stored procedures. To be packaged as simple SQL scripts and installed using a custom-written Perl script.

- *Web Interface*: contains the server-resident user interface components (the WEBINTERFACE component). Installation will be by manual administrative action, copying files into IIS directories according to written instructions.

- *Rental-Tracking Service*: contains the .NET assemblies that implement the services called by the Web and Windows interfaces (the RENTALTRACKER component). Installation will be by manual administrative action, copying files into IIS directories according to written instructions.

- *Reporting Engine*: contains the .NET assemblies that implement the summary reporting engine. Installation will be by manual administrative action, copying files into IIS directories according to written instructions.

Dependencies

- Windows Desktop Client, Web Interface, Rental-Tracking Service, and Reporting Engine depend on Database Schema.

- Windows Desktop Client and Web Interface depend on Rental-Tracking Service.

- Web Interface depends on Reporting Engine.

Constraints

- *Windows Desktop Client*: A restart of the client machine will be required during this installation process.

Backout Strategy

This is the first release of the software, so backout is reasonably straightforward and consists simply of uninstallation. For each installation group, the following action will be required.

- *Windows Desktop Client*: Run the installer with an `uninstall` flag.
- *Database Schema*: A custom Perl script will be supplied to remove all objects created during the installation.
- *Web Interface*: Manual administrative action will be required. The supplied instructions will list the files to be removed.
- *Rental-Tracking Service*: Manual administrative action will be required. The supplied instructions will list the files to be removed.
- *Reporting Engine*: Manual administrative action will be required. The supplied instructions will list the files to be removed.

Migration Models

If a migration process is required, the migration model needs to illustrate the strategy that will be used. Again, a complete plan is not called for in the AD, but rather a succinct definition of the strategies to be employed. This model should allow its reader to understand:

- What overall strategies can (or will) be employed to migrate information and users to the system
- How the new system will be populated with information from the existing environment
- How information in the new and old environments will be kept synchronized (if required)
- How operation could revert to the old system if serious problems emerge with the new one

As with the installation model, the migration model should focus on the requirements and constraints that the current architecture places on the detailed migration process that will be developed later.

NOTATION A migration model is usually documented by using text and tables because no suitable, widely accepted graphical notations are available. Some informal diagrams may help illustrate data migration and synchronization, and particularly complex data migration may require some form of data model to illustrate the transformations involved.

ACTIVITIES

Establish Possible Strategies. Assess your architecture and the existing system(s), and establish which migration strategies (i.e., big bang, parallel run, staged migration) are possible, how each would work, and the tradeoffs among them.

Define the Primary Strategy. In some situations, you will simply define the options and someone else will decide which approach to use (e.g., if you're developing a product and different customers want to migrate in different ways). In other cases, you will be tasked with the responsibility of defining which strategy best meets the needs of your stakeholders and making it happen. If migration is going to take more than a short period of time, you will need to consult with your stakeholders, particularly users, to define an approach that minimizes any business disruption.

Design the Data Migration Approach. Having identified a strategy to use, you need to decide how to populate the system with all of the information in the existing system(s). This doesn't mean you need to spend days mapping fields between databases, but it does mean you have to understand the problem well enough to choose an appropriate approach for the data migration and determine how long it is likely to take and what tasks and resources might be required.

Design the Information Synchronization Approach. Some situations call for information to be synchronized between the old system(s) and the new one. This is particularly the case when using the parallel run migration strategy because information in the old system(s) may continue to be updated after the new system goes live. If synchronization is required, it may be unidirectional (just into the new system) or bidirectional (information changes need to be migrated from new to old as well as old to new). Your task is to identify an overall approach that will allow the required degree of synchronization to be performed within the operational constraints of your environment.

Identify the Backout Strategy. Being able to back out to an existing system (if available) is an attractive risk-reduction option for live operation. The problem is that it isn't always clear how such a backout would work, or if it is even possible (e.g., reverse data migration may not be practical due to the design of the new system). You need to decide whether a backout strategy involving the old system(s) is required and, if so, how it could work.

Configuration Management Models

You may need to create a configuration management model if your system requires complex, regular reconfiguration (e.g., reconfiguring parts of the system to handle different types of workloads according to a calendar-based schedule). This model must explain to its readers:

- The groups of configuration items in the system and how each is managed
- The dependencies that exist among the configuration groups
- The different configuration value sets required for routine system operation (and why each is required)
- How the different sets of configuration values will be applied to the system, taking into account the characteristics of the operational environment(s) that you are using

The aim is to create a model of the system configuration management aproach (rather than identifying lots of individual configuration values). This allows those responsible for system configuration management to understand the problem and plan their solution for it.

Like the installation model, this model is unlikely to be complete in your early AD but can be elaborated and refined as construction of the system progresses and the details of the configuration items required become known.

NOTATION This model is often quite simple and best documented by using text and tables. In more complex cases, it is usually best treated primarily as a data model, and a data-modeling notation, such as entity-relationship diagrams or UML, is a useful addition to the textual description.

ACTIVITIES

Identify the Configuration Groups. Consider all of the configuration values your system requires and break them into cohesive groups with as few intergroup dependencies as possible. This allows you to abstract the problem of managing the individual values to the level of managing large groups as a single unit (think of them as clumps of values). Name each group, explain its purpose, and explain how the configuration group would be managed (how values are defined, collected, applied, and so on).

Identify Any Configuration Group Dependencies. Having identified the groups of configuration information in your system, you can clearly identify and record any dependencies among them. For example, if changing the configuration of your database management system means reconfiguring the operating system, or adding more instances of one of your elements means changing the application server configuration, record these as intergroup dependencies. Identifying these dependencies allows you to start understanding the problem of reconfiguring your system in production.

Identify Configuration Value Sets. Consider your system during its routine operational lifecycle, and establish how many configurations your system will need during it. Define the characteristics of each value set, and identify the configuration groups that change between different configurations. For each set you identify, define its purpose and when it needs to be applied. This allows assessment of the operational impact of your architecture's configuration needs.

Design the Configuration Change Strategy. Once you have identified the configuration your system needs and the changes you need to make to it, design an approach to achieve this in your intended production environment, taking into account any constraints that it imposes. Again, rather than focusing on the minutiae of the administration process, you need to identify a practical overall approach that the production administrators of your system will accept.

EXAMPLE This example shows a configuration management model for the rental-tracking system we described earlier.

Configuration Groups

- *DBMS Parameters*: the SQL Server 2008 parameters that control the initialization, operation, and performance characteristics of the database. These are managed via SQL scripts, applied by database administrators.

- *IIS Parameters*: the IIS parameters that control the initialization, operation, and performance characteristics of the server. These are managed by using a set of PowerShell scripts that will be supplied with the system.

- *Reporting Engine Options*: the Reporting Engine parameters that control what is summarized and when summaries are computed. These are managed as a set of configuration files read by the component.

Configuration Dependencies

- When the IIS parameters are set to allow more connections, the DBMS parameters must be changed to allow for the possible increase in load.

- If the Reporting Engine Options are set for more aggressive summary activity, the DBMS parameters must be set to allow for an increased amount of data cache being required.

Configuration Sets

- *Standard*: normal configuration for planned system workload of up to 1,200 concurrent users with the Reporting Engine producing level 1 summary statistics every 6 hours.

- *High Volume*: configuration to be applied when high client volume is expected. Increases capacity to 2,000 concurrent users and switches off routine operation of the Reporting Engine.

- *Month End*: configuration to be applied during the last two days of the month, limiting concurrent usage to 800 users and allowing the Reporting Engine to run continually to produce complete summary statistics.

Configuration Change Strategy

The configuration sets will be applied as follows.

- The DBMS will be manually reconfigured first, by the database administrator running a single script that sets the parameters for the desired configuration set. (This could involve a DBMS restart.)

- Next, the Reporting Engine Options will be changed by altering the Engine's configuration file parameter and restarting it.

- Finally, the IIS configuration set will be applied by an administrator running the appropriate PowerShell script and restarting the IIS server.

Administration Models

When your system is running in its production environment, it will require some degree of administration to monitor it and keep it running smoothly. The administration model is the section of your AD where you define the operational requirements and constraints of your architecture and the facilities it provides for administrative users.

The administration model must define the following items.

- *Monitoring and control facilities*: In order to support your system's administrators, you may need to provide or use some monitoring and control facilities as part of your architecture. This may involve custom utilities and features and/or integration into one or more existing internal or third-party management environments. It can be as simple as a basic message log or as complex as a full-blown integration with a management or monitoring infrastructure. You need to clearly define the facilities you are going to provide, use, or integrate into; how these address the problem; and whether any limitations in these facilities could constrain their applicability or usefulness.

- *Required routine procedures*: You should also review the architecture you have designed and identify any administrative work that needs to be performed on a regular basis or that may be required in exceptional circumstances. Depending on the system, this can be as basic as a weekly backup and a monthly health check, or it can be a set of complex procedures performed on a round-the-clock basis to keep a critical high-volume system running at peak efficiency. For each procedure, you need to define its purpose, when it is performed, who performs it, and what is involved in performing it. In most cases, you should cross-refer to the relevant monitoring and control facilities provided.

- *Likely error conditions*: Any complex system can suffer unexpected failures due to internal or external faults. From simple situations such as disks filling up to sudden failures of the underlying network causing a cascade of problems, many error conditions that occur can require administrative intervention to rectify them. Some of these conditions are independent of your architecture and are caused by underlying platform failures. The administrators of your system will probably already be experts at diagnosing and recovering from these failures. However, you cannot expect them to understand the possible error conditions that are unique to your architecture, and you need to explain these carefully to help administrators understand the conditions they may need to recover from. Your description should include when the condition can occur, how to recognize it (referencing relevant monitoring facilities provided), how to rectify it (referencing relevant control facilities provided), and possible further failures the condition could trigger.

- *Performance monitoring facilities*: A specialist subset of system monitoring is the ability to monitor the performance of the system. The difference between operational monitoring and performance monitoring tends to be how the data is used. Operational monitoring usually reports by exception and produces little or no output data when everything is going well. In contrast, performance monitoring facilities are usually designed so that performance information can be extracted and analyzed routinely to allow system performance to be tracked over time. We talk more about performance activities in general in Chapter 26. In an administration model, you need to explain the types of performance measures you will make available and how administrators or developers will extract and analyze the information when required.

An important point to note is the strong degree of cross-reference between the administrative facilities you define in this model and the common design model in the Development view. In the Operational view, you define the facilities you will provide for the administrative stakeholders. The Development view needs to define the common processing required across all of the system's elements in order to actually achieve those facilities.

NOTATION The primary customers of the administration model are system administrators, who may not be software developers by training. We have found that the right notation for this model is nearly always text and tables augmented with a few informal diagrams where needed. Extensive use of more formal notation such as UML is less appropriate for this model.

ACTIVITIES

Identify the Routine Maintenance Required. Consider your system running in its production environment and create a list of the types of operational tasks that will need to be performed to keep the system running smoothly. For each task type, define who needs to perform it, when it needs to be performed, and how it should be performed.

Identify Your Likely Error Conditions. Analyze your architecture by considering its primary usage scenarios, and work out what is likely to go wrong during the operational lifecycle (elements failing, data stores filling up, systems running out of memory or other runtime resources). Make sure you think about the ones related to administration and maintenance as well as the ones that end users would be aware of—it is often harder to plan for failures during larger-scale administrative scenarios (such as data maintenance). Identify the classes of error conditions that can occur, what causes them, and how they can be rectified to get the system running again. You should also try to estimate the likely availability impact of the failure to ensure that you can recover the system in a time acceptable to your stakeholders. You may want to consider the error conditions that could occur if routine maintenance *isn't* performed, so that the importance of this maintenance is understood.

Specify Any Custom Utilities. Routine and exceptional procedures may require system-specific utilities to allow administrators to perform them efficiently. Such utilities can range from very simple database or operating system scripts to significant pieces of software in their own right. Consider whether any such utilities are required, and specify any you need.

Identify the Key Performance Scenarios. Some of your architectural usage scenarios will be much more important than others from a performance perspective (look for the scenarios that support time-critical business processes, involve a high workload, are executed very frequently, or are required by key stakeholders). Extract these scenarios from the overall system usage scenarios.

Identify the Performance Metrics. Consider the key performance scenarios and identify metrics that will allow you to measure the performance achieved for each and to analyze where the system spends most of its time and resources. In order to abstract the problem, it may be more useful to identify classes of metrics rather than individual ones. Make sure that you record what each metric or class identified actually means and what it is used for.

Design the Monitoring Facilities. Having established the operational tasks and performance metrics required, you can design monitoring facilities to be used across the system to provide routine system monitoring and error condition recognition and to gather performance metrics from the system's elements. This design will be at the outline level, to be fleshed out later during the development increments of the lifecycle. However, at this stage you should provide enough detail to clarify what needs to be done in each system element to provide the administration facilities required.

EXAMPLE This example shows an administration model for the rental-tracking system.

Monitoring and Control

The monitoring and control facilities are as follows.

- *Server Message Logging*: All server components will write information, warning, and error messages to the Windows Event Log of the machine they are running on.
- *Client Message Logging*: The client software will log messages if an unexpected error is encountered. The log will be written to the hard disk of the client machine for later manual retrieval.
- *Startup and Shutdown*: No system-specific startup and shutdown facilities will be provided because the software will run in the context of the IIS and SQL Server servers, and their facilities are considered to be sufficient.

Operational Procedures

Routine operational procedures are as follows.

- *Backup*: Operational data in the SQL Server database will need to be backed up. This will involve backing up the transaction logs every 15 minutes and backing up the application's databases every day. Details of this procedure will be left to the database administrators.

- *Pruning of Summary Information*: The Reporting Engine does not remove the summary reporting information it creates. This information is left in place and is available to users of the Windows client interface. Database administrators will need to monitor the performance of the Reporting Engine and the management reporting aspects of the Windows client components and manually prune the summary information when its volume starts to impact performance. A written procedure will be supplied to explain how the pruning should be performed.

Error Conditions

The error conditions that administrators should be expected to handle are as follows.

- *Database Out of Log Space*: If transaction volume rises above a certain point, it is possible that the transaction log will fill. This will cause the system to suspend operation. Database administrators will need to recognize log space problems and manually back up the logs to free space. If this happens routinely, the backup interval for the transaction logs should be reduced.

- *Database Out of Data Space*: If the database runs out of data space, the system will stop operating. Again, database administrators will need to recognize this condition and either prune the summary information (see above) or add more data space to the system. A written estimate of the amount of space required for various volumes of workload will be provided.

- *IIS Failure*: If the IIS server fails, the system will completely fail, and Windows clients will lose contact with the server. Administrators need to recognize this condition and restart IIS. The system will recover automatically once IIS is restarted. The Windows clients will automatically reconnect once the server is available again.

Performance Monitoring

No application-specific performance monitoring facilities are planned. System performance monitoring should be achieved by using the following facilities.

- *SQL Server Counters*: The SQL Server 2008 product allows a wide range of performance counters to be collected and viewed via the Windows Server 2008's Reliability & Performance Monitor and the

> SSMS Activity Monitor. These performance metrics should be used
> to assess the volume of workload on the database and the time
> taken for the application's transactions to complete.
>
> ▪ *IIS/ASP.NET Counters*: IIS Server and ASP.NET produce a wide
>   range of performance counters to be collected via the Windows
>   Server 2008's Reliability & Performance Monitor application.
>   These counters should be used to assess the number of Web re-
>   quests being serviced and how long it is taking to service them.
>
> ▪ *.NET Counters*: The .NET runtime allows a wide range of perfor-
>   mance counters to be collected via the Windows Server 2008's
>   Reliability & Performance Monitor application. These counters
>   should be used to establish the amount of non-Web-request work-
>   load that the application is performing and how long it is taking to
>   perform the operations.

Support Models

Once your system is running in production, at least some of the system's
stakeholders are likely to need help using or operating it, and other parties
will need to provide assistance to them. The support model should provide a
clear abstraction of the support that will be provided, who will provide the
support, and how problems can be escalated between parties when searching
for a resolution. This means defining the following in your support model.

▪ *Groups needing support*: The model must clearly define the groups of
  stakeholders who will require support, the nature of the support they
  need, and the appropriate mechanisms for delivering that support.

▪ *Classes of incidents*: The model must also define what sorts of support
  incidents are likely to be encountered and what sort of response is reasonable to expect in each case. The definition of each class of incident
  should clearly state the characteristics of an incident in that class, typically in terms of operational, organizational, or financial impacts.

▪ *Support providers and responsibilities*: Each type of support incident
  needs to be handled by at least one support provider, who must accept
  responsibility for resolving the incident. The model should capture who
  the support providers are and their responsibilities for incident resolution.

▪ *Escalation process*: A serious incident often requires a number of different support providers to resolve the situation because it is too complex or
  specialized for a single provider to handle. Your model should define how

incidents are escalated between support providers and the responsibilities of each when this happens. This will help ensure that incident resolution does not stall because of confusion over responsibilities or a lack of expertise by a particular provider.

As with the other models for the Operational view, the focus of the support model should be to provide an overview of the support problem and a strategy for its solution rather than the definition of detailed procedures.

NOTATION This model needs to be understood by a number of different technical and nontechnical stakeholder groups. The majority of the model should normally be a text-and-tables definition of the support to be provided, with some flow diagrams (such as UML activity diagrams) where required to make the information flow and decision-making processes clear.

ACTIVITIES

Identify the Supported Groups. Identify the groups of stakeholders who will need support, the type of support they will need, and the possible avenues through which that support could be provided.

Identify the Support Providers. Decide who will be providing support to your stakeholders. For each provider (which will probably be an organization), define the support to be provided and how it is to be provided.

Identify Any Incidents Requiring Support. Consider the types of incidents that could trigger the need for assistance by each of your groups of supported stakeholders, and characterize each incident type by likely frequency and severity.

Map the Providers, Incidents, and Groups. Decide which support providers will resolve which incident types for which stakeholder groups, and ensure that each provider can offer suitable support.

Plan the Escalation. Consider your groups of support providers, and identify which of them may need to escalate problems to other internal or external support providers. Define the escalation paths that should be used between providers and the responsibilities of each provider when this happens.

EXAMPLE This example shows a support model for the rental-tracking system.

Supported Groups
- *Web Users*: People using the Web interface to book or manage their rentals may need support if there are problems with the site or if

they have difficulties using the Web interface. Few assumptions may be made about this group, and the primary support channel should be e-mail, with telephone backup.

- *Windows Users*: Internal users using the Windows client may need help with a range of problems including usage issues, system problems, and PC support. Their primary support channel is assumed to be telephone, although they may be prepared to receive support via e-mail.

- *Windows Administrators*: The administrators of the server machines are technically sophisticated and will require assistance only in unexpected failure scenarios. They will need to receive immediate assistance via telephone as well as query resolution via e-mail.

- *Database Administrators*: The database administrators are technically sophisticated and will require assistance only with unfamiliar database behavior. They will need to receive immediate assistance via telephone as well as query resolution via e-mail.

Support Providers

- *Web Services Help Desk*: This organizational group is responsible for resolving all support incidents raised by users of the Web interface. They provide support via e-mail and telephone, six days per week, 20 hours per day.

- *IT Help Desk*: This organizational group is responsible for resolving all support incidents raised by users of the Windows client interface. They provide support via e-mail and telephone and can often provide direct assistance at the end user's desk as well. Support is provided during normal business hours.

- *DBA Group*: This organizational group is responsible for resolving all support incidents related to database management systems. They provide support via e-mail and telephone. Support is normally provided during normal business hours, with the option of using on-call staff outside this period.

- *Windows Administrators*: This organizational group is responsible for resolving all support incidents related to IIS, .NET, and Windows Server 2008 and underlying hardware. They provide support via e-mail and telephone. Support is provided during normal business hours, with the option of using on-call staff outside this period.

- *Microsoft Support*: This is an external organization (the Microsoft Corporation's Support division) that is responsible for assisting with the resolution of support incidents caused by a fault or usage problem with the SQL Server 2008, Windows Server 2008, or IIS products. They provide support via e-mail, newsgroups, Web sites, fax, and telephone. Support is provided 24 hours per day, every day.

- *Development Team*: This is the organizational group that developed the system originally and maintains it on an ongoing basis. They are responsible for resolving any incident that other support providers cannot resolve. They provide support via e-mail, telephone, and site visits during normal business hours, with the ability to reach on-call staff during other times.

Support Incidents and Resolution

- *Web Usage Difficulties*: This class of support incident covers any situation where a user of the Web interface is having problems using the system that are not caused by failure or malfunction of a system component. These incidents should be resolved in a single interaction with the Web Services Help Desk, either by phone or by e-mail. The impact on the organization should be minimal.

- *Windows Usage Difficulties*: This class of support incident covers any situation where a user of the Windows client interface is having problems using the system that are not caused by failure or malfunction of a system component. These incidents should be resolved in a single interaction with the IT Help Desk, either by phone or by e-mail. The impact on the organization should be minimal.

- *End-User System Errors*: This class of support incident covers any situation where a user of the system encounters a problem caused by failure or malfunction of a system component. These incidents should be resolved within 1 working day. The user should interact entirely with staff of the IT or Web Services Help Desk, who will manage problem resolution and deal with other support providers as required. The impact on the organization should be moderate and should not threaten business operations beyond inconvenience.

- *Slow End-User Performance*: This class of support incident covers any situation where end users complain of unacceptably slow performance. These incidents should be resolved within three working days. The user should interact entirely with members of the IT or Web Services Help Desk, who will manage problem resolution and deal with other support providers as required. The impact on the organization should be moderate and should not threaten business operations beyond inconvenience.

- *Database Corruption*: This class of support incident covers any situation where the database system reports internal corruption. These incidents should be resolved within 2 hours (although realistically it is recognized that they could return; however, the original incident should be resolved within 2 hours). The DBA Group is responsible for recognizing and resolving these situations. The impact on the organization should be moderate, but business operations will be interrupted while the problem is resolved.

- *Database Failure*: This class of support incident covers any situation where the database system needs to be recovered from backups. These incidents should be resolved within 4 hours. The DBA Group is responsible for recognizing and resolving these situations. The impact on the organization may be severe during this period, with business operations being interrupted for the whole period of the incident, but should not continue beyond the resolution of the incident.

- *IIS or Windows Server Failure*: This class of support incident covers any situation where the IIS Server, underlying operating system, or underlying hardware suffers a failure. These incidents should be resolved within 1 hour. The Windows Administrators are responsible for recognizing and resolving these situations. The impact on the organization may be severe during this period, with business operations being interrupted for the whole period of the incident, but should not continue beyond the resolution of the incident.

Escalation
The escalation process is as follows.

- Users of the Web interface will report problems to the Web Services Help Desk.
- Users of the Windows client interface will report problems to the IT Help Desk.
- The Help Desks will report system problems to the Windows Administrators.
- The Windows Administrators will report database problems to the DBA Group.

- The Windows Administrators will report other problems to the Development Team.
- The Windows Administrators, DBA Group, and Development Team will report problems with Microsoft software to the Microsoft Support organization.

In each case, the organization accepting the incident must provide the reporter with a unique identifier for the incident and record the reporter's description of it. If the problem is not immediately resolved, the organization accepting the incident must provide the reporter with information on resolution status within 75% of the target resolution time.

PROBLEMS AND PITFALLS

Lack of Engagement with the Operational Staff

In many organizations, a gulf exists between the development staff members who build systems and the operational staff members who deploy and administer them. This can be a significant problem if you want to achieve a smooth, incident-free system rollout.

RISK REDUCTION

- The best solution to this problem is to engage early with the operational groups, stressing how valuable their contribution is. Operational staff often have a legitimate grievance with software developers because systems are frequently passed on to them with very little thought given to operational requirements.
- Use an explicit Operational view to help avoid this situation.

Lack of Backout Planning

Many systems we have seen don't have real backout plans. In fact, many commercial software products don't have graceful recovery mechanisms to cope with situations like failed upgrades. Without a good backout plan, you are relying on a perfect rollout for your entire system, which experience suggests is somewhat optimistic.

RISK REDUCTION

- Make sure that your system can be backed out of its production environment by defining a clear procedure and reviewing it.

Lack of Migration Planning

Many information systems replace a manual system, a previous automated system, or an earlier version of themselves, but many systems are developed without a good migration plan. Migration planning isn't glamorous or, in many cases, even interesting, but without it, you are unlikely to achieve a smooth system deployment.

RISK REDUCTION

- Make sure you understand the migration needs of your architecture as early as possible.
- Address migration needs in your AD.

Insufficient Migration Window

In our experience, data migration *always* takes longer than anticipated, typically because the data does not conform to the level of quality and consistency expected of it and because of the problems associated with handling and manipulating large volumes of data. If you are moving data between geographical locations or between different types of data stores (e.g., importing data from a legacy hierarchical database into a relational database), the process will take longer still.

RISK REDUCTION

- Consider how you will deal with data errors and inconsistencies.
- Develop processes for accepting migrated data, and make sure your stakeholders have bought into them.
- In your hardware sizing models, factor in the storage requirements for transitional data.
- Include adequate elapsed-time contingency in your migration plan.
- Factor in the time needed to reorganize databases, create indexes, and so on.
- When you are migrating data from live systems and the migration time is substantial, create strategies for reconciling any data updates made during the migration period.

Missing Management Tools

Most software developers (and, in fact, many architects) are very focused on the business of building new software. However, successful software spends most of its life in production, not development. This mismatch between focus and lifecycle often manifests itself as a lack of operational facilities, which can result in a system that is difficult to monitor and control. Software developers can monitor or control the system by using primitive tools (operating system commands or simple scripts) because of their detailed knowledge of its internal workings. Operational staff often don't have this knowledge and need more sophisticated tools to automate the required operational procedures. Without such tools, the system is unlikely to be managed well.

RISK REDUCTION

- Understand the needs of your administration stakeholders as early as possible and involve them in the development of the Operational view.

- Ensure that administrators' needs are addressed with standard, system-wide facilities.

Production Environment Constraints

All production environments, whether in-house or external, impose constraints on your application and its operation, so it's important to understand the likely deployment environments you'll be using, and the constraints that each imposes, as soon as you can. If you are using a mixture of environments (for example, hosting in-house but using a cloud environment for short-term "burst" capacity, or using different cloud providers for production and disaster recovery), naturally you need to understand the overall set of constraints across all of the environments.

Production environments may impose constraints on you such as rigid unavailability periods for platform maintenance, particular tools that must be used for deployment or monitoring, limited choices of platform components that are available, procedures that must be adhered to for deployment and operation, and limits to the service-level agreements available. All of these have the ability to affect the system qualities that you may be able to achieve in a particular production environment.

RISK REDUCTION

- Agree on the target production environment(s) for your system as early as possible to allow their constraints to be understood.

- Clearly define what you need and are expecting from a production environment (e.g., reliability, capacity, and availability) as soon as you can so that you can spot possible problems with proposed environments.

- Analyze the planned production environments and what they offer and require so that you understand the opportunities and constraints that they imply and can integrate these into your work.

- Whether in-house or external, obtain definite commitments from the suppliers of your production environments for the service levels that they offer, and test them as much as you can to gain confidence in their realism.

Lack of Integration into the Production Environment

Most information systems are deployed into some sort of existing production environment, even if it is a simple or informal one. Unfortunately, it's common to find that a new system doesn't work with the environment. This can be quite a problem for operational staff who need to learn new interfaces or tools or even totally new ways to manage the system, particularly if you are using a third-party hosting environment for some or all of the system.

RISK REDUCTION

- Make sure that you understand the existing environment and its integration needs early in your system design.
- Involve experts who understand the target production environment as early as possible, and get their advice on how it works and the type and level of integration needed.

Inadequate Backup Models

Backup and restore processes can fail quite spectacularly, and you don't want to find out about problems in your model when you are desperately trying to recover important data.

RISK REDUCTION

- Do not be tempted to skimp on this area or omit it from consideration entirely.
- Incorporate backup and restore as a central part of your architecture rather than trying to add it afterward.
- Make sure that your backup scheme includes all the information you need for data recovery.
- Estimate how long backup and recovery will take, and perform some practical testing under realistic conditions.
- Make sure that your model describes how data will be restored as well as backed up.
- Consider how to maintain data consistency across multiple data stores when you have to restore one of them to an earlier state.
- Consider a "belt-and-braces" approach to backup. For example, many end-user systems—especially older, mainframe-based ones—write copies

of updates received from clients to an audit and recovery area as well as to the main database. This means that if the database is damaged, it is possible to replay these transactions into the database in order to get it in synch again.

Unsuitable Alerting

This pitfall either manifests itself as *alert starvation*, when the system fails to send appropriate alerts when important events occur, or *alert flooding*, when the system sends so many events to the central console that they are ignored or important ones are missed. Either scenario is a significant operational problem since small incidents can soon become big ones and big ones can become catastrophic.

RISK REDUCTION

- Although this pitfall is probably more appropriately addressed during design and build, you can set the scene by defining some suitable architectural principles and approaches in the AD.

CHECKLIST

- Do you know what it takes to install your system?
- Do you have a plan for backing out a failed installation?
- Can you upgrade an existing version of the system (if required)?
- Do you understand the facilities and constraints of the proposed production environment(s) that you plan to use? Can you live with or mitigate these if they are not ideal?
- Do you know how information will be moved from the existing environment into the new system?
- Do you have a clear migration strategy to move workload to the new system? Can you reverse the migration if you need to? How will you deal with data synchronization (if required)?
- Do you know how the system will be backed up? Are you confident that the approach identified will allow reliable system restoration in an acceptable time period?
- Are the administrators confident that they can monitor and control the system in production?
- Do the administrators have a clear understanding of the procedures they need to perform for the system?

- How will performance metrics be captured for the system's elements?
- Can you manage the configuration of all of the system's elements?
- Do you know how support will be provided for the system? Is the support suitable for the stakeholders it is being provided for?
- Have you cross-referenced the requirements of the administration model back to the Development view to ensure that they will be implemented consistently?
- Is the data migration architecture compatible with the amount of time available to perform the data migration? Are there catch-up mechanisms in place where the source data is volatile during the data migration?

FURTHER READING

Little existing literature deals with the operational aspects of a system from the perspective of the application development team. Although there are many books on installing and managing specific pieces of technology, we have found very few books that examine the principles that underpin reliable production systems operation.

Some books that at least partially address this area are [KERN04], [BEHR05], and [JAYA05], and [ALLS10] is an interesting collection of essays written by operations experts that provides a valuable insight into production operations. Also, Dyson and Longshaw [DYSO04] includes a number of patterns useful in the Operational view. It can also be useful to understand how production services are provided, and ITIL has been a very influential model in this area; [BON07] is a concise overview of ITIL v3. A book written from the software development perspective but dealing extensively with the interface to production operations is [NYGA07].

23

ACHIEVING CONSISTENCY ACROSS VIEWS

The use of views addresses one of the biggest challenges you face as an architect: to represent a large and complex system in a way your stakeholders can understand. A view is a way to portray those aspects or elements of the architecture that are relevant to the concerns the view intends to address—and, by implication, the stakeholders for whom those views are important.

Without views, you end up with a single, all-encompassing model that tries (and usually fails) to illustrate all of the aspects of your system. Such a model is complex, uses a mix of notations, and is too hard for anyone to understand—never mind appreciate the subtleties, nuances, and implications of your architectural choices.

However, the problem with partitioning the representation of your architecture through using views is that it is difficult to ensure consistency between them—in other words, to ensure that the structures, features, and elements that appear in one view are compatible and in alignment with the content of your other views. This consistency is a vital characteristic of your AD—without it, the system will not work properly, will not achieve its design goals, and may even be impossible to build.

Unfortunately, although some design tools can simplify the process of creating your models, we are not aware of any currently available tool that will automate such consistency checking to the extent that you need it to. The use of formal modeling languages such as UML only partially addresses this problem, and the tools that support these languages typically provide only basic features for checking one model for consistency against another. And, of course, if you are using an informal notation or one you have developed for your specific situation, the problem is even worse.

Ensuring consistency between views therefore largely comes down to the skill, thoroughness, and diligence of the architect and (to a lesser extent) the stakeholders. We have found the following strategies to be helpful in achieving inter-view consistency.

- *Focus on consistency from the outset*: We saw that trying to apply quality properties after the fact doesn't work—good performance, availability, and resilience have to be designed into your solution from the start. Similarly, it is no good waiting until your models are nearly complete to determine whether they are consistent with one another: More likely than not, they won't be, and you will be faced with a significant piece of rework and additional review.

- *Enumerate model elements*: Assigning each significant model element a unique identifier simplifies the process of asking such questions as "Is element 3 from Model B consistent with element 5 from Model D?"

- *Ensure that consistency checks are a formal part of reviews*: Consistency should be one of the criteria you use to review models and other architectural documentation. This means both *internal consistency* (Is this part of the model consistent with other parts of this model?) and *external consistency* (Is this model consistent with other models that make up the AD?). If you perform such a formal consistency check, you should include its results (and the actions taken) in an appendix to your AD.

RELATIONSHIPS BETWEEN VIEWS

Although all of the views are obviously interrelated, in practice there are *strong* dependencies only between *some* of the views. The UML class diagram in Figure 23–1 shows the most important of these dependencies. The relationships illustrate a strong dependency, which implies that if something changes at the end of the arrow, a change will probably be required at the start of the arrow.

Conversely, if there's no dependency between two views, changing something in one is unlikely to itself necessitate a change in the other. (So changing a Development view element, for example, does not in itself imply any changes to the Functional models—unless you are changing it for a reason not to do with development, of course.)

Note that if you don't develop a particular view—for example, if you encapsulate the concurrency aspects of the architecture in the Functional view, rather than in a separate Concurrency view—it is still useful to apply the checklists presented in this chapter for that view, to ensure that you have addressed its most important concerns.

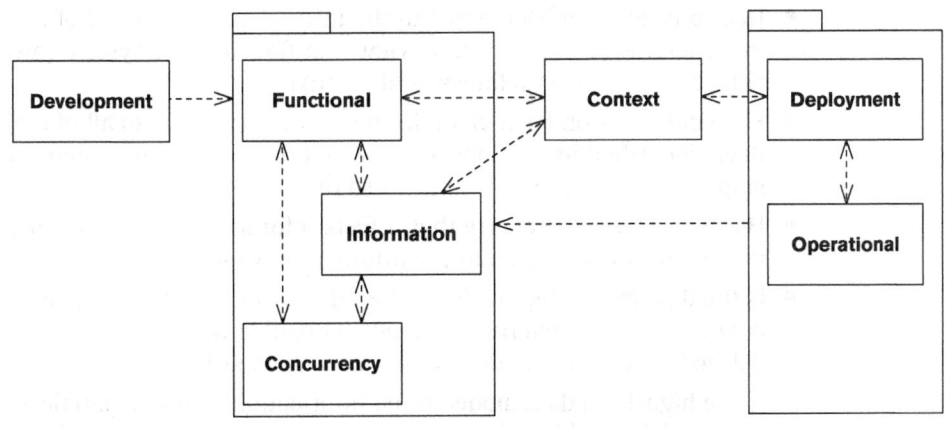

FIGURE 23-1 DEPENDENCIES BETWEEN VIEWS

CONTEXT AND FUNCTIONAL VIEW CONSISTENCY

Goal: To ensure that the system scope and requirements are fully and correctly implemented by the system.

- Does each requirement map to one or more functional elements that implement that requirement?
- Is every functional element necessary (directly or indirectly) in order to implement at least one requirement?
- Has every quality property that affects system functionality been taken into consideration in the system structure defined by the Functional view?
- Is every external entity defined in one view also present in the other view, and do they have the same definition in each view?
- Is every interface defined in one view also present in the other view, and do they have the same definition (responsibilities, nature, and characteristics) in each view?
- Are the interaction scenarios defined in the Context view compatible with the functional structure of the system and the way its elements interact with one another and the outside world?

CONTEXT AND INFORMATION VIEW CONSISTENCY

Goal: To ensure that data flows in and out of the system are compatible with the information management approach defined in the Information view.

- Has consideration been given in the Information view to all of the data items identified in the Context view that flow into the system (ownership, consistency, timeliness, and so on)?

- Has consideration been given in the Information view to all of the data items identified in the Context view that flow out of the system (ownership, consistency, timeliness, and so on)?

- Has every quality property that affects information management been taken into consideration in the Information view?

- Is the data ownership model in the Information view (particularly when data is owned by external entities) compatible with the responsibilities defined for external entities in the Context view?

- Is the high-level data model in the Information view compatible with the data models used by external systems, or if not, have appropriate mechanisms for data transformation been defined?

- If external archiving services are defined in the Information view, are they represented as external entities in the Context view?

CONTEXT AND DEPLOYMENT VIEW CONSISTENCY

Goal: To ensure that external connections between this system and others can be supported in the planned deployment environment.

- Do all external entities that represent systems, interfaces, or other technology-based connections appear consistently in both the Context and the Deployment views?

- Does the Deployment view contain all of the hardware and software required to communicate with the external entities identified in the Context view?

- Is the technology used for each interface in the Deployment view appropriate for its nature and characteristics as defined in the Context view?

- Are system elements that communicate with external entities deployed to parts of the deployment environment where external communication is possible (e.g., to a DMZ in the network)?

- Has every quality objective identified in the Context view that affects the deployment environment been taken into account in the Deployment view?

FUNCTIONAL AND INFORMATION VIEW CONSISTENCY

Goal: To ensure that the functional and information structures are compatible and that nothing is missing in one that is required by the other.

- Does every nontrivial functional element in the Functional view that needs persistent data have corresponding data elements in the Information view?

- Does every nontrivial data element in the Information view have at least one element in the Functional view that is responsible for the maintenance of that data?

- If information flows are described in the Information view, are they consistent with the interelement interactions in the Functional view?

- If the Information view requires specific functional features (e.g., distributed transaction support, redundant logging of updates, and so on), are these features addressed in the Functional view?

- Do the data ownership models in the Information view align with the functional structure in the Functional view?

- If the data ownership characteristics are complex (e.g., multiple creators or updaters), do the functional models reflect the requirements for maintaining distributed data consistency?

- If there are significant issues around the maintenance of distributed identifiers (keys), do the functional models include features to address these problems?

- If the architecture has significant data migration and data quality analysis aspects, are there functional elements for these in the Functional view?

- If the functional structure has loose coupling as an architectural goal, is this reflected (as far as possible) in the static information structure?

FUNCTIONAL AND CONCURRENCY VIEW CONSISTENCY

Goal: To ensure that the functional elements are all mapped to tasks that will allow them to execute and that the interelement interactions are supported by interprocess communication mechanisms if required.

- Is every functional element in the Functional view mapped to a concurrency element (a process or thread) responsible for its execution in the Concurrency view?

- If functional elements are partitioned into separate processes, are suitable interprocess communication mechanisms used to allow all of the interelement interactions shown in the Functional view?

- If multiple functional elements are packaged into a single process, is it clear which element controls the process?

FUNCTIONAL AND DEVELOPMENT VIEW CONSISTENCY

Goal: To ensure that all of the functional elements are mapped to a design-time module and to ensure that the common processing, test approach, and codeline specified are all compatible with and can support the proposed functional structure.

- Does the code module structure include all of the functional elements that need to be developed?
- Does the Development view specify a development environment for each of the technologies used by the Functional view?
- If the Functional view specifies the use of a particular architectural style, does the Development view include sufficient guidelines and constraints to ensure correct implementation of the style?
- Where common processing is specified, can it be implemented in a straightforward manner over all of the elements defined in the Functional view?
- Where reusable functional elements can be identified from the Functional view, are these modeled as libraries or similar features in the Development view?
- If a test environment has been specified, does it meet the functional needs and priorities of the elements defined in the Functional view?
- Can the functional structure described in the Functional view be built, tested, and released reliably using the codeline described in the Development view?

FUNCTIONAL AND DEPLOYMENT VIEW CONSISTENCY

Goal: To ensure that each of the functional elements is correctly mapped to its deployment environment.

- Has each functional element been mapped to a processing node to allow it to be executed?
- Where functional elements are hosted on different nodes, do the network models allow the required element interactions to occur?
- Are functional elements hosted as close as possible to the information they need to process?
- Are functional elements that need to interact extensively hosted as close together as possible?

- Are the specified network connections sufficient for the needs of the interelement interactions that will be carried over them (in terms of capacity, reliability, security, and so on)?
- Is the hardware specified in the Deployment view the most efficient solution for hosting the specified functional elements?

FUNCTIONAL AND OPERATIONAL VIEW CONSISTENCY

Goal: To ensure that each of the specified functional elements can be installed, used, operated, managed, and supported.

- Does the Operational view make it clear how every functional element will be installed (and upgraded if necessary)?
- If migration is required, does the Operational view make it clear how migration will occur to every functional element that needs it?
- Does the Operational view explain how each functional element will be monitored and controlled in the production environment?
- Does the Operational view explain how the configuration of each functional element will be managed in the production environment?
- Does the Operational view explain how the performance of each functional element will be monitored in the production environment?
- Does the Operational view explain how each functional element will be supported in the production environment?
- Are the approaches that the Operational view specifies for installation, migration, monitoring, control, and support the simplest set that will support the needs of the system's functional elements?

INFORMATION AND CONCURRENCY VIEW CONSISTENCY

Goal: To ensure that the concurrency structure of the system does not cause data access problems and that the proposed information structure is compatible with the concurrency structure.

- Does the concurrency design imply concurrent access to any of the system's data elements? If so, have the data elements been protected from concurrent access problems?
- When functional elements are packaged into operating system processes, is the data they require still available to them?
- If functional elements that share data elements are packaged into different operating system processes, has a suitable interprocess data-sharing mechanism been defined?

INFORMATION AND DEVELOPMENT VIEW CONSISTENCY

Goal: To ensure that the proposed development environment can provide the technical resources required to develop the data management aspects of the system.

- Does each data management technology identified in the Information view have development tools and the environment defined for it?
- Does the sizing of the development environments and test data platforms reflect the data volumes created in the Information view?
- If the Information view defines a significant migration data aspect, are there development tools and environments defined to support this?
- If the Information view defines external data components (e.g., for existing systems or external systems under construction), does the Development view take this into account (e.g., the creation of stub environments, realistic test data, and so on)?

INFORMATION AND DEPLOYMENT VIEW CONSISTENCY

Goal: To ensure that the proposed deployment environment provides the resources required to support the defined information structure.

- Does the Deployment view include enough storage (of the appropriate types) to support the information storage approach specified by the Information view?
- If separate storage hardware is used, does the Deployment view specify sufficiently fast and reliable links from the storage to the processing hardware?
- Does the Deployment view reflect the requirements for backup and recovery as addressed by the Information view?
- If large volumes of information need to be moved, is sufficient bandwidth available so that this can be achieved without critically impacting the operation of the system?

INFORMATION AND OPERATIONAL VIEW CONSISTENCY

Goal: To ensure that the system's information structure can be installed, used, operated, managed, and supported.

- Does the Operational view make it clear whether specific installation steps are required for the system's data management technology?
- If migration is required, does the Operational view make it clear how data migration will occur?
- Does the Operational view explain how the data management technology will be monitored and controlled in the production environment?
- Does the Operational view explain how the configuration of the data management technology will be managed in the production environment?
- Does the Operational view explain how the performance of the data management technology will be monitored in the production environment?
- Does the Operational view explain how the data management technology will be supported in the production environment?

CONCURRENCY AND DEVELOPMENT VIEW CONSISTENCY

Goal: To ensure that the concurrency structure specified in the Concurrency view can be built and tested in the development environment specified by the Development view.

- If the concurrency structure is complex, are sufficient design patterns specified in the Development view to guide its implementation?
- Does the codeline defined in the Development view support the packaging of the system's functional elements into the operating system processes specified by the Concurrency view?
- Does the test approach defined in the Development view support testing of the concurrency structure specified in the Concurrency view?
- Does the development environment defined in the Development view allow development and testing of the concurrency structure specified in the Concurrency view?

CONCURRENCY AND DEPLOYMENT VIEW CONSISTENCY

Goal: To ensure that the system's runtime tasks are correctly mapped to execution resources.

- Is every operating system process mapped to a processing node to allow it to run?
- Can the interprocess communication facilities used in the Concurrency view be implemented on and between the processing nodes specified in the Deployment view?

- Are the processing nodes specified in the Deployment view sufficiently powerful to host the processes mapped to them from the Concurrency view?

- Is every processing node in the Deployment view fully used by the processes mapped to it?

DEPLOYMENT AND OPERATIONAL VIEW CONSISTENCY

Goal: To ensure that the deployment environment described in the Deployment view can be installed, used, monitored, managed, and supported.

- Does the Operational view define how each of the elements in the deployment environment will be installed?

- Does the Operational view describe how each of the elements in the deployment environment can be monitored and controlled?

- Does the Operational view make it clear which monitoring and control facilities already exist, which can be bought, and which must be developed?

- Can each of the elements in the deployment environment be supported in the organization?

PART IV

THE PERSPECTIVE CATALOG

24

INTRODUCTION TO THE PERSPECTIVE CATALOG

P art IV is devoted to descriptions of a number of perspectives. We describe the perspectives listed in Table 24–1 in detail, with a chapter devoted to each. We have chosen to explore this set of perspectives more thoroughly because we have found that the quality properties they address are crucial to most information systems.

We outline the perspectives listed in Table 24–2 in the final chapter of Part IV. We have chosen to explore these perspectives more briefly than the others for reasons of space and because, although they are often important, we have not found them as universally applicable as the ones listed in Table 24–1.

TABLE 24–1 PERSPECTIVES DESCRIBED IN DETAIL

Perspective	Desired Quality
Security	The ability of the system to reliably control, monitor, and audit who can perform what actions on which resources and the ability to detect and recover from security breaches
Performance and Scalability	The ability of the system to predictably execute within its mandated performance profile and to handle increased processing volumes in the future if required
Availability and Resilience	The ability of the system to be fully or partly operational as and when required and to effectively handle failures that could affect system availability
Evolution	The ability of the system to be flexible in the face of the inevitable change that all systems experience after deployment, balanced against the costs of providing such flexibility

TABLE 24-2 PERSPECTIVES DESCRIBED IN BRIEF

Perspective	Desired Quality
Accessibility	The ability of the system to be used by people with disabilities
Development Resource	The ability of the system to be designed, built, deployed, and operated within known constraints related to people, budget, time, and materials
Internationalization	The ability of the system to be independent from any particular language, country, or cultural group
Location	The ability of the system to overcome problems brought about by the absolute location of its elements and the distances between them
Regulation	The ability of the system to conform to local and international laws, quasi-legal regulations, company policies, and other rules and standards
Usability	The ease with which people who interact with the system can work effectively

For each perspective, we present the following details:

- The perspective's *applicability to views*—that is, which of your views are most likely to be impacted by applying the perspective
- The most important *concerns* the perspective addresses
- A description of *activities for applying the perspective* to your architecture
- The key *architectural tactics* to be considered as possible solutions when your architecture does not exhibit the required quality properties the perspective addresses
- Some *problems and pitfalls* to be aware of and risk-reduction techniques for mitigating these
- *Checklists* of things to consider when applying the perspective and when reviewing it, to help ensure correctness, completeness, and accuracy

As in our viewpoint catalog, we present only an overview of some complex and detailed topics. Our objective is to provide the fundamental information in each area, so each perspective chapter also includes references to a number of sources of further information.

As we said in Part I, there are many possible perspectives that could apply to a particular architecture, and it is not usually feasible to consider all of them in the context of all of the views. Not every perspective is relevant to every view, or even to every system, and there will be instances where you don't need to consider some of the perspectives at all. The key to getting the most out of them is to consider to what extent each perspective is important to your architecture and to tailor your approach accordingly.

25

THE SECURITY PERSPECTIVE

Desired Quality	The ability of the system to reliably control, monitor, and audit who can perform what actions on which resources and the ability to detect and recover from security breaches
Applicability	Any systems with accessible interfaces, with multiple users where the identity of the user is significant, or where access to operations or information needs to be controlled
Concerns	Resources, principals, policies, threats, confidentiality, integrity, availability, accountability, detection and recovery, and security mechanisms
Activities	Identify sensitive resources, define the security policy, identify threats to the system, design the security implementation, and assess the security risks
Architectural Tactics	Apply recognized security principles, authenticate the principals, authorize access, ensure information secrecy, ensure information integrity, ensure accountability, protect availability, integrate security technologies, provide security administration, and use third-party security infrastructure
Problems and Pitfalls	Complex security policies, unproven security technologies, system not designed for failure, lack of administration facilities, technology-driven approach, failure to consider time sources, overreliance on technology, no clear requirements or models, security as an afterthought, ignoring the insider threat, assuming the client is secure, security embedded in the application code, piecemeal security, and ad hoc security technology

Many factors drive today's need for information systems security, including the increasing trend to distribute systems, the use of public networks (particularly the Internet) as part of system infrastructure, the everyday use of interorganizational computing (such as Web services), and the increasing interest the media and the public have shown in privacy and security. All of these factors point to the fact that today your system's stakeholders are likely to be more interested in the security of the system than they would have been only a couple of years ago.

We define *security* as the set of processes and technologies that allow the owners of resources in the system to reliably control who can access which resources. The *who* refers to the people, pieces of software, and so on that form the set of actors in the system who have a security identity; security specialists normally refer to such actors as *principals*. The *resources* are the parts of the system considered sensitive (i.e., those to which access must be controlled) such as subsystems, data elements, and operations. The *access* to the resources refers to the operations that the principals in the system will want to legitimately perform on the resources (e.g., read them, change them, execute them, and so on), and the fact that access must be limited to principals known to the system.

Resources are at the core of the system's security. *Policies* define the legitimate access allowed to them, which is enforced by *security mechanisms*, which are used by the principals of the system to gain access to the resources that they need. We illustrate the interrelationship of these concepts in Figure 25–1 and discuss them in more detail in the Concerns section of the chapter.

The resources, principals, and policies that need to be considered are often very specific to the system. An Internet service provider is likely to have a totally

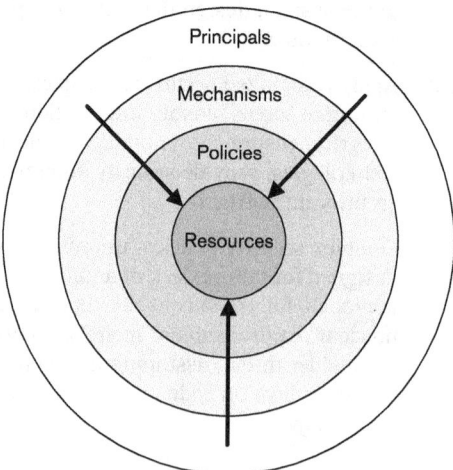

FIGURE 25–1 PRINCIPALS, ACTIONS, AND RESOURCES

different set of security concerns from those of a military intelligence organization, which will be different again from those of an enterprise implementing an internal information system that allows remote access to its employees. However, in all of these cases, security is still the business of allowing the right levels of access to the right resources to the right people.

It is also important to recognize that security is not a simple process of "being secure" or not. Rather than being a binary state, security is really a process of risk management that balances likely security risks against the costs of guarding against them. Bear this in mind to help you set realistic expectations in the minds of your stakeholders and to make intelligent tradeoffs that address the real security risks your system faces.

APPLICABILITY TO VIEWS

Table 25–1 shows how the Security perspective affects each of the views we discussed in Part III.

TABLE 25–1 APPLICABILITY OF THE SECURITY PERSPECTIVE TO THE SEVEN VIEWS

View	Applicability
Context	The Context view allows you to clearly identify the system's external connections and consider how they could become system vulnerabilities and how they will need to be protected from malicious use. It may be the case that considering the security of the system will lead you to change the nature of some of these external connections. The Context view may also reveal possible threats to the system from elements in its immediate environment.
Functional	The Functional view allows you to clearly see which of the system's functional elements need to be protected. Conversely, the functional structure of the system may be impacted by the need to implement your security policies.
Information	The Information view also helps you see what needs to be protected—in this case, the sensitive data in the system. Information models are often modified as a result of security design (e.g., partitioning information by sensitivity).
Concurrency	The Concurrency view defines how functional elements are packaged into runtime elements like processes. Security design may indicate the need to isolate different pieces of the system into different runtime elements, and if so, this will affect the system's concurrency structure.
Development	You may identify guidelines or constraints that the software developers will need to be aware of in order to ensure that the security policy is enforced. You need to include these guidelines or constraints in (or reference them from) the Development view.

Continued on next page

TABLE 25-1 APPLICABILITY OF THE SECURITY PERSPECTIVE TO THE SEVEN VIEWS *(CONTINUED)*

View	Applicability
Deployment	The security design may have a major impact on the system's deployment environment. For example, you may need security-oriented hardware or software, or you may need to change previously assumed deployment arrangements in order to address security risks.
Operational	Enforcing security policy is not just a matter of adding advanced technological features to a system. How the system is operated once it is in production will have a major effect on its security. The Operational view needs to make the security assumptions and responsibilities extremely clear, so that these aspects of the security implementation can be reflected in operational processes.

CONCERNS

Resources

The reason that we need security in our systems is that they contain valuable information and sensitive operations, and we want to be sure these are accessed or executed only by certain people. The items in the system that we are trying to protect are known in security jargon as *resources*, and computer security is the business of designing processes and mechanisms to provide this protection.

Principals

In the security domain, the entities that our system needs to identify for security purposes are known as *principals*. A principal can be a person, a role, a piece of physical equipment, or another computer system. Our security system needs to be able to reliably identify principals (that is, *authenticate* them) in order to allow decisions about their legitimate access rights to be made (*authorization* decisions).

Policies

The security policy for a system defines the system's security needs. It defines the controls and guarantees that the system requires for its resources and identifies which principals (or groups of principals) should be granted which types of access to each resource (or type of resource) within the system. A security policy can be considered to be the security specification for a system, as it defines the set of security-related constraints that the system should be able to enforce.

A typical security policy defines the information access policy in terms of the different types of principals the system contains (e.g., clerks, managers, administrators) and, for each type of information (e.g., payroll records, customer details, invoice information), what sort of access each principal group requires (e.g., whether they can view the information, change it, delete it, share it). A security policy also needs to define how the execution of certain sensitive system operations (e.g., dispatch of payments or system shutdown) will be controlled. The policy also should define information integrity constraints that must be enforced, such as the integrity rules and checking required in data stores and protection of messages from unauthorized changes.

Threats

While the policy defines the security constraints the system requires, the threats the system faces are the possible ways the security constraints might be breached by an attacker who wishes to avoid them. Explicitly considering the security threats the system faces allows you to identify security enforcement mechanisms that can then counter these threats. Adding security mechanisms to a system is never free and often adds significantly to the complexity and cost of the system, while often reducing its usability and making it more difficult to operate in production. Therefore, it is important to select mechanisms appropriate to the threats faced, to ensure that all of the chosen mechanisms counter realistic, credible security threats to the system.

The threats that a system faces are related to the environment into which the system is deployed and how the system is built. Certain threats (such as attackers using "phishing" attacks to gain user names and passwords) are much more likely for an Internet-facing system; others (such as users who hold different security roles colluding to bypass a system control) are much more likely for an enterprise system; and threats relating to the introduction of malicious code into the system are more likely where it is easy to introduce new software into the system (such as those that must support extension through plug-ins).

Common threats that most information systems face include password cracking, network attacks that exploit software or configuration vulnerabilities, and denial-of-service attacks as well as nontechnical, social-engineering attacks that try to trick authorized users of the system to perform operations on behalf of the attacker.

Confidentiality

Confidentiality is normally defined as limiting the disclosure of secrets to those who are legitimately allowed to access them. In practice this usually means keeping information in a system from being disclosed to anyone who has not been granted the right to view it. Confidentiality can be achieved using access control provided that the information can be retained within the confines of the system. When the information cannot be reliably retained within the control of the system (e.g., when it needs to be transmitted to another system), cryptography is usually used to maintain confidentiality when the information passes out of the control of the system.

In classical information security theory, confidentiality is usually considered along with integrity and availability, forming the well-known "CIA" trio of concerns. Nowadays, accountability is often added as a fourth general concern for the security engineer.

Integrity

In the context of information security, integrity is a guarantee that information cannot be changed undetectably, and so we can be sure that information has not been tampered with since it was created or changed by an authorized principal. Ensuring information integrity normally involves "signing" data cryptographically, allowing the data and the cryptographic signature to be compared in order to prove that an unauthorized party has not changed the data.

Availability

Availability is often thought of as a purely operational consideration, but in fact it also has a relationship to security. Ensuring that potential attackers of your system cannot block its availability with denial-of-service attacks is an important part of your security design.

Designing a system for availability involves thinking about planned and unplanned outages that can occur due to the nature of the system itself; designing a system to avoid outages as a result of an external attack involves thinking about risks that can occur as a result of the environment in which the system resides (such as who can access the system and how). Availability security is an area that has rapidly gained importance as systems are routinely connected to public networks like the Internet.

Accountability

Accountability is the means of ensuring that every action can be unambiguously traced back to the principal who performed it.

In centralized server-based systems, the notion of auditing is a common mechanism used to ensure accountability. In distributed systems, cryptographic message signing is typically used to prove that a message originated from a particular principal (a form of accountability also known as *nonrepudiation*).

Detection and Recovery

System security is never perfect, and if a system is attractive enough to an attacker, it is almost inevitable that some sort of security breach will occur eventually. This means that an important security concern is the ability of the system to detect security breaches and recover from them. Addressing this concern is unlikely to be a purely technical matter but is more likely to involve people and processes as well as the technology required to spot a security breach and react to it appropriately.

Security Mechanisms

Security mechanisms are the technologies, configuration settings, and procedures required to enforce the rules established by the security policy and provide the confidentiality, integrity, accountability, and availability guarantees required by the system. Information systems security is a relatively mature field, and many proven security technologies already exist to act as mechanisms in an information system. Examples of commonly used security technologies include user name and password authentication, single-sign-on systems, virtual private networks to secure network links, database access control systems, and SSL/TLS encryption for client/server connections. The broad groups of security mechanisms that are typically found in a modern information system are as follows:

- *Authentication, authorization, and auditing*, which are used to identify principals, grant them rights and privileges, and monitor the use of those rights and privileges, in order to implement effective access control
- *Information privacy and integrity* mechanisms, which use cryptography to prevent information from being accessed by unauthorized parties and allow detection of information tampering
- *Nonrepudiation* mechanisms, such as message signing, which again use cryptography, in this case to prove the provenance of information, such as the identity of a message sender
- *System availability* mechanisms, which aim to keep the system available in the face of malicious or accidental threats (we discuss these technologies primarily in Chapter 27 on the Availability and Resilience perspective)
- *Security monitoring* mechanisms, such as intrusion detection systems and security log monitors, that are used to detect breaches in system security and respond to them

Your challenge as an architect is to select the right set of technologies from the wide array available and to apply them appropriately to the particular system you are building. In particular, it can be difficult to safely combine a number of these different technologies, along with system-wide security configuration settings and a set of secure operational processes, to create a truly secure end-to-end system. Except in the simplest cases, it is usually necessary to involve security specialists in the system design process in order to achieve this. Such specialists

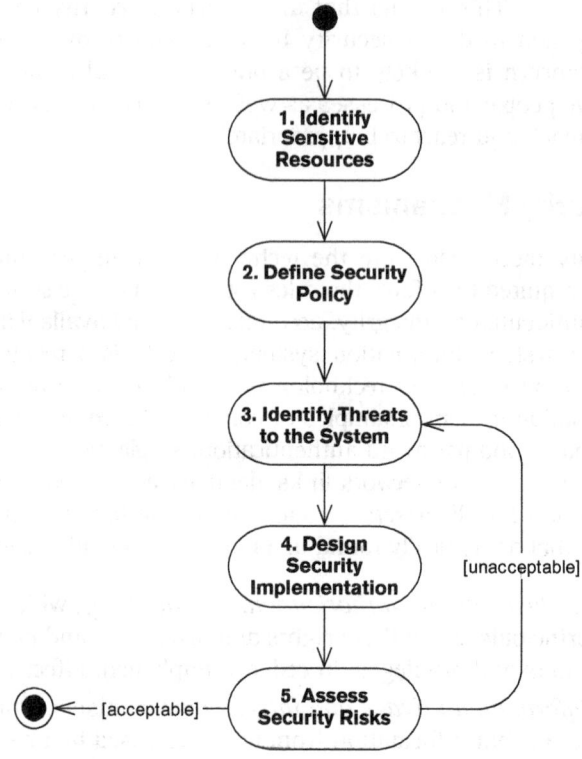

FIGURE 25–2 APPLYING THE SECURITY PERSPECTIVE

will usually also be able to advise you on standards or common practices for your organization or industry.

ACTIVITIES: APPLYING THE SECURITY PERSPECTIVE

The activity diagram in Figure 25–2 illustrates a simple process for applying the Security perspective. In this section, we describe the activities in this process.

Identify Sensitive Resources

Before considering *how* to secure your system, you need to establish *what* needs to be secured. All of the security for your system needs to be driven from this key concern, which you should consider as early in the system's lifecycle as possible.

The information you gather about the security-sensitive resources feeds into all of the other security-related decisions you make.

NOTATION A simple text-and-tables approach is normally sufficient, although you may choose to annotate one of the diagrammatic models of the architecture (typically in the Functional or Information views).

ACTIVITIES

Classify Sensitive Resources. Using the Functional and Information views as primary inputs, along with any security requirements information available, decide what the sensitive resources in the system are—typically, functional operations and data items. For each type of sensitive resource, define the reasons the resource is sensitive, who should be considered its owner, and the type of access controls it requires.

 EXAMPLE Table 25–2 shows a simple example of documenting some of the sensitive resources that might appear in an e-commerce ordering system.

TABLE 25–2 EXAMPLE OF SENSITIVE RESOURCE IDENTIFICATION

Resource	Sensitivity	Owner	Access Control
Customer account records	Personal information of value for identity theft or invasion of privacy	Customer Care Group	No direct data access
Descriptive product catalog entries	Defines what is for sale and its description; if maliciously changed, could harm the business	Stock Management Group	No direct data access
Pricing product catalog entries	Defines pricing for catalog items; if maliciously or accidentally modified, could harm the business or allow fraud	Pricing Team in Stock Management Group	No direct data access
Business operations on customer account records	Needs to be controlled to protect data access and integrity	Customer Care Group	Access to individual record or all records by authenticated principal
Descriptive catalog operations	Needs to be controlled to protect data access and integrity	Stock Management Group	Access to catalog modification operations by authenticated principal
Pricing catalog modification operations	Needs to be controlled to protect data access and integrity	Pricing Team	Access to price modification operations by authenticated principal, with accountability of changes
. . .	. . .	. . .	. . .

If you're fortunate enough to have comprehensive security requirements defined for you, the sensitive resources may have already been identified. In many cases, though, you will need to do this yourself, in conjunction with interested stakeholders (such as auditors and managers of the groups owning the information). Useful inputs into this exercise include organizational security policies and relevant external regulations, as well as the opinions of interested stakeholders.

When performing this exercise, be sure that everyone (including yourself) understands exactly what is included in each resource type as well as the identity of the owner and the type of security the resource type requires.

Define the Security Policy

Having identified the system's sensitive resources and the threats against them, you should be able to define a security policy (also sometimes called a *trust model*) for your system. The security policy is the basis for the security implementation in the system. This model identifies *who* will be trusted with *what* access to *which* system resources (and any constraints on this access such as limiting it to certain times or days of the week), the *integrity* guarantees required within the system, and the *accountability* required when sensitive resources are accessed.

Ideally, you will have a complete, unambiguous, straightforward security policy defined for you by the system's main stakeholders that you can just check and review before proceeding. Alternatively, if it's like every system we've worked on, you'll have nothing of the sort, in which case you'll need to create it and get agreement on it.

The policy should normally be defined in terms of groups of resources and principals (often based on organizational unit and role) rather than enumerating lots of specific cases. Also remember that this is a policy, not a design, so it needs to define what access will be provided to whom rather than defining how this will be achieved.

Work to make the security policy as simple and general as you can, with as few special cases as possible. A straightforward policy model allows the simplest possible implementation of enforcement mechanisms and makes it more likely that the model will be enforced correctly.

The other vital quality of a security policy model is precision. This model is an important deliverable for your system, and it should be approved by all the important stakeholders. If the model isn't precise, each group of stakeholders will interpret it differently, according to their own interests, assumptions, and desires. This is bound to lead to problems when implementing the policy.

NOTATION A security policy is normally defined by using a simple text-and-tables approach to create a structured document. Tables are particularly valuable when defining groups of resources and principals and showing the types of access allowed.

ACTIVITIES

Identify the Principal Classes. In order to make defining the security policy manageable, start by grouping your principals into classes that you can treat as groups for security policy purposes. Partition the principals into sets based on their role and the types of access they require to different types of sensitive resources.

Identify the Resource Classes. Partition the system's sensitive resource types into groups that you can treat uniformly for access control purposes. (The resource types are derived from the resources, as described earlier.)

Identify the Access Control Sets. For each resource class, define the operations that can be performed on members of that class and the principal classes that should be allowed to access each operation on the class.

Identify the Sensitive System Operations. Consider any system-level operations that are independent of the system's managed resources (such as administrative operations), and define which principal classes should be allowed to access these operations.

Identify the Integrity Requirements. Consider any situations in the system where information is or could be changed or sensitive operations performed, and identify the set of integrity guarantees required for them (such as auditing or "four eyes" approval).

 EXAMPLE Table 25–3 shows part of the result of defining the security policy for an e-commerce system.

TABLE 25–3 EXAMPLE OF AN ACCESS CONTROL POLICY

	User Account Records	Product Catalog Records	Pricing Records	User Account Operations	Product Catalog Operations	Price Change Operations
Data administrator	Full with audit	Full with audit	Full with audit	All with approval and audit	All with audit	All with approval from a product price administrator
Catalog clerk	None	None	None	All	Read-only operations	None

Continued on next page

TABLE 25–3 EXAMPLE OF AN ACCESS CONTROL POLICY (*CONTINUED*)

Catalog manager	None	None	None	Read-only operations with audit	All	All with audit
Product price administrator	None	None	None	None	Read-only operations	All with audit
Customer care clerk	None	None	None	All with audit	Read-only operations	None
Registered customer	None	None	None	All on own record	Read-only operations	None
Unknown Website user	None	None	None	None	Read-only operations	None

Seven different classes of principals have been identified (including unauthenticated Web-site users) and six classes of sensitive resources. Only data administrators are allowed access to data directly; all other users can only execute business operations. Data administrators can also execute business operations (on the basis that they can simulate their occurrence anyway by changing data), but all of their activity is audited and some actions need approval. The other classes of principals have been allocated just enough privileges in order to perform their roles in the system.

Identify Threats to the System

In a perfect world, we could now stop and simply publish the list of sensitive resources and the security policy, and everyone would voluntarily follow the policy. However, the reason we need security is that we can't trust everyone to do this, so we need to identify the possible threats to the security policy. Identifying threats provides a clear definition of what needs to be protected and what it needs to be protected from. This makes it clear which threats you are aware of and can try to guard against and also (implicitly) the threats you have not considered.

The result of this process is termed a *threat model*, which builds on the initial list of sensitive resources and should provide a thorough analysis of the threats to which you think the system is subject, the impact of the threat being realized, and the likelihood of the threat occurring.

To create a threat model, ask a number of key questions about your proposed system.

- Who is likely to try to circumvent the security policy?
- What is the attacker's motivation for attacking the system?

- How will an attacker try to circumvent the security policy?
- What are the attacker's main characteristics (such as sophistication, commitment, resources, and so on)?
- What are the consequences of the policy being breached in this way?

When considering the threats your system faces, be sure to consider threats from inside the organization as well as the more obvious "bad guys" who are outside it. Many large organizations have suffered attacks from current or former employees. Employees are often in a trusted position and have a lot of knowledge about the organization's systems, which makes it easier for them than for outsiders to circumvent information systems controls.

It is also important to consider how the environment into which your system is deployed affects the threats it faces. If your system is hosted outside your organization (such as at a hosting provider or in a cloud computing environment), you need to consider the threats it faces from the insiders who run the infrastructure on which it is hosted, as well as the insiders in your own organization. On the other hand, such external providers may be able to provide a level of security technology, expertise, monitoring, and support that is not available within your organization.

Explicitly identifying threats allows specialists from outside your project to provide assistance by reviewing the model and advising you about potential threats that have not been considered at all or threats that may have been incorrectly characterized in the model. Be sure to have it widely reviewed so that you can be confident you have considered all likely threats. The threat model also allows you to systematically consider the set of security facilities your system needs.

NOTATION The threat model is normally presented by using a text-and-tables approach to create a structured document. A graphical alternative is to use an attack tree, which is a tree structure used to categorize and illustrate the threats a system faces and the likely probability of each occurring.

EXAMPLE An attack tree is a useful approach to representing the threat model for your system. The technique is based on the Fault Trees technique used in safety-critical systems design to analyze possible failure modes. In the security domain, you can take a similar approach to represent possible attacks on your system.

An attack tree represents the possible attacks your system may face in order for an attacker to achieve a particular goal. The root of the tree is the goal the attacker is trying to achieve, and the branches of the tree classify the different types of attacks the intruder could attempt in order to achieve the goal.

Attack trees can be represented graphically (as a tree structure with nodes and links) or textually as a "dotted decimal" hierarchy (like nested subheadings in a technical document). The latter form is often more practical because attack trees can get very large as all possible attacks are considered, which can make the graphical form difficult to draw and comprehend.

Here is a possible attack tree for the goal of extracting customer credit card details from an e-commerce Web site.

Goal: Obtain customer credit card details.

1. Extract details from the system database.

   1.1. Access the database directly.

      1.1.1. Crack/guess database passwords.

      1.1.2. Crack/guess operating system passwords that allow database security to be bypassed.

      1.1.3. Exploit a known vulnerability in the database software.

   1.2. Access the details via a member of the database administration staff.

      1.2.1. Bribe a database administrator (DBA).

      1.2.2. Conduct social engineering by phone/e-mail to trick the DBA into revealing details.

2. Extract details from the Web interface.

   2.1. Set up a dummy Web site and e-mail users the URL to trick them into entering credit card details.

   2.2. Crack/guess passwords for user accounts and extract details from the user Web interface.

   2.3. Send users a Trojan horse program by e-mail to record keystrokes/intercept Web traffic.

   2.4. Attack the domain name server to hijack the domain name and use the dummy site attack from 2.1.

   2.5. Attack the site server software directly to try to find loopholes in its security or configuration or to exploit a known vulnerability in the software.

3. Find details outside the system.

   3.1. Conduct social engineering by phone/e-mail to get customer services staff to reveal card details.

   3.2. Direct a social-engineering attack on users by using public details from the site to make contact (see also 2.1).

An attack tree should be created for each of the possible goals that an attacker may have for breaching your system's security. Once you have an attack tree, you can analyze each threat it contains to establish whether the system's security neutralizes the threat.

ACTIVITIES

Identify the Threats. Consider the security threats your system faces from the perspective of the sensitive resources within it, the possible access to these resources that potential attackers might wish to gain, the main characteristics of the potential attackers, and the types of attacks they are likely to carry out.

Characterize the Threats. Characterize each threat in terms of the resources that would be compromised if the attack were successful, the result of this compromise, and the likelihood of the attack occurring.

Design the Security Implementation

Once you understand the sensitive resources and threats, you can consider the technical security design for the system. The goal of this step is to design a system-wide security infrastructure that can enforce the system's security policy in the face of the risks identified in the threat model. In this step, you consider using specific security technologies such as single-sign-on systems, network firewalls, SSL communication link security, cryptographic technology, policy management systems, and so on.

This design process results in a number of design decisions you should incorporate in the architecture. These decisions affect a number of architectural structures, including those likely to be described in the Functional, Information, Deployment, and Operational views.

NOTATION The outputs of this step are a set of design decisions to be reflected in the architectural views, so the notation used for the technical security design depends on the notation used in each view. You may also produce some form of overall security design model, which is typically captured by using a software design notation such as UML (similar to its use in the Functional viewpoint).

EXAMPLE Based on the attack tree shown in the previous example, some of the security measures you might consider for the e-commerce system include the following:

- Isolating the database machines from the public network by using network firewall technology
- Isolating the security-sensitive parts of your system from the public network by using network firewall technology
- Analyzing the paths into your system to check them for possible vulnerabilities
- Arranging penetration testing to see if experts can find ways into your system
- Identifying an intrusion detection strategy that would allow security breaches to be recognized
- Training administration and customer service staff (in fact, probably all staff) to avoid social-engineering attacks and to abide by strict privacy protection procedures for customer information
- Designing your site so that a minimal amount of user information (ideally, none) is publicly viewable
- Designing your site so that sensitive information (e.g., credit card numbers) is never shown in full (e.g., display just the last four digits to allow legitimate users to identify their cards in lists)
- Routinely applying security-related software updates to all third-party software used in the system
- Reviewing the system's code for security vulnerabilities using analysis tools and expert inspection
- Constantly reminding users of security precautions they should take (e.g., not revealing passwords to anyone, including your staff; checking URLs before entering information; and so on)

It is interesting to note how much of a typical security implementation does not involve security technology directly but is about making sure that people act in a secure manner.

ACTIVITIES

Design a Way to Mitigate the Threats. For each of the previously identified threats, design a security mechanism to address the threat. This may include modifying existing architectural decisions, applying one or more security technologies, and designing procedures and processes for the system's operation and use.

Design a Detection and Recovery Approach. Bearing in mind that the security mechanisms you identify are unlikely to be foolproof, design a system-wide approach to detecting violations of the system security policy and recovering from them. This will typically include technical intrusion detection solutions, internal system checks and balances to reveal unexpected inconsistencies, and a set of processes for regularly checking the system for intrusions and reacting to any discovered. Good solutions for intrusion detection are available as proven commercial and open source software packages; however, deciding how to use the packages and design the processes around them are still system-specific activities.

Assess the Technology. One way to address a threat is to use a piece of security technology to provide a security mechanism. This activity involves assessing which candidate security technologies are suitable for addressing a particular threat in a particular context. This includes generic assessment (e.g., checking reliability, ease of use, and so on) as well as context-specific assessment (e.g., checking that the proposed technology can be operated by the system's administrators and is efficient enough to meet the system's performance and scalability goals).

Integrate the Technology. Once you have decided which security technologies to apply to your system, the other important activity is deciding how you will integrate them with the primary system structure and with other security technologies. It is important to spend some time designing the integration approach carefully, to avoid possible security loopholes creeping in due to the unexpected side effects of an ad hoc integration approach.

Assess the Security Risks

No security system is perfect. The process of implementing system security is a balancing act: You balance the risks you believe you face against the cost of implementing mitigations for those risks and the costs you may face if the risks occur.

Having designed a security infrastructure for your system, you now need to reevaluate the risks to consider whether your proposed security infrastructure has achieved an acceptable cost/risk balance. If so, your Security perspective is complete. If not, you need to return to a consideration of the threat model and refine the security infrastructure in order to achieve an acceptable cost/risk balance.

NOTATION The risk assessment delivers a record of the set of risks, the estimated likelihood of each risk occurring given the design of the system, and the notional cost (i.e., the estimated cost adjusted for the probability of occurrence) that each risk implies. This information is usually best presented in a simple tabular form.

TABLE 25-4 EXAMPLE OF RISK ASSESSMENT

Risk	Estimated Cost	Estimated Likelihood	Notional Cost
Attacker gains direct database access	$8,000,000	0.2%	$16,000
Web-site flaw allows free orders to be placed and fulfilled	$800,000	4.0%	$32,000
Social-engineering attack on a customer service representative results in hijacking of customer accounts	$4,000,000	1.5%	$60,000
. . .		. . .	. . .	. . .

EXAMPLE Table 25-4 shows an example, using a tabular presentation style, for a couple of the risks facing our e-commerce system.

A risk presentation in this form allows us to focus on the risks with the highest notional costs (i.e., those that have the highest risk of loss and greatest likelihood of occurrence).

ACTIVITIES

Assess the Risks. The single activity in this step is a process of risk assessment. For each risk in your threat model, reevaluate its likelihood of occurrence and its likely impact given the planned security infrastructure, and compare this against the security needs you established earlier in the process. Assess whether this is an acceptable level of security risk for your particular system's situation. It is worth noting that this can be a lengthy process because it can be difficult and time-consuming to produce reliable estimates for the impact and likelihood of the occurrence of each risk.

ARCHITECTURAL TACTICS

Apply Recognized Security Principles

The field of computer security is relatively mature for a rapidly evolving, high-technology discipline. There is an established body of knowledge, developed and applied by an identifiable professional security community with its own principles, standards, norms, and culture.

This community of researchers and practitioners has established a number of widely accepted and commonly applied principles that are considered important to establishing security within a system. Some of the more important principles include the following.

- *Grant the least amount of privilege possible*: Always grant security principals the smallest set of privileges they require in order to perform their tasks. Consider varying the set of privileges a principal has over time if certain sensitive tasks are executed only intermittently.

- *Secure the weakest link*: The security of a system is only as strong as its weakest element, so understanding the weakest link in your security is an important step toward understanding how secure your system really is. The weakest link could be technological (an unsecured network link), procedural (allowing easy access to a data center), or human (people who write down their passwords). Identify and secure the weakest links in your system's security until you achieve an acceptable level of security risk.

- *Defend in depth*: If you examine physical security systems, you'll find that they rarely rely on just one security measure. Just as medieval castles had moats, drawbridges, and strong walls, banks have alarms, vaults, security guards, surveillance systems, and multiple locks on important doors. These are examples of the principle of defense in depth, where a series of defenses provides a greater level of security than a single one could. Defense in depth is particularly relevant to computer systems, given that many of the security technologies we use may themselves have hidden flaws and that we are also susceptible to human and procedural failures. Rather than relying on one security measure to counter each threat to your system, consider possibilities for layering defenses to provide greater protection.

- *Separate and compartmentalize*: Attempt to clearly separate different responsibilities so that authority for each can be assigned to different principals if required, and compartmentalize responsibilities for different parts of the system so that they can be controlled individually. This makes it easier to control access securely and means that a successful attack on one part of the system does not immediately compromise it entirely. Good examples are separating the "security override" privilege from the "alter audit trail" privilege (with the audit trail being used to record use of the "security override" privilege) and implementing separate security configuration and mechanisms for each major subdivision of a system.

- *Keep security designs simple*: Security engineers often say that complexity is the enemy of security. Complexity in a system is difficult to deal with and makes it very difficult to analyze the system to assess its security. This makes it difficult to know whether the system will be secure or not, and it increases the likelihood of vulnerabilities creeping into the system. Systems with stringent security requirements need to be simple enough to make it possible for them to be secured and verified.

- *Don't rely on obscurity*: Some years ago, it was common for the details of secure systems to be kept secret in an attempt to make them more difficult to attack. An example of this was hiding security secrets, such as cryptographic keys, in obfuscated (and undocumented) computer code for which the source was kept secret. The weaknesses in this approach are that it assumes the attackers aren't smart enough to work past the obscurity and that it may prevent external experts from assessing the real level of security provided. The conventional wisdom in today's security community is total disclosure, where the system is designed assuming that potential attackers know it as well as its implementers do. This principle makes the system's security less reliant on hiding secrets, which is extremely difficult to do successfully.

- *Use secure defaults*: Many systems we have encountered include inherently insecure default settings and behaviors, including empty default passwords, permissive default access control lists, network ports open by default, and so on. Such behavior is very likely to result in real security threats, particularly when exhibited by packaged software products, which are often installed by users who are not familiar with them. Ensuring secure default behavior makes a real contribution to practical systems security.

- *Fail securely*: Another common problem found in many real systems is insecure failure mode behavior, where the system is reasonably secure during normal operation but becomes insecure when things go wrong. Examples include error logs that record sensitive information, audit trails that suspend auditing if the audit logs run out of space, systems that drop back to an insecure mode if security negotiation fails, unprotected recovery consoles that appear after crashes, and so on. System failures are inevitable occasionally, so make sure that if your system fails, it does so securely.

- *Assume external entities are untrusted*: Within your system you should be able to exert a great deal of control over the security environment and the principals within it. This is not the case for external entities who access the system. Ensure that all external entities are totally untrusted until proven otherwise to avoid accidental security breaches in unexpected cases.

- *Audit sensitive events*: Most systems include a number of key security-related events that, if abused, could compromise the security system. Common examples include resetting passwords, assigning powerful roles, and manipulating audit trails. These sensitive events need to be securely audited so that their use can be monitored. This principle often places a number of constraints on your deployment structure to ensure that a reliable audit trail can be implemented.

Make sure that you understand these commonly accepted principles and apply them to your system's security. In the Further Reading section at the end of this chapter, we recommend a number of background references that can provide much more detail on these topics.

Authenticate the Principals

Authentication is the reliable identification of each of the principals who can use the system. These principals could be people, computers, pieces of software, or anything else in the system that has a security identity. Nearly all system security depends on being able to identify the various principals in the system reliably.

Implementing authentication involves reliably binding a unique name of some sort to each principal who can use the system. A wide variety of authentication technologies exist to allow you to identify the principals in your system, including user names with passwords, public/private key systems (such as X.509 digital certificates), and hardware token technologies (such as smart cards). Off-the-shelf products known as single-sign-on systems allow you to delegate the entire system-wide authentication process to them (which is particularly useful in mixed technology environments such as those with both UNIX and Windows authentication). Each of these technologies has its place, but each tends to be suited to different environments and security needs, so you need to select the right ones for your system.

The key decision to be made is how every principal in your system is uniquely identified, via a mechanism that is secure enough to address the particular risks your system faces. You should bear in mind that you may need to use different principal authentication technologies for different principal types, and in some cases, principals may need to be identified by more than one authentication technology (e.g., users in a corporation may have separate digital certificates, operating system logins, database logins, and application logins). When multiple logins are necessary, we strongly recommend some form of single-sign-on technology as a unifying layer on top of the different underlying systems. People simply can't remember more than a couple of passwords, and forcing them to remember more will result in passwords written on notes stuck to terminals!

What is critical at the architectural level is that every principal can be reliably identified when required and that the system you use is simple and usable enough that the system's users will not try to work around it.

Authorize Access

Once you have identified the principals, authorization involves restricting and enforcing what those principals are permitted to do within the system. Conceptually, you define lists of principals and their permitted actions for each controlled resource in the system. This usually involves assigning principals to roles and groups so you can treat them as homogeneous populations. Then you can define permitted actions on resources for the roles and groups in the system.

Most enterprise software technologies already include some form of access control that allows you to limit access to resources based on user identity and credentials (such as group membership). In addition, software developers can code explicit security checks into their software when they implement the system.

In many systems, your key problem as the architect is how to create a coherent access control system from this patchwork of separate, often incompatible authentication and authorization technologies. For system security to be manageable and effective, the system architecture needs to include a clearly defined approach to enforcing principal authorizations, particularly if multiple candidate authorization systems are available in the system's environment.

One solution to this problem is the use of purpose-built access control products. These allow access to many sorts of resources to be controlled through a single product that interfaces to a variety of authentication systems. Another common approach is to standardize all authorization to be the checking of roles against a central enterprise directory (such as an LDAP directory). A simpler approach still would be a simple homegrown access control manager in your system architecture, which may be sufficient for small systems.

Ensure Information Secrecy

Secrecy is the means of ensuring that only owners of information and those with whom they choose to share it can read that information.

Secrecy can be partially achieved by using authorization appropriately, to prevent access to stored information that a principal is not authorized to access. However, access control is rarely sufficient, and it usually needs to be combined with other techniques in order to achieve the secrecy required.

Traditional information systems were highly centralized, with huge information vaults held on central computers. The information was tightly controlled by access control systems (typically as part of database management systems) and was accessible only via custom applications running on terminals directly connected to the central computer.

In contrast, today's information systems are highly distributed, with many computers communicating in order to implement the functions of the system. This means that information may become much less secure than with a traditional centralized system—particularly if public networks are used for communication and the different parts of the system are within different organizations. The ability of most end users to easily access the Internet and its many storage services and the widespread use of very large-capacity personal storage devices (such as USB sticks) make the situation more complicated still.

One of the implications of this shift is that sensitive information needs to be protected once it moves outside the authorization controls of the database servers where it resides. Ensuring secrecy of information outside databases normally involves the use of cryptography, to encrypt information in such a way that only principals who have access to a particular key can decrypt it and read it. In reality, the inherent complexity of cryptography means that it is often implemented by securing network links through the use of communications protocols that include cryptographic protection, like SSL/TLS, rather than by encrypting individual pieces of sensitive information. However, this protects the information only during transmission and leaves it easily accessible at both ends of the network link.

From the architect's point of view, the snag with this neat picture is that extensive use of cryptography in your system is not without cost. It will add significant complexity to many aspects of the system (cryptographic key management alone is a complex problem), and it also tends to have high computational costs, burning up precious computing resources that could be dedicated to useful functional processing. It can be difficult to apply cryptography correctly so that the system is actually secure. It is significantly more complex than just using server-certificate-based SSL to identify your servers because this leaves your system open to any number of alternative attacks (such as intercepting information elsewhere in the system once it has been decrypted).

In general, use your threat model to identify where information needs to be protected, and use the minimum amount of cryptography that leaves your system acceptably secure.

Ensure Information Integrity

Integrity is the name given to the concern of ensuring that information is protected from unauthorized change (particularly during message transmission).

Implementing integrity in most information systems also involves the application of cryptography. We would like the recipients of messages sent over a network to be able to satisfy themselves that they have received each message unchanged and that no one has tampered with it. Ensuring integrity of information usually involves the application of cryptographic hash functions. Hash functions are cryptographic operations that use a secret key to compute a large numeric value for a block of information. They allow the recipient of that block to ensure that the information has not been changed since the hash value was computed. However, useful as this is, the same caveats mentioned for secrecy also apply to integrity, in particular that it adds both complexity and runtime overhead to the system and so needs to be used judiciously.

Ensure Accountability

Many systems require some or all of their users to be accountable for their actions. In some systems (such as certain financial and medical systems), legal requirements mandate user accountability for key operations. There tend to be two distinct forms of accountability required in information systems: *auditing* and *nonrepudiation* of messages.

Auditing is usually used in situations where secure central servers execute the system's primary operations. These servers can record logs of operations performed by the system's users, which can later be used to establish how a particular situation occurred.

In distributed systems without centralized servers, effective auditing is more difficult (due to the lack of a secure store for the audit trail). The analogous concept in these systems is nonrepudiation, the ability to definitively identify a message's creator in a way that she cannot plausibly deny. A common solution to this problem is to use digital signatures on messages that can be generated only by someone with access to the corresponding digital certificate's private key.

Both of these approaches come with their own costs. Auditing has a runtime performance penalty associated with it, as well as management and storage overhead for the records created. Digital signatures are computationally expensive to create and verify, and they can be complex to administer because they require all of the principals in the system to have a unique digital certificate. We are also ignoring other important complexities such as certificate management and revocation and the difficult problem of ensuring that technically sophisticated users do not compromise other users' digital certificates.

Once again, your role as an architect is to balance the cost of these accountability mechanisms against the risks you think your system faces, applying these techniques where the threat model indicates they are really needed.

Protect Availability

When thinking about system availability, it is natural to focus on hardware reliability, software replication, failover, and so on. Such approaches are an important piece of the availability puzzle, as we discuss in Chapter 27 on the Availability and Resilience perspective. However, there is an easily overlooked security aspect related to availability: protecting your system from hostile attacks that aim to reduce its availability.

Such attacks, known as *denial-of-service (DoS) attacks*, have been the subject of increasing interest as systems have started to expose their network interfaces to public networks like the Internet and a number of high-profile DoS attacks have taken place on well-known sites such as the Internet's DNS backbone servers. DoS attacks can range from something as simple as forcing a user to be locked out by repeatedly using an incorrect password with her login,[1] to sophisticated distributed network attacks (so-called DDoS attacks) that use custom software running on many Internet-connected computers to overload systems. DoS attacks can also be physical attacks such as attempting to interrupt a system's power supply.

Work to understand the possible DoS threats your system faces and the impact of any of the threats occurring. This will probably require working with security specialists who understand this area in detail. Once you understand the threats, their costs, their likelihood, and the potential approaches to protect against them, you need to decide the right level of protection for your system by balancing these factors. Be aware, however, that protecting your system from network DoS attacks can be tremendously difficult, and for most systems you may simply have to accept some level of risk of such an attack occurring.

Integrate Security Technologies

Almost inevitably, when you design the security implementation, you will need a number of different technologies in order to fulfill all of the requirements. Similarly, security normally needs to be implemented across a number of distinct parts of your system. Given this situation, you need to make an early design decision about how to achieve end-to-end security in the system. Implementing a large number of unrelated security technologies is highly undesirable because it introduces complexity and the likelihood of creating security vulnerabilities at the boundaries of each technology.

Part of your role in the security design of the system is to ensure that security is implemented consistently and that the different pieces of the technology are put together to form a complete, integrated security system. This will be particularly important if you're using security consultants from a number of sources (such as different product vendors) who will focus on their own parts of the security puzzle.

---

1. This doesn't sound like a terribly serious attack until you consider time-sensitive systems such as online auctions. This attack has allegedly been used on a number of occasions at Internet auction sites to prevent users from bidding on (and so raising the prices of) items that the attacker wishes to buy. Other systems can also be vulnerable to similar DoS attacks—for example, a battlefield system isn't much use if an attacker can lock out all of its users simply by bombarding it with credible user names and random passwords.

Provide Security Administration

Administration is a weakness of many existing security systems, particularly when complex policies need to be enforced or when there is a need to cope with the sort of large user populations found in today's global organizations. This problem can become even more awkward when you need to combine a number of security technologies in order to implement the security policy.

As part of architecture definition, you need to ensure that the planned security implementation can be administered effectively (this will form part of the Operational view). Without good administration, security policy is likely to be ignored simply to "get the job done." Complex security administration facilities can also lead to security loopholes caused by administrators who are unaware of the full ramifications of their actions.

Remember to involve key stakeholders when considering security administration. Your system administrators will be able to provide a lot of feedback about the acceptability of the administration facilities available—testers too often have a perspective on this because they need to reproduce large security configurations automatically to allow reliable, repeatable testing of the security facilities.

Use Third-Party Security Infrastructure

Many of today's infrastructure technologies (such as J2EE and .NET servers, enterprise directories, and e-mail servers) provide a number of standard security functions. Also, specific security infrastructure technologies (such as enterprise access control products) are available that can provide security services to applications. These technologies offer an alternative to the traditional approach to implementing application security—namely, embedding policy enforcement in the application code.

In general, using external security infrastructure is simpler than coding it directly; after all, someone else has done a lot of the work already. This approach is often much more flexible, too. Rather than needing to change program code when the security policy changes, it is often possible to change the configuration of the infrastructure element—a process that can be achieved by the administrators without involving software developers and rereleasing software. Most important, a security infrastructure product is likely to provide more reliable security than application-specific code because it is more widely used and has been written by software developers with specialized interest and training in system security.

We strongly recommend adopting a security approach of pushing as much of your policy enforcement into the underlying infrastructure of your system as possible. We suggest this for three reasons: simplicity, flexibility, and reliability. Security infrastructure products hide much of the complexity of integrating different security systems. They should also provide some degree of abstraction over individual mechanisms, allowing the mechanisms to be changed more easily. Finally, widely deployed infrastructure products have been widely tested, analyzed, and understood, increasing their reliability when compared with custom solutions.

PROBLEMS AND PITFALLS

Complex Security Policies

Security policies have a habit of starting out simple and well defined but becoming complex, full of special cases, and poorly understood as they are reviewed by more and more stakeholders. Implementing system security is difficult during the best of times. If the security policy is not a simple and regular rule set, this job becomes much more difficult during both development and system operation, and the likelihood of flaws in the security implementation is much higher.

RISK REDUCTION

- Make sure that the security policy is as simple as it can be—make functional, performance, and other tradeoffs if appropriate in order to achieve this goal.
- If policies appear to be very complex, consider partitioning the security-sensitive resources or the principals in different ways to make the policy simpler.

Unproven Security Technologies

There are many security technologies available for implementing your security infrastructure. They range from simple, very well-understood technologies such as user names and passwords to large-scale, sophisticated systems in their own right such as many public/private key cryptography implementations.

However, whatever technology you use, your system's security is only as strong as its weakest link. A single weak element in your security infrastructure has the potential to make the rest of the infrastructure irrelevant. The weakness in an element can come from an inherent design or implementation flaw in the underlying product, a mistake made in its application, or indeed a mistake made in operating the technology.

RISK REDUCTION

- Err on the side of caution when selecting your security technology—such technology needs to be well understood and proven in operation before you can consider it a sound choice for a generic piece of infrastructure.

- If you don't have practical experience with a particular technology, find someone who does have such experience to guide you. (And don't assume that everything the vendor says is true!)

System Not Designed for Failure

As any architect knows, things go wrong in the process of designing, building, and operating information systems. Therefore, system elements are often created to fail in certain ways in order to minimize the impact of a particular failure. This is often a sound approach. It allows the system to continue being used (possibly with reduced function) while one or more pieces of it are being fixed. However, when considering security, this is not always the best approach.

To illustrate this, consider the failure of a security element that controls access to a sensitive resource. If the element is unexpectedly unavailable, the high-availability approach to design might suggest that the default behavior in such cases is to simply allow access until the security element is fixed. However, this obviously isn't the right thing to do from a security perspective. Similar but much more subtle examples of this problem can happen when unexpected errors occur and security has not been considered while designing the relevant error-handling code.

RISK REDUCTION

- Design your security infrastructure to cope with failure in a safe way from the beginning so that unexpected element failures do not open security loopholes in the system.

- Ensure that your security infrastructure is configured to fail securely if unexpected situations occur.

- When reviewing your architecture in failure scenarios, be sure to check what impact the failures have on the system's security.

Lack of Administration Facilities

An important but often neglected part of designing security infrastructure is to ensure that it can be effectively administered when the system is in production. Your testers may also have administration needs to ensure that they can reproduce large-scale test scenarios effectively.

Two common problems in this area include administration tools that can be used only for simple test cases (rather than for the thousands of users who can be found in real systems) and the use of a patchwork of administration tools that need to be carefully combined in order to manage the system. Such a situation will likely result in loopholes in security policy enforcement as administrators struggle to use inadequate tools to control access.

RISK REDUCTION

- Review your architecture to ensure that its administration facilities are adequate for the expected size of the user population and the complexity of the security policy.

- Make sure that the administration facilities you are planning to provide are acceptable to the administrators and operators who will have to use them.

- If possible, make sure that administrative security operations can be performed by using one task-driven interface, rather than requiring the use of a number of tools to perform a single task. If many steps are required, the likelihood of omission or error is much higher.

Technology-Driven Approach

A problem we have seen with the security design of some systems occurs when the available technology drives the security design process. You can tell that you have this sort of problem when you inquire whether the designers have considered security yet and you get the reply, "Oh, yes—we're secure; we use SSL." In such situations, although security technology is deployed, you often have no idea whether it addresses the system's security needs.

RISK REDUCTION

- Drive your security design by the resources that need to be protected, the security model that needs to be implemented, and the security threats that the system faces.

- Avoid designing your security architecture around specific pieces of security technology. Don't incorporate security technology that is not justified by the security needs of your system.

Failure to Consider Time Sources

A number of security mechanisms rely on checking the passage of time (e.g., product license timeouts and password expirations). These mechanisms assume that a reliable source of time is readily available. Although the specifics of the mechanisms and the time source they need differ, they all share the characteristic that if the time source is compromised, the mechanism is ineffective.

RISK REDUCTION

- Identify the security mechanisms that require accurate time and the characteristics of the time they need (such as accuracy, absolute or relative, universal or time zone, and so on).

- Incorporate enough secure time sources in your system to meet the needs of your security mechanisms.

- Make sure you understand what will happen if a secure time source is unavailable or is compromised.

- Protect secure time sources against likely threats (using mechanisms such as calling back to secure servers, using external time servers or dedicated hardware devices, using operating system access controls to protect the time source, and so on).

Overreliance on Technology

It is often said by security luminaries like Bruce Schneier and others that security is a process, not a product. Yet you can often find system designers placing great reliance on particular security products to keep their systems secure. Although you certainly do need to use good third-party security products to secure your system, you need to use them intelligently as part of an overall security design that encompasses all of the different aspects of your system.

At a security conference some time ago, an executive of a security product company pointed out that "there is no way you can buy anything, subscribe to anything, and say you are 100% secure." This is sound advice, coming from someone actually in the IT security industry.

RISK REDUCTION

- Use your threat model to drive your security design. Addressing these tangible threats will help you design a system that is secure, rather than a system that just uses security technology.

- Design a sound set of operational procedures to avoid human error exposing the system to security threats.

No Clear Requirements or Models

It is common for systems to have no clear, well-defined security requirements and no formal security models at all. The problem with these systems is that you simply don't know if they are secure because you don't know what "secure" means. Security is an area where it usually isn't possible to be confident that you have met the needs of the stakeholders without firm requirements and formal models. Security can't be seen, and most stakeholders won't test it. You'll find out that you have problems only when the security is breached—at which point you can be pretty certain that the stakeholders won't think their needs are being met.

RISK REDUCTION

- Drive the security design process by using threat and security policy models. Developing these models will help define requirements because they focus the stakeholders' minds on what is valuable, what is likely to be attacked, and what the impact of such attacks would be.

- Use plenty of concrete examples when discussing security with stakeholders. Security is an abstract area that requires some lateral and imaginative thinking in order to be effective. Examples will help your stakeholders think clearly about what they need.

- When identifying your architectural scenarios, consider those related to security as well as to functionality, performance, evolution, and so on. Thinking through security-related scenarios can help identify and clarify important security requirements.

Security as an Afterthought

Because stakeholders often don't think about security requirements explicitly, these requirements don't always get mentioned in the initial requirements analysis. This can lead to the problem where security has to be added to the system at some point during (or even after) development. At best, this is likely to be an expensive and painful process involving a lot of rework. At worst, it won't be possible to introduce the required security without changing the system in some way that upsets a stakeholder group.

RISK REDUCTION

- Start considering the system's security as soon as you start developing its functional and information structure. This will allow you to understand the security needs early in the lifecycle and make sure that the system you design can be secured.

Ignoring the Insider Threat

As noted previously, while it is tempting to treat the system's "insiders" as trusted principals, you need to consider threats from people inside the organization at least as thoroughly as those from principals outside it. Insiders are often trusted and are often privy to knowledge about the organization, its systems, and the security controls that make circumventing a security control rather easier for them than for an outsider. They may also have grievances against their employer for all kinds of reasons, which could motivate them to attempt to damage the organization (e.g., by leaking confidential data). Perhaps it's no surprise, then, that in a 2010 survey[2] nearly 60% of British businesses confirmed that they had dealt with one or more incidents of unauthorized insider access to systems and data.

RISK REDUCTION

- Consider threats to the system that are specific to insiders who have partial or privileged access to it or just thorough knowledge of the system and its controls.

- Work with the enterprise security group, if there is one, to ensure that people do not retain authorizations that they no longer need in the event that their job changes.

- Consider possibilities for collusion between different insiders. Such situations are very difficult to guard against, but it may be worth introducing some form of monitoring for unusual situations that suggest some form of collusion.

- If your system is hosted outside your organization, consider whether insiders in the hosting organization can pose a threat to the system and its resources. Consider protecting externally hosted systems in a way that prevents the hosting company from gaining access to the system (e.g., by encrypting data to prevent its being read by employees of the hosting company who will have administrative access to the hosting environment).

Assuming the Client Is Secure

Years ago, when mainframes and proprietary mini-computers ruled the roost, controlling who could connect to your system was relatively straightforward. Users used proprietary "green screen" terminals to access the system, the terminals were all registered and authorized to connect to the application, and you could be pretty sure that they hadn't been tampered with. Things couldn't be more different today!

Nearly all modern information systems are created in a networked environment, with the main services of the system being accessed by clients of various

---

2. The "Information Security Breaches Survey 2010," available from www.pwc.co.uk/eng/publications/isbs_survey_2010.html.

sorts across a network. Internet-connected systems are obviously the most extreme example of this, with all of their public services being accessed through Web browsers and Web services, by a range of application clients largely outside the architect's control. While most users may be using a market-leading browser on a desktop computer, some may be using mobile phones to access the system, and in a few cases people may even have written their own Web browsers! Even in the corporate environment, it is becoming more common for end users to demand access to applications on a variety of devices including smartphones, tablet computers, and their own computers at home.

In this dynamic and accessible environment we can't reliably assume anything about the client devices that will be used to access our system, and we have to accept that from a security perspective, we have lost control of that part of the system's deployment environment. The only option open to us in many cases is to embrace this diverse client mix as well as we can and to ensure that the system's security does not rely on trusting the client's behavior.

RISK REDUCTION

- Remember that almost anything can be changed on a compromised client device, and reflect this assumption in the system threat model.

- Even if security checks are performed on client devices (e.g., for performance or usability reasons), make sure that the definitive security check is performed in the system's servers that are under your control.

- If it is feasible, consider limiting the devices that can connect to your system by checking their identity and accepting connections only from devices that have been deployed with a verifiable identity.

- If necessary, consider working with your enterprise security group in order to employ mechanisms that prevent data from your application from being saved on client computers (e.g., by preventing users from writing data to local removable storage).

Security Embedded in the Application Code

A problem we have observed in a number of systems occurs when the code that enforces the security model is found sprinkled throughout the application itself. The problems with this approach include reduced reliability, the difficulty of changing the security model being enforced, and the likelihood of introducing security errors in your system.

RISK REDUCTION

- Push as much of the security technology as possible into your underlying infrastructure elements.

- If security does need to be in application code, apply good software engineering judgment to encapsulate as much of it as possible in a single place. Also consider using software technologies (such as aspect-oriented programming or code generation) that would allow the security code to be applied automatically as part of the build process.

Piecemeal Security

To be effective, security needs to be considered on a holistic basis, throughout the system. A problem we have seen in many systems is security being applied to parts of the system but not to others. For example, highly sensitive data is encrypted during transmission but not when stored. This may or may not be a problem depending on the sensitivity of the data and the threats the system is likely to have to withstand. Your role is to make sure that security is implemented everywhere it is needed as revealed by the threat model—not just in the places that immediately spring to mind.

RISK REDUCTION
- The use of an architecture-driven development process will help address this risk. Make sure that you keep considering the architecture and particularly its security as a whole, rather than as a set of separate parts.

Ad Hoc Security Technology

Computer security is a specialized field with its own culture, standards, processes, and background. Security engineers (the people who build security technology and secure systems) tend to have a lot of specialized training and experience. Similarly, cryptographers (the people who study and create ways to encrypt and decrypt data) tend to have advanced degrees in cryptography. Despite this, many software developers without this specialized background fancy themselves as amateur security engineers or cryptographers and decide to create some or all of the security technology in their systems.

In general, we suggest that this is a bad idea—creating truly secure technology is harder than it looks, and without specialized training, most of us can't do it reliably. Given the integrated nature of security, the consequences of one piece of weak security technology can be pretty catastrophic.

RISK REDUCTION
- Use proven, widely accepted security technology from established providers when possible, and get expert help with its use and deployment.
- Make sure you find out what previous users of the possible technologies thought of it and how the security community as a whole rates it.
- If you have to create your own technology, engage expert assistance to help you systematically develop it.

CHECKLISTS

Checklist for Requirements Capture

- Have you identified the sensitive resources contained in the system?
- Have you identified the sets of principals who need access to the resources?
- Have you identified the system's needs for information integrity guarantees?
- Have you identified the system's availability needs?
- Have you established a security policy to define the security needs for the system, including which principals are allowed to perform which operations on which resources and where information integrity needs to be enforced?
- Is the security policy as simple as possible?
- Have you worked through a formal threat model to identify the security risks your system faces?
- Have you considered insider as well as outsider threats to the system?
- Have you considered how the system's deployment environment will alter the threats to the system?
- Have you worked through example scenarios with your stakeholders so that they understand the planned security policy and the security risks the system runs?
- Have you reviewed your security requirements with external experts?

Checklist for Architecture Definition

- Have you addressed each threat identified in the threat model to the extent required?
- Have you used as much third-party security technology as possible?
- Have you produced an integrated overall design for the security solution?
- Have you considered all standard security principles when designing your security infrastructure?
- Is your security infrastructure as simple as possible?
- Have you defined how security breaches will be identified and how to recover from them?
- Have you applied the results of the Security perspective to all of the affected views?
- Have external experts reviewed your security design?

FURTHER READING

You can find a short but thorough and very readable introduction to the main concepts of information systems security in an IEEE magazine article [LAMP04]. A much deeper but still approachable introduction to the process of building secure systems and processes appears in Anderson [ANDE08]; this book provides a comprehensive introduction to many important security topics, as well as being an entertaining read, full of interesting stories from the security field.

A well-known, generally respected, and always colorful figure in the security field is Bruce Schneier. Two books that he authored or coauthored that offer useful background are [FERG10], which provides a good nuts-and-bolts introduction to cryptographic technology for software engineers, and [SCHN01], which moves beyond a technology-focused approach and explains how technology will never provide a complete solution to security problems. This second book is worth reading to understand just how complex the security field is and how broad effective security solutions need to be.

Two good, practical security books aimed at software developers are Viega and McGraw [VIEG02] and Howard and LeBlanc [HOWA04]. Both books explain how to construct software that is secure by design rather than by accident or buzzword compliance. Chapter 5 in the former book also presents and explains a practical and simple set of security principles. Gary McGraw's later book [MCGR06] takes the theme further, explaining how security concerns should be woven into the design process for secure systems. The Fault Trees approach, which forms the basis of the attack trees we introduced in this perspective, is explained in Leveson [LEVE95], and a simple guide to threat modeling can be found in [SWID04].

26

THE PERFORMANCE AND SCALABILITY PERSPECTIVE

Desired Quality	The ability of the system to predictably execute within its mandated performance role and to handle increased processing volumes in the future if required
Applicability	Any system with complex, unclear, or ambitious performance requirements; systems whose architecture includes elements whose performance is unknown; and systems where future expansion is likely to be significant
Concerns	Response time, throughput, scalability, predictability, hardware resource requirements, and peak load behavior
Activities	Capture the performance requirements, create the performance models, analyze the performance models, conduct practical testing, assess against the requirements, and rework the architecture
Architectural Tactics	Optimize repeated processing, reduce contention via replication, prioritize processing, consolidate related workload, distribute processing over time, minimize the use of shared resources, reuse resources and results, partition and parallelize, scale up or scale out, degrade gracefully, use asynchronous processing, relax transactional consistency, and make design compromises
Problems and Pitfalls	Imprecise performance and scalability goals, unrealistic models, use of simple measures for complex cases, inappropriate partitioning, invalid environment and platform assumptions, too much indirection, concurrency-related contention, database contention, transaction overhead, careless allocation of resources, and disregard for network and in-process invocation differences

This chapter discusses two related quality properties for large information systems: performance and scalability. These properties are important because, in large systems, they can cause more unexpected, complex, and expensive problems late in the system lifecycle than most of the other properties combined.

Intel chief Gordon Moore observed in 1965 that the processing power of computer chips doubled approximately every 18 to 24 months (now known as Moore's Law). This remark seems to apply almost as well today as it did in 1965, so one would hope that by now performance and scalability would have receded as major concerns for most computer systems. Unfortunately, this isn't the case, for a couple of reasons.

The fundamental reason for performance concerns is that the tasks we set our systems to perform have become much more complex over time, and the demands we make on the systems (in terms of complexity, numbers of transactions, numbers of users, and so on) have also grown in ways that would have been unimaginable in the 1960s.

To make matters worse, the performance of a computer system depends on much more than the raw processing power of its hardware. The way that hardware is configured and used, the way resources are allocated and managed, and the way the software is written can have significant impacts (good or bad) on the system's ability to meet its performance goals. The simple fact is that we face as many performance challenges today as our predecessors did in the 1960s.

The scalability property of a system is closely related to performance, but rather than considering how quickly the system performs its current workload, scalability focuses on the predictability of the system's performance as the workload increases. Even if your system meets its goals today, how confident are you that it still will in the future? Will it be able to cope with increased numbers of users, transactions, or messages? Will it be able to handle increased complexity of processing? How will it behave when unexpectedly presented with a huge increase in workload?

Applying the Performance and Scalability perspective to your architecture will help you answer all of these questions.

APPLICABILITY TO VIEWS

Table 26–1 shows how the Performance and Scalability perspective affects each of the views we discussed in Part III.

CONCERNS

Response Time

Response time is the length of time it takes for a specified interaction with the system to complete. For a human-oriented system, this could be the length of

TABLE 26-1 APPLICABILITY OF THE PERFORMANCE AND SCALABILITY PERSPECTIVE TO THE SEVEN VIEWS

View	Applicability
Context	The Context view identifies all of the system's external interfaces, and applying this perspective will highlight the performance requirements or potential problems that the use of these interfaces implies. This allows these constraints to be identified early in the design of the system so that their impact on the system can be understood and appropriate mitigating actions identified.
Functional	Applying this perspective may reveal the need for changes and compromises to your ideal functional structure to achieve the system's performance requirements (e.g., by consolidating system elements to avoid communication overhead). The models from this view also provide input to the creation of performance models.
Information	The Information view provides useful input to performance models, identifying shared resources and the transactional requirements of each. As you apply this perspective, you may identify aspects of the Information view as obstacles to performance or scalability. In addition, considering scalability may suggest elements of the Information view that could be replicated or distributed in support of this goal.
Concurrency	Applying this perspective may result in changes to the concurrency design due to identifying problems such as excessive contention on key resources. Alternatively, considering performance and scalability may result in concurrency becoming a more important design element to meet these requirements. Elements of concurrency views (such as interprocess communication mechanisms) can also provide calibration metrics for performance models.
Development	One of the possible outputs of applying this perspective is a set of guidelines related to performance and scalability that should be followed during software development. These guidelines will probably take the form of dos and don'ts (e.g., patterns and antipatterns) that must be followed as the software is developed in order to avoid performance and scalability problems later when it is deployed. You will capture this information in the Development view.
Deployment	The Deployment view is a crucial input to the process of considering performance and scalability. Many parts of the system's performance models are derived from the contents of this view, which also provides a number of critical calibration metrics. In turn, applying this perspective will often suggest changes and refinements to the deployment environment, to allow it to support the performance and scalability needs of the system.
Operational	The application of this perspective highlights the need for performance monitoring and management capabilities.

time between the user initiating the request and the response being available for her use (e.g., the time from clicking a user interface button to seeing the response screen populated with data). For an infrastructure-oriented system such as a database, this could be the time between invoking a service and the service returning a response (e.g., the time from calling a query application programming interface to obtaining the query results).

We define two broad classes of response times you may want to consider separately.

1. *Responsiveness* considers how quickly the system responds to routine workloads such as interactive user requests. The response time for such operations is typically on the order of a few seconds. The key consideration for such workloads is user productivity, ensuring that the system does not slow down its users. The two aspects of responsiveness that usually need to be considered are the responsiveness of the user's device (e.g., how long it takes for a keypress or mouse click to be recognized) and the responsiveness of the system itself (e.g., how long it takes the system to respond to a request when a button is clicked). The latter is usually the focus of our attention, but the former can be important to consider in some circumstances with very resource-limited clients (such as mobile devices), or when users are accessing their devices remotely (such as with remote desktop or thin client technology).

2. *Turnaround time* is the time taken to complete (turn around) larger tasks. This is typically measured in minutes or hours, and the key considerations are whether the task can be completed in the time available to it and the impact the task has on the system responsiveness while it is running. It may also be important to consider how quickly partial results can be produced as part of a long-running task, for example, to provide partial or summary information earlier than the full results.

These two classes of response times can affect different types of stakeholders and often require quite different technical solutions to make sure that requirements of each type are met.

EXAMPLE The following examples show how requirements could be specified for the two classes of response times.

Responsiveness

1. Under a load of 350 update transactions per minute, 95% of transactions should return control to the user within 3 seconds of pressing the submit button.

2. Under the reference load (defined in a separate document), 90% of service requests should return a reply to the calling program within the following times:
   - Open account: 10 seconds
   - Update account details: 5 seconds
   - Retrieve account status: 3 seconds
   - Retrieve balances: 3 seconds, plus 0.5 seconds per account accessed

Turnaround Time

1. Assuming a total daily throughput of 850,000 transactions, the process of establishing a consolidated position against each of the firm's external counterparties should take no longer than 4 hours, including writing the results back to a database. It can be assumed that no other significant system activity will take place during this period.

2. It must be possible to resynchronize the system with all of the production line monitoring stations and reset the database to reflect the current production line state within 5 minutes. It can be assumed that no status updates will be processed during the resynchronization period.

Throughput

Throughput is defined as the amount of workload the system is capable of handling in a unit time period. Throughput and response time have a complex interrelationship in most systems. In general, the shorter your transaction processing time, the higher the throughput your system can achieve. However, as the load on the system increases (and throughput rises), the response time for individual transactions tends to increase. Therefore, it is quite possible to end up with a situation where throughput goals can be met only at the expense of response time goals, or vice versa. We can illustrate this with a simple example.

EXAMPLE A database server can support up to 500 concurrent users performing sales transactions; however, as the number of concurrent users increases, the response time the users see increases as well.

- With 10 concurrent users, a typical transaction is processed in 2 seconds.

- With 100 concurrent users, a typical transaction is processed in 4 seconds.
- With 500 concurrent users, a typical transaction is processed in 14 seconds.

For simplicity, let us assume that it takes 1 second of "thinking time" for a user to enter a transaction.

If we have only 10 users, each user can theoretically perform 20 transactions per minute, and our total possible throughput is a modest 200 transactions per minute.

If the load on the system rises to 100 users, each user can process up to 12 transactions per minute. Our total possible throughput rises to 1,200 transactions per minute, but at the cost of doubling the response time.

If we operate at our peak load of 500 concurrent users, each user can process up to 4 transactions per minute. Our total possible system throughput is 2,000 transactions per minute, but the response time cost has risen significantly for the users.

As the architect, you need to make sure that you and your stakeholders understand these interrelationships and that you have balanced your stakeholders' different performance goals.

Scalability

Most systems are subject to workload growth in some form. Scalability is the ability of a system to handle this increased workload, which may be due to an increase in the number of requests, transactions, messages, or jobs the system is required to process per unit of time or an increase in the complexity of these tasks.

Long-term scalability always has an associated time element that considers how soon the increase in workload is anticipated to arrive. You may also need to consider transient scalability—that is, the ability to handle short bursts of increased workload (such as increased traffic to an Internet news site during an international crisis).

Predictability

In addition to providing acceptable response time and throughput, another desirable property of a computer system is its ability to perform predictably. By this we mean that similar transactions complete in very similar amounts of time regardless of when they are executed. Similarly, the maximum transaction throughput the system can cope with should not vary significantly over time (in particular, it shouldn't decrease).

Predictability is often a more desirable quality than absolute performance.

> **EXAMPLE** Call center agents use a customer service system to answer customer queries over the telephone. Having identified the customer, the agent executes a transaction to retrieve the customer's details. Whether the response time for this transaction is 1 second or 6 seconds probably doesn't matter that much—5 seconds isn't a long pause during such a telephone conversation, and agents can incorporate this delay into their conversations with the customers. Therefore, a predictable transaction time of 6 seconds is acceptable.
>
> However, if the system is unpredictable and produces the result in any time from 1 second to 15 seconds, then even if the average response time is significantly less than 6 seconds, this is still less acceptable to the agents, because it will result in awkward pauses during many of the longer retrievals.

Hardware Resource Requirements

A major part of the performance and scalability puzzle is working out how much (and what type of) hardware your system will need, and this is usually an early concern in any project, being captured as part of the Deployment view. Hardware must be considered early because it costs money, takes time to acquire, often needs people to operate it, and is usually housed in purpose-built environments. Even virtualized environments cost money and need to be carefully planned if intended for production use. The amount of hardware needed for a system usually has a significant and very visible impact on its overall cost.

In general, more hardware means higher throughput and better response times, albeit at higher cost. Given this fundamental tension between cost and performance, your role is often to establish the minimum amount of hardware that will allow the system to meet its performance goals.

Peak Load Behavior

Nearly all computer systems eventually exhibit poor performance as the load on them increases. If you plot a graph of the average transaction response time against the load on the system, it will usually have the shape shown in Figure 26-1.

FIGURE 26-1 THE PERFORMANCE CURVE

The system behaves well for a while: As workload increases, response time increases in a predictable, linear fashion. However, at a certain point things start to go very wrong, and the response times increase sharply. This point is known as the "knee" in the curve. Soon, the graph ends up as a nearly vertical line, indicating that response times have become so long that the system is effectively unusable. This behavior is usually caused by one or more critical resources in the system becoming so overloaded that it can no longer work effectively (e.g., a network card is so swamped by incoming connection requests that it cannot service any of them effectively).

This sort of behavior is exhibited by virtually every system we have come across. However, it obviously isn't acceptable to experience this effect during normal system operation. This means that your challenge is to identify where the "knee" in the performance graph for your system is, to make sure that the corresponding workload level will be irrelevant during normal system operation, and to handle the overload condition gracefully, should it occur.

ACTIVITIES: APPLYING THE PERFORMANCE AND SCALABILITY PERSPECTIVE

The activity diagram in Figure 25–2 illustrates a simple process for applying the Performance and Scalability perspective. In this section, we describe the activities in this process.

Capture the Performance Requirements

Ideally, you will already have a complete, consistent, and credible set of performance and scalability requirements as a result of the initial system requirements

FIGURE 26-2 APPLYING THE PERFORMANCE AND SCALABILITY PERSPECTIVE

work. In reality, this usually isn't the case, and you need to collect these requirements, at least in summary form, as early as possible in the development lifecycle. Even if some requirements do exist, you need to verify their correctness, and your understanding of them, and start to capture this in your Context view.

The performance requirements are often defined in business terms so that they are meaningful to the users of the system rather than the builders. Requirements such as "Be fast enough to support a 20,000-transaction-per-day back-of-fice workload" are common and are useful because they describe the real stakeholder requirement rather than some abstract performance metric. However, at this stage, you need to translate these performance requirements into a set of quantitative performance goals for the system.

Setting specific performance goals involves identifying the underlying performance metrics that are implicitly defined by the business-oriented requirements. From the previous example, you might end up with a definition of 5,000 information lookup requests, 10,000 specific transaction entry requests, and

5,000 report requests distributed over a 9-hour period, with a peak load of 20% of the transactions occurring in 45 minutes. This is a set of specific, quantitative goals, and you can establish whether or not you have met them by measurement and analysis.

A common problem with this process is understanding the business requirements enough to translate them into quantitative goals. Experience, careful analysis, and the knowledge of domain experts who understand the workload can all help to achieve this.

NOTATION Simplicity and clear communication are key goals when communicating performance requirements, and we have found that using text and tables is quite sufficient.

ACTIVITIES

Specify the Response Time Requirements. Response time targets are meaningful only in the context of a defined load. It may be easy for a computer system to process a single transaction in 3 seconds but much harder to achieve this target when it is receiving 500 transactions a second. This means that response time requirements need to specify the context as well as a clearly defined response time goal (which also defines when a transaction starts and ends). In most systems, response time under constant load will vary according to some sort of distribution curve. Most transactions will complete at or near the average response time, but some will take longer, and a few will complete more quickly. In most cases, it isn't reasonable to expect every transaction to complete within the target response time. It is more realistic to require a certain proportion (such as 90% or 95%) of transactions to meet the target.

Specify the Throughput Requirements. Throughput is typically defined in terms of transactions per unit time (second, minute, or hour), where a transaction is a clearly definable unit of work, recognizable to a user of the system. The transactions used for throughput planning should normally be derived from the system's most important usage scenarios (rather than technology-oriented measures such as the number of database insert statements).

Specify the Scalability Requirements. Scalability requirements are usually defined in terms of the increase in workload that the system must be able to absorb over particular time periods while continuing to meet its existing response and throughput goals. Scalability requirements should also make clear any changes to the system that will be needed to meet these increased workload levels.

Create the Performance Models

While data is a key part of the performance engineering process, being able to collect performance data isn't useful in itself. You need to use the data in an effective way to allow you to understand and improve your system's performance. A key part of this process is creating performance models that allow you to gain this insight. Such a model allows you to assess the maximum theoretical workload for your system, supplies useful estimates for capacity planning, and provides a set of measures against which the actual system can be compared to assess its performance.

The types of models you can use for performance analysis vary widely from a few simple calculations on a scrap of paper to sophisticated statistical models to complete online simulations of systems. All these models have their place, but given our degree of expertise and the space available, we will limit our discussion to relatively simple pencil-and-paper performance models involving basic representations of system structure with the simple statistics used to analyze them. The performance engineering books mentioned in the Further Reading section at the end of this chapter provide more information on performance modeling.

NOTATION We have found the following notation methods most helpful when creating performance models.

- *Performance modeling notations*: Specialists in this area have developed several graphical and mathematical performance modeling approaches, including execution graphs, augmented Petri Nets, approaches based on queuing theory, and statistical approaches (see the Further Reading section for more information). Most of the notations used in these approaches are extensions of previously existing notations, with the advantage of being tailored specifically for performance modeling. As with most specialist notations, they often have the disadvantages of complexity and unfamiliarity; many are not widely understood outside the specialist computer measurement community.

- *Ad hoc diagrams*: A simple block diagram notation is probably sufficient for many performance models because they are not terribly complex. In fact, you can use a UML deployment diagram with some ad hoc extensions as the basis for a performance model. Such an approach has the virtue of simplicity but may have limitations for more sophisticated modeling applications.

- *Text and tables*: Some of the performance model will probably need to be captured using text and tables to describe model elements, capture key metrics, and illustrate relationships between elements that the graphical notation does not make clear.

ACTIVITIES

Identify the Performance-Critical Structure. Use the Deployment view of the system as the basis of the model by simplifying it to its essential performance-critical elements—such as processes, nodes, network links, and the main data storage (such as your main databases). Create a new, simple block diagram of the system illustrating the main runtime system elements and how they are connected.

Identify the Key Performance Metrics. Review the block diagram and identify the parts that need to be annotated with performance data to allow the creation of performance estimates. This normally includes the processing time for the main functional elements of the system, the request latency between the main system processes, the length of time taken by a typical database operation, the number of concurrent requests that each major element can handle, and so on.

Estimate the Performance Metrics. At this stage, the values for most of the key performance metrics are probably unclear. For each such metric, you need to derive a reliable estimate of its value. Some may be fairly obvious from previous experiences that you or others on your team have had. For the rest of the metrics, try to create quick prototypes that allow you to derive estimates. If prototypes aren't practical, intelligent guesswork is probably your only remaining option. Whichever approach you use, make sure that the estimates are valid for a realistic workload and not just for a single transaction. When you've completed this process, the result will be a simple performance model you can use for prediction. To estimate the theoretical processing time for an element of system workload, you can trace its execution through the model and piece together the relevant performance estimates.

EXAMPLE Figure 26–3 shows an example of a simple performance model that might be built to investigate the performance of an order-entry process for an order-processing system.

The diagram shows that we have identified five performance-related parts of the system (plus the Browser Client), whose interactions we judge to be the crucial factors determining system performance. For each of the elements that provides any services to others, we have estimated the response times that the element will provide to its clients under defined conditions. We have also estimated the communications latency between the elements, which varies widely (due to different technologies and deployment decisions).

This model provides two valuable insights. First, we can see how long we think a couple of crucial system transactions will take to execute. (We could extend this model or build other similar ones to investigate other aspects of the system's performance.) Second, the model helps us understand the set of performance-related assumptions we are making (such as the invocation latency being minimal between the Order Processor and the Price Calculator), which, if incorrect, may cause us problems later. The model also helps us focus on another step in the process, practical testing.

As we mentioned, the approach illustrated in Figure 26–3 is very simple. Although the model is helpful and provides useful insights, we made a number of important simplifications—for example, we're largely ignoring the modeling of queuing within the system. If you want to create more sophisticated performance models of your system, we again refer you to the books in the Further Reading section.

Analyze the Performance Models

Before you have real measures for key performance metrics, you can start analyzing your performance models by calibrating them with the estimated performance metrics from the previous step and use the results to estimate likely system throughput under different scenarios. The advantage of using performance models is that analysis is cheaper, simpler, and quicker than benchmarking. The disadvantage is obviously that the results are only as good as the models, so they need to be carefully validated by some practical testing as well.

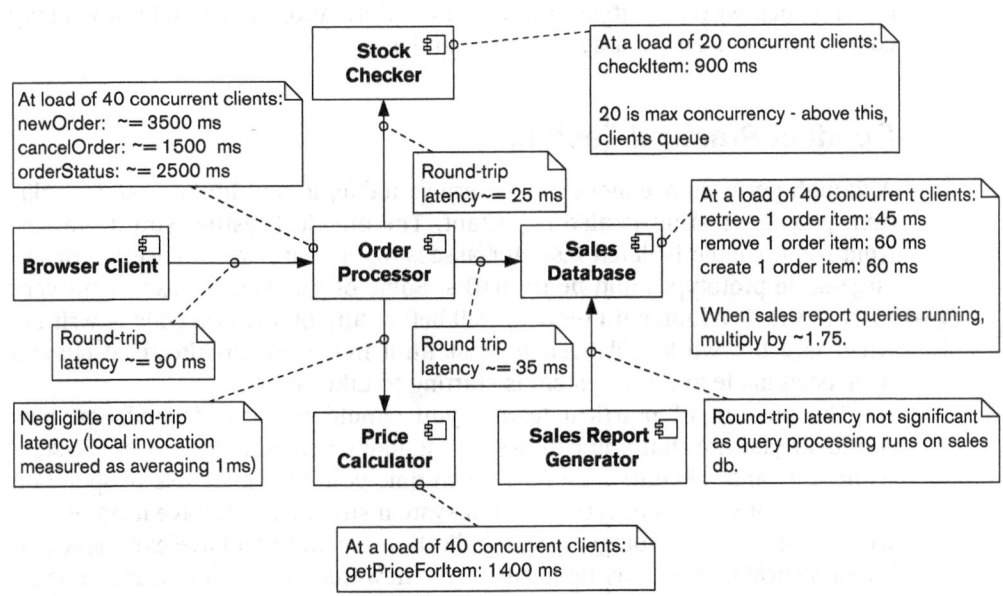

FIGURE 26–3 A SIMPLE PERFORMANCE MODEL

Consider using the performance models to explore a large number of scenarios quickly to find potential trouble spots, and then use this knowledge to drive more time-consuming practical work.

NOTATION Analysis of performance models results in calculated performance data that you can usually represent in tabular form.

ACTIVITIES

Characterize the Workload. The first activity is to establish the "shape" of the workload your system needs to be able to process. This involves prioritizing and estimating the volume of each sort of request the system has been specified to handle, including an estimate of the routine processing needed.

Estimate the Performance. Having identified the kind of workload you expect, you can estimate the processing time of each piece of that workload. This involves using the performance models to identify the elements of the system involved in processing each piece of the workload and to determine how long the likely best- and worse-case durations will be. From this set of inputs, you can establish the estimated best- and worst-case processing times for each element of the expected workload. It is sensible to increase these estimates by a factor that reflects the hidden inefficiencies likely to be present in the system. (A value of 20% is a good starting point for an information system.) At the same time, identify the least scalable element involved in processing each workload item, and use this information to estimate how many concurrent requests your system can handle.

Conduct Practical Testing

Although performance modeling is very valuable, it is of limited use in isolation; practical testing is also important. The practical testing you do ranges from some simple isolated tests for assessing critical performance metrics to large-scale prototypes and benchmarks. Some of this activity can begin very early in the development lifecycle, well before any production code is written, whereas other work will need to wait until important architectural choices have been made and the system is starting to take shape.

The amount of practical testing you should perform depends on how confident you are that you can assess the likely performance of your system without it (and, of course, on how much time you have available to spend on this aspect of your architecture). For a system structure you have used before, with well-tested technology, in an application domain you have experience of, little practical testing may be needed. In a new domain, with new technology, or with a novel system architecture, you will probably want to perform a lot of tests.

NOTATION You can write up test results in a short report if appropriate.

ACTIVITIES

Measure and Estimate the Performance Metrics. To support the process of creating a performance model, you need to measure or estimate values for a number of important performance metrics. A common performance testing activity is to perform a series of practical tests to estimate these metrics accurately. Such testing typically involves quickly prepared trial scenarios that allow a particular performance metric to be empirically tested (such as network response times from a Web server under load). The main pitfall to avoid with such testing is oversimplification of the test scenario, which results in much better performance than would be expected in a real deployment. Make sure that trial scenarios simulate a realistic context for the test metric (such as ensuring a realistic workload on the system element being tested).

Perform Benchmark Tests. Metric estimation is a highly specific activity that focuses on one microlevel metric. It can also be useful to perform more complex practical testing to find out what performance can be expected from a particular configuration of candidate system elements. Such testing is often referred to as *benchmarking* and usually involves creating a trial end-to-end system to allow system-level performance to be estimated. As such, its relationship to metric estimation is similar to the relationship between integration and unit testing. Benchmarking is more involved than simple microlevel performance testing, but the major pitfall is the same: namely, ensuring that the test is valid. Make sure that the limits of the benchmark are understood and that it captures enough of the key characteristics of the planned system to provide a useful insight into its likely performance. (For example, make sure that system elements perform enough processing to be representative of the elements in the system under development.)

Assess against the Requirements

Having completed performance analysis and practical testing, you can compare the results of this process against the performance requirements and draw some initial conclusions. These conclusions may indicate that all should be well or that modifications need to be made to the architecture to resolve potential performance problems. You may also believe that further testing and analysis are required because you made assumptions that you no longer feel comfortable with.

The result of this process should be a decision to either complete this cycle of performance work or circle back through the process. If the latter, you will need to make modifications to your proposed architecture and repeat the analysis and testing cycle, to increase or deepen your knowledge of how the system will behave from a performance perspective.

NOTATION   This activity is a process rather than a model-building activity. However, you do need to clearly capture its outputs so that decisions, assumptions, and assessments are recorded for everyone else to use. Document this activity's outputs as concisely as possible (probably by using plain text), and over time you will create a useful library of performance information that can be applied in other situations.

ACTIVITIES

Identify the Risks. Reconsider the performance risks you believe you are facing, based on your testing and analysis. Clearly record and justify those risks you think are still a problem and those that have been addressed. For those that are still troublesome, identify why they are still present, and use these conclusions to drive the next iteration of performance work, should you decide you need one.

Review the Requirements. Work through each of your performance requirements and demonstrate to your own satisfaction (and the satisfaction of any interested stakeholders) whether or not the proposed architecture will meet each requirement.

Rework the Architecture

The output of this performance work is likely to be a number of cross-view changes you need to make to your candidate architecture. The most likely impact will be to the functional and deployment designs, but other aspects of the architecture (particularly the information- and concurrency-related parts) are also candidates for performance-related changes. Many of the tactics described in the next section imply cross-view changes. In extreme cases, partitioning and parallelization can require changes to the functional, concurrency, information, and deployment structures in order to support effective partitioning and parallel execution of the workload and consolidation of the results.

After changing the architecture, move into the next iteration of the process by modifying your performance model and rerunning or adding practical testing, to establish whether or not the proposed changes have the required effects.

NOTATIONUse the same architectural notations used in your view models.

ACTIVITIES

Any sort of architecture definition activity required to improve performance is relevant here, particularly the tactics discussed in the next section.

ARCHITECTURAL TACTICS

Optimize Repeated Processing

An old software engineering heuristic states that most systems spend 80% of their time running 20% of the system's code. This certainly matches our experience that most systems have a small number of common operations that the system spends most of its time performing.

The resulting performance implication is that you should focus your performance efforts on that core 20% of your system. To state this in slightly more sophisticated terms:

operation total cost = operation invocation cost × operation invocation frequency

We can consider the total cost of a system operation to be the cost of a single invocation multiplied by the number of times we will invoke it during a unit time (e.g., per day). In turn, we can note that:

$$\text{system workload} = \sum_{1..n} \text{operation total cost}$$

The total workload for our system, for a unit time, is the sum of all of the total operation costs over that unit time (where we have n possible operations in our system).

In order to focus your performance engineering effort, rank your system's operations by the total cost metric, and make sure that you optimize the operations at the top of the list first.

Having this information also helps you make intelligent tradeoffs between operation optimizations. In many cases, optimizing for one operation can have a negative impact for another. In general, when you have to make these tradeoffs, the needs of the frequent operations should take precedence.

EXAMPLE A message bus is a piece of software infrastructure that allows applications to exchange messages easily and efficiently. The message bus receives messages from senders, performs any data transformation required, calculates how to route the message to its intended recipients, and delivers the message to them.

In order to process messages efficiently, the message bus could maintain information on its nodes, the routes between them, and the connectivity characteristics of each (such as communication latency). The bus would use this information to derive the most optimal route between message senders and receivers. This speeds up the process of route selection

> (which is a frequent activity), but the tradeoff is that whenever a node or link is added or removed (which happens rarely), the entire set of route tables has to be recalculated, which is a potentially expensive operation.

The goal of the performance engineering process is to minimize the overall system workload; this is one of the few sure ways to improve system performance.

Reduce Contention via Replication

As we discussed in Chapter 19, whenever you have concurrent operations in your system, you have the potential for contention. This contention is often a major source of performance problems, causing reduction in throughput and wasted resources.

Eliminating contention can be a difficult process, particularly when you must deal with a single contention point (such as a shared data structure inside an operating system process). This can occur when the contention is actually within the system's underlying infrastructure (e.g., an application server), rather than in the software over which you have direct control.

A possible solution for some contention problems is to replicate system elements—hardware, software, or data—a tactic that you will often need to combine with the related tactics of partitioning and parallelizing (see the Partition and Parallelize tactic later in the chapter).

EXAMPLE Many large Web sites support many millions of page views per day, far beyond the capacity of even the largest computers. They provide this service by deploying vast server farms, made up of hundreds or even thousands of computers, each running a separate instance of the Web server. Special hardware is used to allocate incoming requests evenly across the Web servers to ensure that response times are consistent and that usage is maximized.

Of course, in this scenario, the network connection into the server farm can still be a bottleneck. By replicating the server nodes, we may just be moving the bottleneck to a different part of the system. This is a very common feature of performance work—solving a problem simply uncovers the next bottleneck in the system!

EXAMPLE A lottery system supports remote point-of-sale terminals in retail locations throughout the country. When a terminal is switched on in the morning, it is necessary to enter a user name and password before the terminal can be used. This authentication is done through a single central database, which experiences very heavy load between 7:00 and 8:30 A.M., resulting in login times of up to a minute.

To alleviate this problem, several regional authorization databases are set up, each one supporting about 10% of the overall terminal population. Programs are written to distribute login information to each database overnight. As a result, login times are significantly improved.

This approach works only in certain situations, and a limiting factor is that the system often needs to be designed to take advantage of replication from the outset. However, where possible, it is worth considering because it can be a lot easier to solve a contention problem by avoiding it completely in this way rather than having to solve it directly.

Prioritize Processing

The workload in your system will vary in terms of its importance, ranging from critical processing that must be performed as quickly as possible to routine work such as housekeeping that can be completed over an extended period.

A problem in many otherwise well-built systems is the overall performance of the system being within target but some important tasks taking too long to execute. In these systems, the underlying hardware is typically busy, and the expected overall throughput is being processed. But critical workload is being processed at the same rate as less important operations, and this leads to the perception of a performance problem.

To avoid this situation, partition the system's workload into priority groups (or classes), and add the ability to prioritize the workload to be processed. This allows you to ensure that your system's resources will be applied to the right task at any point in time, so the perception of performance problems is much less likely. A low-level example of this approach is the priority class-based thread and process scheduling built into most modern operating systems.

When dealing with large information systems, this prioritizing usually involves identifying the business criticality of each class of workload. Those types of workloads that have to complete in a timely manner for business to continue (such as order processing) are naturally prioritized over workloads that, while important, will not immediately impact business operation (such as management reporting).

EXAMPLE A Web-based system to support e-commerce may need to support order capture, customer account management, stock reporting, and sales reporting functions.

Probably all of the customer Web workload (such as order capture and customer account management) should be prioritized over other processing. The customers who use the Web site are extremely important stakeholders because a slow Web site will not only reduce immediate sales but may drive the customers to other retailers, thus damaging the business in the longer term.

In contrast, while the management team members are influential stakeholders, if the management reporting functions run slowly during times of peak load, it is unlikely to directly harm the business. Of course, making such a rational tradeoff can be challenging when dealing with stakeholders who believe their workload is the most important.

The practical problem in most situations is finding the right balance among the different types of workloads. A number of factors need to be taken into account, including the relative importance of different stakeholders, the varying importance that different stakeholders place on different sorts of workloads, and the deadlines for processing various workloads. Finding the right balance for complex situations is often a case of applying your judgment to find an acceptable option, rather than discovering any absolute "right" answer.

Consolidate Related Workload

The processing of most operations in an information system requires a certain amount of context to be available in order for the processing to take place. The management of this context information can itself be a significant overhead when the operation to be performed is small or the context is expensive to locate (e.g., when loaded from a database).

To address this, consolidate related tasks into batches and process groups of related requests together. This pattern of processing normally allows a single initialization step, a number of operation processing steps, and then a single tear-down step—thus saving the initialization and tear-down steps that would be required for each operation if processed separately. Alternatively, consider whether you can reuse resources or results between operations to avoid the overhead of allocating or creating them repeatedly.

EXAMPLE A risk management system for a retail finance organization needs to run every night to update estimations of future credit use by its customers to allow proactive monitoring and management of the risk of individual consumer default. Each such update involves a fairly complicated calculation to estimate the likely future spending of the customer, using both customer-specific and global factors. The simple approach to this would be to perform each calculation separately, but working out the global factors that are needed for the calculation could be a significant overhead. Processing the customers in groups that would share global factor values could significantly improve overall performance, as the global factors could be calculated once for the group rather than for each customer. For example, economic activity based on geographical location could be estimated for one geographical area and then all of the customers in that area processed together.

Such an optimization is inherently related to the structure of the system and the way operations are processed within it, so it is something best considered as part of architecture definition. Doing so can lead to large efficiency gains for some systems.

Distribute Processing over Time

Some systems need to process a similar workload continually at all times of day or night. However, in our experience, such systems are pretty rare (although some Internet-facing systems do fall into this category). Because most internal systems support people at work, and because people work during relatively fixed hours, systems often have different load requirements at different times of day. This means that the workload level for a system varies over time. During busy times (as we have already seen) concurrency tends to cause performance problems, and this can become quite involved for global systems that have users in different time zones. Global systems often need to be available 24 hours a day during the working week and may well experience contention if different sorts of workloads from different regions need to be processed simultaneously (e.g., if the overnight batch processing for Tokyo overlaps with the online day in New York). We talk more about this when we discuss the Location perspective in Chapter 29.

A useful system-level strategy for reducing system load, resource contention, and thus performance problems is to even out peaks and troughs of processing. Some peak workload is simply unavoidable—the result of the way people work. However, consider spending time during the architecture definition process to carefully analyze your system's workload during the peak times. In many cases you will find that some of the workload can be postponed to other times in your processing cycle. By moving these parts of the workload, you will improve performance during peak load times and use idle resources during quieter times.

Minimize the Use of Shared Resources

At any particular time, each nonidle task running on a system is in one of two states:

1. Making use of a resource (e.g., a hardware resource such as a processor, memory, disk, or network or a software resource such as a message service)
2. Waiting for a resource, because it is either busy (e.g., being used by another task) or not in a ready state (e.g., waiting for a head to move over a particular track on a disk or a software service to initialize)

As systems get busier and contention for shared resources increases, the waiting time takes proportionally more of the total elapsed time for tasks and contributes proportionally more to the overall response time.

Increasing the performance of resources that the task uses will help (because in general you have to wait less time for the tasks ahead of you in the queue to finish), although this may not be possible for a number of reasons, perhaps because you have reached the limits of the technology. The other way to alleviate this situation is to minimize the use of shared resources—that is, reduce the situations in which waiting has to occur. This is a complex topic, beyond the scope of this book, but you may want to consider the following strategies.

- Use techniques such as hardware multiplexing to eliminate hardware hot spots in your architecture.
- Favor short, simple transactions over long, complex ones where possible (because transactions tend to lock up resources for extended periods).
- Do not lock resources in human time (e.g., while waiting for a user to press a key).
- Try to access shared resources nonexclusively whenever possible.

Reuse Resources and Results

Some resources involved in processing requests are expensive to obtain because they are computationally expensive to create or they need to be retrieved from a service that takes a significant amount of time to return its results. The judgment as to whether an operation is expensive or not is obviously very context-dependent, because it depends on the percentage of an overall task's execution time that it consumes. In some cases an operation taking 20 milliseconds might be considered significant, while in others an operation taking 10 seconds might be insignificant.

A common tactic when faced with expensive steps in a process is to reuse the results of the expensive operations, by caching them once they are created and reusing them whenever they are required in the future.

EXAMPLE A very simple example of using this tactic is caching the state of Web sessions for interactive Web applications like Web stores. A simplistic solution to storing the session state is simply to write it to a database and retrieve it on every request for that session. However, retrieving the session information from a database can be relatively slow, and so an alternative would be to store it in a distributed cache rather than a database, allowing it to be retrieved quickly when needed.

An application of this tactic for business data would be when foreign exchange conversion rates are required by an application and must be retrieved from an external service. To perform this retrieval every time a foreign exchange rate is needed would dramatically slow down request processing, and so a cache of previously retrieved rates can be kept by the local process and reused repeatedly, avoiding the overhead of the service call.

Partition and Parallelize

If your system involves large, lengthy processes, a possible way to reduce their response time is to partition them into a number of smaller processes, execute these subprocesses in parallel, and, when the last subprocess is complete, consolidate all of the subprocess output into a single result. Whether this approach is likely to be effective in a particular situation depends on four factors:

1. Whether the overall process can be quickly and efficiently partitioned into subprocesses
2. Whether the resulting subprocesses can be executed independently to allow effective parallel processing
3. How much time it will take to consolidate the output of the subprocesses into a single result
4. Whether enough processing capacity is available to process the subprocesses in parallel faster than handling the same workload in a single process

If the overall process cannot be split easily into independent subprocesses, this technique isn't practical. Situations involving lengthy and expensive consolidation of subprocess output are suitable for this technique only if the consolidation cost is still small relative to that of the longer response time for the original process. Finally, if spare processing resources aren't available, parallelization is unlikely to be effective because the subprocesses will be executed one after the other and will be slower than the original design, due to the partitioning and consolidation overheads.

It is also important to remember that this approach is less efficient than using a single linear process (due to the partitioning and consolidation overheads) and achieves a reduction in response time at the price of requiring more processing resources.

EXAMPLE A feature offered by a sales management system is to generate a number of derived measures of sales performance (volume, profitability, average price, and so on) across the company, broken down by region. This feature is likely to involve a lengthy process of calculation over the sales information held in the system but is also likely to be a good candidate for partitioning and parallelization. If the request is partitioned into a process for each sales region (rather than being run as a single process), each region's results can be calculated in parallel and the results consolidated to form the final report. If the underlying data can be efficiently accessed in n parallel streams, assuming similar data volumes per sales region, the parallel process is likely to complete in roughly $1/n$th of the time taken if run as a single process (plus some time for result consolidation, which is likely to be small compared to calculation time). This response time can be greatly reduced, at the cost of some processing efficiency.

Scale Up or Scale Out

When you have reached the limits of your system's current hardware, the obvious solution is to buy more of it. In fact, this is often the first tactic tried when better performance or scalability is required. Nowadays the price of commodity hardware is low enough that just "throwing hardware at the problem" is often the easiest thing to try initially. If you have access to cloud computing services or in-house virtualized environments that allow new virtualized hardware components to be commissioned almost immediately, this tactic is even more attractive.

There are two different ways to add hardware to a system: Either replace the existing hardware with similar but higher-capacity components (e.g., servers with faster processors, more processors, more memory, and so on) or add more components similar to the ones already used by the system (e.g., if the system has two calculation servers already, add another two). The first approach is informally known as "scaling up" and the latter as "scaling out."

In general, scaling up is simpler but more costly (due to the increasing cost of more powerful hardware—a 32-CPU machine is a lot more costly than four 8-CPU ones); scaling up will also eventually hit practical limits when you reach the largest machines available. Scaling out is more complicated and makes more demands on the design of the system, as it adds more processing nodes and the processing must be evenly spread across them all, but it is usually more cost-effective as it uses cheaper commodity hardware. Scaling out also doesn't suffer from arbitrary limits imposed by hardware component size, as proven by the existence of huge Internet sites like Amazon and eBay that use this technique.

The problem with achieving scalability by adding hardware (particularly when scaling out) is that it usually isn't very effective unless the system has been designed to take advantage of the new hardware. If your system's scalability is limited by a single threaded process at its core, adding more CPUs or machines isn't going to help, and increasing the speed of the single CPU on which it runs will be of limited help. Similarly, if you can't partition your workload into many cooperating processes, you won't be able to take advantage of scaling out. You can certainly be lucky, and in certain situations adding some more hardware can save the day, but it is a dangerous tactic to rely on unless the system has been built from the outset with good scalability characteristics.

Degrade Gracefully

It is inevitable that one day your system will be faced with a workload so large that it struggles to keep up. Whether it is a busy day for a trading system, sale time for a retail system, or a major international crisis for a news Web site, it is not cost-effective (or sometimes even possible) to deploy enough hardware to ensure that you never reach the "knee" in the performance curve we described earlier in the chapter.

However, it is important that you design the system so that when this happens, system performance degrades gracefully. You should put proactive monitoring in place and ensure that failures are recognized quickly and handled reliably—in particular, overloading and failures should not ripple destructively throughout the system. One way of achieving this is to design the system so that it contains the software equivalent of "circuit breakers" that prevent internal components from becoming overloaded. Other common tactics are to reject workload when the system is overloaded, perhaps asking the user to try again in a few minutes, and to throttle demand by introducing timeouts for service calls made to the system.

The Further Reading section at the end of this chapter contains references to a number of useful sources of guidance on this topic.

Use Asynchronous Processing

One way to improve perceived response times for users is to carry out some processing asynchronously—that is, in the background, after the system has returned a response to the user.

> **EXAMPLE** Processing a large database query in its entirety may take a significant amount of time, and for some applications it may be necessary to return all of the results to the user interface for display and manipulation by the user (rather than returning a screen of data at a time, which might complete more quickly). The problem with this situation is that if users must wait for the query to complete before returning any data, they will experience a very long delay in processing their request.
>
> A solution to this problem is to process the query asynchronously and to return data to the user interface as it becomes available. The overall execution time of the query will be unaffected by the use of this tactic, but the user will see the data start to arrive fairly quickly and will perceive that the request is being processed more quickly than in the situation where the data is returned synchronously.

You need to use this technique with some care, and only when it is really necessary, for several reasons. First, it is usually significantly more complex to implement, requiring some sort of background service to carry out the asynchronous parts of processing for you. More important, you have to develop strategies for dealing with situations where the background processing fails: It may be minutes or even hours after the transaction was initiated, and the user may not even be available to take corrective action. Finally, asynchronous processing doesn't actually reduce the amount of workload that needs to be performed or make the system more efficient (and thus actually solve the performance issue); it just moves the workload around.

Relax Transactional Consistency

Like many software designers, we were brought up in the era when ACID transactions (providing the familiar guarantees of atomicity, consistency, isolation, and durability) were thought to be the best, and often the only, way of interacting with transactional data stores. More recently, Internet-scale systems that need to be highly scalable and highly available, even when parts of the system suffer failures, have caused some rethinking in this area. The key insight that designers of Internet-scale systems have had is that as long as an individual consumer sees consistent data, the need for immediate system-wide consistency is something that can be relaxed, as long as it happens "eventually" (where your tolerance for the delay until "eventually" depends on your situation).

This insight provides us with another possible tactic for improving the performance and scalability (and in fact the availability) of our systems. If you can design your system such that different parts of the system can receive updates related to a single transaction at slightly different times, this opens up a number of opportunities for partitioning workload and deferring database updates, which can allow a system to be scaled across a number of machines and data stores without the overheads and complexity of full distributed transactions. We address this in a little more detail in Chapter 18 on the Information viewpoint, and the Further Reading section at the end of this chapter suggests a number of references that can provide more depth on this topic.

Make Design Compromises

If other performance tactics you've tried have not resulted in acceptable performance or cannot be applied for some reason, you may need a more extreme approach. Many of the techniques of good architecture definition that we have described in this book can themselves cause performance problems in extreme situations. For example, a loosely coupled, highly modular, and highly coherent system tends to spend more time communicating between its modules than a tightly coupled, monolithic one does.

Although a loosely coupled, always consistent, and highly modular design should always be the goal, you should be aware that the benefits it provides might come at some performance cost. Where performance is a critical concern and other tactics have failed, you might need to compromise the ideal structure of your design. There are many possible design compromises that you can consider making, each with its own tradeoffs, and there are entire books that discuss these options. Architectural choices also evolve over time in the light of technological progress and system design experience. This means that it isn't possible for us to discuss all of the options open to you, and even if we tried to do so, the information would probably be out-of-date quite quickly as new options emerged. Instead, the Further Reading section at the end of the chapter provides some references to some of the best thinking about performance and scalability at the time of writing, and these should provide you with a good starting point for further research.

All that having been said, at a conceptual level, there are certain classical design compromises that have proved to be of lasting value when trying to improve a system's scalability and performance, such as:

- Moving to a more tightly coupled, monolithic design to minimize internal communication delays and contention
- Denormalizing parts of your data model to optimize accesses to data
- Using very coarse-grained operations between distributed system elements
- Relaxing transactional guarantees such as immediate consistency in order to allow partitioning and asynchronous data updates
- Duplicating data or processing locally to minimize traffic over slow communication channels

Making changes like these may improve performance, but they are likely to have costs in terms of maintainability and possibly even ease of use. You should carefully assess the desirability of these tradeoffs before deciding to introduce compromises to your design.

PROBLEMS AND PITFALLS

Imprecise Performance and Scalability Goals

It is far too common for even large projects to have vague, incomplete, or ambiguous performance goals or to have failed to consider the scalability of the system altogether. This is simply storing up trouble for the future—you won't have a suitable framework for designing, tuning, and building the system, and it won't be possible to determine whether or not the system is performing acceptably.

RISK REDUCTION

- Define and obtain approval from your stakeholders for clear, measurable performance and scalability goals.
- Satisfy yourself that your performance and scalability goals are realistic and achievable.

- Communicate the goals to the architecture, design, and build teams so that they can be factored into their work.
- Make sure that acceptance criteria are based only on the agreed-upon goals and do not include other (possibly implied) performance or scalability goals.

Unrealistic Models

The process of building a performance model can be an absorbing one, and the result is often a sophisticated model of the likely performance characteristics of the system. A problem that can result from an impressive model is an overreliance on its abilities. It is easy to be lulled into a false sense of security when a model suggests that no performance problems exist. A lack of problems revealed by a model does not necessarily mean that no problems exist in the real system; the model is an abstraction of reality and only as good as its match with that reality.

RISK REDUCTION

- Balance and augment the performance modeling activity with enough practical testing to make sure that the assumptions underpinning the models are valid and that the conclusions resulting from them are credible.
- Continue practical testing right through the modeling process.
- Always check your modeling results against practical test results.

Use of Simple Measures for Complex Cases

Achieving acceptable performance in a computer system is a complex process, with many variables to consider simultaneously. A common pitfall is to oversimplify the performance testing and modeling process to make it easier, but then to assume that its results will apply to much larger and more complex cases by simple analogy. Practical testing should reflect the real runtime environment you expect for your system, and if your performance models are very simple, the conclusions drawn from them must be used with care.

As a simple example, consider the practical testing you perform to calibrate your model. If these practical tests do not simulate a realistic runtime environment (e.g., by being single-threaded rather than heavily concurrent), the results of these tests are unlikely to reflect the way the real system will behave.

RISK REDUCTION

- Continually question the validity of your analysis and testing conclusions.
- Consider the differences between the test environment and the real system runtime environment to spot critical divergences that are likely to invalidate the performance engineering process.

Inappropriate Partitioning

In Chapter 17, we discussed poor partitioning as a possible pitfall for the Functional view, but it is often also problematic when considering performance. Partitioning becomes a problem when one or more elements appear to be involved in nearly all of the transactions in the system. This often means that these elements become bottlenecks and prevent acceptable performance from being achieved anywhere in the system because of their dominant role. Poor partitioning can also manifest itself as an unexpectedly large amount of intercomponent communication being required for routine operations.

A related problem, which is often a symptom of poor partitioning, is to ignore the performance differences of local and remote processing. We discuss this problem near the end of this chapter when we talk about network and in-process invocation.

RISK REDUCTION

- Watch for functional elements that are highly connected to a large percentage of the system's other functional elements (see the discussion of "God elements" in Chapter 17). These system elements may be your potential bottlenecks.

Invalid Environment and Platform Assumptions

Whenever an innovative system is developed, a level of risk exists because of assumptions that have to be made about its environment or the underlying technology. This risk can result from new technology that has not been widely used before (or perhaps not on this scale), or it can result from assumptions about the system's environment (e.g., peak request volume).

Some of these risks are unavoidable and are simply the result of being first. What is surprising is the number of projects that either run into performance problems in well-understood areas or simply don't control their risks, even when this is perfectly possible.

RISK REDUCTION

- Identify and validate your assumptions, and assess them for risks as part of performance analysis.

- Identify your possible mitigation strategies if your assumptions are proved incorrect.

Too Much Indirection

It has been said that any problem in software engineering can be solved by adding another level of indirection.[1] It is certainly true that indirection is a powerful tool—used wisely, it can make systems more flexible, easier to change, more powerful, and even more elegant. However, another famous adage also applies: There is no such thing as a free lunch!

A problem with indirection is that it introduces hidden work into the system. Some forms of indirection (e.g., object references in an object-oriented language) do not normally introduce enough overhead to cause a problem in anything apart from the most performance-critical situations. However, other forms of indirection can add a significant percentage of overhead for certain sorts of processing. For example, using key-mapping techniques for database access (where complex or structured keys are mapped to more efficient internal identifiers) may lead to some updates requiring two disk writes rather than one, and extra tables having to be included in query join conditions.

RISK REDUCTION

- Be careful how much indirection you introduce into the performance-critical parts of your system.
- If you have a lot of indirection in the implementation of critical path operations, carefully assess the tradeoff between the functional advantages and the performance disadvantages.

Concurrency-Related Contention

Any system with concurrent processing and shared resources has the potential for contention between threads of execution. In its most extreme form, this contention can slow a concurrent system to a crawl as threads spend most of their time "thrashing" in and out of wait states trying to obtain access to shared resources. Even in less extreme cases, such contention can become a significant bottleneck and cause performance problems throughout the system. Careful analysis and design of your system to avoid such bottlenecks is an important part of the performance work for concurrent systems.

---

1. Attributed to Butler Lampson, who in turn credits David Wheeler with originating this famous aphorism, although Wheeler apparently also noted, ". . . but that will often create another problem."

RISK REDUCTION

- Inspect your Functional and Concurrency views to identify the elements of your system that must deal with a significant amount of concurrent processing.

- Investigate the proposed implementation of critical elements as part of your modeling, testing, and analysis process to convince yourself that they will not become bottlenecks that grind your system to a halt.

- During software construction, test the concurrent behavior of critical elements as early as possible.

Database Contention

Most information systems have one or more relational databases at their core, and a problem we have seen time and time again is where database query processing time becomes the dominant determinant of system performance. Sometimes this is just caused by badly written (or generated) database queries or by an overloaded database server that isn't sized correctly for the task. Both of these situations are fairly easy to spot with standard database monitoring tools, and both have fairly obvious solutions (create better queries and increase the size of the database hardware, respectively).

A more subtle cause of poor database performance can be internal database contention, and this is much harder to spot and resolve. The symptoms of internal database contention are usually slow query performance, which slows the system down dramatically, along with a database server that doesn't seem to be very busy, with low CPU utilization and disk I/O. The root cause is often a small number of "hot" database objects that many of the system's operations need to update and read or parts of the database management system's internal infrastructure that have become overloaded (such as transaction logs or particular storage areas). Such objects become major bottlenecks that prevent the system's database operations from performing acceptably quickly.

RISK REDUCTION

- Review the database schema for objects that will be updated very frequently, or for operations that generate a very large number of data changes, and consider ways in which they can be ameliorated (such as partitioning "hot" objects or updating them in batches and decomposing or deferring very large update operations).

- Measure the performance of representative database operations under realistic loads as early in the development process as possible and keep monitoring these measures over time. Look for increasing response times as indicators that contention may be creeping into the database.

▪ Use database monitoring tools (and if possible the services of experts such as a database administration group) to measure contention that occurs within the database server in order to spot potential "hot spots" that need to be addressed.

Transaction Overhead

This pitfall is closely related to the tactic of "Consolidate Related Workload" and reflects what can happen when that tactic is not or cannot be applied. Processing a transaction through an information system always involves a certain amount of overhead in addition to the useful functional processing performed. This overhead can come from a number of sources, including network latency, data serialization, security processing, database access, and so on.

There is a danger that if the overheads are too high and the functional processing is too low, the system will be spending most of its time tied up in processing overheads that are not directly useful, so greatly reducing its performance. This pitfall is particularly common with distributed transactions, where two-phase commit is used to apply updates to two or more database servers as part of a single logical transaction.

RISK REDUCTION

▪ Review the functional transactions being implemented in the system and highlight very small ones, where the overhead of performing a transaction may overwhelm the amount of time taken for the functional processing. For these cases, consider consolidating the workload to perform a number of transactions at once (thus amortizing the overhead over a larger amount of functional processing). You may also be able to reduce the overhead for these transactions, perhaps by simplifying the way in which they are processed (e.g., do they all need fine-grained security authorization checking, or can a simpler coarse-grained approach be used for small transactions?).

▪ Consider whether you can apply one of the techniques for relaxing transactional consistency described earlier in this chapter, so that data becomes "eventually consistent" rather than being immediately consistent in all cases.

▪ Introduce an empty "ping" transaction for each transaction type so that you can measure how long the system takes to do "nothing." Monitor these measures over time and watch them rise as capabilities and complexity are added to the system.

Careless Allocation of Resources

Increases in computing power in recent years mean that, in general, we need to be much less conscious of using hardware resources frugally than used to be the case. However, an often-overlooked problem related to this new freedom is the fact that the process of allocating and freeing runtime resources (such as memory or locks) requires resources itself. As systems scale to millions of users and transactions, this resource management becomes a real problem. This is easy to forget because the process is often implicit (such as the Java language's automatic garbage collection or a relational database's automatic lock allocation). However, this doesn't mean it is free! A good question to ask yourself in any situation involving resource allocation is, "What would happen if this happened a million times?"

An underlying resource allocation problem is often revealed by elements that appear to run much slower than expected without any obvious place where the time is being lost.

RISK REDUCTION

- Avoid large amounts of dynamic resource allocation and deallocation in critical path elements.

- Consider preallocating resources at less critical times (such as at startup or during quiet periods).

- Consider whether allocated resources can be reused more cheaply than freeing and reallocating them.

- Work with software developers to understand the problem and document guidelines and patterns to explain good practice (in the Development view).

Disregard for Network and In-Process Invocation Differences

Modern computing technology provides the option of distributing a system across a number of machines and accessing resources located anywhere on the network. Such distribution is a major feature of many modern information systems. In fact, much of today's information systems technology aims to allow the location of deployed elements to be changed after they have been developed.

It is easy to accidentally ignore the performance differences between invoking operations locally within an address space (process), between two processes on one machine, and between processes on machines located an immense distance apart. In reality, the response times of these different situations can differ by several orders of magnitude.

If you ignore this critical distinction, you run the risk of extremely unpleasant performance surprises when you deploy the system and find that one or more of your critical interelement interactions is much slower than you had assumed due to the locations of key system elements. Consider this pitfall in conjunction with the related pitfall of "Inappropriate Partitioning."

RISK REDUCTION

- Consider interelement distribution and possible remote invocation as part of your fundamental architecture definition process.
- Make sure that the locations of elements and their interelement invocation costs are accurately reflected in your performance model to allow you to take possible invocation latencies into account.

CHECKLISTS

Checklist for Requirements Capture

- Have you identified approved performance targets, at a high level at least, with key stakeholders?
- Have you considered targets for both response time and throughput?
- Do your targets distinguish between observed performance (i.e., synchronous tasks) and actual performance (i.e., taking asynchronous activity into account)?
- Have you assessed your performance targets for reasonableness?
- Have you appropriately set expectations among your stakeholders for what is feasible in your architecture?
- Have you defined all performance targets within the context of a particular load on the system?

Checklist for Architecture Definition

- Have you identified the major potential performance problems in your architecture?
- Have you performed enough testing and analysis to understand the likely performance characteristics of your system?
- Do you know what workload your system can process? Have you prioritized the different classes of work?
- Do you know how far your proposed architecture can be scaled without major changes?

- Have you identified the performance-related assumptions you have made (and validated them if needed)?
- Have you looked for opportunities to relax transactional consistency, especially if you are designing a large-scale or distributed system?
- Have you reviewed your architecture for common performance pitfalls?

FURTHER READING

You can find a very practical yet thorough tutorial on the process of performance engineering for real systems in a book written by two well-known and widely regarded specialists in the field [SMIT02]. We have found this book to be very useful, and it has influenced much of our thinking in this area. A number of our performance pitfalls are similar to performance antipatterns in this book (particularly their God Class, Circuitous Treasure Hunt, One-Lane Bridge, and Excessive Dynamic Allocation), and this book provides valuable advice on recognizing and avoiding these problems.

Another comprehensive, if rather more daunting, explanation of performance engineering focuses on its quantitative aspects [JAIN91]. This book contains more information on statistical and simulation-based performance engineering than most of us will ever be able to apply, but it presents comprehensive explanations of a number of very usable techniques.

A very practical book that provides a lot of good advice about performance and scalability, among other topics, is Michael Nygard's *Release It!* [NYGA07], which includes patterns and antipatterns for performance and scalability.

Professor Eric Brewer's CAP theorem has been very influential in thinking around performance and scalability for very large-scale systems and led to the popularization of the notion of eventual consistency. In short, the theorem says that you can achieve only two of the properties of Consistency, Availability, and Partition tolerance (hence "CAP"). The idea was first introduced in a keynote talk at the Principles of Distributed Computing meeting in 2000 [BREW00]; a more formal treatment was published by Seth Gilbert and Nancy Lynch as [GILB02].

Two articles that explain how large-scale Internet sites have met the challenge embodied in the CAP theorem are Dan Pritchett's description of the BASE architectural style used at eBay [PRIT08] and Werner Vogels's explanation of what "eventually consistent" means in the architecture of Amazon's systems [VOGE08]. Some more general ideas on building systems without distributed transactions can also be found in Pat Helland's well-known paper [HELL07].

There are many good books that cover the topic of performance and scalability as it applies to specific technologies, although they tend to come and go as the technologies they discuss evolve. A search of your favorite online bookstore will allow you to find the most popular for your particular technology platforms.

Finally, if you'd like to check what Moore's Law really says, Intel makes it available via its Web site at www.intel.com/technology/mooreslaw.

27

THE AVAILABILITY AND RESILIENCE PERSPECTIVE

Desired Quality	The ability of the system to be fully or partly operational as and when required and to effectively handle failures that could affect system availability
Applicability	Any system that has complex or extended availability requirements, complex recovery processes, or a high profile (e.g., is visible to the public)
Concerns	Classes of service, planned downtime, unplanned downtime, time to repair, and disaster recovery
Activities	Capture the availability requirements, produce the availability schedule, estimate platform availability, estimate functional availability, assess against the requirements, and apply tactics to rework the architecture
Architectural Tactics	Select fault-tolerant hardware, use high-availability clustering and load balancing, log transactions, apply software availability solutions, select or create fault-tolerant software, design for failure, allow for component replication, relax transactional consistency, and identify backup and disaster recovery solutions
Problems and Pitfalls	Single point of failure, cascading failure, unavailability through overload, overambitious availability requirements, ineffective error detection, overestimation of component resilience, overlooked global availability requirements, and incompatible technologies

In the traditional data processing model of system availability, computers supported the mainstream business of the organization during the day (typically 9:00 A.M. to 5:30 P.M., Monday through Friday) by capturing orders, cash withdrawals, and other sorts of transactions. Then the computers reverted to batch mode during the night to perform tasks such as reconciliation, consolidation, and exchange of information with other systems.

In contrast, companies today routinely run their business on a global basis. This has caused the business day to become longer, often extending into the weekend (the traditional preserve of huge, long-running batch jobs), and near-continuous operation of IT systems is now routinely assumed, with many critical systems needing to be available close to 24 hours per day, five or six days per week.

Today's requirement for many systems, therefore, is to be available for much, if not all, of the 24-hour cycle. With the improved reliability of hardware and, to a lesser extent, software, many expect that failures will be few and far between and that, when these do occur, recovery will be prompt, effective, and largely automated. As the large number of Web-site failures in the early years of Internet e-commerce showed, any system exposed directly to customers must be up and running—if it isn't, the company's reputation will suffer.

This business environment means that underestimating your availability requirements can be very expensive. However, increased online availability comes at a cost, whether in terms of more hardware, increased software sophistication, or redundancy in your telecommunications network.

The Availability and Resilience perspective is important to any system that has complex availability and resilience requirements, is visible to the public in any way, or is complicated enough to warrant special analysis of recovery techniques.

APPLICABILITY TO VIEWS

Table 27–1 shows how the Availability and Resilience perspective affects each of the views we discussed in Part III.

CONCERNS

The fundamental concern of this perspective is system availability: the proportion of time that the system is up and running and available to provide a service to users. However, availability is a bit more complex than it first appears, as we'll discuss in the following subsections.

Classes of Service

When thinking about downtime, you don't need to restrict yourself to a binary available/unavailable model of service. It is often appropriate to consider different levels of service, ranging over a spectrum from full service to none.

TABLE 27-1 APPLICABILITY OF THE AVAILABILITY AND RESILIENCE PERSPECTIVE TO THE SEVEN VIEWS

View	Applicability
Context	Considering availability and resilience is unlikely to result in many changes to the Context view, although it will cause you to consider how your system's availability is affected by the availability of external systems, and it could change the way that you decide to interact with them.
Functional	Availability is a key concern to user and acquirer stakeholders because it may impact the business's ability to operate effectively. Functional changes may sometimes be needed to support availability requirements, such as the ability to operate in an offline mode when a communications network is unavailable.
Information	A key availability consideration is the set of processes and systems for backup and recovery. Systems must be backed up in such a way that they can be recovered in a reasonable amount of time if a disaster occurs. Backups should not impact online availability, or if they do, they may need to be scheduled to occur outside the online day.
Concurrency	Features such as hardware replication and failover in your system may imply changes or enhancements to your concurrency model.
Development	Your approach to achieving availability may impose design constraints on the software modules. For example, all subsystems may have to support start, stop, pause, and restart commands to align with your failover strategy.
Deployment	Availability and resilience can have a big impact on the deployment environment. Availability requirements may mandate a fault-tolerant production environment (i.e., one in which each hardware component is duplicated and failover is automatic) or a separate disaster recovery site that can be quickly activated if the production site goes down. You may also need special software to support hardware redundancy or clustering.
Operational	Processes and mechanisms to allow the identification and recovery of problems in the production environment may be required. There may also be a need for geographically separate disaster recovery facilities. Processes for main site failover, network failover, and data recovery must be designed, tested, and implemented. If the standby site is physically remote from the production site, as it usually is, processes are also required to move production staff from one location to the other or to deploy suitably trained staff at the standby site.

EXAMPLE Consider a self-service banking system that allows users to manage their bank accounts at automated teller machines (ATMs). The ATM communicates in real time with a central computer that maintains information on the customers' accounts. *Full service* implies that customers can query balances and enter all supported types of transactions, and *no service* means that no inquiries or transactions can be done.

> From time to time, the communications network between the ATM and the host computer may fail, may be switched off for maintenance, or may suffer from poor response due to heavy usage. When the network is unavailable or unresponsive, local processing could be carried out on the ATM without reference to the host, allowing the system to offer partial services, such as:
>
> ▪ Restricting transactions to those below a certain limit
> ▪ Requiring increased time to carry out transactions
> ▪ Restricting users to deposits only

Although any system unavailability is usually undesirable, it may be easier (and is probably considerably cheaper) to offer only restricted service during slack times of operation, rather than attempting a solution that offers full service for long periods.

Planned Downtime

In practice, all computer systems require occasional downtime in order to install new or repaired hardware, install operating system or software upgrades, or carry out offline tasks such as backup or data verification.

We call such unavailability *planned downtime* because it occurs according to a predetermined schedule that aligns with the broader requirements of the business. Planned downtime usually occurs overnight or at weekends because the need to access many systems is less at these times.

It's usually possible to make fairly accurate estimates of the length of time such tasks take and the frequency with which they need to be done, so you can usually make reasonable predictions about planned downtime.

Unplanned Downtime

Unplanned downtime, on the other hand, occurs because of a hardware or software fault that renders the system unusable. A CPU or disk may fail, network connectivity may be lost, the operating system may crash, or the application may suffer an error from which it cannot recover.

Compared with planned downtime, it's much harder to predict the time and frequency of unplanned downtime—especially downtime due to software failures. However, most systems suffer from unplanned downtime to a lesser or greater extent, and your analysis must account for this. In particular, if downtime is protracted, you may need to establish contingency procedures (manual or semiautomated) to allow business to continue.

Time to Repair

Failure, of course, is only half of the problem as far as availability is concerned; the other half is how long it takes to rectify the fault.

For hardware, this usually involves swapping out a faulty component for a working one and restarting the affected part of the system. For disks and other persistent storage, you need to add the time required to restore from backup the data that was on the disk. The time required to repair software is harder to quantify. An immediate "repair" may be as simple as restarting the affected part of the system; however, ensuring that the problem does not happen again may be much more complex. Fixing the software itself may involve conducting forensic analysis of the fault; designing, building, and testing the fix; deploying it; and dealing with any lost or damaged data.

Disaster Recovery

If a critical system fails entirely or the physical operational environment becomes unavailable (e.g., due to fire), an entire disaster recovery process may be required in order to restore service. Disaster recovery can involve the re-creation of the entire system environment, including the hardware, communication network, and software platform as well as the system's own application software and data.

> **EXAMPLE** One of us did a study of system availability in the late 1980s for a major UK bank. The bank analyzed its reliance on systems and concluded that if it were to lose its main system (which managed all of the bank's retail accounts), it would go out of business within three days. For this reason, the bank invested in a separate (and very expensive) standby mainframe computer, solely for the purpose of switching over should the main production computer become unavailable.

In our example, the standby mainframe was kept idle in constant anticipation of catastrophe. In reality, it is more common to find standby machines being used for development, testing, training, or some other nonessential activity. However it is done, disaster recovery forms an essential part of any model of service availability. Disasters such as flood or fire are, fortunately, rare, but their impacts can be catastrophic.

Although the system's runtime environment can be replaced, data can't, so your model must also consider how you will recover data in the event of a disaster. You must determine how much data, if any, the business can afford to lose in the event of a disaster and how long it can survive while data is being recovered or repaired.

Many organizations have realized that service availability depends not just on the availability of an operational computing platform but also on the availability of staff, information, a working environment, and an internal and external communications infrastructure. This has developed into the idea of *business continuity*, which extends the system availability concept right into the organization to include people, places, and infrastructure. A discussion of this topic, important as it is, is outside the scope of this book, but we suggest some other books that cover this area in the Further Reading section at the end of this chapter.

ACTIVITIES: APPLYING THE AVAILABILITY AND RESILIENCE PERSPECTIVE

The activity diagram in Figure 27–1 illustrates a simple process for applying the Availability and Resilience perspective. In this section, we describe the activities in this process.

Capture the Availability Requirements

Ideally, your set of availability requirements was defined earlier as part of the system requirements process, but often this isn't the case. If you have the requirements already, you need to analyze, understand, and validate them; if not, you need to capture them as well. In either case, you must work with the stakeholders to understand and validate the system's availability requirements, categorizing them by class of service.

NOTATION A simple text-and-tables approach is usually the most effective and straightforward way to capture availability requirements.

ACTIVITIES

Identify the Types of Services Offered. Consider each of the services your system offers its users. Classify the services into groups based on their criticality to the system users' productivity.

Define the Levels of Services. For each type of service identified, define the availability required in terms of when the service is needed and whether or

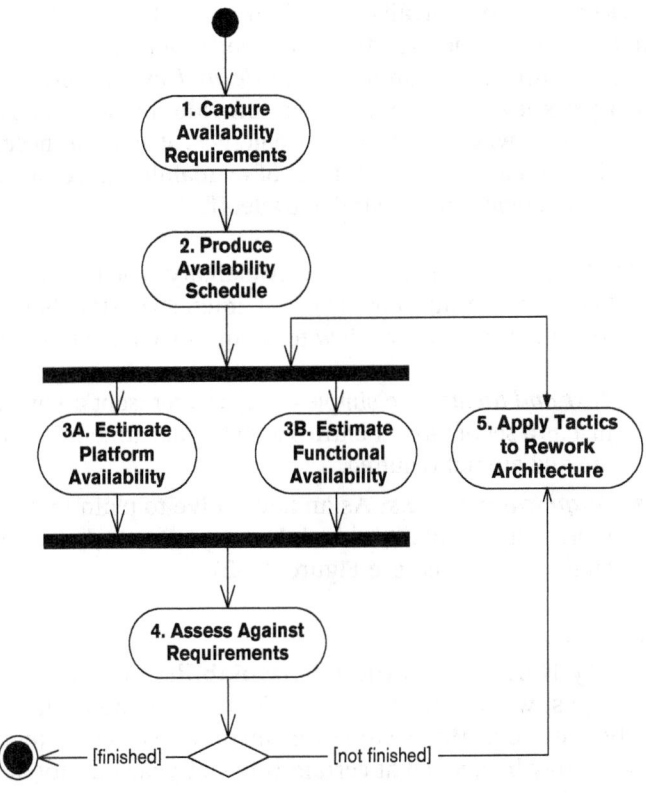

FIGURE 27-1 APPLYING THE AVAILABILITY AND RESILIENCE PERSPECTIVE

not all of its functions are necessary. If possible, identify one or more levels of degraded service that are still useful (e.g., if normal service involves placing an order and confirming a delivery date, a degraded level of service, whereby the order is placed but a delivery date is not available, might still be useful).

Define the Operational Service Levels. Based on the levels of service you aim to provide for each of your service types, define the set of operational service levels that the system as a whole will provide. This involves defining what services need to be available during normal operation and the possible levels of degraded operational availability. Work with the stakeholders to make sure that the levels of service specified are useful to them.

Produce the Availability Schedule

Based on the availability requirements you have validated with your stakeholders, create an availability schedule that defines when the different system services need to be available and any periods when services are not required (and so may not be available). It's worth noting that at this stage of the process, you are really capturing the *desired* availability schedule because you don't yet know what it will cost to provide this level of availability and resilience. Later, when the true cost emerges, it may be necessary to revisit this question and accept a lower level of availability in return for lower cost, complexity, or some other desirable tradeoff.

NOTATION   You can present the availability schedule in a number of ways, the key being to use an approach that interested stakeholders can immediately comprehend. Here we list a few techniques we have found to be effective.

- *Text and tables*: The simplest way to represent an availability schedule is just as a set of tabular entries with textual annotations about when services are and are not required.

- *Graphical notations*: As an alternative to plain text and tables, you can represent availability schedules very effectively by using Gantt charts or similar diagrams (see Figure 27–2).

ACTIVITIES

Identify Normal Operational Availability. For each of the system's service types, work with the stakeholders to identify when this service is normally required. Make sure this includes seasonal availability, when the system may be needed at certain times of year but not at others (e.g., public holidays).

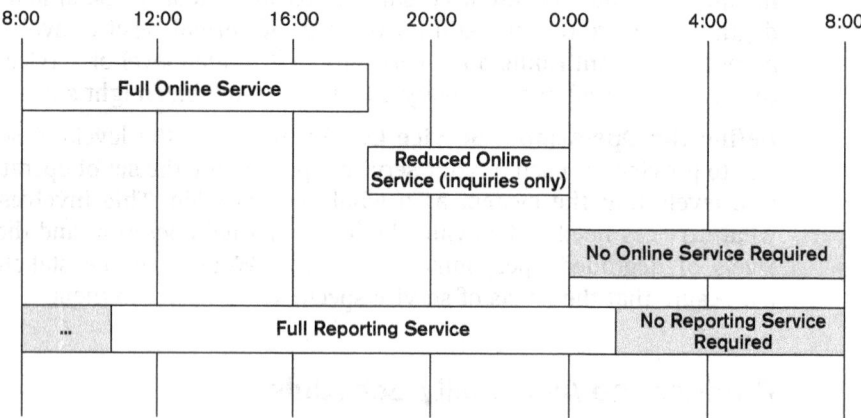

FIGURE 27–2 GANTT CHART OF A REQUIRED AVAILABILITY SCHEDULE

Identify Possible Unavailability. Attempt to identify regular times when services are definitely not required (e.g., weekends). These periods should be marked on the availability schedule as potential unavailability and are useful for scheduling workload that could otherwise reduce system availability if run during normal operational periods.

Estimate Platform Availability

In order to understand the potential availability of your system, you need a reasonably accurate estimate of the availability that your underlying hardware and software platform can provide. This measure is the maximum theoretical availability of your system (before operational constraints are applied, which will reduce availability further).

NOTATION Estimation of platform availability results in a set of statistical measures typically recorded as text and tables, although this information can also be useful for augmenting UML models in the Deployment view with availability information.

ACTIVITIES
Create the System Availability Model. You can predict (and therefore measure) availability by using some basic statistics. Availability models consider system availability on a component-by-component basis and usually consolidate these into an overall availability figure for the system as a whole.

Availability is defined as follows:

$$\text{availability} = \frac{\text{time the system is available}}{\text{elapsed time}}$$

Availability metrics are usually expressed as percentages, such as 99.99%, which represents a downtime of just under an hour a year, or 99.999%, a downtime of 5 minutes a year. (These two values are often shortened to the terms *four nines* and *five nines*, respectively.) A system that is available from 9:00 A.M. to 5:00 P.M., Monday to Friday, for example, has an availability of 40 hours/168 hours, or about 24%.

Unavailability is the converse of availability:

$$\text{unavailability} = \frac{\text{time the system is unavailable}}{\text{elapsed time}}$$

And, obviously:

$$\text{availability} + \text{unavailability} = 100\%$$

For hardware, it is possible to use published *mean time between failures* (MTBF, sometimes known as *mean time before fault*) measures to estimate how often failures are likely to occur. MTBF is defined as follows:

$$\text{MTBF} = \frac{\text{elapsed time}}{\text{number of failures}}$$

Mean time to repair (MTTR) is defined as the average time taken to repair a fault once notified and may be available from hardware manufacturers (or from supplier service-level agreements).

You can combine MTBF and MTTR to estimate hardware availability as follows:

$$\text{hardware availability} = \frac{\text{MTBF}}{\text{MTBF} + \text{MTTR}}$$

You may also be able to obtain reliability data to perform the same sort of calculation for your operating systems and middleware (where "repair" in this case is usually the same as "restart").

Using these formulas and the content of your Deployment view, it is reasonably straightforward to derive predicted measures of hardware (and perhaps system software) availability, although it is often difficult to predict the number of failures for an average site. When combining metrics for multiple components, make sure that you use the rule that the system is only as available as its least-available component.

Unfortunately, there are rarely any reliable metrics that allow you to come up with meaningful estimates for application software availability, except for the most established and unchanging applications. The reason for this is that software doesn't fail according to established failure models, which are based on the degradation of physical materials and assume failure isolation. Software fails because it has to cope with unexpected conditions that it was not designed or tested to meet or as a result of a mistake in its implementation, and worse still, you cannot assume that software failures are isolated. These failures are much harder to predict and require quite different models to characterize them accurately.

However, if you want to try to produce a model of application software availability, you can attempt one by using the models in the Functional, Concurrency, and Deployment views as primary inputs. A number of books provide tutorials on software reliability modeling (see the Further Reading section for suggestions).

When estimating availability, try to present the results in terms of classes of service, for example, "Full service available 95%, at least restricted service available 99.9%." This involves looking at component usage by different types of functionality. (Such information is available primarily from your Functional view.)

Note that your availability model may have some subtleties, especially if the architecture is complex or the unavailability of some internal components of the architecture does not impact the perceived availability of the system as a whole.

> **EXAMPLE** A bank provides leased-line network access for its larger branches and less reliable business-broadband-based connections for smaller or more remote branches. The bank's teller systems are built in such a way that they can work offline if the connection to the central server (which maintains the latest transaction and balance information) goes down for a short period of time.
>
> The perceived availability of this system, from the perspective of tellers and customers, is high, even though the underlying network may not be particularly robust.

Create the Incident Recovery Analysis. Consider the likely incidents that could affect your system's availability. For each, define the failure that could occur, its impact, the remedial actions to be taken, and the likely time needed to rectify the situation.

> **EXAMPLE** Table 27–2 shows an example of incident recovery analysis.

Note that transient failures (e.g., the transient loss of a network connection) are not usually considered in this analysis, although it may be necessary to accommodate these in your architecture (e.g., by automatically retrying failed operations a certain number of times to allow for network recovery).

You may find it useful to walk through some scenarios to validate this analysis. Once the system is developed, you should thoroughly test the remedial actions specified to ensure that they actually work.

Estimate Functional Availability

Estimating the maximum likely availability of your underlying implementation platform provides you with an upper bound on the possible availability of your system. However, it is likely that the system design will impose further unavailability in the guise of planned downtime. Many information systems

TABLE 27-2 SAMPLE INCIDENT RECOVERY SCENARIOS

Incident	Impact	Remedial Action	Time to Repair
Hardware (non-disk) failure	Reduced availability (throughput affected)	Replace the faulty component, and possibly reconfigure the hardware or the operating system	1 hour
Single disk failure	Performance degradation during automated recovery after failed disk is replaced in disk array	Failed disk must be replaced to allow automatic data recovery by disk array	1 hour to replace disk and recover
Disk array failure	Total unavailability (service offline)	Replace the faulty disk array, and possibly recover data from backup and/or other means	6 hours including restore
Nontransient network failure	Temporary service outage, in-flight transactions aborted, some loss of throughput when using backup network	Switch over to the standby network, possibly with reduced bandwidth	5 minutes
Operating system crash	Temporary service outage, normal availability within 5–10 minutes	Reboot, although the crash may be symptomatic of some other problem (such as faulty memory or disk) that needs to be addressed	5 minutes for reboot
Data corruption	Affected accounts and transactions unavailable, failure of end-of-period reconciliation	Recover data from backup and possibly other means (such as replaying transaction logs)	6 hours
Application software failure	Variable, from temporary outage (10 minutes) to total outage due to corruption	Restart, depending on the application and the nature of the failure; may be necessary also to recover data in some way	Not quantified

require some periods when the system cannot provide full operational service because of the need to perform internal processing (such as reconciliation, data maintenance, backups, summary and report processing, and so on).

In order to understand the level of functional availability your system can offer, draw up a functional availability schedule by working through the operational cycle of the system and identifying the periods of operation when the design of the system means that normal service cannot be provided.

You can create this new schedule by starting with the required availability schedule prepared previously and augmenting it with the system operations that may impact availability. When possible, schedule these operations in the periods when the required availability schedule indicates that normal services are not needed.

NOTATION Representing functional availability involves capturing the periods during which different aspects of your system will be available. Here are a couple of techniques we have found effective for achieving this.

- *Text and tables*: The simplest way to represent the system's functional availability is as a set of tabular entries with textual annotations explaining the level of availability that can be provided in each period.
- *Graphical notations*: A graphical notation such as a Gantt chart (see Figure 27–3) is an effective alternative to a tabular presentation.

ACTIVITIES

Design the Functional Availability Schedule. If systems have planned downtime or periods of reduced availability (e.g., to support overnight batch runs), you should draw up schedules to model the offline activity. These will be driven partly by requirements determined by stakeholders (users, operations staff, and so on), as captured in your Operational view, and partly by what is technically

FIGURE 27–3 GANTT CHART OF A FUNCTIONAL AVAILABILITY SCHEDULE

feasible for your architecture, as reflected in your Functional, Information, and Concurrency views.

For the online day periods, availability criteria are typically driven by the business's need to serve its customers. For enterprise systems, online day schedules such as 7:00 A.M. to 8:00 P.M. are common. You also need to consider weekends and holiday periods, when availability may be curtailed (or possibly needs to be extended). If you have an overnight batch run, the most important consideration is whether all batch jobs can be completed during the overnight batch window.

For applications that aim for near 24-hour availability, it is rare to offer a full level of service throughout the period. Although ideally a global or Internet-facing system needs to provide full capacity at all times, the costs of achieving this can be prohibitive, often leading to a tradeoff being made, to accept reduced capability or capacity during periods when less demand is expected. Your analysis needs to balance the costs of very high availability against the benefits it provides. The final decision is usually a business decision and so needs to be made by your acquirer stakeholders.

Define the normal working day in consultation with your users, resisting the temptation to extend this longer than necessary—the longer the working day, the less time available for overnight batch processing (if applicable). When sizing the batch window, consider the worst-case elapsed times, which usually occur at period start or end (the start or end of the month, quarter, financial year, and so on).

Assess against the Requirements

There are two aspects to assessing your architecture against its availability requirements. First, ensure that the overall level of availability you can achieve is acceptable in the context of the system's requirements. Second, ensure that no particular availability risks are unacceptable even when the overall level of availability is sufficient.

If this assessment suggests that your architecture provides sufficient availability, you're done applying this perspective. Otherwise, if the overall level of availability is too low or there appear to be specific availability risks that are too high to be acceptable, the process continues with the next step, reworking the architecture to address the availability limitations in the current architecture.

NOTATION   You can easily capture any outputs of this step by using text and tables, without resorting to special-purpose notations.

ACTIVITIES
Combine the Platform and Functional Availability Estimates. Combine the platform and functional availability estimates you created in the previous steps

to arrive at an overall estimate for your system's availability. The functional availability figure provides you with an estimate of the routine availability of your system, while the platform availability estimate indicates how much unavailability you need to factor in due to unexpected technology failures.

If your functional availability estimate suggests 2 hours of downtime per day (meaning a functional availability of about 91.5%) and your platform availability suggests the loss of 6 days per year to technology failures (giving a platform availability of 98.3%), the overall system availability will be about 90% (.915 × .983 = .899).

Identify Particular Availability Risks. Review the outputs of the platform and functional availability assessments, and review any particular situations you identified that could result in particularly acute availability risks. Things to watch for are situations where particularly long periods of unavailability can occur and situations where the impact of the unavailability is particularly significant (e.g., just after a new product launch or at the end of the financial year). Highlight these particularly significant availability risks, and ensure that they are acceptable to your stakeholders.

Apply Tactics to Rework the Architecture

If the architecture does not provide sufficient availability to meet the system's requirements, you will need to rework aspects of it to increase the availability it can offer. This is likely to center on the Deployment view (where you can add technological availability solutions) and the Functional and Information views (where you can modify the system's design to increase the amount of functional availability the system can offer).

NOTATION The notations used for this activity are the same ones used in the existing models for each view you're modifying.

ACTIVITIES

Reduce Functional Unavailability. Identify each of the features of the architecture that were found to cause a reduction in system availability during the assessment of functional availability. Consider addressing each one by reducing the amount of unavailability (e.g., by reducing or parallelizing tasks) or eliminating unavailability where possible (e.g., using replicated data as input to summary processing). For each, attempt to assess the cost of reducing the availability against the amount of extra availability achieved, and to keep costs under control, implement only those with the most favorable ratios.

Reduce Technology Unavailability. Work through the Deployment view to identify those parts of the deployment environment that are single points of failure and so could reduce the system's availability if they fail. For each

FIGURE 27–4 MIRRORED STORAGE HARDWARE

failure point found, identify a possible solution (such as fault-tolerant hardware or high-availability clustering) that could eliminate that failure point. Again, balance the cost of the solution against the likelihood and impact of the failure, and select those solutions that give the greatest benefit at the lowest cost.

ARCHITECTURAL TACTICS

Select Fault-Tolerant Hardware

Fault-tolerant computing platforms can continue to operate without interruption even if a hardware component fails. These are typically implemented by means of redundant or duplicated hardware: Each component—CPU, memory, disk, I/O port, and so on—is deployed in pairs, and if one of the pair fails, the other continues to operate while the fault is analyzed and the faulty part repaired or replaced. Such platforms, although expensive, deliver a very high level of system availability and often allow hardware upgrades to be performed while the system is online.

Redundant disk architectures (such as RAID[1] or mirrored disks) are a particularly common example. A simple example of disk redundancy is disk mirroring, shown in Figure 27–4. This is known as "RAID 1," which means

---

1. RAID (Redundant Array of Inexpensive or Independent Disks) architectures are available in a variety of configurations, known as RAID levels, which variously provide resilience through mirroring, data redundancy, and error correction and improved performance through striping of data across disks.

that disk writes are applied to each side of the mirror, whereas reads come from only one side (or, in some configurations, whichever side can return the information with the least amount of head movement). If either disk fails, the other can continue on its own until the faulty disk is replaced and resynchronized.

More sophisticated developments of this simple case are the higher levels of RAID storage, as implemented by resilient disk arrays. These units typically implement a variant of RAID 5 or higher, transparently striping data across multiple physical disks and also writing parity information along with the application data, allowing recovery from single disk failure (in the case of RAID 5) or multiple drive failures (in the case of higher levels).

If you are deploying a fault-tolerant platform, remember that availability is only as good as your weakest component. Don't forget to include routers and networks, terminals, PCs, printers, tape drives, and so on in your availability analysis. When fault-tolerant solutions do not exist for these components, you may have to develop strategies of your own (e.g., standby printing facilities).

Use High-Availability Clustering and Load Balancing

High-availability clustering is a technique for protecting against failures by mirroring the whole computer rather than just a disk. In a clustered configuration, two or more identical computers (referred to as *nodes*) are deployed in parallel and share the total workload between them. If any one of the nodes fails, one of the remaining nodes takes over its workload and processing can continue (although the transactions in progress at the failed node may have to be resubmitted). This process is known as *failover*. High-availability clustering is a very effective approach for mitigating local failures within the system's deployment environment (such as the failure of a server node). It can't generally be used across long distances, though, so isn't an effective approach for dealing with site failures, such as total loss of connectivity to a data center. For these cases a more involved disaster recovery approach that migrates the entire system deployment environment to a remote site will be required.

A variety of different clustering configurations are available, depending on how the nodes are connected to shared resources, such as memory, disk, and the communications network, and what failover scenarios are supported. Whatever approach you choose, incoming transactions must be allocated to one of the nodes. A technique called *load balancing* performs this allocation and helps ensure that the nodes are used to their fullest possible extent. Load balancing can be provided via hardware or (less commonly) software. Figure 27–5 illustrates an example configuration, where requests are load balanced between a number of clustered nodes with shared disks, accessed

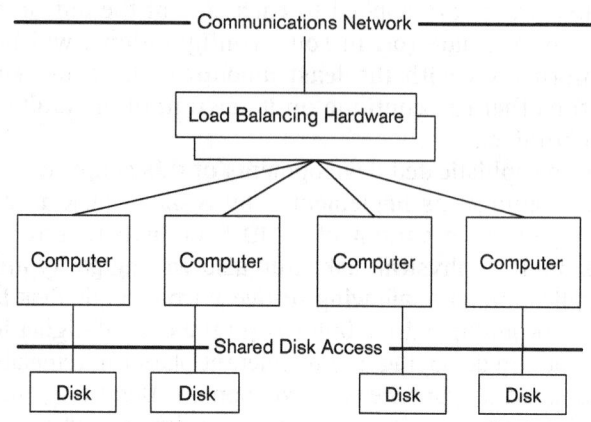

FIGURE 27–5 HIGH-AVAILABILITY CLUSTER

via a high-speed technology such as a storage area network (SAN), to allow failover in case of compute node failure. (The shared storage subsystem needs to be independently resilient to guard against the risk of the failure of one or more of the physical disks.)

Clustering typically requires enhancements to the operating systems, middleware, and application programs that run on them. Special software is also required to manage the cluster. Some types of clusters (scalable clusters) can also be used to enhance performance due to their ability to reduce contention via replication (as we describe for the Performance and Scalability perspective, in Chapter 26).

Log Transactions

While in the case of database or storage failure it may be possible to recover some lost data from backups, that may not be the end of the story. For a number of reasons, backups may not bring data back to the state it was in at the point of failure.

- Backups may have been made only daily or periodically during the day, so the most recent transactions may not be included in the backup.
- It may be necessary to restore multiple databases to a consistent point in time, to maintain cross-database data integrity.
- An up-to-the-minute backup may be available but may have become corrupt due to a fault in the database storage mechanism in use.

In such scenarios, it is extremely useful to have a separate transaction log that can be replayed into the recovered database to bring it completely

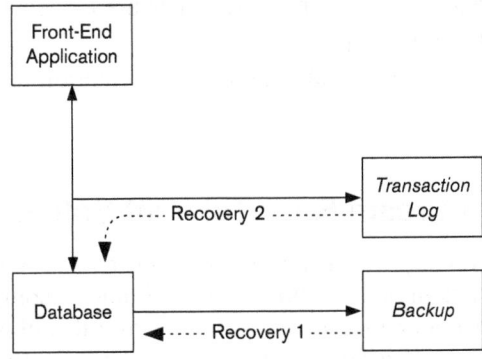

FIGURE 27-6 POINT-IN-TIME RECOVERY WITH A TRANSACTION LOG

up-to-date, as shown in Figure 27–6. Such a capability may be provided by the database or underlying storage mechanism, by underlying transaction management software in your application server or transaction processing monitor, or you may have to develop it yourself as a feature of your application.

An added benefit of such transaction logging is that it may be possible to use it to provide an audit trail.

Apply Software Availability Solutions

Fault-tolerant hardware platforms do not deliver *software* fault tolerance: They are just as vulnerable as ordinary platforms to operating system crashes or application failures. Safety-critical systems, such as aircraft guidance systems, achieve software fault tolerance by using multiplexing software techniques (i.e., independently writing the application several times and employing a real-time "voting" system to compare the outputs of the different versions, allowing inconsistencies between them to be identified). However, the costs of delivering this level of sophistication mean that it is usually not appropriate or affordable for more mainstream systems.

This said, you do still need to develop effective strategies to ensure the reliability and recoverability of your software. While this can be considered a design rather than an architectural concern, the approach for achieving this is a system-wide concern with some architecturally significant aspects, such as:

- A robust strategy for data validation and dealing with rejected data
- A common strategy for detecting, logging, and responding to software errors

- A service to which error messages are logged and from which alerts and errors can be trapped
- The recording of full diagnostic information to help in subsequent analysis and repair

Select or Create Fault-Tolerant Software

Software can also be written to reconfigure itself in response to changing conditions, for example, by allocating itself more resources (such as shared memory) when under load or by automatically disabling certain features if they malfunction and offering only partial service until the problem is rectified. Such technology is still in its relative infancy in mainstream information system development but has been investigated widely by researchers and is appearing in some operating systems and infrastructure software. You can also use these approaches within your own application software to provide a degree of resilience where required.

EXAMPLE A desktop application reads from a preferences file when it starts up in order to restore the user's preferences for presentation (color, font, and so on). If this preferences file is not present, or if it has become damaged or corrupted, the application reverts to a standard, default configuration and creates a clean version of the preferences file.

Design for Failure

When we design systems to be resilient and concentrate on making their components reliable, there is a tendency to forget that no matter what steps we take, we are going to have to deal with partial or total system failure at some point. While modern hardware can be very reliable and we have many approaches for making our software resilient to failure, ultimately enough things can still go wrong that we will encounter a system failure.

It is important to remember this as you design the system's architecture, so that you consider what to do when things go wrong. Even when using resilient and fault-tolerant components, you need to have effective processes and management tools in place to recognize failures and recover from them. Your design work needs to include the ability to recover the system to operation even if one of its highly reliable components fails.

EXAMPLE Modern disk subsystems are very sophisticated and can mask many failures in the physical disks that they contain. However, there are always failure modes that can result in partial or total unavailability of the data managed by the array, but because such failures are rare, there is a tendency to assume that the data in the disk subsystem is safe in all situations. Therefore, it's important to keep reminding yourself of this, and to develop a recovery strategy that does not assume that data from the disk subsystem is available.

Allow for Component Replication

A key tactic for increasing the reliability and resilience of a system is to replicate the components within it. If you can use three servers rather than one, a server failure may still be a dramatic event but is no longer a crisis. Most resilient hardware components, such as high-availability network devices and resilient storage, use this principle extensively by replicating their internal components to allow them to survive the failure of one of them. This approach can also increase the reliability of application software, where the deployment of a number of instances of a component allows the failure of one instance to be masked, with the surviving instances taking over its workload.

The difficulty with applying this tactic in many situations is that you can't blindly replicate most of the components or modules of a typical enterprise application unless they have been designed to allow these multiple instances to cooperate. A system element that hasn't been designed to allow replication may hang, duplicate processing, or even corrupt data, so if you're planning to use this tactic, you must design it into your application from the outset. This normally involves making many of your elements stateless, so that they load the state they need for an incoming request when it arrives and save the resulting state after processing the request.

EXAMPLE A simple example of replicated application components can be found in most Web-based applications, where many instances of the Web and application servers are used to process incoming requests, providing both scalability and resilience benefits for the application. The constraint that this tactic places on the application software is the need for server components to be entirely stateless. This is usually achieved by storing all application state in a shared database and having the server software components load the state they require when a request arrives and write the updated state back to the database afterward.

Relax Transactional Consistency

As discussed with regard to the Performance and Scalability perspective (Chapter 26), the CAP theorem tells us that we can achieve no more than two of the system attributes of consistency, availability, and partition tolerance. If availability is a prime concern, we are likely to choose availability and partition tolerance, and so a possible tactic is to relax the consistency constraints in the system. We introduced this tactic with a slightly different emphasis in the Performance and Scalability perspective, but applying the tactic can benefit availability as well.

Identify Backup and Disaster Recovery Solutions

Every system that manages persistent information (i.e., information that must be stored on stable storage and be available across system restarts) must include mechanisms for backing up this information by writing it to a separate storage medium from which the information can be recovered in the case of system failure (particularly disk failure).

Traditionally, some form of magnetic tape was used for backup, but this method suffers from several constraints: the speed at which data can be written to the backup media, the amount of information a single tape can store, and the reliability of the media. A backup that takes 18 hours and requires 200 tapes will be cumbersome and prone to failure.

High-volume backups are often done to disk, for example, over a very high-speed local- or wide-area network. An alternative solution is to deploy mirrored data disks, unmirroring them temporarily while the backup is done, as shown in Figure 27–7.

While the first mirroring architectures placed the disks physically near one another, you can now mirror onto disks at another location, possibly

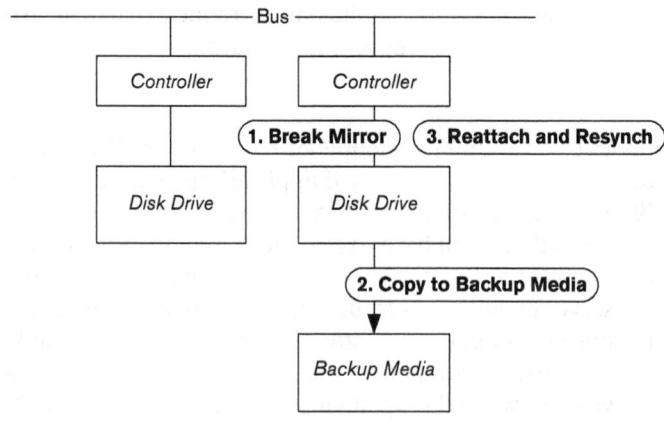

FIGURE 27–7 MIRRORING FOR AVAILABILITY

many miles away, by means of high-bandwidth, highly reliable fiber-optic networks. Such a distributed mirroring solution, while expensive, can also form part of your disaster recovery architecture.

Most backup systems can perform online backups; that is, they can back up data while the system continues to run (with an acceptable degradation in online performance). Others require that the system be taken down in order to perform the backup; if this applies to your situation, you will need to factor this into your recovery plans.

Any backup solution must maintain the transactional integrity of the data so that, when the data is restored, it is left in a transactionally consistent state. We discuss this issue further in Chapter 18 on the Information view.

PROBLEMS AND PITFALLS

Single Point of Failure

A system is only as reliable as its least-reliable component. A *single point of failure* is an individual element in an architecture that, if it fails, causes the whole architecture to fail.

> **EXAMPLE** It is common to improve reliability by deploying mirrored disk configurations of the sort that we described earlier. This is a sensible precaution; disks contain mechanical parts, so they are more prone to failure than other hardware components.
>
> However, in some mirrored configurations, the disk pairs share a common controller (the device that connects the disk to the main computer bus). If a controller fails, access to each disk in the pair is lost. The reliability of the controller thus becomes the key determinant of the reliability of the disk architecture.

The presence of a single point of failure can critically undermine the reliability of the system as a whole.

RISK REDUCTION

- Analyze your architectural models, particularly your Functional and Deployment views, for the presence of any single points of failure. If you find any, determine whether it is cost-effective to enhance these (perhaps by hardware duplication) to improve reliability.

Cascading Failure

A particularly difficult type of failure to deal with is a cascading failure, where the failure of one system component results in failures in other parts of the system, which in turn can cause other components to fail. Cascading failure is well known in many types of complex systems; a prominent example of this outside the computer systems domain is the case of interconnected power grids, where the failure of one grid suddenly results in very high load on the neighboring surviving grids, which can then be pushed beyond their safe capacity, causing further failures.

Complex IT systems can also be vulnerable to cascading failures, such as when the failure of one element within the system causes other elements to fail because of the redistribution of load or internal interdependencies.

Unfortunately, it is easier to talk about this problem in general terms than it is to analyze and address it in real design situations. It can often be difficult to predict how the failure of one component will affect others, and this difficulty increases as the complexity of the system rises. The best advice we can give is to be aware of this problem when designing your system, to keep the design as simple as possible, to isolate components from each other whenever possible, and to ensure that all components handle overload situations gracefully.

EXAMPLE Many Web-based systems track detailed statistics about page views, timings, and other statistics relevant to the user experience and the use of the system. A cascading failure problem that can plague these systems is the failure of the statistics tracking service that all of the page-rendering components call. If the tracking service becomes overloaded and slows down, this can cause all page rendering to slow down too. This in turn results in users canceling requests and hitting the "refresh" button in their browsers, which further increases the load on the site and the struggling tracking service.

The solution to this is to use a more sophisticated approach to invoking the tracking service, so that if it slows down or fails, page rendering is not affected. For example, rather than calling the tracking service via an RPC service call, the information might be sent to it via an asynchronous message.

RISK REDUCTION

- Walk through the design of your system and assess the impact of the failure of each component on the surviving components of the system.

- Design your components to deal with overload situations gracefully, ensuring that sudden high workload does not render them inoperable.
- Consider how you can isolate components from the impact of the failure of others. Can workload be throttled? Are service calls to other components protected by short timeouts? Can processing that depends on other components be skipped if they are not available?

Unavailability through Overload

A measure of success for any system is its widespread use by a large number of people. This is particularly true for Internet-facing systems, the goal of which is often to provide a service to a huge number of people from all over the world. However, the pitfall that lies in wait for successful systems is not being able to deal with large spikes in workload, so that the system becomes unavailable simply because of the number of people trying to use it, rather than any failure within it. This problem is fundamentally a lack of scalability in your system, but as it becomes more serious, it actually results in unavailability rather just poor performance.

This situation can also manifest itself in enterprise systems when a large number of people in the organization try to use a system simultaneously. This might be an authentication service that comes under very heavy load at 9:00 A.M. each day, a retail system that must process huge transaction loads during holiday periods, or an internal HR system that everyone in the organization has to use on the same day to confirm benefit choices for the coming year.

This problem usually appears as a slowing of request processing, eventually resulting in the system becoming unusable as more and more people try to use it. The underlying problem is nearly always application components that were not designed to handle high workloads gracefully. This is often due to internal contention in components, caused by blindly allocating resources (such as memory, threads, or locks) irrespective of how many simultaneous requests are being handled. When the number of requests gets very high, these components spend most of their time trying to allocate and deallocate resources and struggle to perform much useful workload, rapidly leading to system unavailability.

RISK REDUCTION

- Define patterns for request handling that allow your system components to continue to work successfully, or in the worst case reject work gracefully, when load increases sharply. For example, consider creating server component patterns that include timeouts on service calls, messaging for intercomponent connections, and returning errors quickly when components are overloaded. Make sure that your patterns are used throughout the system. We provide some sources of information to help you with this in the Further Reading section.

- Return to your performance model if you have one and use it to analyze the likely behavior of your system if its workload exceeds the limits that you are expecting.

- Test your system under heavy and unpredictable workload so that you understand how it is likely to behave and can identify possible problems that can be rectified before a situation like this happens in production.

Overambitious Availability Requirements

Availability schedules are, of course, driven by the needs of the business. However, like performance requirements, they usually require a tradeoff between necessity and cost. Increasing the length of the online day, for example, reduces the length of the overnight batch; this may necessitate more powerful hardware, or more sophisticated batch systems or scheduling, to complete the overnight batch run.

Many systems, particularly ones that provide services over the Internet, aim for 24/7 availability. This means that the system is never allowed to go down, ever—not even for maintenance or for software or operating system upgrades. This is extremely difficult to achieve and extremely expensive, even with today's very high-availability computing platforms.

RISK REDUCTION

- Validate your high-availability requirements carefully (in particular, challenge requests for 24/7 operation if you hear them). Make sure these requirements are backed by a business need.

- When high availability really is needed, make sure that your proposed technology platforms are suitable (and supported) for this degree of reliability.

- Make your stakeholders (particularly acquirers) aware of the costs of high availability to encourage them to set requirements at a realistic level.

- Tie any third parties into clear, quantitative service-level agreements to ensure that they do not affect your availability.

Ineffective Error Detection

In most systems, more code is devoted to trapping and dealing with errors than to implementing core functionality. It is tempting, especially if there are time pressures, to skimp on error handling, but this can be disastrous in the long run.

EXAMPLE A system collects information on ticket bookings from a number of airlines for the purpose of allocating to customers the bonus points that can be exchanged for free flights. Unfortunately, one of the routines that calculates the point values returns an error code that is not checked. This routine is failing because of a programming error, so customers are not being credited with points they are due.

Eventually, a customer complains that her point values have not been calculated correctly, and a large-scale corruption of data in the database is discovered. The system administrator attempts to restore the database from backup, but because the routine has been failing for a long time, all of the backups are corrupt as well.

The only solution to this situation is to fix the data in the database directly and to eventually write special programs to retrieve the booking information and recalculate the data in the whole database.

Your error-handling strategy (or lack of it) has a wide impact on your system, so you need to clearly define a strategy in the Development view.

RISK REDUCTION

- Define a clear, system-wide error-handling strategy that provides enough information for your availability needs.
- Define design standards for error handling such as the following.
  - All actions that can return an error are checked for success and failure.
  - When errors occur in a low-level routine, they are reported upward to the caller.
  - All errors are logged.
  - At the top level, any reported error either is fixed by the program (e.g., by retrying) or causes a user-visible halt.
- Capture error-handling strategy and standards as part of your Development view to ensure that error detection and handling is implemented consistently throughout the system.

Overestimation of Component Resilience

When incorporating resilient components such as disk arrays into your architecture, it is easy to focus on the resiliency that they provide rather than the possible failure cases that they do not cater for. Most of the documentation you'll find for the high-availability features of software and hardware stresses the cases that the product can survive rather than discussing those that it can't. This can naturally lead to implicit assumptions that a particular component is "bulletproof" when in fact there are perfectly reasonable situations that could occur and cause it to fail. Given that a system is only as resilient as the weakest component, this can lead to dangerous confidence about the system's resilience.

EXAMPLE We tend to think of RAID-based disk arrays as being capable of surviving any likely failure of a disk within them and therefore providing a very high degree of resilience. However, it's important to understand exactly what can fail and still allow the disk array to continue operating. For example, different RAID levels provide different levels of protection against different failures (RAID 5 is able to survive the failure of one disk, and RAID 6 can survive the failure of two), but no level of disk organization will provide resilience in the face of a disk interface failure in the server using the disks or a firmware crash in the disk array. While these seem like obvious statements, in real situations it can be difficult to find out exactly which failures a component is resilient to and which will cause it to fail.

RISK REDUCTION

- Ask detailed questions about the failure modes of your components to understand exactly what happens in each case.
- Test ambiguous cases if you can, or if you cannot, you have to assume the worst case and design your use of the component accordingly.

Overlooked Global Availability Requirements

Any system that has global reach may need to be available around the clock.

EXAMPLE A foreign-exchange trading system is used by traders in Hong Kong, London, and New York. As the trading day is coming to an end in Hong Kong, it is starting in London, and a few hours later, it starts in New York. By the time New York trading has closed, the next day's trading is due to start in Hong Kong again.

However, the system design mandates an end-of-day consolidation run, during which trading cannot take place. It is not possible to fit this run into the timetable at any point because the system is always being used by someone.

Although your system may not have global reach now, you should explore with your stakeholders whether the system might go global in the future. If so, you will save a lot of time by building in some high-availability features now.

RISK REDUCTION

- If required, take a global perspective when considering the availability of your system (also see the discussion of the Location perspective in Chapter 29).
- When continuous uptime is a real requirement, reflect this in your architecture as early and visibly as possible.
- Confirm that your main architectural solutions are compatible with global needs (such as adding hardware to allow the transfer of processing between different servers to "follow the sun").

Incompatible Technologies

Many high-availability solutions have some specific requirements related to the software that will run on them. For example, a database or application server that caches information in shared memory may need to be redesigned to work in a clustered environment where each computer has its own cache.

Unless your software elements have been specifically written to run on such platforms, you may find that they perform badly or just won't work at all. It is particularly important that you make sure that all of the different pieces of third-party software work together perfectly. If they don't, it is very unlikely that they will work correctly during a failover situation.

RISK REDUCTION

- Use supplier data to confirm that your hardware and software elements are compatible with one another.
- If you have any doubt, consider a proof-of-concept, or ask your suppliers to put you in touch with their customers who are running similar configurations.

CHECKLISTS

Checklist for Requirements Capture

- Are availability requirements defined, documented, and approved?
- Are availability requirements driven by business needs?
- Do availability requirements consider different classes of service if appropriate?

- Do availability requirements strike a realistic balance between cost and business needs?
- Do availability requirements consider online and batch availability?
- Do availability requirements take into account variations such as period end?
- Do availability requirements take into account future changes in business operations such as moving to a longer online day?
- Can availability requirements be met by the chosen hardware and software platform?
- Have you defined strategies for disaster recovery and business continuity?
- Do stakeholders have realistic expectations around unplanned downtime?

Checklist for Architecture Definition

- Does the proposed architectural solution meet the availability requirements? Can this be demonstrated, either theoretically or based on previous practical experience?
- Does the solution consider the time taken to recover from failure (e.g., to restore from backup if necessary)?
- Does the backup solution provide for the transactional integrity of restored data?
- Does the backup solution support online backup, with acceptable degradation in performance? If not, is it feasible to take the system down in order to perform backups?
- Has consideration been given to restoring data from corrupt or incomplete backups?
- Will the system respond gracefully to software errors, logging and reporting them appropriately?
- Have you defined a standby site in the architecture if appropriate? Is the standby site configured identically to the production site, or will it offer reduced performance? If the latter, is this reduced performance acceptable to the users?
- Have you defined and tested mechanisms for switching from production to standby environments and back again? If not, when will you do this?
- Have you assessed the impact of the availability solution on functionality and performance? Is this impact acceptable?

- If high availability is particularly important, have you assessed the architecture for single points of failure and other weaknesses?

- If you developed a fault-tolerant model, does this extend to all vulnerable components (such as disk controllers)?

FURTHER READING

Two IT-oriented books on disaster recovery [TOIG02, SNED07] explain how to plan for and cope with system disasters from an IT perspective. An alternative view from the business process perspective can be found in [BARN01] and [WALL10], which provide a lot of useful guidance in areas outside computer systems recovery that are still crucial to achieving effective overall disaster recovery.

A number of approaches exist for modeling and predicting software reliability using statistical models. You can find a readable introduction to these approaches in Neufelder [NEUF92], which explains how to create models to predict the reliability of a piece of software, including a comprehensive description of the various theoretical models available. For an alternative opinion, Butler and Finelli [BUTL93] and Whittaker and Voas [WHIT00] discuss problems with software reliability modeling, and the latter (which is the more accessible of the two) suggests factors that new software reliability models should take into account. When considering disk reliability, it is worth reading Schroeder and Gibson's technical report [SCHR06], which provides some sobering analysis of how reliable disks really are. A large amount of information on RAID-based disk resilience and disk reliability in general can be found at Wikipedia and elsewhere via an Internet search.

You can find a very thorough, practical, and readable discussion of how to create highly available systems using today's mainstream technology in Marcus and Stern [MARC03]. Written for the architect and system administrator, it goes into the practical details of actually getting highly available systems to work. Another more recent book [SCHM06] covers similar ground, in a similarly practitioner-oriented, yet thorough, style. Michael Nygard's book [NYGA07] is written more directly in application design terms and contains a great deal of valuable advice on creating highly available systems, including a number of useful design patterns and antipatterns. Robert Hanmer's book [HANM07] goes into more detail on the software design aspect of this topic, presenting a full pattern language for fault-tolerant software.

Further reading relating to the CAP theorem that we discussed in the Pitfalls section can be found in the Further Reading section of Chapter 26, where we also discuss it in more detail.

No list of availability references would be complete without Pfister [PFIS98], a classic, highly readable, and often entertaining tutorial on the technology of cluster computing, addressing both highly available clusters and scalable clusters. This book manages to make a complex and technical area both approachable and comprehensible, providing a thorough overview of the issues, techniques, and technologies involved in achieving clustered systems.

For those wanting more background on the theory and technology of system availability, a large number of references are available. Examples include the very technical review of the techniques used to create fault-tolerant hardware and software technology found in Jain [JAIN91] and the review and tutorial on achieving fault-tolerant software found in Pullum [PULL01].

28

THE EVOLUTION PERSPECTIVE

Desired Quality	The ability of the system to be flexible in the face of the inevitable change that all systems experience after deployment, balanced against the costs of providing such flexibility
Applicability	Important for all systems to some extent; more important for longer-lived and more widely used systems
Concerns	Product management, magnitude of change, dimensions of change, likelihood of change, timescale for change, when to pay for change, changes driven by external factors, development complexity, preservation of knowledge, and reliability of change
Activities	Characterize the evolution needs, assess the current ease of evolution, consider the evolution tradeoffs, and rework the architecture
Architectural Tactics	Contain change, create extensible interfaces, apply design techniques that facilitate change, apply metamodel-based architectural styles, build variation points into the software, use standard extension points, achieve reliable change, and preserve development environments
Problems and Pitfalls	Prioritization of the wrong dimensions, changes that never happen, impacts of evolution on critical quality properties, overreliance on specific hardware or software, lost development environments, and ad hoc release management

A somewhat overused business maxim tells us that the only constant is change, and most software architects can identify strongly with this. The very ability of software to be "soft" means that stakeholders expect a software-based system to be able to evolve very quickly. Couple this expectation with other common factors such as misunderstood requirements, rapid business change, and the effect that actually delivering a system has on end-user requirements, and it is easy to see why change is such a major factor in the lives of software architects.

The commonly adopted iterative approach to system delivery can make an ability to deal with change all the more important. When a system is delivered in iterations, its users can start using some parts of it much earlier and thus provide early feedback to the developers. This is an extremely valuable process because it allows requirements to be validated early. However, it also means that there is constant pressure during the delivery cycle to change the system's behavior, with a consequent need in some cases to change its architecture.

Although, in principle, software is easy to change, experienced software developers agree that this is true only if change is explicitly considered during its development. Software developed without any concern for the changes that will likely be needed can be much harder to change than anyone expects.

We consider the process of dealing with change in the system development lifecycle under the term *evolution*, by which we mean all of the possible types of changes that a system may experience during its lifetime.

The Evolution perspective addresses the concerns related to dealing with evolution during the lifetime of a system and thus is relevant to most large-scale information systems because of the amount of change that most systems need to handle.

APPLICABILITY TO VIEWS

Table 28–1 shows how the Evolution perspective affects each of the views we discussed in Part III.

TABLE 28–1 APPLICABILITY OF THE EVOLUTION PERSPECTIVE TO THE SEVEN VIEWS

View	Applicability
Context	The Context view may need to show external entities, interfaces, or interactions that will form part of the model only in future versions of the system.
Functional	If the evolution required is significant, the functional structure will need to reflect this.
Information	If environment or information evolution is needed, a flexible information model will be required.
Concurrency	Evolutionary needs may dictate particular element packaging or some constraints on the concurrency structure (e.g., that it must be very simple).
Development	Evolution requirements may have a significant impact on the development environment that needs to be defined (e.g., enforcing portability guidelines).

Deployment	This perspective rarely has a significant impact on the Deployment view because system evolution usually affects structures described in other views.
Operational	This perspective typically has less impact on the Operational view.

CONCERNS

Product Management

In a product development environment, the evolution of a product is usually planned and overseen by a product manager, who is responsible for understanding the needs of the product's customers and the threats and opportunities offered by the market in which the product is sold. The product manager's job is to use this insight to define a roadmap for the future development of the product and to work with the product development organization in order to deliver and evolve the product in line with it.

Agile software development also recognizes the importance of product management, with an analogous role being explicitly recognized in methods like XP, which requires an on-site customer, and Scrum, which identifies the role of product owner. When no such product ownership exists, it is often up to you as the architect to implicitly or explicitly play this role and plot a future course for the system you are developing.

Whether or not it is formally recognized, product management is important because it provides a context and direction for all of the change happening in the system. This helps potential changes to be prioritized systematically and allows them to be considered in the context of a roadmap, to avoid an incoherent feature set developing.

Magnitude of Change

For some systems, potential changes are limited to defect rectification and minor cosmetic adjustments or tweaks to external interfaces. At the other extreme, some widely used, long-lived systems undergo a continual process of major evolution to meet the changing needs of their environments and are effectively rewritten every few years.

The most difficult problems occur when you expect only the former situation but the latter reality emerges during development or deployment. Such cases are likely to be expensive to remedy because the system will probably be hard to change, and complete redevelopment may be your only practical evolution option.

Dimensions of Change

Different types of evolution require different support in the system's architecture and have different costs and risks associated with them. If you can identify the dimensions of change required, you can narrow your system evolution to a more bounded, tractable problem.

We classify the important dimensions of change as follows.

- *Functional evolution*: This includes any change to the functions that the system provides, from simple defect corrections at one end of the scale to the addition or replacement of entire subsystems at the other.
- *Platform evolution*: Many successful systems need to evolve in terms of the software and hardware platforms on which they are deployed. This can include migrating platforms (e.g., from Windows-based servers to Linux-based servers) as well as extending the platforms the system can use (e.g., porting products to new platforms or extending existing PC-based client platforms to include Web-based access).
- *Integration evolution*: Most information systems need to be integrated with a number of other systems to be useful. This may involve retrieving information from systems on demand, processing the outputs of other systems, or providing information for other systems to process. As these other systems are created, evolve, and are removed, this may put evolution pressures on your system, so that although it does not have to change its functionality, it may need to change the way it integrates with other systems.
- *Growth*. As we describe with regard to the Performance and Scalability view, most successful systems undergo a growth in usage during their lifetime. This may be due to many factors, such as an increase in the number or complexity of transactions, an increase in the number of users, or the need to manage and store larger amounts of data. If the system provides an Internet service and proves to be successful, this growth could be substantial and unpredictable.

Likelihood of Change

It is often easy to identify many types of change that could be needed, but assessing the probability that the changes actually will be required may be much harder. Providing facilities for change in your system adds complexity and expense, so it is important to provide support only for changes that are likely to occur.

Timescale for Change

The likely timescale for the required change is also an important concern. The environment of most systems is changing constantly, which means that assumptions that are true today rarely survive intact over time. The further away the need for a change is, the less likely it is that the change will actually be needed in its currently identified form.

Requirements for changes that have no associated delivery date or a far-off delivery date may be of lower priority than changes with firm, short-term dates attached to them.

When to Pay for Change

There are two strategies for planning for change to your system.

1. Design the most flexible system possible now to make it easy to change later. This is perhaps best characterized by the metasystem approach, where the system's information structure and functions are defined at runtime by configuration data.

2. Create the simplest system possible to meet immediate needs and to meet the challenge of making changes only when you absolutely have to. This is perhaps best characterized by the Extreme Programming (XP) mantras of "Do the simplest thing possible" and "You aren't going to need it," which capture the lesson that trying to guess the future and build the most flexible system possible is an expensive, risky, and complex business.

One of the major differences between these two strategies is when you pay for change. Developing highly flexible systems costs a lot more than developing simple, rigid ones, so the cost of change is loaded to the front of the system lifecycle if you follow the first strategy. The tradeoff is that you hope these early costs will be paid back by cheaper and faster changes later. Developing the simplest system possible costs less up front because it is simpler and quicker to deliver, but each later change is likely to cost more because you have no existing mechanism for implementing it.

Getting the balance right between these two extreme positions avoids either wasted early effort or huge change costs later and helps you find a position that minimizes the overall costs of development.

Changes Driven by External Factors

Not all changes are under your control or that of your immediate stakeholders—some may be imposed on you by people or groups outside your sphere of influence. For example, a new CIO may be appointed who wants to take the IT department in a significantly different direction such as adopting a "buy not build" strategy. You still need to cater for such changes, with the added complication that you have less control (or possibly no control at all) over whether and when you do this.

Examples of externally driven change include the following:

- The end-of-life of hardware or software components you plan to use as part of your architecture. This is particularly important if your organization mandates that systems are allowed to run only on hardware and software supported by the vendor. Vendors should be able to supply you with roadmaps for their products that will identify when end-of-life events are likely to occur.

- Changes to interfaces with external entities, such as moving to a new protocol, data format, data content, or interaction model.

- Changes in external regulation, which may drive more stringent requirements for business continuity, validation, data retention, auditing, or control.

- Organizational change that may lead to different priorities, changed requirements, or changes in the user population and transaction profile.

Development Complexity

In nearly all cases, building in support for evolution increases the complexity of a system's design, sometimes by a huge amount. This added complexity costs more to develop (as discussed earlier) and may also bring problems related to system reliability and the time required to deliver early parts of the system. In some cases, complexity can even become an obstacle to system evolution.

Preservation of Knowledge

It is usually fairly obvious how to make changes to a system while it is being built—the people you need are available, knowledge about how the system works is fresh in their minds, and a development environment is available for making and testing the changes. Once the system moves from active development to a more stable deployed state, this may no longer be true.

An important concern for any system is how to preserve the knowledge required to make significant changes to the system as people move to other projects, memories fade, and the available technical environments change.

Reliability of Change

From the simplest bug fix to the most complex subsystem redevelopment, any system change can have a negative impact on the deployed system, so it is essential to have a set of processes and technologies to make this process as reliable as possible.

Automated testing, repeatable and well-understood processes, stable development environments, and effective configuration management are all key factors in addressing this concern as your system evolves.

ACTIVITIES: APPLYING THE EVOLUTION PERSPECTIVE

The activity diagram in Figure 28–1 illustrates a simple process for applying the Evolution perspective. In this section, we describe the activities in this process.

Characterize the Evolution Needs

This step is really one of further requirements analysis, this time to understand the requirements from the perspective of system evolution. The requirements for the system probably focus on what must be delivered, the system's level of

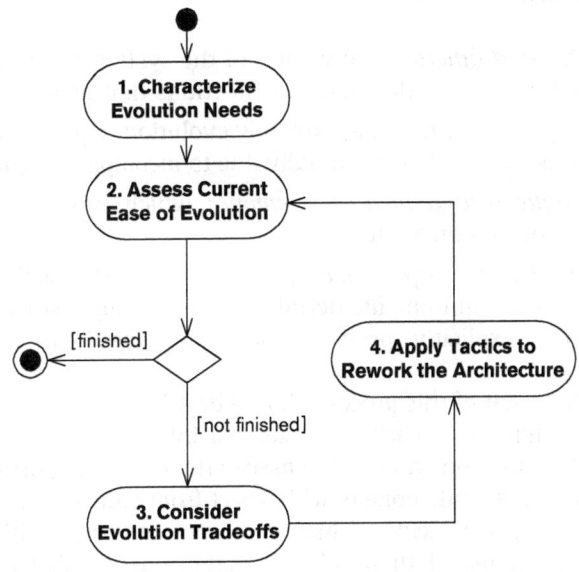

FIGURE 28-1 APPLYING THE EVOLUTION PERSPECTIVE

complexity, technical and project constraints, and so on. Now you must go back to the requirements and work out what will likely need to change over time.

You can characterize your evolution needs as follows.

1. *Type of change required*: Characterize each type of evolution into one of the dimensions described earlier (functional, platform, integration, or growth).

2. *Magnitude of change required*: Establish how much effort each type of evolution will need. Is it just defect correction, or will large-scale, high-risk system changes be required? A useful way to present this is the effort required as a proportion of the initial system development effort.

3. *Likelihood of change*: Assess how likely it is that each of the types of change you have identified will actually be required. This allows you to focus on those that are most likely to occur.

4. *Timescale of required changes*: Are the changes required on an immediate, firm timetable (in effect, a phased delivery)? Or are they vague needs for changes sometime in the future depending on external factors (such as system growth)?

Evolution requirements often are not explicitly recorded, so you need to infer them from the existing documents and validate them through discussions with key stakeholders. When reading the requirements documents, look for elements such as:

- *Deferred functions*, any parts of the system requirements that explicitly define future extensions, or functions that need not be delivered initially

- *Gaps in requirements*, probably evolution requirements in disguise, which could not be defined initially due to incomplete requirements analysis

- *Vague or undefined requirements*, which indicate this area of the system is not well understood

- *Open-ended requirements*, for example, terms such as *like* or *including* in system requirements definitions, which suggest that extensions similar to the explicitly specified cases will be required

The result of this process should be a list of key evolution requirements for your system, with each characterized by its type, magnitude, and timescale. From this list you can quickly assess the overall importance and nature of the evolution that stakeholders will expect from your system.

To help you decide which requirements to prioritize, rank the requirements in terms of their relative magnitude divided by how many months from now you think they'll be needed. (So, for example, a change with an assigned magnitude of 60 needed in 12 months is allocated a score of 5, while a change with a magnitude of 30 needed in 3 months is allocated a value of 10.) Dividing the magnitude of a change by the time until it is needed reflects the fact that things are constantly changing. So investing effort in something not needed for (say) 12 months runs the risk that the effort will be wasted because of the requirement changing or even vanishing during that period. Focus your attention on the top couple of requirements in this list: These are the large changes that are near enough, and so certain enough, to worry about.

NOTATION A simple text-and-tables approach is usually the most effective and straightforward way to present evolution needs.

ACTIVITIES

Analyze the Requirements. Perform a manual review and analysis of the requirements for your system in order to identify these evolution requirements.

Estimate Effort, Nearness, and Priority. Derive a magnitude for each change and divide it by the time until you think it will be needed.

Assess the Current Ease of Evolution

For each of the evolution requirements you have identified, work through a scenario of how you would change your system to meet the requirement when it becomes necessary. For each of these scenarios, note how much of the system must change and how difficult and risky the resulting set of changes is. This assessment allows you to decide whether or not your architecture requires any changes to meet the evolution requirement.

The focus in this step is not to identify all the details of what needs to be done, but rather to assess whether the changes required could be accomplished at reasonable cost during the required timescales.

NOTATION A simple text-based approach is probably sufficient for capturing the results of your assessment.

ACTIVITIES

Assess the Architecture. This step is really a mini architectural evaluation of your system from the perspective of a single quality property (i.e., modifiability). Refer to Chapter 14 for a discussion of architectural assessment.

Perform a Risk Assessment. Given how well (or otherwise) your architecture supports the likely evolution requirements for the system, is this level of risk acceptable enough for your project to go forward?

Consider the Evolution Tradeoffs

If you feel that your architecture needs some changes to support the evolution requirements, consider the options for providing the flexibility you need. The key tradeoff to consider is whether to expend the effort of creating a flexible system during initial development or whether to defer this effort until system changes are actually required. This tradeoff depends very much on the type of system, the likelihood of changes actually being required, and the level of confidence you have about easily making major changes when needed, rather than during initial development.

The result of this step is a strategy for meeting your evolution requirements in terms of how the system will evolve and at what point the support for the evolution will be put into the system.

NOTATION A simple text-based approach is probably sufficient for capturing your strategy for meeting evolution requirements.

ACTIVITIES

Identify the Options. Consider all of the possible approaches to supporting evolution in your system, from doing nothing initially, through designing but not implementing various options, to developing a fully flexible system from the outset. Assess the architectural impact of each possible option.

Assess the Options. Use a mini architectural assessment to consider which option is right for your system, considering the costs, risks, and priorities of your requirements.

Rework the Architecture

Use the best evolution strategy you identified to make the set of changes necessary for your architecture to support the evolution requirements.

NOTATION Reworking the architecture involves changing the views that describe it, so the notations used are dictated by the views you need to change.

ACTIVITIES

Revise the Architectural Design. Revise your architecture in line with the option(s) you selected in the previous step.

ARCHITECTURAL TACTICS

Contain Change

Typically, dealing with change in a small, well-defined part of your system isn't a problem. For example, changing a single software module to deal with a change to its interface to an external system is usually fairly straightforward. A change starts to be a problem when its effects ripple through a number of different parts of the system simultaneously. (For the interface dimension, for example, if the interface change requires a change to internal system interfaces, this is a much more serious problem than changing the single software module that provides the external interface.)

The architectural challenge is to design a system structure so that the required changes are as contained as possible. Normal sound design practice has a lot to offer in meeting this challenge. The following general design principles can help you localize the effects of change.

- *Encapsulation*: If your system elements are strongly encapsulated with well-defined, flexible interfaces, this will go a long way toward helping you isolate change. In particular, making sure that the internal data structures within your system elements are not visible to their callers helps keep those callers isolated from changes that need to be made within an element.

- *Separation of concerns*: Giving each of your system elements a clear and distinct set of responsibilities helps ensure that a change related to one aspect of your system affects only one element. Conversely, if the responsibilities of your system elements are not clear or a number of elements are involved in each part of the system's operation, most changes are likely to affect a large number of pieces of the system and thus will be expensive and risky to implement.

- *Functional cohesion*. As we describe for the Functional viewpoint, functional cohesion is the extent to which all the functions of an element are strongly related to one another. Good cohesion usually makes change easier, since change tends to be contained to a small and well-defined area.

- *Single point of definition*: Make sure that all data types, fundamental values, algorithms, configurations, data schemas, and so on, are defined or implemented only once. This prevents a change to, for example, a system data structure or interface value limit resulting in changes to a number of different parts of the system.

The real trick when containing change is being able to predict which types of changes will need to be contained in which locations. Of course, there is no magic way to do this; the best solution is early analysis.

Create Extensible Interfaces

Of all the changes you might make to a system, changes to interfaces usually have the widest impact and are therefore the most costly. For example, if you add a mandatory parameter to a frequently used function, every piece of code in your system that calls that function will have to be recoded and retested. If you modify the syntax or semantics of a message passed between components, every component that sends or receives a message of that type will be affected.

It is therefore worth investing in designing some level of flexibility into your interfaces if you believe that the system is likely to undergo significant change. Some techniques you can use include the following.

- Replace APIs that have large numbers of individual parameters with ones that pass in objects or other structured data types instead. For example, a `CreateEmployee` method might take as input the employee first and last name, date of birth, and Social Security number. This could be replaced by a method that takes an `Employee` object instead. When members are added to the `Employee` class, they can be given appropriate defaults so that code does not need to be changed everywhere that the method is invoked.

- You can use a similar approach with information interfaces. For example, by using a self-describing message technology such as XML to define message formats, and allowing new message elements to be optional, you can allow messages to be extended with little or no impact on system elements that do not need to use the extended form of the interface.

We should note that such approaches are not without their costs, and you need to evaluate them in the context of your evolution requirements. To take interface flexibility to its logical extreme would involve dropping static typing of your interfaces altogether and establishing the types of all request parameters at runtime. Such a flexible approach can be more difficult to understand and test and may be less efficient too. It can also introduce many subtle system problems because it is hard to check for information that is accidentally missing.

The specifics of how you can create flexible interfaces depend on the technology environment and problem domain of your system. However, considering the degree of flexibility required of your important interfaces and how to achieve it is an important aspect of addressing the evolution concerns of your system.

Apply Design Techniques That Facilitate Change

As we describe in Chapter 11, using styles and patterns allows you to design your system from standard, proven solutions with known capabilities and characteristics.

There are a number of design patterns you can use to help make a system more amenable to change. A detailed consideration of such patterns is outside the scope of this book, but the sorts of patterns you should consider include the following.

- Abstraction and layering patterns make it easier to change one part of the system with minimal impact on others.

- Generalization patterns make it easier to handle new use cases or data types, by just specializing the existing general-purpose functionality in a way that is appropriate to the new use case.

- Inversion of Control (also known as "dependency injection") and Callback patterns help protect higher-level elements in your architecture from the implementation specifics of lower-level elements.

Apply Metamodel-Based Architectural Styles

If you have significant requirements for system evolution, it may be worth considering the adoption of an overall architectural style that is particularly focused on supporting change. Metamodel-based systems (sometimes called metasystems) provide a very high degree of flexibility in some problem domains (particularly database systems requiring significant schema evolution).

Metamodel approaches break down the system's processing and data into their fundamental building blocks and use runtime configurations to assemble these into fully functional components. Changes to requirements can often be made by changing the metamodel, rather than having to change the underlying software components. A detailed explanation of the relevant architectural styles isn't possible here due to space constraints. However, we give a brief example.

EXAMPLE An investment bank needs to capture and process the details of deals involving many sorts of financial instruments, such as bond purchases, foreign exchange transactions, money market transactions, equity trades, derivative transactions, and so on. New types of deals are invented regularly, meaning that there is a significant requirement to support functional evolution.

A traditional architecture for the system might identify a certain number of types of deals that the system can handle—perhaps foreign exchange, money market, and equity transactions. Each of these would be analyzed to work out its characteristics and processing, and the system would be built to support these functions. Perhaps the architect would spot some commonality between these different types of processing during design and would use some generic reusable processing for the common aspects. Later, bond transactions would need to be added, so a similar process would be repeated and the system changed in order to incorporate those functions.

> In contrast, a metamodel-based architecture starts by considering fundamental concepts such as customers (counterparties), currencies, trading and settlement dates, trading limits, collections of trades for a particular trader (books), and so on. Then, instead of developing a system to process a particular set of transaction types, the architect designs a system to provide a set of facilities to implement the underlying concepts and provides a data-based configuration facility to allow the system's implementers to define the types of trades they want to perform in terms of these underlying concepts. Later, when new trade types are required, they are added by changing the configuration data, rather than the system code.

Such metamodel-based systems can provide the ability to support very rapid change because instead of modifying the system implementation to change its behavior, you can just reconfigure it—usually a much faster process.

Of course, there is no such thing as a free lunch—or, for that matter, a free system change. Metamodel-based systems are much more complex to develop and test than systems based on more static architectural styles. They are also inherently less efficient in terms of runtime performance, which can limit their applicability in environments where performance is a major concern.

Build Variation Points into the Software

A less extreme strategy than adopting a complete architectural style is to adopt specific, localized design solutions to support certain types of changes in specific places in the system. This approach involves identifying the locations where supporting a certain type of change is critically important and specifying a mechanism to achieve the change required. We term these places in the system *variation points* (borrowing the term from product-line architecture). Using variation points is an example of the architecture placing specific constraints on the software design process in order to achieve a particular quality property.

A large number of specific software design patterns have been published that attempt to introduce some form of variation point (Façade, Chain of Responsibility, and Bridge, to name only a few). Some of the general approaches we have found useful include the following.

- *Make elements replaceable*: Being able to replace certain elements in your system with an alternative implementation is a very useful mechanism for creating a variation point (and is widely used in commercial software). This typically involves developing the software so that the interface to an element and its implementation are kept separate so that other elements depend only on the interface. This allows you to change the system's behavior by replacing an element at build time or, with some technologies, at runtime.

- *Control behavior using configuration*: Specify that certain aspects of the processing carried out by your software can be parameterized. For example, parameterize the inputs, outputs, and accuracy required of a statistical processing element in the system to allow some aspects of the system's operation to be changed over time without modifying its implementation.

- *Use self-describing data and generic processing*: The simplest approach to processing data is almost always to hard-code the logic required, but this means that changes to the data require changes to the system. However, certain types of processing (e.g., format conversion) can often be performed in a more generic way if the structure of the input data is known. To deal with format changes in such situations, consider specifying the use of a self-describing data stream (such as XML) with the processing code being written in such a way that it uses the structure of the incoming data to guide its processing.

- *Separate physical and logical processing*: In many systems, data formats change frequently, but the actual processing required does not. This is an example of a case where separating the physical processing from the logical processing can create a useful variation point. If the software is partitioned to first process the physical format of the data and then perform the business (or logical) processing on the results, it is much easier to deal with a change in the physical format (e.g., from CSV files to XML files).

- *Break processes into steps*: Business processes are frequently made up of a number of steps that must be performed in sequence. However, the simplest approach to automating the process may be to implement it as a monolithic piece of software. You can introduce a possible variation point to support process change if instead you structure the software as a number of separate elements, one per step, that combine to form a process.

Like other software architecture decisions, you should introduce variation points carefully, balancing the cost involved in creating, maintaining, and using each variation point against the likelihood of its being used and its importance to stakeholder needs.

Use Standard Extension Points

A related approach to building in your own variation points is to consider how you can use extension points built into standard technologies to provide support for changes to your system. Many mainstream information systems technologies provide standard extension points (such as the J2EE platform's ability to easily add support for new types of databases, via the JDBC interface, and external systems, via the JCA interface). If you can use these standard technology solutions, you may find a number of flexible extension points, available for free, that you can adapt and use in a number of ways to meet your evolution requirements.

For example, you could write custom adapters that allow you to use standard application integration facilities to connect to your in-house systems as well as the packaged applications for which they are normally used. This could allow you to avoid designing and building your own mechanism for future integration into in-house systems.

Achieve Reliable Change

A major challenge for the architects, developers, and administrators of many systems is dealing with change in a reliable way. You, like us, have probably seen a supposedly simple change turn out to have a number of serious side effects that caused major problems when deployed.

Change in any system can be risky, but it can be particularly difficult to deal with in software systems, where it often isn't possible to assess the impact visually and the system must be exhaustively tested to confirm your assumptions about postchange behavior.

If your system is one that needs to cope with change (and, of course, nearly all are, whether or not change is actually planned for), you need to make some architectural decisions that allow changes to be made reliably. A number of relevant strategies can help you with this.

- *Software configuration management*: A crucial part of dealing with software change is having a reliable configuration management system that allows you to control changes to the system's software modules and allows formal system versions to be clearly identified and retrieved.

- *Automated build process*: In addition to controlling the versions of the inputs to the software build process, it is important to make the build process itself reliable, consistent, and repeatable, to ensure that building a particular version of the system always ends up with exactly the same result. Inevitably this means creating an automated system so that human error and inconsistency do not creep into the build process.

- *Dependency analysis*: In all but the simplest of systems, working out the effect of a change on other parts of the system can be a challenge. There are many tools available to automate this analysis, and using these once you start building the system can help to highlight dependencies that you might not otherwise have been aware of.

- *Automated release process*: For most systems, taking the outputs of the build process and packaging them for release and deployment isn't a simple process, and you need an automated system to do this reliably. Creating and maintaining the build and release systems takes valuable time and effort, but in our experience it's always cheaper than the alternative.

- *Create mechanisms to roll back unsuccessful deployments*: No matter how much preproduction testing you do, it is not possible to guarantee that the deployment of a change will not cause so many problems that it needs to be reversed back out again. You should ensure that you have some way of doing this in at least a semiautomated way—for example, write scripts to revert to previous versions of software, and to undo data model and state changes introduced by a release. You may even want to make this a release prerequisite.

- *Environment configuration management*: In addition to controlling the versions of the software modules used in your system, you should control the development and production environments used for creating and running the system. These processes may be less well supported by existing tools, but it is important to carefully manage the exact versions of development tools and deployment platforms, as well as the precise configuration information for them, to avoid instability caused by mismatches between different environments.

- *Automated testing*: Testing is a crucial part of managing the process of system change. If you don't have a way to test the system, you won't know whether or not a change to it has been successful. One aspect of this involves making sure that you have a comprehensive set of tests so that you can assess the impact of a change on the system's behavior. The other aspect is automation. If you do have a comprehensive set of tests for a significant system, it will probably amount to hundreds or thousands of tests. It simply isn't possible to run this many tests in a reliable, timely, and efficient way without a high degree of automation.

- *Continuous integration*: When making changes, it is always best to receive bad news as early as possible. Given that large-scale system change often involves bad news, it is sensible to have a process to discover it as soon as you can. A good way to achieve this is to continually integrate the changing parts of your system rather than trying so-called big bang integration at the end of the process. Continuous integration involves bringing system changes together as often as possible and testing the result (at least once per day in most cases). Both the process of integration itself and the tests you run help uncover problems with the proposed changes as quickly as possible. This minimizes wasted effort and allows you to identify possible solutions.

Preserve Development Environments

Once a project has delivered a meaningful amount of functionality, the original development environment is often dismantled or evolved. Over time, you can easily reach the point where no one knows the exact set of compilers, operating systems, patches, libraries, build tools, and so on, used to create the system. This can be a particular problem for product developers who support a wide range of platforms and product versions.

Part of your responsibility as an architect is to preserve the development environment in some way. Clearly record the details of the required development environment, and make sure that enough hardware and software are retained so that the environment can be precisely re-created if the need arises due to an evolution requirement (e.g., if a fault cannot be reproduced in the current development environment).

One way to do this is to use hardware virtualization tools to create an image of the whole software environment. These self-contained images can be saved to disk and brought up later in exactly the same state that they were in when they were saved.

PROBLEMS AND PITFALLS

Prioritization of the Wrong Dimensions

When considering how to allow for change in your architecture, it is easy to focus on dimensions that you know about, or that seem immediately important because they are often mentioned by your more vocal stakeholders. However, the important change dimensions for a system may be found elsewhere. For example, if your background is primarily data-oriented, it is easy to focus on the context dimension, whereas in reality the evolutionary challenge for your system may be to extend the number of client platforms from which users can access the system.

Focusing on the wrong things is a problem throughout architectural design. Focusing on the wrong evolutionary dimensions can result in an architecture that is more complex and expensive to build than simpler alternatives and yet still is not particularly easy to change when needed.

RISK REDUCTION

- If you decide to build in support for system change, do so only after working through enough solid analysis to be confident that you are focusing on the right change dimensions.

Changes That Never Happen

Myriad possible changes could credibly be made to any system. You can't realistically design an architecture that allows for them all, certainly not one that can also be delivered in a cost-effective and timely way with an acceptable level of risk. Any architecture that allows for *all* possible changes would be too complex and unwieldy to build. If you plan for evolution in your architectural design, you are explicitly or implicitly deciding to make some of the possible changes easier than others.

If you build in specific support for a certain type of change that is never actually needed, you end up with design "baggage" that has to be understood and accommodated by its developers until eventually someone is courageous enough to decide that the change is never going to happen and removes the support for it.

Providing support for any future change requires overhead in terms of design, implementation, and often runtime overhead, so supporting a number of changes that don't happen can be a major unnecessary cost for your system.

RISK REDUCTION
- Provide specific support for a type of change in your architecture only when you are confident it will be needed.

Impacts of Evolution on Critical Quality Properties

Building a system to support evolution is not without cost. In particular, highly flexible systems (such as the metamodel-based systems outlined earlier) can bring significant costs in terms of runtime efficiency and performance, as well as the more involved development process that their complexity implies. (Of course, this is not always the case, and a flexible system may actually be easier to tune for performance because it has a well-understood, flexible, modular structure that allows easy monitoring and analysis, varied deployment options, and so on.)

The danger with focusing too heavily on the goal of flexibility is that you could make a system that is very easy to change but fails to meet one or more fundamental quality properties such as performance or availability. Also, it is easy to create such a complex system that all of your energies end up focused on the flexibility problem, and you neglect other properties such as security or internationalization due to lack of time.

RISK REDUCTION
- Having decided on the support for evolution in your architecture, make sure that you maintain the balance between flexibility and the other important quality properties for your system.

- Use a process of continual architectural assessment (discussed in Chapter 14) to achieve this balance.

Overreliance on Specific Hardware or Software

While computers are fairly interchangeable nowadays, there are some cases where you might find yourself critically dependent on a specific hardware or software component. For example, you may install specialized network cards in your servers that implement security features in firmware for speed; you may build your system using a specialized library to perform complex calculations; or you may rely on features in a very specific version and configuration of the operating system or application package.

This approach can be very beneficial but can also be a barrier to change. If you have been forced to write your system in a particular way to deal with the idiosyncrasies of a specialized component, it is much harder to replace that component in the future because it is no longer available or has been superseded by something better or cheaper.

- Assess the use of specialized components in your architecture and ensure that the benefits they bring outweigh the barriers to change.
- Ensure that you are aware of vendor roadmaps and other factors that may limit the life of specialized components.
- Abstract your interfaces to specialized components so that you can interchange them without too much impact.

Lost Development Environments

We have already mentioned that the development (and test) environment is more likely to be lost than the deployment environment. In addition, development environments are often subject to independent change and evolution as development and support priorities and workload naturally change over time.

The problem with trying to re-create a development or test environment is that it often isn't clear exactly what is needed to do so.

- Do you require a specific version of a library, or will a later version be acceptable?
- Other than obvious tools like compilers, what other tools do you need to perform a complete build and release? For example, was a particular scripting language used, and, if so, do you need to install any extensions to it?

- Do any of the major development tools require any software patches? (A common example is the compiler, which may change behavior with certain patches applied.)
- Do you need a particular underlying operating system version or a specific model of a hardware component, or can you substitute them later with supposedly compatible versions?

In our experience, it is quite rare to find that the answers to these questions are known, let alone recorded.

RISK REDUCTION

- Whenever an external element is introduced to the development environment, record its name, version, and origin along with the reason for its inclusion. This doesn't need to be terribly formal; a text file checked into your configuration management system is sufficient.
- Toward the end of the construction phase, try to re-create your development environment in a completely separate location that you haven't used before, and use the information recorded earlier to build the environment. Build your system and run your tests. This process rapidly reveals any elements missing from your list, which you can add to save others (or perhaps yourself) the same problem in the future.
- Use hardware virtualization tools to preserve development environments, and keep spares of critical or hard-to-obtain hardware components.

Ad Hoc Release Management

When deploying to a test environment, it doesn't really matter if the process goes wrong because no one is seriously affected—some tests fail, people realize that deployment has failed and they have to redeploy, but system users are not affected. However, deployment beyond the test environment is much more serious, and any problems at best will be annoying for end users and administrators and at worst may threaten critical operations in the target organization. It is important to orchestrate and manage the release management process just as carefully as the process of building and testing the system.

Release management differs somewhat between turnkey and product development environments, with turnkey developers often being responsible for updating the actual production system, whereas product developers are responsible for creating an installable system for others to install. In reality, though, both of these types of release management can be complex and, if done badly, have a negative impact on important stakeholders (end users and system administrators, respectively).

RISK REDUCTION

- Invest in an automated release process to achieve reliability and repeatability. This will save effort for every release and will also help prevent problems caused by human error during the release process.

CHECKLISTS

Checklist for Requirements Capture

- Have you considered which evolutionary dimensions are most important for your system?
- Are you confident that you have done enough analysis to confirm that your prioritization of evolutionary dimensions is valid?
- Have you identified particular specific changes that will be required and the magnitude of each?
- Have you assessed the likelihood of each of your changes actually being needed?

Checklist for Architecture Definition

- Have you performed an architectural assessment to establish whether your architecture is sufficiently flexible to meet the evolutionary needs of your system?
- When change is likely, does your architectural design contain the change as far as possible?
- Have you considered choosing an inherently change-oriented architectural style? If so, have you assessed the costs of doing so?
- Have you traded off the costs of your support for evolution against the needs of the system as a whole? Are any critical quality properties negatively impacted by the design you have adopted?
- Have you designed the architecture to accommodate only those changes you are confident will be needed?
- Can you re-create your development and test environments reliably?
- Can you reliably and repeatedly build, test, and release your system, including the ability to roll back changes if they go wrong?
- Is your chosen evolutionary approach the cheapest and least risky option of delivering the initial system and the future evolution required?

FURTHER READING

A systematic approach to dealing with change at the implementation level by using a set of well-defined transformations known as refactorings is described in Fowler et al. [FOWL99]. A number of architectural styles are described in Buschmann et al. [BUSC96], including a metamodel-based system style called Reflection, which is particularly amenable to certain types of change.

There isn't much written material on evolution aimed at the architect specifically; however, Bass et al. [BASS03] does include a set of tactics to help achieve architectural modifiability. These tactics are fairly generic but suggest a lot of useful things to consider for your architecture. (The book also provides similar sets of tactics for availability, performance, security, testability, and usability.) When designing APIs, [TULA08] provides a lot of good advice, as does [HENN07] and Joshua Bloch's presentation "How to Design a Good API and Why It Matters," which is easy to find via a Web search. A good resource on product management and ownership in the context of the Scrum method can be found in [PICH10].

In contrast, there are quite a number of books on software design patterns, many of which address change. Some useful ones to start with are Gamma et al. [GAMM95] and Coplien et al. [PLOP95–99, PLOP06]. For a good explanation of the dependency injection pattern, see [FOWL04].

Support for controlled variation and evolution is a major concern of software product-line architecture, and the concept of the variation point, which we mentioned earlier, is borrowed from the techniques used in this discipline. Two books [BASS03, BOSC00] provide introductions to creating software architectures for product lines as well as references to further reading in the area.

One SEI-sponsored book [CLEM02] is a practical guide to performing architectural evaluation including evaluating systems for modifiability, and another SEI book [SEAC03] presents an architecture-based evolution process for modernizing older systems.

Deferring the need to pay for change until it is actually needed is a core principle of the Extreme Programming approach. The original reference for Extreme Programming is Kent Beck's book [BECK00].

29
OTHER PERSPECTIVES

So far, we have defined some important perspectives—Security, Performance and Scalability, Availability and Resilience, and Evolution—in reasonably full detail. We have found the concerns addressed by these perspectives to be relevant to most if not all information systems. If you do not apply these perspectives to your architectural views, you run a serious risk of delivering systems that do not meet the explicit or implicit needs of your stakeholders: They may expose sensitive data to malicious attackers; they may perform poorly under heavy load; they may suffer from frequent and expensive interruptions in service; or they may be very difficult to change.

You may also need to consider a number of other perspectives when designing your architecture. We say "may" for several reasons.

- Not all of these other perspectives are relevant to all situations. For example, a system that operates only in one country is probably unaffected by the Internationalization perspective.
- They may have a less significant impact on the architecture. For example, the concerns of the Usability perspective may not be that relevant to a server-based EAI or data movement system, which is only minimally exposed to users (although the usability needs of system administrators should not be ignored).
- They may relate to less highly visible system properties. A system operating in a lightly regulated business area, for example, is minimally affected by the concerns of the Regulation perspective.

Therefore, in this chapter we define the following *secondary* perspectives and for each one present a subset of the information we provided for the primary ones earlier in Part IV.

- *The Accessibility perspective* ensures that people with disabilities can use the system.

- *The Development Resource perspective* ensures that the system can be built, deployed, and operated within known constraints related to people, budget, time, and materials.

- *The Internationalization perspective* ensures the system's independence from any particular language, country, or cultural group.

- *The Location perspective* ensures that the system can overcome problems brought about by the absolute location of its elements and the distances between them.

- *The Regulation perspective* ensures that the system conforms to local and international laws, quasi-legal regulations, company policies, and other rules and standards.

- *The Usability perspective* ensures that the people who interact with the system can work effectively.

Given that you have only finite time—and probably not very much of that—to develop your AD, you will need to decide which of these perspectives are most relevant to you and how much time you want to spend applying them to your views.

THE ACCESSIBILITY PERSPECTIVE

Desired Quality	The ability of the system to be used by people with disabilities
Applicability	Any system that may be used or operated by people with disabilities or may be subject to legislation regarding disabilities
Concerns	Types of disability, functional availability, and disability regulation
Activities	Identification of system touch points, device independence, and content equivalence
Architectural Tactics	High-contrast visual interfaces, assistive technologies, specialist input devices, and voice recognition
Problems and Pitfalls	Ignoring these needs until too late, lack of knowledge about regulation and legislation, and lack of knowledge about suitable solutions

In recent years, enlightened corporations have come to recognize the contributions that disabled people can make, and many have high-profile programs to encourage their active participation in business operations. Furthermore, many countries have passed legislation that prohibits discrimination against people with disabilities and obliges employers to provide facilities suitable to their needs.

For systems directly exposed to customers (e.g., Internet- or mobile-communications-based systems, public kiosks, or automated teller machines), failing to address the needs of the disabled population can significantly reduce the systems' reach and effectiveness, in addition to reflecting unfavorably on the organization in the eyes of the public.

Accessibility should take into account not only the direct users of the system—that is those sitting at terminals—but the indirect users as well. For example, a financial system may need to provide bank statements in Braille for blind customers.

Consideration of disability aside, addressing accessibility concerns brings benefits in many cases by making systems more usable and efficient in their operation.

It is also important to assess architectures for compliance with legislative requirements and internal standards, as we discuss under the Regulation perspective.

Applicability to Views

Table 29–1 shows how the Accessibility perspective affects each of the views we discussed in Part III.

TABLE 29–1 APPLICABILITY OF THE ACCESSIBILITY PERSPECTIVE TO THE SEVEN VIEWS

View	Applicability
Context	There may be a requirement for the system to interface with specialist devices for use by people with disabilities, such as voice-controlled input devices.
Functional	In theory, the functional structure should not really be affected by accessibility considerations—all functions should be available to disabled users in exactly the same way they are to able-bodied users. In practice, functional compromises may need to be made in some cases. It is particularly important that presentation services be separated from functional components.
Information	The information structure is unlikely to be significantly affected, although it may be necessary, for example, to maintain information about disabilities of customers and/or users.
Concurrency	The concurrency structure of the system is unlikely to impact its accessibility, so the impact on this view is minimal.
Development	The Development view needs to raise awareness that accessibility issues are important. And, of course, you may need to accommodate disabled developers, too.

Continued on next page

TABLE 29–1 APPLICABILITY OF THE ACCESSIBILITY PERSPECTIVE TO THE SEVEN VIEWS *(CONTINUED)*

View	Applicability
Deployment	The deployment environment is likely to be the most affected by this perspective. Special hardware (described in this section) may be needed to support disabled users.
Operational	The Operational view may have to take into account the needs of disabled users requiring support or the needs of disabled support staff themselves.

Concerns

Your system may need to be usable by people with a range of disabilities:

- People who are blind or partially sighted, who cannot read small print or differentiate items on low-contrast displays
- People who are color-blind (this affects up to 10% of the male population)
- People who are totally deaf or hearing-impaired
- People who have difficulty processing information
- People with low levels of literacy or numeracy

Ideally, all functionality should be available to all users regardless of their level of ability. When this is not the case, you should clearly identify the limitations and obtain stakeholder agreement.

Many countries have legal requirements with regard to disability, such as the Americans with Disabilities Act in the United States and the Disability Discrimination Act in the United Kingdom, and at a minimum you should always assess your systems against these. A number of standards, guidelines, and best-practice guides are also available, against which you can assess your architecture. (For more information, see the Further Reading section for this perspective.)

You should be aware of the implications of regulations before you begin architecture definition. It is much easier to design accessibility features into the architecture from the outset than to retrofit them at the end. Specialized knowledge may be required, and you should not be afraid to consult with experts when necessary.

Activities: Applying the Accessibility Perspective

A simple process follows.

- Identify the types of disabilities of users who may need to interact with your system (blind, deaf, movement-impaired, and so on).

- Identify all places where disabled users may interact with the system (*touch points*).
- Use your stakeholders to help identify all relevant regulations and specific concerns related to accessibility.
- At a high level, agree on requirements for the intersection of each type of user with each of the key touch points.
- Develop an architectural approach and, where appropriate, a more detailed solution that meets the requirements.
- Bench-test the solution against the requirements, using prototypes where appropriate.

Architectural Tactics

Hardware and software components that have been designed to meet the needs of disabled users are known as *assistive technologies*. Examples of these include the following.

- Visual interfaces can be made available in *high-contrast, low-resolution* versions. For a Web interface, for example, this can be as simple as providing a different CSS style sheet for use by visually impaired users.
- A *Braille display* is a mechanical device that dynamically raises and lowers dots in a Braille grid. Such devices typically display anything from one character to a whole line at a time.
- A *screen reader* is an adjunct to a visual display that reads the contents of the screen aloud to visually impaired users.
- A *screen magnifier* enlarges a portion of a screen so that users with partial vision can see it more easily.
- A *voice recognition system* provides an alternative to keyboard or mouse data entry by accepting commands spoken by the user.
- *Internet chat* technologies (e.g., Web-based help desks) allow people such as those who are deaf to communicate without using a telephone.
- Many types of specialist input devices are available for mobility-impaired users.

Designing presentation elements to be device-independent is generally a good practice and brings particular benefits when there is a need to support access by disabled users.

Presentation should not rely on one interface capability to convey meaning but should provide alternatives wherever possible. For example, screens and printouts should not rely solely on color or pictures to emphasize elements of text because they may not stand out to color-blind or partially sighted users or those using display devices that do not render color. Instead, use the technique of *content equivalence*—in other words, render content in different ways that convey the same meaning. For example, if a screen uses color to highlight incorrect input, it could also use an annotated arrow that points to the incorrect data.

Similarly, interaction should not rely on a single mechanism but should support alternatives where possible—for example, you could make a graphical user interface operable by both mouse and keyboard.

When interactions involve a number of separate steps or are otherwise complex, aim for navigational simplicity. Screens should be clear in their use, consistent, and well designed. Avoid excessive use of special effects, such as blinking text or sounds, as these may not be perceived by some disabled users.

Problems and Pitfalls

Here are some common pitfalls to keep in mind for the Accessibility perspective.

- *Failure to think about how to address these issues until it's too late*: This can put you at risk of noncompliance with legislation or with the requirements of some key stakeholders.
- *Lack of knowledge about regulations and legislation*: You should consult experts if you are at all unsure.
- *Lack of knowledge about suitable solutions*: If you're unfamiliar with assistive technologies, get advice from specialist stakeholders.

Checklists

CHECKLIST FOR REQUIREMENTS CAPTURE

- Have you identified and obtained stakeholder approval of the extent to which the system must support the needs of disabled users?
- Have you provided for the needs of indirect disabled users, such as customers who need paperwork provided in Braille format?
- Have you identified the disability legislation that affects the system and assessed the system against it?
- Have you ensured that the system meets any internal accessibility standards?
- Have you considered all points at which the system has any human interaction? For example, have you considered operational management and monitoring of the system, or printed forms that are sent to customers to be filled in?

CHECKLIST FOR ARCHITECTURE DEFINITION

- How confident are you that your architectural assumptions are correct? When you are not, are mitigating activities in place (such as a proof-of-concept)?
- Do the interactive elements of your architecture sufficiently separate presentation and content to meet the system's accessibility objectives?
- Are the interfaces between components (particularly those leading in and out of presentation devices) sufficiently generic to be able to take on board new devices without (much) rework?
- Does the architecture allow for presentation alternatives to convey meaning (e.g., text, pictures, and/or sound in a user interface)?
- Are standards for user interface design emphasize simplicity, consistency, and clarity in place? Does the architecture adhere to them?

Further Reading

Many of the references listed later under the Usability perspective also touch on Accessibility.

A number of Web sites are devoted to accessibility. Your best starting point is the Web Accessibility Initiative of the World Wide Web Consortium at www.w3.org/WAI. Also, most hardware and software vendors run disability portals, for example, Microsoft (www.microsoft.com/enable/), IBM (www.ibm.com/able/), and Google (www.google.com/accessibility/). Many governments also maintain online resources that provide best-practice guidelines and explanations of accessibility legislation (such as the www.disabilityinfo.gov site in the United States and the www.disability.gov.uk site in the United Kingdom).

You can assess Web sites for their conformance to accessibility best practices by using online tools such as WAVE (the Web Accessibility Evaluation Tool, maintained by WebAIM at http://wave.webaim.org/).

THE DEVELOPMENT RESOURCE PERSPECTIVE

Desired Quality	The ability of the system to be designed, built, deployed, and operated within known constraints related to people, budget, time, and materials
Applicability	Any system for which development time is limited, technical skills for development or operations are hard to find, or unusual or unfamiliar hardware or software is required

Continued on next page

Concerns	Time constraints, cost constraints, required skill sets, available resources, budgets, and external dependencies
Activities	Cost estimation, development time estimation, development planning, dependency management, scoping, prototyping, and expectation management
Architectural Tactics	Incremental and iterative development, expectation management, descoping, prototyping and piloting, and fitness for purpose
Problems and Pitfalls	Overly ambitious timescales, failure to consider lead times, failure to consider physical constraints, underbudgeting, failure to provide staff training and consider familiarization needs, insufficient resource allocation for testing and rollout, insufficient time for likely rework, overallocation of staff, and difficulty getting access to knowledgeable business stakeholders

In this context, a development resource may be a person, a piece of hardware or software, a building, a timescale, or money. (Note that runtime computing resources are a slightly different topic, which we discuss as part of the Performance and Scalability perspective in Chapter 26.)

All software projects are primarily constrained by time and cost. IT budgets are never unlimited, and although technology capabilities improve from year to year, the costs of building, deployment, and support seem to increase as well. Today's rapidly changing business environments impose substantial pressures to deliver flexible systems ever more quickly. There may even be immovable timescale constraints, such as the arrival of new legislation, new regulations, or a new millennium. (At least that last one is unlikely to recur for another thousand years or so!)

You may think it odd or inappropriate that an architect should get involved in things like time and money. Certainly as an architect, none of these problems are directly yours to solve. However, they all impose constraints on your architectural choices. For example, if you have to wait a month before trained developers are available, you will have less time to build the system and less scope for incorporating complex features. If the budget will not stretch to a mainframe, there is little point in considering it as an architectural candidate. If the data center is full, a server farm is not an option unless space can be found elsewhere.

Applicability to Views

Table 29–2 shows how the Development Resource perspective affects each of the views we discussed in Part III.

TABLE 29-2 APPLICABILITY OF THE DEVELOPMENT RESOURCE PERSPECTIVE TO THE SEVEN VIEWS

View	Applicability
Context	Resource constraints such as short timescales or limitations on available skills may impose constraints on system scope. You may also be dependent on constraints in the development teams for systems that you interact with or interface technologies you need to use.
Functional	Resource constraints often impose restrictions on functionality and on functional qualities such as generality.
Information	Complex or particularly sophisticated information models may require a large staff of specialists to implement; lack of such staff may impose restrictions on your architectural options.
Concurrency	Concurrent architectures are often complex to implement, and you will need to consider the development and testing time and the skills of your developers when designing your architecture.
Development	Cost constraints may limit the number of separate development and test environments available to you, so you may need to formulate strategies for sharing these.
Deployment	Again, cost constraints may limit your options for deployment, particularly where redundancy and resilience are concerned.
Operational	You need to be aware of the cost implications of your proposed operational and support architecture.

Concerns

The constraints of people, budget, time, and materials lead to a number of more specific concerns.

- Appropriately skilled people are always a key resource constraint. If your architecture makes use of a technology unfamiliar to your developers, you will need to provide a large-scale retraining exercise.

- You should also consider the impact of your architecture on the existing support community. Retraining or recruitment may be necessary, and you may need to provide richer tools for operational management, analysis, and repair.

- Your users may need training in new technologies and new applications. This is particularly significant in large-scale rollouts of new or significantly modified applications. If users are unfamiliar with the software they will be using, you may want to put extra effort into usability.

- Deployment of new applications may necessitate large-scale infrastructure upgrades that are not immediately obvious to you. For example, a new application may require more memory than the standard PC desktop provides or more bandwidth than the corporate network can handle. In organizations with a large number of geographically distributed users, this sort of massive cost can kill a project.

- On large-scale programs, you should consider the impact on office space. It may be necessary to quickly commission space to house the development team, the support team, a test center, or the users. Extra data center space may be needed to store a new server farm or large amounts of shared disk storage.

- You should be aware of dependencies between development activities and of the overall critical path (the sequence of activities that, if a delay occurs to any of them, will delay the entire project). Here are some examples.
  - You may have mandated a hardware platform that has a long lead time for procurement and deployment, such as a mainframe computer or specialized hardware built to order.
  - You may be dependent on hardware, software, or services delivered by a third-party supplier.
  - There may be lead times for recruiting and/or training specialized personnel.
  - A large-scale rollout may have to align with other activities.

Consideration of these aspects provides an essential reality check that the system you are proposing will ever see the light of day. You may design the most flawless, performant, and extensible architecture possible, but if building it would take many years or hundreds of programmers, it will probably never get off the drawing board.

Another practical concern is that you may find it hard to get access to stakeholders with specialized business knowledge to help you ensure that the system you design is fit for purpose and to act as representatives of or proxies for your end-user customers. While this may not affect your eventual design, it is bound to elongate the process of requirements validation and architectural definition and will also make it difficult to achieve any real degree of agility in your development processes.

Activities: Applying the Development Resource Perspective

As you develop your architecture, regularly review the development resources likely to be required to realize it. Feed these findings back to the project managers as early as possible—particularly if new or unexpected resources are needed (e.g., specific design skills with a new technology or office space that isn't already available).

Your most important activity here is to not forget anything. If you follow the processes we describe in this book—identifying and engaging stakeholders, creating views, and applying perspectives to these views—you have a much better chance of success.

It may be appropriate to support any controversial architectural decisions with a risk analysis. Discussion of such a risk analysis is outside the scope of this book (see the Further Reading section for this perspective).

Architectural Tactics

Many traditional software engineering techniques, such as component-based development, software reuse, and the use of off-the-shelf software libraries, can contribute to development efficiencies.

An iterative approach to the definition and construction of your system, such as that espoused by the Rational Unified Process (RUP) or all of the mainstream agile approaches, can help mitigate risk and uncertainty and can deliver key benefits early as part of a phased development. In practice, for complex developments, an iterative approach (as opposed to a big bang approach) seems to be the only one that has any chance of success.

Perhaps the most important technique is *expectation management*. Because of the relative immaturity of our profession, many software development projects go over schedule and/or budget, or they fail to deliver all of their promised improvement. It is essential that you communicate clearly with your stakeholders about what will be delivered to them and when and that you obtain their agreement to any compromises you have to make. You might want to present the quality triangle (see Chapter 2) to your stakeholders to help explain the slogan "Quality, speed, cost—pick two!"

Some specific techniques that may be relevant include the following.

- *Descoping*: Reduce the functional scope, or relax some of the required system characteristics such as flexibility or scalability, to reduce development times.
- *Prototyping or piloting*: These can help reduce risk (although they also may set an expectation that the system is more complete than it actually is).
- *Fitness for purpose*: Try not to be tempted to develop a system that is more sophisticated, complex, or flexible than the users actually need. If they want something quick and cheap, that is what you should deliver.

Problems and Pitfalls

In our experience, resource constraints are one of the biggest causes of software project delays or failure. Many factors lead to projects being underresourced or optimistically planned. As an architect, you can draw on your own experience to identify plans that are unlikely to succeed and suggest alternative strategies for them.

In addition to straightforward underbudgeting, keep in mind some other common pitfalls:

- Overly ambitious timescales
- Failure to consider lead times
- Failure to consider physical constraints such as space, power, furniture, and so on
- Failure to provide staff training and consider familiarization needs
- Insufficient time and resources for testing, quality assurance, and rollout
- Insufficient time for rework required due to development mistakes, misunderstood requirements, and unexpected change
- Overallocation of staff, for example, allocating staff to a project five days per week when, realistically, a maximum of about four days of productive work is possible each week
- Difficulty in getting access to stakeholders with the right specialist business knowledge

Checklists

CHECKLIST FOR REQUIREMENTS CAPTURE

- Have you understood the project's key constraints in terms of time and budget, as well as the room for maneuvering if your architecture mandates extra resources?
- Have you considered physical constraints such as existing capacity, office space, and availability of personnel?
- Have you balanced the benefits of new or unfamiliar technologies against the costs and risks of deploying them?
- Have you understood which compromises are more likely to be accepted where resource constraints necessitate this? To what extent would stakeholders consider limiting scope, functionality, or even quality? Are you sufficiently confident that savings would be realized by making such compromises?
- To what extent is there scope for deferring features until future releases of software?
- Do you understand which functional and operational principles absolutely cannot be compromised, no matter what the resource impact? (Examples might include quality, security, user/customer experience, regulatory compliance, and richness of features.)

CHECKLIST FOR ARCHITECTURE DEFINITION

- To what extent did you base your architecture on technologies already familiar to your developer community?
- To what extent did you base your architecture on proven, established technologies as opposed to innovative ones?
- Have you assessed your architecture against existing infrastructure capabilities (desktop platforms, network infrastructure, and so on) to see whether hardware or software upgrades are required?
- Have you included in plans the costs of additional infrastructures for disaster recovery, support, acceptance, and training?
- When new or unfamiliar technologies are used, have you considered the impacts of staff training and support?
- Is your architecture simple enough to be built and supported by development/operations staff who have only recently been trained?

Further Reading

A wealth of material is available on managing projects and risk. The classic text is [BROO95], in which Fred Brooks coined his famous law of software engineering which says that "adding manpower to a late software project makes it later." Hall [HALL98] is a comprehensive guide to identifying and managing risk on complex projects in a structured way. McConnell [MCCO97] is a software project management handbook that focuses on delivering projects on time and within budget. There are many, many books on agile project management, and new ones appear all the time, but a representative group of titles on the popular Scrum approach are [SCHW01] and [COHN09]; [PICH10] provides an interesting perspective, looking at agile development from the product owner's point of view. For guidance on the strengths and weaknesses of agile and plan-driven development, and how to find middle ground between their extremes, [BOEH03] provides a balanced view.

THE INTERNATIONALIZATION PERSPECTIVE

Desired Quality	The ability of the system to be independent from any particular language, country, or cultural group
Applicability	Any system that may need to be accessed by users or operational staff from different cultures or parts of the world, or in multiple languages, either now or in the future

Continued on next page

Concerns	Character sets, text presentation and orientation, specific language needs, cultural norms, automatic translation, currency conversions and exchange rates, and cultural neutrality
Activities	Identification of system touch points, identification of regions of concern, internationalization of code, and localization of resources
Architectural Tactics	Separation of presentation and content, use of message catalogs, system-wide use of suitable character sets (e.g., Unicode), specialized display and presentation hardware, and currency conversion mechanisms
Problems and Pitfalls	Platforms not available in required locales, initial consideration of similar languages only, internationalization performed late in the development process, incompatibilities between locales on servers, insufficient consideration of currency exchange

No longer can we assume that the *lingua franca* of generally available IT systems is English. Even if the users of the system speak English, the customers they are dealing with may not; their names may require support for non-English or non-Western alphabets; and if the system uses the Internet, it may be directly exposed to customers from any part of the world.

The Internationalization perspective is important, therefore, for any system that will have users who speak different languages or come from different countries. If systems are aimed at a specific locale with no plans to move them into a wider area, this perspective has limited relevance.

Because of its length, you may sometimes see the word *internationalization* abbreviated as *I18N*. A related term is *localization* (sometimes abbreviated as *L10N*), which refers to the process of performing the specific work required to use an already internationalized system in a particular locale (e.g., the translation of system messages).

Applicability to Views

Table 29–3 shows how the Internationalization perspective affects each of the views we discussed in Part III.

TABLE 29-3 APPLICABILITY OF THE INTERNATIONALIZATION PERSPECTIVE TO THE SEVEN VIEW

View	Applicability
Context	Specialist display and data entry hardware may be required for non-Western languages.

Continued on next page

TABLE 29-3 APPLICABILITY OF THE INTERNATIONALIZATION PERSPECTIVE TO THE SEVEN VIEW *(CONTINUED)*

View	Applicability
Functional	The functional structure may need to reflect how presentation is separated from content. General functionality should be independent of location.
Information	The Information view defines which stored information needs to be internationalized and how this will be achieved. If data needs to be stored or presented in different units of measurement, you may need to define strategies to do this to an appropriate level of precision. If currency conversion is involved, you will need to identify a source of appropriate exchange rates and define how you will get access to this data.
Concurrency	This perspective has minimal impact on the Concurrency view.
Development	The Development view will need to reflect the impact of these factors on the development environment. For example, internationalized test data may be required, or early access may be needed to specialized devices. User-visible messages must be populated into catalogs.
Deployment	The deployment environment may need to take into consideration such items as internationalized input and presentation devices. Don't forget that your underlying software and hardware platforms need to support the languages you're working with—there is little point in supporting Urdu if your operating system or relational database management system doesn't support it. Similarly, the underlying platform needs to be internationalized (e.g., to have the ability to store Unicode in data stores).
Operational	The Operational view may need to consider what functionality is provided to support the maintenance and administration of localized information and services, and how support will be provided to different locations.

Concerns

This perspective addresses the system's support for the following concerns.

- *Multiple character sets*: A character set is a mapping from a standard set of characters to a list of byte values. Western character sets such as ASCII or EBCDIC encode each letter in a single byte, while more complex character sets such as Kanji (Japanese) require more than one byte per character. Unicode is a two-byte character set that attempts to encapsulate all modern written languages.

- *Differently oriented text presentation* (horizontal, vertical, left to right, right to left): Some non-European languages such as Urdu are written right to left, for example.

- *Language-specific concerns*, such as:
  - Pictographic languages (e.g., Chinese, Japanese), which represent words using pictures or symbols rather than a limited alphabet
  - Use of different languages to present static information (e.g., screen prompts, report headings and titles, error messages, online help and reference documentation, printed documentation such as user manuals and training materials)
  - Different spelling within the same broad language (e.g., British versus American English)
  - Different usage, meaning, or significance of the same words or phrases in different cultures
- *Different cultural norms*, such as:
  - Different units of measurement (metric, imperial, and so on) and automatic conversion of data between these, while maintaining suitable precision
  - Different date, time, and currency display and data entry formats
  - Different output sizes (paper, screens, and so on)
- *Financial and political differences*, particularly different currencies (with varying exchange rates).
- The *automatic translation* of dynamic information for display or printing.
- *Cultural neutrality*, in other words, avoiding concepts that certain groups understand but others do not. This is most difficult to define or measure and is particularly important when systems rely heavily on metaphors or have highly graphical or abstract presentations.

You should consider all of the system's devices (screens, printers, keyboards, and so on) when addressing these concerns.

Activities: Applying the Internationalization Perspective

A simple process follows.

- Identify all places where a person interacts with the system (the touch points).
- Identify the scope of services and information that need to be internationalized at each of these touch points.
- Identify the system's regions of concern (the types of countries and locales from which the system can be touched and the specific set of locales if available).
- Develop an architectural approach and, where appropriate, a more detailed solution that meets these requirements.
- Bench-test the solution against the requirements.

Architectural Tactics

Successful internationalization depends on a clear separation of presentation and content. Screens can be created on the fly with titles, headings, and prompts pulled from library text in the appropriate language.

In many systems, information and error messages are held in dynamic message databases, with variable parameters inserted at runtime. Even if you are not concerned with internationalization, this useful technique gives you much greater flexibility over message content.

To be compatible with the widest range of character sets, you should use a multibyte character set such as Unicode. Note, however, that many rendering devices do not support this fully, and it has sizing implications for the storage of large amounts of text data.

You may need to make use of specialized display and presentation hardware, such as Kanji keyboards for the entry of Japanese text.

If your system needs to deal with different currencies, you will need to provide mechanisms to convert from one to another, automatically or on user request, and will need a source of up-to-date exchange rates (current and possibly historical as well). You may need to store money values in more than one currency rather than calculate them when needed.

Problems and Pitfalls

Here are some common pitfalls to keep in mind for the Internationalization perspective.

- Unavailability of the underlying platform in the correct locale.
- Consideration of only languages similar to your own when planning internationalization (e.g., forgetting about Asian languages and investigating just Western ones or vice versa).
- Attempts to internationalize the system late in the development cycle. This can be very expensive and disruptive. You don't need to do all the localization initially, but it's important to build in the internationalization mechanisms early.
- Incompatibilities between different locales on servers (e.g., some platforms may not support both Chinese and Japanese on the same server).
- Insufficient consideration given to currency conversion (e.g., what exchange rates to use, where to obtain up-to-date rates, failure to store historical rates or historical money values).

Checklists

CHECKLIST FOR REQUIREMENTS CAPTURE

- Have you agreed with stakeholders on the extent to which systems must be operable in different languages or countries, either now or in the future?

- Have you considered all points at which the system has any human interaction? For example, have you considered operational management and monitoring of the system or printed forms sent to customers to be filled in?

- Have you identified whether there is a requirement for non-Western character sets such as Kanji, which have special requirements for entry and presentation of data?

- Does your analysis consider all types of interaction—screens, keyboards, printed reports, and so on?

- If the system needs to convert between different units of measurement, have you considered how this will be done while retaining suitable data precision?

CHECKLIST FOR ARCHITECTURE DEFINITION

- How confident are you that the architecture will meet all the requirements? When you are not, are mitigating activities in place (such as a proof-of-concept)?

- Do the interactive elements of your architecture sufficiently separate presentation and content to meet the system's internationalization objectives?

- If non-Western character sets such as Kanji must be supported, do your input and output devices accommodate these?

- If standard text must be presented in multiple languages, have you designed facilities for maintaining such information?

- Does your system sizing take into consideration the extra capacity (disk storage, network bandwidth, and so on) required for multibyte character sets?

Further Reading

Luong et al. [LUON95] is a thorough explanation of the process required to create internationalized software by a team that worked together at Borland, internationalizing a number of products including C++ and dBase. Microsoft published a comprehensive guide to developing internationalized applications on Microsoft's operating systems [INTE02]. Lund [LUND09] is the definitive book on handling Chinese, Korean, Japanese, and Vietnamese data.

THE LOCATION PERSPECTIVE

Desired Quality	The ability of the system to overcome problems brought about by the absolute location of its elements and the distances between them
Applicability	Any system whose elements (or other systems with which it interacts) are or may be physically far from one another
Concerns	Time zones of operation, network link characteristics, resiliency to link failures, wide-area interoperability, high-volume operations, intercountry concerns (political, commercial, and legal), use of the public Internet, and physical variations between locations
Activities	Geographical mapping, estimation of link quality, estimation of latency, benchmarking, and modeling of geographical characteristics
Architectural Tactics	Avoidance of widely distributed transactions, architectural plans for wide-area link failure, and allowance for offline operation
Problems and Pitfalls	Invalid (wide-area) network assumptions; assumption of single-point administration; assumption of one primary time zone; assumption of end-to-end security; assumption of an overnight batch period; failure to consider political, commercial, or legal differences; assumption that public networks are high-bandwidth, low-latency, and highly available; and assumption of a standard physical environment

The Location perspective addresses the problems that arise when systems or system elements are physically distant from one another. If all elements are located in the same place, you can usually disregard this perspective.

Be aware, however, that the physical separation of elements may not always be immediately obvious. For example, many systems have disaster recovery sites that are physically distant from the main operational site or may rely on links to external, distant systems. Such an architecture presents a number of challenges that you should address through this perspective.

Applicability to Views

Table 29-4 shows how the Location perspective affects each of the views we discussed in Part III.

TABLE 29–4 Applicability of the Location Perspective to the Seven Views

View	Applicability
Context	It may be useful to identify the location of external components in the Context view, to highlight the risk of poor availability or network latency.
Functional	The Functional view is often presented independently of real-world location concerns; typically, these are modeled in the Deployment view.
Information	If data is highly distributed, the Information view should describe how information is kept synchronized, what update latencies are expected, how temporary discrepancies are handled, and how information is transferred between locations.
Concurrency	Concurrent processing across highly distributed parts of the system is likely to be problematic for reliability and latency reasons. The concurrency approach chosen may need to change in order to accommodate location realities.
Development	If system development is spread over multiple locations, the Development view needs to explain how software will be managed, integrated, and tested.
Deployment	The Deployment view must consider how systems are physically rolled out to disparate locations in a controlled, synchronized way and what is needed in order to test and accept this rollout. Significant issues such as latency, lead times, and costs are often associated with the selection and rollout of wide-area networks.
Operational	The Operational view needs to consider how widely distributed systems are monitored, managed, and repaired.

Concerns

The Location perspective addresses a number of concerns.

- If system operation is time-dependent (as virtually all systems are), you must consider the impact on its operation of the different time zones and the overlapping of the operational day in different parts of the world. For example, when it is afternoon in London, it is late evening in Sydney and early morning in New York. The system may need to be able to operate simultaneously in online mode and in overnight mode.

- If elements are geographically very distant but need to communicate efficiently and seamlessly, wide-area network bandwidth, latency, reliability, and resilience become important.

- If elements are distant, connectivity is typically less reliable than when they are nearby. The architecture may need to accommodate situations where wide-area connectivity has been lost for a time, but a (possibly degraded) service must continue to be provided.

- If communications are required over heterogeneous networks between elements in different countries, there may be issues related to compatibility and interoperability of protocols.

- If there is a need to perform high-volume operations remotely over the wide-area network, such as distributed backups or distributed software updates, you must consider the bandwidth and response implications of these.

- You may need to address the political, commercial, and legal implications of your location. For example, systems may be subject to different laws and regulations (which you can also address in the Regulation perspective), taxation regimes, working practices, and so on.

- If your architecture relies on the Internet for some of its interactions, particularly mobile Internet, you can no longer assume you have high-bandwidth, low-latency, highly available connectivity for these components, and you should develop architectural strategies to mitigate this.

- The system may even need to accommodate differences in the physical characteristics of different locations, such as the type or reliability of electrical supply, the availability of telecommunication links, or even extremes of temperature or climate.

Activities: Applying the Location Perspective

A simple process follows.

- Map each physical component to a geographical location.

- Consider the physical distance and the communications infrastructure between each of these components.

- Capture and obtain agreement on operational requirements (response, latency, reliability, and so on) over each of these interfaces.

- Take into account any political, commercial, or legal implications. (We further discuss legal implications in the section on the Regulation perspective later in this chapter).

- Develop an architectural approach and, where appropriate, a more detailed solution that meets these requirements.

- If a system's reach crosses national boundaries, you may want to create some models.

  - You can model the 24-hour day across the time zones in the countries of operation and consider what the system will be doing while it is daytime in one zone and nighttime in another. If you need downtime for overnight batch processing, for example, how will this be accommodated if the system has to provide uninterrupted service?

- You can create a geographical model of system location to help understand the impact of long distances on information flows, multistep processes, and so on. Remember that, in general, the further dispersed the end points are, the worse your latency and reliability will be.
  - Bench-test the solution against requirements.

Architectural Tactics

You should generally avoid transactions that rely on the availability of widely distributed elements. However, this is not always possible, particularly in service-based architectures. In such cases, you can provide resilience in a number of ways. (Note that this area is very complicated and specialized, and we can only skim the surface in this book.)

The simplest approach is to minimize or remove the possibility of network failure by providing standby routes to use if the main route goes down. Modern protocols, particularly IP, provide this rerouting automatically, but your architecture still needs to include the standby network hardware and sufficient emergency bandwidth. When this isn't automated, you also need to consider the processes whereby traffic reroutes from one pipe to another. Essentially, in this model, the network is as much a part of the disaster recovery infrastructure as the computers are and must be designed to support this.

A more sophisticated solution is to provide the ability to work in offline mode. This may be an essential feature if resilient communications cannot be guaranteed, or if you use the Internet as part of your overall network architecture (for example, if your customers are using a Web browser to access your services).

EXAMPLE Banks and other types of retail financial institutions typically operate numerous widely distributed small branches. Although these branches may be semiautonomous, many processes require access to centrally located systems (in the data center or head office).

Financial transactions, for example, may need to be centrally authorized to reduce the risk of fraud; customer or account data may be managed on a central server to make it universally available; regulatory requirements may mandate that information be collated centrally and passed on to the relevant authorities.

The volume of traffic from any one local branch to the central site, however, is probably fairly small. It is not cost-effective, therefore, to use high-bandwidth resilient communications, and typically a solution such as ISDN or even dial-up will be deployed.

However, if communications are interrupted for any reason, the branches must be able to continue operations, possibly with a degraded level of service. If branches cannot accept financial transactions, the bank will soon go out of business.

In such a scenario, it is essential that local systems be able to operate offline, in other words, without connectivity to central servers. Typically this solution will "stack up" transactions to be applied when connectivity is restored.

Problems and Pitfalls

Here are some common pitfalls to keep in mind for the Location perspective:

- Assuming that networks are infinitely fast and have infinite capacity, zero latency, and 100% reliability
- Assuming that one administrator will provide management and support, rather than a team of administrators spread across multiple locations, time zones, and languages
- Assuming a single time zone for all significant operations
- Assuming that the entire end-to-end network is secure, when in reality much of it may run over uncontrolled third-party equipment
- Assuming the availability of an overnight batch period of operation for a system that has worldwide reach
- Failing to investigate (e.g., through expert local advice) the political, legal, and commercial environments of geographical areas unfamiliar to you
- Assuming that public networks are always high-bandwidth, low-latency, and highly available
- Assuming that the physical environment (temperature, physical security, power supply, networking availability, and so on) will match that of the primary site

Checklists

CHECKLIST FOR REQUIREMENTS CAPTURE

- Have you understood and agreed on the physical location of each component of the architecture?

- Do you understand the requirements for throughput, response time, availability, and resilience for all connections between geographically distributed components?

- Are the performance and reliability expectations of the wide-area network realistic and achievable within the time and budget constraints and the capabilities of the available network infrastructures?

- If appropriate, have you understood and agreed on how the system will accommodate simultaneous operation in multiple time zones?

- If there is a requirement for separate online and batch modes of working, is this compatible with the need to operate in multiple time zones around the world?

- Have the bandwidth and response time requirements of high-volume operations such as distributed backups or distributed software updates been understood and approved?

- If there is a requirement to support offline operation when wide-area connectivity is not available, are the service-level requirements for these clear and achievable?

- Do the requirements take into account the legal and political implications of operating in different countries?

- If your architecture relies on the Internet for some of its interactions, are the requirements for bandwidth, latency, and availability realistic?

- Has the network infrastructure between sites been factored into disaster recovery requirements and plans?

CHECKLIST FOR ARCHITECTURE DEFINITION

- How confident are you that the architecture will meet all the requirements? When you are not, are mitigating activities in place (such as a proof-of-concept)?

- If there is a requirement to support offline operation when wide-area connectivity is not available, does the architecture incorporate features to recover and resubmit information when connectivity is restored? Will these complete within an acceptable period of time?

- If your architecture relies on the Internet for some of its interactions, have you developed architectural strategies to mitigate interruptions to service or poor bandwidth or latency?

■ Do the disaster recovery capabilities of the architecture extend to the connectivity between distant locations?

Further Reading

This area doesn't get much attention in the written literature, and we aren't aware of any books that specifically address geographical-location-related concerns for large systems.

THE REGULATION PERSPECTIVE

Desired Quality	The ability of the system to conform to local and international laws, quasi-legal regulations, company policies, and other rules and standards
Applicability	Any system that may be subject to laws or regulations
Concerns	Statutory industry regulation, privacy and data protection, cross-border legal restrictions, data retention and accountability, and organizational policy compliance
Activities	Compliance auditing
Architectural Tactics	Assessment of architecture against regulatory and legislative requirements
Problems and Pitfalls	Not understanding regulations or resulting obligations, and being unaware of statutory regulations

Unlike other system qualities, compliance with the law is an area where you cannot make compromises. Although you may be able to live with a system that is slow, occasionally unreliable, or potentially insecure, a system that does not comply with legal regulations may be prevented from going into production or may expose the organization to risk of prosecution.

Applicability to Views

Table 29–5 shows how the Regulation perspective affects each of the views we discussed in Part III.

TABLE 29-5 Applicability of the Regulation Perspective to the Seven Views

View	Applicability
Context	Application of this perspective may unearth requirements to interface with internal or external auditing or regulatory reporting systems.
Functional	Regulations can have a significant impact on what the system does and how it works.
Information	Especially in Europe, there is a great deal of legislation related to the retention, use, and manipulation of personal information. The impact on the Information view may include privacy, access control, retention and archive, audit, availability, and distribution.
Concurrency	This perspective has little or no impact on the Concurrency view.
Development	This perspective has little or no impact on the Development view, although if production (live) test data is to be used, there may be restrictions on this.
Deployment	This perspective has little or no impact on the Deployment view, although health and safety legislation could have an impact on the hardware deployed.
Operational	Specific operational tools and processes are often required to manage and oversee regulatory reporting activities (e.g., monitor conformance to reporting SLAs).

Concerns

Software systems are potentially subject to a wide range of legislation. Most obvious are any laws that apply directly to the problem the system is intended to solve. For example, an accounting system needs to comply with financial regulations, or a human resources system with employment law.

However, many types of legislation may apply to systems regardless of what they actually do.

- *Company law*: A number of wide-ranging laws on corporate governance and management have been passed in recent years, such as the Sarbanes-Oxley Act in the United States, that may have regulatory implications for your system. This issue is hugely complex and you must seek expert advice if you think you are affected.

- *Finance*: This legislation can be frighteningly complex, with severe penalties for noncompliance. It covers a broad spectrum, including measures against fraud and money laundering, rules about corporate accounting, regulations for local and national taxation, the regulation of banking and credit, and requirements for fair and open treatment of customers.

- *Data protection*: More so in Europe than in North America (e.g., the Data Protection Act of the United Kingdom), this sort of legislation can impose stringent conditions under which personal data can be captured, stored, used, and retained, with severe penalties for noncompliance.

- *Data retention*: This is especially important when financial transactions or contractual agreements are involved. Financial regulations in most countries, for example, impose the requirement to archive financial transactions for a number of years before they can be destroyed. (Note that this does not necessarily mean electronic format, either: It may be necessary to keep paper copies or microfiche.)

- *Disability and antidiscrimination*: We discussed this earlier when we covered the Accessibility perspective.

- *Health and safety*: There is a small but significant category of IT-related industrial injuries such as eyestrain, repetitive stress injuries, and so forth. Incorrect or inappropriate use of computer equipment can cause harm to the users and impose liability on employers.

- *Environment*: These laws may necessitate disposing of waste in an eco-friendly way or reaching targets for the use of recycled materials.

- *Law enforcement*: In recent years, a number of laws (the USA PATRIOT Act in the United States, the Regulation of Investigatory Powers Act in the United Kingdom) have been passed that impose requirements on organizations to support the activities of law enforcement and antiterrorism agencies. Some of these laws have attracted controversy due to their wide-ranging scope.

- *Protection of corporate assets*: This includes areas such as protection of corporate brands, trademarks, and copyright as well as Digital Rights Management, which restricts access to content such as prerecorded music held in digital form.

In addition to considering national and local laws, you also may need to take into account foreign or international laws if your system—particularly if it makes use of the Internet—has a presence in other countries. For example, some countries, particularly the United States, place severe restrictions on the export of some technologies such as encryption, although these constraints have been somewhat relaxed in recent years.

You may also need tools and mechanisms to monitor the regulated aspects of your system; for example, a financial system may need to be able to monitor compliance with SLAs for the time taken to report financial transactions or other activity to regulators and escalate exceptions or degradation in performance for user attention.

Even if your system is completely legal, you need to assess it against the organization's own internal policies for security, backup and restore, disaster recovery, and any business or technology standards that may be mandated or recommended.

Activities: Applying the Regulation Perspective

It is difficult to define a formal process here. You need to identify all relevant regulations (specialist stakeholder involvement will be required) and then assess your architecture for compliance.

Conformance to directly applicable regulations (such as employment law for a human resources system) should be implicit in any specification of requirements. However, although stakeholders will typically understand the law as it applies to their area of interest, you may have to bring in outside experts to consider areas such as data protection, health and safety issues, or environmental protection. Do not complacently assume that these do not apply to software systems; this can be a very costly mistake to make.

Architectural Tactics

There are no solutions specific to this perspective. Rather, you should assess your architecture against regulatory and legislative requirements as we discussed earlier.

Problems and Pitfalls

Here are some common pitfalls to keep in mind for the Regulation perspective:

- Not understanding complex regulations fully
- Not fully understanding the obligations implied by regulations
- Being unaware of regulations entirely because you are new to a domain or because the law is changing so quickly

Checklists

CHECKLIST FOR REQUIREMENTS CAPTURE

- Have you identified all legislation that applies to the functionality the system supports (e.g., employment law for a human resources system, or banking law for a financial system) and assessed the architecture for compliance with these?
- Have you identified the generic legislation that applies to software systems (e.g., health and safety, the environment, data protection) and assessed the architecture for compliance with these?

- Have you determined whether the system can be considered as touching on other countries in any way, and if so, what legislation it may be subject to as a result?

- Have you considered international law such as technology export restrictions?

- Have you identified the relevant internal business and technology regulations and standards? Have you assessed the architecture for compliance with these?

- If legislation requires registration with governmental agencies (e.g., the Data Protection Registrar in the United Kingdom), have you applied for this registration, or do you have plans to make this happen?

- Do your archive and retention plans conform to all applicable legislation?

CHECKLIST FOR ARCHITECTURE DEFINITION

- Does your architecture accommodate any required automated interfaces to regulatory bodies (e.g., automatic upload of accounting or taxation information)? Do these interfaces conform to prescribed business and technical standards?

- Does the architecture conform to any mandated technical standards?

Further Reading

Because regulations can change quickly and vary from country to country, we recommend that you obtain further information from the relevant authorities.

THE USABILITY PERSPECTIVE

Desired Quality	The ease with which people who interact with the system can work effectively
Applicability	Any system that has significant interaction with humans (users, operational staff, and so on) or that is exposed to members of the public
Concerns	User interface usability, business process flow, information quality, alignment of the human–computer interface (HCI) with working practices, alignment of the HCI with users' skills, maximization of the perceived usability, and ease of changing user interfaces
Activities	User interface design, participatory design, interface evaluation, and prototyping

Continued on next page

Architectural Tactics	Separation of user interface from functional processing
Problems and Pitfalls	Failure to consider user capabilities, failure to use human–computer interface specialists, failure to consider how concerns from other perspectives affect usability, overly complex interfaces, assumption of a single type of user access, design based on technology rather than needs, inconsistent interfaces, disregard for organizational standards, and failure to separate interface and processing implementations

Applying the Usability perspective ensures that the system allows those who interact with it to do so effectively. This perspective tends to focus on the end users of the system but should also address the concerns of any others who interact with it directly or indirectly, such as maintainers and support personnel.

Getting usability right can have a significant impact on the success of the system, so it is perhaps surprising that this perspective is all too often neglected. Usability is not just about making life easier for your stakeholders: It can significantly affect the success of your system. If you design a system that is awkward to use, meets users' needs poorly, or fails to help them do their jobs better, your users will do everything in their power not to use it. You may find yourself deploying a white elephant—destined never to see the light of day.

It is easy to get bogged down in details here that are more appropriate to consider during design. With the Usability perspective, focus on architecturally significant issues, that is, ones that involve multiple stakeholders or have far-reaching impact. You should aim to "set the tone" for the way that users will interact with the system and to drive the production of principles, standards, and user interface templates (or you may even need to produce some of them yourself).

Applicability to Views

Table 29–6 shows how the Usability perspective affects each of the views we discussed in Part III.

TABLE 29-6 APPLICABILITY OF THE USABILITY PERSPECTIVE TO THE SEVEN VIEWS

View	Applicability
Context	The Usability perspective does not typically have much of an impact on the Context view.

Continued on next page

TABLE 29-6 APPLICABILITY OF THE USABILITY PERSPECTIVE TO THE SEVEN VIEWS *(CONTINUED)*

View	Applicability
Functional	The functional structure indicates where the system's external interfaces are and thus where usability needs to be considered. It may be impacted by usability needs (e.g., the addition of interface services to support certain interaction styles) but is unlikely to be changed significantly.
Information	Information quality (the provision of accurate, relevant, consistent, and timely data) can have a large impact on usability.
Concurrency	This perspective typically has little or no impact on the Concurrency view.
Development	The results of applying the Usability perspective impact the Development view in terms of the guidelines, standards, and patterns that ensure the creation of a consistent and appropriate set of user interfaces for the system.
Deployment	This perspective has little or no impact on the Deployment view, although usability concerns could require changes to element deployment (e.g., due to response time requirements).
Operational	The Usability perspective should consider the usability needs of the system's administrators. For example, your logging and error-handling strategies should ensure that important information is highlighted in a useful way and that operational staff are not flooded with error messages they end up ignoring.

Concerns

This perspective addresses a wide range of rather loosely related concerns.

- The obvious concern is the usability of the user interface. (Remember that we are considering not only the end users of the system but also any person who interacts with it, such as operations staff, support personnel, maintainers, or trainers.)

- Process flow around the system should be simple, understandable, and consistent, especially when processes are complex, comprise multiple steps, or involve different types of users. Clear and straightforward process flow increases the likelihood of tasks being completed correctly and in a timely manner.

- Information quality has a large impact on usability. The provision of accurate, relevant, consistent, and timely data is essential to the efficient operation of any system. If information cannot be relied on, is not trusted, or is known (or believed) to be of poor quality, systems may not be used or may be used in a way other than the way their designers intended.

- The architecture should align with current (or planned) work practices. When this does not happen, you should rework it, or you may need to drive through some business changes. Business changes are particularly likely when implementing a general-purpose package for areas such as human resources, customer relationship management, or enterprise resource planning. Note that business change driven as a result of technology deployment is a very thorny activity for architects.

- The architecture should align with the current or planned skills of users. When this is not the case, your plans should include provision for staff training.

- You should understand and be aware of *perceived* rather than *actual* system qualities such as reliability and performance. Here are some examples.

  - Making use of asynchronous transactions, where control returns to the user before the transaction has completed in the database, can provide significant improvements in observed response times.

  - Allowing local systems to continue operating in offline mode even though links to remote systems are down can deliver high perceived availability even when the underlying network is of relatively poor quality.

    These approaches add to the complexity of the architecture, however, so you must balance them against the difficulty of repairing data if asynchronous activities fail.

- The ease (or difficulty) of changing user interfaces can impact a system's usability. Difficult-to-change interfaces make it less likely that user feedback will be incorporated through routine modifications.

Activities: Applying the Usability Perspective

A simple process follows.

- Identify all places where people may interact with the system (touch points).

- Understand how users will interact with the system at each touch point. Are they performing quick, atomic transactions such as checking an account balance or the status of an order, or something more measured such as browsing a catalog or doing some research?

- Understand the users' capabilities: How experienced are they at using computers and the interface technologies you have specified in your architecture? How experienced are they in the application or business function your system supports? How much training (if any) will they receive?

- Understand the context in which the system will be used. Is it an internal system that is tightly controlled and managed, or will it be exposed to the general public on a variety of platforms?
- Develop an architectural approach and, where appropriate, a more detailed solution that meets these requirements.
- Bench-test the solution against the requirements.

It is becoming increasingly common to bring in outside expertise (e.g., for graphic design and marketing) when designing interfaces exposed to the public. This helps ensure that the interface is not only functional and easy to use but also aesthetically pleasing and that it conveys the right sales and marketing messages.

Architectural Tactics

The solutions relevant to the Usability perspective depend highly on the type of system being built, the capabilities and experience of the people who will use it, and the means by which they will access it. There are a number of specific approaches to designing particular types of interfaces (see the Further Reading section for this perspective).

One basic architectural principle to keep in mind is separating the implementation of the user interface from the functional processing. If the interface implementation is tangled with the functional processing, it becomes much harder to change or replace the interface than it would be if the two are cleanly separated components. Having the interface as a separate component allows for much easier experimentation and change as a result of user feedback and could also enable simultaneous use of a number of alternative interfaces if desired.

Problems and Pitfalls

Here are some common pitfalls to keep in mind for the Usability perspective:

- Failing to take into account the capabilities, expertise, and experience of your users when designing interfaces
- Failing to bring non-IT professionals (e.g., marketing or graphic design specialists) into the architecture definition process
- Failing to consider how other perspectives—particularly Availability and Resilience, Performance and Scalability, and Internationalization—can impact usability
- Creating overly complex or inappropriately feature-stuffed interfaces

- Assuming a single type of user access (e.g., for Web and mobile platforms, assuming that all users have a high-bandwidth connection, fast processor, high-resolution color display, and so on)
- Crafting the interface around the technology rather than being driven by the business process and the needs of the users
- Using inconsistent or haphazard approaches to data entry validation, error management, user help, and so on
- Failing to comply with strict corporate guidelines for presentation (such as the use of fonts, logos, terminology, and punctuation) for externally visible interfaces such as Web pages
- Implementing the interface and the functional processing together without clear separation between them

Checklists

CHECKLIST FOR REQUIREMENTS CAPTURE

- Have you identified all of the system's key touch points?
- Have you identified all of the different types of users who will interact with the system?
- Do you understand the type of usage (occasional, regular, transactional, unstructured) for each of the touch points?
- Have you taken into account the needs of support and maintenance staff and other second-line users?
- Do you understand the capabilities, experience, and expertise of the system's users? Have you correctly mapped these into requirements for presentation and support?
- Have you taken into account any corporate standards for presentation and interaction, particularly for systems exposed to the public?

CHECKLIST FOR ARCHITECTURE DEFINITION

- For Web and mobile platforms, have you considered the variation in bandwidth, hardware capabilities (screen resolution), and rendering software?
- Do the interface designs align in a sensible way with the business processes they are automating?
- If your system is exposed to the general public, have you obtained any necessary approvals from your marketing department for the use of company logos and so on?

Further Reading

One of the earlier books on the topic, Nielsen [NIEL94], has an extensive bibliography, and the author runs a Web site extolling his practice and principles. The approach of Alan Cooper, another well-known name in the field, can be found in [COOP07]. Shneiderman [SHNE09] is a readable book that takes the jargon and mystery out of the field of human–computer interactions. Bass and John [BASS01] describes a technique for making reasoned decisions about usability tradeoffs in an architectural context.

The Usability Professionals' Association (www.upassoc.org/), which supports the work of professionals in this field, publishes a magazine, a process for usability design, and much other material.

Part V

Putting It All Together

30

WORKING AS A SOFTWARE ARCHITECT

I n Parts I through IV, we explained the principles that underpin the role of the architect, the importance of your role in project delivery, the process of software architecture, and some of the pitfalls you are likely to encounter. We also introduced three key concepts—stakeholders, viewpoints, and perspectives—and explained how to create an effective architecture and capture it in a sound AD.

We have presented a lot of information along the way, and when you consider how to apply it, you may wonder where on earth to start! In this final chapter, we describe how to put into practice the guidance in this book, explaining when it is relevant during different project lifecycles and how to apply it to different types of projects.

ARCHITECTURE IN THE PROJECT LIFECYCLE

As we explained in Part II, you'll be closely involved in the development of your system throughout the project lifecycle, but the nature of your involvement and when it occurs may vary depending on the kind of project you are involved in. Every project is different, but it is possible to classify projects into some broad categories based on attributes like their size and development approach. In this section we discuss some of the common types of projects that we've been involved in and explain the activities that we have found to be most important for each. We suggest your key focus areas and tasks for each project type and refer you to the appropriate parts of the book for further information.

Architecture in Small and Low-Risk Projects

We define small projects (by which we really mean those with relatively low risk) as projects with fewer than ten people who are collocated, where it is possible to deliver working software at least every month, and where the problem being solved is well understood or the impact of project failure on the organization is low.

A "small" project by definition does not involve a lot of time or effort and will have little slack built into its schedule, so there is the danger of architecture work being seen as unnecessary overhead. This means that there is a real need to identify the benefits of the architecture work to the project and to minimize the amount of it by focusing on its specific problems and risks. Unless you discover unexpected risks that will have a significant impact on the organization (in which case you probably no longer have a "small" project), minimalism needs to be the guiding principle for your architecture work.

The way to approach smaller projects is to scale the architecture work to the scale of the risks really facing the project. For example, it is tempting to complete a full security analysis and threat model because it is the "right" thing to do. However, if this is an internal departmental system managing relatively low-risk information, a brief threat assessment and the application of very standard authentication and authorization policies are likely to suffice. Remember that small projects are simpler, are expected to deliver something quickly, and by definition have small downside risks if things go wrong, so there is less need to analyze everything to the degree needed for a larger project.

Dealing with stakeholders is also usually relatively straightforward on a small project because there will be fewer of them (in some cases only one or two) and the decisions and tradeoffs that you are asking them to make are usually much simpler than for a large and complicated project.

Similarly, communication within the development team and with other technical stakeholders can be more direct and less formal than with a large geographically distributed project, where there are more complicated concerns, decisions, and structures to communicate. In a small project you may well be able to capture most of your architectural description using collaborative tools like wikis rather than formal documents.

Finally, bear in mind that unless the purpose of the project is to act as a proof-of-concept for a new technology or approach, small projects can often be designed using fairly conservative, proven technology choices, which further reduce risk and the need for extensive architectural description.

Table 30–1 summarizes the key architectural activities for small projects.

TABLE 30-1 KEY ARCHITECTURE ACTIVITIES FOR SMALL PROJECTS

Description	Further Information
Confirm scope and external interfaces to ensure that the project stays small, with an acceptable level of risk.	Chapter 16
Review the required quality properties to identify any unexpected risk areas that may need more attention.	Part IV
If possible, identify an architectural style, using proven ideas and technologies, to provide the overall architectural structure for the project.	Chapter 11
Create a minimal architectural description for the most important aspects of the architecture, focusing on a small number of key views to address the key risks that the project faces.	Chapter 13 and Part III
Consider a lightweight architectural review, such as a TARA review, in order to assess the system as it is being constructed, and identify any architectural problems that need rectification.	Chapter 14
Ensure that the software development environment is suitable for the scale of the project and that it supports good software engineering practices (e.g., configuration management, automated testing, continuous integration).	Chapter 20
Review the testing that is being performed to ensure its coverage and in particular that the system meets any important quality property requirements that it has.	Bibliography

Architecture in Agile Projects

In recent years, many successful software development teams have adopted an agile approach to software development, following the principles of the *Agile Manifesto* and usually basing their approach on one of the well-known agile methods such as XP or Scrum. Well-run agile projects are characterized by disciplined, self-organizing teams who have a very well-defined set of lightweight ceremonies and an effective set of software development practices that they use in an adaptive and iterative software development approach that allows them to deliver working software very frequently and to rapidly react to changing priorities and circumstances. Scrum is probably the best-known management approach for agile projects, and some of the common technical practices found in agile teams are test-driven development, automated testing, continuous integration, refactoring, and sometimes pair programming.

While agile development is often used on smaller projects, it has been successfully scaled to quite large ones, and so this is why we discuss working with agile teams separately from working with small projects (which may or may not be agile, depending on how the development team is managed).

We briefly discussed working with agile teams in Chapter 7 and Chapter 12. We have found that the key to working with agile teams is to align the architecture work that needs to be done with the culture of the development teams you're working with. Good agile teams are self-organizing and create their own culture and approach, so the most productive way to work with them is to work sympathetically with that approach. Agile teams and software architects should have a lot in common, as they're both interested in efficiently delivering software to meet stakeholder needs, while flexibly allowing for change. There are, however, cultural differences between how many software architects work and the way that agile teams work, not least of which is the tension over the amount of design that needs to be performed early in the lifecycle and the amount of documentation that is needed to capture the design.

The area where software architecture can probably help agile teams the most is in managing the ability of the system to achieve its quality properties. While some agile teams have no problem in creating performant, scalable systems that are highly available and make good tradeoffs between competing quality goals, we have also seen and worked with quite a few agile teams that found this difficult to achieve. While focusing on the end-user stakeholder (the "on-site customer") and functional user stories allows these teams to deliver features quickly, the lack of any systematic system architecture work means that they end up having to do a great deal of expensive and disruptive system-wide refactoring and redesign within a relatively short time, as their systems become successful. This isn't to say that teams following other methods like RUP (for example) sometimes don't have the same problems. However, the snag with many agile approaches is that it isn't clear where design fits in, between the mantras, rules, and dash for functional delivery that often characterize an inexperienced agile team's approach. A sound software architecture for a complex project will not simply emerge unaided from a weekly refactoring cycle, and some sympathetic and diplomatic software architecture assistance can go a long way toward helping these teams avoid a refactoring spiral as time goes on.

Table 30–2 summarizes the key activities that we have found to be important when working with agile teams.

TABLE 30–2 KEY ARCHITECTURE ACTIVITIES FOR AGILE PROJECTS

Description	Further Information
If working with an existing agile team, understand the process that the team is using and agree where software architecture can fit into the process and usefully address risk for the team.	Chapter 7 and Bibliography
Identify how to work in a way that supports the principles of incremental development and iterative delivery, delivering your architecture work in an incremental manner, so that your deliverables are available when they are needed.	Chapter 7 and Bibliography

TABLE 30-2 KEY ARCHITECTURE ACTIVITIES FOR AGILE PROJECTS (CONTINUED)

Draw up a list of key stakeholders and ensure that the importance of each is understood, so that the concerns of the on-site customer do not inadvertently dominate the others.	Chapter 9
Identify the key risks that the project faces, particularly with respect to achieving quality properties and linking to external systems.	Chapter 16 and Part IV
Identify a minimal set of views that will represent the key architectural structures of the system and create "good enough" models to represent them. Consider whether the models can be presented via a collaboration tool such as a wiki.	Chapter 12 and Part III
Select a set of perspectives that will allow you to address the significant quality property risks that the system is facing. Apply the perspectives to the architecture of the system in order to understand and mitigate these risks.	Part IV
Collaboratively define a clear set of design principles to guide the system's design work so that design decisions align with the goals and priorities of the system.	Chapter 8
Collaboratively define the cross-cutting mechanisms that must exist throughout the system (such as the implementation of the system's security mechanisms once you have identified the mechanisms required).	Chapter 20 and Part IV
Work across the teams that you have visibility of to identify possible shared functions across their systems and to encourage knowledge, solution, and software component sharing among them.	Chapter 20 and Bibliography
Whenever possible, work as part of the team and deliver working software or at least proof-of-concept software to validate design ideas.	Chapters 5, 14, and 20
Oversee the acceptance testing of the system to ensure that sufficient validation is performed of the system's important quality properties.	Bibliography

Architecture in Plan-Driven Projects

The term *plan-driven approaches* has been coined to describe structured software development approaches that generally predate the agile movement and that have more emphasis on up-front planning than agile methods. Well-known examples of plan-driven methods would include the Rational Unified Process (RUP) and the Team Software Process. The largely discredited, but unfortunately still widely used, "waterfall" approach is the most extreme example of a plan-driven approach (as it places all of the planning at the start of the project).[1]

---

1. Winston Royce's original paper, "Managing the Development of Large Software Systems," is widely available on the Internet. It is instructive to read it and find that early on he states that a waterfall approach is "risky and invites failure" and stresses the importance of feedback and iteration in the software development lifecycle. It appears that most advocates of the classical waterfall approach didn't actually read the paper!

There isn't a sharp distinction between plan-driven methods and agile methods; indeed, the general term *agile* could be described more as a philosophy or state of mind than a specific method, but plan-driven approaches tend to assume more formal estimation and project management and more early formal design work than agile methods. Their focus is more on predictability and risk management than flexibility and reacting to change (indeed, some classical plan-driven approaches—such as the waterfall approach—are highly resistant to change of any sort late in the delivery lifecycle).

As with our preceding discussion of agile projects, we have separated our discussion of plan-driven projects from the small and large project discussions because plan-driven approaches can be used on the smallest projects as well as the largest programs (where they tend to be the most common approach found).

Plan-driven projects usually follow a formally defined process, and the role of software architecture in the project may well be already defined by this. If not, then you'll need to have additional activities added to the process to allow for software architecture work, and even if there are some architectural activities defined already, you'll need to validate that they are useful, complete, and likely to be effective.

Most plan-driven approaches acknowledge the key role of stakeholders in the project, and they include activities to identify and work with a broad stakeholder group. This activity may be one you can take the lead in performing, or if not you should still be closely involved.

As plan-driven approaches normally include some architectural design activity, there is unlikely to be all that much need to introduce the ideas of software architecture and justify them. However, as we have noted elsewhere, there is a lot of confusion over what software architecture really is, so you will still need to clearly explain to stakeholders what you will be doing, why you will be doing it, and how it reduces risk for them.

Even though nearly all plan-driven approaches advocate iterative processes and incremental delivery, you often see plan-driven projects start to drift back toward a more waterfall approach, where there are very few iterations between inception and delivery, and so there is little iteration, validation, and feedback in the lifecycle. When this happens, it is a cause for concern, because the most dangerous part of a system's lifecycle is the pause between inception and the first production delivery. Minimizing this stage is important in order to start delivering value to the stakeholders and getting their validation and feedback on the system as soon as possible. You can positively influence this aspect of the project by creating an architecture that supports incremental delivery and pushing to deliver parts of it as quickly as possible.

Another factor specific to plan-driven projects is the need to ensure that all of your architecture work (and the other activities in the project lifecycle for that matter) are valuable to the project. Most plan-driven projects adopt a lifecycle model from an existing method (such as RUP), and in many cases people don't spend enough time questioning and understanding each of the activities. This results in their performing time-consuming activities that have little value. This is particularly the case with documentation, and plan-driven teams can often produce large amounts of documentation that no one ever reads. You need to make sure that all of the architecture work you're doing has a customer and is useful to the current project, and it's also worth questioning the value of other activities being performed too if their usefulness is not immediately apparent.

Table 30–3 summarizes the key activities that we have found to be important when working with plan-driven projects.

TABLE 30–3 Key Architecture Activities for Plan-Driven Projects

Description	Further Information
Review the software development process in use, and validate the role of software architecture within it and its relationship to other activities. Work to modify the process if the architecture activities are incorrect or in the wrong place.	Chapter 7 and Bibliography
Work with the stakeholders to make sure that everyone understands your role, the activities you'll be involved in, the deliverables you'll produce, and the purpose of each.	Chapters 7 and 9
Consider whether you should take the lead in the identification of and interaction with the system's stakeholders.	Chapter 9
Ensure that the system's quality property requirements are thoroughly understood and validate them if necessary.	Part IV
Identify the key technical risks that the project faces, focus your architecture work on mitigating these risks, and work to make sure that the riskiest parts of the system are delivered first.	Chapter 7 and Bibliography
Identify and create a set of views and models to represent the important architectural structures of the system, ensuring that the architecture is amenable to incremental delivery.	Part III and Bibliography
Identify a set of perspectives that will allow you to address the system's quality property goals, and apply these to your architectural design in order to meet them.	Part IV
If the system is large or critical enough, perform a scenario-based architectural review of your architecture with its stakeholders; otherwise, consider a simpler evaluation such as a TARA review.	Chapter 14
Work in and with the project team to drive incremental delivery of the system, in alignment with your architecture.	Chapter 20 and Bibliography
Involve yourself in the testing effort to ensure that acceptance testing is effective and in particular that it validates the system's ability to meet its quality goals.	Bibliography

Architecture in Large Programs

Large programs are quite different from individual software development projects, even large ones, as they generally involve creating or changing a system-of-systems rather than an individual system. The scope of a large program like this often spans human systems (such as business process changes) as well as IT systems. Such programs are very common in large organizations as part of organizational change initiatives, in the public sector when making major changes to public service provisions (e.g., tax collection or health care management), and in the defense and emergency management domains.

A major program of this sort necessarily serves a wide and disparate community of stakeholders, and so formal stakeholder identification, management, and communication will be important in order to have a realistic chance of your understanding and meeting their needs.

The scale and complexity of this sort of program mean that architecture will be needed at a number of different levels (e.g., system, business area, enterprise, and CTO) and across a number of different specializations (e.g., software or solution, enterprise, infrastructure, and business process architecture). This means that you will probably be only one of a number of architects working on the program. In this book we focus on software (or solution) architecture for a single system, but you may also have to get involved in broader types of IT architecture (particularly enterprise architecture for an entire business process) and work with architects from a number of specializations. You may be an architectural lead or even the chief architect, in which case your remit will include defining the responsibilities of other architects as well as your own work.

Large development programs are inherently complicated and usually mean long delivery timescales, large numbers of people who need to work together to achieve the overall goal, a number of separate organizations having to coordinate their efforts, and a high degree of risk as they are often trying to solve problems that have not been solved before. It's hardly surprising that cost and time overruns are common, and in fact it's quite amazing that many large programs succeed at all! Part of your role is to understand the risks that the program, or your part of it, is running and to ensure that your architecture work explicitly mitigates these risks, in order to maximize the chances of successful delivery.

Situations like these necessarily need a lot of planning, governance, standardization, and guidance. As well as a number of architects, working both in central teams and directly in the delivery organizations, there will also be a large number of program and project managers working across the program at different levels. Management processes such as formal change management are required to ensure that program-wide decisions are communicated consistently to the whole program team.

In the context of software architecture work, the scale and risk of a large program, and the number of people who need to understand the architecture, usually dictate a fairly formal approach to architectural definition and description.

You will probably use all of the viewpoints and perspectives we define in this book, and you will quite possibly use others, too, that you either define yourself or obtain from other books or papers.

The approach to delivering large programs is usually incremental and iterative, to avoid large amounts of waste if systems aren't validated as early as possible, although it tends to involve a lot more up-front planning than a typical smaller agile development project (being more like the Spiral Model than XP or Scrum).

Due to the scale, and often the novelty, of the problem being solved, the early iterations probably can't deliver directly usable software and instead will focus on defining the architecture, proof-of-concept exercises to test technical decisions, and building one or more system skeletons to validate the architecture and guide software development. Unlike with small projects, until quite a lot of design has been done, it often won't be clear that a solution for a big program is possible, and so building a lot of production software before the architecture has been defined and tested could be quite counterproductive.

Large programs tend to be geographically distributed, and given the involvement of people from different teams and organizations, communication needs to be quite formal, with a lot of information being communicated in written form and explicitly through meetings, reviews, and workshops. As mentioned previously, formal version and change management will be required for most design artifacts to avoid confusion as they evolve through the life of the program.

Finally, at this scale, testing and migration are both major projects in their own right, in order to ensure that the entire end-to-end system works as expected for all of its users and operators, and to make sure that any preexisting workload can be migrated to the new environment without mishap or an unacceptable level of risk.

Table 30–4 summarizes the key software architecture activities for a large program.

TABLE 30–4 KEY ARCHITECTURE ACTIVITIES FOR LARGE PROGRAMS

Description	Further Information
Understand, and if necessary define, the architecture definition process in the program lifecycle and your particular responsibilities within it.	Chapter 7
Understand the program structure and your particular architectural remit, defining the remit of other architects clearly, if this is your responsibility.	Bibliography
Develop resource and time estimates for the planned architecture work and feed them into the overall program plan.	Bibliography

Continued on next page

TABLE 30-4 Key Architecture Activities for Large Programs *(Continued)*

Draw up and validate the list of key business and technology stakeholders and work with them to build good working relationships and to help them understand what involvement you need from them.	Chapters 2 and 9
Review system scope with stakeholders and validate and revise it as necessary.	Chapter 16
Create a Context view of your part of the program, to capture its context and scope.	Chapter 16
Select a set of viewpoints to use to capture the architectural concerns that you are responsible for.	Chapters 2 and 3, Part III
Select a set of perspectives to use to address the key quality requirements that you are responsible for.	Chapters 2 and 4, Part IV
Create an initial architectural design for each major architectural structure within your remit, documenting it as a model in a view.	Part III
Apply your chosen perspectives to your initial architectural design to refine and extend it in order to meet the quality properties that your aspects of the system must meet.	Part IV
Perform formal scenario-based architectural evaluation, to validate your architecture with the key program stakeholders.	Chapters 10 and 14
Ensure that you create an architectural description that effectively provides the information that your stakeholders need in order to understand the architecture and how it meets the program goals.	Chapter 13
Consider creating one or more skeleton systems to implement the main structures of your architecture and to provide a framework for development teams to work within.	Chapters 7 and 14, Bibliography
Create proof-of-concept implementations to validate your design ideas, check assumptions, and prove technology choices.	Chapter 14 and Bibliography
During the construction iterations of the program, work with the implementation teams to ensure the system is implemented in accordance with the architecture, modifying the architecture as needed in the light of implementation experience.	Chapter 14 and Bibliography
Ensure that sufficient user, automated, and acceptance testing is planned to validate the required functions and quality properties that are important to the program's success.	Bibliography
Work with those performing system testing in order to ensure that the planned testing is being performed, that it is effective, and to gain early insight into the quality of what is being delivered.	Bibliography

SUPPORTING DIFFERENT TYPES OF PROJECTS

Information systems architects are involved in many types of system development projects, each with its own unique challenges. Sometimes it is a "greenfield" project, and you must understand the requirements from scratch; in other cases, an existing system needs to be modified, and you must define how the system can be changed at minimum cost and risk; and sometimes, rather than developing a distinct system, your project is to integrate existing systems.

Each of these project types has a different set of priorities, and this is reflected in the viewpoints and perspectives you need to consider. In the following subsections, we outline the architectural priorities for a number of common types of projects and refer back to material elsewhere in the book that is likely to be useful.

In-House System Development

By "in-house" development, we mean a classical information systems project, where a business need leads to the initiation of a system development project to create a new system within an organization. Such development projects require broad architectural involvement, from scoping the new system right through to ensuring that it enters production safely. Table 30–5 summarizes the architectural priorities for this type of project.

New Product Development

Developing a new product involves developing a system in something of a vacuum. Although you may have some ideas about the expected customers

TABLE 30–5 ARCHITECTURAL PRIORITIES FOR IN-HOUSE SYSTEM DEVELOPMENT

Description	Further Information
Understanding the software development methodology being used and your role in it	Chapter 7
Scope and requirements	Chapter 16
Stakeholder identification and engagement	Chapter 9
Design and validation of a new architecture	Parts II, III, and IV
Leading and overseeing construction	Chapter 20
Specification and acquisition of a deployment environment	Chapter 21
Supervision of migration to production	Chapter 22

TABLE 30-6 ARCHITECTURAL PRIORITIES FOR NEW PRODUCT DEVELOPMENT

Description	Further Information
Scope and requirements	Chapter 16
Identification of and engagement with proxy stakeholders	Chapter 9
Design and validation of a new architecture	Parts II, III, and IV
Creation of an architecture that has the ability to evolve over time at low cost	Chapter 28
Assessment of requirements for customer deployment environments	Chapter 21
Creation of a solid development environment for long-term technical integrity	Chapter 20
Leading and overseeing construction	Chapter 20

for the product, you probably don't have any direct contact with them because it hasn't actually been developed yet. This means working extensively with proxy stakeholders (such as user groups and product managers) to understand likely customer needs. The ease of modification of a new product is likely to be paramount because most successful products have long lives spanning many releases. You will also need to lay the groundwork for a solid development environment that can support a sophisticated, multirelease lifecycle in the future. On the other hand, competitive and financial pressures usually mean that the speed of delivery is crucial when developing products, so you will have limited time to get your ideas defined. This means that you will need to focus your attention on the highest risks and most important aspects of the product in order to deliver an architecture quickly. Table 30–6 summarizes the architectural priorities for this type of project.

Enterprise Service

Many organizations deploy enterprise-wide services that provide common capabilities such as enterprise messaging and file transfer, master data management, security authentication, systems management, or a standard user desktop. Developing an enterprise service differs from more traditional systems development because the service doesn't usually provide any user-visible functionality but instead acts as an enabler for the systems that use it. For example, an Enterprise Application Integration (EAI) service links multiple systems together into an integrated information systems environment. A particular architectural challenge in enterprise service development is to find a representative and knowledgeable set of stakeholders. Furthermore, the requirements

TABLE 30-7 ARCHITECTURAL PRIORITIES FOR ENTERPRISE SERVICES

Description	Further Information
Scope and requirements for the service	Chapter 16
Identification of and engagement with stakeholders outside the normal stakeholder community	Chapter 9
Creation of an architecture that is scalable and resilient	Chapters 26 and 27
Creation of an architecture that is easy to monitor and exhibits reliable error handling and failure recovery	Chapter 22
Creation of an architecture that is easy to extend and enhance in the future	Chapter 28

and quality properties of the service may be hard to predict when it is first designed, so it must be easily extendable. Table 30–7 summarizes the architectural priorities for this type of project.

Extension of an Existing System

Extending an existing system can be quite different from creating a new one. The existing system has set stakeholders' expectations, so it is important that any change to the system not come as an unpleasant surprise. Having said this, we should note that extending a system is often an opportunity to revisit and improve weak areas of the existing architecture, and in fact, large system extension projects are sometimes the result of dissatisfaction with the current system, so there may be great opportunities for improvement. Requirements management and scoping are often simpler than with a new system because the stakeholders have probably been identified already, and the requirements can often be specified in terms of enhancements to the existing facilities. Of course, one of the major challenges inherent in extending or changing something that already exists is understanding and dealing with the existing implementation and the decisions that have already been made, particularly if you have not been involved with the system before. Table 30–8 summarizes the architectural priorities for this type of project.

TABLE 30-8 ARCHITECTURAL PRIORITIES FOR EXTENSION OF AN EXISTING SYSTEM

Description	Further Information
Understanding and evaluation of the existing architecture	Chapter 14
Creation of models for the existing system if none exist	Chapter 12

Continued on next page

TABLE 30–8   ARCHITECTURAL PRIORITIES FOR EXTENSION OF AN EXISTING SYSTEM (CONTINUED)

Creation of an architecture that does not cause existing quality properties to be degraded	Part IV
Creation of an architecture that can be implemented without interrupting existing operations	Chapter 22
Management of the change to the system with the lowest risk possible	Chapter 28

Package Implementation

Implementing a software package is another interesting variation of the classical information systems implementation project, and these two types of projects share many common activities. However, when implementing a package, the core activity of the classical project—software development—is largely replaced by configuration and customization of a software package. A large portion of the work for a package implementation involves integrating the package with existing data sources and destinations. Managing requirements and dealing with stakeholder expectations can also be a challenging part of these projects because much of the benefit of implementing a package will be lost if extensive customization is required. Table 30–9 summarizes the architectural priorities for this type of project.

Internet Enablement

Many organizations are starting to make their products and services available directly to the public and to third parties over the public Internet. This is often implemented by putting a Web browser façade in front of existing systems that may have previously been used only by the organization's own staff. This type of project is a special case of a system extension but has many specific concerns, risks, and solution approaches that are not seen in

TABLE 30–9   ARCHITECTURAL PRIORITIES FOR PACKAGE IMPLEMENTATION

Description	Further Information
Scoping and management of stakeholder expectations	Chapters 9 and 16
Understanding and evaluation of the package architecture	Chapter 14
Assurance that the package exhibits suitable quality properties	Part IV
Identification of data sources, destinations, and mappings	Chapter 18
Assurance of the package's manageability	Chapter 22
Design of a deployment environment for the package	Chapter 21

TABLE 30-10 ARCHITECTURAL PRIORITIES FOR INTERNET ENABLEMENT PROJECT

Description	Further Information
Scope and requirements	Chapter 16
Creation of models for the system to be Internet-enabled if none exist	Chapter 12
Creation of an architecture that can scale on demand and is highly resilient (even if the underlying systems aren't)	Chapters 26 and 27
Creation of an architecture that is secure and resistant to malicious attack	Chapter 25
Creation of an architecture that offers an appropriate user experience	The Accessibility, Internationalization, and Usability perspective sections in Chapter 29

other types of development. For example, it is very difficult to predict the number of users of Internet-enabled systems, and if the architecture does not address this concern, a spike in demand can make the Web site unusable with a consequent impact on revenue and reputation. Table 30–10 summarizes the architectural priorities for this type of project.

Decommissioning

All good things come to an end, and eventually even successful systems will be decommissioned, so you may well work on a project to decommission a system at some point. Your skills as an architect can be just as usefully applied to decommissioning a system as to creating one, and you should make sure that you are involved in any decommissioning projects within your remit. Table 30–11 summarizes the architectural priorities for this type of project.

TABLE 30-11 ARCHITECTURAL PRIORITIES FOR DECOMMISSIONING PROJECT

Description	Further Information
Understanding scope and context to understand the implications of decommissioning on other systems	Chapter 16
Functional analysis to ensure that any decommissioned services are now obsolete or are replaced	Chapters 8 and 9

Continued on next page

TABLE 30–11 Architectural Priorities for Decommissioning Project *(Continued)*

Working with stakeholders to ensure that effective migration planning and processes are in place	Chapter 22
Design of suitable data migration and archiving activities to safeguard information when the system is decommissioned	Chapters 18 and 25
Ensuring that all regulatory constraints are met, where appropriate	The Regulation perspective section in Chapter 29

Appendix

Other Viewpoint Sets

The set of viewpoints we present in this book is by no means the only one that could be or has been proposed. While we believe it does a good job of partitioning the AD into a manageable number of sections and ensuring widespread coverage of concerns, we know of a number of other viewpoint sets that approach the problem somewhat differently. In order to allow you to compare and contrast our viewpoints with some of the other viewpoint sets that exist, we summarize a number of other approaches in this appendix. You can find more details of our experiences with some of these viewpoint sets in [WOOD04].

We also include, for comparison, brief descriptions of some enterprise architecture frameworks (which are aimed at the architecture of the whole organization rather than systems within it).

Kruchten "4+1"

When we first started using architectural views, we began with Philippe Kruchten's "4+1" set. The viewpoint set we present in this book is a direct evolution and development of the "4+1" set, so they have a lot in common. Table A–1 outlines the "4+1" viewpoints.

TABLE A–1 Kruchten "4+1" Viewpoint Catalog

Viewpoint	Definition
Logical	The logical representation of the system's functional structure, normally presumed to be a class model (in an object-oriented systems development context). Our Functional viewpoint is a development of this "4+1" viewpoint, renamed to make its content clear (because you could have a number of logical aspects to an architecture).

Continued on next page

TABLE A-1 KRUCHTEN "4+1" VIEWPOINT CATALOG *(CONTINUED)*

Process	The concurrency and synchronization aspects of the architecture. Our Concurrency viewpoint is a development of this "4+1" viewpoint, renamed to avoid confusion with business process modeling.
Development	The design-time software structure, identifying modules, subsystems, and layers and the concerns directly related to software development. Our Development viewpoint is based on this "4+1" viewpoint.
Physical	The identification of the nodes on which the system's software will be executed and the mapping of other architectural elements to these nodes. Our Deployment viewpoint is a development of this "4+1" viewpoint.

This approach also suggests the use of a set of functional usage scenarios (or use cases—the "+1" part of the name) to illustrate how the views work together. We also strongly endorse the use of scenarios for illustration and evaluation (although we suggest spending at least as much time on quality property scenarios as on functional usage scenarios).

In addition to extending and defining the viewpoints outlined in Table A–1, our approach adds three viewpoints to this set: Context, Information, and Operational.

1. We added the Context viewpoint because we have found that there is always a need to clearly define the context, scope, boundaries, and interfaces of systems that we are designing. While much of this information can be captured in other views, we have found it to be more effective to consolidate it in a view dedicated to this aspect of a system.

2. We added the Information viewpoint because the underlying information structure in a large-scale information system may be quite different from the desired functional structure and may be much longer-lived than the processing elements that use it. The Information viewpoint also needs to deal with data-specific concerns such as latency, ownership, distribution, replication, and so on.

3. We added the Operational viewpoint because of our experiences with information systems that were developed with little or no thought given to how they would be installed, migrated to, monitored, controlled, and managed in their production environments. There are often important constraints, stakeholders, and concerns in this area that we believe architects need to take seriously from an early point in the system lifecycle. The Operational viewpoint provides structure and guidance for this process.

You can learn more about these viewpoints in Kruchten [KRUC95].

RM-ODP

The Reference Model for Open Distributed Processing (RM-ODP) is an ISO standard framework for describing and discussing distributed systems technology. The framework is defined using a set of five viewpoints, as shown in Table A–2.

TABLE A–2 RM-ODP VIEWPOINT CATALOG

Viewpoint	Definition
Enterprise	Defines the context for the system and allows capture and organization of requirements.
Information	Describes the information required by the system using static, invariant, and dynamic schemas.
Computational	Contains an object-oriented model of the functional structure of the system, with a particular focus on interfaces and interactions.
Engineering	Describes the systems infrastructure required to implement the desired distribution of the system's elements. This description is performed using a specific reference model.
Technology	Defines the specific technology that will be used to build the system.

While the RM-ODP approach provides an interesting partitioning of the AD, it was actually created to support efforts to standardize distributed systems technology and (as its name suggests) imposes a reference model on the systems being described.

You can find a good tutorial on the use of the RM-ODP approach in Putman [PUTM00].

SIEMENS (HOFMEISTER, NORD, AND SONI)

While working at Siemens Research, Christine Hofmeister, Robert Nord, and Dilip Soni developed a set of four architectural viewpoints based on the way the Siemens software development teams approached software architecture. Table A–3 shows the Siemens viewpoint set.

A strength of this taxonomy is that the viewpoints are presented in fully worked form (rather than just being summaries of the kinds of information they should contain). Unfortunately, we found that this particular viewpoint set didn't work that well for information systems because it is specialized for the needs of embedded and real-time software development.

TABLE A-3 SIEMENS VIEWPOINT CATALOG

Viewpoint	Definition
Conceptual	The conceptual functional structure of the system that defines a set of conceptual components linked by a set of connectors
Module	The concrete structure of the subsystems and modules that will be realized in the system, the interfaces exposed by the modules, the intermodule dependencies, and any layering constraints in the structure
Execution	The runtime structure of the system in terms of processes, threads, interprocess communication elements, and so on, along with a mapping of modules to runtime elements
Code	The design-time layout of the system as source code and the intermediate and delivered binary elements created from it

The Siemens viewpoint set is defined further in Hofmeister et al. [HOFM00].

SEI "VIEWS AND BEYOND" VIEWS

A somewhat different approach to architectural views is the "Views and Beyond" approach defined by a group of well-known software architecture researchers, many of whom are connected to the Software Engineering Institute, which is documented in [CLEM10]. This approach starts by identifying the architectural styles that are appropriate for the design problem that the architect is facing and then applying these to the problem at hand, which results in an architectural view for each. The approach identifies three broad categories of architectural styles, known as *viewtypes* (rather than *viewpoints*), and defines a number of subtypes of each, as shown in Table A-4. The styles define how a particular type of architectural structure should be captured within the overall approach defined by the viewtype.

This set of architectural style definitions is somewhat different from the other viewpoint sets summarized here, primarily containing advice related to documenting, rather than creating, an architecture. Although the style definitions contain less information about the process of software architecture than some of the others, they contain a great deal of useful advice about documenting your architecture, which is likely to be relevant even if you are basing your approach on a different viewpoint set.

TABLE 1-4 SEI VIEWTYPE CATALOG

Style Category	Definition
Component and Connector	The Component and Connector styles are concerned with the system's runtime functional elements, their behaviors, and their interactions. The following styles defined in this category all relate to commonly occurring runtime system organizations: • *Pipe-and-Filter* • *Client-Server* • *Peer-to-Peer* • *Service-Oriented Architecture* • *Publish-Subscribe* • *Shared-Data* • *Multi-Tier*
Module	The Module styles are concerned with how the software comprising the system is structured as a set of implementation (code) units. The following styles are defined for the Module viewtype: • *Decomposition*: for specifying how modules are composed from simpler elements • *Uses*: for capturing *intermodule* usage dependencies • *Generalization*: for capturing commonality and variation (inheritance) relationships between modules • *Layered*: for specifying how modules are arranged in layers according to their level of abstraction • *Aspects*: for isolating the code modules responsible for cross-cutting concerns • *Data Model*: for describing the data elements and relationships of the system's stored data model
Allocation	The Allocation viewtype is concerned with how relationships between the different parts of the system and different aspects of their environment are captured. The following styles are defined for this viewtype: • *Deployment*: for specifying how software elements are mapped to elements of the deployment environment • *Install*: for specifying how the components from a "components-and-connectors" style are mapped to the file system of the production environment • *Work Assignment*: for mapping software modules to those responsible for creating, testing, and deploying them

GARLAND AND ANTHONY

Jeff Garland and Richard Anthony are practicing software architects who have written another practitioner-oriented guide to software architecture for information systems. They also define a viewpoint set, although it's rather different from ours, as shown in Table A–5.

TABLE A–5 GARLAND AND ANTHONY VIEWPOINT CATALOG

Viewpoint	Definition
Analysis Focused	Illustrates how the elements of the system work together in response to a functional usage scenario
Analysis Interaction	Presents the interaction diagram used during problem analysis
Analysis Overall	Consolidates the contents of the Analysis Focused view into a single model
Component	Defines the system's architecturally significant components and their connections
Component Interaction	Illustrates how the components interact in order to make the system work
Component State	Presents the state model(s) for a component or set of closely related components
Context	Defines the context within which the system exists, in terms of external actors and their interactions with the system
Deployment	Shows how software components are mapped to hardware entities in order to be executed
Layered Subsystem	Illustrates the subsystems to be implemented and the layers in the software design structure
Logical Data	Presents the logical view of the architecturally significant data structure
Physical Data	Presents the physical view of the architecturally significant data structure
Process	Defines the runtime concurrency structure (operating system processes that the system's components will be packaged into and interprocess communication mechanisms that will allow communication between them)
Process State	Presents the state transition model for the system's processes
Subsystem Interface Dependency	Defines the dependencies that exist between subsystems and the interfaces of other subsystems

This viewpoint set is much larger than the others; each viewpoint has a narrower scope. The advantage of this is that each view is clearly focused, has a manageable size, and plays an obvious role. The disadvantage is that it is harder to manage the problems of fragmentation in the AD and cross-view consistency.

These viewpoints are defined in Garland and Anthony [GARL03].

IAF

IAF (the Integrated Architecture Framework) is a proprietary architectural framework developed by the French IT services company Capgemini in the 1990s. Its early focus was on systems architecture, but recent versions have also addressed enterprise architecture concerns. It includes an architecture definition methodology as well as an architecture documentation framework.

IAF defines four levels of abstraction: Contextual (Why), Conceptual (What), Logical (How), and Physical (With What). Orthogonal to this, IAF defines four aspect areas, namely, Business Architecture, Information Architecture, Information Systems Architecture, and Technology Infrastructure. There is a third dimension to the metamodel, which includes two common disciplines, Security and Governance.

More information can be obtained from [WOUT10].

ENTERPRISE ARCHITECTURE FRAMEWORKS

Enterprise architecture frameworks are aimed at the architecture of the whole organization (sometimes referred to as the "application landscape"), rather than the systems within it. However, they share many of the concepts with their systems architecture counterparts, and in particular they all have at their core the notion of views.

The Zachman Framework

The Zachman Framework was developed initially as a framework for information systems architecture by John Zachman, then at IBM, in the 1980s. He updated and extended it to address enterprise architecture a few years later, and it is in this incarnation that it is primarily known today.

Zachman organizes architectural artifacts using a two-dimensional grid. The columns of the grid represent six fundamental questions, namely, "What?" (the Data description), "How?" (the Function description), "Where?" (the Network description), "Who?" (the People description), "When?" (the Time description), and "Why?" (the Motivation description). The rows of the grid look at the architecture from the point of view of different stakeholders, as shown in Table A–6.

TABLE A-6 ROWS IN THE ZACHMAN FRAMEWORK

View	Description
Contextual	Planner's view (scope)
Conceptual	Owner's view (enterprise or business model)
Logical	Designer's view (information systems model)
Physical	Builder's view (technology model)
Detailed	Subcontractor's view (detailed specifications)

Each cell of the grid defines the models that can be created for the stakeholders for that row to document the answers to the question for that column. For example, the intersection of the How column with the Logical (information systems) view defines a logical process model for the architecture.

More information can be obtained from http://zachmaninternational.com/.

TOGAF

TOGAF (The Open Group Architecture Framework) is a framework for enterprise architecture that was first published by the Architecture Forum of The Open Group in 1995. New versions of the framework have been published at regular intervals since then. Unlike most of the taxonomies we discuss in this Appendix, TOGAF also includes an architecture methodology called ADM (Architecture Development Method). The framework and its methodology are available to individuals and organizations to use free of charge.

TOGAF defines four architectural domains as shown in Table A–7.

TABLE A-7 TOGAF DOMAINS

Domain	Description
Business architecture	Business strategy, governance, organization, and key business processes
Application architecture	A blueprint for the organization's application systems, the interactions between them, and their relationships to the business processes

Continued on next page

TABLE A–7 TOGAF DOMAINS *(CONTINUED)*

Data architecture	The structure of the organization's logical and physical data assets and associated data management resources
Technical architecture	The hardware, software, and network infrastructure needed to support the deployment of core, mission-critical applications

More information can be obtained from www.opengroup.org/togaf/ and [TOGA09].

OTHER ENTERPRISE ARCHITECTURE FRAMEWORKS

Since John Zachman first developed the concept, a large number of competing enterprise architecture frameworks have been developed by national governments, academic institutions, and commercial organizations. Some frameworks, such as IAF, which originated as systems architecture frameworks, have extended or repositioned themselves to address enterprise architecture concerns. An Internet search will reveal details of many such frameworks.

BIBLIOGRAPHY

[AIEL10]   Aiello, Robert, and Leslie Sachs. *Configuration Management Best Practices: Practical Methods That Work in the Real World.* Boston, MA: Addison-Wesley, 2010.

[ALLS10]   Allspaw, John, and Jesse Robbins. *Web Operations: Keeping the Data on Time.* Sebastopol, CA: O'Reilly, 2010.

[ALUR03]   Alur, Deepak, John Crupi, and Dan Malks. *Core J2EE Patterns: Best Practices and Design Strategies* 2nd ed. Upper Saddle River, NJ: Prentice Hall, 2003.

[AMBL02]   Ambler, Scott. *Agile Modeling: Effective Practices for eXtreme Programming and the Unified Process.* New York: Wiley, 2002.

[AMBL06]   Ambler, Scott, and Pramod Sadalage. *Database Refactoring: Evolutionary Database Design.* Boston, MA: Addison-Wesley, 2006.

[ANDE08]   Anderson, Ross. *Security Engineering: A Guide to Building Dependable Distributed Systems,* 2nd ed. New York: Wiley, 2008.

[BABA04]   Babar, M. A., and Ian Gorton. "Comparison of Scenario-Based Software Architecture Evaluation Methods." In *11th Asia-Pacific Software Engineering Conference, APSEC 2004, Busan, Korea, 30 November–3 December 2004, Proceedings.* Piscataway, NJ: IEEE Computer Society Press, 2004.

[BACH03]   Bachmann, F., Len Bass, and Mark Klein. *Deriving Architectural Tactics: A Step toward Methodical Architectural Design.* Technical Report CMU/SEI-2003-TR-004. Pittsburgh, PA: Software Engineering Institute, Carnegie Mellon University, March 2003.

[BARN01]   Barnes, James. *A Guide to Business Continuity Planning.* New York: Wiley, 2001.

[BASS01]   Bass, Len, and Bonnie John. "Supporting Usability through Software Architecture." *Computer*, 34(10):113–115, October 2001.

[BASS03]   Bass, Len, Paul Clements, and Rick Kazman. *Software Architecture in Practice*, 2nd ed. Boston, MA: Addison-Wesley, 2003.

[BECK00]   Beck, Kent. *Extreme Programming Explained*. Boston, MA: Addison-Wesley, 2000.

[BEED02]   Beedle, Mike, and Ken Schwaber. *Agile Software Development with Scrum*. Upper Saddle River, NJ: Prentice Hall, 2002.

[BEHR05]   Behr, Kevin, Gene Kim, and George Spafford. *The Visible Ops Handbook: Implementing ITIL in 4 Practical and Auditable Steps*. Eugene, OR: Information Technology Process Institute, 2005.

[BON07]   van Bon, Jan. *ITIL V3: A Pocket Guide*. Zaltbommel, The Netherlands: Van Haren Publishing, 2007.

[BERC03]   Berczuk, Stephen P., and Brad Appleton. *Software Configuration Management Patterns: Effective Teamwork, Practical Integration*. Boston, MA: Addison-Wesley, 2003.

[BLOC08]   Bloch, Josh. *Effective Java*, 2nd ed. Boston, MA: Addison-Wesley, 2001.

[BOEH03]   Boehm, Barry, and Richard Turner. *Balancing Agility and Discipline: A Guide for the Perplexed*. Boston, MA: Addison-Wesley, 2003.

[BOSC00]   Bosch, J. *Design and Use of Software Architectures*. Boston, MA: Addison-Wesley, 2000.

[BREN10]   Brent, Mike, and Fiona Dent. *A Leader's Guide to Influence: How to Use Soft Skills to Get Hard Results*. London: Financial Times/Prentice Hall, 2010.

[BRES09]   Breshears, Clay. *The Art of Concurrency*. Sebastopol, CA: O'Reilly, 2009.

[BREW00]   Brewer, Eric A. "Towards Robust Distributed Systems." Invited talk at Principles of Distributed Computing, Portland, OR, July 2000. www.cs.berkeley.edu/~brewer/cs262b-2004/PODC-keynote.pdf.

[BROO95]   Brooks, Fred. *The Mythical Man-Month*, 2nd ed. Boston, MA: Addison-Wesley, 1995.

[BUSC96]   Buschmann, Frank, et al. *Pattern-Oriented Software Architecture: A System of Patterns*. New York: Wiley, 1996.

[BUSC07a]   Buschmann, Frank, Kevlin Henney, and Douglas C. Schmidt. *Pattern-Oriented Software Architecture, Volume 4: A Pattern Language for Distributed Computing*. New York: Wiley, 2007.

[BUSC07b]   Buschmann, Frank, Kevlin Henney, and Douglas C. Schmidt. *Pattern-Oriented Software Architecture, Volume 5: On Patterns and Pattern Languages*. New York: Wiley, 2007.

[BUTL93]   Butler, Ricky, and George Finelli. "The Infeasibility of Quantifying the Reliability of Life-Critical Real-Time Software." *IEEE Transactions on Software Engineering*, 19(1):3–12, January 1993.

[CHEC99]   Checkland, Peter. *Systems Thinking, Systems Practice*. New York: Wiley, 1999.

[CHEE01]   Cheesman, John, and John Daniels. *UML Components*. Boston, MA: Addison-Wesley, 2001.

[CLEM02]   Clements, Paul, Rick Kazman, and Mark Klein. *Evaluating Software Architectures*. Boston, MA: Addison-Wesley, 2002.

[CLEM10]   Clements, Paul, Felix Bachmann, Len Bass, David Garlan, James Ivers, Reed Little, Paulo Merson, Robert Nord, and Judith Stafford. *Documenting Software Architectures: Views and Beyond*. Boston, MA: Addison-Wesley, 2010.

[COCK00]   Cockburn, Alistair. *Writing Effective Use Cases*. Boston, MA: Addison-Wesley, 2000.

[COHN09]   Cohn, Mike. *Succeeding with Agile: Software Development Using Scrum*. Boston, MA: Addison-Wesley, 2009.

[COOK94]   Cook, Steve, and John Daniels. *Designing Object Systems*. Upper Saddle River, NJ: Prentice Hall, 1994.

[COOP07]   Cooper, Alan, Robert Reimann, and David Cronin. *About Face 3: The Essentials of Interaction Design*. New York: Wiley, 2007.

[COPL91]   Coplien, James O. *Advanced C++ Programming Styles and Idioms*. Reading, MA: Addison-Wesley, 1991.

[DATE03]   Date, C. J. *An Introduction to Database Systems*. Boston, MA: Addison-Wesley, 2003.

[DOBR02]   Dobrica, Liliana, and Elia Niemela. "A Survey on Software Architecture Analysis Methods." *IEEE Transactions on Software Engineering*, 28(7):638–653, July 2002.

[DSOU99]   D'Sousa, Desmond, and Alan Wills. *Objects, Components, and Frameworks with UML: The Catalysis Approach*. Reading, MA: Addison-Wesley, 1999.

[DUVA07] Duvall, Paul M., Steve Matyas, and Andrew Glover. *Continuous Integration: Improving Software Quality and Reducing Risk.* Boston, MA: Addison-Wesley, 2007.

[DYSO04] Dyson, Paul, and Andrew Longshaw. *Architecting Enterprise Solutions: Patterns for High-Capability Internet-Based Systems.* New York: Wiley, 2004.

[EELE09] Eeles, Peter, and Peter Cripps. *The Process of Software Architecting.* Upper Saddle River, NJ: Addison-Wesley, 2009.

[ELMA99] Elmasri, Ramez E., and Shamkant B. Navathe. *Fundamentals of Database Systems.* Reading, MA: Addison-Wesley, 1999.

[ESPO08] Esposito, Dino, and Andrea Saltarello. *Microsoft .NET: Architecting Applications for the Enterprise.* Redmond, WA: Microsoft Press, 2008.

[FAIR10] Fairbanks, G. *Just Enough Software Architecture.* Boulder, CO: Marshall and Brainerd, 2010.

[FERG10] Ferguson, Niels, Bruce Schneier, and Tadayoshi Kohno. *Cryptography Engineering: Design Principles and Practical Applications.* New York: Wiley, 2010.

[FISH03] Fisher, Roger, and William Ury. *Getting to Yes: Negotiating an Agreement Without Giving In.* New York: Random House, 2003.

[FOWL97] Fowler, Martin. *Analysis Patterns.* Reading, MA: Addison-Wesley, 1997.

[FOWL99] Fowler, Martin, Kent Beck, John Brant, William Opdyke, and Don Roberts. *Refactoring.* Reading, MA: Addison-Wesley, 1999.

[FOWL03a] Fowler, Martin, and Kendall Scott. *UML Distilled*, 3rd ed. Boston, MA: Addison-Wesley, 2003.

[FOWL03b] Fowler, Martin. *Patterns of Enterprise Application Architecture.* Boston, MA: Addison-Wesley, 2003.

[FOWL04] Fowler, Martin. "Inversion of Control Containers and the Dependency Injection Pattern." http://martinfowler.com/articles/injection.html.

[FOWL10] Fowler, Martin, with Rebecca Parsons. *Domain Specific Languages.* Upper Saddle River, NJ: Prentice Hall, 2010.

[FREE09] Freeman, Steve, and Nat Pryce. *Growing Object-Oriented Software, Guided by Tests.* Boston, MA: Addison-Wesley, 2009.

[GAMM95]   Gamma, Erich, Richard Helm, Ralph Johnson, and John Vlissides. *Design Patterns*. Reading: MA: Addison-Wesley, 1995.

[GARL03]   Garland, Jeff, and Richard Anthony. *Large Scale Software Architecture*. New York: Wiley, 2003.

[GHOS10]   Ghosh, Debasish. *DSLs in Action.* Greenwich, CT: Manning, 2010.

[GILB93]   Gilb, Tom, and Dorothy Graham. *Software Inspection*. Reading, MA: Addison-Wesley, 1993.

[GILB02]   Gilbert, Seth, and Nancy Lynch. "Brewer's Conjecture and the Feasibility of Consistent, Available, Partition-Tolerant Web Services." *ACM SIGACT News,* 33(2):51–59, 2002.

[GIRA02]   Girauld, Claude, and Rudiger Valk. *Petri Nets for Systems Engineering.* Berlin: Springer-Verlag, 2002.

[GORT06]   Gorton, I. *Essential Software Architecture.* Berlin: Springer, 2006.

[HALL98]   Hall, Elaine. *Managing Risk*. Reading, MA: Addison-Wesley, 1998.

[HANM07]   Hanmer, Robert. *Patterns for Fault Tolerant Software.* Chichester, UK: John Wiley & Sons, December 2007.

[HARE87]   Harel, David. "Statecharts: A Visual Formalism for Complex Systems." *Science of Computer Programming*, 8(3):231–274, June 1987.

[HELL07]   Helland, Pat. "Life beyond Distributed Transactions: An Apostate's Opinion." Conference on Innovative Data Systems Research, Pacific Grove, CA, January 2007.

[HENN07]   Henning, Michi. "API Design Matters." *ACM Queue*, 5(4), May–June 2007.

[HOFM00]   Hofmeister, Christine, Robert Nord, and Dilip Soni. *Applied Software Architecture*. Boston, MA: Addison-Wesley, 2000.

[HOWA04]   Howard, Michael, and David LeBlanc. *Writing Secure Code: Practical Strategies and Proven Techniques for Building Secure Applications in a Networked World,* 2nd ed. Redmond, WA: Microsoft Press, 2004.

[HUMB10]   Humble, Jes, and David Farley. *Continuous Delivery: Reliable Software Releases through Build, Test, and Deployment Automation.* Boston, MA: Addison-Wesley, 2010.

[IEEE00]   IEEE Computer Society. *Recommended Practice for Architectural Description*. IEEE Std-1471–2000, October 9, 2000. Available at http://standards.ieee.org/reading/ieee/std_public/description/se/1471-2000_desc.html.

[INMO05]   Inmon, W. H. *Building the Data Warehouse.* New York: Wiley, 2005.

[INTE02]   Dr. International. *Developing International Software*, 2nd ed. Redmond, WA: Microsoft Press, 2002.

[ISO96]   International Organization for Standardization. ISO Standard 11197-3, "Information Technology—Metadata Registries (MDR)—Part 3: Registry Metamodel and Basic Attributes." Available at www. metadata-standards.org/11179/.

[ISO11]   International Organization for Standardization. ISO Standard ISO/IEC 42010:2007, "Systems and Software Engineering— Recommended Practice for Architectural Description of Software-Intensive Systems."

[JACO92]   Jacobson, Ivar. *Object-Oriented Software Engineering: A Use Case Driven Approach.* Boston, MA: Addison-Wesley, 1992.

[JAIN91]   Jain, Raj. *The Art of Computer Systems Performance Analysis*. New York: Wiley, 1991.

[JAYA05]   Jayaswal, Kailash. *Administering Data Centers: Servers, Storage, and Voice over IP.* New York: Wiley, 2005.

[KERN04]   Kern, Harris, Rich Schiesser, and Mayra Muniz. *IT Production Services.* Upper Saddle River, NJ: Prentice Hall, 2004.

[KIMB02]   Kimball, Ralph, and Margy Ross. *The Data Warehouse Toolkit: The Complete Guide to Dimensional Modeling.* New York: Wiley, 2002.

[KIMW99]   Kim, Won (ed.). *Modern Database Management: Object-Oriented and Extended Relational Database Systems*. New York: ACM Press, 1999.

[KIRC04]   Kircher, Michael, and Prashant Jain. *Pattern-Oriented Software Architecture, Volume 3: Patterns for Resource Management (POSA3).* New York: Wiley, 2004.

[KROE02]   Kroenke, David. *Database Processing: Fundamentals of Design.* Upper Saddle River, NJ: Prentice Hall, 2002.

[KRUC95]   Kruchten, Philippe. "Architectural Blueprints—The 4+1 View Model of Software Architecture." *IEEE Software*, 12(6):42–50, November 1995.

[KRUC03]   Kruchten, Philippe. *The Rational Unified Process: An Introduction*, 3rd ed. Boston, MA: Addison-Wesley, 2003.

[LAMP04]   Lampson, Butler. "Computer Security in the Real World." *Computer*, 37(6):37–46, June 2004.

[LEVE95]   Leveson, Nancy. *Safeware: System Safety and Computers*. Reading, MA: Addison-Wesley, 1995.

[LINT03]   Linthicum, David S. *Next Generation Application Integration: From Simple Information to Web Services*. Boston, MA: Addison-Wesley, 2003.

[LUND09]   Lund, Ken. *CKJV Information Processing*, 2nd ed. Sebastopol, CA: O'Reilly, 1998.

[LUON95]   Luong, Tuoc, James Lok, and Kevin Driscoll. *Internationalization: Developing Software for Global Markets*. New York: Wiley, 1995.

[MAGE06]   Magee, Jeff, and Jeff Kramer. *Concurrency: State Models and Java Programs*. New York: Wiley, 2006.

[MAIE09]   Maier, Mark, and Eberhardt Rechtin. *The Art of Systems Architecting*, 3rd ed. Boca Raton, FL: CRC Press, 2009.

[MARC00]   Marco, David. *Building and Managing the Meta Data Repository: A Full Lifecycle Guide*. New York: Wiley, 2000.

[MARC03]   Marcus, Evan, and Hal Stern. *Blueprints for High Availability*, 2nd ed. New York: Wiley, 2003.

[MCCO97]   McConnell, Steve. *Software Project Survival Guide*. Redmond, WA: Microsoft Press, 1997.

[MCGO04]   McGovern, James, et al. *The Practical Guide to Enterprise Architecture*. Upper Saddle River, NJ: Prentice Hall, 2004.

[MCGR06]   McGraw, Gary. *Software Security: Building Security In*. Boston, MA: Addison-Wesley, 2006.

[MEYE00]   Meyer, Bertrand. *Object-Oriented Software Construction*, 2nd ed. Upper Saddle River, NJ: Prentice Hall, 2000.

[MILE06]   Miles, Russ, and Kim Hamilton. *Learning UML 2*. Sebastopol, CA: O'Reilly, 2006.

[MILN89]   Milner, Robin. *Communication and Concurrency*. Upper Saddle River, NJ: Prentice Hall, 1989.

[MITC02]   Mitchell, Richard, and Jim McKim. *Design by Contract by Example*. Boston, MA: Addison-Wesley, 2002.

[NEUF92]   Neufelder, Ann Marie. *Ensuring Software Reliability*. New York: Marcel Dekker, 1992.

[NIEL94]   Nielsen, Jakob. *Usability Engineering*. San Diego, CA: Academic Press, 1994.

[NORD09]   Nord, Robert, Paul Clements, David Emery, and Rich Hilliard. *A Structured Approach to Reviewing Architecture Documentation.* Technical Report CMU/SEI-2009-TN-030. Pittsburgh, PA: Software Engineering Institute, Carnegie Mellon University, December 2009.

[NUSE01]   Nuseibeh, Bashar. "Weaving Together Requirements and Architectures." *IEEE Computer*, 34(3):115–117, March 2001.

[NYGA07]   Nygard, Michael. *Release It!* Raleigh, NC: Pragmatic Bookshelf, 2007.

[OMG10a]   Object Management Group. *OMG Unified Modelling Language Infrastructure,* version 2.3. Available from www.omg.org/spec/UML/2.3/Infrastructure.

[OMG10b]   Object Management Group. *OMG Unified Modelling Language Superstructure*, version 2.3. Available from www.omg.org/spec/UML/2.3/Superstructure.

[PALM02]   Palmer, Steven, and Mac Felsing. *A Practical Guide to Feature Driven Development*. Upper Saddle River, NJ: Prentice Hall, 2002.

[PELL09]   Pellerin, Charles J. *How NASA Builds Teams: Mission Critical Soft Skills for Scientists, Engineers, and Project Teams.* Hoboken, NJ: Wiley, 2009.

[PERK03]   Perks, Col, and Tony Beveridge. *Guide to Enterprise IT Architecture.* Berlin: Springer-Verlag, 2003.

[PERR92]   Perry, Dewayne, and Alexander Wolf. "Foundations for the Study of Software Architecture." *ACM SIGSOFT Software Engineering Notes*, 17(4):40–52, October 1992.

[PFIS98]   Pfister, Greg. *In Search of Clusters*, 2nd ed. Upper Saddle River, NJ: Prentice Hall, 1998.

[PICH10]   Pichler, Roman. *Agile Product Management with Scrum: Creating Products That Customers Love.* Boston, MA: Addison-Wesley, 2010.

[PLOP95–99]   Coplien, James, et al. *Pattern Languages of Program Design 1–4.* Reading, MA: Addison-Wesley, 1995–1999.

[PLOP06]   Manolescu, Dragos, Markus Voelter, and James Noble. *Pattern Languages of Program Design 5 (Software Patterns).* Boston, MA: Addison-Wesley, 2006.

[POPP03]   Poppendieck, Mary, and Tom Poppendieck. *Lean Software Development: An Agile Toolkit.* Boston, MA: Addison-Wesley, 2003.

[PRIT08]   Pritchett, Dan. "BASE: An ACID Alternative." *ACM Queue,* 6(3), May/June 2008.

[PULL01]   Pullum, Laura. *Software Fault Tolerance Techniques and Implementation.* Norwood, MA: Artech House, 2001.

[PUTM00]   Putman, J. *Architecting with RM-ODP.* Upper Saddle River, NJ: Prentice Hall, 2000.

[REDM97]   Redman, Thomas C. *Data Quality for the Information Age.* Norwood, MA: Artech House, 1997.

[ROSC97]   Roscoe, A. W. *The Theory and Practice of Concurrency.* Upper Saddle River, NJ: Prentice Hall, 1997.

[RUHW00]   Ruh, William A., Francis X. Maginnis, and William J. Brown. *Enterprise Application Integration: A Wiley Tech Brief.* New York: Wiley, 2000.

[RUMB99]   Rumbaugh, James, Ivar Jacobson, and Grady Booch. *The Unified Modeling Language Reference Manual.* Reading, MA: Addison-Wesley, 1999.

[SARA02]   SARA Working Group. "Software Architecture Review and Assessment (SARA) Report," v1.0.

[SCHM00]   Schmidt, Douglas, Michael Stal, Hans Rohnert, and Frank Buschmann. *Pattern Oriented Software Architecture, Volume 2: Patterns for Concurrent and Networked Objects.* New York: Wiley, 2000.

[SCHM06]   Schmidt, Klaus. *High Availability and Disaster Recovery: Concepts, Design, Implementation.* Berlin: Springer, 2006.

[SCHN01]   Schneier, Bruce. *Secrets and Lies.* New York: Wiley, 2001.

[SCHR06]   Schroeder, Bianca, and Garth Gibson. *Disk Failures in the Real World.* Technical Report CMU-PDL-06-111. Pittsburgh, PA: Parallel Data Laboratory, Carnegie Mellon University, September 2006.

[SCHW01]   Schwaber, Ken, and Mike Beedle. *Agile Software Development with Scrum.* Upper Saddle River, NJ: Prentice Hall, 2001.

[SDL02]   The SDL Forum Society Web site, www.sdl-forum.org.

[SEAC03]   Seacord, Robert, Daniel Plakosh, and Grace A. Lewis. *Modernizing Legacy Systems.* Boston, MA: Addison-Wesley, 2003.

[SHAR08]   Sharp, Alec, and Patrick McDermott. *Workflow Modeling: Tools for Process Improvement and Application Development.* Norwood, MA: Artech House, 2008.

[SHAW94]   Shaw, Mary. "Procedure Calls Are the Assembly Language of Software Interconnection: Connectors Deserve First-Class Status." Technical Report CMU-CS-94-107, CMU/SEI, 1994.

[SHAW96]   Shaw, Mary, and David Garlan. *Software Architecture—Perspectives on an Emerging Discipline*. Upper Saddle River, NJ: Prentice Hall, 1996.

[SHNE09]   Shneiderman, Ben, Catherine Plaisant, Maxine Cohen, and Steve Jacobs. *Designing the User Interface: Strategies for Effective Human-Computer Interaction,* 5th ed. Boston, MA: Addison-Wesley, 2009.

[SMIT02]   Smith, Connie, and Lloyd Williams. *Performance Solutions: A Practical Guide to Creating Responsive, Scalable Software*. Boston, MA: Addison-Wesley, 2002.

[SNED07]   Snedaker, Susan. *Business Continuity and Disaster Recovery Planning for IT Professionals.* Waltham, MA: Syngress, 2007.

[SOMM97]   Sommerville, Ian, and Pete Sawyer. *Requirements Engineering: A Good Practice Guide*. New York: Wiley, 1997.

[SWID04]   Swiderski, Frank, and Window Snyder. *Threat Modelling.* Redmond, WA: Microsoft Press, 2004.

[TAYL09]   Taylor, R. N., N. Medvidovic, and E. M. Dashofy. *Software Architecture: Foundations, Theory, and Practice.* New York: Wiley, 2009.

[TOGA09]   TOGAF Version 9. Reading, UK: The Open Group, 2009.

[TOIG02]   Toigo, Jon William, Margaret Toigo, and Jon Toigo. *Disaster Recovery Planning: Preparing for the Unthinkable,* 3rd ed. Upper Saddle River, NJ: Prentice Hall, 2002.

[TUCK65]   Tuckman, Bruce W. "Developmental Sequence in Small Groups." *Psychological Bulletin*, 63, 384–399, reprinted in *Group Facilitation: A Research and Applications Journal*, Number 3, Spring 2001.

[TULA08]   Tulach, Jaroslav. *Practical API Design.* New York: Apress, July 2008.

[TYRE05]   Tyree, Jeff, and Art Akerman. "Architecture Decisions: Demystifying Architecture." *IEEE Software*, March/April 2005.

[VIEG02]   Viega, Gary, and John McGraw. *Building Secure Software*. Boston, MA: Addison-Wesley, 2002.

[VOGE08]   Vogels, Werner. "Eventually Consistent." *ACM Queue*, 6(6), October 2008.

[WAGN10]   Wagner, Bill. *Effective C#: 50 Specific Ways to Improve Your C#.* Reading, MA: Addison-Wesley, 2010.

[WALL10]   Wallace, Michael, and Lawrence Webber. *The Disaster Recovery Handbook.* New York: AMACOM, 2010.

[WHIT00]   Whittaker, James, and Jeffrey Voas. "Toward a More Reliable Theory of Software Reliability." *IEEE Computer*, 33(12):36–42, December 2000.

[WIRF90]   Wirfs-Brock, Rebecca, Brian Wilkerson, and Lauren Weiner. *Designing Object-Oriented Software*. Upper Saddle River, NJ: Prentice Hall, 1990.

[WIRF02]   Wirfs-Brock, Rebecca, and Alan McKean. *Object Design: Roles, Responsibilities, and Collaborations.* Boston, MA: Addison-Wesley, 2002.

[WOOD04]   Woods, Eoin. "Experiences Using Viewpoints for Information Systems Architecture: An Industrial Experience Report." In F. Oquendo et al. (eds.), *Software Architecture: First European Workshop, EWSA 2004, St. Andrews, UK, May 21–22, 2004, Proceedings.* Springer Lecture Notes in Computer Science 3047, pp. 182–193. Berlin: Springer-Verlag, 2004.

[WOOD11]   Woods, Eoin. "Industrial Architectural Assessment Using TARA." In *9th Working IEEE Conference on Software Architecture, WICSA 2011, Colorado, USA, 20–24 June 2011, Proceedings.* Piscataway, NJ: IEEE Computer Society Press, 2010.

[WOUT10]   Van't Wout, Jack, Maarten Waage, Herman Hartman, Max Stahlecker, and Aaldert Hofman. *The Integrated Architecture Framework Explained: Why, What, How.* Berlin: Springer-Verlag, 2010.

ABOUT THE AUTHORS

Nick Rozanski is the functional architect for a front-office IT department in a major British bank. He has oversight of the systems landscape for the whole department and also provides architectural guidance and support for key systems and projects. He produces some of the department's architecture descriptions himself, which requires him to create all types of views and address concerns in almost every perspective described in this book.

Nick has worked in IT since 1980 for several large and small systems integrators, including Logica, Capgemini, and Sybase, and end-user organizations including Marks and Spencer and Barclays Global Investors. He has taken senior roles on a wide range of programs in finance, retail, manufacturing, and government. His technology background includes enterprise application integration, package implementation, relational database, data replication, and object-oriented software development. He is also an experienced technical instructor and certified internal project auditor.

Nick was educated at the Universities of Cambridge and Manchester, United Kingdom. He is a chartered engineer and a Chartered Fellow of the British Computer Society.

Eoin Woods is a lead system architect in the equities technology group of a major European investment bank with architecture and design responsibility for a number of the organization's key systems. He has been working in software engineering since 1990 and during that time has worked for a number of technology companies, consultancies, and financial services firms.

Eoin has worked throughout the system delivery lifecycle and has led applied research, server product development, and large-scale information systems implementation projects. His main professional interests are software architecture, distributed systems, computer security, and data management.

Eoin holds B.Sc. and M.Sc. degrees in Software Engineering from Brunel and Manchester universities. He is a chartered member of the Institution of Engineering and Technology, and a chartered engineer and a Chartered Fellow of the British Computer Society.

INDEX

FREE Online Edition

Your purchase of *Software Systems Architecture, Second Edition,* includes access to a free online edition for 45 days through the Safari Books Online subscription service. Nearly every Addison-Wesley Professional book is available online through Safari Books Online, along with more than 5,000 other technical books and videos from publishers such as Cisco Press, Exam Cram, IBM Press, O'Reilly, Prentice Hall, Que, and Sams.

SAFARI BOOKS ONLINE allows you to search for a specific answer, cut and paste code, download chapters, and stay current with emerging technologies.

Activate your FREE Online Edition at
www.informit.com/safarifree

> **STEP 1:** Enter the coupon code: JIGMNVH.

> **STEP 2:** New Safari users, complete the brief registration form.
> Safari subscribers, just log in.

If you have difficulty registering on Safari or accessing the online edition, please e-mail customer-service@safaribooksonline.com